1,000,000 Books

are available to read at

www.ForgottenBooks.com

Read online
Download PDF
Purchase in print

ISBN 978-1-330-96039-4
PIBN 10126679

This book is a reproduction of an important historical work. Forgotten Books uses state-of-the-art technology to digitally reconstruct the work, preserving the original format whilst repairing imperfections present in the aged copy. In rare cases, an imperfection in the original, such as a blemish or missing page, may be replicated in our edition. We do, however, repair the vast majority of imperfections successfully; any imperfections that remain are intentionally left to preserve the state of such historical works.

Forgotten Books is a registered trademark of FB &c Ltd.
Copyright © 2018 FB &c Ltd.
FB &c Ltd, Dalton House, 60 Windsor Avenue, London, SW19 2RR.
Company number 08720141. Registered in England and Wales.

For support please visit www.forgottenbooks.com

1 MONTH OF FREE READING

at
www.ForgottenBooks.com

By purchasing this book you are eligible for one month membership to ForgottenBooks.com, giving you unlimited access to our entire collection of over 1,000,000 titles via our web site and mobile apps.

To claim your free month visit:
www.forgottenbooks.com/free126679

* Offer is valid for 45 days from date of purchase. Terms and conditions apply.

English
Français
Deutsche
Italiano
Español
Português

www.forgottenbooks.com

Mythology Photography **Fiction**
Fishing Christianity **Art** Cooking
Essays Buddhism Freemasonry
Medicine **Biology** Music **Ancient Egypt** Evolution Carpentry Physics
Dance Geology **Mathematics** Fitness
Shakespeare **Folklore** Yoga Marketing
Confidence Immortality Biographies
Poetry **Psychology** Witchcraft
Electronics Chemistry History **Law**
Accounting **Philosophy** Anthropology
Alchemy Drama Quantum Mechanics
Atheism Sexual Health **Ancient History**
Entrepreneurship Languages Sport
Paleontology Needlework Islam
Metaphysics Investment Archaeology
Parenting Statistics Criminology
Motivational

ISAIAH:

A
NEW TRANSLATION;

WITH

A PRELIMINARY DISSERTATION,

AND

NOTES,

CRITICAL, PHILOLOGICAL, AND EXPLANATORY.

By ROBERT LOWTH, D.D. F.R.SS. Lond. & Goet.
LORD BISHOP OF LONDON.

FROM THE TENTH ENGLISH EDITION,
CAREFULLY CORRECTED AND REVISED.

BOSTON:
WILLIAM HILLIARD, 14 WATER STREET.
CAMBRIDGE:
JAMES MUNROE AND COMPANY.

1834.

THE
PRELIMINARY DISSERTATION.

The design of the following translation of Isaiah, is not only to give an exact and faithful representation of the words and of the sense of the Prophet, by adhering closely to the letter of the text, and treading as nearly as may be in his footsteps; but, moreover, to imitate the air and manner of the author, to express the form and fashion of the composition, and to give the English reader some notion of the peculiar turn and cast of the original. The latter part of this design coincides perfectly well with the former: it is indeed impossible to give a just idea of the Prophet's manner of writing, otherwise than by a close literal version. And yet, though so many literal versions of this Prophet have been given, as well of old as in later times, a just representation of his manner, and of the form of his composition, has never been attempted, or even thought of, by any translator, in any language, whether ancient or modern. Whatever of that kind has appeared in former translations, (and much indeed must appear in every literal translation), has been rather the effect of chance than of design, of necessity than of study: for what room could there be for study or design in this case, or at least for success in it, when the translators themselves had but a very imperfect notion, an inadequate or even false idea, of the real character of the author as a writer; of the general nature, and of the peculiar form, of the composition?

It has, I think, been universally understood, that the Prophecies of Isaiah are written in prose. The style, the thoughts, the images, the expressions, have been allowed to be poetical, and that in the highest degree; but that they are written in verse, in measure, or rhythm, or whatever it is that distinguishes, as poetry, the composition of those books of the Old Testament which are allowed to be poetical, such as Job, the Psalms, and the Proverbs, from the historical books, as mere prose; this has never been supposed, at least has not been at any time the prevailing opinion. The opinions of the learned concerning Hebrew verse have been various; their ideas of the nature of it vague, obscure, and imperfect: yet still there has been a general persuasion, that some books of the Old Testament are written' in verse; but that the writings of the prophets are not of that number.

The learned Vitringa says,* that Isaiah's composition has a sort of numbers, or measure; "esse orationem suis adstrictam numeris:" he means, that it has a kind of oratorial number, or measure, as he afterwards explains it; and he quotes Scaliger as being of the same opinion, and as adding, that "however upon this account it could not rightly be called poetry." † About the beginning of this century, Herman Von der Hardt, ‡ the Hardouin of Germany, attempted to reduce Joel's Elegies, as he called them, to iambic verse: and, consistently with his hypothesis, he affirmed, that the prophets wrote in verse. This is the only exeption I meet with to the universality of the contrary opinion. It was looked upon as one of his paradoxes, and little attention was paid to it. But what was his success in making out Joel's iambics, and in helping his readers to form in consequence a more just idea of the character of the prophetic style, I cannot say, having never seen his treatise on that subject.

The Jews of early times were of the same opinion, that the books of the prophets are written in prose, as far as we have any evidence of their judgment on this subject. Jerome § certainly speaks the sense of his Jewish preceptors as to this matter. Having written his translation of Isaiah from the Hebrew Verity in *stichi*, or lines divided according to the *cola* and *commata*, after the manner of verse, which was ‖ often done in the prophetic writings for the

* Prolegom." in Iesaiam, p. 8.
† Scaliger, Animadvers. in Chron. Eusebii, p. 6.
‡ See Wolfii Biblioth. Hebr. tom. ii. p. 169.
§ Præf. in Transl. Esaiæ ex Heb. Veritate.
‖ See Grabe, Proleg. in LXX Intt. tom. i. cap. i. § 6.

sake of perspicuity, he cautions his reader "not to mistake it for metre, as if it were any thing like the Psalms, or the writings of Solomon; for it was nothing more than what was usual in the copies of the prose works of Demosthenes and Cicero." The later Jews have been uniformly of the same opinion; and the rest of the learned world seem to have taken it up on their authority, and have generally maintained it.

But if there should appear a manifest conformity between the prophetical style and that of the books supposed to be metrical,—a conformity in every known part of the poetical character, which equally discriminates the prophetical and the metrical books from those acknowledged to be prose—it will be of use to trace out and to mark this conformity with all possible accuracy; to observe how far the peculiar characteristics of each style coincide; and to see whether the agreement between them be such as to induce us to conclude, that the poetical and the prophetical character of style and composition, though generally supposed to be different, yet are really one and the same.

This I purpose to do in the following dissertation; and I the more readily embrace the present opportunity of resuming this subject, as what I have formerly written* upon it seems to have met with the approbation of the learned. And here I shall endeavour to treat it more at large; to pursue it further, and to a greater degree of minuteness; and to present it to the English reader in the easiest and most intelligible form that I am able to give it. The examples with which I shall illustrate it, shall be more numerous, and all (a very few excepted) different from those already given; that they may serve by way of supplement to that part of the former work, as well as of themselves to place the subject in the fullest and clearest light.

Now, in order to make this comparison between the prophetical and the poetical books, it will be necessary, in the first place, to state the true character of the poetical or metrical style, to trace out carefully whatever plain signs or indications yet remain of metre, or rhythm, or whatever else it was that constituted Hebrew verse; to separate the true, or at least the probable, from the manifestly false; and to

* De Sacra Poësi Hebræorum Prælect. xviii. xix.

give as clear and satisfactory an explanation of the matter as can now reasonably be expected, in the present imperfect state of the Hebrew language, and on a subject which for near two thousand years has been involved in great obscurity, and only rendered still more obscure by the discordant opinions of the learned, and the various hypotheses which they have formed concerning it.

The first and most manifest indication of verse in the Hebrew poetical books, presents itself in the acrostic or alphabetical poems; of which there happily remain many examples, and those of various kinds; so that we could not have hoped, or even wished, for more light of this sort to lead us on in the very entrance of our inquiry. The nature, or rather the form, of these poems is this: The poem consists of twenty-two lines, or of twenty-two systems of lines, or periods, or stanzas, according to the number of the letters of the Hebrew alphabet; and every line, or every stanza, begins with each letter in its order, as it stands in the alphabet; that is, the first line, or first stanza, begins with א, the second with ב, and so on. This was certainly intended for the assistance of the memory, and was chiefly employed in subjects of common use, as maxims of morality, and forms of devotion; which being expressed in detached sentences, or aphorisms, (the form in which the sages of the most ancient times delivered their instructions,) the inconvenience arising from the subject, the want of connexion in the parts, and of a regular train of thought carried through the whole, was remedied by this artificial contrivance in the form. There are still extant, in the books of the Old Testament, twelve* of these poems; (for I reckon the four first chapters of the Lamentations of Jeremiah as so many distinct poems); three of them perfectly † alphabetical, in which every line is marked by its initial letter; the other nine less perfectly alphabetical, in which every stanza only is so distinguished. Of the three former it is to be remarked, that not only every single line is distinguished by its initial letter, but that the whole poem is laid out into stanzas; two ‡ of these

---

* Psal. xxv. xxxiv. xxxvii. cxi. cxii. cxix. cxlv.   Prov. xxxi. 10—31. Lam. i. ii. iii. iv.
† Psal. cxi. cxii.   Lam. iii.   ‡ Psal. cxi. cxii.

poems each into ten stanzas, all of two lines, except the two last stanzas in each, which are of three lines: in these, the sense and the construction manifestly point out the division into stanzas, and mark the limit of every stanza. The third* of these perfectly alphabetical poems consists of twenty-two stanzas of three lines; but in this the initial letter of every stanza is also the initial letter of every line of that stanza; so that both the lines and the stanzas are infallibly limited: And in all the three poems, the pauses of the sentences coincide with the pauses of the lines and stanzas.

It is also further to be observed of these three poems, that the lines so determined by the initial letters in the same poem, are remarkably equal to one another in length, in the number of words nearly, and probably in the number of syllables; and that the lines of the same stanza have a remarkable congruity one with another, in the matter and the form, in the sense and the construction.

Of the other nine poems less perfectly alphabetical, in which the stanzas only are marked with initial letters, six † consist of stanzas of two lines, two ‡ of stanzas of three lines, and one § of stanzas of four lines; not taking into the account at present some irregularities, which in all probability are to be imputed to the mistakes of transcribers. And these stanzas likewise naturally divide themselves into their distinct lines, the sense and the construction plainly pointing out their limits; and the lines have the same congruity one with another in matter and form, as was above observed in regard to the poems more perfectly alphabetical.

Another thing to be observed of the three poems perfectly alphabetical is, that in two ‖ of them the lines are shorter than those of the third ** by about one-third part, or almost half; and of the other nine poems, the stanzas only of which are alphabetical, that three†† consist of the longer lines, and the six others of the shorter.

Now from these examples, which are not only curious, but of real use, and of great importance in the present

---

* Lam. iii.
† Psal. xxv. xxxiv. cxix. cxlv.   Prov. xxxi.   Lam. iv.
‡ Lam. i. ii.   § Psal. xxxvii.
‖ Psal. cxi. cxii.   ** Lam. iii.
†† Lam. i. ii. iv.

inquiry, we may draw some conclusions, which plainly follow from the premises, and must be admitted in regard to the alphabetical poems themselves; which also may by analogy be applied with great probability to other poems, where the lines and stanzas are not so determined by initial letters, yet which appear in other respects to be of the same kind.

In the first place, we may safely conclude that the poems perfectly alphabetical consist of verses properly so called; of verses regulated by some observation of harmony or cadence; of measure numbers, or rhythm. For it is not at all probable in the nature of the thing, or from examples of the like kind in other languages, that a portion of mere prose, in which numbers and harmony are totally disregarded, should be laid out according to a scale of division, which carries with it such evident marks of study and labour, of art in the contrivance, and exactness in the execution. And I presume it will be easily granted in regard to the other poems which are divided into stanzas by the initial letters, which stanzas are subdivided by the pauses of the sentence into lines easily distinguished one from another, commonly the same number of lines to a stanza in the same poem, that these are of the same kind of composition with the former, and that they equally consist of verses: And, in general, in regard to the rest of the poems of the Hebrews, bearing evidently the same marks and characteristics of composition with the alphabetical poems in other respects, and falling into regular lines, often into regular stanzas, according to the pauses of the sentences; which stanzas and lines have a certain parity or proportion to one another; that these likewise consist of verse,—of verse distinguished from prose, not only by the style, the figures, the diction, by a loftiness of thought and richness of imagery, but by being divided into lines, and sometimes into systems of lines; which lines, having an apparent equality, similitude, or proportion one to another, were in some sort measured by the ear, and regulated according to some general laws of metre, rhythm, harmony, or cadence.

Further, we may conclude, from the example of the perfectly alphabetical poems, that whatever it might be that constituted Hebrew verse, it certainly did not consist in rhyme, or similar and correspondent sounds at the ends of the verses; for, as the ends of the verses in those poems are infallibly marked, and it plainly appears that the final syllables of the correspondent verses, whether in distichs or triplets, are not similar in sound to one another, it is manifest that rhymes, or similar endings, are not an essential part of Hebrew verses. The grammatical forms of the Hebrew language in the verbs, and pronouns, and the plurals of nouns, are so simple and uniform, and bear so great a share in the termination of words, that similar endings must sometimes happen, and cannot well be avoided; but, so far from constituting an essential or principal part of the art of Hebrew versification, they seem to have been no object of attention and study, nor to have been industriously sought after as a favourite accessary ornament.

That the verses had something regular in their form and composition, seems probable from their apparent parity and uniformity, and the relation which they manifestly bear to the distribution of the sentence into its members. But as to the harmony and cadence, the metre or rhythm, of what kind they were, and by what laws regulated, these examples give us no light, nor afford us sufficient principles on which to build any theory, or to form any hypothesis. For harmony arises from the proportion, relation, and correspondence of different combined sounds; and verse, from the arrangement of words, and the disposition of syllables, according to number, quantity, and accent;—therefore the harmony and true modulation of verse depends upon a perfect pronunciation of the language, and a knowledge of the principles and rules of versification; and metre supposes an exact knowledge of the number and quantity of syllables, and, in some languages, of the accent. But the true pronunciation of Hebrew is lost,—lost to a degree far beyond what can ever be the case of any European language preserved only in writing; for the Hebrew language, like most of the other Oriental languages, expressing only the consonants, and being destitute of its vowels, has lain now for two thousand years in a manner mute and incapable of utterance: the number of syllables is in a great many words uncertain, the quantity and accent wholly unknown. We are ignorant of all these particulars, and incapable of acquiring any certain knowledge concerning them; how then is it possible for us to attain to the knowledge of Hebrew verse? That we know nothing of the quantity of the syllables in Hebrew, and of the number of them in many words, and of the accent, will hardly now be denied by any man;

but if any should still maintain the authority of the Masoretical punctuation, (though discordant in many instances from the imperfect remains of a pronunciation of much earlier date, and of better authority, that of the Seventy, of Origen, and other writers,) yet it must be allowed, that no one, according to that system, hath been able to reduce the Hebrew poems to any sort of harmony.* And indeed it is not to be wondered, that rules of pronunciation, formed, as it is now generally admitted, above a thousand years after the language ceased to be spoken, should fail of giving us the true sound of Hebrew verse. But if it was impossible for the Masoretes, assisted in some measure by a traditionary pronunciation delivered down from their ancestors, to attain to a true expression of the sounds of the language, how is it possible for us at this time, so much further removed from the only source of knowledge in this case, the audible voice, to improve or to amend their system, or to supply a more genuine system in its place, which may answer our purpose better, and lay open to us the laws of Hebrew versification? The pursuit is vain; the object of it lies beyond our reach; it is not within the compass of human reason or invention. The question concerning Hebrew metre is now pretty much upon the same footing with that concerning the Greek accents. That there were certain laws of ancient Hebrew metre is very probable; and that the living Greek language was modulated by certain rules of accent is beyond dispute: but a man born deaf may as reasonably pretend to acquire an idea of sound, as the critic of these days to attain to the true modulation of Greek by accent, and of Hebrew by metre.†

Thus much then, I think, we may be allowed to infer from the alphabetical poems; namely, that the Hebrew poems are written in verse, properly so called; that the harmony of the verses does not arise from rhyme, that is, from similar corresponding sounds terminating the verses, but from some sort of rhythm, probably from some sort of metre, the laws of which are now altogether unknown, and wholly undiscoverable;—yet that there are evident marks of a certain correspondence of the verses with one another, and of a certain relation between the composition of the verses and

---

* See Hare, Prolegomena in Psalmos, p. xl. &c.
† See A Larger Confutation of Bishop Hare's Hebrew Metre; London, 1766; where I have fully treated of this subject.

the composition of the sentences,—the formation of the former depending in some degree upon the distribution of the latter,—so that generally periods coincide with stanzas, members with verses, and pauses of the one with pauses of the other; which peculiar form of composition is so observable, as plainly to discriminate in general the parts of the Hebrew Scriptures which are written in verse, from those which are written in prose. This will require a larger and more minute explication, not only as a matter necessary to our present purpose, that is, to ascertain the character of the prophetical style in general, and of that of the Prophet Isaiah in particular, but as a principle of considerable use, and of no small importance, in the interpretation of the poetical parts of the Old Testament.

The correspondence of one verse or line with another, I call parallelism. When a proposition is delivered, and a second is subjoined to it, or drawn under it, equivalent, or contrasted with it in sense, or similar to it in the form of grammatical construction, these I call parallel lines; and the words or phrases, answering one to another in the corresponding lines, parallel terms.

Parallel lines may be reduced to three sorts,—parallels synonomous, parallels antithetic, and parallels synthetic. Of each of these I shall give a variety of examples, in order to shew the various forms under which they appear; first, from the books-universally acknowledged to be poetical; then, correspondent examples from the Prophet Isaiah, and sometimes also from the other prophets, to shew that the form and character of the composition is in all the same.

As some of the examples which follow are of many lines, the reader may perhaps note a single line or two intermixed, which do not properly belong to that class under which they are ranged. These are retained, to preserve the connexion and harmony of the whole passage; and it is to be observed, that the several sorts of parallels are perpetually mixed with one another, and this mixture gives a variety and beauty to the composition.

First, of parallel lines synonomous; that is, which correspond one to another, by expressing the same sense in different but equivalent terms; when a proposition is delivered, and is immediately repeated, in the whole or in part, the expression being varied, but the sense entirely or nearly the same. As in the following examples:—

"O-Jehovah, in-thy-strength the-king shall-rejoice;
And-in-thy-salvation how greatly shall-he-exult!
The-desire of-his-heart thou-hast-granted unto-him;
And-the-request of-his-lips thou-hast-not denied."
Psal. xxi. 1, 2.

"Because I-called, and-ye-refused;
I-stretched-out my-hand, and-no-one regarded;
But-ye-have-defeated all my-counsel;
And-would-not incline to-my-reproof:
I also will-laugh at-your-calamity;
I-will-mock, when-what-you-feared cometh;
When-what-you-feared cometh like-a-devastation;
And-your-calamity advanceth like-a-tempest;
When-distress and-anguish come upon-you:
Then shall-they-call-upon-me, but-I-will-not answer;
They-shall seek-me-early, but-they-shall not find-me;
Because they-hated knowledge;
And-did-not choose the-fear of-Jehovah;
Did-not incline to-my-counsel;
Contemptuously-rejected all my-reproof:
Therefore-shall-they-eat of-the-fruit of-their-ways;
And-shall-be-satiated with-their-own-devices.
For the-defection of-the-simple shall-slay-them;
And-the-security of-fools shall-destroy them."
Prov. i. 24—32.

"Seek-ye Jehovah, while-he-may-be-found;
Call-ye-upon-him, while-he-is-near;
Let-the-wicked forsake his-way;
And-the-unrighteous man his-thoughts:
And-let-him-return to Jehovah, and-he-will-compassionate him;
And-unto our-God, for he-aboundeth in forgiveness."
Isa. lv. 6, 7.

"Fear not, for thou-shalt-not be-ashamed;
And-blush not, for thou-shalt-not be-brought-to-reproach:
For thou-shalt-forget the-shame of-thy-youth;
And-the-reproach of-thy-widowhood thou-shalt-remember no more."
Isa. liv. 4.

"Hearken unto-me, ye-that-know righteousness;
The-people in-whose-heart is-my-law:
Fear not the-reproach of-wretched-man;
Neither be-ye-borne-down by-their-revilings;

"For the-moth shall-consume-them like-a-garment;
And-the-worm shall-eat-them like wool:
But-my-righteousness shall-endure for-ever;
And-my-salvation to-the-age of-ages."   Isa. li. 7, 8.

"Like-mighty-men shall-they-rush-on;
Like-warriors shall-they mount the-wall:
And-every-one in-his-way shall-they-march;
And-they-shall-not turn-aside from-their paths."   Joel, ii. 7.

"Blessed-is the-man, that-feareth Jehovah;
That-greatly delighteth in-his-commandments."   Psal. cxii. 1.

"Hearken unto me, O-house of-Jacob;
And-all the-remnant of-the-house of-Israel.   Isa. xlvi. 3.

"Honour Jehovah with-thy-riches;
And-with-the-first-fruits of-all thine-increase."   Prov. iii. 9.

"Incline your-ear, and-come unto-me;
Hearken, and-your-soul shall-live."   Isa. lv. 3.

In the foregoing* examples may be observed the different degrees of synonymous parallelism. The parallel lines sometimes consist of three or more synonymous terms; sometimes of two, which is generally the case when the verb, or the nominative case of the first sentence is to be carried on to the second, or understood there; sometimes of one only, as in the four last examples. There are also among the foregoing a few instances, in which the lines consist each of double members, or two propositions. I shall add one or two more of these, very perfect in their kind:—

"Bow thy heavens, O Jehovah, and descend;
Touch the mountains, and they shall smoke:
Dart forth lightning, and scatter them;
Shoot out thine arrows, and destroy them." Psal. cxliv. 5, 6.

"And they shall build houses, and shall inhabit them;
And they shall plant vineyards, and shall eat the fruit thereof:
They shall not build, and another inhabit;
They shall not plant, and another eat:
For as the days of a tree, shall be the days of my people;
And they shall wear out the works of their own hands."
    Isa. lxv. 21, 22.

---

* The terms in English, consisting of several words, are hitherto distinguished with marks of connexion,—to shew, that they answer to single words in Hebrew.

Parallels are also sometimes formed by a repetition of part of the first sentence:—

"My voice is unto God, and I cry aloud;
My voice is unto God, and he will hearken unto me."
"I will remember the works of Jehovah;
Yea, I will remember thy wonders of old."
"The waters saw thee, O God!
The waters saw thee; they were seized with anguish."
Psal. lxxvii. I. 11. 16.

"For he hath humbled those that dwell on high;
The lofty city, he hath brought her down:
He hath brought her down to the ground,
He hath levelled her with the dust.
The foot shall trample upon her;
The feet of the poor, the steps of the needy."
Isa. xxvi. 5, 6.

"What shall I do unto thee, O Ephraim!
What shall I do unto thee, O Judah!
For your goodness is as the morning cloud,
And as the early dew it passeth away."
Hosea, vi. 4.

Sometimes in the latter line a part is to be supplied from the former to complete the sentence:—

"And those that persecute me thou wilt make to turn their backs to me;
Those that hate me,* and I will cut them off."
2 Sam. xxii. 41.

"The mighty dead tremble from beneath;
The waters, and they that dwell therein.
Job, xxvi. 5.

"And I looked, and there was no man;
Even among the idols,† and there was no one that gave advice;"
"And I inquired of them, and [there was no one] that returned an answer."
Isa. xli. 28.

Further, there are parallel triplets—when three lines correspond together, and form a kind of stanza, of which, however, only two commonly are synonymous:—

---

* In the parallel place, Psal. xviii. the poetical form of the sentence is much hurt, by the removing of the conjunction from the second to the first word in this line; but a MS. in that place reads as here.
† See the note on the place.

"The wicked shall see it and it shall grieve him;
He shall gnash his teeth, and pine away;
The desire of the wicked shall perish."   Psal. cxii. 10.

"That day, let it become darkness;
Let not God from above inquire after it;
Nor let the flowing light radiate upon it.
That night, let utter darkness seize it.
Let it not be united with the days of the year;
Let it not come into the number of the months.
Let the stars of its twilight be darkened;
Let it look for light, and may there be none;
And let it not behold the eyelids of the morning."
                                             Job, iii. 4. 6. 9.

"And he shall snatch on the right, and yet be hungry;
And he shall devour on the left, and not be satisfied;
Every man shall devour the flesh of his neighbour."*
                                             Isa. ix. 20.

"Put ye in the sickle, for the harvest is ripe;
Come away, get you down, for the wine-press is full;
The vats overflow; for great is their wickedness."
                                             Joel, iii. 13.

There are likewise parallels consisting of four lines; two distichs being so connected together, by the sense and the construction, as to make one stanza. Such is the form of the xxxviith Psalm, which is evidently laid out by the initial letters in stanzas of four lines; though in regard to that disposition some irregularities are found in the present copies. From this Psalm, which gives a sufficient warrant for considering the union of two distichs as making a stanza of four lines, I shall take the first example:—

"Be not moved with indignation against the evil-doers;
Nor with zeal against the workers of iniquity:
For like the grass they shall soon be cut off;
And like the green herb they shall wither.
                                             Psal. xxxvii. 1, 2.

"The ox knoweth his possessor;
And the ass the crib of his lord:
But Israel doth not know Me;*
Neither doth my people consider."   Isa. i. 3.

"And I said, I have laboured in vain;
For nought and for vanity I have spent my strength:

---
* See the note on the place.

Nevertheless my cause is with Jehovah;
And the reward of my work with my God.   Isa. xlix. 4.

" Jehovah shall roar from Sion;
And shall utter his voice from Jerusalem:
And the habitations of the shepherds shall mourn;
And the head of Carmel shall wither."   Amos, i. 2.

In like manner, some periods may be considered as making stanzas of five lines, in which the odd line or member either comes in between two distichs, or after two distichs makes a full close:—

" If thou wouldst seek early unto God;
And make thy supplication to the Almighty;
If thou wert pure and upright;
Verily now would he rise up in thy defence;
And make peaceable the dwelling of thy righteousness.
Job, viii. 5, 6.

" They bear him on the shoulder; they carry him about;
They set him down in his place, and he standeth;
From his place he shall not remove;
To him, that crieth unto him, he will not answer;
Neither will he deliver him from his distress."
Isa. xlvi. 7.

" Who is wise, and will understand these things?
Prudent, and will know them?
For right are the ways of Jehovah;
And the just shall walk in them;
But the disobedient shall fall therein."   Hosea, xiv. 9.

" And Jehovah shall roar out of Sion;
And from Jerusalem shall utter his voice;
And the heavens and the earth shall tremble:
But Jehovah will be the refuge of his people;
And a strong defence to the sons of Israel."   Joel, iii. 16.

" Who establisheth the word of his servant;
And accomplisheth the counsel of his messengers:
Who sayeth to Jerusalem, Thou shalt be inhabited;
And to the cities of Judah, Ye shall be built;
And her desolate places I will restore."   Isa. xliv. 26.

In stanzas of four lines, sometimes the parallel lines answer to one another alternately; the first to the third, and the second to the fourth:—

" As the heavens are high above the earth ;
   So high* is his goodness over them that fear him:
As remote as the east is from the west;
   So far hath he removed from us our transgressions."
                                                    Psal. ciii. 11, 12.

" And ye said, Nay, but on horses will we flee;
   Therefore shall ye be put to flight:
And on swift coursers will we ride;
   Therefore shall they be swift, that pursue you."
                                                    Isa. xxx. 16.

And a stanza of five lines admits of the same elegance :—

" Who is there among you that feareth Jehovah?
   Let him hearken unto the voice of his servant:
That walketh in darkness, and hath no light?
   Let him trust in the name of Jehovah;
   And rest himself on the support of his God."   Isa. l. 10.

The second sort of parallels are the antithetic,—when two lines correspond with one another by an opposition of terms and sentiments; when the second is contrasted with the first, sometimes in expressions, sometimes in sense only. Accordingly the degrees of antithesis are various; from an exact contraposition of word to word through the whole sentence, down to a general disparity, with something of a contrariety, in the two propositions.

Thus, in the following examples :—

" A wise son rejoiceth his father ;
   But a foolish son is the grief of his mother."   Prov. x. 1.

Where every word hath its opposite; for the terms *father* and *mother* are, as the logicians say, relatively opposite.

" The memory of the just is a blessing ;
   But the name of the wicked shall rot."   Prov. x. 7.

Here there are only two antithetic terms; for *memory* and *name* are synonymous.

"There is that scattereth, and still increaseth ;
   And that is unreasonably sparing, yet groweth poor."
                                                    Prov. xi. 24.

* גבה ; compare the next verse; and see Isaiah, lv. 9, and the note there.

Here there is a kind of double antithesis; one between the two lines themselves; and likewise a subordinate opposition between the two parts of each.

"Many seek the face of the prince;
But the determination concerning a man is from Jehovah."
Prov. xxix. 26.

Where the opposition is chiefly between the single terms, the Prince and Jehovah: but there is an opposition likewise in the general sentiment; which expresses, or intimates, the vanity of depending on the former, without seeking the favour of the latter. In the following, there is much the same opposition of sentiment, without any contraposition of terms at all:—

"The lot is cast into the lap;
But the whole determination of it is from Jehovah."
Prov. xvi. 33.

That is, the event seems to be the work of chance, but is really the direction of Providence.

The foregoing examples are all taken from the Proverbs of Solomon, where they abound: for this form is peculiarly adapted to that kind of writing—to adages, aphorisms, and detached sentences. Indeed, the elegance, acuteness, and force of a great number of Solomon's wise sayings, arise in a great measure from the antithetic form, the opposition of diction and sentiment. We are not therefore to expect frequent instances of it in the other poems of the Old Testament; especially those that are elevated in the style, and more connected in the parts. However, I shall add a few examples of the like kind from the higher poetry.

"These in chariots, and those in horses;
But we in the name of Jehovah our God will be strong.*
They are bowed down, and fallen;
But we are risen, and maintain ourselves firm." Psal. xx. 7, 8.

"For his wrath is but for a moment, his favour for life;
Sorrow may lodge for the evening, but in the morning gladness." Psal. xxx. 5.

"Yet a little while, and the wicked shall be no more;
Thou shalt look at his place, and he shall not be found:

---

* נגביר, so LXX, Syr. Æthiop.

But the meek shall inherit the land;
And delight themselves in abundant prosperity."
Psal. xxxvii. 10, 11.

In the last example the opposition lies between the two parts of a stanza of four lines, the latter distich being opposed to the former. So likewise the following:—

" For the mountains shall be removed;
And the hills shall be overthrown:
But my kindness from thee shall not be removed;
And the covenant of my peace shall not be overthrown."
Isa. liv. 10.

" The bricks are fallen, but we will build with hewn stone;
The sycamores are cut down, but we will replace them with cedars."
Isa. ix. 10.

Here the lines themselves are synthetically parallel; and the opposition lies between the two members of each.

The third sort of parallels I call synthetic or constructive —where the parallelism consists only in the similar form of construction; in which word does not answer to word, and sentence to sentence, as equivalent or opposite; but there is a correspondence and equality between different propositions, in respect of the shape and turn of the whole sentence, and of the constructive parts—such as noun answering to noun, verb to verb, member to member, negative to negative, interrogative to interrogative.

" Praise ye Jehovah, ye of the earth;
Ye sea-monsters, and all deeps:
Fire and hail, snow and vapour;
Stormy wind, executing his command:
Mountains, and all hills;
Fruit-trees, and all cedars:
Wild beasts, and all cattle;
Reptiles, and birds of wing:
Kings of the earth, and all peoples;
Princes, and all judges of the earth:
Youths, and also virgins;
Old men, together with the children:
Let them praise the name of Jehovah;
For his name alone is exalted;
His majesty, above earth and heaven." Psal. cxlviii. 7—13.

"With him is wisdom and might;
To him belong counsel and understanding.
Lo! he pulleth down, and it shall not be built;
He encloseth a man, and he shall not be set loose.
Lo! he withholdeth the waters, and they are dried up;
And he sendeth them forth, and they overturn the earth.
With him is strength, and perfect existence;
The deceived, and the deceiver, are his." Job, xii. 13—16.

" Is such then the fast which I choose;
That a man should afflict his soul for a day?
Is it, that he should bow down his head like a bulrush;
And spread sackcloth and ashes for his couch?
Shall this be called a fast;
And a day acceptable to Jehovah?—
Is not this the fast that I choose?
To dissolve the bands of wickedness;
To loosen the oppressive burthens;
To deliver those that are crushed by violence;
And that ye should break asunder every yoke?
Is it not to distribute thy bread to the hungry;
And to bring the wandering poor into thy house?
When thou seest the naked, that thou clothe him;
And that thou hide not thyself from thine own flesh?
Then shall thy light break forth like the morning;
And thy wounds shall speedily be healed over:
And thy righteousness shall go before thee;
And the glory of Jehovah shall bring up thy rear."
Isa. lxiii. 5—8.

Of the constructive kind is most commonly the parallelism of stanzas of three lines; though they are sometimes synonymous throughout, and often have two lines synonymous; examples of both which are above given. The following are constructively parallel:—

" Whatsoever Jehovah pleaseth,
That doeth he in the heavens, and in the earth;
In the sea, and in all the deeps:
Causing the vapours to ascend from the ends of the earth;
Making the lightnings with the rain;
Bringing forth the wind out of his treasures."
Psal. cxxxv 6, 7

" The Lord Jehovah hath opened mine ear.
And I was not rebellious;
Neither did I withdraw myself backward,—
I gave my back to the smiters,

And my cheeks to them that plucked off the hair;
My face I hid not from shame and spitting." Isa. l. 5, 6.

" Thou shalt sow, but shall not reap;
Thou shalt tread the olive, but shalt not anoint thee with oil;
And the grape, but shalt not drink wine." Micah, vi. 15.

Of the same sort of parallelism are those passages frequent in the poetic books, where a definite number is twice put for an indefinite; this being followed by an enumeration of particulars, naturally throws the sentences into a parallelism, which cannot be of any other than the synthetic kind. This seems to have been a favourite ornament. There are many elegant examples of it in the xxxth chapter of Proverbs, to which I refer the reader; and shall here give one or two from other places.

" These six things Jehovah hateth;
And seven are the abomination of his soul:—
Lofty eyes, and a lying tongue;
And hands shedding innocent blood:
A heart fabricating wicked thoughts;
Feet hastily running to mischief:
A false witness breathing out lies;
And the sower of strife between brethren." Prov. vi. 16—19.

" Give a portion to seven, and also to eight;
For thou knowest not what evil shall be upon the earth."
Eccl. xi. 2.

" These two things have befallen thee; who shall bemoan thee?
Desolation and destruction, the famine and the sword; who shall comfort thee?" Isa. li. 19.

that is, taken alternately, desolation by famine, and destruction by the sword. Of which alternate construction I shall add a remarkable example or two, where the parallelism arises from the alternation of the members of the sentences:—

" I am black, but yet beautiful, O daughters of Jerusalem:
Like the tents of Kedar; like the pavilions of Solomon."
Cant. i. 5.

that is, black as the tents of Kedar, (made of dark-coloured goats hair); beautiful as the pavilions of Solomon.

" On her house-tops, and to her open streets,
Every one howleth, descendeth with weeping." Isa. xv. 3.

that is, every one howleth on her house-tops, and descendeth with weeping to her open streets.

The reader will observe in the foregoing examples, that though there are perhaps no two lines corresponding one with another as equivalent, or opposite in terms; yet there is a parallelism equally apparent, and almost as striking, which arises from the similar form and equality of the lines, from the correspondence of the members and the construction; the consequence of which is a harmony and rhythm little inferior in effect to that of the two kinds preceding.

The degrees of the correspondence of the lines in this last sort of parallels must, from the nature of it, be various. Sometimes the parallelism is more, sometimes less exact; sometimes hardly at all apparent. It requires indeed particular attention, much study of the genius of the language, much habitude in the analysis of the construction, to be able in all cases to see and to distinguish the nice rests and pauses which ought to be made, in order to give the period or the sentence its intended turn and cadence, and to each part its due time and proportion. The Jewish critics, called the Masoretes, were exceedingly attentive to their language in this part, even to a scrupulous exactness and subtile refinement, as it appears from that extremely complicated system of grammatical punctuation, more embarrassing than useful, which they have invented. It is therefore not improbable, that they might have had some insight into this matter; and, in distinguishing the parts of the sentence by accents, might have had regard to the harmony of the period and the proportion of the members, as well as to the strict grammatical disposition of the constructive parts. Of this, I think, I perceive evident tokens; for they sometimes seem to have more regard in distributing the sentence to the poetical or rhetorical harmony of the period, and the proportion of the members, than to the grammatical construction. To explain what I mean, I shall here give some examples, in which the Masoretes, in distinguishing the sentence into its parts, have given marks of pauses perfectly agreeable to the poetical rhythm, but such as the grammatical construction does not require, and scarcely admits. Though it is a difficult matter to know the precise quantity of time which they allot to every distinctive point; for it depends on the relation and proportion which it bears to the whole arrangement of points throughout the sentence;

and though it is impossible to express the great variety of them by our scanty system of punctuation,—yet I shall endeavour to mark them out to the English reader, in a rude manner, so as to give him some notion of what I imagine it to have been their design to express. Thus then they distinguish the following sentences:—

"And they that recompense evil for good ;*
Are mine adversaries, because I follow what is good."
Psal. xxxviii. 20.

"Upon Jehovah, in my distress ;*
I called, and he heard me."
"Long hath my soul had her dwelling ;*
With him that hateth peace." Psal. cxx. 1. 6.

"I love Jehovah, for he hath heard ;*
The voice of my supplication.
I will walk, before Jehovah ;*
In the land of the living.
What shall I return unto Jehovah ;*
For all the benefits which he hath bestowed on me?
My vows I will pay to Jehovah ;*
Now in the presence of all his people.
Precious in the eyes of Jehovah ;*
Is the death of his saints." Psal. cxvi. 1. 9. 12. 14, 15.

"Yea the stars of heaven and the constellations thereof,†
Shall not send forth their light." Isa. xiii. 10.

"In that day, shall his strongly fenced cities become,‡
Like the desertion of the Hivites and the Amorites."
Isa. xvii. 9.

"For the glorious name of Jehovah shall be unto us,†
A place of confluent streams, of broad rivers."
Isa. xxxiii. 21.

"That she hath received at the hand of Jehovah,†
Double of the punishment of all her sins." Isa. xl. 2.

Of the three different sorts of parallels, as above explained, every one hath its peculiar character and proper effect;

---

* Athnac. † Zakeph-katon. ‡ Rebiah.

Athnac in the three metrical books, as the Jews account them, is but the third in order of power among the distinctive points; but, however, always takes place when the period is of two members only; in all the other books he is second: in the latter, therefore, *Rebiah* and *Zakeph-katon*, which come next to Athnac, have nearly the same distinctive power as Athnac has in the former. They will scarce be thought over-rated at a comma.

and therefore they are differently employed on different occasions; and that sort of parallelism is chiefly made use of which is best adapted to the nature of the subject and of the poem. Synonymous parallels have the appearance of art and concinnity, and a studied elegance: they prevail chiefly in shorter poems; in many of the Psalms; in Balaam's prophecies; frequently in those of Isaiah which are most of them distinct poems of no great length. The antithetic parallelism gives an acuteness and force to adages and moral sentences; and therefore, as I observed before, abounds in Solomon's Proverbs, and elsewhere is not often to be met with. The poem of Job, being on a large plan, and in a high tragic style, though very exact in the division of the lines, and in the parallelism, and affording many fine examples of the synonymous kind, yet consists chiefly of the constructive. A happy mixture of the several sorts gives an agreeable variety; and they serve mutually to recommend and set off one another.

I mentioned above, that there appeared to be two sorts of Hebrew verses, differing from one another in regard to their length: the examples hitherto given are all, except one, of the shorter kind of verse. The longer, though they admit of every sort of parallelism, yet belonging for the most part to the last class, that of constructive parallels, I shall treat of them in this place, and endeavour to explain the nature, and to point out the marks of them, as fully and exactly as I can.

This distinction of Hebrew verses into longer and shorter, is founded on the authority of the alphabetical poems; one third of the whole number of which are manifestly of the longer sort of verse, the rest of the shorter. I do not presume exactly to define by the number of syllables, supposing we could with some probability determine it, the limit that separates one sort of verse from the other, so that every verse exceeding or falling short of that number should be always accounted a long or a short verse; all that I affirm is this,—that one of the three poems perfectly alphabetical, and therefore infallibly divided into its verses; and three of the nine other alphabetical poems, divided into their verses, after the manner of the perfectly alphabetical, with the greatest degree of probability; that these four poems, being the four first Lamentations of Jeremiah, fall into verses about one-third longer, taking them one with another than those of the other eight alphabetical poems. I shall first give an example of these long verses from a poem perfectly alphabetical, in which therefore the limits of the verses are unerringly defined :—

"I am the man that hath seen affliction, by the rod of his anger:
He hath led me, and made me walk, in darkness, not in light:
Even again turneth he his hand against me, all the day long.
He hath made old my flesh and my skin, he hath broken my bones:
He hath built against me, and hath compassed me, with gall and travail:
He hath made me dwell in dark places, as the dead of old."
Lam. iii. 1—6.

The following is from the first Lamentation, in which the stanzas are defined by initial letters, and are, like the former, of three lines :—

"How doth the city solitary sit, she that was full of people!
How is she become a widow, that was great among the nations!
Princess among the provinces, how is she become tributary!
She weepeth sore in the night, and her tear is upon her cheek:
She hath none to comfort her, among all her lovers:
All her friends have betrayed her, they became her enemies."
Lam. i. 1, 2.

I shall now give examples of the same sort of verse, where the limits of the verses are to be collected only from the poetical construction of the sentences ;—and first from the books acknowledged on all hands to be poetical ; and of these we must have recourse to the Psalms only, for I believe there is not a single instance of this sort of verse to be found in the poem of Job, and scarce any in the Proverbs of Solomon.

"The law of Jehovah is perfect, restoring the soul;
The testimony of Jehovah is sure, making wise the simple:
The precepts of Jehovah are right, rejoicing the heart;
The commandment of Jehovah is clear, enlightening the eyes:
The fear of Jehovah is pure, enduring for ever;

The judgments of Jehovah are truth; they are altogether righteous:
More desirable than gold, and than much fine gold;
And sweeter than honey, and the dropping of honey-combs."
Psal. xix. 7—10.

" That our sons may be like plants, growing up in their youth;
Our daughters like the corner-pillars, carved for the structure of a palace:
Our store-houses full, producing all kinds of provision:
Our flocks bringing forth thousands, ten thousands in our fields:
Our oxen strong to labour; no irruption, no captivity;
And no outcry in our streets." Psal. cxliv. 12—14.

" Oh! how great is thy goodness which thou hast treasured up, for them that fear thee;
Which thou hast wrought for them that trust in thee, before the sons of men!
Thou wilt hide them in the secret place of thy presence, from the vexations of man;
Thou wilt keep them safe in the tabernacle, from the strife of tongues." Psal. xxxi. 19, 20.

" A sound of a multitude in the mountains, as of many people;
A sound of the tumult of kingdoms, of nations gathered together:
Jehovah God of Hosts mustereth the host for the battle.
They come from a distant land, from the end of heaven;
Jehovah and the instruments of his wrath, to destroy the whole land." Isa. xiii. 4, 5.

" They are turned backward, they are utterly confounded, who trust in the graven image;
Who say unto the molten image, ye are our gods!"
Isa. xlii. 17.

" They are ashamed, they are even confounded, his * adversaries all of them;
Together they retire in confusion, the fabricators of images:
But Israel shall be saved in Jehovah, with eternal salvation;
Ye shall not be ashamed, neither shall ye be confounded, to the ages of eternity." Isa. xlv. 16, 17.

These examples, all except the two first, are of long verses thrown in irregularly, but with design, between

---

* See the note on the place.

verses of another sort; among which they stand out, as it were, somewhat distinguished in regard to their matter as well as their form.

I think I perceive some peculiarities in the cast and structure of these verses, which mark them, and distinguish them from those of the other sort. The closing pause of each line is generally very full and strong; and in each line, commonly towards the end, at least beyond the middle of it, there is a small rest or interval, depending on the sense and grammatical construction, which I would call a half-pause.

The conjunction ו, the common particle of connexion, which abounds in the Hebrew language, and is very often used without any necessity at all, seems to be frequently and studiously omitted at the half-pause; the remaining clause being added, to use a grammatical term, by apposition to some word preceding; or coming in as an adjunct, or circumstance depending on the former part, and completing the sentence. This gives a certain air to these verses, which may be esteemed in some sort as characteristic of the kind.

The first four Lamentations are four distinct poems, consisting uniformly and entirely of * the long verse, which may therefore be properly called the Elegiac verse—from those elegies, which give the plainest and the most undoubted examples of it. There may perhaps be found many other very probable examples in the same kind; but this is what I cannot pretend to determine with any certainty. Such, I think, are the 42d and 43d Psalms; which I imagine make

---

* In the second Lamentation, the second line of the fourth period is deficient in length; and so likewise is the 31st verse of the third Lamentation. In the former, two words are lost out of the text; in the latter, one. This will plain appear by supplying those words from the Chaldee paraphrase, which has happily preserved them. They prove their own genuineness by making the line of a just length, and by completely restoring the sense; which in the former is otherwise not unexceptionable, in the latter manifestly imperfect. I will ad the lines, with the words supplied included in crotchets.

ויהרג [כל נער] כל מחמדי־עיז

"And he slew [every youth] all that were desirable to the eye."

כי לא יונח לעולם [עבדיו] אדני

"For the Lord will not cast off [his servants] forever."

one entire poem,* and ought not to have been divided into two Psalms: the lines are all of the longer kind, except the third line of the intercalary stanza three times inserted; which third line, like that at the close of an example given above from the 144th Psalm, is of the shorter kind of verse, somewhat like the Parœmiac verse of the Greeks, which commonly makes the close of a set of Anapæstic verses. Such likewise may perhaps be the 101st Psalm, which seems to consist of fourteen long verses, or seven distichs, thus divided:—

" Mercy and judgment will I celebrate; to thee, O Jehovah, will I sing.
I will act circumspectly in the perfect way; when wilt thou come unto me?
I will walk with a perfect heart, in the midst of my house;
I will not set before mine eyes, a wicked thing;
Him that dealeth unfaithfully, I hate; he shall not cleave unto me;
A perverse heart shall remove from me; the wicked I will not know.
Whoso slandereth in secret his friend, him will I destroy.
The lofty of eyes, and the proud of heart, him I will not endure.
Mine eyes shall be on the faithful of the land, that they may dwell with me:
Whoso walketh in the perfect way, he shall minister unto me.
He shall not dwell within my house, who practiseth deceit.
He that speaketh falsehood, shall not be established in my sight.
Every morning will I destroy all the wicked of the land;
To cut off, from the city of Jehovah, all the workers of iniquity."

The sublime ode of Isaiah in the 14th chapter is all of this kind of verse, except, perhaps, a verse or two towards the end; and the prophecy against Senacherib in the 37th chapter, as far as it addressed Senacherib himself.

I venture to submit to the judgment of the candid reader the preceding observations, upon a subject which hardly admits of proof and certainty; which is rather a matter of opinion and of taste, than of science; especially in the latter

---

* This conjecture, offered some years ago, has since been confirmed by twenty-two MSS, which join them together.

part, which endeavours to establish, and to point out the difference of two sorts of verse, the longer and the shorter. For though the third Lamentation of Jeremiah gives a clear and indubitable example of the elegiac or long verse, and the two Psalms perfectly alphabetical of the shorter; yet the whole art of Hebrew versification, except only what appears in the construction of the sentences, being totally lost, it is not easy to try by them other passages of verse, so as to draw any certain conclusion in all cases, whether they are of the same kind or not: And that, for this among other reasons; because what I call the half-pause, which I think prevails for the most part in the longer verses, is sometimes so strong and so full in the middle of the line, that it seems naturally to resolve it into a distich of two short verses. I readily therefore acknowledge, that in settling the distribution of the lines, or verses, in the following translation, I have had frequent doubts and particularly in determining the long and short verses. I am still uncertain in regard to many places, whether two lines ought not to be joined to make one, or one line divided into two. But whatever doubts may remain concerning particulars, yet, upon the whole, I should hope that the method of distribution here proposed, of sentences into stanzas and verses in the poetical books of Scripture, will appear to have some foundation, and even to carry with it a considerable degree of probability. Though no complete system of rules concerning this matter can perhaps be formed, which will hold good in every particular; yet this way of considering the subject may have its use, in furnishing a principle of interpretation of some consequence, in giving a general idea of the style and character of the Hebrew poetry, and in shewing the close conformity of style and character between great part of the prophetical writings, and the other books of the Old Testament universally acknowledged to be poetical.

And that the reader may not think his pains wholly lost, in labouring through this long disquisition concerning sentences, and members of sentences, in weighing words and balancing periods, I shall endeavour to shew him something of the use and application of the preceding observations; and to convince him, that this branch of criticism, minute as it may appear, yet merits the attention of the translator and of the interpreter of the Holy Scriptures; so large a part of which is entirely poetical, and where occasional pieces of poetry are interspersed through the whole.

It is incumbent on every translator to study the manner of his author; to mark the peculiarities of his style, to imitate his features, his air, his gesture, and, as far as the difference of language will permit, even his voice; in a word, to give a just and expressive resemblance of the original. If he does not carefully attend to this, he will sometimes fail of entering into his meaning; he will always exhibit him unlike himself,—in a dress, that will appear strange and unbecoming to all that are in any degree acquainted with him. Sebastian Castellio stands in the first rank for critical abilities and theological learning, among the modern translators of Scripture; but, by endeavouring to give the whole composition of his translation a new cast, to throw it out of the Hebrew idiom, and to make it adopt the Latin phrase and structure in its stead, he has given us something that is neither Hebrew nor Latin: the Hebrew manner is destroyed, and the Latin manner is not perfectly acquired; we regret the loss of the Hebrew simplicity, and we are disgusted with the perpetual affectation of Latin elegance. This is in general the case, but chiefly in the poetical parts. Take the following for a specimen.

" Quum Israelitæ ex Ægypto, quum Jacobæa domus emigraret
    ex populo barbaro,
Judæi Israelitæ Deo fuere sanctitati atque potestati.
Quo viso, mare fugit, et Jordanis retrocessit.
Montes arietum, colles ove natorum ritu exiliverunt."

Surely to this even the barbarism of the Vulgate is preferable; for though it has no elegance of its own, yet it still retains the form, and gives us some idea of the force and spirit of the Hebrew. I will subjoin it here, for it needs not fear the comparison.

" In exitu Israel de Ægypto, domûs Jacob de populo barbaro,
Facta est Judæa sanctificatio ejus, Israel potestas ejus.
Mare vidit, et fugit: Jordanis conversus est retrorsum.
Montes exultaverunt ut arietes: et colles sicut agni ovium."

Flatness and insipidity will generally be the consequence of a deviation from the native manner of an original, which has a real merit and a peculiar force of its own: for it will be very difficult to compensate the loss of this by any adventitious ornaments. To express fully and exactly the sense of the author is indeed the principal, but not the whole duty of the translator. In a work of elegance and genius, he is not only to inform, he must endeavour to please; and to please by the same means, if possible, by which his author pleases. If this pleasure arises in a great measure from the shape of the composition and the form of the construction, as it does in the Hebrew poetry perhaps beyond any other example whatsoever, the translator's eye ought to be always intent upon this: to neglect this, is to give up all chance of success, and all pretension to it. The importance of the subject, and the consequent necessity of keeping closely to the letter of the original, has confined the translators of Scripture within such narrow limits, that they have been forced, whether they designed it or not, and even sometimes contrary to their design, as in the case of Castellio, to retain much of the Hebrew manner. This is remarkably the case in our vulgar translation, the constant use of which has rendered this manner familiar and agreeable to us. We have adopted the Hebrew taste; and what is with judgment, and upon proper occasion, well expressed in that taste, hardly ever fails to suggest the ideas of beauty, solemnity, and elevation. To shew the difference in this respect, I shall here give an example or two of a free and loose translation, yet sufficiently well expressing the sense, contrasted with another translation of the same, as strictly literal as possible.

1. "The merciful and gracious Lord hath so done his marvellous works, that they ought to be had in remembrance."
Psal. cxi. 4. Old Version.

2. "Lo! children and the fruit of the womb are an heritage and gift, that cometh from the Lord." Psal. cxxvii. 4. O. V.

3. "O put not your trust in princes, nor in any child of man; for there is no help in them.
"For when the breath of man goeth forth, he shall turn again to his earth; and then all his thoughts perish.
4. "The Lord thy God, O Sion, shall be king for evermore, and throughout all generations. Psal. cxlvi. 2, 3. 10. O. V.

1. "He hath made a memorial of his wonders: gracious and of tender mercy is Jehovah."
2. "Behold, an heritage from Jehovah are children; a reward, the fruit of the womb."

3. "Trust ye not in princes; in the son of man, in whom is no salvation.

"His breath goeth forth; he returneth to his earth; in that day his thoughts perish.

4. "Jehovah shall reign for ever; thy God, O Sion, from age to age."

The former examples are mere prose; the latter retain the outlines and the features of the original Hebrew, and from that cause alone are still poetry.

But this strict attention to the form and fashion of the composition of the sacred writings of the Old Testament is not only useful, and even necessary, in the translator who is ambitious of preserving in his copy the force, and spirit, and elegance of the original; it will be of great use to him likewise merely as an interpreter, and will often lead him into the meaning of obscure words and phrases: sometimes it will suggest the true reading, where the text in our present copies is faulty; and will verify and confirm a correction offered on the authority of MSS, or of the ancient versions. I shall add a few examples, as evidences of what is here advanced. One short passage of Isaiah will furnish a number sufficient for our purpose; and the observant reader will find several more in the version and notes subjoined.

" Wherefore hear ye the word of Jehovah, ye scoffers;
Ye who to this people in Jerusalem utter sententious speeches.
Who say, We have entered into a covenant with death;
And with the grave we have made a treaty.——
But your covenant with death shall be broken;
And your treaty with the grave shall not stand."

Isa. xxviii. 14, 15. 18.

משלי, ye that *rule* this people, says our version; and so the generality of interpreters ancient and modern. But this prophecy is not addressed to the rulers of the people; nor is it at all concerned with them in particular, but is directed to the Ephraimites in general; and this part to the scoffers among them, who ridiculed the denunciations of the prophets, by giving out parabolical sentences, and solemn speeches, somewhat in the prophetic style, in opposition to their prophecies; of which speeches he gives specimens in the next verse, as he had done before in the 9th and 10th verses. משלי therefore is parallel and synonymous to אנשי לצון,

scoffers; and is not to be translated *rulers,* but to be taken in the other sense of the word, and rendered, "those that speak parables." And Iarchi in this place very properly explains it, "qui dicunt verba irrisionis parabolicè."

The next verse gives us an instance still more remarkable of the influence which the parallelism has in determining the sense of words:

> "We have entered into a covenant with death;
> And with the grave we have made ———"

what? Every one must answer immediately, an agreement, a bargain, a treaty, or something to the same sense: and so in effect say all the versions, ancient and modern. But the word חזה means no such thing in any part of the Bible; (except in the 18th verse of this chapter, here quoted, where it is repeated in the same sense, and nearly in the same form); nor can the lexicographers give any satisfactory account of the word in this sense; which however they are forced to admit from the necessity of the case; " Rectè verto vocem חזה, perinde ac חזות, v. 18. *transactionem,* licet neutra hac significatione alibi occurrat: circumstantia enim orationis eam necessariò exigit;" says the learned Vitringa upon the place. It could not otherwise have been known that the word had this meaning; it is the parallelism alone that determines it to this meaning; and that so clearly, that no doubt at all remains concerning the sense of the passage.

Again:—

> "And your covenant with death shall *be broken:*"

But כפר means to *cover,* to *cover sin,* and so to *expiate,* &c. and is never used in the sense of *breaking* or *dissolving* a covenant, though that notion so often occurs in the Scriptures; nor can it be forced into this sense, but by a great deal of far-fetched reasoning. Besides, it ought to be כפרה, or תכפר, in the feminine form, to agree with ברית. So that the word, as it stands, makes neither grammar nor sense. There is great reason therefore to suspect some mistake in our present copy. The true reading is probably תפר, differing by one letter. So conjectured Houbigant; and so Archbishop Secker: and I find their conjecture confirmed by the Chaldee paraphrast, who renders it by בטל, the word which he generally uses in rendering this common phrase, הֵפִיר בְּרִית. And this reading is still further confirmed by the parallelism; for הֻפַר, *shall be broken*, in the first line, is parallel and synonymous to לֹא תקוּם, *shall not stand*, in the second.

The very same phrases are parallel and synonymous, Isa. viii. 10.

" Take counsel together, and it shall come to nought, וְתֻפָר;
Speak the word, and it shall not stand, וְלֹא יָקוּם."

I shall add one example more; and that of a reading suggested by the parallelism, and destitute of all authority of MSS, or ancient versions.

" But mine enemies *living* are numerous;
And they that hate me wrongfully are multiplied."
Psal. xxxviii. 19.

The word חַיִּים, *living*, seems not to belong to this place; besides, that the construction of it in the Hebrew is very unusual and inelegant. The true reading in all probability is חִנָּם, *without cause*; parallel and synonymous to שֶׁקֶר, *wrongfully*, in the next line, (as in Psal. xxxv. 19.); which completes the parallelism through both lines. Let the reader compare Psal. lxix. 5. where the very same three terms in each line are set parallel to one another, just in the same manner as I suppose they must have been originally here. Which place likewise furnishes another example in the same kind: for a fourth term being there introduced in each line, the fourth term in the last line has been corrupted by the small mistake of inserting a י in the middle of it. It has been well restored by a conjecture of the learned and ingenious Bishop Hare.

" They that hate me without cause are multiplied beyond the hairs of my head;
They that are mine enemies wrongfully are more numerous then the hairs of my locks."

For מַצְמִיתַי, *who destroy me*, read מִצַּמַּת, *more than my locks*, parallel to מִשַּׂעֲרוֹת רֹאשִׁי, *more than the hairs of my head*, in the first line. The Bishop's conjecture is since confirmed by seven MSS.

Thus two inveterate mistakes, which have disgraced the text above two thousand years, (for they are prior to the version of the seventy,) are happily corrected, and that, I think, beyond a doubt, by the parallelism supported by the example of similar passages.

RABBI AZARIAS,* a learned Jew of the sixteenth century, has treated of the ancient Hebrew versification upon principles similar to those above proposed, and partly coincident with them: he makes the form of the verse to depend on the structure of the sentence, and the measures in every verse to be determined by the several parts of the proposition. As he is the only one of the Jewish writers, who appears to have had any just idea at all of this matter; as his system seems to be well founded; and as his observations may be of use on the present occasion, both by giving some degree of authority to the hypothesis above explained, and by setting the subject in a light somewhat different,—I shall here give the reader at large his opinion upon it.

This author in a large work entitled *Meor Enajim*, (that is, *The light of the Eyes*,) containing a great variety of matter, historical, critical, and philosophical, takes occasion to treat of the Hebrew poetry in a separate chapter; of which the younger Buxtorf has given a Latin translation. †

" Azarias finding little satisfaction in what former writers had said upon the subject; whether those who make the Hebrew verse consist of a certain number of syllables and certain feet, like that of the Greeks and Latins; or those who exclude all metre, and make the harmony of their verse to arise from accents, tones, and musical modulations; which latter opinion he thinks agreeable to truth;—and having consulted the most learned of his nation without being able to obtain any solution of his difficulties; for they allowed that there was a sensible difference between the songs and the other parts of the Hebrew Scriptures when they were read;

---

* R. Azarias Min Haadumim, *i.e.* de Rubeis, or Rossi, of Ferrara, finished his treatise entitled *Meor Enajim*, A. D. 1573, and published it at Mantua, the place of his birth, 1574. Wolfii Biblioth. Hebræa, vol. i. p. 944.

† Mantissa Dissertationum, p. 415. at the end of his edition of Cosri. Suspecting, from some obscurities, that Buxtorf's translation was not very accurate, I procured the original edition; and having carefully examined it, I corrected from it this account of the author's sentiments.

a kind of metrical sweetness in the former, which the latter had not; but whence that difference arose no one could explain;—in this state of uncertainty, he long considered the matter, endeavouring to obtain some satisfaction in his inquiries. He at last came to the following determination upon it:—That the sacred songs have undoubtedly certain measures and proportions; which, however, do not consist in the number of syllables, perfect or imperfect, according to the form of the modern verse which the Jews make use of, and which is borrowed from the Arabians; (though the Arabic prosody, he observes, is too complicated to be applied to the Hebrew language); but in the number of things, and of the parts of things,—that is, the subject, and the predicate, and their adjuncts, in every sentence and proposition. Thus a phrase, containing two parts of a proposition, consists of two measures; add another containing two more, and they become four measures; another again, containing three parts of a proposition, consists of three measures; add to it another of the like, and you have six measures.

" For example; in the Song of Moses, " Thy-right-hand, O-Jehovah," is a phrase consisting of two terms, or parts of a proposition; to which is connected, " is-glorious in-power," consisting likewise of two terms: these joined together make four measures, or a tetrameter: " Thy-right-hand, O-Jehovah," repeated, makes two more; " hath-crushed the-enemy," two more; which, together, make four measures, or a second tetrameter. So likewise,

" The-enemy said, I-will-pursue, I-will overtake;
I-will-divide the-spoil; my-lust shall-be-satisfied-upon-them;
I-will-draw my-sword; my-hand shall-destroy-them;
Thou-didst-blow with-thy-wind; the-sea covered-them."

" The Song of Deuteronomy consists of propositions of three parts, or three measures; which, doubled in the same manner, make six, or hexameters: thus,

" Hearken, O-heavens, and-I-will-speak; and-let-the-earth hear the-words-of-my-mouth :*
My-doctrine shall-drop, as-the-rain; my-word shall-distil, as the-dew."

* Two words joined together by *maccaph* are considered as a single word, according to the laws of punctuation; so אמרי־פי is one word.

"Sometimes in the same period, much more in the same song, these two kinds meet together, according to the divine impulse moving the prophet, and as the variety suited his design, and the nature of the subject. For example,—

"And-by the-blast of-thy-nostrils, the-waters were-compressed;"

These are each two measures, which together make a tetrameter: it follows,—

"The-floods stood-upright, as-in-a-heap:
The-deeps were-congealed in-the-heart-of-the-sea:"*

These are two trimeters, which make an hexameter. So the Song of the Well begins with trimeters; to which are afterwards subjoined † dimeters. So in the prayer of Habakkuk the verses are trimeters:—

"God came from-Teman;
And-the-Holy-One from the-mount-of-Paran.‡ Selah.
His-glory covered the-heavens;
And-his-splendour filled the-earth."

"The author proceeds to observe, that in some verses certain words occur, which make no part of the measures, or are not taken into the account of the verse; as in the Song of Deuteronomy:—

"And-he-said,
I-will-hide my-face from-them:"

The word, "And-he-said," ‖ stands by itself,—and the remaining words make a trimeter:—

---

* בלביּם, one word.
† The Song of the Well, Numb. xxi. 17, 18., according to our way of fixing the conclusion of it, and if we measure it by Azarias's rules, consist of three trimeters and one dimeter only. But the Targum of Onkelos continues the song to the end of the 20th verse, taking in the catalogue of stations, (as we understand it), which immediately follows, as part of the song; and interpreting it as such. Azarias follows his authority: so Aben Tybbon, (see Cozri, p. 431.), and Iarchi upon the place. At this rate we shall have half a dozen dimeters more.
‡ מהר־פארן, (from-the-mount-of-Paran,) being joined by *maccaph*, and so making but one word, the author is obliged to take in *Selah* as part of the verse, to make out his third term or measure. The authority of the Masoretic maccaph has led him into an error. The verse without *Selah* is a trimeter; as it ought to be in conformity with the rest.
‖ So far the observation seems to be just; and perhaps there may be two more examples of it in the same poem, ver. 26. and 37.; where, according to

" I-will-see, what-is their-latter-end,"

is the trimeter answering to it. So in the prayer of Habakkuk:—

" O-Jehovah,
I-have-heard thy-speech ; I-was-afraid ;
O-Jehovah,
Revive thy-work in-the-midst-of-the years :" *

The word, " O-Jehovah," is twice to be read separate; and the words added to it make a trimeter. But this verse,

" Though the-fig-tree shall-not blossom,"

is of a different sort, consisting of the subject and predicate: " Though the fig-tree," being the subject; " shall not blossom," the predicate. So in a verse containing twelve terms, those terms may be reduced to six measures. For you are not to be reckon, either the syllables, or the words, but only the things. And for this reason a particle is often joined to the word next to it. The verses of the Psalms observe the same order:—

" Have-mercy-upon-me, O-God, according-to-thy-goodness ;
According-to-the-multitude-of-thy-mercies, † blot-out my-transgressions."

Azarias's doctrine, the words, *I said, And he shall say*, may conveniently enough be considered as making no part of the verse. So in Isaiah, the common forms, *Thus saith Jehovah, And it shall come to pass in that day*, and the like, probably are not always to be reckoned as making part of the measure. The period ס in the 4th Lamentation cannot well be divided into two lines, as it ought to be; but if the words קראו למו, *they cried unto them*, and אמרו בגוים, *they said among the heathen*, are excluded from the measure, the remainder will make two lines of just length:—

" Depart, ye are polluted, depart; depart ye, forbear to touch :
Yea, they are fled, they are removed ; they shall dwell here no more."

Or perhaps they may be two marginal interpretations, which by mistake have got into the text; which, I think, is better without them. So likewise, Lam. ii. 15. the word שאמרו, *of-which-they-said*, either does not reckon in the verse, which with it is too long; or, as I rather think, should be omitted, as an interpolation.

* In order to make out the trimeter, it is necessary to suppose that Azarias reads בקרב־שנים as one word.

† Azarias takes the liberty of joining the two words כרב רחמיך together by a *maccaph*, which is not to be found in our editions, in order to bring the verse within his rules. The reader will observe, that this distich, which in the Hebrew contains but seven words, cannot be rendered in English in less than

These are trimeters. So likewise,

" In-God I-will-praise his-word ;
In-Jehovah I-will-praise his-word."

So likewise the Proverbs of Solomon,

" Wisdom crieth without ;
In-the-streets she-uttereth her-voice."

"I am aware, adds he, that some verses are to be found, which I cannot accommodate to these rules and forms; and perhaps a great number. But by observing these things, the intelligent may perhaps receive new light, and discover what has escaped me. However, they may be assured, that all the verses that are found in the Sacred Writings; such as the song at the Red Sea, of the Well, of Moses, of Deborah, of David, of the Book of Job, the Psalms, and the Proverbs; all of them have an established order and measure, different in different places, or even sometimes different in one and the same poem;—as we may perceive, in reading them, an admirable propriety and fitness, though we cannot arrive at the true method of measuring or scanning them.

"It is not to be wondered, that the same song should consist of different measures; for the case is the same in the poetry of the Greeks and Romans: they suited their measures to the nature of the subject and the argument; and the variations which they admitted, were accommodated to the motions of the body, and the affections of the soul. Every kind of measure is not proper for every subject; and an ode, a panegyric, or a prayer, should not be composed in the same measure with an elegy. Do not you observe, says he, in the Book of Lamentations of Jeremiah, that the periods of the first and second chapters each of them consist of three propositions; and every one of these of a subject, and a predicate, and of the adjuncts belonging to them? The third chapter follows the same method; and for this reason is placed next to them in order: but of this chapter every period is distributed into three initial letters. But the fourth chapter does not perfect the senses in every

one-and-twenty words. By this he will judge, under what great disadvantage all the foregoing examples, whether of the parallelism or of the metre of things, must appear in an English version, in which many words are almost always necessary to render what is expressed by one word in Hebrew.

verse; * but consists of two and two, which make four. But the fifth chapter, which contains a prayer, you will find to be built on another plan; that is, one and one, which make two,† or a dimeter; like the verses of the Books of Job, Psalms, and Proverbs. So the Song of Moses, and the Song of Deborah, have a different form; consisting of three and three, which make six; that is, hexameters; like the heroic measure, which is the noblest of all measures.

"Upon the whole, the author concludes, that the poetical parts of the Hebrew Scriptures are not composed according to the rules and measures of certain feet, dissyllables, trisyllables, or the like, as the poems of the modern Jews are; but nevertheless have undoubtedly other measures which depend on things,‡ as above explained. For which reason, they are more excellent than those which consist of certain feet, according to the number and quantity of syllables. Of this, says he, you may judge yourself in the Songs of the Prophets. For do you not see, if you translate some of them into another language, that they still keep and retain their measure, if not wholly, at least in part? which cannot be the case in those verses, the measures of which arise from a certain quantity and number of syllables."

---

* He said above, that in the 1st and 2d chapters each separate verse, or line, was a single proposition: he now says, that this is not the case in the 4th chapter; for it does not perfect the sense in every verse; that is, each verse does not consist of one single proposition. As, for example the line or verse,—

"How is obscured the gold! changed the fine gold!"

"How is obscured | the gold!" makes one proposition, and two measures; "changed | the fine gold!" another proposition, and two other measures; which, according to him make a tetrameter. This, he says, makes the difference between the three first and the 4th chapter. But there seems to be no such difference; many single lines in the three first containing two propositions, and many in the 4th containing only one.

† According to the author's own definition of his terms, *one and one which make two*, should mean, one term and one term making two measures, or a dimeter: but the 5th chapter does not at all seem to answer that description. Besides, he says, the verses of it are like those of Job, Psalms, and Proverbs, of two of which books he said before, that the verses were trimeters. I know not what he means, unless it be that one and one sentences make two, that is a distich; and that this chapter consists of distichs, of two short lines, as the Books of Job, Psalms, and Proverbs, for the most part do; which is true.

‡ Perhaps the harmony might depend in some degree on both; for it may be often observed, that where the words of an hemistich happen to be longer, and consequently to consist of more syllables than the words of the adjoining hemistich, there the things expressed are fewer. See, for example, Psal. cviii. 4, 5. Which seems to prove, that the measures of the verses did not depend on the things expressed only, but on the syllables also.

Such is R. Azarias's hypothesis of the rhythmus of things; that is, of terms and of senses; of the grammatical parts of speech, and of the logical parts of propositions. The principle seems to be right; but, I think, he has not made the best use, of which it was capable, in the application. He acknowledges, that it will not hold in all cases. I believe, there is no such thing to be found in the Hebrew Bible, as a whole poem consisting of trimeters, tetrameters, or hexameters only, measured and scanned according to his rules. The Song of Moses, Deut. xxxii. is a very apt example for his purpose; but will not in all parts fall in with his measures. Besides, there is no sort of reason for his making it to consist of hexameters, rather than trimeter distichs; such, as he says, the Psalms and Proverbs consist of. Examine the cxith and cxiith Psalms by his rules; and though they will fall into his trimeters for the most part pretty well, yet we are sure, that these were not to be coupled together to make hexameters; for they are necessarily divided into twenty-two distinct short lines by the initial letters. The Hebrew poetry, consisting for the most part of short sentences, must in general naturally fall into such measures as Azarias establishes; or with some management may be easily reduced to his rules. Every proposition must consist of a subject and a predicate, joined together by a copula; and the predicate including the copula will generally consist of two terms, expressing the action, and the thing acted upon. In Hebrew, sometimes the subject is combined with the copula in one word, and sometimes the predicate; sometimes all three make but one term. In these cases, the addition of a simple adjunct (for the shortness of the style will not admit of much more) to the subject, or the predicate, or both, furnishes a second, a third, and sometimes a fourth term; that is, makes the verse a dimeter, trimeter, or tetrameter. For instance, in dimeters,—

" They-made-him-jealous, with-strange-Gods ;
They-provoked-him, with-abominations." Deut. xxxii. 16.

In trimeters,—

" I-will-bless Jehovah, at-all-time ;
His-praise [shall be] in my mouth, continually.
My-soul shall-make-her-boast, in-Jehovah ;
The meek shall-hear-it, and-rejoice.

O-magnify-ye Jehovah, with-me ;
And-let-us-praise his-name, together." Psal. xxxiv. 1—3.

In these examples, the first part of every line makes an entire proposition, and the last is an adjunct making the second, or the third, term. In the following, the subject, and the predicate, with their adjuncts, consist of two terms, each of them: that is, of two measures; and, being joined together, make a tetrameter:—

" The-counsel of-Jehovah shall-stand for-ever."

The next line is in the same form, except that the verb is understood, and the latter adjunct divided into two terms; and makes a second tetrameter to pair, with the first:—

" The-thoughts of-his-heart, from-age to-age."

Something of this kind must necessarily be the result of this sententious way of writing: it is what comes of course, without much study. But whatever attention the Hebrew poets might give to the scanning of their verses by the number of terms, it does not appear to have been their design to confine all the verses of the same poem to any set number of terms; whereas they do plainly appear to have studied to throw the corresponding lines of the same distich into the same number of terms, into the same form of construction, and still more into an identity, or opposition, or a general conformity of sense. I agree therefore with Azarias in his general principle of a rhythmus of things: but instead of considering terms, or phrases, or senses, in single lines, as measures; determining the nature and denomination of the verse, as dimeter, trimeter, or tetrameter; I consider only that relation and proportion of one verse to another, which arises from the correspondence of terms, and from the form of construction; from whence results a rhythmus of propositions, and a harmony of sentences.

This peculiar conformation of sentences; short, concise, with frequent pauses, and regular intervals, divided into pairs, for the most part, of corresponding lines; is the most evident characteristic now remaining of poetry among the Hebrews, as distinguished from prose: and this, I suppose, is what is implied in the name, *Mizmor ;** which I under-

---

* מזמור. זמר signifies to *cut*, to *prune*, to *sing*, to *play* on a musical instrument. *Cæsura* is the common idea, which prevails in all.

stand to be the proper name for verse; that is, for numerous, rhythmical, or metrical language. This form made their verse peculiarly fit for music and dance; which with them were the usual concomitants of poetry, on occasions of public joy, and in the most solemn offices of religion.* Both their dance and song were on such occasions performed by two choirs† taking their parts alternately in each: the regular form of the stanzas, chiefly distichal, and the parallelism of the lines, were excellently well suited to this purpose, and fell in naturally with the movements of the body, of the voice, and of the instruments, and with the division of the parts between the two sets of performers.

But, besides the poetical structure of the sentences, there are other indications of verse in the poetical and prophetical parts of the Hebrew Scriptures: such are, peculiarities of language; unusual and foreign words; phrases, and forms of words, uncommon in prose; bold elliptical expression; frequent and abrupt change of persons, and an use of the tenses out of the common order; and lastly, the poetical dialect, consisting chiefly in certain anomalies peculiar to poetry; in letters and syllables added to the ends of words; a kind of license commonly permitted to poetry in every language. But as these cannot be explained by a few examples, nor perfectly understood without some knowledge of Hebrew; I must beg leave to refer the learned reader, who would inquire further into this subject, to what I have said upon it in another place;‡ or rather, to recommend it to his own observation, in reading the sacred poets in their own language.

Thus far of the genuine form and character of the Prophet's composition; which it has been the translator's endeavour closely to follow, and as exactly to express, as the difference of the languages would permit: in which indeed he has had great advantage in the habit, which our language has acquired, of expressing with ease, and not without elegance, Hebrew ideas and Hebrew forms of speaking, from

---

* See Exod. xv. 20. 21. 2 Sam. vi. 14. 16.

† See 1 Sam. xviii. 6, 7. Ezra iii. 11. Nehem. xii. 24. and Philo's Observations (Περι Γεωργιας) on the Song at the Red Sea.

‡ De Sacra Poesi Hebræorum, Prælect. iii. xiv. xv.

our constant use of a close verbal translation of both the Old and New Testament; which has by degrees moulded our language into such a conformity with that of the original Scriptures, that it can upon occasion assume the Hebrew character without appearing altogether forced and unnatural. It remains to say something of the Translation in regard to its fidelity; and of the principles of interpretation by which the translator has been guided in the prosecution of it.

THE first and principal business of a translator, is to give the plain literal and grammatical sense of his author; the obvious meaning of his words, phrases, and sentences; and to express them in the language into which he translates, as far as may be, in equivalent words, phrases, and sentences. Whatever indulgence may be allowed him in other respects; however excusable he may be, if he fail of attaining the elegance, the spirit, the sublimity of his author,—which will generally be in some degree the case, if his author excels at all in those qualities; want of fidelity admits of no excuse, and is entitled to no indulgence. This is peculiarly so in subjects of high importance, such as the Holy Scriptures, in which so much depends on the phrase and expression; and particularly in the prophetical books of Scripture; where from the letter are often deduced deep and recondite senses, which must owe all their weight and solidity to the just and accurate interpretation of the words of the prophecy. For whatever senses are supposed to be included in the Prophet's words, spiritual, mystical, allegorical, analogical, or the like, they must all entirely depend on the literal sense. This is the only foundation upon which such interpretations can be securely raised; and if this is not firmly and well established, all that is built upon it will fall to the ground.

For example; if כתוא מכמר, Isa. li. xx. does not signify ὡς σευτλιον ἡμιεφθον, *like parboiled bete*, as the LXX render it; but *like an oryx* (a large, fierce, wild beast) *in the toils;* what becomes of Theodoret's explication of this image? [Καθευδονἰες ὡς σευτλιον ἡμιεφθον] Εδειξεν αυτων δια μεν τȣ ὑπνȣ το ῥαθυμον, δια δε τȣ λαχανȣ το ανανδρον. According to this interpretation, the Prophet would express the drowsiness and flaccidity, the slothfulness and want of spirit, of his countrymen: whereas his idea was impotent rage, and obstinate violence, subdued by a superior power; the Jews taken in the snares of their own wickedness, struggling in vain, till, overspent and exhausted, they sink under the weight of God's judgments. And Procopius's explication of the same passage, according to the rendering of the words by Aquila, Symmachus, and Theodotion, which is probably the true one, is almost as foreign to the purpose: "He compares, saith he, the people of Jerusalem to the oryx, that is, to a *bird ;* because they are taken in the snares of the devil, and therefore are delivered over to wrath." Such strange and absurd deductions of notions and ideas, foreign to the author's drift and design, will often arise from the invention of commentators who have nothing but an inaccurate translation to work upon. This was the case of the generality of the Fathers of the Christian Church, who wrote comments on the Old Testament: and it is no wonder, that we find them of little service in leading us into the true meaning and the deep sense of the prophetical writings.

It being then a translator's indispensable duty faithfully and religiously to express the sense of his author, he ought to take great care that he proceed upon just principles of criticism, in a rational method of interpretation ; and that the copy from which he translates be accurate and perfect in itself, or corrected as carefully as possible by the best authorities, and on the clearest result of critical inquiry.

The method of studying the Scriptures of the Old Testament has been very defective hitherto in both these respects. Beside the difficulties attending it, arising from the nature of the thing itself, from the language in which it is written, and the condition in which it is come down to us through so many ages ; what we have of it being the scanty relics of a language formerly copious, and consequently the true meaning of many words and phrases being obscure and dubious, and perhaps incapable of being clearly ascertained ; beside these impediments, necessarily inherent in the subject, others have been thrown in the way of our progress in the study of these writings, from prejudice, and an ill-founded opinion of the authority of the Jews, both as interpreters and conservators of them.

The Masoretic punctuation, by which the pronunciation of the language is given, the forms of the several parts of speech, the construction of the words, the distribution and limits of the sentences, and the connexion of the several members are fixed, is in effect an interpretation of the Hebrew text made by the Jews of late ages, probably not earlier than the eighth century; and may be considered as their translation of the Old Testament. Where the words unpointed are capable of various meanings, according as they may be variously pronounced and constructed, the Jews by their pointing have determined them to one meaning and construction; and the sense which they thus give, is their sense of the passage: just as the rendering of a translator into another language is his sense; that is, the sense in which, in his opinion, the original words are to be taken; and it has no other authority, than what arises from its being agreeable to the rules of just interpretation. But because in the languages of Europe the vowels are essential parts of written words, a notion was too hastily taken up by the learned at the revival of letters, when the original Scriptures began to be more carefully examined, that the vowel points were necessary appendages of the Hebrew letters, and therefore coeval with them; at least, that they became absolutely necessary when the Hebrew was become a dead language, and must have been added by Ezra, who collected and formed the canon of the Old Testament, in regard to all the books of it in his time extant. On this supposition, the points have been considered as part of the Hebrew text, and as giving the meaning of it on no less than divine authority. Accordingly our public translations in the modern tongues for the use of the church among Protestants, and so likewise the modern Latin translations, are for the most part close copies of the Hebrew pointed text, and are in reality only versions at second hand, translations of the Jews' interpretation of the Old Testament. We do not deny the usefulness of this interpretation, nor would we be thought to detract from its merit by setting it in this light: it is perhaps, upon the whole, preferable to any one of the ancient versions; it has probably the great advantage of having been formed upon a traditionary explanation of the text, and of being generally agreeable to that sense of Scripture which passed current, and was commonly received by the Jewish nation in ancient times; and it has certainly been of great service to the moderns, in leading them into the knowledge of the Hebrew tongue. But they would have made a much better use of it, and a greater progress in the explication of the Scriptures of the Old Testament, had they consulted it, without absolutely submitting to its authority;

had they considered it as an assistant, not as an infallible guide.

To what a length an opinion lightly taken up, and embraced with a full assent, without due examination, may be carried, we may see in another example of much the same kind. The learned of the Church of Rome, who have taken the liberty of giving translations of Scripture in the modern languages, have for the most part subjected and devoted themselves to a prejudice equally groundless and absurd. The Council of Trent declared the Latin translation of the Scriptures called the Vulgate, which had been for many ages in use in their church, to be authentic,—a very ambiguous term, which ought to have been more precisely defined than the Fathers of this Council chose to define it. Upon this ground many contended, that the Vulgate version was dictated by the Holy Spirit; at least was providentially guarded against all error; was consequently of divine authority, and more to be regarded than even the original Hebrew and Greek texts. And in effect the decree of the Council, however limited and moderated by the explanation of some of their judicious divines, has given to the Vulgate such a high degree of authority, that, in this instance at least, the translation has taken place of the original: for these translators, instead of the Hebrew and Greek texts, profess to translate the Vulgate. Indeed, when they find the Vulgate very notoriously deficient in expressing the sense, they do the original Scriptures the honour of consulting them, and take the liberty, by following them, of departing from their authentic guide; but in general the Vulgate is their original text, and they give us a translation of a translation; by which second transfusion of the Holy Scriptures into another tongue, still more of the original sense must be lost, and more of the genuine spirit must evaporate.

The other prejudice, which has stood in the way, and obstructed our progress in the true understanding of the Old Testament,—a prejudice even more unreasonable than the former, is the notion that has prevailed of the great care and skill of the Jews in preserving the text, and transmitting it down to the present times pure, and entirely free from all mistakes, as it came from the hands of the authors. In opposition to which opinion it has been often observed, that such a perfect degree of integrity no human skill or care could warrant; it must imply no less than a constant miraculous superintendence of divine Providence, to guide the hand of the copyist, and to guard him from error, in respect to every transcript that has been made through so long a succession of ages. And it is universally acknowledged, that Almighty God has not thought such a miraculous interposition necessary in regard to the Scriptures of the New Testament, at least of equal authority and importance with those of the Old: We plainly see, that he has not exempted them from the common lot of other books; the copies of these, as well as of other ancient writings, differing in some degree from one another, so that no one of them has any just pretension to be a perfect and entire copy, truly and precisely representing in every word and letter the originals, as they came from the hands of the several authors. All writings transmitted to us, like these, from early times, the original copies of which have long ago perished, have suffered in their passage to us by the mistakes of many transcribers through whose hands we have received them; errors continually accumulating in proportion to the number of transcripts, and the stream generally becoming more impure, the more distant it is from the source. Now, the Hebrew writings of the Old Testament being for much the greater part the most ancient of any; instead of finding them absolutely perfect, we may reasonably expect to find, that they have suffered in this respect more than others of less antiquity generally have done.

But beside this common source of errors, there is a circumstance very unfavourable in this respect to these writings in particular, which makes them peculiarly liable to mistakes in transcribing; that is, the great similitude which some letters bear to others in the Hebrew alphabet: such as ב to כ, ד to ר, ה to ח, ג to נ; ו, ז, and ך, to one another; more perhaps than are to be found in any other alphabet whatsoever; and in so great a degree of likeness, that they are hardly distinguishable even in some printed copies; and not only these letters, but others likewise beside these, are not easily distinguished from one another in many manuscripts. This must have been a perpetual cause of frequent mistakes; of which, in regard to the two first pairs of letters above noted, there are many undeniable examples; insomuch that a change of one of the similar letters for the other, when it remarkably clears up the sense, may be fairly allowed to criticism, even without any other authority than that of the context to support it.

But to these natural sources of error, as we may call them, the Jewish copyists have added others, by some absurd practices which they have adopted in transcribing;—such as their consulting more the fair appearance of their copy than the correctness of it; by wilfully leaving mistakes uncorrected, lest by erasing they should diminish the beauty and the value of the transcript; (for instance, when they had written a word, or part of a word, wrongly, and immediately saw their mistake, they left the mistake uncorrected, and wrote the word anew after it): their scrupulous regard to the evenness and fulness of their lines; which induced them to cut off from the ends of lines a letter or letters, for which there was not sufficient room, (for they never divided a word so that the parts of it should belong to two lines); and to add to the ends of lines letters wholly insignificant, by way of expletives, to fill up a vacant space: their custom of writing part of a word at the end of a line, where there was not room for the whole, and then giving the whole word at the beginning of the next line. These and some other like practices manifestly tended to multiply mistakes: they were so many traps and snares laid in the way of future transcribers, and must have given occasion to frequent errors.

These circumstances considered, it would be the most astonishing of all miracles, if, notwithstanding the acknowledged fallibility of transcribers, and their proneness to error, from the nature of the subject itself on which they were employed, the Hebrew writings of the Old Testament had come down to us through their hands absolutely pure, and free from all mistakes whatsoever.

If it be asked, what then is the real condition of the present Hebrew text; and of what sort, and in what number, are the mistakes which we must acknowledge to be found in it? it is answered, That the condition of the Hebrew text is such as, from the nature of the thing, the antiquity of the writings themselves, the want of due care, or critical skill, (in which latter at least the Jews have been exceedingly deficient,) might in all reason have been expected; that the mistakes are frequent, and of various kinds; of letters, words, and sentences; by variation, omission, transposition; such as often injure the beauty and elegance, embarrass the construction, alter or obscure the sense, and sometimes render it quite unintelligible. If it be objected, that a concession so large as this is, tends to invalidate the authority of Scripture; that it gives up in effect the certainty and authenticity of the doctrines contained in it, and exposes our religion naked and defenceless to the assaults of its enemies; this, I think, is a vain and groundless apprehension. Casual errors may blemish parts, but do not destroy, or much alter, the whole. If the Iliad or the Æneid had come down to us with more errors in all the copies than are to be found in the worst manuscript now extant of either, without doubt many particular passages would have lost much of their beauty; in many the sense would have been greatly injured; in some rendered wholly unintelligible; but the plan of the poem in the whole and in its parts, the fable, the mythology, the machinery, the characters, the great constituent parts, would still have been visible and apparent, without having suffered any essential diminution of their greatness. Of all the precious remains of antiquity, perhaps Aristotle's treatise on Poetry is come down to us as much injured by time as any: as it has been greatly mutilated in the whole, some considerable members of it being lost; so the parts remaining have suffered in proportion, and many passages are rendered very obscure, probably by the imperfection and frequent mistakes of the copies now extant. Yet, notwithstanding these disadvantages, this treatise, so much injured by time and so mutilated, still continues to be the great code of criticism; the fundamental principles of which are plainly deducible from it: we still have recourse to it for the rules and laws of epic and dramatic poetry, and the imperfection of the copy does not at all impeach the authority of the legislator. Important and fundamental doctrines do not wholly depend on single passages; an universal harmony runs through the Holy Scriptures; the parts mutually support each other, and supply one another's deficiencies and obscurities. Superficial damages and partial defects may greatly diminish the beauty of the edifice, without injuring its strength, and bringing on utter ruin and destruction.*

* " Librariorum discordiam ostendunt varia exemplaria, in quibus idem locus aliter atque aliter legitur. Sed ea discordia offendere nos non debet; primum, quia autorum non est, sed librariorum, quorum culpam præstare

" The copies of the Holy Scriptures of the Old Testament being then subject, like all other ancient writings, to mistakes arising from the unskilfulness or inattention of transcribers,—a plain matter of fact, which cannot be denied, and needs not be 'palliated; it is to be considered, what remedy can be applied in this case; how such mistakes can be corrected upon certain or highly probable grounds? Now the case being the same, the method which has been used with good effect in correcting the ancient Greek and Latin authors, ought in all reason to be applied to the ' Hebrew writings. At the revival of literature, critics and editors finding the Greek and Latin authors full of mistakes, set about correcting them, by procuring different copies, and the best that they could meet with: these they compared together, and the mistakes not being the same in all, one copy corrected another; and thus they easily got rid of such errors as had not obtained possession in all the copies: and generally the more copies they had to compare, the more errors were corrected, and the more perfect the text was rendered. This, which common sense dictated in the first place as necessary to be done in order to the removing of difficulties in reading ancient Greek and Latin

autores nec possunt nec debent. Deinde, quia plerumque ejusmodi discordia unius aut alterius verbi est, in quo nihil læditur sententia; aut si quid forte læditur, aliunde corrigi potest; quandoquidem autorum sententiæ non semper ex singulis verbis superstitiosius observandis, sed plerumque ex orationis tenore, aut similium locorum observatione, aut mentis ratiocinatione sunt investigandæ. Ac tales librariorum discordiæ etiam in profanis autoribus inveniuntur; ut in Platone, in Aristotele, in Homero, in Cicerone, in Virgilio, et cæteris. Quamvis enim summo in pretio semper fuerint apud gentiles hi autores, summaque cum diligentia describi soliti, tamen caveri non potuit, quin multa scripturæ menda et discrepantiæ annorum longitudine obrepserint; nec tamen ea res studiosos deterret; nec facit, ut qui libri Ciceronis habentur, ii aut non boni aut non Ciceronis esse ducantur: sicut enim detorti aut etiam decussi ramuli agricolam non offendunt, nec arborem vitiant, quippe quæ ramorum infinita multitudine sic abundet, ut tantulam jacturam alibi sine ullo detrimento resarciat; ita si in autore pauculis in locis simile quidpiam usu venit, id nec bonum lectorem offendit, nec autorem vitiat. Manet enim ipsa stirps, et, ut ita loquar, corpus autoris, ex cujus perpetuo tenore dictorumque ubertate percipi possunt sine ullo detrimento fructus pleni.

Ad scrupulum eorum, qui metuunt, ne, si hoc concessum fuerit, labescat sacrarum literarum autoritas, hoc respondeo; non esse scriptorum autoritatem in paucis quibusdam verbis, quæ vitiari detrahive potuerunt, sed in perpetuo orationis tenore, qui mansit incorruptus, positam. Itaque quemadmodum Cicero apud sui studiosos nihilo minoris est autoritatis propter paucula quædam mutilata aut depravata, quam esset, si id non accidisset; ita debet et sacrarum literarum autoritati nihil detrahi, si quid in eis tale, quale ostendimus, contigit." Sebast. Castellio, quoted by Wetstein, Nov. Test. tom. ii. p. 856.

authors, we have had recourse to in the last place in regard to the ancient Hebrew writers. Hebrew manuscripts have at length been consulted and collated, notwithstanding the unaccountable opinion which prevailed, that they all exactly agreed with one another, and formed precisely one uniform text. An infinite number of variations have been collected, from above six hundred manuscripts, and some ancient printed editions, collated or consulted, in most parts of Europe; and have been in part published, and the publication of the whole will I hope soon be completed, by the learned Dr. Kennicott, in his edition of the Hebrew Bible with various readings; a work, the greatest and most important that has been undertaken and accomplished since the revival of letters.

But the Hebrew text of the Old Testament, compared with the text of ancient Greek and Latin authors, has in one respect greatly the disadvantage. There are manuscripts of the latter, which are much nearer in time to the age of the authors; and have suffered much less in proportion to the shorter space of time intervening. For example, the Medicean manuscript of Virgil was written probably within four or five hundred years after the time of the poet; whereas the oldest of the Hebrew manuscripts now known to be extant, do not come within many centuries of the times of the several authors; not nearer than about fourteen centuries to the age of Ezra, one of the latest of them, who is supposed to have revised the books of the Old Testament than extant, and to have reduced them to a perfect and correct standard: so that we can hardly expect much more from this vast collection of variations, taken in themselves as correctors of the text, exclusively of other consequences, than to be able by their means to discharge and eliminate the errors that have been gathering and accumulating in the copies for about a thousand years past; and to give us now as good and correct a text as was commonly current among the Jews, or might easily have been obtained, so long ago. Indeed, some of the oldest manuscripts, from which these variations have been collected, may possibly be faithful transcripts of select manuscripts at that time very ancient, and so may really carry us nearer to the age of Ezra; but this is an advantage which we cannot be assured of, and upon which we must not presume. But to get so far nearer to the source, as we plainly do by the assistance of manuscripts, though of comparatively late date, is an advantage by no means inconsiderable, or lightly to be regarded.

On the other hand, we have a great advantage in regard to the Hebrew text, which the Greek and Latin authors generally want, and which in some degree makes up for the defect of age in the present Hebrew manuscripts; that is, from the several ancient versions of the Old Testament in different languages, made in much earlier times, and from manuscripts in all probability much more correct and perfect than any now extant. These versions, for the most part, being evidently intended for exact literal renderings of the Hebrew text, may be considered in some respects as representatives of the manuscripts from which they were taken: and when the version gives a sense better in itself, and more agreeable to the context, than the Hebrew text offers, and at the same time answerable to a word or words similar to those of the Hebrew text, and only differing from it by the change of one or more similar letters, or by the different position of the same letters, or by some other inconsiderable variation; we have good reason to believe, that the similar Hebrew words answering to the version, were indeed the very reading that stood in the manuscript from which the translation was made. To add strength to this way of reasoning, it is to be observed, that the manuscripts now extant frequently confirm such supposed reading of those manuscripts from which the ancient versions were taken, in opposition to the authority of the present printed Hebrew text; and make the collection of variations, now preparing for the public, of the highest importance; as they give a new evidence of the fidelity of the ancient versions, and set them upon a footing of authority which they never could obtain before. They were looked upon as the work of wild and licentious interpreters, who often departed from the text, which they undertook to render, without any good reason, and only followed their own fancy and caprice. The present Hebrew manuscripts so often justify the versions in such passages, that we cannot but conclude, that in many others likewise the difference of the version from the present original is not to be imputed to the licentiousness of the translator, but to the carelessness of the Hebrew copyist; and this affords a just and reasonable ground for correcting the Hebrew text on the authority of the ancient versions.

But the assistance of manuscripts and ancient versions united will be found very insufficient perfectly to correct the Hebrew text. Passages will sometimes occur, in which neither the one nor the other give any satisfactory sense; which has been occasioned probably by very ancient mistakes of the copy, antecedent to the date of the oldest of them. On these occasions, translators are put to great difficulties, through which they force their way as well as they can: they invent new meanings for words and phrases, and put us off either with what makes no sense at all, or with a sense that apparently does not arise out of the words of the text. The renderings of such desperate places, when they carry any sense with them, are manifestly conjectural; and full as much so, as the conjectures of the critic who hazards an alteration of the text itself. The fairest way of proceeding in these cases seems to be, to confess the difficulty, and to lay it before the reader; and to leave it to his judgment to decide, whether the conjectural rendering, or the conjectural emendation, be more agreeable to the context, to the exigence of the place, to parallel and similar passages, to the rules and genius of the language, and to the laws of sound and temperate criticism.

The condition of the present text of Isaiah in particular is answerable to the representation above given of the Hebrew text in general. It is, I presume, considerably injured and stands in need of frequent emendation. Nothing is more apt to affect, and sometimes utterly to destroy, the meaning of a sentence, than the omission of a word; than which no sort of mistake is more frequent. I reckon, that in the book of Isaiah, the words omitted in different places amount to the number of fifty. I mean whole words, not including particles, prepositions, and pronouns affixed; and I speak of such as I am well persuaded are real omissions; much the greater part of which, I flatter myself, the reader will find supplied in the translation and notes, with a good degree of probability, from manuscripts and ancient versions. Beside these, there are some other places, in which I suspect some omission, though there may be no evidence to prove it. If there be any truth in this account of words omitted, the reader will easily suppose, that mistakes of other kinds must be frequent in proportion, and amount all together to a considerable number.

The manuscripts and ancient versions afford the proper means of remedying these and other defects of the present copy. It is manifest, that the ancient interpreters had before them copies of the Hebrew text different in many places from that which passes current at present; and the manuscripts even now extant frequently vary from that, and from one another. Neither is there any one manuscript or edition whatever, that has the least pretension to a superior authority, so as to claim to be a standard to which the rest ought to be reduced. A true text, as far as it is possible to recover it, is to be gathered from the manuscripts now extant, and from the evidence furnished by the ancient versions of the readings of manuscripts of much earlier times. This being the case, the first care of the translator should be, especially in places obscure and difficult, to consider whether the words which he is to render be indeed the genuine words of the Prophet, and to ascertain, as far as may be, the true reading of the text.

The ancient versions above-mentioned as the principal sources of emendation, and highly useful in rectifying, as well as in explaining, the Hebrew text, are contained in the London Polyglott.

The Greek version, commonly called the Septuagint, or of the seventy interpreters, probably made by different hands, (the number of them uncertain,) and at different times, as the exigence of the Jewish church at Alexandria and in other parts of Egypt required, is of the first authority, and of the greatest use in correcting the Hebrew text; as being the most ancient of all; and as the copy, from which it was translated, appears to have been free from many errors, which afterwards by degrees got into the text. But the version of Isaiah is not so old as that of the Pentateuch by a hundred years and more; having been made in all probability after the time of Antiochus Epiphanes, when the reading of the Prophets in the Jewish synagogues began to be practised; and even after the building of Onias's temple, to favour which there seems to have been some artifice employed in a certain passage of Isaiah * in this version. And it unfortunately happens, that Isaiah has had the hard fate to meet with a translator very unworthy of him, there being hardly any book of the Old Testament so ill rendered in that version as this of Isaiah. Add to this, that the version of Isaiah, as well as other parts of the Greek version, is come down to us in a bad condition, incorrect, and with frequent omissions and interpolations. Yet, with all these disadvantages, with all its faults and imperfections, this version is of more use in correcting the Hebrew text than any other whatsoever.

The Arabic version is sometimes referred to as verifying the reading of the LXX, being, for the most part at least, taken from that version.

The learned Mr. Woide, to whom we are indebted for the publication of a Coptic lexicon and grammar, very useful and necessary for the promotion of that part of literature, has very kindly communicated to me his extracts from the fragments of a manuscript of a Coptic version of Isaiah, made from the LXX, with which he has collated them. They are preserved in the Library of St. Germain de Prez at Paris. He judges this Coptic version to be of the second century. The manuscript was written in the beginning of the fourteenth century. The same gentleman has had the goodness, at my request, to collate with Bos's edition of the LXX, through the book of Isaiah, two manuscripts of the King's Library, now in the British Museum, the one marked I. B. II. the other I. D. II. The former manuscript, containing the Prophets of the version of the LXX, was written in the eleventh or twelfth century, according to Grabe; (in the tenth or eleventh century, in Mr. Woide's opinion); and by a note on the back of the first leaf appears to have belonged to Pachomius, patriarch of Constantinople in the beginning of the sixteenth century. Grabe highly valued this manuscript; and intended to write a dissertation on the superiority of this and of the Alexandrian manuscript to that of the Vatican; but did not live to execute his design. See Prolegom. ad tom. 3tium, LXX Interp. edit. Grabe, sect. iii. and v., and Grabe de Vitiis LXX Interp. p. 118. I quote this manuscript by the title of MS Pachom. for the reason above given.

* Chap. xix. 18. See the note there.

The latter manuscript 1. D. 11. above-mentioned, contains many of the historical books, beginning with Ruth, and ending with Ezra, according to the order of the books in our English Bible; and also the prophet Isaiah, of the version of the LXX. This manuscript in the book of Isaiah consists of two different parts: the first from the beginning to the word τυφλων, chap. xxxv. 5. written in a more ancient and better character, and upon better vellum; which Mr. Woide judges to be of the eleventh or twelfth century: the remaining part he refers to the beginning of the fourteenth century; which Grabe supposes to be the age of the whole: See Grabe de Vitiis, LXX Interp. p. 104. This manuscript seems to have been taken from a good copy, as it frequently agrees with the best and most ancient manuscripts, and in particular with the manuscript of Pachomius.

The Coptic fragments above-mentioned, and these manuscripts, are useful for the same purpose of authenticating the reading of the LXX; and, in consequence, of ascertaining or correcting the Hebrew text in some places.

My examination of Mr. Woide's collation of the two Greek manuscripts of Isaiah, has been confined to this single view in respect of the Hebrew text. Were these manuscripts to be applied more extensively, and to their proper use, that of correcting the text of the LXX, through all the parts of it which they contain, I am persuaded they would be found to be of very great importance, and would contribute largely to the revision and emendation of that ancient and very valuable version: a work, which may be now considered as one of the principal desiderata of sacred criticism; and which ought to follow that arduous undertaking, which has so happily succeeded, the collation of Hebrew manuscripts; to which it stands next in order of importance and usefulness towards our attaining a more perfect knowledge of the Holy Scriptures.

The Chaldee paraphrase of Jonathan Ben Uziel, made about or before the time of our Saviour, though it often wanders from the text in a wordy allegorical explanation, yet very frequently adheres to it closely, and gives a verbal rendering of it; and accordingly is sometimes of great use in ascertaining the true reading of the Hebrew text.

The Syriac version stands next in order of time, but is superior to the Chaldee in usefulness and authority, as well in ascertaining as in explaining the Hebrew text. It is a close translation of the Hebrew into a language of near affinity to it. It is supposed to have been made as early as the first century.

The fragments of the three Greek versions of Aquila, Symmachus, and Theodotion, all made in the second century, which are collected in the Hexapla of Montfaucon, are of considerable use for the same purpose.

The Vulgate, being for the most part the translation of Jerome, made in the fourth century, is of service in the same way, in proportion to its antiquity.

I am greatly obliged to several learned friends for their observations on particular passages: To one great person more especially, whom I had the honour to call my friend, the late excellent Archbishop Secker; whose marginal notes on the Bible, deposited by his order in the library at Lambeth, I had permission to consult by the favour of his most worthy successor. There are two Bibles with his notes: one a folio English Bible interleaved, containing chiefly corrections of the English translation; the other a Hebrew Bible of the edition of Michaelis, Halle, 1720, in 4to.; the large margins of which are filled with critical remarks on the Hebrew text, collations of the ancient versions, and other short annotations; which stand an illustrious monument of the learning, judgment and indefatigable industry of that excellent person: I add also, of his candour and modesty; for there is hardly a proposed emendation, however ingenious and probable, to which he has not added the objections which occurred to him against it. These valuable remains of that great and good man will be of infinite service, whenever that necessary work, a new translation, or a revision of the present translation, of the Holy Scriptures, for the use of our church, shall be undertaken. To his observations I have set his name. And to the remarks of others of my learned friends, I have likewise subjoined in the notes their names respectively. Among these I must here particularly mention the late learned Dr. Durell, Principal of Hertford College in Oxford; who some years ago communicated to me his manuscript remarks on the Prophets. With his leave I took short memorandums of some of his corrections of the text; and had his permission to make what use I pleased of them.

I am in a more particular manner obliged to my learned friend Dr. Kennicott, for his singular favour in frequently communicating to me his collations while they were collecting, and the printed copy of the book of Isaiah itself, as soon as it was finished at the press, for my private use, while the remainder of the volume is in hand and preparing for the public. These I have examined with some attention; and I hope the reader, whose expectations do not exceed the bounds of reason and moderation, will be satisfied with the assistance and benefit which he will find they have afforded me. But I must beg to have it well understood, that I do by no means pretend to have exhausted these valuable stores: many things may have escaped me, which may strike the eye of another observer; many a variation, which appears at first sight very minute and trifling, and manifestly false and absurd, may by some side-light tend to useful discoveries. To apply these materials to all the uses which can possibly be made of them, will require much labour and consideration, much judgment and sagacity, and repeated trials by a variety of examiners, to whose different views they may shew themselves in every possible light. Some critics may be very forward and hasty in pronouncing their judgments; but it must be left to time and experience to establish their real and full value.

In regard to the character and authority of the several manuscripts which have been collated and which in the notes are referred to, we must wait for the information which Dr. Kennicott will give us in his general Dissertation. The knowledge of Hebrew manuscripts is almost a new subject in literature: little progress has been made in it hitherto; and no wonder, when they were esteemed uniformly consonant one with another, and with the printed text; consequently useless, and not worth the trouble of examining. Dr. Kennicott, and his worthy and very able assistant Mr. Bruns, who have been more conversant with Hebrew manuscripts, and have had more experience, and more insight into the subject, than any, or than all, of the learned of the present age, will give us the best information concerning it that can yet be obtained. It must be left to the attentive observation, and mature experience, of the learned of succeeding times, to perfect a part of knowledge which, like others, must, in its nature, wait the result of diligent inquiry, and be carried on by gradual improvements.

In referring to Dr. Kennicott's Variations, I have given the whole number of manuscripts or editions which concur in any particular reading: what proportion that number bears to the whole number of collated copies which contain the book of Isaiah, may, I hope, soon be seen by comparing it with the catalogue of copies collated, which will be given at the end of that book. But that the reader in the mean time, till he can have more full information concerning the value and authority of the several manuscripts, may at least have some mark to direct his judgment in estimating the credit due to the manuscripts quoted, I have, from the kind communication of Dr. Kennicott concerning the dates of the manuscripts, whether certain or probable, given some general intimation of their value in this respect: for though antiquity is no certain mark of the goodness of a manuscript, yet it is one circumstance that gives it no small weight and authority, especially in this case; the Hebrew manuscripts being in general more pure and valuable in proportion to their antiquity; those of later date having been more studiously rendered conformable to the Masoretic standard.* Among the manuscripts which have been collated, I consider those of the tenth, eleventh, and twelfth centuries, as ancient, comparatively and in respect of the rest. Therefore in quoting a number of manuscripts, where the variation is of some importance, I have added, that so many of that number are ancient, that is, are of the centuries above mentioned.

I have ventured to call this a New Translation, though much of our vulgar translation is retained in it. As the style of that translation is not only excellent in itself, but has taken possession of our ear, and of our taste, to have endeavoured to vary from it, with no other design than that of giving something new instead of it, would have been to disgust the reader, and to represent the sense of the Prophet in a more unfavourable manner; besides that it is impossible for a verbal translator to follow an approved verbal translation, which has gone before him, without frequently treading in the very footsteps of it. The most obvious, the properest, and perhaps the only terms which the language affords, are already occupied; and without going out of his way to find worse, he cannot avoid them. Every translator has taken this liberty with his predecessors: it is no more

---

* See Kennicott, State of the Printed Heb. Text, Dissert. ii. p. 470.

than the laws of translation admit, nor indeed than the necessity of the case requires. And as to the turn and modification of the sentences, the translator, in this particular province of translation, is, I think, as much confined to the author's manner, as to his words: so that too great liberties taken in varying either the expression or the composition, in order to give a new air to the whole, will be apt to have a very bad effect. For these reasons, whenever it shall be thought proper to set forth the Holy Scriptures for the public use of our church to better advantage, than as they appear in the present English translation, the expediency of which grows every day more and more evident, a revision or correction of that translation may perhaps be more advisable, than to attempt an entirely new one: For as to the style and language, it admits of but little improvement; but, in respect of the sense and the accuracy of interpretation, the improvements of which it is capable are great and numberless.

The translation here offered will perhaps be found to be in general as close to the text, and as literal, as our English version. When it departs at all from the Hebrew text on account of some correction, which I suppose to be requisite, I give notice to the reader of such correction, and offer my reasons for it: if those reasons should sometimes appear insufficient, and the translation to be merely conjectural, I desire the reader to consider the exigence of the case, and to judge, whether it is not better, in a very obscure and doubtful passage, to give something probable by way of supplement to the author's sense, apparently defective, than either to leave a blank in the translation, or to give a merely verbal rendering, which would be altogether unintelligible. I believe that every translator whatever of any part of the Old Testament, has taken sometimes the liberty, or rather has found himself under the necessity, of offering such renderings as, if examined, will be found to be merely conjectural. But I desire to be understood as offering this apology in behalf only of translations designed for the private use of the reader; not as extended, without proper limitations, to those that are made for the public service of the church.

The design of the Notes is to give the reasons and authorities on which the translation is founded; to rectify or to explain the words of the text; to illustrate the ideas, the images, and the allusions of the Prophet, by referring to objects, notions, and customs, which peculiarly belong to his age and his country; and to point out the beauties of particular passages. I sometimes indeed endeavour to open the design of the prophecy, to shew the connexion between its parts, and to point out the event which it foretells. But in general I must entreat the reader to be satisfied with my endeavours faithfully to express the literal sense, which is all that I undertake. If he would go deeper into the mystical sense, into theological, historical, and chronological disquisitions, there are many learned expositors to whom he may have recourse, who have written full commentaries on this Prophet; to which title the present work has no pretensions. The sublime and spiritual uses to be made of this peculiarly evangelical Prophet, must, as I have observed, be all founded on a faithful representation of the literal sense which his words contain. This is what I have endeavoured closely and exactly to express. And within the limits of this humble, but necessary province, my endeavours must be confined. To proceed further, or even to execute this in the manner I could wish, were it within my abilities, yet would hardly be consistent with my present engagements; which oblige me to offer rather prematurely to the public, what further time, with more leisure, might perhaps enable me to render more worthy of their attention.

ISAIAH.

CHAP. I.

1 THE VISION OF ISAIAH THE SON OF AMOTS, WHICH HE SAW CONCERNING JUDAH AND JERUSALEM; IN THE DAYS OF UZZIAH, JOTHAM, AHAZ, HEZEKIAH, KINGS OF JUDAH.

2 Hear, O ye heavens; and give ear, O earth!
For it is JEHOVAH that speaketh.
I have nourished children, and brought them up;
And even they have revolted from me.
3 The ox knoweth his possessor;
And the ass the crib of his lord:
But Israel knoweth not Me;
Neither doth my people consider.
4 Ah, sinful nation! a people laden with iniquity!
A race of evil doers! children degenerate!
They have forsaken JEHOVAH;
They have rejected with disdain the Holy One of Israel;
They are estranged from him; they have turned their back upon him.
5 On what part will ye smite again, will ye add correction?
The whole head is sick, and the whole heart faint:
6 From the sole of the foot even to the head, there is no soundness therein;
It is wound, and bruise, and putrefying sore:

It hath not been pressed, neither hath it been bound;
Neither hath it been softened with ointment.
7 Your country is desolate, your cities are burnt with fire;
Your land, before your eyes strangers devour it;
And it is become desolate, as if destroyed by an inundation.
8 And the daughter of Sion is left, as a shed in a vineyard;
As a lodge in a garden of cucumbers, as a city taken by siege.
9 Had not JEHOVAH God of Hosts left us a remnant,
We had soon become as Sodom; we had been like unto Gomorrah.

10   Hear ye the word of JEHOVAH, O ye princes of Sodom!
Give ear to the law of our God, ye people of Gomorrah!
11 What have I to do with the multitude of your sacrifices? saith JEHOVAH:
I am cloyed with the burnt-offerings of rams, and the fat of fed beasts;
And in the blood of bullocks, and of lambs, and of goats, I have no delight.
12 When you come to appear before me,
Who hath required this at your hands?
13 Tread my courts no more; bring no more a vain oblation:
Incense! it is an abomination unto me.
The new moon, and the sabbath, and the assembly proclaimed,
I cannot endure; the fast, and the day of restraint.
14 Your months, and your solemnities, my soul hateth:
They are a burthen upon me; I am weary of bearing them.
15 When ye spread forth your hands, I will hide mine eyes from you;.
Even when ye multiply prayer, I will not hear;
For your hands are full of blood.
16 Wash ye, make ye clean; remove ye far away
The evil of your doings from before mine eyes:
17 Cease to do evil; learn to do well;
Seek judgment; amend that which is corrupted;
Do justice to the fatherless; defend the cause of the widow.

18   Come on now, and let us plead together, saith JE-
       HOVAH:
    Though your sins be as scarlet, they shall be as white
       as snow;
    Though they be red as crimson, they shall be like wool.
19 If ye shall be willing and obedient,
    Ye shall feed on the good of the land;
20 But if ye refuse, and be rebellious,
    Ye shall be food for the sword of the enemy:
    For the mouth of JEHOVAH hath pronounced it.

21   How is the faithful city become a harlot!
    She that was full of judgment, righteousness dwelled in
       her;
    But now murtherers!
22 Thy silver is become dross; thy wine is mixed with
       water.
23 Thy princes are rebellious, associates of robbers;
    Every one of them loveth a gift, and seeketh rewards:
    To the fatherless they administer not justice;
    And the cause of the widow cometh not before them.

24   Wherefore saith the Lord JEHOVAH God of Hosts, the
       Mighty One of Israel;
    Aha! I will be eased of mine adversaries;
    I will be avenged of mine enemies.
25 And I will bring again mine hand over thee;
    And I will purge in the furnace thy dross;
    And I will remove all thine alloy.
26 And I will restore thy judges, as at the first;
    And thy counsellors, as at the beginning:
    And after this thy name shall be called,
    The city of righteousness, the faithful metropolis.
27 Sion shall be redeemed in judgment,
    And her captives in righteousness:
28 But destruction shall fall at once on the revolters and
       the sinners;
    And they that forsake JEHOVAH shall be consumed.
29 For ye shall be ashamed of the ilexes, which ye have
       desired;
    And ye shall blush for the gardens, which ye have
       chosen:

30 When ye shall be as an ilex, whose leaves are blasted;
   And as a garden, wherein is no water.
31 And the strong shall become tow, and his work a spark
     of fire;
   And they shall both burn together, and none shall
     quench them.

CHAP. II.
1   THE WORD, WHICH WAS REVEALED TO ISAIAH, THE
   SON OF AMOTS, CONCERNING JUDAH AND JERUSALEM.

2   IT shall come to pass in the latter days;
   The mountain of the house of JEHOVAH shall be estab-
     lished on the top of the mountains;
   And it shall be exalted above the hills:
   And all nations shall flow unto it.
3 And many peoples shall go, and shall say,
   Come ye, and let us go up to the mountain of JEHO-
     VAH;
   To the house of the God of Jacob;
   And he will teach us of his ways;
   And we will walk in his paths:
   For from Sion shall go forth the law;
4 And the word of JEHOVAH from Jerusalem.
   And he shall judge among the nations;
   And shall work conviction in many peoples:
   And they shall beat their swords into ploughshares,
   And their spears into pruning-hooks:
   Nation shall not lift up sword against nation;
   Neither shall they learn war any more.

5   O house of Jacob, come ye,
   And let us walk in the light of JEHOVAH!
6 Verily thou hast abandoned thy people, the house of
     Jacob:
   Because they are filled with diviners from the east;
   And with soothsayers like the Philistines;
   And they multiply a spurious brood of strange children.
7 And his land is filled with silver and gold;
   And there is no end to his treasures:
   And his land is filled with horses;
   Neither is there any end to his chariots.

8 And his land is filled with idols;
   He boweth himself down to the work of his hands;
   To that which his fingers have made:
9 Therefore shall the mean man be bowed down, and the mighty man shall be humbled;
   And thou wilt not forgive them.

10 Go into the rock, and hide thyself in the dust;
    From the fear of JEHOVAH, and from the glory of his majesty,
    When he ariseth to strike the earth with terror.
11 The lofty eyes of men shall be humbled;
   The highth of mortals shall bow down:
   And JEHOVAH alone shall be exalted in that day.
12 For the day of JEHOVAH God of Hosts is against every thing great and lofty;
   And against every thing that is exalted, and it shall be humbled.
13 Even against all the cedars of Lebanon, the high and the exalted;
   And against all the oaks of Basan:
14 And against all the mountains, the high ones;
   And against all the hills, the exalted ones;
15 And against every tower, high-raised;
   And against every mound, strongly fortified.
16 And against all the ships of Tarshish;
   And against every lovely work of art.
17 And the pride of man shall bow down;
   And the highth of mortals shall be humbled;
   And JEHOVAH alone shall be exalted in that day:
18 And the idols shall totally disappear:
19 And they shall go into caverns of rocks, and into holes of the dust;
   From the fear of JEHOVAH, and from the glory of his majesty,
   When he ariseth to strike the earth with terror.
20 In that day shall a man cast away his idols of silver,
   And his idols of gold, which they have made to worship;
   To the moles and to the bats:
21 To go into caves of the rocks, and into clefts of the craggy rocks;

From the fear of JEHOVAH, and from the glory of his majesty,
When he ariseth to strike the earth with terror.

22 Trust ye no more in man, whose breath is in his nostrils;
For of what account is he to be made?

CHAP. III.
1 For behold the Lord JEHOVAH God of Hosts
Removeth from Jerusalem, and from Judah,
Every stay and support;
The whole stay of bread, and the whole stay of water;
2 The mighty man, and the warrior;
The judge, and the prophet, and the diviner, and the sage:
3 The ruler of fifty, and the honourable person;
And the counsellor, and the skilful artist, and the powerful in persuasion.
4 And I will make boys their princes;
And infants shall rule over them.
5 And the people shall be oppressed, one man by another:
And every man shall behave insolently towards his neighbour;
The boy towards the old man, and the base towards the honourable.
6 Therefore shall a man take his brother, of his father's house, by the garment;
Saying, Come, and be thou ruler over us;
And let thine hand support our ruinous state.
7 Then shall he openly declare, saying,
I will not be the healer of your breaches;
For in my house is neither bread, nor raiment:
Appoint not me ruler of the people.
8 For Jerusalem tottereth, and Judah falleth;
Because their tongues, and their hands, are against JEHOVAH;
To provoke by their disobedience the cloud of his glory.
9 The stedfastness of their countenance witnesseth against them;
For their sin, like Sodom, they publish, they hide it not:
Wo to their souls! for upon themselves have they brought down evil.

10 Pronounce ye a blessing on the just: verily good [shall
    be to him];
   For the fruit of his deeds shall he eat.
11 Wo to the wicked: evil [shall be his portion];
   For the work of his hands shall be repaid unto him.
12 As for my people, children are their oppressors;
   And women bear rule over them.
   O my people, thy leaders cause thee to err;
   And pervert the way of thy paths.

13   JEHOVAH ariseth to plead his cause;
   He standeth up to contend with his people.
14 JEHOVAH will meet in judgment,
   The elders of his people, and their princes:
   As for you, ye have consumed my vineyard;
   The plunder of the poor is in your houses.
15 What mean ye, that ye crush my people;
   And grind the faces of the poor?
   Saith JEHOVAH, the Lord of Hosts.

16   Moreover JEHOVAH hath said:
   Because the daughters of Sion are haughty;
   And walk displaying the neck,
   And falsely setting off their eyes with paint;
   Mincing their steps as they go,
   And with their feet lightly tripping along:
17 Therefore will the Lord humble the head of the daughters
    of Sion;
   And JEHOVAH will expose their nakedness.
18 In that day will the Lord take from them the ornaments
   Of the feet-rings, and the net-works, and the crescents;
19 The pendents, and the bracelets, and the thin veils;
20 The tires, and the fetters, and the zones,
   And the perfume-boxes, and the amulets;
21 The rings, and the jewels of the nostril;
22 The embroidered robes, and the tunics;
   And the cloaks, and the little purses;
23 The transparent garments, and the fine linen vests;
   And the turbans, and the mantles:
24 And there shall be, instead of perfume, a putrid ulcer;
   And, instead of well-girt raiment, rags;
   And, instead of high-dressed hair, baldness;

And, instead of a zone, a girdle of sackcloth :
A sun-burnt skin, instead of beauty.
25 Thy people shall fall by the sword ;
And thy mighty men in the battle.
26 And her doors shall lament and mourn ;
And desolate shall she sit on the ground.

CHAP. IV.
1 And seven women shall lay hold on one man in that day, saying :
Our own bread will we eat,
And with our own garments will we be clothed ;
Only let us be called by thy name ;
Take away our reproach.

2   In that day shall the branch of JEHOVAH
Become glorious and honourable ;
And the produce of the land excellent and beautiful,
For the escaped of the house of Israel.
3 And it shall come to pass, whosoever is left in Sion,
And remaineth in Jerusalem,
Holy shall he be called ;
Every one that is written among the living in Jerusalem.
4 When the Lord shall have washed away the filth of the daughters of Sion ;
And the blood of Jerusalem shall have removed from the midst of her,
By a spirit of judgment, and by a spirit of burning :
6 Then shall JEHOVAH create upon the station of Mount Sion,
And upon all her holy assemblies,
A cloud by day, and smoke ;
And the brightness of a flaming fire by night :
Yea, over all shall the Glory be a covering.
6 And a tabernacle it shall be, for shade by day from the heat ;
And for a covert, and a refuge, from storm and rain.

CHAP. V.
1. LET me sing now a song to my Beloved ;
A song of loves concerning his vineyard.
My Beloved had a vineyard,
On a high and fruitful hill :
2 And he fenced it round, and be cleared it from the stones,

And he planted it with the vine of Sorek;
And he built a tower in the midst of it,
And he hewed out also a lake therein:
And he expected, that it should bring forth grapes,
But it brought forth poisonous berries.
3 And now, O inhabitants of Jerusalem, and ye men of Judah,
Judge, I pray you, between me and my vineyard:
4 What could have been done more to my vineyard,
Than I have done unto it?
Why, when I expected that it should bring forth grapes,
Brought it forth poisonous berries?
5 But come now, and I will make known unto you,
What I purpose to do to my vineyard:
To remove its hedge, and it shall be devoured;
To destroy its fence, and it shall be trodden down.
6 And I will make it a desolation:
And it shall not be pruned, neither shall it be digged;
But the briar and the thorn shall spring up in it;
And I will command the clouds,
That they shed no rain upon it.
7 Verily, the vineyard of JEHOVAH GOD of Hosts is the house of Israel;
And the men of Judah the plant of his delight:
And he looked for judgment, but behold tyranny;
And for righteousness, but behold the cry of the oppressed.

8 Wo unto you, who join house to house;
Who lay field unto field together;
Until there be no place, and ye have your dwelling
Alone to yourselves, in the midst of the land.
9 To mine ear hath JEHOVAH GOD of Hosts revealed it:
Surely many houses shall become a desolation;
The great and the fair ones, without an inhabitant.
10 Yea, ten acres of vineyard shall yield a single bath of wine,
And a chomer of seed shall produce an ephah.
11 Wo unto them, who rise early in the morning, to follow strong drink;
Who sit late in the evening, that wine may inflame them:
12 And the lyre, and the harp, the tabor, and the pipe,
And wine, are their entertainments:

But the works of JEHOVAH they regard not;
And the operation of his hands they do not perceive.
13 Therefore my people goeth into captivity for want of knowledge;
And their nobles have died with hunger;
And their plebeians are parched up with thirst.
14 Therefore Hades hath enlarged his appetite;
And hath stretched open his mouth without measure:
And down go her nobility, and her populace;
And her busy throng, and all that exult in her.
15 And the mean man shall be bowed down, and the great man shall be brought low;
And the eyes of the haughty shall be humbled:
16 And JEHOVAH God of Hosts shall be exalted in judgment;
And God the Holy One shall be sanctified by displaying his righteousness.
17 Then shall the sheep feed without restraint;
And the kids shall depasture the desolate fields of the luxurious.
18 Wo unto them, who draw out iniquity, as a long cable;
And sin, as the thick traces of a wain:
19 Who say, let him make speed then, let him hasten
His work, that he may see it;
And let the counsel of the Holy One of Israel
Draw near, and come to pass, that we may know it.
20 Wo unto them who call evil good, and good evil;
Who put darkness for light, and light for darkness;
Who put bitter for sweet and sweet for bitter.
21 Wo unto them, who are wise in their own eyes,
And prudent in their own conceit.
22 Wo unto them, who are powerful to drink wine;
And men of might to mingle strong drink:
23 Who justify the guilty for reward,
And take away the righteousness of the righteous from him.
24 Therefore, as the tongue of fire licketh up the stubble,
And as the flame dissolveth the chaff;
So shall their root become like touchwood,
And their blossom shall go up like the dust:
Because they have despised the law of JEHOVAH God of Hosts;
And scornfully rejected the word of the Holy One of Israel.

25 Wherefore the anger of JEHOVAH is kindled against his
    people;
And he hath stretched out his hand against them:
And he smote them; and the mountains trembled;
And their carcasses became as the dung in the midst of
    the streets.
For all this his anger is not turned away;
But still is his hand stretched out.
25 And he will erect a standard for the nations afar off;
And he will hist every one of them from the ends of the
    earth;
And behold, with speed swiftly shall they come.
27 None among them is faint, and none stumbleth;
None shall slumber, nor sleep:
Nor shall the girdle of their loins be loosed;
Nor shall the latchet of their shoes be unbound.
28 Whose arrows are sharpened;
And all their bows are bent:
The hoofs of their horses shall be counted as adamant;
And their wheels as a whirlwind.
29 Their growling is like the growling of the lioness;
Like the young lions shall they growl:
They shall roar and shall seize the prey;
And they shall bear it away, and none shall rescue it.
30 In that day, shall they roar against them, like the roaring of the sea;
And these shall look to the heaven upward, and down to
    the earth;
And lo! darkness, distress!
And the light is obscured by the gloomy vapour.

CHAP. VI.
1 In the year in which Uzziah the king died, I saw JEHOVAH sitting on a throne high and lofty; and the train
2 of his robe filled the temple. Above him stood seraphim: each one of them had six wings: with two of them he covereth his face, with two of them he covereth his feet, and
3 two of them he useth in flying. And they cried alternately, and said:
    Holy, holy, holy, JEHOVAH God of Hosts!
    The whole earth is filled with his glory.

4 And the pillars of the vestibule were shaken with the voice
   of their cry; and the temple was filled with smoke. And
5 I said, Alas for me! I am struck dumb: for I am a man
   of polluted lips; and in the midst of a people of polluted
   lips do I dwell: for mine eyes have seen the King, JE-
6 HOVAH God of Hosts. And one of the seraphim came
   flying unto me; and in his hand was a burning coal,
   which he had taken with the tongs from off the altar. And
7 he touched my mouth, and said —
   Lo! this hath touched thy lips;
   Thine iniquity is removed, and thy sin is expiated.
8 And I heard the voice of JEHOVAH, saying: Whom shall
   I send; and who will go for us? And I said: Behold,
9 Here am I; send me. And he said:—
   Go, and say thou to this people:
   Hear ye indeed, but understand not;
   See ye indeed, but perceive not:
   Make gross the heart of this people;
   Make their ears dull, and close up their eyes;
   Lest they see with their eyes, and hear with their ears,
   And understand with their hearts, and be converted;
   and I should heal them.
11 And I said: How long, O JEHOVAH? And he said:—
   Until cities be laid waste, so that there be no inhabitant;
   And houses, so that there be no man:
   And the land be left utterly desolate.
12 Until JEHOVAH remove man far away;
   And there be many a deserted woman in the midst of
   the land.
13 And though there be a tenth part remaining in it,
   Even this shall undergo a repeated destruction;
   Yet, as the ilex, and the oak, though cut down, hath its
   stock remaining,
   A holy seed shall be the stock of the nation.

CHAP. VII.
1 In the days of Ahaz, the son of Jotham, the son of
   Uzziah king of Judah, Retsin king of Syria, and Pekah,
   the son of Remaliah, king of Israel, came up against
   Jerusalem, to besiege it; but they could not overcome
2 it. And when it was told to the house of David, that
   Syria was supported by Ephraim; the heart of the king,

and the heart of his people, was moved; as the trees of the forest are moved before the wind.
3 And JEHOVAH said to Isaiah: Go out now to meet Ahaz; thou and Shearjashub thy son; at the end of the aqueduct of the upper pool, at the causeway of the ful-
4 ler's field. And thou shalt say unto him:—
Take heed, and be still; fear not, neither let thy heart be faint,
Because of the two tails of these smoking firebrands;
For the fierce wrath of Retsin, and of the son of Remaliah.
5 Because Syria hath devised evil against thee;
Ephraim, and the son of Remaliah, saying:
6 Let us go up against Judah, and harass it;
And let us rend off a part of it for ourselves;
And let us set a king to reign in the midst of it;
Even the son of Tabeal.
7 Thus saith the Lord JEHOVAH:
It shall not stand, neither shall it be.
8 Though the head of Syria be Damascus,
And the head of Damascus, Retsin;
Yet within threescore and five years
Ephraim shall be broken, that he be no more a people:
9 Though the head of Ephraim be Samaria;
And the head of Samaria, Remaliah's son.
If ye believe not in me, ye shall not be established.
10 And JEHOVAH spake yet again to Ahaz, saying:
11 Ask thee a sign from JEHOVAH thy God:
Go deep to the grave, or high to the heaven above.
12 And Ahaz said: I will not ask; neither will I tempt
13 JEHOVAH. And he said:
Hear ye now, O house of David:
Is it a small thing for you to weary men,
That you should weary my God also?
14 Therefore JEHOVAH himself shall give you a sign:
Behold, the Virgin conceiveth, and beareth a son;
And she shall call his name, Immanuel.
15 Butter and honey shall he eat,
When he shall know to refuse what is evil, and to choose what is good:
16 For before this child shall know

To refuse the evil, and to choose the good;
The land shall become desolate,
By whose two kings thou art distressed.
17 But Jehovah shall bring upon thee,
And upon thy people, and upon thy father's house,
Days, such as have not come,
From the day that Ephraim departed from Judah.
18 And it shall come to pass in that day;
Jehovah shall hist the fly,
That is in the utmost part of the rivers of Egypt;
And the bee, that is in the land of Assyria:
19 And they shall come, and they shall light all of them
On the desolate vallies, and on the craggy rocks,
And on all the thickets, and on all the caverns.
20 In that day, Jehovah shall shave by the hired razor,
By the people beyond the river, by the king of Assyria,
The head and the hair of the feet;
And even the beard itself shall be destroyed.
21 And it shall come to pass in that day,
That if a man shall feed a young cow, and two sheep;
22 From the plenty of milk, which they shall produce, he shall eat butter:
Even butter and honey shall he eat,
Whosoever is left in the midst of the land.
23 And every vineyard, that hath a thousand vines,
Valued at a thousand pieces of silver,
Shall become in that day briers and thorns.
24 With arrows and with the bows shall they come thither;
For the whole land shall become briers and thorns.
25 And all the hills, which were dressed with the mattock,
Where the fear of briers and thorns never came,
Shall be for the range of the ox, and for the treading of sheep.

CHAP. VIII.
1 And Jehovah said unto me: Take unto thee a large mirror, and write on it with a workman's graving tool;
2 To hasten the spoil, to take quickly the prey. And I called unto me for a testimony faithful witnesses; Uriah the priest, and Zachariah the son of Jeberechiah.

3 And I approached unto the prophetess; and she conceived, and bare a son. And JEHOVAH said unto me: Call his name Maher-shalal hash-baz;
4   For before the child shall know
To pronounce, My father and My mother,
The riches of Damascus shall be borne away,
And the spoil of Samaria, before the king of Assyria.
5 Yet again JEHOVAH spake unto me, saying:
6   Because this people hath rejected
The waters of Siloah, which flow gently;
And rejoiceth in Retsin, and the son of Remaliah:
7   Therefore behold the Lord bringeth up upon them
The waters of the river, the strong and the mighty;
Even the king of Assyria, and all his force.
And he shall rise above all their channels,
And shall go over all their banks,
8   And he shall pass through Judah, overflowing and spreading,
Even to the neck shall he reach:
And the extension of his wings shall be
Over the full breadth of thy land, O Immanuel!

9   Know ye this, O ye peoples, and be struck with consternation;
And give ear to it, all ye of distant lands:
Gird yourselves, and be dismayed; gird yourselves, and be dismayed.
10   Take counsel together, and it shall come to nought;
Speak the word, and it shall not stand:
For God is with us.
11   For thus said JEHOVAH unto me;
As taking me by the hand he instructed me,
That I should not walk in the way of this people, saying:
12 Say ye not, It is holy,
Of every thing of which this people shall say, It is holy:
And fear ye not the object of their fear, neither be ye terrified.
13 JEHOVAH God of Hosts, sanctify ye him;
And let him be your fear, and let him be your dread:
14 And he shall be unto you a sanctuary;
But a stone of stumbling, and a rock of offence,
To the two houses of Israel;

A trap and a snare to the inhabitants of Jerusalem.
15 And many among them shall stumble.
And shall fall, and be broken; and shall be ensnared and caught.
16 Bind up the testimony, seal the command, among my disciples.
17 I will therefore wait for JEHOVAH, who hideth his face
From the house of Jacob; yet will I look for him.
18 Behold, I, and the children,
Whom JEHOVAH hath given unto me;
For signs and for wonders in Israel,
From JEHOVAH God of Hosts,
Who dwelleth in the mountain of Sion.
19 And when they shall say unto you:
Seek unto the necromancers and the wizards;
To them that speak inwardly, and that mutter:
Should not a people seek unto their God?
Should they seek, instead of the living, unto the dead?
20 Unto the command, and unto the testimony, let them seek:
If they will not speak according to this word,
In which there is no obscurity;
21 Every one of them shall pass through the land distressed and famished:
And when he shall be famished, and angry with himself,
He shall curse his king and his God.
22 And he shall cast his eyes upwards, and look down to the earth:
And lo! distress and darkness!
Gloom, tribulation, and accumulated darkness!

23 But there shall not hereafter be darkness in the land which was distressed:
In the former time he debased
The land of Zebulon, and the land of Naphthali;
But in the latter time he hath made it glorious:
Even the way of the sea, beyond Jordan, Galilee of the nations.

CHAP. IX.
1 The people, that walked in darkness,
Have seen a great light;
They that dwelled in the land of the shadow of death,
Unto them hath the light shined.

2 Thou hast multiplied the nation, thou hast increased their joy:
They rejoice before thee, as with the joy of harvest;
As they rejoice, who divide the spoil.
3 For the yoke of his burthen, the staff laid on his shoulder,
The rod of his oppressor, hast thou broken, as in the day of Midian.
4 For the greaves of the armed warrior in the conflict,
And the garment rolled in much blood,
Shall be for a burning, even fuel for the fire.
5 For unto us a Child is born; unto us a Son is given;
And the government shall be upon his shoulder:
And his name shall be called Wonderful, Counsellor,
The mighty God, the Father of the everlasting age, the Prince of peace.
6 Of the increase of his government and peace there shall be no end;
Upon the throne of David, and upon his kingdom;
To fix it, and to establish it
With judgment and with justice, henceforth and for ever:
The zeal of JEHOVAH God of Hosts will do this.

7 JEHOVAH hath sent a word against Jacob;
And it hath lighted upon Israel.
8 Because the people all of them carry themselves haughtily;
Ephraim, and the inhabitant of Samaria;
In pride and arrogance of heart, saying:
9 The bricks are fallen, but we will build with hewn stone;
The sycamores are cut down, but we will replace them with cedars:
10 Therefore will JEHOVAH excite the princes of Retsin against him:
And raise up his enemies together:
11 The Syrians from the east, and the Philistines from the west;
And they shall devour Israel on every side.
For all this his anger is not turned away;
But his hand is still stretched out.

7*

12   Yet this people have not turned unto him that smote them;
    And JEHOVAH God of Hosts they have not sought.
13 Therefore shall JEHOVAH cut off from Israel the head and the tail;
    The branch and the rush, in one day:
14 The aged, and the honourable person, he is the head;
    And the prophet that teacheth falsehood, he is the tail.
15 For the leaders of this people lead them astray;
    And they that are led by them shall be devoured.
16 Wherefore JEHOVAH shall not rejoice over their young men;
    And on their orphans, and their widows, he shall have no compassion.
    For every one of them is a hypocrite and evil-doer;
    And every mouth speaketh folly.
        For all this his anger is not turned away;
        But his hand is still stretched out.

17   For wickedness burneth like a fire;
    The brier and the bramble it shall consume:
    And it shall kindle the thicket of the wood;
    And they shall mount up in volumes of rising smoke.
18 Through the wrath of JEHOVAH God of Hosts is the land darkened;
    And the people shall be as fuel for the fire:
    A man shall not spare his brother.
19 But he shall snatch on the right, and yet be hungry;
    And he shall devour on the left, and not be satisfied:
    Every man shall devour the flesh of his neighbour.
20 Manasseh shall devour Ephraim, and Ephraim Manasseh;
    And both of them shall be united against Judah.
        For all this his anger is not turned away;
        But his hand is still stretched out.

CHAP. X.
1   Wo unto them, that decree unrighteous decrees;
    Unto the scribes, that prescribe oppression:
2 To turn aside the needy from judgment;
    To rob of their right the poor of my people:

That the widows may become their prey;
And that they may plunder the orphans.
3 And what will ye do in the day of visitation?
And in the desolation, which shall come from afar?
To whom will ye flee for succour?
And where will ye deposit your wealth?
4 Without me, they shall bow down under the bounden,
And under the slain shall they fall.
   For all this his anger is not turned away;
   But his hand is still stretched out.

5   Ho! to the Assyrian, the rod of mine anger,
The staff in whose hand is the instrument of mine indignation!
6 Against a dissembling nation will I send him;
And against a people the object of my wrath will I give him a charge:
To gather the spoil, and to bear away the prey;
And to trample them under foot like the mire of the streets.
7 But he doth not so purpose;
And his heart doth not so intend:
But to destroy is in his heart;
And to cut off nations not a few.
8 For he saith, Are not my princes altogether kings?
9 Is not Calno as Carchemish?
Is not Hamath as Arphad?
Is not Samaria as Damascus?
10 As my hand hath seized the kingdoms of the idols,
Whose graven images were superior to those of Samaria and Jerusalem;
11 As I have done unto Samaria and her idols,
Shall I not likewise do unto Jerusalem, and her images?
12   But it shall be, when JEHOVAH hath accomplished his whole work
Upon Mount Sion, and upon Jerusalem;
I will punish the effect of the proud heart of the king of Assyria;
And the triumphant look of his haughty eyes.
13 For he hath said, By the strength of my hand have I done it;
  And by my wisdom; for I am endowed with prudence.

I have removed the bounds of the peoples;
And I have plundered their hoarded treasures;
And I have brought down those, that were strongly
  seated.
14 And my hand hath found, as a nest, the riches of the
  peoples;
And as one gathereth eggs deserted,
So have I made a general gathering of the earth:
And there was no one, that moved the wing;
That opened the beak, or that chirped.
15 Shall the axe boast itself against him, that heweth
    therewith?
Shall the saw magnify itself against him, that moveth it?
As if the rod should wield him, that lifteth it;
As if the staff should lift up its master.
16 Wherefore JEHOVAH the Lord of Hosts shall send
Upon his fat ones leanness;
And under his glory shall he kindle
A burning as of a conflagration.
17 And the light of Israel shall become a fire,
And his Holy One a flame;
And he shall burn, and consume his thorn
And his brier in one day.
18 Even the glory of his forest, and of his fruitful field,
From the soul even to the flesh, shall he consume;
And it shall be, as when one fleeth out of the fire.
19 And the remainder of the trees of his forest shall be a small
  number,
So that a child may write them down.

20   And it shall come to pass in that day,
No more shall the remnant of Israel,
And the escaped of the house of Jacob,
Lean upon him, that smote them:
But shall lean upon JEHOVAH,
The Holy One of Israel, in truth.
21 A remnant shall return, a remnant of Jacob,
Unto God the Mighty.
22 For though thy people, O Israel, shall be as the sand of the
  sea,
A remnant of them only shall return.
The consummation decided, overfloweth with strict jus-
  tice;

23 For a full and decisive decree
   Shall JEHOVAH the Lord of Hosts accomplish in the midst
      of the land.
24   Wherefore thus saith Jehovah the Lord of Hosts:
   Fear not, O my people, that dwellest in Sion, because of
      the Assyrian:
   With his staff indeed shall he smite thee,
   And his rod shall he lift up against thee, in the way of
      Egypt.
25 But yet a very little time, and mine indignation shall
      cease;
   And mine anger in their destruction:
26 And JEHOVAH God of Hosts shall raise up against him a
      scourge,
   Like the stroke upon Midian at the rock of Oreb,
   And like the rod which he lifted up over the sea;
   Yea he will lift it up, after the manner of Egypt.
27 And it shall come to pass in that day,
   His burthen shall be removed from off thy shoulder,
   And his yoke from off thy neck:
   Yea the yoke shall perish from off your shoulders.

28 He is come to Aiath; he hath passed to Migron;
   At Michmas he will deposit his baggage.
29 They have passed the strait; Geba is their lodging for
      the night:
   Ramah is frightened; Gibeah of Saul fleeth.
30 Cry aloud with thy voice, O daughter of Gallim;
   Hearken unto her, O Laish; answer her, O Anathoth.
31 Madmena is gone away; the inhabitants of Gebim flee
      amain.
32 Yet this day shall he abide in Nob:
   He shall shake his hand against the mount of the daugh-
      ter of Sion;
   Against the hill of Jerusalem.
33   Behold JEHOVAH, the Lord of Hosts,
   Shall lop the flourishing branch with a dreadful crash;
   And the high of stature shall be cut down,
   And the lofty shall be brought low:
34 And he shall hew the thickets of the forest with iron,
   And Lebanon shall fall by a mighty hand.

CHAP. XI.
1 But there shall spring forth a rod from the trunk of Jesse;
And a scion from his roots shall become fruitful.
2 And the spirit of Jehovah shall rest upon him;
The spirit of wisdom, and understanding;
The spirit of counsel, and strength;
The spirit of the knowledge, and the fear of Jehovah.
3 And he shall be of quick discernment in the fear of Jehovah:
So that not according to the sight of his eyes shall he judge;
Nor according to the hearing of his ears shall he reprove.
4 But with righteousness shall he judge the poor,
And with equity shall he work conviction in the meek of the earth.
And he shall smite the earth with a blast of his mouth,
And with the breath of his lips he shall slay the wicked one.
5 And righteousness shall be the girdle of his loins;
And faithfulness the cincture of his reins.
6 Then shall the wolf take up his abode with the lamb;
And the leopard shall lie down with the kid:
And the calf, and the young lion, and the fatling shall come together;
And a little child shall lead them.
7 And the heifer and the she-bear shall feed together;
Together shall their young ones lie down;
And the lion shall eat straw like the ox.
8 And the suckling shall play upon the hole of the aspic;
And upon the den of the basilisk shall the new-weaned child lay his hand.
9 They shall not hurt, nor destroy, in all my holy mountain;
For the earth shall be full of the knowledge of Jehovah,
As the waters that cover the depths of the sea.
10 And it shall come to pass in that day,
The root of Jesse, which standeth for an ensign to the peoples,
Unto him shall the nations repair,
And his resting-place shall be glorious.

11 And it shall come to pass in that day,
   JEHOVAH shall again the second time put forth his hand,
   To recover the remnant of his people
   That remaineth, from Assyria, and from Egypt;
   And from Pathros, and from Cush, and from Elam;
   And from Shinear, and from Hamath, and from the western regions.
12 And he shall lift up a signal to the nations;
   And he shall gather the outcasts of Israel,
   And the dispersed of Judah shall he collect,
   From the four extremities of the earth.
13 And the jealousy of Ephraim shall cease;
   And the enmity of Judah shall be no more:
   Ephraim shall not be jealous of Judah;
   And Judah shall not be at enmity with Ephraim.
14 But they shall invade the borders of the Philistines westward;
   Together shall they spoil the children of the east:
   On Edom and Moab they shall lay their hand;
   And the sons of Ammon shall obey them.
15 And JEHOVAH shall smite with a drought the tongue of the Egyptian sea;
   And he shall shake his hand over the river with his vehement wind;
   And he shall strike it into seven streams,
   And make them pass over it dry-shod.
16 And there shall be a high-way for the remnant of his people,
   Which shall remain from Assyria:
   As it was unto Israel,
   In the day when he came up from the land of Egypt.

CHAP. XII.

1   AND in that day thou shalt say:
    I will give thanks unto thee, O JEHOVAH; for though thou hast been angry with me,
    Thine anger is turned away, and thou hast comforted me.
2   Behold, God is my salvation;
    I will trust, and will not be afraid:
    For my strength, and my song, is JEHOVAH;
    And he is become unto me salvation.
3 And when ye shall draw waters with joy from the foun-
4 tains of salvation; in that day ye shall say:
    Give ye thanks to JEHOVAH; call upon his name;

Make known among the peoples his mighty deeds:
Record ye, how highly his name is exalted.
5 Sing ye Jehovah; for he hath wrought a stupendous work:
This is made manifest in all the earth.
6 Cry aloud, and shout for joy, O inhabitress of Sion;
For great in the midst of thee is the Holy One of Israel.

CHAP. XIII.
1 The oracle concerning Babylon, which was revealed to Isaiah, the son of Amots.

2 Upon a lofty mountain erect the standard;
Exalt the voice; beckon with the hand;
That they may enter the gates of princes.
3 I have given a charge to mine enrolled warriors;
I have even called my strong ones to execute my wrath;
Those that exult in my greatness.
4 A sound of a multitude in the mountains, as of a great people;
A sound of the tumult of kingdoms, of nations gathered together!
Jehovah, God of Hosts, mustereth the host for the battle.
5 They come from a distant land, from the end of the heavens;
Jehovah, and the instruments of his wrath, to destroy the whole land.
6 Howl ye, for the day of Jehovah is at hand:
As a destruction from the Almighty shall it come.
7 Therefore shall all hands be slackened;
And every heart of mortal shall melt; and they shall be terrified:
8 Torments and pangs shall seize them;
As a woman in travail, they shall be pained:
They shall look one upon another with astonishment;
Their countenances shall be like flames of fire.
9 Behold, the day of Jehovah cometh, inexorable;
Even indignation, and burning wrath:
To make the land a desolation;
And her sinners he shall destroy from out of her.

10 Yea the stars of heaven, and the constellations thereof,
Shall not send forth their light :
The sun is darkened at his going forth,
And the moon shall not cause her light to shine.
11 And I will visit the world for its evil,
And the wicked for their iniquity :
And I will put an end to the arrogance of the proud ;
And I will bring down the haughtiness of the terrible.
12 I will make a mortal more precious than fine gold ;
Yea a man, than the rich ore of Ophir.
13 Wherefore I will make the heavens tremble ;
And the earth shall be shaken out of her place:
In the indignation of JEHOVAH God of Hosts ;
And in the day of his burning anger.
14 And the remnant shall be as a roe chased ;
And as sheep, when there is none to gather them to-
gether ;
They shall look, every one towards his own people ;
And they shall flee every one to his own land.
15 Every one, that is overtaken, shall be thrust through ;
And all that are collected in a body shall fall by the
sword.
16 And their infants shall be dashed before their eyes ;
Their houses shall be plundered, and their wives ravished.
17   Behold, I raise up against them the Medes ;
Who shall hold silver of no account ;
And as for gold, they shall not delight in it.
18 Their bows shall dash the young men ;
And on the fruit of the womb they shall have no mercy ;
Their eye shall have no pity even on the children.
19 And Babylon shall become, she that was the beauty of
kingdoms,
The glory of the pride of the Chaldeans,
As the overthrow of Sodom and Gomorrah by the hand of
God.
20 It shall not be inhabited for ever ;
Nor shall it be dwelt in from generation to generation :
Neither shall the Arabian pitch his tent there ;
Neither shall the shepherds make their folds there.
21 But there shall the wild beasts of the deserts lodge ;
And howling monsters shall fill their houses :
And there shall the daughters of the ostrich dwell ;
And there shall the satyrs hold their revels.

22 And wolves shall howl to one another in their palaces;
And dragons in their voluptuous pavilions.
And her time is near come;
And her days shall not be prolonged.

CHAP. XIV.
1   For JEHOVAH will have compassion on Jacob,
And will yet choose Israel.
And he shall give them rest upon their own land:
And the stranger shall be joined unto them,
And shall cleave unto the house of Jacob.
2 And the nations shall take them, and bring them into their own place;
And the house of Israel shall possess them in the land of JEHOVAH,
As servants and as handmaids:
And they shall take them captive, whose captives they were;
And they shall rule over their oppressors.
3 And it shall come to pass in that day, that JEHOVAH shall give thee rest from thine affliction, and from thy disquiet, and from the hard servitude which was laid
4 upon thee; and thou shalt pronounce this parable upon the king of Babylon; and shalt say:

How hath the oppressor ceased! the exactress of gold ceased!
5 JEHOVAH hath broken the staff of the wicked, the sceptre of the rulers.
6 He that smote the peoples in wrath, with a stroke unremitted;
He that ruled the nations in anger, is persecuted, and none hindereth.
7 The whole earth is at rest, is quiet; they burst forth into a joyful shout:
8 Even the fir-trees rejoice over thee, the cedars of Libanus:
Since thou art fallen, no feller hath come up against us.
9   Hades from beneath is moved because of thee, to meet thee at thy coming:
He rouseth for thee the mighty dead, all the great chiefs of the earth;
He maketh to rise up from their thrones, all the kings of the nations.

10 All of them shall accost thee, and shall say unto thee:
Art thou, even thou too, become weak as we? art thou
made like unto us?
11 Is then thy pride brought down to the grave; the sound of
thy sprightly instruments?
Is the vermin become thy couch, and the earth-worm thy
covering?
12 How art thou fallen from heaven, O Lucifer, son of the
morning!
Art cut down to the earth, thou that didst subdue the nations!
13 Yet thou didst say in thy heart: I will ascend the heavens;
Above the stars of God I will exalt my throne;
And I will sit upon the mount of the divine presence on
the sides of the north:
14 I will ascend above the highths of the clouds; I will be like
the Most High.
15 But thou shalt be brought down to the grave, to the sides
of the pit.
16 Those that see thee shall look attentively at thee; they
shall well consider thee:
Is this the man, that made the earth to tremble; that
shook the kingdoms?
17 That made the world like a desert; that destroyed the
cities?
That never dismissed his captives to their own home?
18 All the kings of the nations, all of them,
Lie down in glory, each in his own sepulchre:
19 But thou art cast out of the grave, as the tree abominated;
Clothed with the slain, with the pierced by the sword,
With them that go down to the stones of the pit; as a
trodden carcass.
20 Thou shalt not be joined unto them in burial;
Because thou hast destroyed thy country, thou hast slain
thy people:
The seed of evil doers shall never be renowned.
21 Prepare ye slaughter for his children, for the iniquity of
their fathers;
Lest they rise, and possess the earth; and fill the face of
the world with cities.

22 For I will arise against them, saith Jehovah God of
    Hosts:
    And I will cut off from Babylon the name, and the remnant;
    And the son, and the son's son, saith Jehovah.
23 And I will make it an inheritance for the porcupine, and
    pools of water;
    And I will plunge it in the miry gulf of destruction, saith
    Jehovah God of Hosts.
24   Jehovah God of Hosts hath sworn, saying:
    Surely as I have devised, so shall it be;
    And as I have purposed, that thing shall stand:
25 To crush the Assyrian in my land, and to trample him on
    my mountains.
    Then shall his yoke depart from off them;
    And his burthen shall be removed from off their shoulder.
26 This is the decree, which is determined on the whole
    earth;
    And this the hand, which is stretched out over all the nations:
27 For Jehovah God of Hosts hath decreed; and who shall
    disannul it?
    And it is his hand that is stretched out; and who shall
    turn it back?

28   In the year in which Ahaz the king died, this oracle was delivered.

29   Rejoice not, O Philistia, with one consent,
    Because the rod that smote thee is broken:
    For from the root of the serpent shall come forth a basilisk;
    And his fruit shall be a flying fiery serpent.
30 For the poor shall feed on my choice first-fruits;
    And the needy shall lie down in security:
    But he will kill thy root with drought:
    And thy remnant he will slay.
31   Howl, O gate; cry out, O city!
    O Philistia, thou art altogether sunk in consternation!
    For from the north cometh a smoke;
    And there shall not be a straggler among his levies.

23 And what answer shall be given to the ambassadors of the nations?
That JEHOVAH hath laid the foundation of Sion;
And the poor of his people shall take refuge in her.

CHAP. XV.
1 THE ORACLE CONCERNING MOAB.

BECAUSE in the night Ar is destroyed, Moab is un done!
Because in the night Kiris destroyed, Moab is undone!
2 He goeth up to Beth-Dibon, to the high places to weep:
Over Nebo, and over Medeba, shall Moab howl:
On every head there is baldness; every beard is shorn.
3 In her streets they gird themselves with sackcloth:
On her house-tops, and to her open places,
Every one howleth, descendeth with weeping.
4 And Heshbon and Eleale cry out aloud;
Unto Jabats is their voice heard:
Yea the very loins of Moab cry out;
Her life is grievous unto her.
5 The heart of Moab crieth within her;
To Tsoar [she crieth out] like the lowing of a young heifer:
Yea the ascent of Luhith with weeping shall they ascend;
Yea in the way of Horonaim they raise a cry of destruction.
9 For the waters of Nimrim shall become desolate:
For the pasture is withered, the tender plant faileth, the green herb is no more.
7 Wherefore the riches, which they have gained, shall perish;
And what they have deposited, to the valley of willows shall be carried away.
8 For the cry encompasseth the border of Moab:
To Eglaim reacheth her moan; and to Beer-Elim her howling.
9 Yea the waters of Dimon are full of blood:
Yet will I bring more evils upon Dimon;
Upon the escaped of Moab and Ariel, and the remnant of Admah.

CHAP. XVI.

1 I will send forth the son of the ruler of the land,
From Selah of the desert to the mount of the daughter of Sion.
2 And as wandering birds, driven from the nest,
So shall be the daughters of Moab at the fords of Arnon.
3 Impart counsel; interpose with equity;
Make thy shadows as the night in the midst of noon-day.
Hide the outcasts; discover not the fugitive.
4 Let the outcasts of Moab sojourn with thee, [O Sion];
Be thou to them a covert from the destroyer.
For the oppressor is no more, the destroyer ceaseth;
He that trampled you under foot is perished from the land.
5 And the throne shall be established in mercy,
And in truth shall One sit thereon;
In the tabernacle of David a judge;
Carefully searching out the right, and dispatching justice.
6 We have heard the pride of Moab; he is very proud;
His haughtiness, and his pride, and his anger: vain are his lies.
7 Therefore shall Moab lament aloud;
For the whole people of Moab shall he lament;
For the men of Kirhares shall ye make a moan.
8 For the fields of Heshbon are put to shame;
The vine of Sibmah languisheth,
Whose generous shoots overpowered the mighty lords of the nations;
They reached unto Jazer; they strayed to the desert;
Her branches extended themselves, they passed over the sea.
9 Wherefore I will weep, as with the weeping of Jazer, for the vine of Sibmah;
I will water thee with my tears, O Heshbon and Elealeh!
For upon thy summer fruits, and upon thy vintage, the destroyer hath fallen.
10 And joy and gladness is taken away from the fruitful field;
And in the vineyards they shall not sing, they shall not shout:
In the vats the treader shall not tread out the wine;
An end is put to the shouting.

11 Wherefore my bowels for Moab like a harp shall sound;
   And my entrails for Kirhares.
12 ' And it shall be, when Moab shall see,
   That he hath wearied himself out on the high place,
   That he shall enter his sanctuary,'
   To intercede: but he shall not prevail.
13 This is the word, which JEHOVAH spake concerning
14 Moab long ago; but now JEHOVAH hath spoken, saying:
   After three years, as the years of an hireling,
   The glory of Moab shall be debased, in all his great multitude;
   And the remnant shall be few, small, and without strength.

CHAP. XVII.
1 THE ORACLE CONCERNING DAMASCUS.

   BEHOLD Damascus is removed, so as to be no more a city:
   It shall even become a ruinous heap.
2 The cities are deserted for ever;
   They shall be given up to the flocks,
   And they shall lie down, and none shall scare them away.
3 And the fortress shall cease from Ephraim,
   And the kingdom from Damascus:
   And the pride of Syria shall be as the glory of the sons of Israel;
   Saith JEHOVAH the God of Hosts.
4 And it shall come to pass in that day,
   The glory of Jacob shall be diminished,
   And the fatness of his flesh shall become lean.
5 And it shall be, as when one gathereth the standing harvest,
   And his arm reapeth the ears of corn:
   Or as when one gleaneth ears in the valley of Rephaim.
6 A gleaning shall be left in it, as in the shaking of the olive tree;
   Two or three berries on the top of the uppermost bough;
   Four or five on the straggling fruitful branches:
   Saith JEHOVAH the God of Israel.

7 In that day shall a man regard his Maker,
And toward the Holy One of Israel shall his eyes look:
8 And he shall not regard the altars dedicated to the work
   of his hands;
And what his fingers have made, he shall not respect;
Nor the groves, nor the solar statues.
9 In that day shall his strongly fenced cities become
Like the desertion of the Hivites and the Amorites,
When they deserted the land before the face of the
   sons of Israel;
And the land shall become a desolation.
10 Because thou hast forgotten the God of thy salvation,
And hast not remembered the rock of thy strength;
Therefore, when thou shalt have planted pleasant plants,
And shalt have set shoots from a foreign soil;
11 In the day when thou shalt have made thy plants to
   grow;
And in the morning, when thou shalt have made thy shoots
   to spring forth;
Even in the day of possession shall the harvest be taken
   away,
And there shall be sorrow without hope.

12 Wo to the multitude of the numerous peoples,
Who make a sound like the sound of the seas:
And to the roaring of the nations,
Who make a roaring like the roaring of mighty waters.
13 Like the roaring of mighty waters do the nations roar;
But he shall rebuke them, and they shall flee far away;
And they shall be driven like the chaff of the hills before
   the wind,
And like the gossamer before the whirlwind.
14 At the season of evening, behold terror!
Before the morning, and he is no more!
This is the portion of those that spoil us;
And the lot of those that plunder us.

CHAP. XVIII.
1   Ho! to the land of the winged cymbal,
Which borders on the rivers of Cush;
2 Which sendeth ambassadors on the sea,
And in vessels of papyrus on the face of the waters.

Go, ye swift messengers,
To a nation stretched out in length, and smoothed;
To a people terrible from the first, and hitherto;
A nation meted out by line, and trodden down;
Whose land the rivers have nourished.
3 Yea, all ye that inhabit the world, and that dwell on the earth,
When the standard is lifted up on the mountains, behold!
And when the trumpet is sounded, hear!
4 For thus hath JEHOVAH said unto me:
I will sit still, and regard my fixed habitation;
Like the clear heat after rain,
Like the dewy cloud in the day of harvest.
5 Surely before the vintage, when the bud is perfect,
And the blossom is become a swelling grape;
He shall cut off the shoots with pruning-hooks,
And the branches he shall take away, he shall cut down.
6 They shall be left together to the rapacious bird of the mountains;
And to the wild beasts of the earth:
And the rapacious bird shall summer upon it;
And every wild beast of the earth shall winter upon it.
7 At that time shall a gift be brought to JEHOVAH the God of Hosts,
From a people stretched out in length, and smoothed;
A nation meted out by line, and trodden down;
And from a people terrible from the first, and hitherto;
Whose land the rivers have nourished;
To the place of the name of JEHOVAH God of Hosts, to Mount Sion.

CHAP. XIX.
1 THE ORACLE CONCERNING EGYPT.

BEHOLD, JEHOVAH rideth
On a swift cloud, and cometh to Egypt!
And the idols of Egypt shall be moved at his presence;
And the heart of Egypt shall melt in the midst of her.
2 And I will excite Egyptians against Egyptians,
And they shall fight, every man against his brother, and every man against his neighbour:

City against city, kingdom against kingdom.
3 And the spirit of Egypt shall fail in the midst of her;
And I will swallow up her counsel:
And they shall seek to the idols, and to the sorcerers,
And to the necromancers, and to the wizards.
4 And I will give up Egypt bound into the hands of cruel lords,
And a fierce king shall rule over them;
Saith the Lord JEHOVAH God of Hosts.
5 Then shall the waters fail from the sea,
And the river shall be wasted and dried up.
6 And the streams shall become putrid;
The canals of Egypt shall be emptied and dried up.
The reed and the lotus shall wither:
7 The meadow by the canal, even at the mouth of the canal,
And all that is sown by the canal,
Shall wither, be blasted, and be no more.
8 And the fishers shall mourn, and lament;
All those that cast the hook in the river,
And those that spread nets on the face of the waters, shall languish.
9 And they that work the fine flax shall be confounded,
And they that weave net-work.
10 And her stores shall be broken up,
Even of all that make a gain of pools for fish.
11 Surely, the princes of Zoan are fools;
The wise counsellors of Pharaoh have counselled a brutish counsel.
How will ye boast unto Pharaoh:
I am the son of the wise, the son of ancient kings?
12 Where are they; where, thy wise men? let them come;
And let them tell thee now, and let them declare,
What JEHOVAH God of Hosts hath determined against Egypt.
13 The princes of Zoan are become fools, the princes of Noph are deceived;
They have caused Egypt to err, even the chief pillars of her tribes.
14 JEHOVAH hath mingled in the midst of them a spirit of giddiness;
And they have caused Egypt to err in all her works,
As a drunkard staggereth in his vomit:

15 Nor shall there be any work in Egypt,
   Which the head or tail, the branch or rush, may perform.
16 In that day the Egyptians shall be as women:
   And they shall tremble and fear,
   At the shaking of the hand of JEHOVAH God of Hosts,
   Which he shall shake over them.
17 And the land of Judah shall become a terror to the Egyptians:
   If any one mention it unto them, they shall fear;
   Because of the counsel of JEHOVAH God of Hosts,
   Which he hath counselled against them.
18 In that day, there shall be five cities in the land of Egypt,
   Speaking the language of Canaan,
   And swearing unto JEHOVAH God of Hosts:
   One of them shall be called the City of the Sun.
19 In that day, there shall be an altar to JEHOVAH
   In the midst of the land of Egypt;
   And a pillar by the border thereof to JEHOVAH:
20 And it shall be for a sign, and for a witness,
   To JEHOVAH God of Hosts in the land of Egypt:
   That, when they cried unto JEHOVAH because of oppressors,
   He sent unto them a saviour, and a vindicator, and he delivered them.
21 And JEHOVAH shall be known to Egypt,
   And the Egyptians shall know JEHOVAH in that day;
   And they shall serve him with sacrifice and oblation,
   And they shall vow a vow unto JEHOVAH, and shall perform it.
22 And JEHOVAH shall smite Egypt, smiting and healing her;
   And they shall turn unto JEHOVAH, and he will be entreated by them, and will heal them.
23 In that day, there shall be a high-way from Egypt to Assyria;
   And the Assyrian shall come into Egypt, and the Egyptian into Assyria:
   And the Egyptian shall worship with the Assyrian.
24 In that day, Israel shall be reckoned a third,
   Together with Egypt and Assyria;
   A blessing in the midst of the earth:

25 Whom JEHOVAH God of Hosts hath blessed, saying:
    Blessed be my people, Egypt;
    And Assyria, the work of my hands;
    And Israel, mine inheritance.

CHAP. XX.

1 IN the year that Tharthan marched to Ashdod; whither he was sent by Sargon king of Assyria; (and he fought against Ashdod, and took it); at that time JE-
2 HOVAH spake by Isaiah, the son of Amots, saying:
    Go, loose the sackcloth from off thy loins;
    And put off thy shoes from thy feet.
3 And he did so, walking naked and barefoot. And JEHOVAH said:
    As my servant Isaiah hath walked naked and barefoot;
    A sign and a prodigy of three years,
    Upon Egypt and upon Cush:
4   So shall the king of Assyria lead
    The captives of Egypt, and the exiles of Cush,
    The young and the old, naked and barefoot;
    With their hind-parts discovered, to the shame of the Egyptians.
5   And they [of Ashdod] shall be terrified, and ashamed of Cush in whom they trusted,
    And of Egypt, in whom they gloried.
6   And the inhabitant of this country shall say, in that day:
    Behold, such is the object of our trust,
    To whom we fled for succour,
    That we might be delivered from the king of Assyria!
    How then shall we escape?

CHAP. XXI.

1   THE ORACLE CONCERNING THE DESERT OF THE SEA.

    LIKE the southern tempests violently rushing along,
    From the desert he cometh, from the terrible country.
2 A dreadful vision! it is revealed unto me:
    The plunderer is plundered, and the destroyer is destroyed!

Go up, O Elam ; from the siege, O Media !
I have put an end to all her vexations.
3 Therefore are my loins filled with pain :
Anguish hath seized me, as the anguish of a woman in travail.
I am convulsed, so that I cannot hear ; I am astonished, so that I cannot see.
4 My heart is bewildered ; terrors have scared me :
The evening, for which I longed, hath he turned into horror.
5 The table is prepared, the watch is set ; they eat, they drink :
Rise, O ye princes ; anoint the shield.
6 For thus hath the Lord said unto me :
Go, set a watchman on his station ;
Whatever he shall see, let him report unto thee.
7 And he saw a chariot with two riders ;
A rider on an ass, a rider on a camel.
And he observed diligently with extreme diligence.
8 And he that looked out on the watch cried aloud :
O my Lord, I keep my station all the day long ;
And on my ward have I continued every night.
9 And behold, here cometh a man, one of the two riders :
And he answereth, and sayeth, Babylon is fallen, is fallen ;
And all the graven idols of her gods are broken to the ground.
10 O my threshing, and the corn of my floor !
What I have heard from JEHOVAH God of Hosts, the God of Israel,
That I have declared unto you.

11   THE ORACLE CONCERNING DUMAH.

A VOICE crieth unto me from Seir :
Watchman, what from the night ?
Watchman, what from the night ?
12. The watchman replieth :
The morning cometh, and also the night.
If ye will inquire, inquire ye : come again.

13   THE ORACLE CONCERNING ARABIA.

    IN the forest, at even, shall ye lodge,
    O ye caravans of Dedan!
14 To meet the thirsty bring ye forth water,
    O inhabitants of the southern country;
    With bread prevent the fugitive.
15 For from the face of the sword they shall flee:
    From the face of the drawn sword;
    And from the face of the bended bow;
    And from the face of the grievous war.
16 For thus hath the Lord said unto me:
    Within yet â year, as the years of an hireling,
    Shall all the glory of Kedar be consumed;
17 And the remainder of the number of the mighty bowmen,
    Of the sons of Kedar, shall be diminished:
    For JEHOVAH the God of Israel hath spoken it.

CHAP. XXII.
1   THE ORACLE CONCERNING THE VALLEY OF VISION.

    WHAT aileth thee now, that all thine inhabitants are gone up to the house-tops?
2 O thou, that wast full of noise,
    A tumultuous city, a joyous city!
    Thy slain were not slain by the sword,
    Neither did they die in battle.
3 All thy leaders are gone off together; they are fled from the bow;
    All that were found in thee are fled together, they are gone far away.
4 Wherefore I said: Turn away from me; I will weep bitterly:
    Strive not to comfort me for the desolation of the daughter of my people.
5 For it is a day of trouble, and of treading down, and of perplexity;
    The day of the Lord JEHOVAH God of Hosts in the valley of vision:

Breaking down the wall, and crying to the mountain.
6 And Elam beareth the quiver;
With chariots cometh the Syrian, and with horsemen;
And Kir uncovereth the shield.
7 And thy choicest valleys shall be filled with chariots;
And the horsemen shall set themselves in array against the gate;
8 And the barrier of Judah shall be laid open:
Then thou shalt look towards the arsenal of the house of the forest.
9 And the breaches of the city of David, ye shall see that they are many;
And ye shall collect the waters of the lower pool;
10 And the houses of Jerusalem ye shall number;
And ye shall break down the houses to fortify the rampart:
11 And ye shall make a lake between the two walls,
To receive the waters of the old pool.
But ye look not to him, that hath disposed this:
And him that formed it of old, ye regard not.
12 And the Lord JEHOVAH God of Hosts called in that day,
To weeping, and to lamentation;
And to baldness, and to girding with sackcloth:
13 But, behold, joy and gladness,
Slaying of oxen, and killing of sheep;
Eating of flesh, and drinking of wine:
Let us eat, and drink; for to-morrow we die.
14 And the voice of JEHOVAH God of Hosts was revealed to mine ears:
Surely this your iniquity shall not be expiated, till ye die,
Saith the Lord JEHOVAH God of Hosts.

15 THUS saith the the Lord JEHOVAH God of Hosts: Go, get thee to this treasurer, unto Shebna, who is over the household; and say unto him:
16 What hast thou here? and whom hast thou here?
That thou hast hewn out here a sepulchre for thyself?
O thou that hewest out thy sepulchre on high,
That gravest in the rock an habitation for thyself!

17 Behold JEHOVAH will cast thee out,
  Casting thee violently out, and will surely cover thee:
18 He will whirl thee round and round, and cast thee away,
  Like a ball [from a sling] into a wide country:
  There shalt thou die; and there shall thy glorious chariots
  Become the shame of the house of thy lord.
19 And I will drive thee from thy station,
  And from thy state will I overthrow thee.
20 And in that day I will call my servant,
  Even Eliakim the son of Hilkiah:
21 And I will clothe him with thy robe,
  And with thy baldric will I strengthen him:
  And thy government will I commit to his hand;
  And he shall be a father to the inhabitants of Jerusalem,
  And to the house of Judah:
22 And I will lay the key of the house of David upon his shoulder;
  And he shall open, and none shall shut;
  And he shall shut, and none shall open.
23 And I will fasten him as a nail in a sure place;
  And he shall become a glorious seat for his father's house.
24 And they shall hang upon him all the glory of his father's house,
  The offspring of high and of low degree;
  Every small vessel; from every sort of goblets,
  To every sort of meaner vessels.
25 In that day, saith JEHOVAH God of Hosts,
  The nail once fastened in a sure place shall be moved;
  And it shall be hewn down, and it shall fall;
  And the burthen which was upon it, shall be cut off:
  For JEHOVAH hath spoken it.

CHAP. XXIII.
1 THE ORACLE CONCERNING TYRE.

  Howl, O ye ships of Tarshish!
  For she is utterly destroyed both within and without:
  From the land of Chittim the tidings are brought unto them.

2 Be silent, O ye inhabitants of the sea-coast:
The merchants of Sidon, they that pass over the sea, crowded thee.
3 And the seed of the Nile, growing from abundant waters;
The harvest of the river, was her revenue:
And she became the mart of the nations.
4 Be thou ashamed, O Sidon; for the sea hath spoken,
Even the mighty fortress of the sea, saying:
I am as if I had not travailed, nor brought forth children;
As if I had not nourished youths, nor educated virgins.
5 When the tidings shall reach Egypt,
They shall be seized with anguish at the tidings of Tyre.
6 Pass ye over to Tarshish; howl, O ye inhabitants of the sea-coast!
7 Is this your triumphant city; whose antiquity is of the earliest date?
Her own feet bear her far away to sojourn.
8 Who hath purposed this against Tyre, who dispensed crowns;
Whose merchants were princes; whose traders were nobles of the land?
9 JEHOVAH God of Hosts had counselled it;
To stain the pride of all beauty;
To make contemptible all the nobles of the earth.
10 Overflow thy land, like a river,
O daughter of Tarshish; the mound [that kept in thy waters] is no more.
11 He hath stretched his hand over the sea; he hath shaken the kingdoms:
JEHOVAH hath issued a command concerning Canaan, that they should destroy her strong places.
12 And he hath said: Thou shalt triumph no more,
O thou defloured virgin, the daughter of Sidon!
To Chittim arise, pass over; even there thou shalt have no rest.
13 Behold the land of the Chaldeans;
This people was of no account;
(The Assyrian founded it for the inhabitants of the desert;

They raised the watch-towers, they set up the palaces
thereof) :
This people hath reduced her to a ruin.
14 Howl, O ye ships of Tarshish ; for your stronghold is destroyed.
15   And it shall come to pass in that day ;
That Tyre shall be forgotten seventy years,
According to the days of one king :
At the end of seventy years,
Tyre shall sing, as the harlot singeth.
16 Take thy lyre, go about the city, O harlot long forgotten ;
Strike the lyre artfully ; multiply the song ; that thou
mayest again be remembered.
17 And at the end of seventy years,
JEHOVAH will take account of Tyre :
And she shall return to her gainful practice ;
And she shall play the harlot with all the kingdom of the
world,
That are upon the face of the earth.
18 But her traffic, and her gain, shall be holy to JEHOVAH :
It shall not be treasured, nor shall it be kept in store ;
For her traffic shall be for them, that dwell before JEHOVAH,
For food sufficient, and for durable clothing.

CHAP. XXIV.
1   BEHOLD, JEHOVAH emptieth the land, and maketh it
waste ;
He even turneth it upside down, and scattereth abroad the
inhabitants.
2 And it shall be, as with the people, so with the priest ;
As with the servant, so with his master ;
As with the handmaid, so with her mistress ;
As with the buyer, so with the seller ;
As with the borrower, so with the lender ;
As with the usurer, so with the giver of usury.
3 The land shall be utterly emptied, and utterly spoiled ,
For JEHOVAH hath spoken this word.
4 The land mourneth, it withereth ;
The world languisheth, it withereth ;
The lofty people of the land do languish.

5 The land is even polluted under her inhabitants;
   For they have transgressed the law, they have changed
     the decree;
6 They have broken the everlasting covenant.
   Therefore hath a curse devoured the land;
   Because they are guilty, that dwell in her.
   Therefore are the inhabitants of the land destroyed;
   And few are the mortals that are left in her.
7 The new wine mourneth; the vine languisheth;
   All, that were glad of heart, sigh.
8 The joyful sound of the tabour ceaseth;
   The noise of exultation is no more;
   The joyful sound of the harp ceaseth:
9 With songs they shall no more drink wine;
   The palm-wine shall be bitter to them that drink it.
10 The city is broken down; it is desolate:
   Every house is obstructed, so that no one can enter.
11 There is a cry in the streets for wine;
   All gladness is passed away;
   The joy of the whole land is banished.
12 Desolation is left in the city;
   And with a great tumult the gate is battered down.
13 Yea thus shall it be in the very centre of the land, in
     the midst of the people;
   As the shaking of the olive; as the gleaning, when the
     vintage is finished.
14 But these shall lift up their voice, they shall sing;
   The waters shall resound with the exaltation of JEHO-
     VAH.
15 Wherefore in the distant coasts, glorify ye JEHOVAH;
   In the distant coasts of the sea, the name of JEHOVAH,
     the God of Israel.
16 From the uttermost part of the land, we have heard
     songs, Glory to the righteous!
   But I said, Alas, my wretchedness, my wretchedness!
   Wo is me! the plunderers plunder;
   Yea the plunderers still continue their cruel depreda-
     tions.
17 The terror, the pit, and the snare,
   Are upon thee, O inhabitant of the land:
18 And it shall be, that whoso fleeth from the terror,
   He shall fall into the pit;
   And whoso escapeth from the pit,

He shall be taken in the snare:
For the flood-gates from on high are opened;
And the foundations of the earth tremble.
19 The land is grievously shaken;
The land is utterly shattered to pieces;
The land is violently shaken out of its place;
20 The land reeleth to and fro like a drunkard;
And moveth this way and that, like a lodge for a night:
For her iniquity lieth heavy upon her;
And she shall fall, and rise no more.
21 And it shall come to pass in that day,
Jehovah shall summon on high the host that is on high;
And on earth the kings of the earth:
And they shall be gathered together, as in a bundle for the pit;
22 And shall be closely imprisoned in the prison:
And after many days, account shall be taken of them.
23 And the moon shall be confounded, and the sun shall be ashamed;
For Jehovah God of Hosts shall reign
On Mount Sion, and in Jerusalem;
And before his ancients shall he be glorified.

CHAP XXV.
1 O Jehovah, thou art my God:
I will exalt thee; I will praise thy name:
For thou hast effected wonderful things;
Counsels of old time, promises immutably true.
2 For thou hast made the city an heap;
The strongly fortified citadel a ruin:
The palace of the proud ones, that it should be no more a city;
That it never should be built up again.
3 Therefore shall the fierce people glorify thee;
The city of the formidable nations shall fear thee;
4 For thou hast been a defence to the poor;
A defence to the needy in his distress:
A refuge from the storm, a shadow from the heat;
When the blast of the formidable rages like a winter storm.
5 As the heat in a parched land, the tumult of the proud shalt thou bring low;

As the heat by a thick cloud, the triumph of the formidable shall be humbled.
6 And JEHOVAH God of Hosts shall make,
For all the peoples, in this mountain,
A feast of delicacies, a feast of old wines:
Of delicacies exquisitely rich, of old wines perfectly refined.
7 And on this mountain shall he destroy
The covering, that covered the face of all the peoples;
And the vail, that was spread over all the nations.
8 He shall utterly destroy death forever;
And the Lord JEHOVAH shall wipe away the tear from off all faces;
And the reproach of his people shall he remove from off the whole earth
For JEHOVAH hath spoken it.
9 In that day shall they say:
Behold, this is our God;
We have trusted in him, and he hath saved us:
This is JEHOVAH; we have trusted in him;
We will rejoice, and triumph, in his salvation.
10 For the hand of JEHOVAH shall give rest upon this mountain;
And Moab shall be threshed in his place,
As the straw is threshed under the wheels of the car.
11 And he shall stretch out his hands in the midst thereof,
As he, that sinketh, stretcheth out his hands to swim:
But God shall bring down his pride with the sudden gripe of his hands.
12 And the bulwark of thy high walls shall he lay low:
He shall bring them down to the ground; he shall lay them in the dust.

CHAP. XXVI.
1 IN that day shall this song be sung:
In the land of Judah we have a strong city;
Salvation shall he establish for walls and bulwarks.
2 Open ye the gates, and let the righteous nation enter;
3 Constant in the truth, stayed in mind:
Thou shalt preserve them in perpetual peace,
Because they have trusted in thee.

4 Trust ye in JEHOVAH for ever;
  For in JEHOVAH is never-failing protection.
5 For he hath humbled those, that dwell on high;
  The lofty city, he hath brought her down;
  He hath brought her down to the ground:
  He hath levelled her with the dust.
6 The foot shall trample upon her;
  The feet of the poor, the steps of the needy.
7 The way of the righteous is perfectly straight;
  Thou most exactly levellest the path of the righteous.
8 Even in the way of thy laws, O JEHOVAH,
  We have placed our confidence in thy name;
  And in the remembrance of thee is the desire of our soul.
9 With my soul have I desired thee in the night;
  Yea with my inmost spirit in the morn have I sought thee.
  For when thy judgments are in the earth,
  The inhabitants of the world learn righteousness.
10 Though mercy be shewn to the wicked, yet will he not learn righteousness:
   In the very land of rectitude he will deal perversely;
   And will not regard the majesty of JEHOVAH.
11 JEHOVAH, thy hand is lifted up, yet will they not see:
   But they shall see, with confusion, thy zeal for thy people;
   Yea the fire shall burn up thine adversaries.
12 JEHOVAH, thou wilt ordain for us peace:
   For even all our mighty deeds thou hast performed for us.
13 O JEHOVAH, our God!
   Other lords, exclusive of thee, have had dominion over us:
   Thee only, and thy name, henceforth will we celebrate.
14 They are dead, they shall not live;
   They are deceased tyrants, they shall not rise.
   Therefore hast thou visited and destroyed them;
   And all memorial of them thou hast abolished.
15 Thou hast added to the nation, O JEHOVAH;
   Thou hast added to the nation; thou art glorified:
   Thou hast extended far all the borders of the land.
16 O JEHOVAH, in affliction have we sought thee;
   We have poured out humble supplication, when thy chastisement was upon us.

CHAP. XXVI.　　　ISAIAH.　　　47

17 As a woman, that hath conceived, when her delivery approacheth,
　　Is in anguish, crieth out aloud, in her travail;
　　Thus have we been before thee, O JEHOVAH.
18 We have conceived; we have been in anguish; we have, as it were, brought forth wind:
　　Salvation is not wrought in the land;
　　Neither are the inhabitants of the world fallen.
19 Thy dead shall live; my deceased, they shall rise:
　　Awake, and sing, ye that dwell in the dust!
　　For thy dew is as the dew of the dawn;
　　But the earth shall cast forth, as an abortion, the deceased tyrants.
20 Come, O my people; retire into thy secret apartments;
　　And shut thy door after thee:
　　Hide thyself for a little while, for a moment;
　　Until the indignation shall have passed away.
21 For behold, JEHOVAH issueth forth from his place;
　　To punish for his iniquity the inhabitant of the earth:
　　And the earth shall disclose the blood that is upon her;
　　And shall no longer cover her slain.

CHAP. XXVII.
1 In that day shall JEHOVAH punish with his sword;
　　His well-tempered, and great, and strong sword;
　　Leviathan the rigid serpent,
　　And Leviathan the winding serpent:
　　And shall slay the monster, that is in the sea.

2 　　IN that day,
　　To the beloved Vineyard, sing ye a responsive song.
3 J. It is I, JEHOVAH, that preserve her:
　　I will water her every moment;
　　I will take care of her by night;
　　And by day I will keep guard over her.
4 V. I have no wall for my defence:
　　O that I had a fence of the thorn and brier!
　J. Against them should I march in battle,
　　I should burn them up together.

5 Ah! let her rather take hold of my protection.
 V. Let him make peace with me!
 Peace let him make with me!
6 J. They that come from the root of Jacob shall flourish,
  Israel shall bud forth;
 And they shall fill the face of the world with fruit.

7 Hath he smitten him, as he smiteth those that smote
  him?
 And like the slaughter of those, that slew him, is he
  slain?
8 In just measure, when thou inflictest the stroke, wilt
  thou debate with her;
 With due deliberation, even in the rough tempest, in
  the day of the east wind.
9 Wherefore on this condition shall the iniquity of Jacob
  be expiated;
 And so shall he reap the whole benefit of the removal
  of his sin;
 If he shall render all the stones of the altar,
 Like the limestones scattered abroad;
 And if the groves and the images rise no more.
10 But the strongly fortified city shall be desolate;
 An habitation forsaken, and deserted as a wilderness.
 There shall the bullock feed, and there shall he lie down;
 And he shall browse on the tender shoots thereof.
11 When her boughs are withered, they shall be broken:
 Women shall come, and set them on a blaze.
 Surely it is a people void of understanding;
 Wherefore he, that made him, shall not have pity on
  him;
 And he, that formed him, shall shew him no favour.
12 And it shall come to pass in that day,
 JEHOVAH shall make a gathering of his fruit, from the
  flood of the river,
 To the stream of Egypt;
 And ye shall be gleaned up,
 One by one, O ye sons of Israel.
13 And it shall come to pass in that day,
 The great trumpet shall be sounded;
 And those shall come, who were perishing in the land
  of Assyria;
 And who were dispersed in the land of Egypt:

And they shall bow themselves down before JEHOVAH,
In the holy mountain, in Jerusalem.

CHAP. XXVIII.
1   Wo to the proud crown of the drunkards of Ephraim,
And to the fading flower of their glorious beauty!
To those, that are at the head of the rich valley, that are stupified with wine!
2 Behold the mighty one, the exceedingly strong one!
Like a storm of hail, like a destructive tempest;
Like a rapid flood of mighty waters pouring down;
He shall dash them to the ground with his hand.
3 They shall be trodden under foot,
The proud crowns of the drunkards of Ephraim:
4 And the fading flower of their glorious beauty,
Which is at the head of the rich valley,
Shall be as the early fruit before the summer;
Which whoso seeth, he plucketh it immediately;
And it is no sooner in his hand, than he swalloweth it.

5   In that day shall JEHOVAH God of Hosts become a beauteous crown,
And a glorious diadem, to the remnant of his people:
6. And a spirit of judgment, to them that sit in judgment;
And strength to them, that repell the war to the gate [of the enemy].
7 But even these have erred through wine, and through strong drink they have reeled;
The priest and the prophet have erred through strong drink;
They are overwhelmed with wine; they have reeled through strong drink:
They have erred in vision, they have stumbled in judgment.
8 For all their tables are full of vomit;
Of filthiness, so that no place is free.

9   " Whom [say they] would he teach knowledge; and to
    " whom would he impart instruction?
    " To such as are weaned from the milk, as are kept back
    " from the breast?
10 " For it is command upon command; command upon
    " command;

"Line upon line; line upon line:
"A little here, and a little there."
11 Yea verily, with a stammering lip, and a strange tongue,
He shall speak unto this people.
12 For when he said unto them:
This is the true rest; give ye rest unto the weary;
And this is the refreshment; they would not hear.
13 Therefore shall the word of JEHOVAH be indeed unto them,
Command upon command, command upon command;
Line upon line, line upon line;
A little here, and a little there:
That they may go on, and fall backward;
And be broken, and snared, and caught.
14 Wherefore hear ye the word of JEHOVAH, ye scoffers;
Ye of this people in Jerusalem, who utter sententious speeches:
15 Who say, we have entered into a covenant with death;
And with the grave we have made a treaty:
The overflowing plague, when it passeth through, shall not reach us:
For we have made falsehood our refuge;
And under deceit we have hidden ourselves.
16 Wherefore thus saith the Lord JEHOVAH:
Behold, I lay in Sion for a foundation a stone, an approved stone;
A corner-stone, precious, immoveably fixed:
He, that trusteth in him, shall not be confounded.
17 And I will mete out judgment by the rule;
And strict justice, by the plummet:
And the hail shall sweep away the refuge of falsehood;
And the hiding-place the waters shall overwhelm.
18 And your covenant with death shall be broken;
And your treaty with the grave shall not stand:
When the overflowing plague passeth through,
By it shall ye be beaten down.
19 As soon as it passeth through, shall it seize you;
Yea morning after morning shall it pass through, by day and by night;
And even the report alone shall cause terror.
20 For the bed is too short, for one to stretch himself out at length;

And the covering is too narrow, for one to gather himself up under it.
21 For as in Mount Peratsim, JEHOVAH will arise;
As in the valley of Gibeon, shall he be moved with anger;
That he may execute his work, his strange work;
And effect his operation, his unusual operation.
22 And now, give yourselves up to scoffing no more,
Lest your chastisements become more severe:
For a full and decisive decree have I heard,
From the Lord JEHOVAH God of Hosts, on the whole land.

23 Listen ye, and hear my voice;
Attend, and hearken unto my words.
24 Doth the husbandman plough every day that he may sow,
Opening, and breaking the clods of his field?
25 When he hath made even the face thereof,
Doth not he then scatter the dill, and cast abroad the cummin;
And sow the wheat in due measure;
And the barley, and the rye, hath its appointed limit?
26 For his God rightly instructeth him; he furnisheth him with knowledge.
27 The dill is not beaten out with the corn-drag;
Nor is the wheel of the wain made to turn upon the cummin:
But the dill is beaten out with the staff;
28 And the cummin with the flail: but the bread-corn with the threshing-wain.
But not for ever will he continue thus to thresh it;
Nor to vex it with the wheel of his wain;
Nor to bruise it with the hoofs of his cattle.
29 This also proceedeth from JEHOVAH God of Hosts:
He sheweth himself wonderful in counsel, great in operation.

CHAP. XXIX.
1   Wo to Ariel, to Ariel, the city which David besieged!
    Add year to year; let the feasts go round in their course.
2   Yet will I bring distress upon Ariel;
    And there shall be continual mourning and sorrow:
    And it shall be unto me as the hearth of the great altar.
3   And I will encamp against thee, like David;
    And I will lay siege against thee with a mound;
    And I will erect towers against thee.
4   And thou shalt be brought low; thou shalt speak as from beneath the earth:
    And from out of the dust thou shalt utter a feeble speech;
    And thy voice shall come out of the ground, like that of a necromancer:
    And thy words from out of the dust shall give a small shrill sound.
5   But the multitude of the proud shall be like the small dust;
    And like the flitting chaff the multitude of the terrible:
    Yea, the effect shall be momentary, in an instant.
6   From JEHOVAH God of Hosts there shall be a sudden visitation,
    With thunder, and earthquake, and a mighty voice;
    With storm, and tempest, and flame of devouring fire.
7   And like as a dream, a vision of the night,
    So shall it be with the multitude of all the nations, that fight against Ariel;
    And all their armies, and their towers, and those that distress her.
8   As when a hungry man dreameth; and lo! he seemeth to eat;
    But he awaketh, and his appetite is still unsatisfied:
    And as a thirsty man dreameth; and lo! he seemeth to drink;
    But he awaketh, and he is still faint, and his appetite still craving:
    So shall it be with the multitude of all the nations,
    Which have set themselves in array against Mount Sion.

9   They are struck with amazement, they stand astonished;
   They stare with a look of stupid surprise:
   They are drunken, but not with wine;
   They stagger, but not with strong drink.
10 For JEHOVAH hath poured upon you a spirit of profound sleep;
   And hath closed up your eyes;
   The prophets, and the rulers; the seers hath he blindfolded.
11 So that all the vision is to you, as the words of a book sealed up;
   Which if one delivers to a man, that knoweth letters,
   Saying, Read this, I pray thee;
   He answereth, I cannot read it; for it is sealed up:
12 Or should the book be given to one, that knoweth not letters,
   Saying, Read this, I pray thee;
   He answereth, I know not letters.
13 Wherefore JEHOVAH hath said:
   Forasmuch as this people draweth near with their mouth,
   And honoureth me with their lips,
   While their heart is far from me;
   And vain is their fear of me,
   Teaching the commandments of men:
14 Therefore behold, I will again deal with this people,
   In a manner so wonderful and astonishing;
   That the wisdom of the wise shall perish,
   And the prudence of the prudent shall disappear.

15   Wo unto them, that are too deep for JEHOVAH in forming secret designs;
   Whose deeds are in the dark; and who say,
   Who is there, that seeth us; and who shall know us?
16 Perverse as ye are! shall the potter be esteemed as the clay?
   Shall the work say of the workman, He hath not made me?
   And shall the thing formed say of the former of it, He hath no understanding?
17 Shall it not be but a very short space,
   Ere Lebanon become like Carmel,
   And Carmel appear like a desert?

18 Then shall the deaf hear the words of the book;
  And the eyes of the blind, covered before with clouds
    and darkness, shall see.
19 The meek shall increase their joy in JEHOVAH;
  And the needy shall exult in the Holy One of Israel.
20 For the terrible one faileth, the scoffer is no more;
  And all that were vigilant in iniquity are utterly cut off:
21 Who bewildered the poor man in speaking;
  And laid snares for him, that pleaded in the gate;
  And with falsehood subverted the righteous.
22   Therefore thus saith JEHOVAH the God of the house
    of Jacob,
  He who redeemed Abraham:
  Jacob shall no more be ashamed;
  His face shall no more be covered with confusion:
23 For when his children shall see the work of my hands,
  Among themselves shall they sanctify my name:
  They shall sanctify the Holy One of Jacob,
  And tremble before the God of Israel.
24 Those, that were led away with the spirit of error, shall
    gain knowledge;
  And the malignant shall attend to instruction.

CHAP. XXX.
 1   Wo unto the rebellious children, saith JEHOVAH;
  Who form counsels, but not from me;
  Who ratify covenants, but not by my spirit:
  That they may add sin to sin.
 2 Who set forward to go down to Egypt;
  But have not inquired at my mouth:
  To strengthen themselves with the strength of Pharaoh
  And to trust in the shadow of Egypt.
 3 But the strength of Pharaoh shall be your shame;
  And your trust in the shadow of Egypt your confusion.
 4 Their princes were at Tsoan;
  And their ambassadors arrived at Hanes:
 5 They were all ashamed of a people, that profited them
    not;
  Who were of no help, and of no profit;
  But proved even a shame, and a reproach unto them.
 6   The burthen of the beasts travelling southward,
  Through a land of distress and difficulty:
  Whence come forth the lioness, and the fierce lion;
  The viper, and the flying fiery serpent:

They carry on the shoulder of the young cattle their
 wealth;
And on the bunch of the camel their treasures:
To a people, that will not profit them.
7 For Egypt is a mere vapour; in vain shall they help:
Wherefore have I called her, Rahab the inactive.

8 Go now, write it before them on a tablet;
And record it in letters upon a book:
That it may be for future times;
For a testimony for ever.
9 For this is a rebellious people, lying children;
Children who choose not to hear the law of JEHOVAH:
10 Who say to the seers, See not;
And to the prophets, Prophesy not right things:
Speak unto us smooth things, prophesy deceits.
11 Turn aside from the way; decline from the straight path;
Remove from our sight the Holy One of Israel.
12 Wherefore thus saith the Holy One of Israel:
Because ye have rejected this word;
And have trusted in obliquity, and perversion;
And have leaned entirely upon it:
13 Therefore shall this offence be unto you,
Like a breach threatening ruin; a swelling in a high
 wall;
Whose destruction cometh suddenly, in an instant.
14 It shall be broken, as when one breaketh a potter's
 vessel:
He dasheth it to pieces, and spareth it not;
So that there shall not be found a sherd among its frag-
 ments,
To take up fire from the hearth,
Or to dip up water from the cistern.
15 Verily thus saith the Lord JEHOVAH, the Holy one of
 Israel:
By turning from your ways, and by abiding quiet, ye
 shall be saved;
In silence, and in pious confidence, shall be your strength:
But ye would not hearken.
16 And ye said: Nay, but on horses will we flee;
Therefore shall ye be put to flight:
And on swift coursers will we ride;
Therefore shall they be swift, that pursue you.

17 One thousand, at the rebuke of one;
At the rebuke of five, ten thousand of you shall flee:
Till ye be left as a standard on the summit of a mountain;
And as a beacon on a high hill.
18 Yet for this shall JEHOVAH wait to shew favour unto you;
Even for this shall he expect in silence, that he may have mercy upon you:
(For JEHOVAH is a God of judgment;
Blessed are all they that trust in him):
19 When a holy people shall dwell in Sion;
When in Jerusalem thou shalt implore him with weeping:
At the voice of thy cry he shall be abundantly gracious unto thee;
No sooner shall he hear, than he shall answer thee.
20 Though JEHOVAH hath given you bread of distress, and water of affliction;
Yet the timely rain shall no more be restrained;
But thine eyes shall behold the timely rain.
21 And thine ears shall hear the word prompting thee behind:
Saying, This is the way; walk ye in it;
Turn not aside, to the right, or to the left.

22 And ye shall treat as defiled the covering of your idols of silver;
And the clothing of your molten images of gold:
Thou shalt cast them away like a polluted garment;
Thou shalt say unto them, Be gone from me.
23 And he shall give rain for thy seed,
With which thou shalt sow the ground;
And bread of the produce of the ground:
And it shall be abundant and plenteous.
Then shall thy cattle feed in large pasture;
24 And the oxen, and the young asses, that till the ground,
Shall eat well-fermented maslin,
Winnowed with the van and the sieve.
25 And on every lofty mountain,
And on every high hill,
Shall be disparting rills, and streams of water,
In the day of the great slaughter, when the mighty fall.

26 And the light of the moon shall be as the light of the meridian sun;
And the light of the meridian sun shall be seven-fold:
In the day when JEHOVAH shall bind up the breach of his people;
And shall heal the wound, which his stroke hath inflicted.

27 Lo! the name of JEHOVAH cometh from afar;
His wrath burneth, and the flame rageth violently:
His lips are filled with indignation;
And his tongue is as a consuming fire.
28 His spirit is like a torrent overflowing;
It shall reach to the middle of the neck:
He cometh to toss the nations with the van of perdition;
And there shall be a bridle, to lead them astray, in the jaws of the people.
29 Ye shall utter a song, as in the night when the feast is solemnly proclaimed;
With joy of heart, as when one marcheth to the sound of the pipe;
To go to the mountain of JEHOVAH, to the rock of Israel.
30 And JEHOVAH shall cause his glorious voice to be heard,
And the lighting down of his arm to be seen;
With wrath indignant, and a flame of consuming fire;
With a violent storm, and rushing showers, and hailstones.
31 By the voice of JEHOVAH the Assyrian shall be beaten down;
He, that was ready to smite with his staff.
32 And it shall be, that wherever shall pass the rod of correction,
Which JEHOVAH shall lay heavily upon him;
It shall be accompanied with tabrets and harps;
And with fierce battles shall he fight against them.
33 For Tophet is ordained of old;
Even the same for the king is prepared:
He hath made it deep; he hath made it large;
A fiery pyre, and abundance of fuel;
And the breath of JEHOVAH, like a stream of sulphur, shall kindle it.

CHAP. XXXI.
1 Wo unto them, that go down to Egypt for help;
Who trust in horses for their support:
Who confide in chariots, because they are many;
And in horsemen, because they are very strong:
But look not unto the Holy One of Israel;
And of JEHOVAH they ask not counsel.
2 But he in his wisdom will bring evil upon them;
And he will not set aside his word:
But will rise against the house of the wicked;
And against the helpers of those that work iniquity.
3 For the Egyptians are man, and not God;
And their horses are flesh, and not spirit:
And JEHOVAH shall stretch forth his hand;
And the helper shall fall, and the holpen shall be overthrown;
And together shall all of them be destroyed.
4 For thus hath JEHOVAH said unto me:
Like as the lion growleth,
Even the young lion, over his prey;
Though the whole company of shepherds be called together against him:
At their voice he will not be terrified,
Nor at their tumult will he be humbled
So shall JEHOVAH God of Hosts descend to fight
For Mount Sion, and for his own hill.
5 As the mother birds, hovering over their young,
So shall JEHOVAH God of Hosts protect Jerusalem;
Protecting, and delivering; leaping forward, and rescuing her.

6 Return unto him, from whom ye have so deeply engaged in revolt,
O ye sons of Israel!
7 Verily in that day shall they cast away with contempt,
Every man his idols of silver, and his idols of gold;
The sin, which their own hands have made.
8 And the Assyrian shall fall by a sword not of man;
Yea a sword not of mortal shall devour him.
And he shall betake himself to flight from the face of the sword;
And the courage of his chosen men shall fail.

9 And through terror he shall pass beyond his stronghold;
And his princes shall be struck with consternation at his flight.
Thus saith JEHOVAH, who hath his fire in Sion,
And his furnace in Jerusalem.

CHAP. XXXII.
1 BEHOLD, a king shall reign in righteousness;
And princes shall rule with equity:
2 And the man shall be as a covert from the storm, as a refuge from the flood;
As canals of waters in a dry place;
As the shadow of a great rock in a land fainting with heat:
3 And him the eyes of those, that see, shall regard;
And the ears of those, that hear, shall hearken.
4 Even the heart of the rash shall consider, and acquire knowledge;
And the stammering tongue shall speak readily and plainly.
5 The fool shall no longer be called honourable;
And the niggard shall no more be called liberal:
6 For the fool will still utter folly;
And his heart will devise iniquity:
Practising hypocrisy, and speaking wrongfully against JEHOVAH;
To exhaust the soul of the hungry,
And to deprive the thirsty of drink.
7 As for the niggard, his instruments are evil:
He plotteth mischievous devices;
To entangle the humble with lying words;
And to defeat the assertions of the poor in judgment.
8 But the generous will devise generous things;
And he by his generous purposes shall be established.

9 O YE women, that sit at ease, arise, hear my voice!
O ye daughters, that dwell in security, give ear unto my speech!
10 Years upon years shall ye be disquieted, O ye careless women:
For the vintage hath failed, the gathering of the fruits shall not come.

11 Tremble, O ye that are at ease; be ye disquieted, O ye
   careless ones!
   Strip ye, make ye bare; and gird ye sackcloth
12 Upon your loins, upon your breasts;
   Mourn ye for the pleasant field, for the fruitful vine.
13 Over the land of my people the thorn and the brier
   shall come up;
   Yea, over all the joyous houses, over the exulting city.
14 For the palace is deserted, the populous city is left desolate;
   Ophel and the watch-tower shall for a long time be a den,
   A joy of wild asses, a pasture for the flocks:
15 Till the spirit from on high be poured out upon us;
   And the wilderness become a fruitful field;
   And the fruitful field be esteemed a forest:
16 And judgment shall dwell in the wilderness;
   And in the fruitful field shall reside righteousness.
17 And the work of righteousness shall be peace;
   And the effect of righteousness perpetual quiet and security.
18 And my people shall dwell in a peaceful mansion,
   And in habitations secure,
   And in resting places undisturbed.
19 But the hail shall fall, and the forest be brought down;
   And the city shall be laid level with the plain.
20 Blessed are ye, who sow your seed in every well-watered place;
   Who send forth the foot of the ox and the ass.

CHAP. XXXIII.

1 Wo unto thee, thou spoiler, who hast not been spoiled thyself;
   And thou plunderer, who hast not been plundered:
   When thou hast ceased to spoil, thou shalt be spoiled;
   When thou art weary of plundering, they shall plunder thee.

2 O Jehovah, have mercy on us; we have trusted in thee;
   Be thou our strength every morning;
   Even our salvation in the time of distress.

3   From thy terrible voice the peoples fled;
    When thou didst raise thyself up, the nations were dispersed.
4· But your spoil shall be gathered, as the locust gathereth;
    As the caterpillar runneth to and fro, so shall they run, and seize it.

5   JEHOVAH is exalted; yea, he dwelleth on high:
    He hath filled Sion with judgment and justice.
6   And wisdom and knowledge shall be the stability of thy times,
    The possession of continued salvation;
    The fear of JEHOVAH, this shall be thy treasure.

7   Behold the mighty men raise a grievous cry;
    The messengers of peace weep bitterly.
.8 The highways are desolate; the traveller ceaseth:
    He hath broken the covenant; he hath rejected the offered cities;
    Of men he maketh no account.
9   The land mourneth, it languisheth;
    Libanus is put to shame, it withereth:
    Sharon is become like a desert;
    And Bashan and Carmel are stripped of their beauty.

10 Now will I arise, saith JEHOVAH;
    Now will I lift myself up on high; now will I be exalted.
11 Ye shall conceive chaff; ye shall bring forth stubble;
    And my spirit like fire shall consume you.
12 And peoples shall be burned, as the lime is burned;
    As the thorns are cut up, and consumed in the fire.
13   Hear, O ye that are afar off, my doings;
    And acknowledge, O ye that are near, my power.
14 The sinners in Sion are struck with dread;
    Terror hath seized the hypocrites:
    Who among us can abide this consuming fire?
    Who among us can abide these continued burnings?
15 He who walketh in perfect righteousness, and speaketh right things:
    Who detesteth the lucre of oppression;
    Who shaketh his hands from bribery;
    Who stoppeth his ears to the proposal of bloodshed;

Who shutteth his eyes against the appearance of evil:
16 His dwelling shall be in the high places;
The strongholds of the rocks shall be his lofty fortress:
His bread shall be duly furnished; his waters shall not fail.
17 Thine eyes shall see the king in his beauty;
They shall see thine own land far extended.
18 Thine heart shall reflect on the past terror:
Where is now the accomptant? where the weigher of tribute?
Where is he, that numbered the towers?
19 Thou shalt see no more that barbarous people;
The people of a deep speech, which thou couldst not hear;
And of a stammering tongue, which thou couldst not understand.
20 Thou shalt see Sion, the city of our solemn feasts;
Thine eyes shall behold Jerusalem,
The quiet habitation, the tabernacle unshaken:
Whose stakes shall not be plucked up for ever,
And of whose cords none shall be broken.
21 But the glorious name of JEHOVAH shall be unto us,
A place of confluent streams, of broad rivers;
Which no oared ship shall pass,
Neither shall any mighty vessel go through.
22 For JEHOVAH is our judge; JEHOVAH is our lawgiver;
JEHOVAH is our king: he shall save us.

23 Thy sails are loose; they cannot make them fast:
Thy mast is not firm; they cannot spread the ensign.
Then shall a copious spoil be divided;
Even the lame shall seize the prey.
24 Neither shall the inhabitant say, I am disabled with sickness:
The people, that dwelleth therein, is freed from the punishment of their iniquity.

CHAP. XXXIV.
1 DRAW near, O ye nations, and hearken;
And attend unto me, O ye peoples!
Let the earth hear, and the fulness thereof;
The world, and all that spring from it.

2 For the wrath of JEHOVAH is kindled against all the nations;
And his anger against all the orders thereof:
He hath devoted them; he hath given them up to slaughter.
3 And their slain shall be cast out;
And from their carcasses their stink shall ascend;
And the mountains shall melt down with their blood.
4 And all the host of heaven shall waste away;
And the heavens shall be rolled up like a scroll:
And all their host shall wither;
As the withered leaf falleth from the vine,
And as the blighted fruit from the fig-tree.
5 For my sword is made bare in the heavens:
Behold, on Edom it shall descend;
And on the people justly by me devoted to destruction.
6 The sword of JEHOVAH is glutted with blood;
It is pampered with fat:
With the blood of lambs, and of goats;
With the fat of the reins of rams:
For JEHOVAH celebrateth a sacrifice in Botsrah,
And a great slaughter in the land of Edom.
7 And the wild goats shall fall down with them;
And the bullocks, together with the bulls:
And their own land shall be drunken with their blood,
And their dust shall be enriched with fat.
8 For it is the day of vengeance to JEHOVAH;
The year of recompense to the defender of the cause of Sion.
9 And her torrents shall be turned into pitch,
And her dust into sulphur;
And her whole land shall become burning pitch:
10 By night or by day it shall not be extinguished
For ever shall her smoke ascend:
From generation to generation she shall lie desert;
To everlasting ages no one shall pass through her;
11 But the pelican and the porcupine shall inherit her;
And the owl and the raven shall inhabit there:
And he shall stretch over her the line of devastation,
And the plummet of emptiness over her scorched plains.
12 No more shall they boast the renown of the kingdom;
And all her princes shall utterly fail.

13 And in her palaces shall spring up thorns;
   The nettle and the bramble, in her fortresses:
   And she shall become an habitation for dragons,
   A court for the daughters of the ostrich.
14 And the jackals and the mountain-cats shall meet one another;
   And the satyr shall call to his fellow:
   There also the screech-owl shall pitch;
   And shall find for herself a place of rest.
15 There shall the night-raven make her nest, and lay her eggs;
   And she shall hatch them, and gather her young under her shadow:
   There also shall the vultures be gathered together;
   Every one of them shall join her mate.
16 Consult ye the book of JEHOVAH, and read:
   Not one of these shall be missed;
   Not a female shall lack her mate:
   For the mouth of JEHOVAH hath given the command;
   And his spirit itself hath gathered them.
17 And he hath cast the lot for them;
   And his hand hath meted out their portion by the line:
   They shall possess the land for a perpetual inheritance;
   From generation to generation shall they dwell therein.

CHAP. XXXV.
1   THE desert, and the waste, shall be glad;
   And the wilderness shall rejoice, and flourish:
2 Like the rose shall it beautifully flourish;
   And the well-watered plain of Jordan shall also rejoice:
   The glory of Lebanon shall be given unto it,
   The beauty of Carmel and of Sharon:
   These shall behold the glory of JEHOVAH,
   The majesty of our God.
3   Strengthen ye the feeble hands,
   And confirm ye the tottering knees.
4 Say ye to the faint-hearted: Be ye strong;
   Fear ye not; behold your God!
   Vengeance will come; the retribution of God:
   He himself will come, and will deliver you.
5 Then shall be unclosed the eyes of the blind;
   And the ears of the deaf shall be opened:
6 Then shall the lame bound like the hart,
   And the tongue of the dumb shall sing:

For in the wilderness shall burst forth waters,
And torrents in the desert :
7 And the glowing sand shall become a pool,
And the thirsty soil bubbling springs :
And in the haunt of dragons shall spring forth
The grass, with the reed, and the bulrush.
8 And a highway shall be there ;
And it shall be called the way of holiness :
No unclean person shall pass through it :
But He himself shall be with them, walking in the way,
And the foolish shall not err therein.
9 No lion shall be there ;
Nor shall the tyrant of the beasts come up thither :
Neither shall he be found there ;
But the redeemed shall walk in it.
10 Yea the ransomed of JEHOVAH shall return :
They shall come to Sion with triumph ;
And perpetual gladness shall crown their heads.
Joy and gladness shall they obtain ;
And sorrow and sighing shall flee away.

CHAP. XXXVI.
1 IN the fourteenth year of king Hezekiah, Senacherib king of Assyria came up against all the fenced cities of
2 Judah, and took them. And the king of Assyria sent Rabshakeh, from Lachish to Jerusalem, to the king Hezekiah, with a great body of forces : and he presented himself at the conduit of the upper pool, in the highway
3 that leads to the fuller's field. Then came out unto him Eliakim, the son of Hilkiah, who was over the household, and Shebna the scribe, and Joah, the son of Asaph,
4 the recorder. And Rabshakeh said unto them : Say ye to Hezekiah ; Thus saith the great king, the king of Assyria : What is this ground of confidence, in which
5 thou confidest ? Thou hast said, (but they are vain words), I have counsel and strength sufficient for the war. Now in whom dost thou confide, that thou re-
6 bellest against me ? Thou certainly confidest in the support of this broken reed, in Egypt; on which if a man lean, it will pierce his hand, and go through it: such is Pharaoh king of Egypt to all that confide in
7 him. But if ye say to me, We confide in JEHOVAH our

God; is it not He, whose high places and whose altars Hezekiah hath removed; and hath commanded Judah 8 and Jerusalem to worship only before this altar? Enter now, I pray thee, into an engagement with my lord the king of Assyria; and I will give thee two thousand horses, on condition, that thou canst on thy part provide 9 riders for them. How then wilt thou turn back any one commander, among the least of my lord's servants, advancing against thee? And trustest thou, that Egypt 10 will supply thee with chariots and with horsemen? And am I now come up without JEHOVAH against this land to destroy it? JEHOVAH hath said unto me, Go thou up against this land, and destroy it.

11 Then said Eliakim, and Shebna, and Joah, unto Rabshakeh: Speak, we beseech thee, to thy servants in the Syrian language, for we understand it; and speak not to us in the Jewish language, in the hearing of the 12 people, who are upon the wall. And Rabshakeh said, Hath my lord sent me to thy lord and to thee, to speak these words? and not to the men, that sit on the wall, destined to eat their own dung, and drink their own 13 urine, together with you? Then Rabshakeh stood, and cried with a loud voice in the Jewish language, and said: Hear ye the words of the great king, the king of 14 Assyria. Thus saith the king: Let not Hezekiah de- 15 ceive you; for he will not be able to deliver you. And let not Hezekiah persuade you to trust in JEHOVAH; saying, JEHOVAH will certainly deliver us; this city shall not be given up into the hand of the king of 16 Assyria. Hearken not unto Hezekiah; for thus saith the king of Assyria: Make peace with me, and come out unto me. And eat ye every one of his own vine, and every one of his own fig-tree; and drink ye every 17 one the waters of his own cistern: until I come and take you to a land like your own land; a land of corn 18 and of wine, a land of bread and of vineyards. Nor let Hezekiah seduce you, saying, JEHOVAH will deliver us. Have the gods of the nations delivered each his own 19 land from the hand of the king of Assyria? Where are the gods of Hamath, and of Arphad? where are the gods of Sepharvaim? have they delivered Samaria out 20 of my hand? Who are there among all the gods of

these lands, that have delivered their own lands out of
my hand; that JEHOVAH should deliver out of my hand
21 Jerusalem? But the people held their peace, and answered him not a word: for the king's command was,
Answer him not.
22 Then came Eliakim, the son of Hilkiah, who was
over the household, and Shebna the scribe, and Joah,
the son of Asaph, the recorder, to Hezekiah, with their
clothes rent; and reported unto him the words of Rabshakeh.

CHAP. XXXVII.

1 And when king Hezekiah heard it, he rent his clothes,
and covered himself with sackcloth, and went into the
2 house of JEHOVAH. And he sent Eliakim, who was
over the household, and Shebna the scribe, and the
elders of the priests, covered with sackcloth, to Isaiah,
3 the son of Amots, the prophet. And they said unto
him: Thus saith Hezekiah; This day is a day of distress, and of rebuke, and of contumely: for the children
are come to the birth, and there is not strength to bring
4 forth. O that JEHOVAH thy God would hear the words
of Rabshakeh, whom his lord the king of Assyria hath
sent to reproach the living God! and that he would
refute the words, which JEHOVAH thy God hath heard!
And do thou offer up thy prayer for the poor remains
5 of the people. And the servants of king Hezekiah came
6 to Isaiah. And Isaiah said unto them; Thus shall ye
say to your lord: Thus saith JEHOVAH, Be not afraid,
because of the words which thou hast heard, with which
the servants of the king of Assyria have blasphemed me.
7 Behold, I will infuse a spirit into him; and he shall
hear a rumour, and return to his own land; and I will
cause him to fall by the sword in his own land.

8 But Rabshakeh returned; and found the king of
Assyria besieging Libnah: for he had heard, that he
9 had decamped from Lachish. And when Senacherib
had received advice concerning Tirhakah king of Cush,
that he was advancing to give him battle; he sent mes-
10 sengers again to Hezekiah, saying; Thus shall ye say
to Hezekiah king of Judah: Let not thy God, in whom
thou confidest, deceive thee; by assuring thee, that Jerusalem shall not be given up into the hand of the king

11 of Assyria. Thou hast certainly heard, what the kings of Assyria have done to all lands, which they have ut-
12 terly destroyed: and shalt thou be delivered? Have the gods of the nations delivered those, which my fathers have destroyed? Gozan, and Haran, and Retseph; and
13 the sons of Eden, which were in Thelassar? Where is the king of Hamath, and the king of Arphad, and the king of the city of Sepharvaim, of Henah, and of Ivah?

14 And Hezekiah received the letters from the hand of the messengers, and read them; and he went up to the house of JEHOVAH: and Hezekiah spread them before
15 the presence of JEHOVAH. And Hezekiah prayed be-
16 fore JEHOVAH, saying: O JEHOVAH, God of Hosts, thou God of Israel, who art seated on the cherubim! Thou art the God, thou alone, to all the kingdoms of the earth! Thou hast made the heavens, and the earth!
17 Incline, O JEHOVAH, thine ear, and hear; open, O JEHOVAH, thine eyes, and see: yea, hear all the words of Senacherib, which he hath sent to reproach the living
18 God. In truth, O JEHOVAH, the kings of Assyria have destroyed all the nations, and their lands; and have
19 cast their gods into the fire: for they were not gods, but the work of the hands of man, wood and stone;
20 therefore they have destroyed them. And now, O JEHOVAH, our God, save us, we beseech thee, from his hand; that all the kingdoms of the earth may know, that thou JEHOVAH art the only God.

21 Then Isaiah the son of Amots sent unto Hezekiah, saying: Thus saith JEHOVAH the God of Israel: Thy prayer unto me, concerning Senacherib king of Assyria,
22 I have heard. This is the word, which JEHOVAH hath spoken concerning him:

> THE virgin daughter of Sion hath despised thee,
>   she hath laughed thee to scorn;
> The daughter of Jerusalem hath shaken her head behind thee.
23 Whom hast thou reproached, and reviled; and against whom hast thou exalted thy voice?
> And hast lifted up thine eyes on high? Even against the Holy One of Israel.

24   By thy messengers hast thou reproached JEHOVAH, and said:
By the multitude of my chariots have I ascended
The highth of the mountains, the sides of Lebanon;
And I will cut down his tallest cedars, his choicest fir-trees;
And I will penetrate into his extreme retreats, his richest forests.
25   I have digged, and I have drunk strange waters;
And I have dried up with the sole of my feet all the canals of fenced places.
26   Hast thou not heard, of old, that I have disposed it?
And, of ancient times, that I have formed it?
Now have I brought it to pass, that thou shouldst be to lay waste
Warlike nations, strong-fenced cities.
27   Therefore were their inhabitants of small strength; they were dismayed and confounded:
They were as the grass of the field, and as the green herb;
The grass of the house-top; and as the corn blasted before it groweth up.
28   But thy sitting down, and thy going out, and thy coming in,
And thy rage against me, I have known.
29   Because thy rage against me, and thy insolence, is come up into mine ears;
Therefore will I put my hook in thy nose, and my bridle in thy jaws;
And I will turn thee back by the way in which thou earnest.
30   And this shall be a sign unto thee:
Eat this year that which groweth of itself;
And the second year, that which springeth up of the same;
And in the third year sow ye, and reap;
And plant vineyards, and eat the fruit thereof.
31   And again shall the escaped, the remnant of the house of Judah,
Strike root downward, and bear fruit upward.
For from Jerusalem shall go forth the remnant;
And the part escaped from Mount Sion:
The zeal of JEHOVAH God of Hosts shall effect this.

32 Therefore thus saith JEHOVAH concerning the king of
    Assyria:
    He shall not enter into this city;
    Nor shall he shoot an arrow there;
    Nor shall he present a shield before it;
    Nor shall he cast up a mound against it.
33 By the way, in which he came, by the same shall he
      return;
    And into this city shall he not come; saith JEHOVAH.
34 And I will protect this city to deliver it;
    For mine own sake, and for the sake of David my
      servant.

35 And the angel of JEHOVAH went forth, and smote in
the camp of the Assyrians an hundred and fourscore and
five thousand men: and when the people arose early in
36 the morning, behold, they were all dead corpses. Then
Senacherib king of Assyria decamped, and departed, and
37 returned; and dwelt at Nineveh. And as he was worshipping in the temple of Nisroc his god, Adramelec and
Sharetser, his sons, smote him with the sword: and they
escaped into the land of Armenia; and Esarhaddon his
son reigned in his stead.

CHAP. XXXVIII.
1 AT that time Hezekiah was seized with a mortal sickness: and Isaiah the prophet, the son of Amots, came
unto him; and said unto him: Thus saith JEHOVAH:
Give orders concerning the affairs of thy family; for
2 thou must die; thou shalt no longer live. Then Hezekiah turned his face to the wall; and made his suppli-
3 cation to JEHOVAH. And he said: I beseech thee, O
JEHOVAH, remember now, how I have endeavoured to
walk before thee in truth, and with a perfect heart; and
have done that which is good in thine eyes. And He-
4 zekiah wept, and lamented grievously. Now [before
Isaiah was gone out into the middle court,] the word of
JEHOVAH came unto him, saying: Go [back], and say
5 unto Hezekiah: Thus saith JEHOVAH, the God of David
thy father: I have heard thy supplication; I have seen
thy tears. Behold [I will heal thee; and on the third
day thou shalt go up into the house of JEHOVAH. And]
6 I will add unto thy days fifteen years. And I will de-

liver thee, and this city, from the hand of the king of
22 Assyria; And I will protect this city. And [Hezekiah
said: By what sign shall I know, that I shall go up into
7 the house of JEHOVAH? And Isaiah said:] This shall
be the sign unto thee from JEHOVAH, that JEHOVAH will
8 bring to effect this word which he hath spoken. Behold,
I will bring back the shadow of the degrees, by which
the sun is gone down on the degrees of Ahaz, ten degrees backward. And the sun returned backward ten degrees, on the degrees by which it had gone down.
21 And Isaiah said: Let them take a lump of figs: and they
bruised them, and applied them to the boil; and he recovered.

9   THE WRITING OF HEZEKIAH KING OF JUDAH, WHEN
HE HAD BEEN SICK, AND WAS RECOVERED FROM HIS
SICKNESS.

10   I said, when my days were just going to be cut off,
I shall pass through the gates of the grave;
I am deprived of the residue of my years!
11   I said, I shall no more see JEHOVAH in the land of
the living!
I shall no longer behold man, with the inhabitants of
the world!
12   My habitation is taken away, and is removed from me,
like a shepherd's tent:
My life is cut off, as by the weaver; he will sever me
from the loom;
In the course of the day thou wilt finish my web.
13   I roared until the morning, like the lion;
So did he break to pieces all my bones.
14   Like the swallow, like the crane did I twitter;
I made a moaning like the dove.
Mine eyes fail with looking upward:
O Lord, contend thou for me; be thou my surety.
15   What shall I say? he hath given me a promise, and
he hath performed it.
Through the rest of my years will I reflect on this
bitterness of my soul.
16   For this cause shall it be declared, O JEHOVAH, con-
concerning thee,
That thou hast revived my spirit;

That thou hast restored my health, and prolonged my life.
17 Behold my anguish is changed into ease!
Thou hast rescued my soul from perdition;
Yea thou hast cast behind thy back all my sins.
18 Verily the grave shall not give thanks unto thee; death shall not praise thee;
They that go down into the pit shall not await thy truth:
19 The living, the living, he shall praise thee, as I do this day;
The father to the children shall make known thy faithfulness.
20 JEHOVAH was present to save me: therefore will we sing our songs to the harp,
All the days of our life, in the house of JEHOVAH.

CHAP. XXXIX.
1 At that time Merodach Baladan, the son of Baladan king of Babylon, sent letters, and ambassadors, and a present to Hezekiah; for he had heard that he had been
2 sick, and was recovered. And Hezekiah was rejoiced at their arrival: and he shewed them his magazines, the silver, and the gold, and the spices, and the precious ointment, and his whole arsenal, and all that was contained in his treasures: there was not any thing in his house, and in all his dominion, that Hezekiah did not shew them.
3 And Isaiah the prophet came unto king Hezekiah, and said unto him: What say these men? and from whence came they unto thee? And Hezekiah said: They are come to me from a distant country; from Babylon.
4 And he said: What have they seen in thy house? And Hezekiah said: They have seen every thing in my house: there is nothing in my treasures, which I have
5 not shewn them. And Isaiah said unto Hezekiah: Hear thou the word of JEHOVAH God of Hosts.
6 Behold, the day shall come, when all that is in thy house, and that thy fathers have treasured up unto this day, shall be carried away to Babylon: there shall not
7 any thing be left, saith JEHOVAH. And of thy sons, which shall issue from thee, which thou shalt beget, shall they take: and they shall be eunuchs in the palace of

8 the king of Babylon. And Hezekiah said unto Isaiah :
Gracious is the word of JEHOVAH, which thou hast delivered! For, added he, there shall be peace, according to his faithful promise, in my days.

CHAP. XL.

1 COMFORT ye, comfort ye my people, saith your God:
2 Speak ye animating words to Jerusalem, and declare unto her,
That her warfare is fulfilled; that the expiation of her iniquity is accepted;
That she shall receive at the hand of JEHOVAH
[Blessings] double to the punishment of all her sins.

3 A voice crieth: In the wilderness prepare ye the way of JEHOVAH!
Make straight in the desert a highway for our God!
4 Every valley shall be exalted, and every mountain and hill be brought low;
And the crooked shall become straight, and the rough places a smooth plain:
5 And the glory of JEHOVAH shall be revealed;
And all flesh shall see together the salvation of our God:
For the mouth of JEHOVAH hath spoken it.
6 A voice sayeth: Proclaim! And I said, What shall I proclaim?
All flesh is grass, and all its glory like the flower of the field:
7 The grass withereth, the flower fadeth;
When the wind of JEHOVAH bloweth upon it.
Verily this people is grass.
8 The grass withereth, the flower fadeth;
But the word of our God shall stand for ever.
9 Get thee up upon a high mountain, O daughter that bringest glad tidings to Sion:
Exalt thy voice with strength, O daughter that bringest glad tidings to Jerusalem.
Exalt it; be not afraid:
Say to the cities of Judah, Behold your God!
10 Behold, the Lord JEHOVAH shall come against the strong one,
And his arm shall prevail over him.

Behold, his reward is with him, and the recompense of
his work before him.
11 Like a shepherd shall he feed his flock ;
In his arm shall he gather up the lambs,
And shall bear them in his bosom ; the nursing ewes
shall he gently lead.

12 Who hath measured the waters in the hollow of his
hand ;
And hath meted out the heavens by his span ;
And hath comprehended the dust of the earth in a tierce ;
And hath weighed in scales the mountains, and the hills
in a balance ?
13 Who hath directed the spirit of JEHOVAH ;
And, as one of his council, hath informed him ?
14 Whom hath he consulted, that he should instruct him,
And teach him the path of judgment;
That he should impart to him science,
And inform him in the way of understanding ?
15 Behold, the nations are as a drop from the bucket;
As the small dust of the balance shall they be accounted:
Behold, the islands he taketh up as an atom.
16 And Lebanon is not sufficient for the fire ;
Nor his beasts sufficient for the burnt-offering.
17 All the nations are as nothing before him ;
They are esteemed by him as less than nought, and
vanity.

18 To whom therefore will ye liken God ?
And what is the model of resemblance, that ye will prepare for him ?
19 The workman casteth an image ;
And the smith overlayeth it with plates of gold ;
And forgeth for it chains of silver.
20 He that cannot afford a costly oblation, chooseth a piece
of wood that will not rot ;
He procureth a skilful artist,
To erect an image, which shall not be moved.
21 Will ye not know ? will ye not hear ?
Hath it not been declared to you from the beginning ?
Have ye not understood it from the foundations of the
earth ?
22 It is He, that sitteth on the circle of the earth ;

And the inhabitants are to him as grasshoppers :
That extendeth the heavens, as a thin veil ;
And spreadeth them out, as a tent to dwell in :
23 That reduceth princes to nothing ;
That maketh the judges of the earth a mere inanity.
24 Yea they shall not leave a plant behind them, they shall not be sown,
Their trunk shall not spread its root in the ground :
If he but blow upon them, they instantly wither ;
And the whirlwind shall bear them away like the stubble.
25 To whom then will ye liken me ?
And to whom shall I be equalled ? saith the Holy One.
26 Lift up your eyes on high ;
And see, who hath created these.
He draweth forth their armies by number ;
He calleth them all by name :
Through the greatness of his strength, and the mightiness of his power,
Not one of them faileth to appear.

27 Wherefore sayest thou then, O Jacob,
And why speakest thou thus, O Israel,
My way is hidden from JEHOVAH,
And my cause passeth unregarded by my God.
28 Hast thou not known, hast thou not heard,
That JEHOVAH is the everlasting God,
The Creator of the bounds of the earth ?
That he neither fainteth, nor is wearied ;
And that his understanding is unsearchable !
29 He giveth strength to the faint,
And to the infirm he multiplieth force.
30 The young men shall faint and be wearied ;
And the chosen youths shall stumble and fall :
31 But they that trust in JEHOVAH shall gather new strength ;
They shall put forth fresh feathers like the moulting eagle :
They shall run, and not be wearied ;
They shall march onward, and shall not faint.

CHAP. XLI.

1 LET the distant nations repair to me with new force of mind ;
And let the peoples recover their strength.

Let them draw near; then let them speak;
Let us enter into solemn debate together.

2   Who hath raised up the righteous man from the east
Hath called him to attend his steps?
Hath subdued nations at his presence;
And given him dominion over kings?
Hath made them like the dust before his sword;
And like the driven stubble before his bow?
3 He pursueth them; he passeth in safety;
By a way never trodden before with his feet.
4 Who hath performed, and made these things,
Calling the several generations from the beginning?
I Jehovah, the first;
And with the last, I am the same.

5   The distant nations saw, and they were afraid;
The remotest parts of the earth, and they were terrified.
They drew near, they came together;
6 Every one assisted his neighbour,
And said to his brother, Be of good courage.
7 The carver encourageth the smith;
He that smootheth with the hammer, him that smiteth on the anvil;
Saying of the solder, It is good;
And he fixeth the idol with nails, that it shall not move.

8   But thou, Israel, my servant;
Thou, Jacob, whom I have chosen;
The seed of Abraham my friend:
9 Thou, whom I have led by the hand from the ends of the earth;
And called from the extremities thereof;
And I said unto thee, Thou art my servant;
I have chosen thee, and will not reject thee:
10 Fear not, for I am with thee;
Be not dismayed, for I am thy God.
I have strengthened thee, I have assisted thee;
I have even supported thee with my faithful right hand.
11 Behold, they, that were enraged against thee, shall be ashamed and confounded;

They, that contended with thee, shall become as nothing,
  and shall utterly perish.
12 Thou shalt seek them, and shalt not find them, even the
  men that strove with thee :
  They shall become as nothing, and as mere nought,
  even the men that opposed thee in battle.
13 For I am JEHOVAH thy God, that hold thee fast by thy
  right hand;
  That say unto thee, Fear not; I am thy helper.
14 Fear not, thou worm Jacob; ye mortals of Israel:
  I am thy helper, saith JEHOVAH;
  And thine avenger is the Holy One of Israel.
15 Behold, I have made thee a thrashing wain;
  A new corn-drag armed with pointed teeth:
  Thou shalt thrash the mountains, and beat them small;
  And reduce the hills to chaff:
16 Thou shalt winnow them, and the wind shall bear them
  away;
  And the tempest shall scatter them abroad:
  But thou shalt rejoice in JEHOVAH;
  In the Holy One of Israel shalt thou triumph.

17 The poor and the needy seek for water, and there is
  none;
  Their tongue is parched with thirst:
  I JEHOVAH will answer them;
  The God of Israel, I will not forsake them.
18 I will open in the high places rivers;
  And in the midst of the vallies, fountains:
  I will make the desert a standing pool;
  And the dry ground streams of waters.
19 In the wilderness I will give the cedar;
  The acacia, the myrtle, and the tree producing oil:
  I will plant the fir-tree in the desert;
  The pine, and the box together:
20 That they may see, and that they may know;
  And may consider, and understand at once,
  That the hand of JEHOVAH hath done this,
  And that the Holy One of Israel hath created it.

21 Draw near, produce your cause, saith JEHOVAH:
  Produce these your mighty powers, saith the king of
  Jacob.

22 Let them approach, and tell us the things that shall
   happen;
   The things that shall first happen, what they are, let
   them tell us:
   And we will consider them; and we shall know the event.
   Or declare to us things to come hereafter:
23 Tell us the things, that will come to pass in later times;
   Then shall we know that ye are Gods.
   Yea, do good, or do evil;
   Then shall we be struck at once with admiration and
   terror.
24 But, behold, ye are less than nothing;
   And your operation is less than nought;
   Abhorred be the man that chooseth you!

25 I have raised up one from the north, and he shall
   come;
   From the rising of the sun he shall invoke my name:
   And he shall trample on princes, like the mortar;
   Even as the potter treadeth down the clay.
26 Who hath declared this from the beginning, that we
   should know it?
   And beforehand, that we might say, The prediction is
   true?
   There was not one, that foretold it; not one, that declared it;
   There was not one, that heard your words:
27 I first to Sion [give the word], Behold they are here;
   And to Jerusalem I give the messenger of glad tidings.
28 But I looked, and there was no man;
   And among the idols, and there was no one that gave
   warning;
29 And I inquired of them, and [there was no one] that
   could return an answer.
   Behold, they are all of them vanity; their works are
   nought:
   Mere wind and emptiness are their molten images.

CHAP. XLII.
 1 BEHOLD my servant, whom I will uphold;
    My chosen, in whom my soul delighteth:
    I will make my spirit rest upon him;
    And he shall publish judgment to the nations.

2 He shall not cry aloud, nor raise a clamour,
Nor cause his voice to be heard in the public places:
3 The bruised reed he shall not break;
And the dimly burning flax he shall not quench:
He shall publish judgment, so as to establish it perfectly.
4 His force shall not be abated, nor broken;
Until he hath firmly seated judgment in the earth:
And the distant nations shall earnestly wait for his law.

5 Thus saith the God, even JEHOVAH,
Who created the heavens, and stretched them out;
Who spread abroad the earth, and the produce thereof;
Who giveth breath to the people upon it,
And spirit to them that tread thereon:
6 I JEHOVAH have called thee for a righteous purpose;
And I will take hold of thy hand, and will preserve thee;
And I will give thee for a covenant to the people, for a light to the nations:
7 To open the eyes of the blind;
To bring the captive out of confinement;
And from the dungeon, those that dwell in darkness.
8 I am JEHOVAH, that is my name;
And my glory will I not give to another,
Nor my praise to the graven images.
9 The former predictions, lo! they are come to pass;
And new events I now declare:
Before they spring forth, I make them known unto you.

10 Sing unto JEHOVAH a new song;
His praise, from the ends of the earth:
Ye that go down upon the sea, and all that fill it;
Ye distant sea-coasts, and ye that dwell therein:
11 Let the desert cry aloud, and the cities thereof;
The villages, and they that dwell in Kedar:
Let the inhabitants of the rocky country utter a joyful sound;
Let them shout aloud from the top of the mountains:
12 Let them ascribe glory to JEHOVAH;
And among the distant nations make known his praise.
13 JEHOVAH shall march forth like a hero;
Like a mighty warrior shall he rouse his vengeance:

He shall cry aloud; he shall shout amain;
He shall exert his strength against his enemies.
14 I have long holden my peace; shall I keep silence for ever?
Shall I still contain myself? I will cry out like a woman in travail;
Breathing short, and drawing in my breath with violence.
15 I will make barren the mountains and hills;
And burn up all the grass, that is upon them:
I will make the rivers dry deserts;
And scorch up the pools of water.
16 I will lead the blind in a way, which they have not known;
And through paths, which they have not known, will I make them go:
I will turn darkness into light before them;
And the rugged ways into a smooth plain.
These things will I do for them, and will not forsake them.

17 They are turned backward, they are utterly confounded, who trust in the graven image;
Who say unto the molten image, Ye are our gods!

18 Hear, O ye deaf;
And, ye blind, look attentively, that ye may see!
19 Who is blind, but my servant;
And deaf, as he to whom I have sent my messengers?
Who is blind, as he who is perfectly instructed;
And deaf, as the servant of JEHOVAH?
20 Thou hast seen indeed, yet thou dost not regard;
Thine ears are open, yet thou wilt not hear.
21 Yet JEHOVAH was gracious unto him, for his truth's sake:
He hath exalted his own praise, and made it glorious.
22 But this is a people spoiled and plundered:
All their chosen youths are taken in the toils,
And are plunged in the dark dungeons:
They are become a spoil, and there was none to rescue them;
A plunder, and no one said, Restore.

23   Who is there among you, that will listen to this;
    That will hearken, and attend to it, for the future?
24 Who hath given Jacob for a spoil;
    And Israel to the plunderers?
    Was it not JEHOVAH; He, against whom they have sinned;
    In whose ways they would not walk;
    And whose law they would not obey?
25 Therefore poured he out upon them the heat of his wrath, and the violence of war:
    And it kindled a flame round about him, yet he did not regard it;
    And it set him on fire, yet he did not consider it.

CHAP. XLIII.
1   Yet now, thus saith JEHOVAH;
    Who created thee, O Jacob; and who formed thee, O Israel:
    Fear thou not, for I have redeemed thee;
    I have called thee by thy name; thou art mine.
2 When thou passest through waters, I am with thee;
    And through rivers, they shall not overwhelm thee:
    When thou walkest in the fire, thou shalt not be scorched;
    And the flame shall not take hold of thee.
3 For I am JEHOVAH, thy God;
    The Holy One of Israel, thy redeemer:
    I have given Egypt for thy ransom;
    Cush, and Saba, in thy stead.
4 Because thou hast been precious in my sight,
    Thou hast been honoured, and I have loved thee:
    Therefore will I give men instead of thee;
    And peoples instead of thy soul.
5 Fear thou not, for I am with thee:
    From the east I will bring thy children,
    And from the west I will gather thee together:
6 I will say to the north, Give up;
    And to the south, Withhold not:
    Bring my sons from afar;
    And my daughters from the ends of the earth:
7 Every one that is called by my name,
    Whom for my glory I have created;
    Whom I have formed, yea whom I have made.

8 Bring forth the people, blind, although they have eyes;
And deaf, although they have ears.
9 Let all the nations be gathered together,
And let the peoples be collected.
Who among them will declare this;
And will tell us, what first shall come to pass?
Let them produce their witnesses, that they may be justified:
Or let them hear in their turn, and say, This is true.
10 Ye are my witnesses, saith JEHOVAH;
Even my servant, whom I have chosen:
That ye may know, and believe me;
And understand, that I am He.
Before me no god was formed;
And after me none shall exist.
11 I, even I, am JEHOVAH;
And beside me there is no saviour.
12 I declared my purpose, and I have saved:
I made it known; nor was it any strange god among you:
And ye are my witnesses, saith JEHOVAH, that I am God.
13 Even before time was, I am He;
And there is none that can rescue out of my hand:
I work; and who shall undo what I have done?

14 Thus saith JEHOVAH,
Your redeemer, the Holy One of Israel:
For your sake have I sent unto Babylon;
And I will bring down all her strong bars;
And the Chaldeans, exulting in their ships:
15 I am JEHOVAH, your Holy One;
The creator of Israel, your king.

16 Thus saith JEHOVAH;
Who made a way in the sea,
And a path in the mighty waters;
17 Who brought forth the rider and the horse, the army and the warrior;
Together they lay down, they rose no more;
They were extinguished, they were quenched like tow:

18 Remember not the former things;
And the things of ancient times regard not;
19 Behold, I make a new thing;
Even now shall it spring forth : will ye not regard it?
Yea I will make in the wilderness a way;
In the desert, streams of water.
20 The wild beast of the field shall glorify me;
The dragons, and the daughters of the ostrich:
Because I have given waters in the wilderness;
And flowing streams in the desert;
To give drink to my people, my chosen:
21 This people, whom I have formed for myself;
Who shall recount my praise.

22 But thou hast not invoked me, O Jacob;
Neither on my account hast thou laboured, O Israel.
23 Thou hast not brought to me the lamb of thy burnt-offering;
Neither hast thou honoured me with thy sacrifices:
I have not burthened thee with exacting oblations;
Nor wearied thee with demands of frankincense:
24 Thou hast not purchased for me with silver the aromatic reed;
Neither hast thou satiated me with the fat of thy sacrifices.
On the contrary, thou hast burthened me with thy sins;
Thou hast wearied me with thine iniquities.
25 I, even I, am He;
I blot out thy transgressions for mine own sake;
And thy sins I will not remember.
26 Remind me of thy plea: let us be judged on equal terms:
Set forth thine own cause, that thou mayest clear thyself.
27 Thy chief leader hath sinned;
And thy public teachers have revolted from me;
28 And thy princes have profaned my sanctuary:
Therefore will I give up Jacob for a devoted thing,
And Israel to reproach.

CHAP. XLIV.
1 But hear now, O Jacob, my servant;
And Israel, whom I have chosen:
2 Thus saith JEHOVAH, thy maker;

And he that formed thee from the womb, and will help
    thee:
Fear thou not, O my servant Jacob;
And, O Jeshurun, whom I have chosen:
3 For I will pour out waters on the thirsty;
And flowing streams on the dry ground:
I will pour out my spirit on thy seed;
And my blessing on thine offspring.
4 And they shall spring up as the grass among the waters;
As the willows beside the aqueducts.
5 One shall say; I belong to JEHOVAH;
And another shall be called by the name of Jacob:
And this shall inscribe his hand to JEHOVAH;
And shall be surnamed by the name of Israel.

6   Thus saith JEHOVAH, the king of Israel;
And his redeemer, JEHOVAH God of Hosts:
I am the first, and I am the last;
And beside me there is no God.
7 And who is like me, that he should call forth this event,
And make it known beforehand, and dispose it for me,
From the time that I appointed the people of the destined
    age?
The things that are now coming, and are to come hereaf-
   ter, let them declare unto us.
8 Fear ye not, neither be ye afraid:
Have I not declared it unto you from the first?
Yea, I have foreshewn it; and ye are my witnesses.
Is there a God beside me?
Yea, there is no other sure protector; I know not any.
9 They that form the graven image are all of them vanity;
And their most curious works shall not profit.
Yea, their works themselves bear witness to them,
That they see not, and that they understand not:
10 That every one may be ashamed, that he hath formed a
    god,
And cast a graven image, that profiteth not.
11 Behold, all his associates shall be ashamed;
Even the workmen themselves shall blush:
They shall assemble all of them; they shall present
    themselves;
They shall fear, and be ashamed together.

12   The smith cutteth off a portion of iron :
     He worketh it in the coals, and with hammers he formeth it;
     And he exerteth upon it the force of his arm.
     Yea, he is hungry, and his strength faileth him;
     He drinketh no water, and he is faint.
13   The carpenter stretcheth his line;
     He marketh out the form of it with red ochre:
     He worketh it with the sharp tool;
     He figureth it with the compass:
     He maketh it according to the fashion of a man;
     According to the beauty of the human form, that it may abide in the house.
14   He heweth down cedars for his use :
     And he taketh the pine, and the oak;
     And layeth in good store of the trees of the forest.
     He planteth the ash, and the rain nourisheth it;
15   That it may be for the use of man, for fuel:
     And he taketh thereof, and warmeth himself;
     Yea he beateth the oven with it, and baketh bread:
     He also formeth a god, and worshippeth it:
     He maketh of it a graven image, and boweth down unto it.
16   Part of it he burneth in the fire ;
     And with part of it he dresseth flesh, and eateth :
     He roasteth meat, and his hunger is satisfied;
     He also warmeth himself, and sayeth,
     Aha! I am warmed, I have enjoyed the fire :
17   And the remainder thereof he maketh a god, even his graven image;
     He boweth down to it, and worshippeth it :
     And he prayeth unto it, and sayeth;
     Deliver me, for thou art my God!
18   They know not, neither do they understand:
     Verily their eyes are closed up, that they cannot see;
     And their heart, that they cannot rightly-discern :
19   Neither doth he consider in his heart;
     Neither hath he knowledge, nor understanding, to say :
     Part of it I have burned in the fire;
     I have also baked bread on the coals thereof;
     I have roasted flesh, and I have eaten :
     And shall I make the remnant an abomination ?

    Shall I bow myself down to the stock of a tree?
20 He feedeth on ashes; a deluded heart leadeth him aside;
    So that he cannot deliver his own soul, nor say,
    Is there not a lie in my right hand?

21   Remember these things, O Jacob;
    And, Israel; for thou art my servant:
    I have formed thee; thou art a servant unto me;
    O Israel, by me thou shalt not be forgotten.
22 I have made thy transgressions vanish away like a cloud;
    And thy sins like a vapour:
    Return unto me; for I have redeemed thee.

23   Sing, O ye heavens, for JEHOVAH hath effected it;
    Utter a joyful sound, O ye depths of the earth:
    Burst forth into song, O ye mountains;
    Thou, forest, and every tree therein!
    For JEHOVAH hath redeemed Jacob;
    And will be glorified in Israel.

24   Thus saith JEHOVAH, thy redeemer;
    Even he, that formed thee from the womb:
    I am JEHOVAH, who make all things;
    Who stretch out the heavens alone;
    Who spread the firm earth by myself:
25 I am he, who frustrateth the prognostics of the impostors;
    And maketh the diviners mad:
    Who reverseth the devices of the sages,
    And infatuateth their knowledge:
26 Who establisheth the word of his servant;
    And accomplisheth the counsel of his messengers:
    Who sayeth to Jerusalem, Thou shalt be inhabited;
    And to the cities of Judah, Ye shall be built;
    And her desolated places I will restore:
27 Who sayeth to the deep, Be thou wasted;
    And I will make dry thy rivers:
28 Who sayeth to Cyrus, Thou art my shepherd!
    And he shall fulfil all my pleasure:
    Who sayeth to Jerusalem, Thou shalt be built;
    And to the temple, Thy foundations shall be laid.

CHAP. XLV.
1   Thus saith JEHOVAH to his anointed;
    To Cyrus, whom I hold fast by the right hand:
    That I may subdue nations before him;
    And ungird the loins of kings:
    That I may open before him the valves;
    And the gates shall not be shut.
2   I will go before thee;
    And make the mountains level :
    The valves of brass I will break in sunder;
    And the bars of iron will I hew down.
3   And I will give unto thee the treasures of darkness,
    And the stores deep hidden in secret places:
    That thou mayest know, that I am JEHOVAH;
    He that calleth thee by thy name, the God of Israel.
4   For the sake of my servant Jacob;
    And of Israel, my chosen;
    I have even called thee by thy name;
    I have surnamed thee, though thou knowest me not.
5   I am JEHOVAH, and none else;
    Beside me there is no God:
    I will gird thee, though thou hast not known me.
6   That they may know, from the rising of the sun,
    And from the west, that there is none beside me :
    I am JEHOVAH, and none else;
7   Forming light, and creating darkness;
    Making peace, and creating evil :
    I JEHOVAH am the author of all these things.

8   Drop down, O ye heavens, the dew from above;
    And let the clouds shower down righteousness:
    Let the earth open her bosom, and let salvation produce her fruit;
    And let justice push forth her bud together :
    I JEHOVAH have created it.

9   Wo unto him, that contendeth with the power that formed him;
    The potsherd with the moulder of the clay !
    Shall the clay say to the potter, What makest thou
    And to the workman, Thou hast no hands ?
10 Wo unto him that sayeth to his father, What begettest thou?
    And to his mother, What dost thou bring forth ?

11   Thus saith JEHOVAH, the Holy One of Israel;
And he that formeth the things, which are to come:
Do ye question me concerning my children?
And do ye give me directions concerning the works of
   my hands?
12 I have made the earth;
And man upon it I have created:
My hands have stretched out the heavens;
And to all the host of them I have given command:
13 I have raised him up in righteousness;
And I will make level all his ways.
He shall build my city, and release my captives;
Not for price, nor for reward:
Saith JEHOVAH God of Hosts.

14   Thus saith JEHOVAH:
The wealth of Egypt, and the merchandise of Cush,
And the Sabeans tall of stature,
Shall come over to thee, and shall be thine:
They shall follow thee; in chains shall they pass along;
They shall bow down to thee, and in suppliant guise ad-
   dress thee:
In thee alone is God;
And there is no God besides whatever.
15   Verily, thou art a God that hidest thy counsels,
O God of Israel, the saviour!

16   They are ashamed, they are even confounded, his adversaries, all of them;
Together they retire in confusion, the fabricators of images.
17 But Israel shall be saved in JEHOVAH with eternal salvation:
Ye shall not be ashamed, neither shall ye be confounded,
   to the ages of eternity.

18   For thus saith JEHOVAH,
Who created the heavens; he is God:
Who formed the earth and made it; he hath established
   it:
He created it not in vain; for he formed it to be inha-
   bited:

I am JEHOVAH, and none besides :
19 I have not spoken in secret, in a dark place of the earth;
I have not said to the seed of Jacob, Seek ye me in vain:
I am JEHOVAH, who speak truth; who give direct answers.
20 Assemble yourselves together, and come;
Gather yourselves together, ye that are escaped from among the nations.
They know nothing, that carry about the wood, which they have carved;
That address themselves in prayer to a god, which cannot save.
21 Publish it abroad, and bring them near; and let them consult together:
Who hath made this known long before, hath declared it from the first?
Is it not I JEHOVAH, than whom there is no other God?
A God, that uttereth truth, and granteth salvation; there is none beside me?
22 Look unto me, and be saved, O all ye remote people of the earth;
For I am God, and there is none else.
23 By myself have I sworn; truth is gone forth from my mouth;
The word, and it shall not be revoked:
Surely to me shall every knee bow, shall every tongue swear:
24 Saying, Only to JEHOVAH belongeth salvation and power:
To him they shall come; they shall be ashamed, all that are incensed against him:
25 In JEHOVAH shall be justified, and make their boast, all the seed of Israel.

CHAP. XLVI.
1 BEL boweth down, Nebo croucheth;
Their idols are laid on the beasts and the cattle;
Their burthens are heavy, a grievous weight to the weary beast.
2 They crouched, they bowed down together:
They could not deliver their own charge;
Even they themselves are gone into captivity.

3 Hearken unto me, O house of Jacob;
And all ye the remnant of the house of Israel:

Ye that have been borne by me from the birth;
That have been carried from the womb.
4 And even to your old age, I am the same;
And even to your grey hairs, I will carry you.
I have made, and I will bear;
I will carry, and will deliver you.

5   To whom will ye liken me, and equal me?
And to whom will ye compare me, that we may be like?
6 Ye that lavish gold out of the bag;
And that weigh silver in the balance?
They hire a goldsmith, and he maketh it a god:
They worship him; yea they prostrate themselves before him.
7 They bear him on the shoulder; they carry him about;
They set him down in his place, and he standeth:
From his place he shall not remove;
To him that crieth unto him, he will not answer;
Neither will he deliver him from his distress.

8   Remember this, and shew yourselves men:
Reflect on it deeply, O ye apostates.
9 Remember the former things, of old time:
Verily I am God, and none else;
I am God, nor is there any thing like me.
10 From the beginning making known the end;
And from early times, the things that are not yet done;
Saying, My counsel shall stand;
And whatever I have willed, I will effect.
11 Calling from the east the eagle;
And from a land far distant, the man of my counsel:
As I have spoken, so will I bring it to pass;
I have formed the design, and I will execute it.
12   Hearken unto me, O ye stubborn of heart;
Ye that are far distant from deliverance:
13 I bring my promised deliverance near, it shall not be far distant;
And my salvation shall not be delayed.
And I will give in Sion salvation;
To Israel I will give my glory.

CHAP. XLVII.

1 Descend, and sit on the dust, O virgin daughter of Babylon;
Sit on the bare ground without a throne, O daughter of the Chaldeans:
For thou shalt no longer be called the tender, and the delicate.
2 Take the mill, and grind the corn:
Uncover thy locks, disclose thy flowing hair;
Make bare thy leg; wade through the rivers.
3 Thy nakedness shall be uncovered; even thy shame shall be seen:
I will take full vengeance; neither will I suffer man to intercede with me.

4 Our avenger, JEHOVAH God of Hosts,
The Holy One of Israel, is his name!

5 Sit thou in silence, go into darkness, O daughter of the Chaldeans;
For thou shalt no longer be called the lady of the kingdoms.
6 I was angry with my people; I profaned my heritage;
And I gave them up into thy hand:
Thou didst not shew mercy unto them;
Even upon the aged didst thou greatly aggravate the weight of thy yoke.
7 And thou saidst, I shall be a lady for ever:
Because thou didst not attentively consider these things;
Thou didst not think on what was in the end to befall thee.
8 But hear now this, O thou voluptuous, that sittest in security;
Thou that sayest in thy heart, I am, and there is none else;
I shall not sit a widow; I shall not know the loss of children.
9 Yet shall these two things come upon thee in a moment;
In one day, loss of children and widowhood:
On a sudden shall they come upon thee;
Notwithstanding the multitude of thy sorceries, and the great strength of thine enchantments.

10 But thou didst trust in thy wickedness, and saidst, None seeth me:
Thy wisdom and thy knowledge have perverted thy mind';
So that thou hast said in thy heart, I am, and there is none besides.
11 Therefore evil shall come upon thee, which thou shalt not know how to deprecate;
And mischief shall fall upon thee, which thou shalt not be able to expiate;
And destruction shall come upon thee suddenly, of which thou shalt have no apprehension.
12 Persist now in thine enchantments;
And in the multitude of thy sorceries, in which thou hast laboured from thy youth:
If peradventure thou mayest be profited, if thou mayest be strengthened by them.
13 Thou art wearied in the multiplicity of thy counsels:
Let them stand up now, and save thee;
The observers of the heavens, the gazers on the stars;
They that prognosticate at every new moon,
What are the events, that shall happen unto thee.
14 Behold they shall be like stubble; the fire shall burn them up:
They shall not deliver their own souls from the power of the flame;
Not a coal to warm one, not a fire to sit by, shall be left of them.
15 Such shall these be unto thee, with whom thou hast laboured;
Thy negociators, with whom thou hast dealt from thy youth:
Every one shall turn aside to his own business; none shall deliver thee.

CHAP. XLVIII.
1 Hear this, O house of Jacob;
Ye that are called by the name of Israel:
Ye that flow from the fountain of Judah;
Ye that swear by the name of Jehovah,
And publicly acknowledge the God of Israel;
But not in sincerity, nor in truth:
2 Who take their name from the Holy City,

And make the God of Israel their support;
Jehovah God of Hosts is his name:
3 The former things I shewed unto you from the first;
And from my mouth they proceeded, and I declared them:
On a sudden I effected them, and they came to pass.
4 Because I knew, that thou wast obstinate,
And that thy neck was a sinew of iron,
And that thy front was brass:
5 Therefore I shewed them unto thee from the first;
Before they should come to pass, I made thee hear them:
Lest thou shouldst say, Mine idol hath caused them;
And my graven and my molten image hath directed them.
6 Thou didst hear it beforehand; behold, the whole is accomplished:
And will ye not openly acknowledge this?
From this time I make thee hear new things,
Kept secret hitherto, and of which thou hast no knowledge:
7 They are produced now, and not of old;
And before this day thou hast not heard them:
Lest thou shouldst say, Lo! I knew them.
8 Yea, thou hast not heard, thou hast not known,
Yea, from the first thine ear was not opened to receive them:
For I knew, that thou wouldst certainly deal falsely,
And that Apostate was thy name from thy birth.
9 For the sake of my name I will defer mine anger;
And for the sake of my praise I will restrain it from thee,
That I may not utterly cut thee off.
10 Behold, I have purified thee in the fire, but not as silver;
I have tried thee in the furnace of affliction.
11 For mine own sake will I do it; for how would my name be blasphemed?
And my glory I will not give to another.

12 Hearken unto me, O Jacob my servant;
And Israel, whom I have called.
I am He; I am the first, and I am the last:
13 Yea my hand hath founded the earth;
And my right hand hath spanned the heavens:
I summon them; they present themselves together.

14   Gather yourselves together all of you, and hear:
Who among you hath predicted these things?
He, whom Jehovah hath loved, will execute
His will on Babylon, and his power on the Chaldeans.
15 I, even I, have spoken; yea I have called him:
I have brought him, and his way shall prosper.
16   Draw near unto me, and hear ye this:
From the beginning I have not spoken in secret;
Before the time when it began to exist, I had decreed it.
And now the Lord Jehovah hath sent me, and his
   Spirit.

17   'Thus saith Jehovah,
Thy redeemer, the Holy One of Israel:
I am Jehovah, thy God;
Who teacheth thee what will tend to thy profit;
Who directeth thee in the way wherein thou shouldst go.
18 O that thou hadst attended to my commands!
Then had thy prosperity been like the river;
And thy blessedness, as the floods of the sea:
19 And thy seed had been as the sand;
And the issue of thy bowels, like that of the bowels
   thereof
Thy name should not be cut off, nor destroyed from before me.

20   Come ye forth from Babylon; flee ye from the land of
   the Chaldeans with the voice of joy:
Publish ye this, and make it heard; utter it forth even to
   the end of the earth:
Say ye, Jehovah hath redeemed his servant Jacob;
21 They thirsted not in the deserts, through which he made
   them go;
Waters from the rock be caused to flow for them;
Yea he clave the rock, and forth gushed the waters.
22   There is no peace, saith Jehovah, to the wicked.

CHAP. XLIX.
1   Hearken unto me, O ye distant lands;
And ye peoples, attend from afar.
Jehovah from the womb hath called me;

From the bowels of my mother hath he mentioned my name.
2 And he hath made my mouth a sharp sword;
In the shadow of his hand he hath concealed me:
Yea he hath made me a polished shaft;
He hath laid me up in store in his quiver:
3 And he hath said unto me, Thou art my servant;
Israel, in whom I will be glorified.
4 And I said: I have laboured in vain;
For nought, and for vanity, I have spent my strength:
Nevertheless my cause is with JEHOVAH;
And the reward of my work with my God.
5 And now thus saith JEHOVAH,
(Who formed me from the womb to be his servant,
To bring back again Jacob unto him,
And that Israel unto him may be gathered:
Therefore am I glorious in the eyes of JEHOVAH,
And my God is my strength):
6 It is a small thing for thee, that thou shouldst be my servant,
To raise up the scions of Jacob,
And to restore the branches of Israel:
I will even give thee for a light to the nations,
To be my salvation to the end of the earth.

7 Thus saith JEHOVAH,
The redeemer of Israel, his Holy One;
To him, whose person is despised, whom the nation holds in abhorrence;
To the subject of rulers:
Kings shall see him, and rise up;
Princes, and they shall worship him:
For the sake of JEHOVAH, who is faithful;
Of the Holy One of Israel, for he hath chosen thee.
8 Thus saith JEHOVAH:
In the season of acceptance have I heard thee,
And in the day of salvation have I helped thee;
And I will preserve thee, and give thee for a covenant of the people;
To restore the land, to give possession of the desolate heritages.
9. Saying to the bounden, Go forth;
And to those that are in darkness, Appear:

They shall feed beside the ways,
And on all the eminences shall be their pasture.
10 They shall not hunger, neither shall they thirst;
Neither shall the glowing heat, or the sun, smite them:
For he, that hath compassion on them, shall lead them;
And shall guide them to the bursting springs of water.
11 And I will make all my mountains an even way;
And my causeways shall be raised on high.
12 Lo! these shall come from afar;
And lo! these from the north and the west;
And these from the land of Sinim.

13 Sing aloud, O ye heavens; and rejoice, O earth;
Ye mountains, burst forth into song:
For JEHOVAH hath comforted his people,
And will have compassion on his afflicted.

14 But Sion sayeth: JEHOVAH hath forsaken me;
And my Lord hath forgotten me.
15 Can a woman forget her sucking infant;
That she should have no tenderness for the son of her womb?
Even these may forget;
But I will not forget thee.
16 Behold, on the palms of my hands have I delineated thee:
Thy walls are for ever in my sight.
17 They, that destroyed thee, shall soon become thy builders;
And they, that laid thee waste, shall become thine offspring.
18 Lift up thine eyes around, and see;
All these are gathered together, they come to thee.
As I live, saith JEHOVAH,
Surely thou shalt clothe thyself with them all, as with a rich dress;
And bind them about thee, as a bride her jewels.
19 For thy waste, and thy desolate places,
And thy land laid in ruins;
Even now it shall be straitened with inhabitants;
And they, that devoured thee, shall be removed far away.
20 The sons, of whom thou wast bereaved, shall yet say in thine ears:

This place is too strait for me; make room for me, that
    I may dwell.
21 And thou shalt say in thine heart: Who hath begotten
    me these?
I was bereaved of my children, and solitary;
An exile, and an outcast; who then hath nursed these up?
Lo! I was abandoned, and alone; these then, where
    were they?
22   Thus saith the Lord JEHOVAH:
Behold, I will lift up my hand to the nations;
And to the peoples will I exalt my signal;
And they shall bring thy sons in their bosom,
And thy daughters shall be borne on their shoulder:
23 And kings shall be thy foster-fathers,
And their queens thy nursing mothers:
With their faces to the earth they shall bow down unto
    thee,
And shall lick the dust of thy feet.
And thou shalt know, that I am JEHOVAH;
And that they, who trust in him, shall not be ashamed.

24   Shall the spoil be taken away from the mighty?
Or shall the prey seized by the terrible be rescued?
25 Yea, thus saith JEHOVAH:
Even the prey of the mighty shall be retaken;
And the spoil seized by the terrible shall be rescued:
For with those, that contend with thee, I will contend;
And thy children I will deliver.
26 And I will gorge thine oppressors with their own flesh;
And with their own blood, as with new wine, will I
    drench them:
And all flesh shall know,
That I JEHOVAH am thy saviour;
And that thy redeemer is the Mighty One of Jacob.

CHAP. L.
1   THUS saith JEHOVAH:
Where is this bill of your mother's divorcement,
By which I dismissed her?
Or who is he among my creditors,
To whom I have sold you?
Behold, for your iniquities are ye sold;
And for your transgressions is your mother dismissed.

2 Wherefore came I, and there was no man?
   Called I, and none answered?
   Is then my hand so greatly shortened, that I cannot redeem?
   And have I no power to deliver?
   Behold, at my rebuke I make dry the sea;
   I make the rivers a desert:
   Their fish is dried up, because there is no water;
   And dieth away for thirst.
3 I clothe the heavens with blackness;
   And sackcloth I make their covering.

4   THE Lord JEHOVAH hath given me the tongue of the learned;
   That I might know how to speak a seasonable word to the weary.
   He wakeneth, morning by morning,
   He wakeneth mine ear, to hearken with the attention of a learner.
5 The Lord JEHOVAH hath opened mine ear;
   And I was not rebellious;
   Neither did I withdraw myself backward.
6 I gave my back to the smiters,
   And my cheeks to them that plucked off the hair:
   My face I hid not from shame and spitting.
7 For the Lord JEHOVAH is my helper;
   Therefore I am not ashamed.
   Therefore have I set my face as a flint;
   And I know, that I shall not be confounded.
8 He that justifieth me is near at hand:
   Who is he that will contend with me? let us stand forth together:
   Who is mine adversary? let him come on to the contest.
9 Behold, the Lord JEHOVAH is my advocate:
   Who is he that shall condemn me?
   Lo! all of them shall wax old as a garment;
   The moth shall consume them.

10   Who is there among you, that feareth JEHOVAH?
   Let him hearken unto the voice of his servant:
   That walketh in darkness, and hath no light?
   Let him trust in the name of JEHOVAH;

And rest himself on the support of his God.
11 Behold, all ye who kindle a fire;
Who heap the fuel round about:
Walk ye in the light of your fire,
And of the fuel, which ye have kindled.
This ye shall have at my hand;
Ye shall lie down in sorrow.

CHAP. LI.
1 HEARKEN unto me, ye that pursue righteousness,
Ye that seek JEHOVAH.
Look unto the rock, from whence ye were hewn;
And to the hollow of the cave, whence ye were digged.
2 Look unto Abraham your father;
And unto Sarah, who bore you:
For I called him, being a single person,
And I blessed him, and I multiplied him.
3 Thus therefore shall JEHOVAH console Sion;
He shall console all her desolations:
And he shall make her wilderness like Eden;
And her desert like the garden of JEHOVAH:
Joy and gladness shall be found in her;
Thanksgiving, and the voice of melody.

4 Attend unto me, O ye peoples;
And give ear unto me, O ye nations:
For the law from me shall proceed;
And my judgment will I cause to break forth for a light to the peoples.
5 My righteousness is at hand; my salvation goeth forth;
And mine arm shall dispense judgment to the peoples:
Me the distant lands shall expect;
And to mine arm shall they look with confidence.
6 Lift up unto the heavens your eyes;
And look down unto the earth beneath:
Verily the heavens shall dissolve, like smoke;
And the earth shall wax old, like a garment;
And its inhabitants shall perish, like the vilest insect:
But my salvation shall endure for ever;
And my righteousness shall not decay.

7 Hearken unto me, ye that know righteousness;
The people, in whose heart is my law:
Fear not the reproach of wretched man;

Neither be ye borne down by their revilings.
8 For the moth shall consume them, like a garment;
And the worm shall eat them, like wool:
But my righteousness shall endure for ever;
And my salvation to the age of ages.

9   Awake, awake, clothe thyself with strength, O arm of Jehovah!
Awake, as in the days of old, the ancient generations.
Art thou not the same that smote Rahab, that wounded the dragon?
10 Art thou not the same, that dried up the sea, the waters of the great deep?
That made the depths of the sea a path for the redeemed to pass through?
11 Thus shall the ransomed of Jehovah return,
And come to Sion with loud acclamation:
And everlasting gladness shall crown their heads;
Joy and gladness shall they obtain,
And sorrow and sighing shall flee away.
12 I, even I, am he that comforteth you:
Who art thou, that thou shouldst fear wretched man, that dieth;
And the son of man, that shall become as the grass?
13 And shouldst forget Jehovah thy maker,
Who stretched out the heavens, and founded the earth;
And shouldst every day be in continued fear,
Because of the fury of the oppressor,
As if he were just ready to destroy?
And where now is the fury of the oppressor?
14 He marcheth on with speed, who cometh to set free the captive;
That he may not die in the dungeon,
And that his bread may not fail.
15 For I am Jehovah thy God;
He, who stilleth at once the sea, though the waves thereof roar;
Jehovah God of Hosts is his name.
16 I have put my words in thy mouth;
And with the shadow of my hand have I covered thee:
To stretch out the heavens, and to lay the foundations of the earth;
And to say unto Sion, Thou art my people.

17 Rouse thyself, rouse thyself up; arise, O Jerusalem!
Who hast drunken from the hand of JEHOVAH the cup of
' his fury:
The dregs of the cup of trembling thou hast drunken,
thou hast wrung them out.
18 There is not one to lead her, of all the sons which she
hath brought forth;
Neither is there one to support her by the hand, of all the
sons which she hath educated.
19 These two things have befallen thee; who shall bemoan
thee?
Desolation, and destruction; the famine, and the sword;
who shall comfort thee?
20 Thy sons lie astounded; they are cast down;
At the head of all the streets, like the oryx taken in the
toils;
Drenched to the full with the fury of JEHOVAH, with the
rebuke of thy God.
21 Wherefore hear now this, O thou afflicted daughter;
And thou drunken, but not with wine.
22 Thus saith thy Lord JEHOVAH;
And thy God, who avengeth his people:
Behold, I take from thy hand the cup of trembling;
The dregs of the cup of my fury;
Thou shalt drink of it again no more.
33 But I will put it into the hand of them who oppress
thee;
Who say to thee, Bow down thy body, that we may go
over:
And thou layedst down thy back, as the ground;
And as the street, to them that pass along.

CHAP. LII.
1 AWAKE, awake; be clothed with thy strength, O Sion:
Clothe thyself with thy glorious garments, O Jerusalem,
thou holy city!
For no more shall enter into thee the uncircumcised and
the polluted.
2 Shake thyself from the dust, ascend thy lofty seat, O Jerusalem:
Loose thyself from the bands of thy neck, O captive
daughter of Sion!

3   For thus saith JEHOVAH:
For nought were ye sold;
And not with money shall ye be ransomed.
4 For thus saith the Lord JEHOVAH:
My people went down to Egypt,
At the first, to sojourn there;
And the Assyrian, at the last, hath oppressed them.
5 And now, what have I more to do, saith JEHOVAH:
Seeing that my people is taken away for nought;
And they, that are lords over them, make their boast of it, saith JEHOVAH;
And continually every day is my name exposed to contempt?
6 Therefore shall my people know my name in that day:
For I am he, JEHOVAH, that promised; and lo! here I am!
7   How beautiful appear on the mountains
The feet of the joyful messenger; of him, that announceth peace!
Of the joyful messenger of good tidings; of him, that announceth salvation!
Of him, that sayeth unto Sion, Thy God reigneth!
8 All thy watchmen lift up their voice; they shout together:
For face to face shall they see, when JEHOVAH returneth to Sion.
9 Burst forth into joy, shout together, ye ruins of Jerusalem!
For JEHOVAH hath comforted his people; he hath redeemed Israel.
10 JEHOVAH hath made bare his holy arm, in the sight of all the nations;
And all the ends of the earth have seen the salvation of our God.

11   Depart, depart ye, go ye out from thence; touch no polluted thing:
Go ye out from the midst of her; be ye clean, ye that bear the vessels of JEHOVAH!
12 Verily not in haste shall ye go forth;
And not by flight shall ye march along:
For JEHOVAH shall march in your front;
And the God of Israel shall bring up your rear.

13 Behold, my servant shall prosper;
   He shall be raised aloft, and magnified, and very highly exalted.
14 As many were astonished at him;
   (To such a degree was his countenance disfigured, more than that of man;
   And his form, more than the sons of men);
15 So shall he sprinkle many nations:
   Before him shall kings shut their mouths;
   For what was not before declared to them, they shall see,
   And what they had not heard, they shall attentively consider.

CHAP. LIII.
1 Who hath believed our report;
   And to whom hath the arm of JEHOVAH been manifested?
2 For he groweth up in their sight like a tender sucker;
   And like a root from a thirsty soil:
   He hath no form, nor any beauty, that we should regard him;
   Nor is his countenance such, that we should desire him.
3 Despised, nor accounted in the number of men;
   A man of sorrows, and acquainted with grief;
   As one that hideth his face from us:
   He was despised, and we esteemed him not.
4 Surely our infirmities he hath borne;
   And our sorrows, he hath carried them:
   Yet we thought him judicially stricken;
   Smitten of God, and afflicted.
5 But he was wounded for our transgressions;
   Was smitten for our iniquities:
   The chastisement, by which our peace is effected, was laid upon him;
   And by his bruises we are healed.
6 We all of us like sheep have strayed;
   We have turned aside, every one to his own way;
   And JEHOVAH hath made to light upon him the iniquity of us all.
7 It was exacted, and he was made answerable; and he opened not his mouth:
   As a lamb that is led to the slaughter,

    And as a sheep before her shearers
    Is dumb; so he opened not his mouth.
8 By an oppressive judgment he was taken off;
    And his manner of life who would declare?
    For he was cut off from the land of the living;
    For the transgression of my people he was smitten to death.
9 And his grave was appointed with the wicked;
    But with the rich man was his tomb.
    Although he had done no wrong,
    Neither was there any guile in his mouth;
10 Yet it pleased JEHOVAH to crush him with affliction.
    If his soul shall make a propitiatory sacrifice,
    He shall see a seed, which shall prolong their days,
    And the gracious purpose of JEHOVAH shall prosper in his hands.
11 Of the travail of his soul he shall see [the fruit], and be satisfied:
    By the knowledge of him shall my servant justify many;
    For the punishment of their iniquities he shall bear.
12 Therefore will I distribute to him the many for his portion;
    And the mighty people shall he share for his spoil:
    Because he poured out his soul unto death;
    And was numbered with the transgressors:
    And he bare the sin of many;
    And made intercession for the transgressors.

CHAP. LIV.

1   SHOUT for joy, O thou barren, that didst not bear;
    Break forth into joyful shouting, and exult, thou that didst not travail:
    For more are the children of the desolate,
    Than of the married woman, saith JEHOVAH.
2 Enlarge the place of thy tent;
    And let the canopy of thy habitation be extended:
    Spare not; lengthen thy cords,
    And firmly fix thy stakes:
3 For on the right hand, and on the left, thou shalt burst forth with increase;
    And thy seed shall inherit the nations;
    And they shall inhabit the desolate cities.
4 Fear not, for thou shalt not be confounded;
    And blush not, for thou shalt not be brought to reproach:

For thou shalt forget the shame of thy youth;
And the reproach of thy widowhood thou shalt remember no more.
5 For thy husband is thy maker;
JEHOVAH God of Hosts is his name:
And thy redeemer is the Holy One of Israel;
The God of the whole earth shall he be called.
6 For as a woman forsaken, and deeply afflicted, hath JEHOVAH recalled thee;
And as a wife, wedded in youth, but afterwards rejected, saith thy God.
7 In a little anger have I forsaken thee;
But with great mercies will I receive thee again:
8 In a short wrath I hid my face for a moment from thee;
But with everlasting kindness will I have mercy on thee;
Saith thy redeemer JEHOVAH.
9 The same will I do now, as in the days of Noah, when I sware,
That the waters of Noah should no more pass over the earth:
So have I sworn, that I will not be wroth with thee, nor rebuke thee.
10 For the mountains shall be removed;
And the hills shall be overthrown:
But my kindness from thee shall not be removed;
And the covenant of my peace shall not be overthrown;
Saith JEHOVAH, who beareth towards thee the most tender affection.
11 O thou afflicted, beaten with the storm, destitute of consolation!
Behold I lay thy stones in cement of vermilion,
And thy foundations with sapphires:
12 And I will make of rubies thy battlements;
And thy gates of carbuncles;
And the whole circuit of thy walls shall be of precious stones.
13 And all thy children shall be taught by JEHOVAH;
And great shall be the prosperity of thy children.
14 In righteousness shalt thou be established:
Be thou far from oppression; yea thou shalt not fear it;
And from terror; for it shall not approach thee.
15 Behold, they shall be leagued together, but not by my command;

Whosoever is leagued against thee, shall come over to thy
    side.
16 Behold, I have created the smith,
Who bloweth up the coals into a fire,
And produceth instruments according to his work;
And I have created the destroyer to lay waste.
17 Whatever weapon is formed against thee, it shall not prosper;
And against every tongue, that contendeth with thee,
    thou shalt obtain thy cause.
This is the heritage of JEHOVAH's servants;
And their justification from me, saith JEHOVAH.

CHAP. LV.
1   Ho! every one that thirsteth, come ye to the waters!
And that hath no silver, come ye, buy, and eat!
Yea, come, buy ye without silver;
And without price, wine and milk.
2 Wherefore do ye weigh out your silver for that which is
    no bread?
And your riches, for that which will not satisfy?
Attend, and hearken unto me; and eat that which is truly
    good;
And your soul shall feast itself with the richest delicacies.
Incline your ear, and come unto me;
Attend, and your soul shall live:
And I will make with you an everlasting covenant;
I will give you the gracious promises made to David,
    which shall never fail.
4 Behold, for a witness to the peoples I have given him;
A leader, and a lawgiver to the nations.
5 Behold, the nation, whom thou knewest not, thou shalt
    call;
And the nation, who knew not thee, shall run unto thee,
For the sake of JEHOVAH thy God;
And for the Holy One of Israel, for he hath glorified
    thee.

6   Seek ye JEHOVAH, while he may be found;
Call ye upon him, while he is near at hand:
7 Let the wicked forsake his way,
And the unrighteous man his thoughts;

And let him return unto Jehovah, for he will receive him
   with compassion ;
And unto our God, for he aboundeth in forgiveness.
8 For my thoughts are not your thoughts ;
Neither are your ways my ways, saith Jehovah.
9 For as the heavens are higher than the earth ;
So are my ways higher than your ways,
And my thoughts than your thoughts.
10   Verily, like as the rain descendeth,
And the snow, from the heavens ;
And thither it doth not return ;
But moisteneth the earth,
And maketh it generate, and put forth its increase ;
That it may give seed to the sower, and bread to the
   eater :
11 So shall be the word, which goeth forth from my mouth ;
It shall not return unto me fruitless ;
But it shall effect what I have willed ;
And make the purpose succeed, for which I have sent it.
12 Surely with joy shall ye go forth,
And with peace shall ye be led onward :
The mountains and the hills shall burst forth before you
   into song ;
And all the trees of the field shall clap their hands.
13 Instead of the thorny bushes shall grow up the fir-tree ;
And instead of the bramble shall grow up the myrtle :
And it shall be unto Jehovah for a memorial ;
For a perpetual sign, which shall not be abolished.

CHAP. LVI.
 1   Thus saith Jehovah :
Keep ye judgment, and practise righteousness ;
For my salvation is near, just ready to come ;
And my righteousness, to be revealed.
2 Blessed is the mortal that doeth this ;
And the son of man that holdeth it fast ;
That keepeth the sabbath, and profaneth it not ;
And restraineth his hand from doing evil.

 3   And let not the son of the stranger speak,
That cleaveth unto Jehovah, saying :
Jehovah hath utterly separated me from his people.

Neither let the eunuch say:
Behold, I am a dry tree.
4 For thus saith JEHOVAH to the eunuchs:
Whoever of them shall have kept my sabbaths,
And shall have chosen that in which I delight,
And shall have steadfastly maintained my covenant;
5 To them I will give in my house,
And within my walls, a memorial and a name,
Better than that of sons and daughters:
An everlasting name will I give them,
Which shall never be cut off.
6 And the sons of the stranger, who cleave unto JEHOVAH;
To minister unto him, and to love the name of JEHOVAH,
And to become his servants:
Every one that keepeth the sabbath, and profaneth it not;
And that steadfastly maintaineth my covenant;
7 Them will I bring unto my holy mountain;
And I will make them rejoice in my house of prayer:
Their burnt-offerings and their sacrifices shall be accepted
on mine altar;
For my house shall be called, The house of prayer for all
the peoples.
8 Thus saith the Lord JEHOVAH,
Who gathereth together the outcasts of Israel:
Yet will I gather others unto him, beside those that are
already gathered.

9 O ALL ye beasts of the field, come away;
Come to devour, O all ye beasts of the forest!
10 His watchmen are blind, all of them; they are ignorant;
They are all of them dumb dogs, they cannot bark:
Dreamers, sluggards, loving to slumber.
11 Yea these dogs are of untamed appetite;
They know not to be satisfied.
And the shepherds themselves cannot understand:
They all of them turn aside to their own way;
Each to his own lucre, from the highest to the lowest.
12 Come on, let us provide wine;
And let us swill strong drink:
And as to-day, so shall be the cheer of to-morrow;
Great, even far more abundant.

CHAP. LVII.

1 The righteous man perisheth, and no one considereth;
And pious men are taken away, and no one understandeth,
That the righteous man is taken away, because of the evil.
2 He shall go in peace: he shall rest in his bed;
Even the perfect man; he that walketh in the strait path.
3 But ye, draw ye near hither, O ye sons of the sorceress;
Ye seed of the adulterer, and of the harlot!
4 Of whom do ye make your sport?
At whom do ye widen the mouth, and loll the tongue?
Are ye not apostate children, a false seed?
5 Burning with the lust of idols under every green tree;
Slaying the children in the vallies, under the clefts of the rocks?
6 Among the smooth stones of the valley is thy portion;
These, these are thy lot:
Even to these hast thou poured out thy libation,
Hast thou presented thine offering.
Can I see these things with acquiescence?
7 Upon a high and lofty mountain hast thou set thy bed:
Even thither hast thou gone up to offer sacrifice.
8 Behind the door and the door-posts hast thou set thy memorial:
Thou hast departed from me, and art gone up; thou hast enlarged thy bed;
And thou hast made a covenant with them:
Thou hast loved their bed; thou hast provided a place for it.
9 And thou hast visited the king with a present of oil;
And hast multiplied thy precious ointments:
And thou hast sent thine ambassadors afar;
And hast debased thyself even to Hades.
10 In the length of thy journeys thou hast wearied thyself;
Thou hast said, There is no hope:
Thou hast found the support of thy life by thy labour:
Therefore thou hast not utterly fainted.
11 And of whom hast thou been so anxiously afraid, that thou shouldst thus deal falsely?
And hast not remembered me, nor revolved it in thy mind?

    Is it not because I was silent, and winked; and thou fearest me not?
12 But I will declare my righteousness;
And thy deeds shall not avail thee.
13 When thou criest, let thine associates deliver thee:
But the wind shall bear them away; a breath shall take them off.
But he that trusteth in me shall inherit the land,
And shall possess my holy mountain.

14   Then will I say: Cast up, cast up the causeway; make clear the way;
Remove every obstruction from the road of my people.
15 For thus saith JEHOVAH, the high, and the lofty;
Inhabiting eternity; and whose name is the Holy One:
The high and the holy place will I inhabit;
And with the contrite, and humble of spirit:
To revive the spirit of the humble;
And to give life to the heart of the contrite.
16 For I will not alway contend;
Neither for ever will I be wroth:
For the spirit from before me would be overwhelmed;
And the living souls, which I have made.
17 Because of his iniquity for a short time I was wroth:
And I smote him; hiding my face in mine anger.
And he departed, turning back in the way of his own heart.
18 I have seen his ways; and I will heal him, and will be his guide;
And I will restore comforts, to him, and to his mourners.
19 I create the fruit of the lips:
Peace, peace, to him that is near,
And to him that is afar off, saith JEHOVAH; and I will heal him.
20   But the wicked are like the troubled sea;
For it never can be at rest;
But its waters work up filth and mire.
21 There is no peace, saith my God, to the wicked.

CHAP. LVIII.
1   CRY aloud; spare not:
Like a trumpet lift up thy voice:
And declare unto my people their transgression;
And to the house of Jacob their sin.

2 Yet me day after day they seek ;
And to know my ways they take delight:
As a nation that doeth righteousness,
And hath not forsaken the ordinance of their God.
They continually inquire of me concerning the ordinances
 of righteousness ;
They take delight to draw nigh unto God.
3 Wherefore have we fasted, and thou seest not ?
Have we afflicted our souls, and thou dost not regard ?
Behold, in the day of your fasting, ye enjoy your pleas-
 ure ;
And all your demands of labour ye rigorously exact.
4 Behold, ye fast for strife and contention ;
And to smite with the fist the poor.
Wherefore fast ye unto me in this manner ;
To make your voice to be heard on high ?
5 Is such then the fast which I choose ;
That a man should afflict his soul for a day ?
Is it, that he should bow down his head like a bulrush ;
And spread sackcloth and ashes for his couch ?
Shall this be called a fast,
And a day acceptable to JEHOVAH ?
6 Is not this the fast which I choose ?
To dissolve the bands of wickedness ;
To loosen the oppressive burthens ;
To deliver those that are crushed by violence ;
And that ye should break asunder every yoke ?
7 Is it not to distribute thy bread to the hungry ;
And to bring the wandering poor into thy house ?
When thou seest the naked, that thou clothe him ;
And that thou hide not thyself from thine own flesh ?
8 Then shall thy light break forth like the morning
And thy wounds shall speedily be healed over :
And thy righteousness shall go before thee ;
And the glory of JEHOVAH shall bring up thy rear.
9 Then shalt thou call, and JEHOVAH shall answer ;
Thou shalt cry, and he shall say, Lo I am here !
If thou remove from the midst of thee the yoke ;
The pointing of the finger, and the injurious speech :
10 If thou bring forth thy bread to the hungry,
And satisfy the afflicted soul ;
Then shall thy light rise in obscurity,
And thy darkness shall be as the noon-day.

11 And Jehovah shall lead thee continually,
   And satisfy thy soul in the severest drought;
   And he shall renew thy strength:
   And thou shalt be like a well-watered garden, and like a flowing spring,
   Whose waters shall never fail.
12 And they that spring from thee shall build the ancient ruins;
   The foundations of old times shall they raise up:
   And thou shalt be called the repairer of the broken mound;
   The restorer of paths to be frequented by inhabitants.
13 If thou restrain thy foot from the sabbath;
   From doing thy pleasure on my holy day:
   And shalt call the sabbath, a delight;
   And the holy feast of Jehovah, honourable:
   And shalt honour it, by refraining from thy purpose;
   From pursuing thy pleasure, and from speaking vain words:
14 Then shalt thou delight thyself in Jehovah;
   And I will make thee ride on the high places of the earth;
   And I will feed thee on the inheritance of Jacob thy father:
   For the mouth of Jehovah hath spoken it.

CHAP. LIX.

1   Behold, the hand of Jehovah is not contracted, so that he cannot save;
    Neither is his ear grown dull, so that he cannot hear.
2   But your iniquities have made a separation
      Between you and your God;
    And your sins have hidden
      His face from you, that he doth not hear.
3   For your hands are polluted with blood,
      And your fingers with iniquity;
    Your lips speak falsehood,
      And your tongue muttereth wickedness.
4   No one preferreth his suit in justice,
      And no one pleadeth in truth:
    Trusting in vanity, and speaking lies;
      Conceiving mischief, and bringing forth iniquity.

5 They hatch the eggs of the basilisk,
   And weave the web of the spider:
  He that eateth of their eggs dieth;
   And when it is crushed, a viper breaketh forth.
6 Of their webs no garment shall be made;
   Neither shall they cover themselves with their works:
  Their works are works of iniquity,
   And the deed of violence is in their hands.
7 Their feet run swiftly to evil,
   And they hasten to shed innocent blood:
  Their devices are devices of iniquity;
   Destruction and calamity is in their paths.
8 The way of peace they know not;
   Neither is there any judgment in their tracks:
  They have made to themselves crooked paths;
   Whoever goeth in them, knoweth not peace.
9 Therefore is judgment far distant from us;
   Neither doth justice overtake us:
  We look for light, but behold darkness;
   For brightness, but we walk in obscurity.
10 We grope for the wall, like the blind;
   And we wander, as those that are deprived of sight:
  We stumble at mid-day, as in the twilight;
   In the midst of delicacies, as among the dead.
11 We groan all of us, like the bears;
   And like the doves, we make a continued moan.
  We look for judgment, and there is none;
   For salvation, and it is far distant from us.
12 For our transgressions are multiplied before thee;
   And our sins bring an accusation against us:
  For our transgressions cleave fast unto us;
   And our iniquities we acknowledge.
13 By rebelling, and lying, against JEHOVAH;
   And by turning backward from following our God:
  By speaking injury, and conceiving revolt;
   And by meditating from the heart lying words.
14 And judgment is turned away backwards;
   And justice standeth aloof:
  For truth hath stumbled in the open street;
   And rectitude hath not been able to enter.
15 And truth is utterly lost;
   And he that shunneth evil, exposeth himself to be plundered:

And JEHOVAH saw it,
And it displeased him, that there was no judgment.
16 And he saw, that there was no man;
And he wondered, that there was no one to interpose:
Then his own arm wrought salvation for him;
And his righteousness, it supported him.
17 And he put on righteousness, as a breast-plate;
And the helmet of salvation was on his head:
And he put on the garments of vengeance for his clothing;
And he clad himself with zeal, as with a mantle.
18 He is mighty to recompense;
He that is mighty to recompense will requite:
Wrath to his adversaries, recompense to his enemies;
To the distant coasts a recompense will he requite.
19 And they from the west shall revere the name of JEHOVAH;
And they from the rising of the sun, his glory;
When he shall come, like a river straitened in his course,
Which a strong wind driveth along.
20 And the Redeemer shall come to Sion;
And shall turn away iniquity from Jacob; saith JEHOVAH.
21 And this is the covenant, which I make with them, saith JEHOVAH:
My spirit, which is upon thee,
And my words, which I have put in thy mouth;
They shall not depart from thy mouth,
Nor from the mouth of thy seed,
Nor from the mouth of thy seed's seed, saith JEHOVAH;
From this time forth for ever.

CHAP. LX.
1 ARISE, be thou enlightened; for thy light is come;
And the glory of JEHOVAH is risen upon thee.
2 For behold, darkness shall cover the earth;
And a thick vapour the nations:
And upon thee shall JEHOVAH arise;
And his glory upon thee shall be conspicuous.
3 And the nations shall walk in thy light;
And kings in the brightness of thy sun-rising.
4 Lift up thine eyes round about, and see;
All of them are gathered together, they come unto thee:

Thy sons shall come from afar;
And thy daughters shall be carried at the side.
5 Then shalt thou fear, and overflow with joy;
And thy heart shall be ruffled, and dilated;
When the riches of the sea shall be poured in upon thee;
When the wealth of the nations shall come unto thee.
6 An inundation of camels shall cover thee;
The dromedaries of Midian and Epha;
All of them from Saba shall come:
Gold and frankincense shall they bear;
And the praise of JEHOVAH shall they joyfully proclaim.
7 All the flocks of Kedar shall be gathered unto thee;
Unto thee shall the rams of Nebaioth minister:
They shall ascend with acceptance on mine altar;
And my beauteous house I will yet beautify.
8 Who are these, that fly like a cloud?
And like doves upon the wing?
9 Verily the distant coasts shall await me;
And the ships of Tarshish among the first:
To bring thy sons from afar;
Their silver and their gold with them:
Because of the name of JEHOVAH thy God;
And of the Holy One of Israel; for he hath glorified thee.
10 And the sons of the stranger shall build up thy walls;
And their kings shall minister unto thee:
For in my wrath I smote thee;
But in my favour I will embrace thee with the most tender affection.
11 And thy gates shall be open continually;
By day, or by night, they shall not be shut:
To bring unto thee the wealth of the nations;
And that their kings may come pompously attended.
12 For that nation, and that kingdom,
Which will not serve thee, shall perish;
Yea, those nations shall be utterly desolated.
13 The glory of Lebanon shall come unto thee;
The fir-tree, the pine, and the box together:
To adorn the place of my sanctuary;
And that I may glorify the place, whereon I rest my feet.
14 And the sons of thine oppressors shall come bending before thee;

And all, that scornfully rejected thee, shall do obeisance to
the soles of thy feet:
And they shall call thee, The City of JEHOVAH;
The Sion of the Holy One of Israel.
15 Instead of thy being forsaken,
And hated, so that no one passed through thee;
I will make thee an everlasting boast;
A subject of joy for perpetual generations.
16 And thou shalt suck the milk of nations;
Even at the breast of kings shalt thou be fostered:
And thou shalt know, that I JEHOVAH am thy saviour;
And that thy redeemer is the Mighty One of Jacob.
17 Instead of brass, I will bring gold;
And instead of iron, I will bring silver:
And instead of wood, brass;
And instead of stones, iron.
And I will make thine inspectors peace;
And thine exactors, righteousness.
18 Violence shall no more be heard in thy land;
Destruction and calamity, in thy borders:
But thou shalt call thy walls, Salvation;
And thy gates, Praise.
19 No longer shalt thou have the sun for a light by day;
Nor by night shall the brightness of the moon enlighten
thee:
For JEHOVAH shall be to thee an everlasting light,
And thy God shall be thy glory.
20 Thy sun shall no more go down;
Neither shall thy moon wane:
For JEHOVAH shall be thine everlasting light;
And the days of thy mourning shall be ended.
21 And thy people shall be all righteous;
For ever shall they possess the land:
The cion of my planting, the work of my hands, that I
may be glorified.
22 The little one shall become a thousand;
And the small one a strong nation:
I JEHOVAH in due time will hasten it.

CHAP. LXI.

1 The spirit of JEHOVAH is upon me,
  Because JEHOVAH hath anointed me.
  To publish glad tidings to the meek hath he sent me;
  To bind up the broken hearted:
  To proclaim to the captives freedom;
  And to the bounden, perfect liberty:
2 To proclaim the year of acceptance with JEHOVAH;
  And the day of vengeance of our God.
  To comfort all those that mourn;
3 To impart [gladness] to the mourners of Sion:
  To give them a beautiful crown, instead of ashes;
  The oil of gladness instead of sorrow;
  The clothing of praise, instead of the spirit of heaviness.
  That they may be called trees approved;
  The plantation of JEHOVAH for his glory.
4 And they that spring from thee shall build up the ruins of old times;
  They shall restore the ancient desolations
  They shall repair the cities laid waste;
  The desolations of continued ages.
5 And strangers shall stand up and feed your flocks;
  And the sons of the alien shall be your husbandmen and vine-dressers.
6 But ye shall be called the priests of JEHOVAH;
  The ministers of our God, shall be your title.
  The riches of the nations shall ye eat;
  And in their glory shall ye make your boast.
7 Instead of your shame, ye shall receive a double inheritance;
  And of your ignominy, ye shall rejoice in their portion:
  For in their land a double share shall ye inherit;
  And everlasting gladness shall ye possess.
8 For I am JEHOVAH, who love judgment;
  Who hate rapine and iniquity:
  And I will give them the reward of their work with faithfulness;
  And an everlasting covenant I will make with them:
9 And their seed shall be illustrious among the nations;
  And their offspring, in the midst of the peoples.
  And they that see them shall acknowledge them,
  That they are a seed which JEHOVAH hath blessed.

10 I will greatly rejoice in Jehovah;
My soul shall exult in my God.
For he hath clothed me with the garments of salvation;
He hath covered me with the mantle of righteousness:
As the bridegroom decketh himself with a priestly crown;
And as the bride adorneth herself with her costly jewels.
11   Surely, as the earth pusheth forth her tender shoots;
And as a garden maketh her seed to germinate:
So shall the Lord Jehovah cause righteousness to spring forth;
And praise, in the presence of all the nations.

CHAP. LXII.
1 For Sion's sake I will not keep silence;
And for the sake of Jerusalem I will not rest:
Until her righteousness break forth as a strong light;
And her salvation, like a blazing torch.
2 And the nations shall see thy righteousness;
And all the kings, thy glory:
And thou shalt be called by a new name,
Which the mouth of Jehovah shall fix upon thee.
3 And thou shalt be a beautiful crown in the hand of Jehovah;
And a royal diadem in the grasp of thy God.
4 No more shall it be said unto thee, Thou forsaken!
Neither to thy land shall it be said any more, Thou desolate!
But thou shalt be called, The object of my delight;
And thy land, The wedded matron:
For Jehovah shall delight in thee;
And thy land shall be joined in marriage.
5 For as a young man weddeth a virgin,
So shall thy restorer wed thee:
And as the bridegroom rejoiceth in his bride,
So shall thy God rejoice in thee.

6   Upon thy walls, O Jerusalem,
Have I set watchmen all the day;
And all the night long they shall not keep silence.
O ye, that proclaim the name of Jehovah!
7 Keep not silence yourselves, nor let him rest in silence;

Until he establish, and until he render,
Jerusalem a praise in the earth.
8 JEHOVAH hath sworn by his right hand, and by his powerful arm :
I will no more give thy corn for food to thine enemies ;
Nor shall the sons of the stranger drink thy must, for which thou hast labored :
9 But they, that reap the harvest, shall eat it, and praise JEHOVAH ;
And they, that gather the vintage, shall drink it in my sacred courts.

10 Pass ye, pass through the gates ; prepare the way for the people !
Cast ye up, cast up the causeway ; clear it from the stones !
Lift up on high a standard to the nations !
11 Behold, JEHOVAH hath thus proclaimed to the end of the earth :
Say ye to the daughter of Sion, Lo thy saviour cometh !
Lo ! his reward is with him, and the recompense of his work before him.
And they shall be called, The holy people, the redeemed of JEHOVAH ;
12 And thou shalt be called, The much desired, The city unforsaken.

CHAP. LXIII.
1 CHO. WHO is this, that cometh from Edom ?
With garments deeply dyed from Botsra ?
This, that is magnificent in his apparel ;
Marching on in the greatness of his strength ?
MES. I, who publish righteousness, and am mighty to save.
2 CHO. Wherefore is thine apparel red ?
And thy garments, as of one that treadeth the wine-vat ?
3 MES. I have trodden the vat alone ;
And of the peoples there was not a man with me.
And I trod them in mine anger ;
And I trampled them in mine indignation :
And their life-blood was sprinkled upon my garments ;

And I have stained all mine apparel.
4 For the day of vengeance was in my heart;
And the year of my redeemed was come.
5 And I looked, and there was no one to help;
And I was astonished, that there was no one to uphold:
Therefore mine own arm wrought salvation for me,
And mine indignation itself sustained me.
6 And I trod down the peoples in mine anger;
And I crushed them in mine indignation;
And I spilled their life-blood on the ground.

7 THE mercies of JEHOVAH will I record, the praise of JEHOVAH;
According to all that JEHOVAH hath bestowed upon us:
And the greatness of his goodness to the house of Israel;
Which he hath bestowed upon them, through his tenderness and great kindness.
8 For he said: Surely they are my people, children that will not prove false;
And he became their saviour in all their distress.
9 It was not an envoy, nor an angel of his presence, that saved them:
Through his love, and his indulgence, he himself redeemed them;
And he took them up, and he bare them, all the days of old.
10 But they rebelled, and grieved his holy spirit;
So that he became their enemy; and he fought against them.
11 And he remembered the days of old, Moses his servant;
How he brought them up from the sea, with the shepherd of his flock;
How he placed in his breast his holy spirit:
12 Making his glorious arm to attend Moses on his right hand in his march;
Cleaving the waters before them, to make himself a name everlasting;
13 Leading them through the abyss, like a courser in the plain, without obstacle.
14 As the herd descendeth to the valley, the spirit of JEHOVAH conducted them:

So didst thou lead thy people, to make thyself a name illustrious.
15 Look down from heaven, and see, from thy holy and glorious dwelling:
Where is thy zeal, and thy mighty power;
The yearning of thy bowels, and thy tender affections?
are they restrained from us?
16 Verily, Thou art our father; for Abraham knoweth us not,
And Israel doth not acknowledge us.
Thou, O JEHOVAH, art our father:
O deliver us for the sake of thy name!
17 Wherefore, O JEHOVAH, dost thou suffer us to err from thy ways?
To harden our hearts from the fear of thee?
Return for the sake of thy servants;
For the sake of the tribes of thine inheritance.
18 It is little, that they have taken possession of thy holy mountain;
That our enemies have trodden down thy sanctuary:
19 We have long been as those, whom thou hast not ruled;
Who have not been called by thy name.

CHAP. LXIV.
1 O! that thou wouldst rend the heavens, that thou wouldst descend;
That the mountains might flow down at thy presence!
2 As the fire kindleth the dry fuel;
As the fire causeth the waters to boil:
To make known thy name to thine enemies;
That the nations might tremble at thy presence.
3 When thou didst wonderful things, which we expected not;
Thou didst descend; at thy presence the mountains flowed down.
4 For never have men heard, nor perceived by the ear,
Nor hath eye seen, a God beside thee,
Who doeth such things for those that trust in him.
5 Thou meetest with joy those who work righteousness;
Who in thy ways remember thee.
Lo! Thou art angry; for we have sinned:
Because of our deeds; for we have been rebellious.
6 And we are all of us as a polluted thing;
And like a rejected garment are all our righteous deeds:

And we are withered away, like a leaf, all of us;
And our sins, like the wind, have borne us away.
7 There is no one that invoketh thy name;
That rouseth himself up to lay hold on thee:
Therefore thou hast hidden thy face from us;
And hast delivered us up into the hand of our iniquities.
8 But thou, O JEHOVAH, thou art our father;
We are the clay, and thou hast formed us:
We are all of us the work of thy hands.
9 Be not wroth, O JEHOVAH, to the uttermost;
Nor forever remember iniquity.
Behold, look upon us, we beseech thee; we are all thy people.
10 Thy holy cities are become a wilderness;
Sion is become a wilderness; Jerusalem is desolate.
11 Our holy and glorious temple,
Wherein our fathers praised thee,
Is utterly burnt up with fire;
And all the objects of our desire are become a devastation.
12 Wilt thou contain thyself at these things, O JEHOVAH?
Wilt thou keep silence, and still grievously afflict us?

CHAP. LXV.
1 I AM made known to those, that asked not for me;
I am found of those, that sought me not:
I have said: Behold me, here I am,
To the nation, which never invoked my name:
2 I have stretched out my hands all the day to a rebellious people,
Who walk in an evil way, after their own devices.
3 A people, who provoke me to my face continually;
Sacrificing in the gardens, and burning incense on the tiles:
4 Who dwell in the sepulchres, and lodge in the caverns;
Who eat the flesh of the swine;
And the broth of abominable meats is in their vessels:
5 Who say: Keep to thyself; come not near me; for I am holier than thou.
These kindle a smoke in my nostrils, a fire burning all the day long.
6 Behold, this is recorded in writing before me:
I will not keep silence, but will certainly requite;

7 I will requite into their bosom their iniquities;
And the iniquities of their fathers together, saith Jehovah:
Who burnt incense on the mountains, and dishonoured me upon the hills:
Yea, I will pour into their bosom the full measure of their former deeds.

8   Thus saith Jehovah:
As when one findeth a good grape in the cluster;
And sayeth, Destroy it not; for a blessing is in it:
So will I do for the sake of my servants; I will not destroy the whole.
9 So will I bring forth from Jacob a seed;
And from Judah an inheritor of my mountain:
And my chosen shall inherit the land;
And my servants shall dwell there.
10 And Sharon shall be a fold for the flock,
And the valley of Achor a resting for the herd;
For my people, who have sought after me.

11   But ye, who have deserted Jehovah;
And have forgotten my holy mountain:
Who set in order a table for Gad;
And fill out a libation to Meni:
12 You will I number out to the sword;
And all of you shall bow down to the slaughter.
Because I called, and ye answered not;
I spake, and ye would not hear:
But ye did that, which is evil in my sight;
And that, in which I delighted not, ye chose.
13   Wherefore thus saith the Lord Jehovah:
Behold, my servants shall eat, but ye shall be famished;
Behold, my servants shall drink, but ye shall be thirsty;
Behold, my servants shall rejoice, but ye shall be confounded:
14 Behold, my servants shall sing aloud, for gladness of heart;
But ye shall cry aloud, for grief of heart;
And in the anguish of a broken spirit shall ye howl.
15 And ye shall leave your name for a curse to my chosen:
And the Lord Jehovah shall slay you;
And his servants shall he call by another name.

16 Whoso blesseth himself upon the earth,
Shall bless himself in the God of truth;
And whoso sweareth upon the earth,
Shall swear by the God of truth.
Because the former provocations are forgotten;
And because they are hidden from mine eyes.
17 For behold, I create new heavens, and a new earth:
And the former ones shall not be remembered,
Neither shall they be brought to mind any more.
18 But ye shall rejoice and exult in the age to come, which I create:
For lo! I create Jerusalem a subject of joy, and her people of gladness;
19 And I will exult in Jerusalem, and rejoice in my people.
And there shall not be heard any more therein,
The voice of weeping, and the voice of a distressful cry:
20 No more shall be there an infant short-lived;
Nor an old man who hath not fulfilled his days:
For he, that dieth at an hundred years, shall die a boy;
And the sinner that dieth at an hundred years, shall be deemed accursed.
21 And they shall build houses, and shall inhabit them;
And they shall plant vineyards, and shall eat the fruit thereof.
22 They shall not build, and another inhabit;
They shall not plant, and another eat:
For as the days of a tree shall be the days of my people;
And they shall wear out the works of their own hands.
23 My chosen shall not labour in vain;
Neither shall they generate a short-lived race:
For they shall be a seed blessed of JEHOVAH;
They, and their offspring with them.
24 And it shall be, that before they call, I will answer;
They shall be yet speaking, and I shall have heard.
25 The wolf and the lamb shall feed together;
And the lion shall eat straw like the ox:
But as for the serpent, dust shall be his food.
They shall not hurt, neither shall they destroy,
In all my holy mountain, saith JEHOVAH.

CHAP. LXVI.

1 Thus saith Jehovah:
The heavens are my throne; and the earth is my footstool:
Where is this house, which ye build for me?
And where is this place of my rest?
2 For all these things my hand hath made;
And all these things are mine, saith Jehovah.
But such a one will I regard, even him that is humble,
And of a contrite spirit, and that revereth my word.
3 He that slayeth an ox, killeth a man;
That sacrificeth a lamb, beheadeth a dog;
That maketh an oblation, [offereth] swine's blood;
That burneth incense, blesseth an idol:
Yea, they themselves have chosen their own ways;
And in their abominations their soul delighteth.
4 I will also choose their calamities;
And what they dread, I will bring upon them;
Because I called, and no one answered;
I spake, and they would not hear:
And they have done what is evil in my sight;
And that, in which I delighted not, they have chosen.

5 Hear ye the word of Jehovah, ye that revere his word:
Say ye to your brethren, that hate you;
And that thrust you out, for my name's sake:
Jehovah will be glorified, and he will appear;
To your joy [will he appear], and they shall be confounded.

6 A voice of tumult from the city! a voice from the temple!
The voice of Jehovah! rendering recompense to his enemies.

7 Before she was in travail, she brought forth;
Before her pangs came, she was delivered of a male.
8 Who hath heard such a thing? and who hath seen th like of these things?
Is a country brought forth in one day?
Is a nation born in an instant?

For no sooner was Sion in travail, than she brought
    forth her children.
9 Shall I bring to the birth, and not cause to bring forth?
    saith JEHOVAH:
Shall I, who beget, restrain the birth? saith thy God.
10 Rejoice with Jerusalem, and exult on her account, all ye
    that love her;
Be exceedingly joyful with her, all ye that mourn over
    her:
11 That ye may suck, and be satisfied, from the breast of
    her consolations;
That ye may draw forth the delicious nourishment from
    her abundant stores.

12   For thus saith JEHOVAH:
Behold, I spread over her prosperity, like the great
    river;
And like the overflowing stream the wealth of the na-
    tions:
And ye shall suck at the breast;
Ye shall be carried by the side;
And on the knees shall ye be dandled.
13 As one, whom his mother comforteth,
So will I comfort you:
And in Jerusalem shall ye receive consolation.
14 And ye shall see it, and your heart shall rejoice;
And your bones shall flourish, like the green herb:
And the hand of JEHOVAH shall be manifested to his
    servants;
And he will be moved with indignation against his ene-
    mies.
15 For, behold! JEHOVAH shall come, as a fire;
And his chariot, as a whirlwind:
To breathe forth his anger in a burning heat,
And his rebuke in flames of fire.
16 For by fire shall JEHOVAH execute judgment;
And by his sword, upon all flesh:
And many shall be the slain of JEHOVAH.

17   They who sanctify themselves, and purify themselves,
In the gardens, after the rites of Achad;
In the midst of those who eat swine's flesh,
And the abomination, and the field-mouse;

    Together shall they perish, saith Jehovah.
18 For I know their deeds, and their devices:
    And I come to gather all the nations and tongues together;
    And they shall come, and shall see my glory.
19 And I will impart to them a sign;
    And of those that escape I will send to the nations:
    To Tarshish, Phul, and Lud, who draw the bow;
    Tubal, and Javan, the far distant coasts:
    To those, who never heard my name;
    And who never saw my glory:
    And they shall declare my glory among the nations.
20 And they shall bring all your brethren,
    From all the nations, for an oblation to Jehovah;
    On horses, and in litters, and in counes;
    On mules, and on dromedaries;
    To my holy mountain Jerusalem, saith Jehovah:
    Like as the sons of Israel brought the oblation,
    In pure vessels, to the house of Jehovah.
21 And of them will I also take,
    For priests, and for Levites, saith Jehovah.
22 For like as the new heavens,
    And the new earth, which I make,
    Stand continually before me, saith Jehovah;
    So shall continue your seed, and your name.
23 And it shall be, from new moon to new moon,
    And from sabbath to sabbath;
    All flesh shall come to worship before me, saith Jehovah.
24 And they shall go forth, and shall see
    The carcasses of the men who rebelled against me.
    For their worm shall not die,
    And their fire shall not be quenched;
    And they shall be an abhorrence to all flesh.

NOTES

ON

ISAIAH.

Isaiah exercised the prophetical office during a long period of time, if he lived to the reign of Manasseh; for the lowest computation, beginning from the year in which Uzziah died, when some suppose him to have received his first appointment to that office, brings it to 61 years. But the tradition of the Jews, that he was put to death by Manasseh, is very uncertain; and one of their principal rabbins (Aben Ezra, Com. in Isa. i. 1.) seems rather to think, that he died before Hezekiah; which is indeed more probable. It is however certain, that he lived at least to the 15th or 16th year of Hezekiah: this makes the least possible term of the duration of his prophetical office about 48 years. The time of the delivery of some of his prophecies is either expressly marked, or sufficiently clear from the history to which they relate: that of a few others may with some probability be deduced from internal marks; from expressions, descriptions, and circumstances interwoven. It may therefore be of some use in this respect, and for the better understanding of his prophecies in general, to give here a summary view of the history of his time.

The kingdom of Judah seems to have been in a more flourishing condition during the reigns of Uzziah and Jotham, than at any other time after the revolt of the ten tribes. The former recovered the port of Elath on the Red Sea, which the Edomites had taken in the reign of Joram: he was successful in his wars with the Philistines, and took from them several cities, Gath, Jabneh, Ashdod; as likewise against some people of Arabia Deserta; and against the Ammonites, whom he compelled to pay him tribute. He repaired and improved the fortifications of Jerusalem; and had a great army well appointed and disciplined. He was no less attentive to the arts of peace; and very much encouraged agriculture, and the breeding of cattle. Jotham maintained the establishments and improvements made by his father; added to what Uzziah had done in strengthening the frontier places; conquered the Ammonites, who had revolted, and exacted from them a more stated and probably a larger tribute. However, at the latter end of his time, the league between Pekah king of Israel and Retsin king of Syria was formed against Judah; and they began to carry their designs into execution.

But in the reign of Ahaz his son, not only all these advantages were lost, but the kingdom of Judah was brought to the brink of destruction. Pekah king of Israel overthrew the army of Ahaz, who lost in battle 120,000 men; and the Israelites carried away captives 200,000 women and children; which however were released, and sent home again, upon the remonstrance of the prophet Oded. After this, as it should seem, (see Vitringa on chap. vii. 2.), the two kings of Israel and Syria, joining their forces, laid siege to Jerusalem; but in this attempt they failed of success. In this distress Ahaz called in the assistance of Tiglath-Pileser king of Assyria; who invaded the kingdoms of Israel and Syria, and slew Retsin: but he was more in danger than ever from his too powerful ally; to purchase whose forbearance, as he had before bought his assistance, he was forced to strip himself and his people of all the wealth he could possibly raise, from his own treasury, from the temple, and from the country. About the time of the seige of Jerusalem, the Syrians took Elath, which was never after recovered. The Edomites likewise, taking advantage of the distress of Ahaz, ravaged Judea, and carried away many captives. The Philistines recovered what they had before lost; and took many places in Judea, and maintained themselves there. Idolatry was established by the command of the king in Jerusalem, and throughout Judea; and the service of the temple was either intermitted, or converted into an idolatrous worship.

Hezekiah, his son, at his accession to the throne, immediately set about the restoration of the legal worship of God, both in Jerusalem and through Judea. He cleansed and repaired the temple, and held a solemn passover. He improved the city, repaired the fortifications; erected magazines of all sorts, and built a new aqueduct. In the fourth year of his reign, Shalmaneser king of Assyria invaded the kingdom of Israel, took Samaria, and carried away the Israelites into captivity; and replaced them by different people sent from his own country; and this was the final destruction of that kingdom, in the sixth year of the reign of Hezekiah.

Hezekiah was not deterred by this alarming example from refusing to pay the tribute to the king of Assyria, which had been imposed on Ahaz. This brought on the invasion of Senacherib in the fourteenth year of his reign; an account of which is inserted among the prophecies of Isaiah. After a great and miraculous deliverance from so powerful an enemy, Hezekiah continued his reign in peace: he prospered in all his works, and left his kingdom in a flourishing state to his son Manasseh; a son in every respect unworthy of such a father.

CHAPTER I.

1. *The vision of Isaiah*—] It seems doubtful, whether this title belong to the whole book, or only to the prophecy contained in this chapter. The former part of the title seems properly to belong to this particular prophecy: the latter part, which enumerates the kings of Judah, under whom Isaiah exercised his prophetical office, seems to extend it to the whole collection of prophecies delivered in the course of his ministry. Vitringa (to whom the world is greatly indebted for his learned labours on this Prophet; and to whom we should have owed much more, if he had not so totally devoted himself to Masoretic authority) has, I think, very judiciously resolved this doubt. He supposes, that the former part of the title was originally prefixed to this single prophecy; and that, when the collection of all Isaiah's prophecies was made, the enumeration of the kings of Judah was added, to make it at the same time a proper title to the whole book. As such it is plainly taken in 2 Chron. xxxii. 32. where the book of Isaiah is cited by this title: "The vision of Isaiah the Prophet, the son of Amots."

The prophecy contained in this first chapter stands single and unconnected, making an entire piece of itself. It contains a severe remonstrance against the corruptions prevailing among the Jews of that time; powerful exhortations to repentance; grievous threatenings to the impenitent; and gracious promises of better times, when the nation shall have been reformed by the just judgments of God. The expression upon the whole is clear; the connexion of the several parts easy; and, in regard to the images, sentiments, and style, it gives a beautiful example of the Prophet's elegant manner of writing; though perhaps it may not be equal in these respects to many of the following prophecies.

2. *Hear, O ye heavens*—] God is introduced as entering upon a solemn and public action, or pleading, before the whole world, against his disobedient people. The prophet, as herald, or officer to proclaim the summons to the court, calls upon all created beings, celestial and terrestrial, to attend, and bear witness to the truth of his plea, and the justice of his cause. The same scene is more fully displayed in the noble exordium of Psalm l. where God summons all mankind, from east to west, to be present to hear his appeal; and the solemnity is held on Sion, where he is attended with the same terrible pomp that accompanied him on mount Sinai:—

"A consuming fire goes before him,
And round him rages a violent tempest:
He calleth the heavens from above,
And the earth, that he may contend in judgment with his people." Psal. l. 3, 4.

By the same bold figure, Micah calls upon the mountains, that is, the whole country of Judea, to attend to him: Chap. vi. 1, 2.

"Arise, plead thou before the mountains,
And let the hills hear thy voice.
Hear, O ye mountains, the controversy of JEHOVAH;
And ye, O ye strong foundations of the earth:
For JEHOVAH hath a controversy with his people,
And he will plead his cause against Israel."

With the like invocation Moses introduces his sublime song; the design of which was the same as that of this prophecy, "to testify, as a witness, against the Israelites," for their disobedience, Deut. xxxi. 21.

"Give ear, O ye heavens, and I will speak;
And let the earth hear the words of my mouth."
Deut. xxxii. 1.

This in the simple yet strong oratorical style of Moses is, "I call heaven and earth to witness against thee this day:

life and death have I set before thee; the blessing and the curse: choose now life, that thou mayest live, thou and thy seed." Deut. xxx. 19. The poetical style, by an apostrophe, sets the personification in a much stronger light.

Ibid.—*that speaketh*] I render it in the present time, pointing it דֹבֵר. There seems to be an impropriety in demanding attention to a speech already delivered.

Ibid. *I have nourished*—] The LXX have ἐγέννησα, *I have begotten*. Instead of גדלתי, they read ילדתי; a word little differing from the other, and perhaps more proper: which the Chaldee likewise seems to favour; " vocavi eos filios." See Exod. iv. 22. Jer. xxxi. 9.

3. *The ox knoweth*—] An amplification of the gross insensibility of the disobedient Jews, by comparing them with the most heavy and stupid of all animals, yet not so insensible as they. Bochart has well illustrated the comparison, and shewn the peculiar force of it. " He sets them lower than the beasts, and even than the stupidest of all beasts; for there is scarce any more so than the ox and the ass. Yet these acknowledge their master; they know the manger of their lord: by whom they are fed, not for their own, but for his good; neither are they looked upon as children, but as beasts of burthen; neither are they advanced to honours, but oppressed with great and daily labours: While the Israelites, chosen by the mere favour of God, adopted as sons, promoted to the highest dignity, yet acknowledged not their Lord and their God; but despised his commandments, though in the highest degree equitable and just." Hieroz. i. col. 409.

Jeremiah's comparison to the same purpose is equally elegant; but has not so much spirit and severity as this of Isaiah :—

" Even the stork in the heavens knoweth her season ;
 And the turtle, and the swallow, and the crane, observe the
   time of their coming :
 But my people doth not know the judgment of JEHOVAH."
                                                           Jer. viii. 7.

Hosea has given a very elegant turn to the same image, in the way of metaphor or allegory :
" I drew them with human cords, with the bands of love:
 And I was to them, as he that lifteth up the yoke upon their
   cheek;
 And I laid down their fodder before them." Hosea, xi. 4.

Salomo ben Melech thus explains the middle part of the verse, which is somewhat obscure: "I was to them at their desire, as they that have compassion on a heifer, lest she be over-worked in ploughing; and that lift up the yoke from off her neck, and rest it upon her cheek, that she may not still draw, but rest from her labour an hour or two in the day."

Ibid. *But Israel*—] The LXX, Syriac, Aquila, Theodotion, and Vulgate, read וישראל, adding the conjunction; which, being rendered as an adversative, sets the opposition in a stronger light.

Ibid, *Me.*] The same ancient versions agree in adding this word; which very properly answers, and indeed is almost necessarily required to answer, the words *possessor* and *lord* preceding. Ισραηλ δε ΜΕ ȣκ εγνω, LXX. "Israel autem ΜΕ non cognovit," Vulg. Ισραηλ δε ΜΟΥ ȣκ εγνω, Aq. Theod. The testimony of so scrupulous an interpreter as Aquila is of great weight in this case. And both his and Theodotion's rendering is such, as shews plainly, that they did not add the word ΜΟΥ to help out the sense; for it only embarrasses it. It also clearly determines what was the original reading in the old copies, from which they translated. It could not be ידעני, which most obviously answers to the version of LXX and Vulg. for it does not accord with that of Aquila and Theodotion. The version of these latter interpreters, however injudicious, clearly ascertains both the phrase, and the order of the words, of the original Hebrew: it was וישראל אותי לא ידע. The word אותי has been lost out of the text. The very same phrase is used by Jeremiah, chap. iv. 22. עמי אותי לא ידעו: and the order of the words must have been as above represented; for they have joined ישראל with אותי, as *in regimine:* they could not have taken it in this sense, *Israel ΜΕUS non cognovit*, had either this phrase, or the order of the words, been different. I have endeavoured to set this matter in a clear light, as it is the first example of a whole word lost out of the text; of which the reader will find many other plain examples in the course of these notes.

The LXX, Syr. Vulg. read ועמי, "*and* my people;" and so likewise sixteen MSS.

4. *degenerate*] Five MSS (one of them ancient) read משחתים without the first י; in Hophal, *corrupted*, not

corrupters. See the same word, in the same form, in the same sense, Prov. xxv. 26.

Ibid.—*are estranged*] Thirty-two MSS. (five ancient) and two editions, read נזורו: which reading determines the word to be from the root זור, *to alienate,* not from נזר, *to separate:* so Kimchi understands it. See also Annotat. in Noldium, 68.

Ibid. *they have turned their backs upon him*] So Kimchi explains it: "they have turned unto him the back, and not the face:" see Jer. ii. 27. vii. 24. I have been forced to render this line paraphrastically; as the verbal translation "they are estranged backward," would have been unintelligible.

5. *On what part*—] The Vulgate renders על מה, *super quo,* (see Job xxxviii. 6. 2 Chron. xxxii. 10.), *upon what part:* and so Abendana, on Sal. b. Melech: "There are some who explain it thus: Upon what limb shall you be smitten, if you add defection? for already for your sins have you been smitten upon all of them; so that there is not to be found in you a whole limb, on which you can be smitten." Which agrees with what follows: "From the sole of the foot even to the head, there is no soundness therein:" and the sentiment and image is exactly the same with that of Ovid, Pont. ii. 7. 42.

"Vix habet in nobis jam nova plaga locum."

Or that still more expressive line of Euripides; the great force and effect of which Longinus ascribes to its close and compressed structure, analogous to the sense which it expresses:—

Γεμω κακων δη· κ᾽ ουκετ᾽ εσθ᾽ οπη τεθη.
I'm full of miseries: there's no room for more.
Herc. Fur. 1245. Long. sect. 40.

"On what part will ye strike again; will ye add correction?" This is addressed to the instruments of God's vengeance; those that inflicted the punishment, who or whatsoever they were. "Ad verbum certæ personæ intelligendæ sunt, quibus ista actio [quae per verbum exprimitur] competit:" as Glassius says in a similar case, Phil. Sacr. i. 3. 22. See chap. viii. 4.

As from ידע, דעה, knowledge; from יעץ, עצה, counsel; from ישן, שנה, sleep, &c.; so from יסר is regularly derived סרה, correction.

6. *It hath not been pressed*—] The art of medicine in the East consists chiefly in external applications: accordingly the Prophet's images in this place are all taken from surgery. Sir John Chardin, in his note on Prov. iii. 8. "It shall be health to thy navel, and marrow to thy bones," observes, that "the comparison is taken from the plasters, ointments, oils, frictions, which are made use of in the East upon the belly and stomach in most maladies. Being ignorant in the villages of the art of making decoctions and potions, and of the proper doses of such things, they generally make use of external medicines." Harmer's Observations on Scripture, vol. ii. p. 488. And in surgery their materia medica is extremely simple; oil making the principal part of it. "In India," says Tavernier, "they have a certain preparation of oil and melted grease, which they commonly use for the healing of wounds." Voyage Ind. So the good Samaritan poured oil and wine on the wounds of the distressed Jew: wine, cleansing and somewhat astringent, proper for a fresh wound; oil, mollifying and healing. Luke x. 34.

Of the three verbs in this sentence, one is in the singular number in the text, another is singular in two MSS (one of them ancient) חבשה; and Syr. and Vulg. render all of them in the singular number.

7—9. *Your country is desolate*—] The description of the ruined and desolate state of the country in these verses, does not suit with any part of the prosperous times of Uzziah and Jotham. It very well agrees with the time of Ahaz, when Judea was ravaged by the joint invasion of the Israelites and Syrians, and by the incursions of the Philistines and Edomites. The date of this prophecy is therefore generally fixed to the time of Ahaz. But on the other hand it may be considered, whether those instances of idolatry, which are urged in the 29th verse, (the worshipping in groves and gardens), having been at all times too commonly practised, can be supposed to be the only ones which the Prophet would insist upon in the time of Ahaz; who spread the grossest idolatry through the whole country, and introduced it even into the temple; and, to complete his abominations, made his son pass through the fire to Moloch. It is said, 2 Kings xv. 37. that in Jotham's time "the Lord began to send against Judah Retsin and Pekah:" If we may suppose any invasion from that quarter to have been actually made at the latter end of Jotham's reign, I should choose to refer this prophecy to that time.

7. זרים, (at the end of the verse). This reading, though confirmed by all the ancient versions, gives us no good sense; for, your land is devoured by "strangers; and is desolate, as if overthrown by *strangers;*" is a mere tautology, or, what is as bad, an identical comparison. Aben Ezra thought, that the word, in its present form, might be taken for the same with זרם, *an inundation*: Schultens is of the same opinion, (see Taylor's Concord.); and Schindler in his Lexicon explains it in the same manner: and so, says Kimchi, some explain it. Abendana endeavours to reconcile it to grammatical analogy in the following manner:—"זרים is the same with זרם; that is, as overthrown by an *inundation of waters:* and these two words have the same analogy as קדם and קדים. Or it may be a concrete, of the same form with שכיר; and the meaning will be, as overthrown by rain pouring down violently, and causing a flood." On Sal. b. Melech, in loc. But I rather suppose the true reading to be זרם, and have translated it accordingly: the word זרים, in the line above, seems to have caught the transcriber's eye and to have led him into this mistake.

8. *as a shed in a vineyard*—] A little temporary hut covered with boughs, straw, turf, or the like materials, for a shelter from the heat by day, and the cold and dews by night, for the watchman that kept the garden, or vineyard, during the short season while the fruit was ripening; (see Job xxvii. 18.): and presently removed, when it had served that purpose. See Harmer, Obser. . 454. They were probably obliged to have such a constant watch, to defend the fruit from the jackals." "The jackal," (chical of the Turks,) says Hasselquist, (Travels, p. 277.), "is a species of mustela which is very common in Palestine, especially during the vintage, and often destroys whole vineyards, and gardens of cucumbers." "There is also plenty of the canis vulpes, the fox, near the convent of St. John in the desert, about vintage time; for they destroy all the vines, unless they are strictly watched." Ibid. p. 184. See Cant. ii. 15.

Fruits of the gourd kind, melons, water-melons, cucumbers, &c. are much used, and in great request, in the Levant, on account of their cooling quality. The Israelites in the wilderness regretted the loss of the cucumbers and the melons, among the other good things of Egypt; Numb. xi. 5.

In Egypt, the season of water-melons, which are most in request, and which the common people then chiefly live upon, lasts but three weeks. See Hasselquist, p. 256. Tavernier makes it of longer continuance :—" L'on y void de grands carreaux de melons et de concombres ; mais beaucoup plus des derniers, dont les Levantins font leur delices. Le plus souvent ils les mangent sans les peler, après quoy ils vont boire une verre d'eau. Dans toute l'Asie c'est la nourriture ordinaire du petit peuple pendant trois ou quatre mois; toute la famille en vit, et quand un enfant demande à manger, au lieu qu'en France ou ailleurs nous luy donnerions du pain, dans le Levant on luy presente un concombre, qu'il mange cru comme on le vient de cueillir.—Les concombres dans le Levant ont une bonté particulière, et quoyqu' on les mange crus, ils ne font jamais de mal." Tavernier, Relat. du Serrail, c. xix.

Ibid. *a city taken by seige.*] So LXX and Vulg.

9. *Jehovah God of Hosts*] As this title of God צבאות יהוה, "JEHOVAH of Hosts," occurs here for the first time, I think it proper to note, that I translate it always, as in this place, "JEHOVAH God of Hosts;" taking it as an elliptical expression for יהוה אלהי צבאות. This title imports, that JEHOVAH is the God, or Lord, of hosts or armies; as he is the Creator, and supreme Governor of all beings in heaven and earth ; and disposeth and ruleth them all in their several orders and stations ; the Almighty, Universal Lord.

10. *Ye princes of Sodom*—] The incidental mention of Sodom and Gomorrah in the preceding verse, suggested to the Prophet this spirited address to the rulers and inhabitants of Jerusalem, under the character of princes of Sodom and people of Gomorrah. Two examples of a sort of elegant turn of the like kind may be observed in St. Paul's Epistle to the Romans, xv. 4, 5. and 12, 13. See Locke on the place ; and see 29, 30. of this chapter ; which gives another example of the same.

11. —*the fat of fed beasts ; And in the blood*—] The fat and the blood are particularly mentioned, because these were in all sacrifices set apart to God. The fat was always burnt upon the altar ; and the blood was partly sprinkled, differently on different occasions, and partly poured out at the bottom of the altar. See Lev. iv.

11—16. *What have I to do*—] The prophet Amos has expressed the same sentiments with great elegance:

" I hate, I despise your feasts;
And I will not delight in the odour of your solemnities;
Though ye offer unto me burnt-offerings:
And your meat-offerings I will not accept;
Neither will I regard the peace-offerings of your fatlings.
Take away from me the noise of your songs;
And the melody of your viols I will not hear.
But let judgment roll down like waters;
And righteousness like a mighty stream." Amos, v. 21—24.

12. *Tread my courts no more*—] So the LXX divide the sentence; joining the end of this verse to the beginning of the next.

13. *The fast and the day of restraint*] און ועצרה. These words are rendered in many different manners by different interpreters; to a good and probable sense by all; but, I think, by none in such a sense as can arise from the phrase itself, agreeably to the idiom of the Hebrew language. Instead of און, the LXX manifestly read צום, νηϛειαν, "the fast." This Houbigant has adopted. The Prophet could not well have omitted the fast in the enumeration of their solemnities; nor the abuse of it, among the instances of their hypocrisy, which he has treated at large with such force and elegance in his 58th chapter. Observe also, that the prophet Joel twice joins together the fast, and the day of restraint:

קרשו צום קראו עצרה

" Sanctify a fast; proclaim a day of restraint." Joel i. 14. ii. 15. Which shews how properly they are here joined together. עצרה, *the restraint*, is rendered, both here and in other places in our English translation, *the solemn assembly*. Certain holy days, ordained by the law, were distinguished by a particular charge, that " no servile work should be done therein." Lev. xxiii. 36. Numb. xxix. 35. Deut. xvi. 8. This circumstance clearly explains the reason of the name, *the restraint*, or *the day of restraint*, given to those days.

If I could approve of any translation of these two words, which I have met with, it should be that of the Spanish version of the Old Testament, made for the use of the Spanish Jews: " tortura y detenimiento," " it is a pain and a constraint unto me." But I still think, that the reading of the LXX is more probably the truth.

15. *When ye spread*—] The Syr. LXX, and MS, read בפרשכם, without the conjunction ו.

Ibid. *For your hands*—] Αι γαρ χειρες. LXX. Manus enim vestræ. Vulg. They seem to have read כי ידיכם.

16. *Wash ye*—] Referring to the preceding verse, "your hands are full of blood;" and alluding to the legal washings commanded on several occasions. See Lev. xiv. 8, 9, 47.

17. *amend that which is corrupted*] אשרו חמוץ. In rendering this obscure phrase I follow Bochart, (Hieroz. Part. I. lib. ii. cap. 7.), though I am not perfectly satisfied with his explication of it.

18. *Though your sins were as scarlet*—] שני, "scarlet, or crimson," *dibaphum, twice dipped*, or *double-dyed;* from שנה, *iterare, to double*, or *to do a thing twice*. This derivation seems much more probable than that which Salmasius prefers, from שנן, *acucre*, from the *sharpness* and strength of the colour; οξυφοινικον. תלע, the same; properly the *worm, vermiculus,* (from whence *vermeil*); for this colour was produced from a worm, or insect, which grew in a coccus, or excrescence, of a shrub of the ilex kind, (see Plin. Nat. Hist. xvi. 8.); like the cochineal worm in the opuntia of America, (see Ulloa's Voyage, b. v. ch. 2. note to p. 342.) There is a shrub of this kind, that grows in Provence and Languedoc, and produces the like insect, called the *kermes oak*, (see Miller, Dict. *Quercus*); from *kermez*, the Arabic word for this colour; whence our word *crimson* is derived.

> "Neque amissos colores
> Lana refert medicata fuco."

says the poet; applying the same image to a different purpose. To discharge these strong colours is impossible to human art or power; but to the grace and power of God, all things, even much more difficult, are possible and easy.

19. *Ye shall feed on the good of the land*] Referring to ver. 7.; it shall not be "devoured by strangers."

20. *Ye shall be food for the sword*] The LXX and Vulg. read האכלכם, "the sword *shall devour you;*" which is of much more easy construction than the present reading of the text.

"The Chaldee seems to read בחרב אויב תאכלו; 'ye shall be consumed *by* the sword *of the enemy.*' Syr. also reads בחרב, and renders the verb passively. And the rhythmus seems to require this addition." Dr. JUBB.

21. —*become a harlot*] See Lowth, Comment. on the place; and De S. Poes. Hebr. Præl. xxxi.

22. *wine mixed with water*] An image used for the *adulteration* of wine, with more propriety than may at first appear, if what Thevenot says of the people of the Levant of late times was true of them formerly: He says, "they never mingle water with their wine to drink; but drink by itself what water they think proper for abating the strength of the wine." "Lorsque les Persans boivent du vin, ils le prennent tout pur, à la façon des Levantins, qui ne le mêlent jamais avec de l'eau; mais en beuvant du vin, de temps en temps ils prennent un pot d'eau, et en boivent de grand traits." Voyage, Part. II. liv. ii. chap. 10. "Ils (les Turcs) n'y melent jamais d'eau, et se moquent des Chrestiens, qui en mettent, ce qui leur semble tout-a-fait ridicule." Ibid. Part. I. chap. 24.

It is remarkable, that whereas the Greeks and Latins by *mixed* wine always understood wine diluted and lowered with water, the Hebrews on the contrary generally mean by it wine made stronger and more inebriating, by the addition of higher and more powerful ingredients; such as honey, spices, defrutum, (or wine inspissated by boiling it down to two-thirds, or one-half, of the quantity), myrrh, mandragora, opiates, and other strong drugs. Such were the exhilarating, or rather stupifying, ingredients, which Helen mixed in the bowl together with the wine for her guests oppressed with grief, to raise their spirits; the composition of which she had learned in Egypt:

Αυτικ' αρ εις οινον βαλε φαρμακον, ενθεν επινον,
Νηπενθες τ' αχολον τε, κακων επιληθον απαντων. Hom. Odys. iv. 220.

" Mean while, with genial joy to warm the soul,
Bright Helen mix'd a mirth-inspiring bowl;
Temper'd with drugs of sovereign use, t' assuage
The boiling bosom of tumultuous rage :
Charm'd with that virtuous draught, th' exalted mind
All sense of woe delivers to the wind." Pope.

Such was "the spiced wine and the juice of pomegranates," mentioned Cant. viii. 2. And how much the eastern people to this day deal in artificial liquors of prodigious strength, the use of wine being forbidden, may be seen in a curious chapter of Kempfer upon that subject. Amœn. Exot. Fasc. iii. Obs. 15.

Thus the drunkard is properly described, (Prov. xxiii. 30.), as one "that seeketh *mixt* wine;" and is "mighty to *mingle* strong drink:" Isaiah, v. 22. And hence the Psalmist took that highly poetical and sublime image of the cup of God's wrath, called by Isaiah, (li. 17.) "the cup of trembling," (causing intoxication and stupefaction; see Chappelow's note on Hariri, p. 33.); containing, as St. John expresses in Greek this Hebrew idea, with the utmost precision, though with a seeming contradiction in terms, κεκερασμενον ακρατον, *merum mixtum*, pure wine made yet stronger by a mixture of powerful ingredients: Rev. xiv. 10. "In the hand of JEHOVAH," saith the Psalmist, (Psal. lxxv. 9.), "there is a cup, and the wine is turbid: it is full of a mixed liquor, and he poureth out of it: (or rather, "he poureth it out of one vessel into another," to mix it perfectly; according to the reading expressed by the ancient versions, מזח אל זה ויגר): verily the dregs thereof, (the thickest sediment of the strong ingredients mingled with it), all the ungodly of the earth shall wring them out, and drink them."

23. *associates*—] The LXX, Vulg. and four MSS. read חברי, without the conjunction ו.

24. *Aha! I will be eased*—] Anger, arising from a sense of injury and affront, especially from those who, from every consideration of duty and gratitude, ought to have behaved far otherwise, is an uneasy and painful sensation; and revenge, executed to the full on the offenders, removes that uneasiness, and consequently is pleasing and quieting, at least for the present. Ezekiel introduces God expressing himself in the same manner:

" And mine anger shall be fully accomplished:
And I will make my fury rest upon them;
And I will give myself ease." Chap. v. 13.

This is a strong instance of the metaphor called Anthropopathia; by which, throughout the Scriptures, as well the historical as the poetical parts, the sentiments, sensations, and affections, the bodily faculties, qualities, and members of men, and even of brute animals, are attributed to God; and that with the utmost liberty and latitude of application. The foundation of this is obvious; it arises from necessity: we have no idea of the natural attributes of God, of his pure essence, of his manner of existence, of his manner of acting: when therefore we would treat on these subjects, we find ourselves forced to express them by sensible images. But necessity leads to beauty: this is true of metaphor in general, and in particular of this kind of metaphor; which is used with great elegance and sublimity in the sacred poetry: and what is very remarkable, in the grossest instances of the application of it, it is generally the most striking and the most sublime. The reason seems to be this: When the images are taken from the superior faculties of the human nature, from the purer and more generous affections, and applied to God, we are apt to acquiesce in the notion; we overlook the metaphor, and take it as a proper attribute: but when the idea is gross and offensive, as in this passage of Isaiah, where the impatience of anger, and the pleasure of revenge, is attributed to God; we are immediately shocked at the application; the impropriety strikes us at once; and the mind, casting about for something in the divine nature analogous to the image, lays hold on some great, obscure, vague idea, which she endeavours in vain to comprehend, and is lost in immensity and astonishment. See De S. Poesi Hebr. Præl. xvi. sub fin. where this matter is treated and illustrated by examples.

25. *in the furnace*] The text has כבר; which some render, "*as with soap;*" as if it were the same with כבורית; so Kimchi: but soap can have nothing to do with the purifying of metals: others, "*according to purity,* or *purely,*" as our version. Le Clerc conjectured, that the true reading is ככור, "*as in the furnace:*" see Ezek. xxii. 18. 20. Dr. Durell proposes only a transposition of letters בכר; to the same sense: and so likewise Archbishop Secker. That this is the true reading is highly probable.

26. *And after this*—] The LXX, Syr. Chald. and eighteen MSS, add the conjunction ו.

27.—*in judgment;*] by the exercise of God's strict justice in destroying the obdurate, (see ver. 28.), and delivering the penitent: *in righteousness;* by the truth and faithfulness of God in performing his promises.

29, 30. *For ye shall be ashamed of the ilexes*—] Sacred groves were a very ancient and favourite appendage of idolatry. They were furnished with the temple of the god to whom they were dedicated; with altars, images, and every thing necessary for performing the various rites of worship offered there; and were the scenes of many impure ceremonies, and of much abominable superstition. They made a principal part of the religion of the old inhabitants of Canaan; and the Israelites were commanded to destroy their groves, among other monuments of their false worship.

The Israelites themselves became afterward very much addicted to this species of idolatry.

" When I had brought them into the land,
Which I sware that I would give unto them ;
Then they saw every high hill, and every thick tree:
And there they slew their victims ;
And there they presented the provocation of their offerings;
- And there they placed their sweet savour;
And there they poured out their libations." Ezek. xx. 28.

" On the tops of the mountains they sacrifice;
And on the hills they burn incense:
Under the oak, and the poplar;
And the ilex, because her shade is pleasant." Hosea, iv. 13.

Of what particular kinds the trees here mentioned are, it cannot be determined with certainty. In regard to אלה, in this place of Isaiah, as well as in Hosea, Celsius (Hierobot.) understands it of the terebinth; because the most ancient interpreters render it so; in the first place the LXX. He quotes eight places; but in three of these eight places the copies vary, some having δρυς instead of τερεβινθος. And he should have told us, that these same LXX render it in sixteen other places by δρυς: so that their authority is really against him; and the LXX *stant pro quercu*, contrary to what he says at first setting out. Add to this, that Symmachus, Theodotion, and Aquila, generally render it by δρυς; the latter only once rendering it by τερεβινθος. His other arguments seem to me not very conclusive: he says, that all the qualities of אלה agree to the terebinth; that it grows in mountainous countries; that it is a strong tree; long-lived; large and high; and deciduous. All these qualities agree just as well to the oak, against which he contends; and he actually attributes them to the oak in the very next section. But, I think, neither the oak nor the terebinth will do in this place of Isaiah, from the last circumstance which he mentions, their being deciduous; where the Prophet's design seems to me to require an ever-green: otherwise the casting of its leaves would be nothing out of the common established course of nature, and no proper image of extreme distress, and total desolation ; parallel to that of a garden without water, that is, wholly burnt up and destroyed. An ancient, who was an inhabitant and a native of this country, understands it, in like manner, of a tree blasted with uncommon and immoderate heat:—"velut arbores, cum frondes æstu torrente decusserunt." Ephræm Syr. in loc. edit. Assemani. Compare Psal. i. 4. Jer. xvii. 8. Upon the whole, I have chosen to make it the ilex; which word Vossius (Etymolog.) derives from the Hebrew אלה; that, whether the word itself be rightly rendered or not, I might at least preserve the propriety of the poetical image.

29. *For ye shall be ashamed*] תבושו, in the second person, Vulg. Chald. two MSS, and one edition; and in agreement with the rest of the sentence.

30. —*whose leaves*] Twenty-six MSS and three editions read עליה, in its full and regular form. This is worth remarking, as it accounts for a great number of anomalies of the like kind, which want only the same authority to rectify them.

30. —*a garden wherein is no water.*] In the hotter parts of the eastern countries, a constant supply of water is so absolutely necessary for the cultivation, and even for the preservation and existence of a garden, that should it want water but for a few days, every thing in it would be burnt up with the heat, and totally destroyed. There is therefore no garden whatever in those countries, but what has such a certain supply; either from some neighbouring river, or from a reservoir of water collected from springs, or filled with rain-water in the proper season, in sufficient quantity to afford ample provision for the rest of the year.

Moses, having described the habitation of man newly created, as a garden, planted with every tree pleasant to the sight and good for food, adds, as a circumstance necessary to complete the idea of a garden, that it was well supplied with water: (Gen. ii. 10. and see xiii. 10.) "And a river went out of Eden to water the garden."

That the reader may have a clear notion of this matter, it will be necessary to give some account of the management of their gardens in this respect.

"Damascus, (says Maundrell, p. 122.), is encompassed with gardens, extending no less, according to common estimation, than thirty miles round; which makes it look like a city in a vast wood. The gardens are thick set with fruit-trees of all kinds, kept fresh and verdant by the waters of Barrady, (the Chrysorrhoas of the ancients), which supply both the gardens and city in great abundance. This river, as soon as it issues out from between the cleft of the mountain before mentioned into the plain, is immediately divided into three streams; of which the middlemost and biggest runs directly to Damascus, and is distributed to all the cisterns and fountains of the city. The other two (which I take to be the work of art) are drawn round, one to the right hand, and the other to the left, on the borders of the gardens, into which they are let as they pass, by little currents, and so dispersed all over the vast wood; insomuch, that there is not a garden but has a fine quick stream running through it. Barrady is almost wholly drunk up by the city and gardens. What small part of it escapes is united, as I was informed, in one channel again, on the south-east side of the city; and, after about three or four hours' course, finally loses itself in a bog there, without ever arriving at the sea." This was likewise the case in former times, as Strabo, lib. xvi. Pliny, v. 18. testify; who say, "that this river was expended in canals, and drunk up by watering the place."

"The best sight (says the same Maundrell, p. 39.) that the palace [of the Emir of Beroot, anciently Berytus] affords, and the worthiest to be remembered, is the orange garden. It contains a large quadrangular plat of ground, divided into sixteen lesser squares, four in a row, with walks between them. The walks are shaded with orange-trees, of a large spreading size. Every one of these sixteen lesser squares in the garden was bordered with stone; and in the stone-work were troughs, very artificially contrived, for conveying the water all over the garden: there being little outlets cut at every tree, for the stream, as it passed by, to flow out, and water it." The royal gardens at Ispahan are watered just in the same manner, according to Kempfer's description, Amœn. Exot. p. 193.

This gives us a clear idea of the פלגי מים, mentioned in the first Psalm, and other places of Scripture, "the divisions of waters," the waters distributed in artificial canals; for so the phrase properly signifies. The prophet Jeremiah has imitated, and elegantly amplified, the passage of the Psalmist above referred to:—

"He shall be like a tree planted by the water-side,
And which sendeth forth her roots to the aqueduct:
She shall not fear, when the heat cometh;
But her leaf shall be green;
And in the year of drought she shall not be anxious,
Neither shall she cease from bearing fruit." Jer. xvii. 8.

From this image the son of Sirach has most beautifully illustrated the influence and the increase of religious wisdom in a well-prepared heart:—

"I also come forth as a canal from a river,
And as a conduit flowing into a paradise.
I said: I will water my garden,
And I will abundantly moisten my border:
And lo! my canal became a river,
And my river became a sea." Eccl'us, xxiv. 30, 31.

This gives us the true meaning of the following elegant proverb:—

"The heart of the king is like the canals of waters in the hand of JEHOVAH;
Whithersoever it pleaseth him, he inclineth it." Prov. xxi. 1.

The direction of it is in the hand of JEHOVAH, as the distribution of the water of the reservoir, through the garden, by different canals, is at the will of the gardener:—

"Et, quum exustus ager morientibus æstuat herbis,
Ecce supercilio clivosi tramitis undam
Elicit: illa cadens raucum per levia murmur
Saxa ciet, scatebrisque arentia temperat arva."
Virg. Georg. i. 107.

Solomon mentions his own works of this kind:

"I made me gardens, and paradises;
And I planted in them all kinds of fruit-trees.
I made me pools of water,
To water with them the grove flourishing with trees."
Eccles. ii. 5. 6.

Maundrell (p. 88.) has given a description of the remains, as they are said to be, of these very pools made by Solomon, for the reception and preservation of the waters of a spring, rising at a little distance from them; which will give us a perfect notion of the contrivance and design of such reservoirs. "As for the pools, they are three in number, lying in a row above each other; being so disposed, that the waters of the uppermost may descend into the second, and those of the second into the third. Their figure is quadrangular; the breadth is the same in all, amounting to about ninety paces: in their length there is some difference between them; the first being one hundred and sixty paces long; the second two hundred; the third two hundred and twenty. They are all lined with wall, and plastered: and contain a great depth of water."

The immense works which were made by the ancient kings of Egypt, for receiving the waters of the Nile when it overflowed, for such uses, are well known. But there never was a more stupendous work of this kind, than the reservoir of Saba, or Merab, in Arabia Felix. According to the tradition of the country, it was the work of Balkis, that queen of Sheba who visited Solomon. It was a vast lake formed by the collection of the waters of a torrent in a valley, where, at a narrow pass between two mountains, a very high mole, or dam, was built. The water of the lake so formed had near twenty fathom depth; and there were three sluices at different heights, by which, at whatever height the lake stood, the plain below might be watered. By conduits and canals from these sluices the water was constantly distributed in due proportion to the several lands; so that the whole country for many miles became a perfect paradise. The city of Saba, or Merab, was situated immediately below the great dam: a great flood came, and raised the lake above its usual height: the dam gave way in the middle of the night; the waters burst forth at once, and overwhelmed the whole city, with the neighbouring towns, and people. The remains of eight tribes were forced to abandon their dwelling, and the beautiful valley became a morass and a desert. This fatal catastrophe happened long before the time of Mohammed, who mentions it in the Koran, chap. xxxiv. See also Sale, Prelim. sect. i.; and Michaelis, Questions aux Voyageurs Danois, No. 94.; Niebuhr, Descrip. de l'Arabie, p. 240.

CHAPTER II.

The prophecy contained in the second, third, and fourth chapters, makes one continued discourse. The first five verses of chapter second foretell the kingdom of Messiah, the conversion of the Gentiles, and their admission into it. From the sixth verse to the end of the second chapter is foretold the punishment of the unbelieving Jews, for their idolatrous practices, their confidence in their own strength, and distrust of God's protection; and moreover the destruction of idolatry, in consequence of the establishment of Messiah's kingdom. The whole third chapter, with the first verse of the fourth, is a prophecy of the calamities of the Babylonian invasion and captivity; with a particular amplification of the distress of the proud and luxurious daughters of Sion. Chap. iv. 2—6. promises to the remnant, which shall have escaped this severe purgation, a future restoration to the favour and protection of God.

This prophecy was probably delivered in the time of Jotham, or perhaps in that of Uzziah; as Isaiah is said to have prophesied in his reign; to which time not any of his prophecies is so applicable as that of these chapters. The seventh verse of the second, and the latter part of the third chapter, plainly point out times in which riches abounded, and luxury and delicacy prevailed. Plenty of silver and gold could only arise from their commerce; particularly from that part of it which was carried on by the Red Sea. This circumstance seems to confine the prophecy within the limits above mentioned, while the port of Elath was in their hands: it was lost under Ahaz, and never recovered.

2. —*in the latter days*—] " Wherever the latter times are mentioned in Scripture, the days of the Messiah are always meant;" says Kimchi on this place: and, in regard to this place, nothing can be more clear and certain. The Prophet Micah (chap. iv. 1—4.) has repeated this prophecy of the establishment of the kingdom of Christ, and of its progress to universality and perfection, in the same words, with little and hardly any material variation: for as he did not begin to prophesy till Jotham's time, and this seems to be one of the first of Isaiah's prophecies, I suppose Micah to have taken it from hence. The variations, as I said, are of no great importance. Verse 2. הוא after ונשא, a word of some emphasis, may be supplied from Micah, if dropt in Isaiah: an ancient MS has it here in the margin: It has in like manner been lost in chap. liii. 4. (see note on the place); and in Psal. xxii. 29. where it is supplied by Syr. and LXX. Instead of כל הגוים, *all the nations*, Micah has only עמים, *peoples;* where Syr. has כל עמים, *all peoples*, as probably it ought to be. Verse 3. for the 2d אל read ואל, seventeen MSS, two editions, LXX, Vulg. Syr. Chald. and so Micah iv. 2. Verse 4. Micah adds, עד רחק, *afar off*, which the Syriac also reads in this parallel place of Isaiah. It is also to be observed, that Micah has improved the passage by adding a verse, or sentence, for imagery and expression worthy even of the elegance of Isaiah:—

" And they shall sit, every man under his vine,
And under his fig-tree, and none shall affright them:
For the mouth of JEHOVAH God of Hosts hath spoken it."

The description of well-established peace, by the image of " beating their swords into ploughshares, and their spears into pruning-hooks," is very poetical. The Roman poets have employed the same image: Martial, xiv. 34. " Falx ex ense."

" Pax me certa ducis placidos curvavit in usus:
Agricolæ nunc sum; militis ante fui."

The Prophet Joel hath reversed it, and applied it to war prevailing over peace:—

" Beat your ploughshares into swords;
And your pruning-hooks into spears." Joel, iii. 10.

And so likewise the Roman poet:—

" Non ullus aratro
Dignus honos: squalent abductis arva colonis,
Et curvæ rigidum falces conflantur in ensem."
Virg. Georg. i. 506.

" Bella diu tenuere viros: erat aptior ensis
Vomere: cedebat taurus arator equo.
Sarcula cessabant; versique in pila ligones;
Factaque de rastri pondere cassis erat." Ovid. Fast. i. 697.

The Prophet Ezekiel has presignified the same great event with equal clearness, though in a more abstruse form, in an allegory; from an image, suggested by the former part of the prophecy, happily introduced, and well pursued:—

" Thus saith the Lord JEHOVAH:
I myself will take from the shoot of the lofty cedar;
Even a tender cion from the top of his cions will I pluck off:
And I myself will plant it on a mountain high and eminent.
On the lofty mountain of Israel will I plant it;
And it shall exalt its branch and bring forth fruit;
And it shall become a majestic cedar:
And under it shall dwell all fowl of every wing;
In the shadow of its branches shall they dwell:
And all the trees of the field shall know,
That I JEHOVAH have brought low the high tree;
Have exalted the low tree;
Have dried up the green tree;
And have made the dry tree to flourish:
I JEHOVAH have spoken it, and will do it." Ezek. xvii. 22-24.

The word ונתתי in this passage, verse 22. as the sentence now stands, seems incapable of being reduced to any proper construction or sense; none of the ancient versions acknowledge it, except Theodotion and Vulg.; and all but the latter vary very much from the present reading of this clause. Houbigant's correction of the passage, by reading, instead of ויונקת, ונתתי, (*and a tender cion*), which is not very unlike it, (perhaps better יונק, with which the adjective רך will agree without alteration), is ingenious and probable; and I have adopted it in the above translation.

6. *they are filled with diviners*—] Heb. *They are filled from the east;* or, *more than the east.* The sentence is manifestly imperfect. The LXX, Vulg. and Chaldee, seem to have read כמקדם; and the latter, with another word before it signifying *idols: They are filled with idols as from of old.* Houbigant for מקדם, reads מקסם, as Brentius had proposed long ago. I rather think, that both words together give us the true reading: מקסם, מקדם, *with divination from the east;* and that the first word has been by mistake omitted, from its similitude to the second.

Ibid. *And they multiply*—] Seven MSS and one edition read יספיקו. "Read יספיחו; *and have joined themselves to the children of strangers;* that is, in marriage, or worship." Dr. JUBB. So Vulg. *adhæserunt.* Compare chap. xiv. 1. But the very learned professor Chevalier Michaelis has explained the word יספחו, Job, xxx. 7. (German translation, note on the place) in another manner; which perfectly well agrees with that place, and perhaps will be found to give as good a sense here. ספיח, the noun, means corn springing up, not from the seed regularly sown on cultivated land, but in the untilled field, from the scattered grains of the former harvest. This, by an easy metaphor, is applied to a spurious brood of children irregularly and casually begotten. The LXX seem to have understood the verb here in this sense, reading it as Vulg. seems to have done: this justifies their version, which it is hard to account for in any other manner: καὶ τεκνα πολλα αλλοφυλα εγενηθη αυτοις. Compare Hos. v. 7. and LXX there.

7. *And his land is filled with horses*] This was in direct contradiction to God's command in the law: "But he [the king] shall not multiply horses to himself; nor cause the people to return to Egypt, to the end that he should multiply horses:—neither shall he greatly multiply to himself silver and gold:" Deut. xvii. 16, 17. Uzziah seems to have followed the example of Solomon, (see 1 Kings x. 26,

—29.), who first transgressed in these particulars: be recovered the port of Elath on the Red Sea, and with it that commerce, which, in Solomon's days, had "made silver and gold as plenteous at Jerusalem as stones:" 2 Chron. i. 15. He had an army of 307,500 men; in which, as we may infer from this testimony of Isaiah, the chariots and horse made a considerable part. "The law above-mentioned was to be a standing trial of prince and people, whether they had trust and confidence in God their deliverer." See Bp. Sherlock's Discourses on Prophecy, Dissert. iv. where he has excellently explained the reason and effect of the law and the influence which the observance or neglect of it had on the affairs of the Israelites.

8. *And his land is filled with idols*] Uzziah and Jotham are both said (2 Kings xv. 3, 4. and 34, 35.) "to have done that which was right in the sight of the Lord;" (that is, to have adhered to, and maintained the legal worship of God, in opposition to idolatry, and all irregular worship; for to this sense the meaning of that phrase is commonly to be restrained); "save that the high places were not removed, where the people still sacrificed and burned incense." There was hardly any time when they were quite free from this irregular and unlawful practice; which they seem to have looked upon as very consistent with the true worship of God; and which seems in some measure to have been tolerated, while the tabernacle was removed from place to place, and before the temple was built. Even after the conversion of Manasseh, when he had removed the strange gods, and commanded Judah to serve Jehovah the God of Israel; it is added, "Nevertheless the people did sacrifice still on the high places, yet unto Jehovah their God only:" 2 Chron. xxxiii. 17. The worshipping on the high places therefore does not necessarily imply idolatry: and from what is said of these two kings, Uzziah and Jotham, we may presume, that the public exercise of idolatrous worship was not permitted in their time. The idols therefore here spoken of, must have been such as were designed for a private and secret use. Such probably were the Teraphim so often mentioned in Scripture; a kind of household gods, of human form, as it should seem, (see 1 Sam. xix. 13. and compare Gen. xxxi. 34.), of different magnitude, used for idolatrous and superstitious purposes; particularly for divination, and as oracles, which they consulted for direction in their affairs.

9. —*shall be bowed down*] This has reference to the preceding verse: they bowed themselves down to their idols; therefore shall they be bowed down and brought low under the avenging hand of God.

10. *When he ariseth to strike the earth with terror.*] On the authority of LXX, confirmed by the Arabic and an ancient MS, I have here added to the text a line, which in the 19th and 21st verses is repeated together with the preceding line, and has, I think, evidently been omitted by mistake in this place. The MS here varies only in one letter from the reading of the other two verses: it has באריץ instead of הארץ.

11. —*be humbled*] "For שפל ושח, read שפלו שח." Dr. Durell. Which rectifies the grammatical construction.

13—16. *Even against all the cedars—*] These verses afford us a striking example of that peculiar way of writing, which makes a principal characteristic of the parabolical or poetical style of the Hebrews, and in which their prophets deal so largely; namely, their manner of exhibiting things divine, spiritual, moral, and political, by a set of images taken from things natural, artificial, religious, historical; in the way of metaphor or allegory. Of these, nature furnishes much the largest and the most pleasing share; and all poetry has chiefly recourse to natural images, as the richest and most powerful source of illustration. But it may be observed of the Hebrew poetry in particular, that in the use of such images, and in the application of them in the way of illustration and ornament, it is more regular and constant than any other poetry whatever; that it has, for the most part, a set of images appropriated in a manner to the explication of certain subjects. Thus you will find, in many other places beside this before us, that cedars of Libanus and oaks of Basan are used, in the way of metaphor and allegory, for kings, princes, potentates, of the highest rank; high mountains and lofty hills, for kingdoms, republics, states, cities; towers and fortresses, for defenders and protectors, whether by counsel or strength, in peace or war; ships of Tarshish, and works of art and invention employed in adorning them, for merchants, men enriched by commerce, and abounding in all the luxuries and elegancies of life; such as those of Tyre and Sidon: for it appears from the course of the whole passage, and from the train of ideas, that the fortresses and the ships are to be taken metaphorically, as well as the high trees and the lofty mountains.

Ships of Tarshish are in Scripture frequently used by a metonymy for ships in general, especially such as are employed in carrying on traffic between distant countries; as Tarshish was the most celebrated mart of those times, frequented of old by the Phenicians, and the principal source of wealth to Judea and the neighbouring countries. The learned seem now to be perfectly well agreed, that Tarshish is Tartessus, a city of Spain, at the mouth of the river Bætis; whence the Phenicians, who first opened this trade, brought silver and gold, (Jer. x. 9. Ezek. xxvii. 12.), in which that country then abounded; and pursuing their voyage still further to the Cassiterides, [Bochart. Canaan, I. cap. 39. Huet, Hist. de Commerce, p. 194.), the islands of Scilly and Cornwall, they brought from thence lead and tin.

Tarshish is celebrated in Scripture (2 Chron. viii. 17, 18. ix. 21.) for the trade which Solomon carried on thither, in conjunction with the Tyrians. Jehosaphat (1 Kings xxii. 48. 2 Chron. xx. 36.) attempted afterward to renew that trade; and from the account given of his attempt it appears, that his fleet was to sail from Eziongeber on the Red Sea: they must therefore have designed to sail round Africa, as Solomon's fleet probably had done before, (see Huet, Histoire de Commerce, p. 32.); for it was a three years' voyage, (2 Chron. ix. 21.); and they brought gold from Ophir, probably on the coast of Arabia, silver from Tartessus, and ivory, apes, and peacocks from Africa. "אופיר, Afri, *Africa*, the Roman termination, *Africa terra*. תרשיש, some city, or country, in Africa. So Chald. on 1 Kings xxii. 49. where he renders תרשיש, by אפריקה; and compare 2 Chron. xx. 36. from whence it appears, that to go to Ophir and to Tarshish is one and the same thing." Dr. JUBB. It is certain, that under Pharaoh Necho, about two hundred years afterward, this voyage was made by the Egyptians. (Herodot. iv. 42.) They sailed from the Red Sea, and returned by the Mediterranean, and they performed it in three years; just the same time that the voyage under Solomon had taken up. It appears likewise from Pliny, (Nat. Hist. ii. 67.), that the passage round the Cape of Good Hope was known and frequently practised before his time; by Hanno the Carthaginian, when Carthage was in its glory; by one Eudoxus, in the time of Ptolemy Lathyrus king of Egypt; and Cælius Antipater, an historian of good credit, somewhat earlier than Pliny, testifies, that he had seen a merchant, who had made the voyage from Gades to Æthio ia. The Portuguese under Vasco de Gama, near three hundred years ago, recovered this navigation, after it had been intermitted and lost for many centuries.

18. —*shall disappear*] The ancient versions, and an ancient MS, read חלפי, plural.

19—21. *into caverns of rocks*—] The country of Judea, being mountainous and rocky, is full of caverns; as it appears from the history of David's persecution under Saul. At Engedi, in particular, there was a cave so large, that David with six hundred men hid themselves in the sides of it; and Saul entered the mouth of the cave without perceiving that any one was there: 1 Sam. xxiv. Josephus (Antiq. lib. xiv. cap. 15.; and Bell. Jud. lib. i. cap. 16.) tells us of a numerous gang of banditti, who, having infested the country, and being pursued by Herod with his army, retired into certain caverns, almost inaccessible, near Arbela in Galilee, where they were with great difficulty subdued. Some of these were natural, others artificial. "Beyond Damascus," says Strabo, lib. xvi. "are two mountains called Trachones; [from which the country has the name of Trachonitis]: and from hence, towards Arabia and Iturea, are certain rugged mountains, in which there are deep caverns; one of which will hold four thousand men." Tavernier (Voyage de Perse, Part II. chap. 4.) speaks of a grot, between Aleppo and Bir, that would hold near three thousand horse. Three hours distant from Sidon, about a mile from the sea, there runs along a high rocky mountain; in the sides of which are hewn a multitude of grots, all very little differing from each other. They have entrances about two feet square: on the inside, you find in most or all of them a room of about four yards square. There are of these subterraneous caverns two hundred in number. It may, with probability at least, be concluded that these places were contrived for the use of the living, and not of the dead. Strabo describes the habitations of the Troglodytæ to have been somewhat of this kind:" Maundrell, p. 118. The Horites, who dwelt in Mount Seir, were Troglodytes, as their name חרים imports. But those mentioned by Strabo were on each side of the Arabian Gulf. Mohammed (Koran, chap. xv. and xxvi.) speaks of a tribe of Arabians, the tribe of Thamud, "who hewed houses out of the mountains," to secure themselves." Thus, " because of the Midianites, the children of Israel made them the dens which are in the mountains, and caves, and strongholds." Judges, vi. 2. To these they betook themselves for refuge in times of distress and hostile invasion: " When the men of Israel saw that they were in a strait, (for the people were distressed), then the people did hide themselves in caves, and in thickets, and in rocks, and in high places, and in pits;" 1 Sam. xiii. 6. and see Jer. xli. 9. Therefore, " to enter into the rock; to go into the holes of the rocks, and into the caves of the earth," was to them a very proper and familiar image to express terror and consternation. The Prophet Hosea hath carried the same image further, and added great strength and spirit to it: Chap. x. 8.

" They shall say to the mountains, Cover us;
And to the hills, Fall on us."

Which image, together with these of Isaiah, is adopted by the sublime author of the Revelation, (chap. vi. 15, 16.), who frequently borrows his imagery from our Prophet.

20. —*which they have made to worship*—] The word לו, *for himself,* is omitted by an ancient MS, and is unnecessary. It does not appear that any copy of LXX has it, except MS Pachom. and MS I. D. II. and they have ἑαυτοῖς, להם, plural.

Ibid. —*to the moles*—] They shall carry their idols with them into the dark caverns, old ruins, or desolate places, to which they shall flee for refuge; and so shall give them up, and relinquish them to the filthy animals that frequent such places, and have taken possession of them as their proper habitation. Bellonius, Greaves, P. Lucas, and many other travellers, speak of bats of an enormous size as inhabiting the great Pyramid. See Harmer, Obser. vol. ii. 455. Three MSS express הפרפרות, *the moles,* as one word.

CHAPTER III.

1. *Every stay and support*—] Heb. " the support masculine, and the support feminine;" that is, every kind of support, whether great or small, strong or weak: " *Al kanîtz, wal-kanîtzah;* the wild beast, male and female: Preverbially applied both to fishing and hunting; *i. e.* I seized the prey, great or little, good or bad. From hence, as

Schultens observes, is explained Isa. iii. 1. literally the *male and female stay: i. e.* the strong and weak, the great and small." Chappelow, note on Hariri, Assembly I. Compare Eccles. ii. 8.

The two following verses, 2, 3. are very clearly explained by the sacred historian's account of the event, the captivity of Jehoiachin by Nebuchadnezzar king of Babylon: "And he carried away all Jerusalem, and all the princes, and all the mighty men of valour, even ten thousand captives, and all the craftsmen and smiths: none remained, save the poorest sort of the people of the land:" 2 Kings xxiv. 14.

4. *I will make boys their princes*—] This also was fully accomplished in the succession of weak and wicked princes, from the death of Josiah to the destruction of the city and temple, and the taking of Zedekiah, the last of them, by Nebuchadnezzar.

6. —*of his father's house*] For בית, the ancient interpreters seem to have read מבית: τε οικεια τε πατρος αυτε; LXX: domesticum patris sui; Vulg. which gives no good sense. (But LXX, MS 1. D. 11. for οικεια, has οικε.) And, *his brother, of his father's house*, is little better than a tautology. The case seems to require, that the man should apply to a person of some sort of rank and eminence; one that was the *head* of his father's house, (see Josh. xxii. 14.); whether of the house of him who applies to him, or of any other; ראש בית אביו. I cannot help suspecting, therefore, that the word ראש has been lost out of the text.

Ibid. —*saying*—] Before שמלה, *garment*, two MSS (one ancient), and the Babylonish Talmud, have the word לאמר: and so LXX, Vulg. Syr. Chald. I place it with Houbigant, after שמלה.

Ibid. —*take by the garment.*] That is, shall entreat him in an humble and supplicating manner. "Ten men shall take hold of the skirt of him that is a Jew; saying, Let us go with you; for we have heard that God is with you:" Zech. viii. 23. And so in Isaiah, chap. iv. 1. the same gesture is used to express earnest and humble entreaty. The behaviour of Saul towards Samuel was of the same kind, when he laid hold on the skirt of his raiment: 1 Sam. xv. 27. The preceding and following verses shew, that his whole deportment, in regard to the prophet, was full of submission and humility.

Ibid. *And let thy hand support*—] Before תחת ידי a

MS adds תהיה; another MS adds in the same place בירך תקח, which latter seems to be a various reading of the two preceding words, making a very good sense; "take into thy hand our ruinous state." Twenty-one MSS, and three editions, and the Babylonish Talmud, have יָדְיִ, plural.

7. *Then shall he openly declare*—] The LXX, Syr. and Jerom. read וישא, adding the conjunction; which seems necessary in this place.

Ibid. *For in my house is neither bread nor raiment.*] "It is customary through all the East," says Sir J. Chardin, "to gather together an immense quantity of furniture and clothes; for their fashions never alter." Princes and great men are obliged to have a great stock of such things in readiness for presents upon all occasions. "The kings of Persia," says the same author, "have great wardrobes, where there are always many hundreds of habits ready, designed for presents, and sorted." Harmer, Observ. ii. 11. and 88. A great quantity of provision for the table was equally necessary. The daily provision for Solomon's household, whose attendants were exceedingly numerous, was proportionably great: 1 Kings, iv. 22, 23. Even Nehemiah, in his strait circumstances, had a large supply daily for his table; at which were received an hundred and fifty of the Jews and rulers, beside those that came from among the neighbouring heathens: Neh. v. 17, 18.

This explains the meaning of the excuse made by him that is desired to undertake the government: he alleges, that he has not wherewithal to support the dignity of the station by such acts of liberality and hospitality as the law of custom required of persons of superior rank. See Harmer's Observations, i. 340. ii. 88.

8. —*the cloud*] This word appears to be of very doubtful form, from the printed editions, the MSS, and the ancient versions. The first jod in עיני, which is necessary, according to the common interpretation, is in many of them omitted: the two last letters are upon a rasure in two MSS. I think it should be ענן, as the Syriac reads; and that the allusion is to the cloud, in which the glory of the Lord appeared above the tabernacle. See Exod. xvi. 9, 10. xl. 34—38. Numb. xvi. 41, 42.

10. *Pronounce ye*—] The reading of this verse is very dubious. The LXX for אמרו read נאסר; or both, נאסר אמרו: and כי לא טוב לנו. Δησωμεν τον δικαιον, οτι δυσχρησος ημιν

11. Perhaps, for אמרו, the true reading may be אשרו, *bless ye:* or אמרו אשרי, *say ye, blessed is*—. Vulg. and an ancient MS read, in the singular number, יאכל, *comedet.*

12. *Pervert*] בלע, *swallow.* Among many unsatisfactory methods of accounting for the unusual meaning of this word in this place, I chose Jarchi's explication, as making the best sense. "Read בללו, *confound.* Syr." Dr. JUBB. "Read בהלו, *disturb* or *trouble.*" SECKER. So LXX.

13. —*his people*] עמו, LXX.

14. —*my vineyard*] כרמי, LXX, Chald. Jerom.

15. *And grind the faces*] The expression and the image is strong, to denote grievous oppression; but is exceeded by the prophet Micah:

> "Hear, I pray you, ye chiefs of Jacob;
> And ye princes of the house of Israel:
> Is it not yours to know what is right?
> Ye that hate good, and love evil:
> Who tear their skin from off them;
> And their flesh from off their bones:
> Who devour the flesh of my people;
> And flay from off them their skin:
> And their bones they dash in pieces;
> And chop them asunder, as morsels for the pot;
> And as flesh thrown into the midst of the cauldron."
>
> Micah, iii. 1—3.

In the last line but one, for כאשר, read, by the transposition of a letter, כשאר with the LXX, and Chald.

16. *And falsely setting off their eyes with paint*] Heb. *falsifying* their eyes. I take this to be the true meaning and literal rendering of the word; from שָׁקַר. The Masoretes have pointed it, as if it were from שָׁקַף, a different word. This arose, as I imagine, from their supposing that the word was the same with סקר, Chald. *intueri, innuere oculis;* or that it had an affinity with the noun סיקרא, which the Chaldeans, or the Rabbins at least, use for *stibium,* the mineral which was commonly used in colouring the eyes. See Jarchi's comment on the place. Though the colouring of the eyes with stibium be not particularly here expressed, yet I suppose it to be implied: and so the Chaldee paraphrase explains it; "*stibio linitis oculis.*" This fashion sems to have prevailed very generally among the eastern people in ancient times; and they retain the very same to this day.

Pietro della Valle, giving a description of his wife, an Assyrian lady, born in Mesopotamia, and educated at Baghdad, whom he married in that country, (Viaggi, tom. i. lettera 17.), says, "Her eye-lashes, which are long, and, according to the custom of the East, dressed with stibium, (as we often read in the Holy Scriptures of the Hebrew women of old, Jer. iv. 30. Ezek. xxiii. 40.; and in Xenophon of Astyages the grandfather of Cyrus, and of the Medes of that time, Cyropæd. lib. i.), give a dark, and at the same time a majestic shade to the eyes." "Great eyes (says Sandys, Travels, p. 67., speaking of the Turkish women) they have in principal repute; and of those, the blacker they be, the more amiable: insomuch that they put between the eye-lids and the eye a certain black powder, with a fine long pencil, made of a mineral brought from the kingdom of Fez, and called *alcohole;* which, by the not disagreeable staining of the lids, doth better set forth the whiteness of the eye; and though it be troublesome for a time, yet it comforteth the sight, and repelleth ill humours." " Vis ejus [stibii] astringere ac refrigerare, principalis autem circa oculos; namque ideo etiam plerique Platyophthalmon id appellavere, quoniam in calliblepharis mulierum dilatat oculos; et fluxiones inhibet oculorum exulcerationesque." Plin. Nat. Hist. xxxiii. 6.

"Ille supercilium madida fuligine tinctum
Obliqua producit acu, pingitque trementes
Attollens oculos." Juv. Sat. ii. 92.

"But none of those [Moorish] ladies," says Dr. Shaw, (Travels, p. 294. fol.), "take themselves to be completely dressed, till they have tinged the hair and edges of their eye-lids with *al-kahol,* the powder of lead ore. This operation is performed by dipping first into the powder a small wooden bodkin of the thickness of a quill, and then drawing it afterwards through the eye-lids, over the ball of the eye." Ezekiel (xxiii. 40.) uses the same word in the form of a verb, כחלת עיניך, "thou didst dress thine eyes with *al-cahol;*" which the LXX render ἐστίβιζου τοὺς ὀφθαλμούς σου, "thou didst dress thine eyes with *stibium;*" just as they do when the word פוך is employed: (compare 2 Kings ix. 30. Jer. iv. 30.): they supposed therefore, that פוך and כחל, or; in the Arabic form, *al-cahol,* meant the same thing; and probably the mineral used of old, for this purpose, was the same that is used now; which Dr. Shaw (Ibid. note) says,

is "a rich lead ore, pounded into an impalpable powder."
Alcoholados; the word משקרות, in this place, is thus rendered in an old Spanish translation. Sanctius. See also Russell's Nat. Hist. of Aleppo, p. 102.

The following inventory, as one may call it, of the wardrobe of a Hebrew lady, must, from its antiquity, and from the nature of the subject, have been very obscure, even to the most ancient interpreters which we have of it; and, from its obscurity, must have been also peculiarly liable to the mistakes of transcribers: however, it is rather matter of curiosity than of importance; and indeed it is, upon the whole, more intelligible, and less corrupted, than one might have reasonably expected. Clemens Alexandrinus (Pædag. lib. ii. cap. 12.) and Julius Pollux (lib. vii. cap. 22.) have each of them preserved, from a comedy of Aristophanes, now lost, a similar catalogue of the several parts of the dress and ornaments of a Grecian lady; which though much more capable of illustration from other writers, though of later date, and quoted and transmitted down to us by two different authors; yet seems to be much less intelligible, and considerably more corrupted, than this passage of Isaiah. Salmasius has endeavoured, by comparing the two quotations, and by much critical conjecture and learned disquisition, to restore the true reading, and to explain the particulars; with what success, I leave to the determination of the learned reader, whose curiosity shall lead him to compare the passage of the comedian with this of the Prophet, and to examine the critic's learned labours upon it. Exercit. Plinian. p. 1148.; or see Clem. Alex. as cited above, edit. Potter, where the passage as corrected by Salmasius is given.

Nich. Guil. Schroederus, professor of Oriental languages in the university of Marpurg, has published a very learned and judicious treatise upon this passage of Isaiah. The title of it is, "Commentarius Philologico-Criticus De Vestitu Mulierum Hebræarum ad Iesai, iii. ver. 16—24. Lugd. Bat. 1745." 4to. As I think no one has handled this subject with so much judgment and ability as this author, I have for the most part followed him, in giving the explanation of the several terms denoting the different parts of dress, of which this passage consists; signifying the reasons of my dissent, where he does not give me full satisfaction.

17.—*will the Lord humble*—] Ταπεινωσει, LXX; and so Syr. and Chald. For שפח they read שפל.

Ibid. —*expose their nakedness*] It was the barbarous custom of the conquerors of those times to strip their captives naked, and to make them travel in that condition, exposed to the inclemency of the weather; and the worst of all, to the intolerable heat of the sun. But this to the women was the height of cruelty and indignity; and especially to such as those here described, who had indulged themselves in all manner of delicacies of living, and all the superfluities of ornamental dress; and even whose faces had hardly ever been exposed to the sight of man. This is always mentioned as the hardest part of the lot of captives. Nahum, denouncing the fate of Nineveh, paints it in very strong colours:

> " Behold, I am against thee, saith JEHOVAH God of Hosts:
> And I will discover thy skirts upon thy face;
> And I will expose thy nakedness to the nations;
> And to the kingdoms thy shame.
> And I will throw ordures upon thee;
> And I will make thee vile, and set thee as a gazing-stock."
> Nahum, iii. 5, 6.

18. —*the ornaments of the feet rings*—] The late learned Dr. Hunt, professor of Hebrew and Arabic in the university of Oxford, has very well explained the word עכס, both verb and noun, in his very ingenious Dissertation on Prov. vii. 22, 23. The verb means to skip, to bound, to dance along; and the noun, those ornaments of the feet which the eastern ladies wore; chains, or rings, which made a tinkling sound as they moved nimbly in walking. Eugene Roger, Description de la Terre Sainte, liv. ii. chap. 2. speaking of the Arabian women of the first rank in Palestine, says, " Au lieu de brasselets elles ont de menottes d'argent, qu'elles portent aux poignets et aux pieds; où sont attachez quantité de petits annelets d'argent, qui font un cliquetis comme d'une cymbale, lorsqu'elles cheminent ou se mouvent quelque peu." See Dr. Hunt's Dissertation; where he produces other testimonies to the same purpose from authors of travels.

Ibid.—*the net-works*] I am obliged to differ from the learned Schroederus, almost at first setting out; he renders the word שביסים by *soliculi*, little ornaments, bullæ, or studs in shape representing the *sun*, and so answering to the following word שהרנים, *lunulæ*, crescents. He supposes the word to be the same with שמשים, the י in the second syllable making the word diminutive, and the letter מ being changed for ב, a letter of the same organ. How just and well-founded his authorities for the transmutation of these letters in the Arabic language are, I cannot pretend to judge; but, as I know of no such instance in Hebrew, it seems to me a very forced etymology. Being dissatisfied with this account of the matter, I applied to my good friend above-mentioned, the late Dr. Hunt, who very kindly returned the following answer to my inquiries :—

"I have consulted the Arabic lexicons, as well MS as printed, but cannot find שביסים in any of them, nor any thing belonging to it. So that no help is to be had from that language towards clearing up the meaning of this difficult word. But what the Arabic denies, the Syriac perhaps may afford; in which I find the verb שבש to *entangle*, or *interweave*, an etymology which is equally favourable to our marginal translation, *net-works*, with שבץ, to *make chequer-work*, or *embroider*, (the word by which Kimchi and others have explained שבים), and has moreover this advantage over it, that the letters ש and ס are very frequently put for each other, but צ and ס scarce ever. Aben Ezra joins שביסים. and עכסים (which immediately precedes it) together; and says, that שבים *was the ornament of the legs*, as עכם *was of the feet*. His words are, שוקים של תכשיט שביס רגלים של עכם כמו."

21. *The jewels of the nostril*—] נזמי האף. Schroederus explains this, as many others do, of jewels, or strings of pearl, hanging from the forehead, and reaching to the upper part of the nose. But it appears from many passages of Holy Scripture, that the phrase is to be literally and properly understood of nose-jewels, rings set with jewels hanging from the nostrils, as ear-rings from the ears, by holes bored to receive them.

Ezekiel, enumerating the common ornaments of women of the first rank, has not omitted this particular, and is to be understood in the same manner; chap. xvi. 11, 12. (See also Gen. xxiv. 47.)

> " And I decked thee with ornaments;
> And I put bracelets upon thine hands,
> And a chain on thy neck:
> And I put a jewel on thy nose,
> And ear-rings on thine ears,
> And a splendid crown upon thine head."

And in an elegant proverb of Solomon there is a manifest allusion to this kind of ornament, which shews it to have been used in his time:

" As a jewel set in gold in the snout of a swine;
So is a woman beautiful, but wanting discretion."
Prov. xi. 22.

This fashion, however strange it may appear to us, was formerly, and is still, common in many parts of the East, among women of all ranks. Paul Lucas, speaking of a village, or clan, of wandering people, a little on this side of the Euphrates; "The women," says he, (2d Voyage du Levant, tom. i. art. 24.), "almost all of them, travel on foot: I saw none handsome among them. They have almost all of them the nose bored, and wear in it a great ring, which makes them still more deformed." But in regard to this custom, better authority cannot be produced than that of Pietro della Valle, in the account which he gives of the lady before-mentioned, Signora Maani Gioerida, his own wife. The description of her dress, as to the ornamental parts of it, with which he introduces the mention of this particular, will give us some notion of the taste of the eastern ladies for finery. "The ornaments of gold, and of jewels, for the head, for the neck, for the arms, for the legs, and for the feet, (for they wear rings even on their toes), are indeed, unlike those of the Turks, carried to great excess, but not of great value; for in Baghdad jewels of high price either are not to be had, or are not used; and they wear such only as are of little value; as turquoises, small rubies, emeralds, carbuncles, garnets, pearls, and the like. My spouse dresses herself with all of them according to their fashion; with exception, however, of certain ugly rings of very large size, set with jewels, which in truth, very absurdly, it is the custom to wear fastened to one of their nostrils, like buffaloes: an ancient custom however in the East, which, as we find in the Holy Scriptures, prevailed among the Hebrew ladies even in the time of Solomon: Prov. xi. 22. These nose-rings in complaisance to me she has left off; but I have not yet been able to prevail with her cousin and her sisters to do the same: so fond are they of an old custom, be it ever so absurd, who have been long habituated to it." Viaggi, tom. i. lett. 17.

23. *The transparent garments—*] הגליונים, τα διαφανη λακωνικα, LXX. A kind of silken dress, transparent, like

gauze; worn only by the most delicate women, and such as dressed themselves "elegantius, quam necesse esset probis." This sort of garments was afterwards in use among the Greeks. Prodicus, in his celebrated fable. (Xenoph. Memorab. Socr. lib. ii.) exhibits the personage of Sloth in this dress: εσθητα δε, εξ 'ης αν μαλιϛα αρα διαλαμποι.

"Her robe betray'd
Through the clear texture every tender limb,
Height'ning the charms it only seemed to shade;
And as it flow'd adown so loose and thin,
Her stature shew'd more tall, more snowy white her skin."

They were called Multitia and Coa (sc. vestimenta) by the Romans, from their being invented, or rather introduced into Greece, by one Pamphila of the island of Cos. This, like other Grecian fashions, was received at Rome when luxury began to prevail under the Emperors; it was sometimes worn even by the men, but looked upon as a mark of extreme effeminacy: (see Juvenal, Sat. ii. 65, &c.) Publius Syrus, who lived when the fashion was first introduced, has given a humorous satirical description of it in two lines, which by chance have been preserved:

"Æquum est, induere nuptam ventum textilem?
Palam prostare nudam in nebula lineâ?"

24. *Instead of perfume*—] A principal part of the delicacy of the Asiatic ladies consists in the use of baths, and of the richest oils and perfumes: an attention to which is, in some degree, necessary in those hot countries. Frequent mention is made of the rich ointments of the spouse in the Song of Solomon:—

"How beautiful are thy breasts, my sister, my spouse!
How much more excellent than wine;
And the odour of thine ointments than all perfumes!
Thy lips drop as the honey-comb, my spouse!
Honey and milk are under thy tongue:
And the odour of thy garments is as the odour of Lebanon."
Cant. iv. 10, 11.

The preparation for Esther's being introduced to King Ahasuerus was a course of bathing and perfuming for a whole year; "Six months with oil of myrrh, and six months with sweet odours:" Esth. ii. 12. A diseased and loathsome habit of body, instead of a beautiful skin, softened and made agreeable with all that art could devise, and all that nature, so prodigal in those countries of the richest perfumes, could supply, must have been a punishment the most severe, and the most mortifying to the delicacy of these haughty daughters of Sion.

Ibid. *A sun-burnt skin*—] Gaspar Sanctius thinks the words כי תחת an interpolation, because the Vulgate has omitted them. The clause כי תחת יפי seems to me rather to be imperfect at the end. Not to mention that כי, taken as a noun, for *adustio, burning*, is without example, and very improbable: the passage ends abruptly, and seems to want a fuller conclusion.

In agreement with which opinion of the defect of the Hebrew text in this place, the LXX, according to MSS Pachom. and I. D. II. and Marchal. which are of the best authority, express it with the same evident marks of imperfection at the end of the sentence; thus, ταυτα σοι αντι καλλωπισμȣ— The two latter add σȣ. This chasm in the text, from the loss probably of three or four words, seems therefore to be of long standing.

Taking כי in its usual sense, as a particle, and supplying לך from σοι of the LXX, it might possibly have been originally somewhat in this form:—

כי תחת יפי תהיה לך רעת מראה:

"Yea, instead of beauty, thou shalt have an ill-favoured countenance."

כי תחת יפי [q. יחת] "for beauty *shall be destroyed*." Syr. from חתת, or גחת. Dr. DURELL.

May it not be כחי, "*wrinkles* instead of beauty?" as from יפה is formed יפי; from מרה, מרי, &c. so from כהה, *to be wrinkled*, כהי." Dr. JUBB.

25. *thy mighty men*—] For גבורתך, an ancient MS has גבורך. The true reading from LXX, Vulg. Syr. Chald. seems to be גבוריך.

26 —*sit on the ground.*] Sitting on the ground was a posture that denoted mourning and deep distress. The Prophet Jeremiah has given it the first place, among many indications of sorrow, in the following elegant description of the same state of distress of his country:—

"The elders of the daughter of Sion sit on the ground, they are silent:
They have cast up dust on their heads; they have girded themselves with sackcloth:
The virgins of Jerusalem have bowed down their heads to the ground." Lam. ii. 10.

" We find Judea," says Mr. Addison, (on Medals, Dial. ii.) " on several coins of Vespasian and Titus, in a posture that denotes sorrow and captivity.—I need not mention her sitting on the ground, because we have already spoken of the aptness of such a posture to represent an extreme affliction. I fancy the Romans might have an eye on the customs of the Jewish nation, as well as those of their country, in the several marks of sorrow they have set on this figure. The Psalmist describes the Jews lamenting their captivity in the same pensive posture. " By the waters of Babylon we sat down and wept, when we remembered thee, O Sion.". But what is more remarkable, we find Judea represented as a woman in sorrow sitting on the ground, in a passage of the Prophet that foretells the very captivity recorded on this medal." Mr. Addison, I presume, refers to this place of Isaiah ; and therefore must have understood it as foretelling the destruction of Jerusalem and the Jewish nation by the Romans: whereas it seems plainly to relate, in its first and more immediate view at least, to the destruction of the city by Nebuchadnezzar, and the dissolution of the Jewish state under the captivity at Babylon.

CHAPTER IV.

1. *And seven women*—] The division of the chapters has interrupted the Prophet's discourse, and broken it off almost in the midst of the sentence. " The numbers slain in battle shall be so great, that seven women shall be left to one man." The Prophet has described the greatness of this distress by images and adjuncts the most expressive and forcible. The young women, contrary to their natural modesty, shall become suitors to the men : they will take hold of them, and use the most pressing importunity to be married: in spite of the natural suggestions of jealousy, they will be content with a share only of the rights of marriage in common with several others; and that on hard conditions, renouncing the legal demands of the wife on the husband, (see, Exod. xxi. 10.), and begging only the name and credit of wedlock, and to be freed from the reproach of celibacy, (see chap. liv. 4, 5.) Like Marcia, on a different occasion, and in other circumstances,—

" Da tantum nomen inane
Connubii: liceat tumulo scripsisse, Catonis
Marcia." Lucan. ii 342.

Ibid. —*in that day*—] These words are omitted in LXX and MS.

Ibid. *The branch of* JEHOVAH—] The Messiah of JEHOVAH, says the Chaldee. The branch is an appropriated title of the Messiah; and the fruit of the land means the great Person to spring from the house of Judah, and is only a parallel expression signifying the same; or perhaps the blessings consequent upon the redemption procured by him. Compare chap. xlv. 8. where the same great event is set forth in similar images; and see the note there.

Ibid. —*the house of Israel.*] A MS has בית ישראל.

3. —*written among the living.*] That is, whose name stands in the enrolment or register of the people; or every man living, who is a citizen of Jerusalem. See Ezek. xiii. 9. where "they shall not be written in the writings of the house of Israel," is the same with what immediately goes before, "they shall not be in the assembly of my people." Compare Psal. lxxxvii. 6. lxix. 28; Exod. xxxii. 32. To number and register the people was agreeable to the law of Moses, and probably was always practised; being, in sound policy, useful and even necessary. David's design of numbering the people was of another kind; it was to enrol them for his army. Michaelis, Mosaisches Recht, Part III. p. 227. See also his Dissert. de Censibus Hebræorum.

4. "*The spirit of burning,*"] means the fire of God's wrath, by which he will prove and purify his people; gathering them into his furnace, in order to separate the dross from the silver, the bad from the good. The severity of God's judgments, the fiery trial of his servants, Ezekiel (chap. xxii. 18—22.) has set forth at large, after his manner, with great boldness of imagery and force of expression. God threatens to gather them into the midst of Jerusalem, as into the furnace; to blow the fire upon them, and to melt them. Malachi (chap. iii. 2, 3.) treats the same subject, and represents the same event under the like images :—

"But who may abide the day of his coming?
And who shall stand when he appeareth?
For he is like the fire of the refiner,
And like the soap of the fullers.
And he shall sit refining and purifying the silver;
And he shall purify the sons of Levi,
And cleanse them like gold, and like silver;
That they may be JEHOVAH's ministers,
Presenting unto him an offering in righteousness."

5. *—the station—*] The Hebrew text has, *every station;* but four MSS (one ancient) omit כל; very rightly, as it should seem; for the station was Mount Sion itself, and no other. See Exod. xv. 17. And the LXX and MS add the same word כל before מקראיה, probably right: the word has only changed its place by mistake. מקראיה, "the place where they were gathered together in their holy assemblies," says Sal. b. Melec.

Ibid. *A cloud by day—*] This is a manifest allusion to the pillar of a cloud and of fire, which attended the Israelites in their passage out of Egypt, and to the glory that rested on the tabernacle, Exod. xiii. 21. xl. 38. The prophet Zechariah applies the same image to the same purpose:—

"And I will be unto her a wall of fire round about;
And a glory will I be in the midst of her." Zech. ii. 5.

That is, the visible presence of God shall protect her. Which explains the conclusion of this verse of Isaiah; where the makkaph between כל and כבוד, connecting the two words in construction, which ought not to be connected, has thrown an obscurity upon the sentence, and misled most of the translators.

6. *And a tabernacle—*] In countries subject to violent tempests, as well as to intolerable heat, a portable tent is a necessary part of a traveller's baggage, for defence and shelter.

CHAPTER V.

This chapter likewise stands single and alone, unconnected with the preceding or following. The subject of it is nearly the same with that of the first chapter. It is a general reproof of the Jews for their wickedness: but it exceeds that chapter in force, in severity, in variety, and elegance; and it adds a more express declaration of vengeance, by the Babylonian invasion.

1. *Let me sing now a song*] A MS, respectable for its antiquity, adds the word שיר *(a song)* after נא; which gives so elegant a turn to the sentence by the repetition of it in the next member, and by distinguishing the members so exactly in the style and manner of the Hebrew poetical composition, that I am much inclined to think it genuine.

Ibid. *A song of loves*] דודי, for דודים; *status constructus pro absoluto*, as the grammarians say, as Micah, vi. 16.; Lament. iii. 14. and 66.; so Archbishop Secker. Or rather, in all these and the like cases, a mistake of the transcribers, by not observing a small stroke, which in many MSS is made to supply the ם of the plural, thus דודי׳. שירת דודים is the same with שיר ידידת, Psal. xlv. 1. In this way of understanding it, we avoid the great impropriety of making the author of the song, and the person to whom it is addressed, to be the same.

Ibid. *On a high and fruitful hill*] Heb. " on a horn the son of oil." The expression is highly descriptive and poetical. " He calls the land of Israel a horn, because it is higher than all lands; as the horn is higher than the whole body: and the son of oil, because it is said to be a land flowing with milk and honey." Kimchi on the place. The parts of animals are, by an easy metaphor, applied to parts of the earth, both in common and poetical language. A promontory is called a cape, or head; the Turks call it a nose. " Dorsum immane mari summo ; " Virg. a back, or ridge of rocks.

" Hanc latus angustum jam se cogentis in arctum
 Hesperiæ tenuem producit in æquora *linguam*,
 Adriacas flexis claudit quæ *cornibus* undas."

Lucan. ii. 612. of Brundusium, *i. e.* Βρεντεσιον, which, in the ancient language of that country, signifies stag's-head, says Strabo. A horn is a proper and obvious image for a mountain, or mountainous country. Solinus, cap. viii. says, " Italiam, ubi longius processerit, in *cornua* duo scindi : " that is, the high ridge of the Alps, which runs through the whole length of it, divides at last into two ridges, one going through Calabria, the other through the country of the Brutii. " Cornwall is called by the inhabitants in the British tongue *Kernaw*, as lessening by degrees like a horn, running out into promontories like so many horns. For the Britains call a horn *corn*, in the plural *kern:* " Camden. " And Sammes is of opinion, that the country had this name originally from the Phenicians, who traded hither for tin ; *keren*, in their language, being a *horn:* " Gibson.

Here the precise idea seems to be that of a high mountain standing by itself: " vertex montis, aut pars montis ab aliis divisa ; " which signification, says I. H. Michaelis, (Bibl. Hallens. Not. in loc.) the word has in Arabic.

Judea was in general a mountainous country; whence Moses sometimes calls it the Mountain :—" Thou shalt plant them in the Mountain of thine inheritance ; " Exod. xv. 17. " I pray thee let me go over, and see the good land that is beyond Jordan; that goodly Mountain, and Lebanon;" Deut. iii. 25. And in a political and religious view it was detached and separated from all the nations round it. Whoever has considered the descriptions given of Mount Tabor, (see Reland, Palæstin.; Eugene Roger, Terre Sainte, p. 64.), and the views of it which are to be seen in books of travels, (Maundrell, p. 114. Egmont and Heyman, vol. ii. p. 25. Thevenot, vol. i. p. 429.); its regular conic form, rising singly in a plain to a great height from a base small in proportion; its beauty and fertility to the very top; will have a good idea of " a horn the son of oil;" and will perhaps be induced to think, that the Prophet took his image from that mountain.

2. *and he cleared it from the stones.*] This was agreeable to the ancient husbandry: " Saxa, summa parte terræ, et vites et arbores lædunt; ima parte, refrigerant;" Columell. De Arb. 4. " Saxosum facile est expedire lectione lapidum;" Id. ii. 2. "Lapides, qui supersunt, [al. insuper sunt] bieme rigent, æstate fervescunt; idcirco satis, arbustis, et vitibus nocent;" Pallad. i. 6. A piece of ground thus cleared of the stones, Persius, in his hard way of metaphor, calls " Exossatus ager;" Sat. vi. 52.

Ibid. *Sorek.*] Many of the ancient interpreters, LXX, Aq. Theod. have retained this word as a proper name; I think very rightly. Sorek was a valley lying between Ascalon and Gaza, and running far up eastward in the tribe of Judah. Both Ascalon and Gaza were anciently famous for wine: the former is mentioned as such by Alexander Trallianus; the latter by several authors: (quoted by Reland, Palæst. p. 589. and 986.) And it seems, that the upper part of the valley of Sorek, and that of Eshcol, where the spies gathered the single cluster of grapes which they were obliged to bear between two upon a staff, being both near to Hebron, were in the same neighbourhood; and that all this part of the country abounded with rich vineyards. Compare Numb. xiii. 22, 23. Judg. xvi. 3, 4. P. Nau supposes Eshcol and Sorek to be only different names for the same valley: Voyage Nouveau de la Terre Sainte, liv. iv. chap. 18. So likewise De Lisle's posthumous map of the Holy Land; Paris, 1763. See Bochart, Hieroz. ii. col. 725. Thevenot, i. p. 406. Michaelis (note on Judg. xvi. 4. German translation) thinks it probable, from some circumstances of the history there given, that Sorek was in the tribe of Judah, not in the country of the Philistines.

The vine of Sorek was known to the Israelites, being mentioned by Moses (Gen. xlix. 11.) before their coming out of Egypt. Egypt was not a wine country. " Throughout this country there are no wines;" Sandys, p. 101. At least in very ancient times they had none. Herodotus, ii. 77. says, it had no vines; and therefore used an artificial wine made of barley. That is not strictly true; for the vines of Egypt are spoken of in Scripture, (Psal. lxxviii. 47. cv. 33., and see Gen. xl. 11. by which it should seem, that they drank only the fresh juice pressed from the grape, which was called οινος αμπελινος, Herodot. ii. 37.); but they had no large vineyards; nor was the country proper for them, being little more than one large plain, annually overflowed by the Nile. The Mareotic in later times is, I think, the only celebrated Egyptian wine which we meet with in history. The vine was formerly, as Hasselquist tells us it is now, "cultivated in Egypt for the sake of eating the grapes, not for wine; which is brought from Candia," &c. "They were supplied with wine from Greece, and likewise from Phenicia;" Herod. iii. 6. The vine and the wine of Sorek, therefore, which lay near at hand for importation into Egypt, must, in all probability, have been well known to the Israelites when they sojourned there. There is something remarkable in the manner in which Moses makes mention of it, which, for want of considering this matter, has not been attended to: It is in Jacob's prophecy of the future prosperity of the tribe of Judah :—

> " Binding his foal to the vine,
> And his ass's colt to his own Sorek;
> He washeth his raiment in wine,
> And his cloak in the blood of grapes." Gen. xlix. 11.

I take the liberty of rendering שרקה, for שרקו, *his* Sorek, as the Masoretes do of pointing עירה, for עירו, *his* foal. עיר might naturally enough appear in the feminine form, but it is not at all probable that שרק ever should. By naming particularly the vine of Sorek, and as the vine belonging to Judah, the prophecy intimates the very part of the country which was to fall to the lot of that tribe. Sir John Chardin says, "That at Casbin, a city in Persia, they turn their cattle into the vineyards, after the vintage, to browse on the vines." He speaks also of vines in that country, so large that he could hardly compass the trunks of them with his arms. Voyages, tom. iii. p. 12. 12mo. This shews, that the ass might be securely bound to the vine; and without danger of damaging the tree by browsing on it.

Ibid. *And he built a tower in the midst of it.*] Our Saviour, who has taken the general idea of one of his parables (Matt. xxi. 33. Mark xii. 1.) from this of Isaiah, has likewise inserted this circumstance of building a tower; which is generally explained by commentators, as designed for the keeper of the vineyard to watch and defend the fruits. But for this purpose it was usual to make a little temporary hut, (Isa. i. 8.), which might serve for the short season while the fruit was ripening, and which was removed afterwards. The tower, therefore, should rather mean a building of a more permanent nature and use; the farm, as we may call it, of the vineyard, containing all the offices and implements, and the whole apparatus necessary for the culture of the vineyard, and the making of the wine. To which image in the allegory, the situation, the manner of building, the use, and the whole service of the temple, exactly answered. And so the Chaldee paraphrast very rightly expounds it:—" Et statui eos (Israelitas) ut plantam vineæ selectae, et aedificavi *sanctuarium meum* in medio illorum." So also Hieron. in loc. " Ædificavit quoque turrim in medio ejus: templum videlicet in media civitate." That they have still such towers or buildings, for use or pleasure, in their gardens in the East, see Harmer's Observations, ii. p. 241.

Ibid. *And hewed out a lake therein.*] This image also our Saviour has preserved in his parable. יקב, LXX render it here προληνιον; and in four other places υποληνιον; Isa. xvi. 10. Joel, iii. 13. Hagg. ii. 17. Zech. xiv. 10.; I think, more properly: and this latter word St. Mark uses. It means, not the wine-press itself, or *calcatorium*, which is called גת, or פורה, but what the Romans called *lacus*, the *lake;* the large open place, or vessel, which, by a conduit or spout, received the must from the wine-press. In very hot countries it was perhaps necessary, or at least very convenient, to have the lake under ground, or in a cave hewed out of the side of the rock, for coolness; that the heat might not cause too great a fermentation, and sour the must. " Vini confectio instituitur in cella, vel intimae domus camera quadam, a ventorum ingressu remota:" Kempfer, of Schiras wine; Amœn. Exot. p. 376: For the hot wind, to which that country is subject, would injure the wine. " The wine-presses in Persia," says Sir John Chardin, "are formed by making hollow places in the ground, lined with mason's work." Harmer's Observations, i. p. 392. See a print of one in Kempfer, p. 377. Nonnus describes, at large, Bacchus hollowing the inside of the rock, and hewing out a place for the wine-press, or rather the lake:—

Και σκοπελης ελαχηνε· πεδοσκαφεος δε σιδηρου
Θηγαλεη γλωχινι μυχον κοιληνατο πετρης·
Λειηνας δε μεἶωπα βαθυνομενων κενεωνων
Αφρον [f. ακρον.] εὐςαφυλοιο τυπον ποιησατο ληνου.

"He pierc'd the rock; and with the sharpen'd tool
Of steel well temper'd, scoop'd its inmost depth:
Then smooth'd the front, and form'd the dark recess
In just dimension for the foaming lake." Dionysiac. lib. xii.

Ibid. *And he expected*—] Jeremiah uses the same image, and applies it to the same purpose, in an elegant paraphrase of this part of Isaiah's parable, in his flowing and plaintive manner:

" But I planted thee a Sorek, a cion perfectly genuine:
How then art thou changed, and become to me the degenerate shoots of the strange vine! " Chap. ii. 21.

Ibid. *poisonous berries*] באושים, not merely useless unprofitable grapes, such as wild grapes; but grapes offensive to the smell, noxious, poisonous. By the force and intent of the allegory, to good grapes ought to be opposed fruit of a dangerous and pernicious quality; as, in the explication of it, to judgment is opposed tyranny, and to righteousness oppression. גפן, the vine, is a common name, or genus, including several species under it; and Moses, to distinguish the true vine, or that from which wine is made, from the rest, calls it, Numb. vi. 4. גפן היין, the wine-vine. Some of the other sorts were of a poisonous quality; as appears from the story related among the miraculous acts of Elisha, 2 Kings iv. 39—41. " And one went out into the field to gather pot-herbs; and he found a field-vine: and he gathered from it wild fruit, his lapful; and he went, and shred them into the pot of pottage: for they knew them not. And they poured it out for the men to eat: and it came to pass, as they were eating of the pottage, that they cried out, and said, There is death in the pot, O man of God! and they could not eat of it. And he said, Bring meal; (leg. קח, nine MSS, one edition); and he threw it into the pot. And he said, Pour out for the people, that they may eat. And there was nothing hurtful in the pot."

From some such sorts of poisonous fruits, of the grape kind, Moses has taken those strong and highly poetical images, with which he has set forth the future corruption and extreme degeneracy of the Israelites, in on allegory which has a near relation, both in its subject and imagery, to this of Isaiah:—

"Their vine is from the vine of Sodom,
And from the fields of Gomorrah:
Their grapes are grapes of gall;
Their clusters are bitter:
Their wine is the poison of dragons,
And the cruel venom of aspics."   Deut. xxxii. 32, 33.

"I am inclined to believe, (says Hasselquist), that the Prophet here (Isa. v. 2. and 4.) means the hoary nightshade, *solanum incanum*; because it is common in Egypt, Palestine, and the East; and the Arabian name agrees well with it. The Arabs call it *aneb el dib*, i. e. *wolf-grapes*. The Prophet could not have found a plant more opposite to the vine than this; for it grows much in the vineyards, and is very pernicious to them; wherefore they root it out: it likewise resembles a vine by its shrubby stalk:" Travels, p. 289. See also Michaelis, Questions aux Voyageurs Danois, No. 64.

3. —*inhabitants*] ישבי, in the plural number; three MSS, (two ancient); and so likewise LXX and Vulg.

6. *the horns shall spring up in it.*] A MS has בשמיר; the true reading seems to be בר שמיר: which is confirmed by LXX, Syr. Vulg.

7. *And he looked for judgment*—] The paronomasia, or play on the words, in this place, is very remarkable: *mispat, mispach; zedakah, zeakah*. There are many examples of it in the other Prophets; but Isaiah seems peculiarly fond of it: see chap. xiii. 6. xxiv. 17. xxvii. 7. xxxiii. 1. lvii, 6. lxi. 3. lxv. 11, 12. The Rabbins esteem it a great beauty: their term for it is צחות הלשון, "elegance of language."

Ibid. —*tyranny*] משפח, from שפח, servum fecit, Arab. Houbigant: שפחה, is serva, a handmaid, or female slave. מספח, eighteen MSS.

8. *You who lay field*—] Read תקריבו, in the second person; to answer to the verb following; so Vulg.

9. *To mine ear*—] The sentence in the Hebrew text seems to be imperfect in this place; as likewise in chap. xxii. 14. where the very same sense seems to be required

as here. See the note there: and compare 1 Sam. ix. 15. In this place LXX supply the word ηκυσθη, and Syr. אשתמע, *auditus est* JEHOVAH in auribus meis: *i. e.* נגלה, as in chap. xxii. 14.

9, 10. —*many houses*—] This has reference to what was said in the preceding verse: " In vain are ye so intent upon joining house to house, and field to field: your houses shall be left uninhabited, and your fields shall become desolate and barren; so that a vineyard of ten acres shall produce but one bath (not eight gallons) of wine, and the husbandman shall reap but a tenth part of the seed which he has sown."

11. —*to follow strong drink*] Theodoret and Chrysostom on this place, both Syrians, and unexceptionable witnesses in what belongs to their own country, inform us, that שכר, (σικερα in the Greek of both Testaments, rendered by us by the general term *strong drink*), meant properly palm-wine, or date-wine, which was and is still much in use in the eastern countries. Judea was famous for the abundance and excellence of its palm-trees; and consequently had plenty of this wine. " Fiunt (vina) et è pomis: —primumque è palmis, quo Parthi et Indi utuntur, et Oriens totus: maturarum modio in aquæ congiis tribus macerato expressoque:" Plin. xiv. 19. " Ab his *cariotæ* [palmæ] maxime celebrantur; et cibo quidem, sed et succo, uberrimæ. Ex quibus præcipua vina Orienti; iniqua capiti, unde pomo nomen:" Id. xiii. 9. Καρος. signifies *stupefaction:* and in Hebrew likewise, the wine has its name from its remarkable *inebriating* quality.

11, 12. *Wo unto them who rise early*—] There is a likeness between this and the following passage of the Prophet Amos, who probably wrote before Isaiah: if the latter is th copyer, he seems hardly to have equalled the elegance of the original:—

" Ye that put far away the evil day,
And affect the seat of violence;
Who lie upon beds of ivory,
And stretch yourselves upon your couches;
And eat the lambs from the flock,
And calves from the midst of the stall;
Who chant to the sound of the viol,
And like David invent for yourselves instruments of music;
Who quaff wine in large bowls,
And are anointed with the choicest ointments:
But are not grieved for the affliction of Joseph." Amos vi. 3-6.

13, 14. *And their nobles*—] These verses have likewise a reference to the two preceding. They, that indulged in feasting and drinking, shall perish with hunger and thirst; and Hades shall indulge his appetite as much as they had done, and devour them all. The image is strong, and expressive in the highest degree. Habakkuk uses the same image with great force: the ambitious and avaricious conqueror

"Enlargeth his appetite like Hades;
And he is like death, and will never be satisfied." Hab. ii. 5.

But, in Isaiah, Hades is introduced, to much greater advantage, in person; and placed before our eyes in the form of a ravenous monster, opening wide his unmeasurable jaws, and swallowing them all together.

17. —*without restraint*—] כדברם, secundum ductum eorum: *i. e.* suo ipsorum ductu; as their own will shall lead them.

Ibid. *And the kids*—] Heb. גרים, *strangers*. The LXX read, more agreeably to the design of the Prophet, כרים, ἄρνες, *the lambs:* גדים, *the kids*, Dr. DURELL; nearer to the present reading: and so Archbishop Secker. The meaning is, their luxurious habitations shall be so entirely destroyed, as to become a pasture for flocks.

18. —*as a long cable*] The LXX, Aquila, Sym. and Theod. for בחבלי read כחבלי, ὡς σχοινίῳ, or σχοινίοις: and the LXX, instead of שוא, read some other word signifying *long*; ὡς σχοινίῳ μακρῷ: and so likewise the Syriac, אריכא. Houbigant conjectures, that the word which the LXX had in their copies was שרוע, which is used, Lev. xxi. 18. xxii. 23. for something in an animal body superfluous, lengthened beyond its natural measure. And he explains it of sin added to sin, and one sin drawing on another, till the whole comes to an enormous length and magnitude; compared to the work of a rope-maker, still increasing and lengthening his rope, with the continued addition of new materials. "Eos propheta similes facit homini restiario, qui funem torquet, cannabe addita et contorta, eadem iterans, donec funem in longum duxerit, neque eum liceat protrahi longius." "An evil inclination (says Kimchi on the place, from the ancient Rabbins) is at the beginning like a fine hair-string, but at the finishing like a thick cart-rope." By a long progression n iniquity, and a continued accumulation of sin, men arrive at length to the highest degree of wickedness; bidding open

defiance to God, and scoffing at his threatened judgments, as it is finely expressed in the next verse. The Chaldee paraphrast explains it in the same manner, of wickedness increasing from small beginnings, till it arrives to a great magnitude.

23. —*the righteous*] צדיק, singular, LXX, Vulg. and two editions.

24. —*the tongue of fire*] "The flame, because it is in the shape of a tongue; and so it is called metaphorically:" Sal. b. Melec. The metaphor is so exceedingly obvious, as well as beautiful, that one may wonder that it has not been more frequently used. Virgil very elegantly intimates, rather than expresses, the image: Æn. ii. 682.

" Ecce levis summo de vertice visus Iuli
Fundere lumen apex; tractuque innoxia molli
Lambere flamma comas, et circum tempora *pasci*."

And more boldly of Ætna darting out flames from its top: Æn. iii. 574.

" Attollitque globos flammarum, et sidera *lambit*."

The disparted tongues, as it were, of fire, (Acts ii. 3.), which appeared at the descent of the Holy Spirit on the apostles, give the same idea; that is, of flames shooting diversely into pyramidal forms, or points, like tongues. It may be further observed, that the Prophet in this place has given the metaphor its full force, in applying it to the action of fire in eating up and devouring whatever comes in its way, like a ravenous animal, whose tongue is principally employed in taking in his food or prey; which image Moses has strongly exhibited in a most expressive comparison:—" And Moab said to the elders of Midian, Now shall this collection of people lick up all that are round about us, as the ox licketh up the grass of the field;" Numb. xxii. 4. See also 1 Kings xviii. 38.

25. —*and the mountains trembled*—] Probably referring to the great earthquakes in the days of Uzziah king of Judah, in, or not long before, the time of the Prophet himself: recorded as a remarkable era in the title of the Prophecies of Amos, chap. i. 1. and by Zechariah, chap. xiv. 5.

26. —*he will hist*—] "The metaphor is taken from the practice of those that keep bees; who draw them out of their hives into the fields, and lead them back again, συρισμασι, by a hiss, or a whistle:" Cyril, on the place; and to the same purpose, Theodoret, ibid. In chap. vii. 18. the metaphor is

more apparent, by being carried further; where the hostile armies are expressed by the fly and the bee :—

" JEHOVAH shall hist the fly,
That is in the utmost parts of Egypt;
And the bee, that is in the land of Assyria."

On which place see Deut. i. 44. Psal. cxviii. 12.; and God calls the locusts his great army, Joel, ii. 25. Exod. xxiii. 28. See Huet. Quæst. Alnet. ii. 12.

Ibid. —*with speed*—] This refers to the 19th verse. As the scoffers had challenged God to make speed and to hasten his work of vengeance; so now God assures them, that with speed and swiftly it shall come.

27. *Nor shall the girdle*—] The eastern people, wearing long and loose garments, were unfit for action or business of any kind, without girding their clothes about them: when their business was finished, they took off their girdles. A girdle therefore denotes strength and activity; and to unloose the girdle, is to deprive of strength, to render unfit for action. God promises to unloose the loins of kings before Cyrus, chap. xlv. 1. The girdle is so essential a part of a soldier's accoutrement, being the last that he puts on to make himself ready for action, that *to be girded*, ζωννυσθαι, with the Greeks, means to be completely armed, and ready for battle :—

Ατρειδης δ' εβοησεν, ιδε ζωννυσθαι ανωγεν
Αργειυς. Il. xi. 15.

Το δε ενδυναι τα οπλα εκαλυν οι παλαιοι ζωννυσθαι. Pausan. Bœot.

It is used in the same manner by the Hebrews :—" Let not him, that girdeth himself, boast, as he that unlooseth his girdle," 1 Kings xx. 11.; that is, "triumph not, before the war is finished."

28. *The hoofs of their horses shall be counted as adamant.*] The shoeing of horses with iron plates nailed to the hoof is quite a modern practice, and unknown to the ancients; as appears from the silence of the Greek and Roman writers, especially those that treat of horse-medicine; who could not have passed over a matter so obvious, and of such importance, that now the whole science takes its name from it, being called by us Farriery. The horse-shoes of leather and of iron, which are mentioned; the silver and the gold shoes with which Nero and Poppea shod their mules, used occasionally to preserve the hoofs of delicate cattle, or for vanity,

were of a very different kind; they inclosed the whole hoof as in a case, or as a shoe does a man's foot, and were bound or tied on. For this reason, the strength, firmness, and solidity of a horse's hoof was of much greater importance with them than with us; and was esteemed one of the first praises of a fine horse. Xenophon says, that a good horse's hoof is hard, hollow, and sounds upon the ground like a cymbal. Hence the χαλκοποδες ιπποι of Homer; and Virgil's "solido graviter sonat ungula cornu." And Xenophon gives directions for hardening the horse's hoofs, by making the pavement, on which he stands in the stable, with round-headed stones. For want of this artificial defence to the foot, which our horses have, Amos (vi. 12.) speaks of it as a thing as much impracticable to make horses run upon a hard rock, as to plough up the same rock with oxen:—

" Shall horses run upon a rock?
Shall one plough it up with oxen?"

These circumstances must be taken into consideration, in order to give us a full notion of the propriety and force of the image, by which the Prophet sets forth the strength and excellence of the Babylonish cavalry; which made a great part of the strength of the Assyrian army. Xenoph. Cyrop. lib. ii.

27, 28. *None among them*—] Kimchi has well illustrated this continued exaggeration, or hyperbole, as he rightly calls it, to the following effect:—" Through the greatness of their courage, they shall not be fatigued with their march; nor shall they stumble, though they march with the utmost speed: they shall not slumber by day, nor sleep by night; neither shall they ungird their armour, or put off their sandals, to take their rest: their arms shall be always in readiness, their arrows sharpened, and their bows bent: the hoofs of their horses are hard as a rock; they shall not fail, or need to be shod with iron: the wheels of their carriages shall move as rapidly as a whirlwind."

30. *And these shall look to the heaven upward, and down to the earth.*] ונבט לארץ. Και εμβλεψονται εις την γην. So the LXX, according to Vat. and Alex. copies; but the Compl. and Ald. editions have it more fully thus, Και εμβλεψονται εις τον ερανον ανω, και κατω: and the Arabic, from the LXX, as if it had stood thus, Και εμβλεψονται εις τον ερανον, και εις την γην κατω: both of which are plainly defective; the words εις την γην being wanted in the former, and the word ανω in the

latter. But an ancient Coptic version from the LXX, supposed to be of the 2d century, some fragments of which are preserved in the library of St. Germain des Prez at Paris, completes the sentence; for, according to this version, it stood thus in LXX, Καὶ ἐμβλεψονταί εἰς τὸν ϋρανον ανω, καὶ εἰς την γην κατω; and so it stands in LXX, MSS Pachom. and 1. D. 11. according to which they must have read in their Hebrew text in this manner: ונבט לשמים למעלה ולארץ למטה. This is probably the true reading; with which I have made the translation agree. Compare chap. viii. 22. where the same sense is expressed in regard to both particulars, which are here equally and highly proper, the looking upwards, as well as down to the earth; but the form of expression is varied. I believe the Hebrew text in that place to be right, though not so full as I suppose it was originally here; and that of the LXX there to be redundant, being as full as the Coptic version, and MSS Pachom. and 1. D. 11. represent it in this place, from which I suppose it has been interpolated.

Ibid. *the gloomy vapour*] Syr. and Vulg. seems to have read בערפלה. But Jarchi explains the present reading as signifying darkness; and so possibly Syr. and Vulg. may have understood it in the same manner.

CHAPTER VI.

As this vision seems to contain a solemn designation of Isaiah to the prophetical office, it is by most interpreters thought to be the first in order of his prophecies. But this perhaps may not be so: for Isaiah is said, in the general title of his Prophecies, to have prophesied in the time of Uzziah; whose acts first and last he wrote, 2 Chron. xxvi. 22. which was usually done by a contemporary Prophet: and the phrase, "in the year when Uzziah died," probably means after the death of Uzziah; as the same phrase, chap. xiv. 28. means after the death of Ahaz. Not that Isaiah's prophecies are placed in exact order of time: chapters ii. iii. iv. v. seem by internal marks to be antecedent to chap. i.; they suit the time of Uzziah, or the former part of Jotham's reign; whereas chap. i. can hardly be earlier than the last years of Jotham. See note on chap. i. 7. and ii. 1. This might be a new designation, to introduce more solemnly a general declaration of the whole course of God's dispensations in regard to his people, and the fates of the nation; which are even now still depending, and will not be fully accomplished till the final restoration of Israel.

In this vision the ideas are taken in general from royal majesty, as displayed by the Monarchs of the East; for the Prophet could not represent the ineffable presence of God by any other than sensible and earthly images. The particular scenery of it is taken from the temple. God is represented as seated on his throne above the ark in the most holy place, where the glory appeared above the cherubim, surrounded by his attendant ministers. This is called by God himself, "The place of his throne, and the place of the soles of his feet;" Ezek. xliii. 7. "A glorious throne, exalted of old, is the place of our sanctuary," saith the Prophet Jeremiah, chap. xvii. 12. The very posture of sitting is a mark of state and solemnity: "Sed et ipsum verbum *sedere* regni significat potestatem," saith Jerome, Comment. in Ephes. i. 20. See note on chap. lii. 2. St. John, who has taken many sublime images from the Prophets of the Old Testament, and in particular from Isaiah, hath exhibited the same scenery, drawn out into a greater number of particulars, Rev. chap. iv.

The veil, separating the most holy place from the holy, or outermost part of the temple, is here supposed to be taken away; for the Prophet, to whom the whole is exhibited, is manifestly placed by the altar of burnt-offering, at the entrance of the temple, (compare Ezek. xliii. 5, 6.), which was filled with the train of the robe, the spreading and overflowing of the divine glory. The Lord upon the throne, according to St. John, xii. 41. was Christ; and the vision related to his future kingdom; when the veil of separation was to be removed, and the whole earth was to be filled with the glory of God, revealed to all mankind: which is likewise implied in the hymn of the seraphim; the design of which is, saith Jerom on the place, 'ut mysterium Trinitatis in una Divinitate demonstrent; et nequaquam templum Judaicum, sicut prius, sed omnem terram illius gloria plenam esse testentur." It relates indeed primarily to the Prophet's own time, and the obduration of the Jews of that age, and their punishment by the Babylonish captivity; but extends in its full latitude to the age of Messiah, and the blindness of the Jews to the gospel; (see Matt. xiii. 14. John xii. 40. Acts xxviii. 26. Rom. xi. 8.); the desolation of their country by the Romans, and their being rejected by God: that nevertheless a holy seed, a remnant should be preserved, and that the nation should sprout out and flourish again from the old stock.

In the first verse, fifty-one MSS, and one edition ; in the 8th verse, forty-four MSS, and one edition ; and in the 11th verse, thirty-three MSS, and one edition, for אדני, "the Lord," read יהוה, " Jehovah ;" which is probably the true reading, (compare verse 6th) ; as in many other places, in which the superstition of the Jews has substituted אדני for יהוה.

2. *he covereth his feet.*] By the *feet* the Hebrews mean all the lower parts of the body. But the people of the East generally wearing long robes reaching to the ground, and covering the lower parts of the body down to the feet, it may hence have been thought want of respect and decency to appear in public, and on solemn occasions, with even the feet themselves uncovered. Kempfer, speaking of the king of Persia giving audience, says ; "Rex in medio supremi atrii cruribus more patrio inflexis sedebat : corpus tunica investiebat flava, ad suras cum staret protensa ; discumbentis vero *pedes discalceatos pro urbanitate patria operiens:*" Amœn. Exot. p. 227. Sir John Chardin's MS note on this place of Isaiah is as follows : " Grande marque de respect en Orient de se cacher les pieds, quand on est assis, et de baisser le visage. Quand le soverain se. monstre en Chine et à Japon, chacun se jette le visage contre terre, et il n'est pas permis de regarder le roi."

3. *Holy, holy, holy*—] This hymn, performed by the seraphim, divided into two choirs, the one singing responsively to the other, which Gregory Nazian. Carm. 18. very elegantly calls Συμφωνον, αντιφωνον, αἰγελων ϛασιν, is formed upon the practice of alternate singing, which prevailed in the Jewish church from the time of Moses, whose ode at the Red Sea was thus performed, (see Exod. xv. 20, 21.), to that of Ezra, under whom the priests and Levites sung alternately,

"O praise Jehovah, for he is gracious;
For his mercy endureth for ever."

Ezra iii. 11. See De S. Poes. Hebr. Præl. 'xix. at the beginning.

5. *I am struck dumb.*] נדמרי, twenty-eight MSS (five ancient) and three editions. I understand it as from דום, or דמם, *silere*; and so it is rendered by Syr. Vulg. Sym. and

by some of the Jewish interpreters, apud. Sal. b. Melec. The rendering of the Syriac is, תויר אני, stupens, attonitus sum. He immediately gives the reason why he was struck dumb; because he was a man of polluted lips, and dwelt among a people of polluted lips; and was unworthy either to join the seraphim in singing praises to God, or to be the messenger of God to his people. Compare Exod. iv. 10. vi. 12. Jer. i. 6.

6. *from off the altar.*] That is, from the altar of burnt-offering, before the door of the temple; on which the fire that came down at first from heaven, Lev. ix. 24. 2 Chron. vii. 1. was perpetually kept burning: it was never to be extinguished, Lev. vi. 12, 13.

9. Thirteen MSS have ראה, in the regular form.

10. *Make gross—*] The Prophet speaks of the event, the fact as it would actually happen; not of God's purpose and act by his ministry. The Prophets are in other places said to perform the thing which they only foretell:—

"Lo! I have given thee a charge this day,
Over the nations, and over the kingdoms;
To pluck up, and to pull down;
To destroy, and to demolish;
To build, and to plant." Jer. i. 10.

And Ezekiel says, "when I came to destroy the city;" that is, as it is rendered in the margin of our version, "when I came to prophesy, that the city should be destroyed;" chap. xliii. 3. To hear, and not understand; to see, and not perceive; is a common saying in many languages. Demosthenes uses it, and expressly calls it a proverb: ὥστε τὸ τῆς παροιμίας ὁρῶντας μὴ ὁρᾷν, καὶ ἀκούοντας μὴ ἀκούειν: Contra Aristogit. i. sub fin. The Prophet, by the bold figure in the sentiment above-mentioned, and the elegant form and construction of the sentence, has raised it from a common proverb into a beautiful *mashal*; and given it the sublime air of poetry.

Ibid. —*close up*] הׁשע: this word Sal. b. Melec. explains to this sense, in which it is hardly used elsewhere, on the authority of Onkelos. He says, it means closing up the eyes, so that one cannot see; that the root is שׁע, by which word the Targum has rendered the word טח, Lev. xiv. 42. וטח את בית, "and shall plaster the house." And the word טח is used in the same sense, Isa. xliv. 18. So that it signifies to close up the eyes by some matter spread upon the lids. Mr. Harmer very ingeniously applies to this passage a practice of sealing up the eyes as a ceremony, or as a kind of punishment, used in the East, from which the image may possibly be taken. Observations, ii. 278.

Ibid. —*with their hearts.*] ובלבבו, fifteen MSS, and two editions.

Ibid. —*and I should heal.*] וארפא, LXX, Vulg. So likewise Matt. xiii. 14. John xii. 40. Acts xxviii. 27.

11. —*be left.*] For תשאה, LXX and Vulg. read תשאר.

13. —*a tenth part*] This passage, though somewhat obscure, and variously explained by various interpreters, yet, I think, has been made so clear by the accomplishment of the prophecy, that there remains little room to doubt of the sense of it. When Nebuchadnezzar had carried away the greater and better part of the people into captivity, there was yet a tenth remaining in the land, the poorer sort, left to be vine-dressers and husbandmen, under Gedaliah, 2 Kings xxv. 12. 22.; and the dispersed Jews gathered themselves together, and returned to him, Jer. xl. 12.: yet even these, fleeing into Egypt after the death of Gedaliah, contrary to the warning of God given by the Prophet Jeremiah, miserably perished there. Again, in the subsequent and more remarkable completion of the prophecy, in the destruction of Jerusalem and the dissolution of the commonwealth by the Romans, when the Jews, after the loss of above a million of men, had increased from the scanty residue that was left of them, and had become very numerous again in their country; Hadrian, provoked by their rebellious behaviour, slew above half a million more of them, and a second time almost extirpated the nation. Yet after these signal and almost universal destructions of that nation, and after so many other repeated exterminations and massacres of them, in different times and on various occasions since, we yet see, with astonishment, that the stock still remains, from which God, according to his promise, frequently given by his Prophets, will cause his people to shoot forth again, and to flourish.

For בם, above seventy MSS (eleven ancient) read בה; and so LXX.

CHAPTER VII.

The confederacy of Retsin king of Syria, and Pekah king of Israel, against the kingdom of Judah, was formed in the time of Jotham; and perhaps the effects of it were felt in the latter part of his reign: see 2 Kings xv. 37. and note on chap. i. 7—9. However, in the very beginning of the reign of Ahaz, they jointly invaded Judah with a powerful army, and threatened to destroy, or to dethrone, the house of David. The king and royal family being in the utmost consternation on receiving advices of their designs, Isaiah is sent to them to support and comfort them in their present distress, by assuring them, that God would make good his promises to David and his house. This makes the subject of this, and the following, and the beginning of the ninth chapters; in which there are many and great difficulties.

Chapter vii. begins with an historical account of the occasion of this prophecy; and then follows, ver. 4—16. a prediction of the ill success of the designs of the Israelites and Syrians against Judah; and, from thence to the end of the chapter, a denunciation of the calamities to be brought upon the king and people of Judah by the Assyrians, whom they had now hired to assist them. Chapter viii. has a pretty close connexion with the foregoing: it contains a confirmation of the prophecy before given of the approaching destruction of the kingdoms of Israel and Syria by the Assyrians; of the denunciation of the invasion of Judah by the same Assyrians: ver. 9, 10. give a repeated general assurance, that all the designs of the enemies of God's people shall be in the end disappointed, and brought to nought: ver. 11, &c. admonitions and threatenings, (I do not attempt a more particular explanation of this very difficult part), concluding with an illustrious prophecy (chap. ix. 1—6.) of the manifestation of Messiah; the transcendent dignity of his character; and the universality and eternal duration of his kingdom.

4. The Syriac omits וארם; Vulg. reads מלך ארם: one or the other seems to be the true reading. I prefer the former; or, instead of וארם ובן, read ופקח בן, MS.

8, 9. Though the head of Syria be Damascus,
    And the head of Damascus, Retsin;
    Yet within threescore and five years
    Ephraim shall be broken, that he be no more a people:
    And the head of Ephraim be Samaria;
    And the head of Samaria, Remaliah's son.]

"Here are six lines, or three distichs, the order of which seems to have been disturbed by a transposition, occasioned by three of the lines beginning with the same word וראש;

which three lines ought not to have been separated by any other line intervening; but a copyist, having written the first of them, and casting his eye on the third, might easily proceed to write, after the first line beginning with ורֹאשׁ, that which ought to have followed the third line beginning with ורֹאשׁ. Then, finding his mistake, to preserve the beauty of his copy, added at the end the distich which should have been in the middle; making that the second distich which ought to have been the third. For the order as it now stands is preposterous: the destruction of Ephraim is denounced, and then their grandeur is set forth; whereas naturally the representation of the grandeur of Ephraim should precede that of their destruction. And the destruction of Ephraim has no coherence with the grandeur of Syria, simply as such, which it now follows; but it naturally and properly follows the grandeur of Ephraim, joined to that of Syria their ally.

"The arrangement then of the whole sentence seems originally to have been thus:

" Though the head of Syria be Damascus;
And the head of Damascus, Retsin:
And the head of Ephraim be Samaria;
And the head of Samaria, Remaliah's son:
Yet within threescore and five years
Ephraim shall be broken, that he be no more a people."

Dr. Jubb.

8. —*threescore and five years*] It was sixty-five years from the beginning of the reign of Ahaz, when this prophecy was delivered, to the total depopulation of the kingdom of Israel by Esarhaddon, who carried away the remains of the ten tribes which had been left by Tiglath Pileser and Shalmaneser, and who planted the country with new inhabitants. That the country was not wholly stripped of its inhabitants by Shalmaneser, appears from many passages of the history of Josiah; where Israelites are mentioned as still remaining there, 2 Chron. xxxiv. 6, 7. 33. and xxxv. 18. 2 Kings xxiii. 19, 20. This seems to be the best explanation of the chronological difficulty in this place, which has much embarrassed the commentators: see Usserii Annal. V. T. ad an. 3327; and Sir I. Newton, Chronol. p. 283.

"That the last deportation of Israel by Esarhaddon was in the sixty-fifth year after the second of Ahaz, is probable, for the following reasons: The Jews, in Seder Olam Rabba, and the Talmudists, in D. Kimchi on Ezek. iv. say, that Manasseh king of Judah was carried to Babylon by the king of Assyria's captains, 2 Chron. xxxiii. 11. in the twenty-second year of his reign; that is, before Christ 676, according to Dr. Blair's tables. And they are probably right in this. It could not be much earlier; as the king of Assyria was not king of Babylon till 680; ibid. As Esarhaddon was then in the neighbourhood of Samaria, it is highly probable that he did then carry away the last remains of Israel; and brought those strangers thither, who mention him as their founder, Ezra iv. 2. But this year is just the sixty-fifth year from the second of Ahaz, which was 740 before Christ. Now the carrying away of the last remains of Israel, (who, till then, though their kingdom was destroyed forty-five years before, and though small in number, yet might keep up some form of being a people, by living according to their own laws), entirely put an end to the people of Israel, as a people separate from all others: for from this time they never returned to their own country in a body, but were confounded with the people of Judah in the captivity; and the whole people, the ten tribes included, were called Jews." Dr. JUBB.

9. *If ye believe not*—] "This clause is very much illustrated, by considering the captivity of Manasseh as happening at the same time with this predicted final ruin of Ephraim as a people. The near connexion of the two facts makes the prediction of the one naturally to cohere with the prediction of the other. And the words are well suited to this event in the history of the people of Judah. "If ye believe not, ye shall not be established;" that is, unless ye believe this prophecy of the destruction of Israel, ye Jews also, as well as the people of Israel, shall not remain established as a kingdom and people; ye also shall be visited with punishment at the same time: As our Saviour told the Jews in his time, "unless ye repent, ye shall all likewise perish;" intimating their destruction by the Romans; to which also, as well as to the captivity of Manasseh, and to the Babylonish captivity, the views of the Prophet might here extend. The close connexion of this threat to the Jews, with the prophecy of the destruction of Israel, is another strong proof, that the order of the preceding lines above proposed is right." Dr. JUBB.

Ibid. *If ye believe not in me*—] The exhortation of Jehoshaphat to his people, when God had promised to them, by the Prophet Jahaziel, victory over the Moabites and Ammonites, is very like this, both in sense and expression, and seems to be delivered in verse:

" Hear me, O Judah ; and ye inhabitants of Jerusalem!
Believe in JEHOVAH your God, and ye shall be established:
Believe his prophets, and ye shall prosper." 2 Chron xx. 20.

Where both the sense and construction render very probable a conjecture of Archbishop Secker on this place ; that instead of כי we should read בי. "If ye will not believe *in me*, ye shall not be established." So likewise Dr. Durell. The Chaldee has, "If ye will not believe in the words of the Prophet," which seems to be a paraphrase of the reading here proposed. In favour of which it may be further observed, that in one MS כי is upon a rasure; and another for the last לא reads ולא; which would properly follow כי, but could not follow בי.

11. *Go deep to the grave*—] So Aquila, Sym. Theodot. Vulg.

14. *JEHOVAH*] For אדני, twenty-five MSS (nine ancient) read יהוה. And so ver. 20. eighteen MSS.

14—16. *When he shall know*—] " Though so much has been written on this important passage, there is an obscurity and inconsequence which still attends it, in the general run of all the interpretations given to it by the most learned. And this obscure incoherence is given to it by the false rendering of a Hebrew particle, viz. ל in לרעתו. This has been generally rendered, either "that he may know," or "till he know." It is capable of either version, without doubt. But either of these versions makes ver. 15. incoherent and inconsistent with ver. 16. For ver. 16. plainly means to give a reason for the assertion in ver. 15.; because it is subjoined to it by the particle כי, *for*. But it is no reason why a child should eat butter and honey *till* he was at an age to distinguish, that *before* that time the land of his nativity should be free from its enemies. This latter supposition indeed implies what is inconsistent with the preceding assertion : For it implies, that in part of that time of the infancy spoken of, the land should not be free from enemies, and consequently these species of delicate food could not be attainable, as they are in times of peace. The other version, " that he may know," has no meaning at all : For what sense is there in asserting, that a child shall eat butter and honey, *that* he may know to refuse evil and choose good? Is there any such effect in this food? Surely no. Besides, the child is thus represented to eat those things, which only a state of peace produces, during its whole infancy, inconsistently with ver. 16. which promises a relief from enemies only before the *end* of this infancy; implying plainly, that part of it would be passed in distressful times of war and siege; which was the state of things when the prophecy was delivered.

" But all these objections are cut off, and a clear coherent sense is given to this passage, by giving another sense to the particle ל; which never occurred to me till I saw it in Harmer's Observat. vol. i. p. 299. See how coherent the words of the Prophet run, with how natural a connexion one clause follows another, by properly rendering this one particle :—" Behold this virgin shall conceive and bear a son, and thou shalt call his name Immanuel: Butter and honey shall he eat, *when* he shall know to refuse evil, and choose good. For, before this child shall know to refuse evil, and choose good, the land shall be desolate, by whose two kings thou art distressed." Thus ver. 16. subjoins a plain reason why the child should eat butter and honey, the food of plentiful times, *when* he came to a distinguishing age; viz. because before that time the country of the two kings, who now distressed Judea, should be desolated; and so Judea should recover that plenty which attends peace. That this rendering, which gives perspicuity and rational connexion to the passage, is according to the use of the Hebrew particle is certain. Thus, לפנות בקר, " *at* the appearing of morning, or, *when* morning appeared;" Exod. xiv. 27. לעת האכל, "*at* meal-time, or, *when* it was time to eat;" Ruth. ii. 14. In the same manner, לדעתו, "*at* his knowing, that is, *when* he knows."

" Harmer (Ibid.)) has clearly shewn, that these articles of food are delicacies in the East; and as such denote a state of plenty. See also Josh. v. 6. They therefore naturally express the plenty of the country, as a mark of peace restored to it. Indeed, ver. 22. it expresses a plenty arising from the thinness of the people; but that it signifies, ver. 15. a plenty arising from deliverance from war then present, is evident; because otherwise there is no expression of this deliverance. And that a deliverance was intended to be here expressed is plain, from calling the child, which should be born, Immanuel, God with us. It is plain, also, because it is before given to the Prophet in charge to make a declaration of the deliverance, ver. 3—7.; and it is there made; and this prophecy must undoubtedly be conformable to that in this matter." Dr. JUBB.

The circumstance of the child's eating butter and honey is explained by Jarchi as denoting a state of plenty: " Butyrum et mel comedet infans iste, quoniam terra nostra plena erit omnis boni : " Comment. in locum. The infant Jupiter, says Callimachus, was tenderly nursed with goat's milk and honey: Hymn. in Jov. 48. Homer, of the orphan daughters of Pandareus,

" Κομισσε δε δι' Αφροδιτη
Τυρω, και μελιτι γλυκερω, και ηδει οινω." Odyss. xx. 68.

" Venus in tender delicacy rears
With honey, milk, and wine, their infant years." Pope.

Τρυφης εςιν ενδειξις· " This is a description of delicate food," says Eustathius on the place.

Agreeably to the observations communicated by the learned person above-mentioned, which perfectly well explain the historical sense of this much-disputed passage, not excluding a higher secondary sense, the obvious and literal meaning of the prophecy is this : ' That within the time that a young woman, now a virgin, should conceive and bring forth a child, and that child should arrive at such an age as to distinguish between good and evil, that is, within a few years, (compare chap. viii. 4), the enemies of Judah should be destroyed.' But the prophecy is introduced in so solemn a manner; the sign is so marked, as a sign selected and given by God himself, after Ahaz had rejected the offer of any sign of his own choosing out of the whole compass of nature; the terms of the prophecy are so peculiar, and the name of the child so expressive, containing in them much more than the circumstances of the birth of a common child required, or even admitted ; that we may easily suppose, that, in minds prepared by the general expectation of a great Deliverer to spring from the house of David, they raised hopes far beyond what the present occasion suggested ; especially when it was found, that in the subsequent prophecy, delivered immediately afterward, this child, called Immanuel, is treated as the Lord and Prince of the land of Judah. Who could this be, other than the heir of the throne of David? under which character a great and even a divine person had been promised. No one of that age answered to this character, except Hezekiah; but he was certainly born nine or ten years before the delivery of this prophecy. That this was so understood at that time, is collected, I think, with great probability, from a passage of Micah, a Prophet contemporary with Isaiah, but who began to prophesy after him; and who, as I have already observed, imitated him, and sometimes used his expressions. Micah, having delivered that remarkable prophecy, which determines the place of the birth of Messiah, "the ruler of God's people, whose goings forth have been of old, from everlasting;" that it should be Bethlehem Ephrata; adds immediately, that nevertheless, in the mean time, God would deliver his people into the hands of their enemies: "he will give them up, till she, who is to bear a child, shall bring forth;" Micah. v. 3. This obviously and plainly refers to some known prophecy concerning a woman to bring forth a child; and seems much more properly applicable to this passage of Isaiah, than to any others of the same Prophet, to which some interpreters have applied it. St. Matthew, therefore, in applying this prophecy to the birth of Christ, does it not merely in the way of accommodating the words of the Prophet to a suitable case not in the Prophet's view; but takes it in its strictest, clearest, and most important sense, and applies it according to the original design and principal intention of the Prophet.

17. But *JEHOVAH will bring*] Houbigant reads ויבא, from LXX; αλλα επαξει ὁ Θεος: to mark the transition to a new subject.

Ibid. *Even the king of Assyria—*] Houbigant supposes these words to have been a marginal gloss, brought into the text by mistake; and so likewise Archbp. Secker. Besides their having no force or effect here, they do not join well in construction with the words preceding; as may be seen by the strange manner in which the ancient interpreters have taken them; and they very inelegantly forestall the mention of the king of Assyria, which comes in with great propriety in the 20th verse. I have therefore taken the liberty of omitting them in the translation.

18. —*hist the fly*] See note on chap. v. 26.

Ibid. *Egypt and Assyria*] Senacherib, Esarhaddon, Pharao Necho, and Nebuchadnezzar, who one after another desolated Judea.

19. —*caverns*] So LXX, Syr. Vulg. whence Houbigant supposes the true reading to be הנחללים.

20. —*the river*] That is, the Euphrates; הנוזר, so read the LXX, and two MSS.

Ibid. *JEHOVAH shall shave by the hired rasor*—] To shave with the hired rasor the head, the feet, and the beard, is an expression highly parabolical; to denote the utter devastation of the country from one end to the other, and the plundering of the people, from the highest to the lowest, by the Assyrians; whom God employed as his instrument to punish the Jews. Ahaz himself, in the first place, hired the king of Assyria to come to help him against the Syrians, by a present made to him of all the treasures of the temple, as well as his own: And God himself considered the great nations, whom he thus employed, as his mercenaries, and paid them their wages: thus he paid Nebuchadnezzar for his services against Tyre, by the conquest of Egypt; Ezek. xxix. 18—20. The hairs of the head are those of the highest order in the state; those of the feet, or the lower parts, are the common people; the beard is the king, the highpriest, the very supreme in dignity and majesty. The eastern people have always held the beard in the highest veneration, and have been extremely jealous of its honour. To pluck a man's beard is an instance of the greatest indignity that can be offered. See Isa. l. 6. The king of the Ammonites, to shew the utmost contempt of David, "cut off half the beards of his servants; and the men were greatly ashamed: and David bade them tarry at Jericho till their beards were grown;" 2 Sam. x. 4, 5. Niebuhr, Arabie, p. 275. gives a modern instance of the very same kind of insult. "The Turks," says Thevenot, "greatly esteem a man who has a fine beard: it is a very great affront to take a man by his beard, unless it be to kiss it: they swear by the beard;" Voyages, i. p. 57. D'Arvieux gives a remarkable instance of an Arab, who, having received a wound in his jaw, chose to hazard his life, rather than suffer his surgeon to take off his beard. Mémoires, tom. iii. p. 214. See also Niebuhr, Arabie, p. 61.

The remaining verses of this chapter, 21—25. contain an elegant and very expressive description of a country depopulated, and left to run wild, from its adjuncts and circumstances: the vineyards and corn-fields, before well cultivated, now overrun with briers and thorns; much grass, so that the few cattle that are left, a young cow and two sheep, have their full range, and abundant pasture, so as to yield milk in plenty to the scanty family of the owner; the thinly scattered people, living not on corn, wine and oil, the produce of cultivation, but on milk and honey, the gifts of nature; and the whole land given up to the wild beasts; so that the miserable inhabitants are forced to go out armed with bows and arrows, either to defend themselves against the wild beasts, or to supply themselves with necessary food by hunting.

CHAPTER VIII.

The prophecy in the foregoing chapter relates directly to the kingdom of Judah only: the first part of it promises them deliverance from the united invasion of the Israelites and Syrians; the latter part, from ver. 17. denounces the desolation to be brought upon the kingdom of Judah by the Assyrians. The 6th, 7th, and 8th verses of this chapter, seem to take in both the kingdoms of Israel and Judah. "This people, that refuseth the waters of Siloah," may be meant of both: the Israelites despised the kingdom of Judah, which they had deserted, and now attempted to des roy ; the people of Judah, from a consideration of their own weakness, and a distrust of God's promises, being reduced to despair, applied to the Assyrians for assistance against the two confederate kings. But how could it be said of Judah, that they rejoiced in Retsin and the son of Remaliah, the enemies confederated against them? If some of the people were inclined to revolt to the enemy, which however does not clearly appear from any part of the history or the prophecy, yet there was nothing like a tendency to a general defection. This, therefore, must be understood of Israel. The Prophet denounces the Assyrian invasion, which should overwhelm the whole kingdom of Israel under Tiglath Pileser and Shalmaneser: and the subsequent invasion of Judah by the same power under Senacherib, which would bring them into the most imminent danger, like a flood reaching to the neck, in which a man can but just keep his head above water. The two next verses, 9, 10. are addressed by the Prophet, as a subject of the kingdom of Judah, to the Israelites and Syrians; and perhaps to all the enemies of God's people; assuring them, that their attempts against that kingdom shall be fruitless; for that the promised Immanuel, to whom he alludes by using his name to express the signification of it, *for God is with us,* shall be the defence of the house of David, and deliver the kingdom of Judah out of their hands. He then proceeds to warn the people of Judah against idolatry, divination, and the like forbidden practices; to which they were much inclined, and which would soon bring down God's judgments upon Israel. The prophecy concludes, at the 6th verse of chap. ix. with promises of blessings in future times, by the coming of the great Deliverer already pointed out by the name of Immanuel, whose person and character is set forth in terms the most ample and magnificent.

And here it may be observed, that it is almost the constant practice of the Prophet to connect in like manner deliverances temporal with spiritual. Thus the xith chapter, setting forth the kingdom of Messiah, is closely connected with the xth, which foretells the destruction of Senacherib. So likewise the destruction of nations, enemies to God, in the xxxivth chapter, introduces the flourishing state of the kingdom of Christ in the xxxvth. And thus the chapters, from xl. to xlix. inclusive, plainly relating to the deliverance from the captivity of Babylon, do in some parts as plainly relate to the great deliverance by Christ.

1. *Take unto thee a large mirror*—] The word גליון is not regularly formed from גלל, *to roll,* but from גלה; as פדיון from פדה, כליון from כלה, נקיון from נקה, עליון from עלה, &c. the י supplying the place of the radical ה. גלה signifies to shew, to reveal; properly, as Schroederus says, (De Vestitu Mulier. Hebr. p. 294.), to render clear and bright by rubbing, to polish: גליון, therefore, according to this derivation, is not a roll, or volume, but may very well signify a polished tablet of metal, such as anciently was used for a mirror: the Chaldee paraphrast renders it by לוח, a tablet; and the same word, though somewhat differently pointed, the Chaldee paraphrast and the Rabbins render a mirror, chap. iii. 23. The mirrors of the Israelitish women were made of brass finely polished, Exod. xxxviii. 8.; from which place it likewise appears, that what they used were little hand-mirrors, which they carried with them, even when they assembled at the door of the tabernacle. I have a metalline mirror, found in Herculaneum, which is not above three inches square. The prophet is commanded to take a

mirror, or brazen polished tablet, not like these little hand-mirrors, but a large one; large enough for him to engrave upon it, in deep and lasting characters, חרט אנוש, with a workman's graving tool, the prophecy which he was to deliver. חרט in this place certainly signifies an instrument to write, or to engrave with; but חריט, the same word, only differing a little in the form, means something belonging to a lady's dress, chap. iii. 22. (where however five MSS leave out the י, whereby only it differs from the word in this place); either a crisping-pin, which might be not unlike a graving tool, as some will have it; or a purse, as others infer from 2 Kings v. 23. It may therefore be called here חרט אנוש, a workman's instrument, to distinguish it from הרט אשה, an instrument of the same name used by the women. In this manner he was to record the prophecy of the destruction of Damascus and Samaria by the Assyrians: the subject and sum of which prophecy is here expressed with great brevity in four words, *maher shalal, hash baz;* i. e. "to hasten the spoil, to take quickly the prey:" which are afterwards applied as the name of the Prophet's son, who was made a sign of the speedy completion of it: Maher-shalal Hash-baz; Haste-to-the-spoil Quick-to-the-prey. And that it might be done with the greater solemnity, and to preclude all doubt of the real delivery of the prophecy before the event, he calls witnesses to attest the recording of it.

4. *For before the child—*] The prophecy was accordingly accomplished within three years; when Tiglath Pileser, king of Assyria, went up against Damascus, and took it, and carried the people of it captive to Kir, and slew Retsin; and also took the Reubenites, and the Gadites, and the half tribe of Manasseh, and carried them captive to Assyria; 2 Kings xvi. 9. xv. 29. 1 Chron. v. 26.

6, 7. *Because this people have rejected—*] The gentle waters of Siloah, a small fountain and brook just without Jerusalem, which supplied a pool within the city for the use of the inhabitants, is an apt emblem of the state of the kingdom and house of David, much reduced in its apparent strength, yet supported by the blessing of God: and is finely contrasted with the waters of the Euphrates, great, rapid, and impetuous; the image of the Babylonian empire, which God threatens to bring down, like a mighty flood, upon all these apostates of both kingdoms, as a punishment for their manifold iniquities, and their contemptuous disregard of his promises. The brook and the river are put for the kingdoms to which they belong, and the different states of which respectively they most aptly represent. Juvenal, inveighing against the corruption of Rome by the importation of Asiatic manners, says, with great elegance, that the Orontes has been long discharging itself into the Tiber:—

"Jampridem Syrus in Tiberim defluxit Orontes."

And Virgil, to express the submission of some of the eastern countries to the Roman arms, says, that the waters of Euphrates now flowed more humbly and gently:—"Euphrates ibat jam mollior undis:" Æn. viii. 726. But the happy contrast between the brook and the river gives a peculiar beauty to this passage of the Prophet, with which the simple figure in the Roman poets, however beautiful, yet uncontrasted, cannot contend.

8. *Even to the neck shall he reach*] He compares Jerusalem (says Kimchi) to the head in the human body: as when the waters come up to a man's neck, he is very near drowning; for a little increase of them would go over his head: so the king of Assyria coming up to Jerusalem was like a flood reaching to the neck; the whole country was overflowed, and the capital was in imminent danger. Accordingly the Chaldee renders reaching to the neck, by reaching to Jerusalem.

9. *Know ye this*] God by his Prophet plainly declares to the confederate adversaries of Judah, and bids them regard and attend to his declaration, that all their efforts shall be in vain. The present reading רעו, is subject to many difficulties: I follow that of the LXX, דעו, γνωτε. Archbishop Secker approves this reading. דעו, *know ye this*, is parallel and synonymous to האזינו, *give ear to it*, in the next line. The LXX have likewise very well paraphrased the conclusion of this verse: "When ye have strengthened yourselves, ye shall be broken; and though ye again strengthen yourselves, again shall ye be broken:" taking חתו as meaning the same with נשברו.

11. *As taking me by the hand*] Eleven MSS (two ancient) read כחזקת: and so Sym. Syr. Vulg.

12. *Say ye not, It is holy—*] קשר. Both the reading and the sense of this word are doubtful. The LXX manifestly read קשה; for they render it by σκληρον, *hard*. Syr. and Chald. render it מרדא and מרוד, *rebellion*. How they came by this sense of the word, or what they read in their

copies, is not so clear. But the worst of it is, that neither of these readings or renderings, gives any clear sense in this place: For why should God forbid his faithful servants to say, with the unbelieving Jews, it is *hard;* or, there is a *rebellion;* or, as our translators render it, a *confederacy*? And how can this be called, "walking in the way of this people," ver. 11. which usually means, following their example; joining with them in religious worship? Or what confederacy do they mean? The union of the kingdoms of Syria and Israel against Judah? That was properly a league between two independent states; not an unlawful conspiracy of one part against another in the same state; for this is the meaning of the word קשר. For want of any satisfactory interpretation of this place, that I can meet with, I adopt a conjecture of Archbishop Secker, which he proposes with great diffidence; and even seems immediately to give up, as being destitute of any authority to support it. I will give it in his own words: "Videri potest ex cap. v. 16. et hujus cap. 13, 14. 19. legendum קדש, vel קדוש, eadem sententia, qua אלחינו, Hos. xiv. 3. Sed nihil necesse est. Vide enim Jer. xi. 9. Ezek. xxii. 25. Optimè tamen sic responderent huic versiculo versiculi 13, 14." The passages of Jeremiah and Ezekiel, above referred to, seem to me not at all to clear up the sense of the word קשר in this place. But the context greatly favours the conjecture here given, and makes it highly probable: "Walk not in the way of this people; call not their idols holy; nor fear ye the object of their fear: (that is, the σεβασματα, or gods of the idolaters; for so *fear* here signifies, to wit, the thing feared; so God is called "the fear of Isaac," Gen. xxxi. 42. 53.): but look up to JEHOVAH as your Holy One; and let Him be your fear, and let Him be your dread; and He shall be a holy refuge unto you." Here there is a harmony and consistency running through the whole sentence; and the latter part naturally arises out of the former, and answers to it. Observe, that the difference between קשר and קדש is chiefly in the transposition of the two last letters; for the letters ר and ד are hardly distinguishable in some copies, printed as well as MS; so that the mistake, in respect of the letters themselves, is a very easy and a very common one.

14. *And He shall be unto you a sanctuary.*] The word לכם, *unto you,* absolutely necessary, as I conceive, to the sense, is lost in this place: it is preserved by the Vulgate;

" et erit *vobis* in sanctificationem : " the LXX have it in the singular number ; εςαι σοι εις αγιασμον. Or else, instead of מקרש, *a sanctuary*, we must read מוקש, *a snare*, which would then be repeated, without any propriety or elegance, at the end of the verse. The Chaldee reads instead of it משפט, *judgment ;* for he renders it by פורען ; which word frequently answers to משפט in his paraphrase. A MS has (instead of מקרש ולאבן) להם לאבן ; which clears the sense and construction. But the reading of the Vulgate is, I think, the best remedy to this difficulty ; and is in some degree authorized by להם, the reading of the MS above mentioned.

16. *among my disciples*] בלמרי. " The LXX render it, τȣ μη μαθειν. Bishop Chandler, Defence of Christianity, p. 308. " thinks they read מלמד, *that it be not understood ;* and approves this reading : " Archbishop SECKER.

18. *God of Hosts*] A MS reads אלהי צבאות.

19. *Should they seek—*] After ידרש, the LXX, repeating the word, read הידרש : Ουκ εθνος προς θεον αυτȣ εκζητησȣσι; τι εκζητησȣσι περι των ζωντων τȣς νεκρȣς ; and this repetition of the verb seems necessary to the sense ; and, as Procopius on the place observes, it strongly expresses the Prophet's indignation at their folly.

20. *Unto the command, and unto the testimony—*] " Is not תעורה here the attested prophecy, ver. 1—4.? and perhaps תורה the command, ver. 11—15.? for it means sometimes a particular, and even a human command ; see Prov. vi. 20. and vii. 2, 3. where it is ordered to be hid, that is, secretly kept : " Archbishop SECKER. So Deschamps in his translation, or rather paraphrase, understands it : " Tenons-nous à l'instrument authentique, mis en dépôt par ordre du Seigneur." If this be right, the 16th verse must be understood in the same manner.

Ibid. *In which there is no obscurity*] שחר, as an adjective, frequently signifies *dark, obscure ;* and the noun שחר signifies *darkness, gloominess,* Joel ii. 2. if we may judge by the context :

" A day of darkness and obscurity ;
Of cloud, and of thick vapour ;
As the gloom spread upon the mountains :
A people mighty and numerous ; "

Where the *gloom,* שחר, seems to be the same with the cloud and thick vapour, mentioned in the line preceding : see Lam. iv. 8. Job xxx. 30. See this meaning of the word

שחר well supported in Christ. Muller Satura Observationum Philolog. p. 53. Ludg. Bat. 1752. The *morning* seems to be an idea wholly incongruous in the passage of Joel: And in this of Isaiah, the words, " in which there is no morning," (for so it ought to be rendered, if שחר in this place signifies, according to its usual sense, *morning*), seem to give no meaning at all. " It is because there is no light in them," says our translation: If there be any sense in these words, it is not the sense of the original; which cannot justly be so translated. Qui n'a rien d'obscur; Deschamps. The reading of LXX and Syr. שחר, *gift*, affords not any assistance towards the clearing up of this difficult place.

21. —*distressed*—] Instead of נקשה, *distressed*, the Vulg. Chald. and Sym. manifestly read נכשל, *stumbling, tottering through weakness, ready to fall;* a sense which suits very well with the place.

22. *And he shall cast his eyes upward*—] The learned professor Michaelis, treating of this place, (Not. in De S. Poes. Hebr. Præl. ix.), refers to a passage in the Koran, which is similar to it. As it is a very celebrated passage, and on many accounts remarkable, I shall give it here at large, with the same author's further remarks upon it in another place of his writings. It must be noted here, that the learned professor renders נבט in this and the parallel place, chap. v. 30. which I translate *he looketh*, by *it thundereth*, from Schultens, Orig. Ling. Hebr. lib. i. chap. 2.; of the justness of which rendering I much doubt. This brings the image of Isaiah more near, in one circumstance, to that of Mohammed, than it appears to be in my translation.

" Labid, contemporary with Mohammed, the last of the seven Arabian poets who had the honour of having their poems, one of each, hung up in the entrance of the Temple of Mecca, struck with the sublimity of a passage in the Koran, became a convert to Mohammedism; for he concluded, that no man could write in such a manner, unless he were divinely inspired.

" One must have a curiosity to examine a passage which had so great an effect upon Labid. It is, I must own, the finest that I know in the whole Koran; but I scarce think it will have a second time the like effect, so as to tempt any one of my readers to submit to circumcision. It is in the second chapter; where he is speaking of certain apostates from the faith. ' They are like,' saith he, ' to a man who

kindleth a light. As soon as it begins to shine, God takes
from them the light, and leaves them in darkness, that they
see nothing. They are deaf, dumb, and blind; and return
not into the right way. Or they fare, as when a cloud, full
of darkness, thunder, and lightning, covers the heaven:
when it bursteth, they stop their ears with their fingers, with
deadly fear; and God hath the unbelievers in his power.
The lightning almost robbeth them of their eyes: as often
as it flasheth, they go on by its light; and when it vanisheth
in darkness, they stand still. If God pleased, they would retain neither hearing nor sight.' That the thought is beautiful, no one will deny; and Labid, who had probably a mind
to flatter Mohammed, was lucky in finding a passage in the
Koran, so little abounding in poetical beauties, to which his
conversion might with any propriety be ascribed. It was
well that he went no further; otherwise his taste for poetry
might have made him again an infidel." Michaelis, Erpenii
Arabische Grammatik abgekurzt, Vorrede, s. 32.

23. —*accumulated darkness*] Either מנדחה, fem. to agree
with אבלה; or אבל הכנדח, alluding perhaps to the palpable
Egyptian darkness, Exod. x. 21.

Ibid. *The land of Zebulon*—] Zebulon, Naphthali, Manasseh, that is, the country of Galilee, all round the Sea of
Genesareth, were the parts that principally suffered in the
first Assyrian invasion under Tiglath Pileser: see 2 Kings
xv. 29. 1. Chron. v. 26.: and they were the first that en-
joyed the blessing of Christ's preaching the gospel, and exhibiting his miraculous works among them. See Mede's
Works, p. 101. and 457.

CHAPTER IX.

2. *Thou hast increased their joy*] Eleven MSS (two
ancient) read לו, according to the Masoretical correction.

Ibid. —*as with the joy of harvest*] כשמחת בקציר. For
בקציר a MSS has קציר, and another הקציר: one of which
seems to be the true reading, as the noun preceding is *in regimine*.

4. *The greaves of the armed warrior*] סאון סאן. This
word, occurring only in this place, is of very doubtful signification. Schindler fairly tells us, that we must guess at
it by the context. The Jews have explained it, by guess I

believe, as signifying *battle, conflict:* the Vulgate renders it *violenta prædatio.* But it seems as if something was rather meant, which was capable of becoming fuel for the fire together with the garments mentioned in the same sentence. In Syriac, the word, as a noun, signifies a *shoe* or a *sandal*, as a learned friend suggested to me some years ago: see Luke xv. 22. Acts xii. 8. I take it therefore to mean that part of the armour which covered the legs and feet, and I would render the two words in Latin by *caliga caligati.* The burning of heaps of armour, gathered from the field of battle, as an offering made to the god supposed to be the giver of victory, was a custom that prevailed among some heathen nations; and the Romans used it as an emblem of peace: which perfectly well suits with the design of the Prophet in this place. A medal, struck by Vespasian on finishing his wars both at home and abroad, represents the goddess Peace, holding an olive branch in one hand, and with a lighted torch in the other setting fire to a heap of armour. Virgil mentions the custom:

"Cum primam aciem Præneste sub ipsa
Stravi, scutorumque incendi victor acervos." Æn. viii. 561.

See Addison on Medals, Series ii. 18. And there are notices of some such practice among the Israelites, and other nations of the most early times. God promises to Joshua victory over the kings of Canaan: "To-morrow I will deliver them up all slain before Israel: thou shalt hough their horses, and burn their chariots with fire;" Josh. xi. 6. See also Nahum ii. 13. And the Psalmist employs this image to express complete victory, and a perfect establishment of peace:

"He maketh wars to cease, even to the end of the land:
He breaketh the bow, and cutteth the spear in sunder;
And burneth the chariots in the fire." Psal. xlvi. 9.

עגלות, properly *plaustra,* the *baggage-waggons;* which however the LXX and Vulg. render *scuta, shields,* and Chald. *round shields,* to shew the propriety of that sense of the word from the etymology; which, if admitted, makes the image the same with that used by the Romans

Ezekiel, in his bold manner, has carried this image to a degree of amplification, which, I think, hardly any other of the Hebrew poets would have attempted. He describes the burning of the arms of the enemy, in consequence of the complete victory to be obtained by the Israelites over Gog and Magog:

"Behold, it is come to pass, and it is done;
Saith the Lord JEHOVAH.
This is the day, of which I spake
And the inhabitants of the cities of Israel shall go forth;
And shall set on fire the armour, and the shield,
And the buckler, and the bow, and the arrows,
And the clubs, and the lances;
And they shall set them on fire for seven years;
And they shall not bear wood from the field;
Neither shall they hew from the forest:
For of the armour shall they make their fires;
And they shall spoil their spoilers,
And they shall plunder their plunderers." Ezek. xxxix 8–10.

5. *The government shall be upon his shoulder.*] That is, the ensign of government; the sceptre, the sword, the key, or the like, which was borne upon or hung from the shoulder. See note on chap. xxii. 22.

Chap. ix. 7.—Chap. x. 4.] This whole passage, reduced to its proper and entire form, and healed of the dislocation which it suffers by the absurd division of the chapters, makes a distinct prophecy, and a just poem, remarkable for the regularity of its disposition, and the elegance of its plan. It has no relation to the preceding or the following prophecy; though the parts, violently torn asunder, have been, on the one side and the other, patched on to them. Those relate principally to the kingdom of Judah; this is addressed exclusively to the kingdom of Israel. The subject of it is a denunciation of vengeance awaiting their crimes. It is divided into four parts, each threatening the particular punishment of some grievous offence,—of their pride; of their perseverance in their vices; of their impiety; and of their injustice. To which is added a general denunciation of a further reserve of divine wrath, contained in a distich, before used by the Prophet on a like occasion, chap. v. 25. and here repeated after each part: this makes the intercalary verse of the poem, or, as we call it, the burthen of the song.

"Post hoc comma (chap. x. 4.) interponitur spatium unius lineæ, in cod. 2. et 3.: idemque observatur in 245. in quo nullum est spatium ad finem capitis ix." Kennicott, Var. Lect.

7. *JEHOVAH.*] For אדני, thirty MSS and three editions read יהוה.

8. —*carry themselves haughtily*] וירעו, *and they shall know:* so ours, and the versions in general. But what is it that they shall know? The verb stands destitute of its object; and the sense is imperfect. The Chaldee is the only one, as far as I can find, that expresses it otherwise. He renders the verb in this place by ואתרברבו, *they exalt themselves*, or *carry themselves haughtily;* the same word by which he renders נכהו, chap. iii. 16. He seems therefore in this place to have read ויגבהו; which agrees perfectly well with what follows, and clears up the difficulty. Archbishop Secker conjectured וידברו, referring it to לאמר in the next verse; which shews, that he was not satisfied with the present reading. Houbigant reads וירעו, *et pravi facti sunt;* which is found in a MS; but I prefer the reading of the Chaldee, which suits much better with the context.

9. *The bricks—*] "The eastern bricks, (says Sir John Chardin, see Harmer, Obser. i. p. 176.), are only clay well moistened with water, and mixed with straw, and dried in the sun." So that their walls are commonly no better than our mud-wall: see Maundrell, p. 124. That straw was a necessary part in the composition of this sort of bricks, to make the parts of the clay adhere together, appears from Exodus, chap. v. These bricks are properly opposed to hewn stone, so greatly superior in beauty and durableness. The sycamores, which, as Jerom on the place says, are timber of little worth, with equal propriety are opposed to the cedars. "As the grain and texture of the sycamore is remarkably coarse and spongy, it could therefore stand in no competition at all (as it is observed, Isa. ix. 10.) with the cedar for beauty and ornament:" Shaw, Supplement to Travels, p. 96. We meet with the same opposition of cedars to sycamores, 1 Kings x. 27. where Solomon is said to have made silver as the stones, and cedars as the sycamores in the vale, for abundance. By this *mashal*, or figurative and sententious speech, they boast, that they shall easily be able to repair their present losses, suffered perhaps by the first Assyrian invasion under Tiglath Pileser; and to bring their affairs to a more flourishing condition than ever.

10. —*the princes of Retsin against him*] For צרי, *enemies*, Houbigant by conjecture reads שרי, *princes;* which is confirmed by twenty-one MSS (two ancient), and nine more have צ upon a rasure, and therefore had probably at first שרי. The princes of Retsin, the late ally of Israel, that is,

the Syrians, expressly named in the next verse, shall now be excited against Israel.

The LXX in this place gives us another variation: for רצין, they read הר ציון, ὄρος Σιων, *Mount Sion;* of which this may be the sense: But JEHOVAH shall set up the adversaries of Mount Sion against him (*i. e.* against Israel), and will *strengthen* his enemies together: the Syrians,—the Philistines,—who are called the adversaries of Mount Sion. See Simonis Lex. in voce סכך.

11. —*on every side*] בכל פה, in every corner; in every part of their country, pursuing them to the remotest. extremities, and the most retired parts. So the Chald. בכל אתר, in every place.

13. —*in one day*] Eight MSS read ביום; and another has a rasure in the place of the letter ב.

16. JEHOVAH] For אדני, eighteen MSS read יהוה.

17. *For wickedness—*] Wickedness rageth like a fire, destroying and laying waste the nation: but it shall be its own destruction, by bringing down the fire of God's wrath, which shall burn up the briers and the thorns; that is, the wicked themselves. Briers and thorns are an image frequently applied in Scripture, when set on fire, to the rage of the wicked, violent yet impotent, and of no long continuance, —" they are extinct as the fire of thorns;" Psal. cxviii. 12.; —to the wicked themselves, as useless and unprofitable, proper objects of God's wrath, to be burned up, or driven away by the wind,—" as thorns cut up, they shall be consumed in the fire;" Isa. xxxiii. 12. Both these ideas seem to be joined in Psal. lviii. 9.

" Before your pots shall feel the thorn,
 As well the green as the dry, the tempest shall bear them away."

The green and the dry is a proverbial expression, meaning all sorts of them, good and bad, great and small, &c.; so Ezekiel: —" Behold, I will kindle a fire, and it shall devour every green tree, and every dry tree;" chap. xx. 47. D'Herbelot quotes a Persian poet describing a pestilence under the image of a conflagration:—" This was a lightning that, falling upon a forest, consumed there the green wood with the dry." See Harmer, Obser. ii. p. 187.

19. —*the flesh of his neighbour*] " Τοῦ βραχίονος τοῦ ἀδελφοῦ αὐτοῦ, LXX, Alexand. Duplex Versio, quarum altera legit רעו, quæ vox extat Jer. vi. 21. Nam רע, ἀδελφός, Gen. xliii.

33. Recte, ni fallor:" Secker. I add to this excellent remark, that the Chaldee manifestly reads רֵעוֹ, not זְרֹעוֹ; for he renders it by קריביה, *his neighbour*. And Jeremiah has the very same expression: ואיש בשר רעהו יאכלו, "And every one shall eat the flesh of his neighbour;" chap. xix. 9. This observation, I think, gives the true reading and sense of this place; and the context strongly confirms it, by explaining the general idea by particular instances, in the following verse: "Every man shall devour the flesh of his neighbour; (that is, they shall harass and destroy one another); Manasseh shall devour Ephraim, and Ephraim Manasseh; (which two tribes were most closely connected both in blood and situation, as brothers and neighbours); and both of them in the midst of their own dissensions shall agree in preying upon Judah." The common reading, "shall devour the flesh of his own *arm*," in connexion with what follows, seems to make either an inconsistency, or an anticlimax; whereas by this correction the following verse becomes an elegant illustration of the foregoing.

CHAPTER X.

4. *Without me*—] That is, without my aid, they shall be taken captive even by the captives, and shall be subdued by the vanquished. "The י in בלתי is a pronoun, as in Hos. xiii. 4. :" Kimchi on the place.

5. *Ho to the Assyrian*—] Here begins a new and distinct prophecy; continued to the end of the xiith chapter: and it appears, from ver. 9—11. of this chapter, that this prophecy was delivered after the taking of Samaria by Shalmaneser; which was in the sixth year of the reign of Hezekiah: and as the former part of it foretells the invasion of Senacherib, and the destruction of his army, which makes the whole subject of this chapter, it must have been delivered before the fourteenth of the same reign.

Ibid. *The staff in whose hand*] The word הוא in this place seems to embarrass the sentence. I omit it on the authority of the Alexandrine copy of LXX; and five MSS, (two ancient), for ומטה הוא, read מטהו. Archbishop Secker was not satisfied with the present reading: he proposes another method of clearing up the sense, by reading בים instead of בידם: "And he is a staff *in the day* of mine indignation."

12. *JEHOVAH*] For אדני, fourteen MSS, and three editions, read יהוה.

Ibid. —*the effect*—] "פרי, f. צבי, vid. xiii. 19. sed confer Prov. i. 31. xxxi. 16. 31:" SECKER. The Chaldee renders the word פרי by עובדי, *opera ;* which seems to be the true sense ; and I have followed it.

13. —*strongly*—] Twelve MSS agree with the Keri in reading כביר without the א. And S. b. Melec and Kimchi thus explain it : " Them, who dwelled in a great and strong place, I have brought down to the ground."

15. —*its master*] I have here given the meaning, without attempting to keep to the expression of the original : לא עץ, " the no-wood ;" that which is not wood like itself, but of a quite different and superior nature. The Hebrews have a peculiar way of joining the negative particle לא to a noun, to signify in a strong manner a total negation of the thing expressed by the noun.

" How hast thou given help, ללא כח, to the no-strength?
And saved the arm, לא עז, of the no-power?
How hast thou given counsel, ללא חכמה, to the no-wisdom?"

that is, to the man totally deprived of strength, power, and wisdom : Job xxvi. 2. 3.

" Ye that rejoice, ללא דבר, in no-thing : "

that is, in your fancied strength, which is none at all, a mere nonentity : Amos vi. 13.

" For I am God, ולא איש, and no-man;
The Holy One in the midst of thee, yet do not frequent cities." Hosea xi. 9.

" And the Assyrians shall fall by a sword, לא איש, of no-man;
And a sword of, לא אדם, no-mortal shall devour him."
Isa. xxxi. 8.

" Wherefore do ye weigh out your silver, בלוא לחם, for the no-bread." Isa. lv. 2.

So here לא עץ means him who is far from being an inert piece of wood, but is an animated and active being ; not an instrument, but an agent.

16. *JEHOVAH*] For אדני, fifty-two MSS, and six editions, read יהוה.

Ibid. *And under his glory*] That is, all that he could boast of as great and strong in his army ; (Sal. b. Melec in loc.); expressed afterwards, ver. 18. by the glory of his forest, and of his fruitful field.

17, 18. *And he shall burn and consume his thorn*—] The briers and thorns are the common people; the glory of his forest are the nobles, and those of highest rank and importance. See note on chap. ix. 17. and compare Ezek. xx. 47. The fire of God's wrath shall destroy them both great and small, it shall consume them *from the soul to the flesh:* a proverbial expression; *soul and body,* as we say; it shall consume them entirely and altogether. And the few that escape shall be looked upon as having escaped from the most imminent danger; " as a firebrand plucked out of the fire; " Amos iv. 11. Ὡς διὰ πυρός, 1 Cor. iii. 15. as a man, when a house is burning, is forced to make his escape by running through the midst of the fire.

I follow here the reading of the LXX; כנס נאכם, ὡς ὁ φευγων ἀπο φλογος καιομενης. Symmachus also renders the latter word by φευγων.

22, 23. *For though thy people, O Israel*—] I have endeavoured to keep to the letter of the text, as nearly as I can, in this obscure passage. But it is remarkable, that neither the LXX, nor St Paul, Rom. ix. 28. who, except in a few words of no great importance, follows them nearly in this place, nor any one of the ancient versions, take any notice of the word שטף, *overflowing;* which seems to give an idea not easily reconcileable with those with which it is here joined. I. S. Mœrlius (Schol. Philolog. ad Selecta S. Cod. loca) conjectures, that the two last letters of this word are by mistake transposed, and that the true reading is שפט, *judging* with strict justice. The LXX might think this sufficiently expressed by ἐν δικαιοσυνη. A MS, with St Paul and LXX Alex. omits בי in the 22d verse; sixty-nine MSS, and six editions, omit כל in the 23d verse: and so St. Paul, Rom. ix. 28.

The learned Dr. Bagot, dean of Christchurch, Oxford, in some observations on this place, which he has been so kind as to communicate to me, and which will appear in their proper light when he himself shall give them to the public, renders the word כליון by *accomplishment,* and makes it refer to the predictions of Moses; the blessing and the curse which he laid before the people; both conditional, and depending on their future conduct. They had by their disobedience incurred those judgments which were now to be fully executed upon them. His translation is: " The accomplishment determined overflows with justice; for it is accomplished, and that which is determined the Lord God of Hosts doeth in the midst of the land."

24. and 26. —*in the way of Egypt*] I think there is a designed ambiguity in these words. Senacherib, soon after his return from his Egyptian expedition, which, I imagine, took him up three years, invested Jerusalem. He is represented by the Prophet as lifting up his rod in his march from Egypt, and threatening the people of God, as Pharaoh and the Egyptians had done when they pursued them to the Red Sea. But God in his turn will lift up his rod over the sea, as he did at that time, in the way, or after the manner of Egypt: and as Senacherib has imitated the Egyptians in his threats, and came full of rage against them from the same quarter; so God will act over again the same part that he had taken formerly in Egypt, and overthrow their enemies in as signal a manner. It was all to be, both the attack and the deliverance, בדרך, or כדרך, as a MS has it in each place, in the way, or after the manner, of Egypt.

25. *mine indignation*] Indignatio mea, Vulg.; ἡ οργη, LXX; μὴ 'η οργη ἡ κατα σε, MS. Pachom.; μὴ ἡ οργη κατα σε, MS I. D. II.: so that ימי, or הועם, as a MS has it, seems to be the true reading.

26. *And like his rod which he lifted up over the sea*] The Jewish interpreters suppose here an ellipsis of כ, the particle of similitude, before מטה, to be supplied from the line above: so that here are two similitudes; one comparing the destruction of the Assyrians to the slaughter of the Midianites at the rock of Oreb; the other to that of the Egyptians at the Red Sea. Aben Ezra, Kimchi, Salomo b. Melec.

27. —*from off your shoulders*] I follow here the LXX, who, for מפני שמן, read משכמיכם, απο των ωμων υμων; not being able to make any good sense out of the present reading. I will add here the marginal conjectures of Archbishop Secker, who appears, like all others, to have been at a loss for a probable interpretation of the text as it now stands. "ὅ· leg. שכם; forte legend. מבני שמן, vid. cap. v. 1. Zech. iv. 14. Et possunt intelligi Judæi uncti Dei; Psal. cv. 15. vel Assyrii משמנים, hic ver. 16. ut dicat Propheta depulsum iri jugum ab his impositum: sed hoc durius. Vel potest legi מפני שמי:" SECKER.

28—32. *He is come to Aiath*—] A description of the march of Senacherib's army approaching Jerusalem in order to invest it, and of the terror and confusion spreading and increasing through the several places as he advanced; expressed with great brevity, but finely diversified. The places here mentioned are all in the neighbourhood of Jerusalem; from Ai northward, to Nob westward of it; from which last place he might probably have a prospect of Mount Sion. Anathoth was within three Roman miles of Jerusalem; according to Eusebius, Jerom, and Josephus: Onomast. Loc. Hebr. et. Antiq. Jud. x. 7. 3. Nob probably still nearer. And it should seem from this passage of Isaiah, that Senacherib's army was destroyed near the latter of these places. In coming out of Egypt, he might perhaps join the rest of his army at Ashdod, after the taking of that place, which happened about that time, (see chap. xx.); and march from thence near the coast by Lachish and Libnah, which lay in his way, from south to north, and both which he invested, till he came to the north-west of Jerusalem; crossing over to the north of it, perhaps by Joppa and Lydda, or still more north through the plain of Esdraelon.

29. *They have passed the strait—*] The strait here mentioned is that of Michmas, a very narrow passage between two sharp hills of rocks, (see 1 Sam. xiv. 4, 5.), where a great army might have been opposed with advantage by a very inferior force. The author of the book of Judith might perhaps mean this pass, at least among others: " Charging them to keep the passages of the hill country; for by them there was an entrance into Judea, and it was easy to stop them that would come up; because the passage was strait, for two men at the most:" Judith iv. 7. The enemies having passed the strait without opposition, shews that all thoughts of making a stand in the open country were given up, and that their only resource was in the strength of the city.

Ibid. *—their lodging—*] The sense seems necessarily to require, that we read למו instead of לנו. These two words are in other places mistaken one for the other. Thus Isa. xliv. 7. for למו read לנו, with the Chaldee: and in the same manner Psal. lxiv. 6. with Syr. and Psal. lxxx. 7. on the authority of LXX and Syr. beside the necessity of te sense.

30. *Hearken unto her, O Laish; answer her, O Anathoth!*] I follow in this the Syriac version. The Prophet plainly alludes to the name of the place; and with a peculiar propriety, if it had its name from its remarkable echo.

"עֲנָתוֹת, *responsiones*: eadem ratio nominis, quæ in עֲנָת בֵּית, *locus echûs*; nam hodienum ejus rudera ostenduntur in valle, scil. in medio montium, ut referunt Robertus in Itiner. p. 70. et Monconnysius, p. 301." Simonis Onomasticon Vet. Test.

CHAPTER XI.

The Prophet had described the destruction of the Assyrian army under the image of a mighty forest, consisting of flourishing trees, growing thick together, and of a great height—of Lebanon itself crowned with lofty cedars; but cut down and laid level with the ground by the axe, wielded by the hand of some powerful and illustrious agent. In opposition to this image he represents the great person, who makes the subject of this chapter, as a slender twig, shooting out from the trunk of an old tree, cut down, lopped to the very root, and decayed; which tender plant, so weak in appearance, should nevertheless become fruitful and prosper. This contrast shows plainly the connexion between this and the preceding chapter; which is moreover expressed by the connecting particle: And we have here a remarkable instance of that method so common with the Prophets, and particularly with Isaiah, of taking occasion, from the mention of some great temporal deliverance, to launch out into the display of the spiritual deliverance of God's people by the Messiah: for that this prophecy relates to the Messiah, we have the express authority of St. Paul, Rom. xv. 12. " Conjungit Parasciam hanc, quæ respicit dies futuros Messiæ, cum fiducia, quae fuit in diebus Ezekiae:" Kimchi in ver. 1. Thus, in the latter part of Isaiah's prophecies, the subject of the great redemption, and of the glories of Messiah's kingdom, arises out of the restoration of Judah by the deliverance from the captivity of Babylon, and is all along connected and intermixed with it.

4. *By the blast of his mouth*] For בשבט, by the *rod*, Houbigant reads בשבת, by the *blast* of his mouth, from נשב, *to blow*. The conjecture is ingenious and probable; and seems to be confirmed by the LXX and Chaldee, who render it, by the *word* of his mouth; which answers much better to the correction than to the present reading. Add to this, that the *blast of his mouth*, is perfectly parallel to *the breath of his lips* in the next line.

5.—*the cincture*—] All the ancient versions, except that of Symmachus, have two different words for *girdle* in the two hemistichs. It is not probable that Isaiah would have repeated אזר, when a synonymous word so obvious as חגור occurred. The tautology seems to have arisen from the mistake of some transcriber. The meaning of this verse is, that a zeal for justice and truth shall make him active and strong in executing the great work which he shall undertake. See note on chap. v. 27.

6—8. *Then shall the wolf*—] The idea of the renewal of the golden age, as it is called, is much the same in the oriental writers with that of the Greeks and Romans: the wild beasts grow tame ; serpents and poisonous herbs become harmless ; all is peace and harmony, plenty and happiness :

>" Occidet et serpens, et fallax herba veneni
>   Occidet."
>———" Nec magnos metuent armenta leones."
>" Nec lupus insidias pecori———."   Virg.
>" Nec vespertinus circumgemit ursus ovile,
>   Nec intumescit alta viperis humus."   Hor.
>" Εσται δη τυτ' αμαρ, οπηνικα νεβρον εν ευνα
>   Καρχαροδων σινεσθαι ιδων λυκος ουκ εθελησει."   Theoc.

I have laid before the reader these common passages from the most elegant of the ancient poets, that he may see how greatly the Prophet on the same subject has the advantage upon the comparison ; how much the former fall short of that beauty and elegance, and variety of imagery, with which Isaiah has set forth the very same ideas. The wolf and the leopard not only forbear to destroy the lamb and the kid, but even take their abode and lie down together with them. The calf, and the young lion, and the fatling, not only come together, but are led quietly in the same band, and that by a little child. The heifer and the she-bear not only feed together, but even lodge their young ones, for whom they used to be most jealously fearful, in the same place. All the serpent kind is so perfectly harmless, that the sucking infant, and the newly weaned child, puts his hand on the basilisk's den, and plays upon the hole of the aspic. The lion not only abstains from preying on the weaker animals, but becomes tame and domestic, and feeds on straw like the ox. These are all beautiful circumstances, not one of which has been touched upon by the ancient poets.

The Arabian and Persian poets elegantly apply the same ideas, to shew the effects of justice impartially administered, and firmly supported, by a great and good king:

" Rerum dominus Mahmud, rex potens;
Ad cujus aquam potum veniunt simul agnus et lupus."
Ferdusi.

" Justitia, a qua mansuetus fit lupus fame astrictus,
Esuriens, licet hinnuleum candidum videat." Ibn Onein.
Jones, Poes. Asiat. Comment. p. 380.

The application is extremely ingenious and beautiful; but the exquisite imagery of Isaiah is not equalled.

7. *Together*—] Here a word is omitted in the text, יחדו, *together;* which ought to be repeated in the second hemistich, being quite necessary to the sense. It is accordingly twice expressed by the LXX, and Syr.

10. *The root of Jesse, which standeth*—] St. John hath taken this expression from Isaiah, Rev. v. 5. and xxii. 16. where Christ hath twice applied it to himself. Seven MSS have עומד, the present participle. " Radix Isæi dicitur jam stare, et aliquantum stetisse, in signum populorum:" Vitringa. Which rightly explains either of the two readings.

11. *JEHOVAH*] For אדני, thirty-three MSS, and two editions, read יהוה.

11—16. *And it shall come to pass in that day*—] This part of the chapter contains a prophecy, which certainly remains yet to be accomplished. See Lowth on the place.

13. *And the enmity of Judah*—] צררים. " Postulat pars posterior versus, ut intelligantur *inimicitiæ* Judæ in Ephraimum:—et potest צררים inimicitiam notare, ut נחמים pœnitentiam, Hos. xi. 8;" SECKER.

15. *smite with a drought*—] The Chaldee reads החריב; and so perhaps LXX, who have ερημωσει, the word by which they commonly render it. Vulg. *desolabit.* The LXX, Vulg. and Chald. read הדריכהו, " shall make *it* passable," adding the pronoun, which is necessary.

Here is a plain allusion to the passage of the Red Sea. And the Lord's shaking his hand over the river with his vehement wind, refers to a particular circumstance of the same miracle: for " he caused the sea to go back by a strong east wind all that night, and made the sea dry land:" Exod. xiv. 21. The tongue; a very apposite and descriptive expression for a bay, such as that of the Red Sea: it is used in the same sense, Josh. xv. 2. 5. xviii. 19. The Latins gave the same name to a narrow strip of land running into the sea: "tenuem producit in æquora linguam:" Lucan, ii. 613.

Herodotus, i. 189. tells a story of his Cyrus, (a very different character from that of the Cyrus of the Scriptures and Xenophon), which may somewhat illustrate this passage; in which it is said, that God would inflict a kind of punishment and judgment on the Euphrates, and render it fordable, by dividing it into seven streams. "Cyrus being impeded in his march to Babylon by the Gyndes, a deep and rapid river which falls into the Tigris, and having lost one of his sacred white horses that attempted to pass it, was so enraged against the river, that he threatened to reduce it, and make it so shallow, that it should be easily fordable even by women, who should not be up to their knees in passing it. Accordingly, he set his whole army to work; and, cutting three hundred and sixty trenches, from both sides of the river, turned the waters into them, and drained them off."

CHAPTER XII.

This hymn seems, by its whole tenor, and by many expressions in it, much better calculated for the use of the Christian church, than for the Jewish in any circumstances, or at any time that can be assigned. The Jews themselves seem to have applied it to the times of Messiah. On the last day of the feast of tabernacles, they fetched water in a golden pitcher from the fountain of Siloah, springing at the foot of Mount Sion without the city: they brought it through the water-gate into the temple, and poured it, mixed with wine, on the sacrifice as it lay upon the altar, with great rejoicing. They seem to have taken up this custom, for it is not ordained in the law of Moses, as an emblem of future blessings, in allusion to this passage of Isaiah, "Ye shall draw waters with joy from the fountains of salvation:" expressions, that can hardly be understood of any benefits afforded by the Mosaic dispensation. Our Saviour applied the ceremony, and the intention of it, to himself, and to the effusion of the Holy Spirit, promised, and to be given, by him. The sense of the Jews in this matter is plainly shewn by the following passage of the Jerusalem Talmud: "Why is it called the place, or house, of drawing?" (for that was the term for this ceremony, or for the place where the water was taken up): "Because from thence they draw the Holy Spirit; as it is written, And ye shall draw water with joy from the fountains of salvation." See Wolf. Curæ Philol. in N. T. on John vii. 37. 39.

1. *for, though thou hast been angry*—] The Hebrew phrase, to which the LXX, Vulg. and our translation, have too closely adhered, is exactly the same with that of St. Paul, Rom. vi. 17. " But thanks be to God, that ye were the slaves of sin; but have obeyed from the heart"—that is, " that, whereas, or though, ye were the slaves of sin; yet ye have now obeyed from the heart the doctrine, on the model of which ye were formed."

2. —*my song*—] The pronoun is here necessary; and it is added by LXX, Vulg. Syr. who read זמרתי ; as it is in a MS. Two MSS omit יה : See Houbigant, not. in loc. Another MS has it in one word, זמרתיה. Seven others omit יהוה. See Exod. xv. 2. with Var. Lect. Kennicott.

CHAPTERS XIII. & XIV.

These two chapters (striking off the five last verses of the latter, which belong to a quite different subject), contain one entire prophecy, foretelling the destruction of Babylon by the Medes and Persians; delivered probably in the reign of Ahaz, (see Vitringa, i. 380.), about 200 years before the completion of it. The captivity itself of the Jews at Babylon, (which the Prophet does not expressly foretell, but supposes, in the spirit of prophecy, as what was actually to be effected), did not fully take place till about 130 years after the delivery of this prophecy: and the Medes, who are expressly mentioned, chap. xiii. 17. as the principal agents in the overthrow of the Babylonian monarchy, by which the Jews were released from that captivity, were at this time an inconsiderable people; having been in a state of anarchy ever since the fall of the great Assyrian Empire, of which they had made a part, under Sardanapalus, and did not become a kingdom under Deioces till about the 17th of Hezekiah.

The former part of this prophecy is one of the most beautiful examples, that can be given, of elegance of composition, variety of imagery, and sublimity of sentiment and diction, in the prophetic style; and the latter part consists of an ode of supreme and singular excellence.

The prophecy opens with the command of God to gather together the forces which he had destined to this service, ver. 2, 3. Upon which the Prophet immediately hears the tumultuous noise of the different nations crowding together to his standard; he sees them advancing, prepared to execute the divine wrath, ver. 4, 5. He proceeds to describe the dreadful consequences of this visitation; the consternation which will seize those that are the objects of it; and, transferring unawares the speech from himself to God, ver. 11. sets forth, under a variety of the most striking images, the dreadful destruction of the inhabitants of Babylon which will follow, ver. 11—16.; and the everlasting desolation to which that great city is doomed, ver. 17—22.

The deliverance of Judea from captivity, the immediate consequence of this great revolution, is then set forth, without being much enlarged upon, or greatly amplified; chap. xiv. 1, 2. This introduces, with the greatest ease, and the utmost propriety, the triumphant song on that subject, ver. 4—28. The beauties of which, the various images, scenes, persons introduced, and the elegant transitions from one to another, I shall here endeavour to point out in their order; leaving a few remarks upon particular passages of these two chapters to be given, after these general observations on the whole.

A chorus of Jews is introduced, expressing their surprise and astonishment at the sudden downfall of Babylon, and the great reverse of fortune that had befallen the tyrant, who, like his predecessors, had oppressed his own, and harassed the neighbouring kingdoms. These oppressed kingdoms, or their rulers, are represented under the image of the fir-trees and the cedars of Libanus, frequently used to express any thing in the political or religious world that is supereminently great and majestic: the whole earth shouteth for joy; the cedars of Libanus utter a severe taunt over the fallen tyrant, and boast their security now he is no more.

The scene is immediately changed; and a new set of persons is introduced: The regions of the dead are laid open, and Hades is represented as rousing up the shades of the departed monarchs: they rise from their thrones to meet the king of Babylon at his coming; and insult him on his being reduced to the same low estate of impotence and dissolution with themselves. This is one of the boldest prosopopœias that ever was attempted in poetry; and is executed with astonishing brevity and perspicuity, and with that peculiar force which in a great subject naturally results from both. The image of the state of the dead, or the Infernum Poeticum of the Hebrews, is taken from their custom of burying, those at least of the higher rank, in large sepulchral vaults hewn in the rock. Of this kind of sepulchres there are remains at Jerusalem now extant; and some that are said to be the sepulchres of the kings of Judah: see Maundrell, p. 76. You are to form to yourself an idea of an immense subterraneous vault, a vast gloomy cavern, all round the sides of which there are cells to receive the dead bodies: Here the deceased monarchs lie in a distinguished sort of state, suitable to their former rank, each on his own couch, with his arms beside him, his sword at his head, and the bodies of his chiefs and companions round about him: see Ezek. xxxii. 27. On which place Sir John Chardin's MS note is as follows:—" En Mingrelie ils dorment tous leur epée sous leurs têtes, et leurs autres armes à leur coté; et on les enterre de mesme, leurs armes posées, de cette façon." These illustrious shades rise at once from their couches, as from their thrones; and advance to the entrance of the cavern to meet the king of Babylon, and to receive him with insults on his fall.

The Jews now resume the speech: They address the king of Babylon as the morning-star fallen from heaven, as the first in splendour and dignity in the political world fallen from his high state; they introduce him as uttering the most extravagant vaunts of his power and ambitious designs in his former glory: these are strongly contrasted in the close with his present low and abject condition.

Immediately follows a different scene, and a most happy image, to diversify the same subject, to give it a new turn and an additional force. Certain persons are introduced, who light upon the corpse of the king of Babylon, cast out and lying naked on the bare ground, among the common slain, just after the taking of the city; covered with wounds, and so disfigured, that it is some time before they know him. They accost him with the severest taunts, and bitterly reproach him with his destructive ambition, and his cruel usage of the conquered; which have deservedly brought upon him this ignominious treatment, so different from that which those of his rank usually meet with, and which shall cover his posterity with disgrace.

To complete the whole, God is introduced, declaring the fate of Babylon, the utter extirpation of the royal family, and the total desolation of the city; the deliverance of his people, and the destruction of their enemies; confirming the irreversible decree by the awful sanction of his oath.

I believe it may with truth be affirmed, that there is no poem of its kind extant in any language, in which the subject is so well laid out, and so happily conducted, with such a richness of invention, with such variety of images, persons, and distinct actions, with such rapidity and ease of transition, in so small a compass, as in this ode of Isaiah. For beauty of disposition, strength of colouring, greatness of sentiment, brevity, perspicuity, and force of expression, it stands among all the monuments of antiquity unrivaled.

2. *Exalt the voice*—] The word להם, *to them*, which is of no use, and rather weakens the sentence, is omitted by an ancient MS and Vulg.

4. *for the battle*] The Bodley MS has למלחמה. Cyrus's army was made up of many different nations. Jeremiah calls it "an assembly of great nations from the north country," chap. l. 9. And afterwards mentions the kingdoms of "Ararat, Minni, and Ashchenaz, (*i. e.* Armenia, Corduene, Pontus vel Phrygia; Vitring.), with the kings of the Medes;" chap. li. 27, 28. See Xenophon. Cyrop.

8. —*and they shall be terrified*] I join this verb, ונבהלו, to the preceding verse, with Syr. and Vulg.

Ibid. *pangs shall seize* them—] The LXX, Syr. and Chald. read אחזום, instead of אחזון, which does not express the pronoun *them*, necessary to the sense.

10. *Yea the stars of heaven*—] The Hebrew poets, to express happiness, prosperity, the instauration and advancement of states, kingdoms, and potentates, make use of images taken from the most striking parts of nature,—from the heavenly bodies, from the sun, moon, and stars; which they describe as shining with increased splendour, and never setting; the moon becomes like the meridian sun, and the sun's light is augmented sevenfold; see Isa. xxx. 26.: new heavens and a new earth are created, and a brighter age commences. On the contrary, the overthrow and destruction of kingdoms is represented by opposite images: the stars are ob-

scured, the moon withdraws her light, and the sun shines no more; the earth quakes, and the heavens tremble; and all things seem tending to their original chaos. See Joel ii. 10. iii. 15, 16. Amos viii. 9. Matth. xxiv. 29. and De S. Poes. Hebr. Præl. vi. and ix.

11. *I will visit the world*] That is, the Babylonish empire: as ἡ οἰκȣμενη, for the Roman empire, or for Judea; Luke ii. 1. Acts xi. 28. So, universus orbis Romanus, for the Roman empire; Salvian. lib. v. Minos calls Crete his world: " Creten, quæ meus est orbis;" Ovid. Metamorph. viii. 99.

14. *And the remnant*—] Here is plainly a defect in this sentence, as it stands in the Hebrew text; the subject of the proposition is lost. What is it, that shall be like a roe chased? The LXX happily supply it: οἱ καταλελειμμενοι, שאר, *the remnant*. A MS here supplies the word יושב, *the inhabitant*, which makes a tolerably good sense; but I much prefer the reading of the LXX.

Ibid. *They shall look*—] That is, the forces of the king of Babylon, destitute of their leader, and all his auxiliaries, collected from Asia Minor and other distant countries, shall disperse, and flee to their respective homes.

15. *Every one that is overtaken*—] That is, none shall escape from the slaughter; neither they who flee singly, dispersed and in confusion; nor they who endeavour to make their retreat in a more regular manner, by forming compact bodies,—they shall all be equally cut off by the sword of the enemy. The LXX have understood it in this sense; which they have well expressed:—

" Ὅς γαρ αν ἁλω ηττηθησεται,
  Και οἱτινες συνηγμενοι εἰσι πεσȣνται μαχαιρα."

Where for ηττηθησεται, MS Pachom. has εκκεντηθησεται; and οἱ Γ Cod. Marchal. in margine, and MS 1. D. 11. εκκεντηθησεται: which seems to be right, being properly expressive of the Hebrew.

17. *Who shall hold silver of no account*] That is, who shall not be induced, by large offers of gold and silver for ransom, to spare the lives of those whom they have subdued in battle: their rage and cruelty will get the better of all such motives. We have many examples in the Iliad and in the Æneid of addresses of the vanquished to the pity and avarice of the vanquishers, to induce them to spare their lives.

"Est domus alta: jacent penitus defossa talenta
Cælati argenti: sunt auri pondera facti
Infectique mihi: non hic victoria Teucrûm
Vertitur; aut anima una dabit discrimina tanta.
Dixerat: Æneas contra cui talia reddit:
Argenti atque auri memoras quæ multa talenta
Gnatis parce tuis." Æn. x. 526.

"High in my dome are silver talents roll'd,
With piles of labour'd and unlabour'd gold:
These, to procure my ransom, I resign;
The war depends not on a life like mine:
One, one poor life can no such difference yield,
Nor turn the mighty balance of the field.
Thy talents, (cried the prince), thy treasur'd store,
Keep for thy sons." Pitt.

It is remarkable, that Xenophon makes Cyrus open a speech to his army, and in particular to the Medes, who made the principal part of it, with praising them for their disregard of riches. Ανδρες Μηδοι, και παντες οι παροντες, εγω υμας οιδα σαφως, οτι ετε χρηματων δεομενοι συν εμοι εξηλθετε:—"Ye Medes, and others who now hear me, I well know that you have not accompanied me in this expedition with a view of acquiring wealth:" Cyrop. lib. v.

18. *Their bows shall dash*—] Both Herodotus, i. 61. and Xenophon, Anab. iii. mention, that the Persians used large bows, τοξα μεγαλα: and the latter says particularly, that their bows were three cubits long; Anab. iv. They were celebrated for their archers: see chap. xxii. 6. Jer. xlix. 35. Probably their neighbours and allies, the Medes, dealt much in the same sort of arms. In Psal. xviii. 35. and Job. xx. 24. mention is made of a bow of brass: If the Persian bows were of metal, we may easily conceive, that with a metalline bow of three cubits length, and proportionably strong, the soldiers might dash and slay the young men, the weaker and unresisting part of the inhabitants, (for they are joined with the fruit of the womb and the children), in the general carnage on taking the city.

18. *And on the fruit*—] A MS reads ויגל פרי. And nine MSS (three ancient) and two editions, with LXX, Vulg. Syr. add likewise the conjunction ו to על afterward.

19. *And Babylon*] The great city of Babylon was at this time rising to its height of glory, while the Prophet Isaiah, was repeatedly denouncing its utter destruction. From the first of Hezekiah to the first of Nebuchadnezzar, under

whom it was brought to the highest degree of strength and splendour, are about one hundred and twenty years. I will here very briefly mention some particulars of the greatness of the place, and note the several steps by which this remarkable prophecy was at length accomplished in the total ruin of it.

It was, according to the lowest account given of it by ancient historians, a regular square, forty-five miles in compass, enclosed by a wall two hundred feet high, fifty broad; in which there were a hundred gates of brass. Its principal ornaments were the temple of Belus, in the middle of which was a tower of eight stories of building, upon a base of a quarter of a mile square; a most magnificent palace; and the famous hanging gardens; which were an artificial mountain, raised upon arches, and planted with trees of the largest as well as the most beautiful sorts.

Cyrus took the city by diverting the waters of the Euphrates, which ran through the midst of it, and entering the place at night by the dry channel. The river, being never restored afterward to its proper course, overflowed the whole country, and made it little better than a great morass: This, and the great slaughter of the inhabitants, with other bad consequences of the taking of the city, was the first step to the ruin of the place. The Persian monarchs ever regarded it with a jealous eye; they kept it under, and took care to prevent its recovering its former greatness. Darius Hystaspis not long afterward most severely punished it for a revolt, greatly depopulated the place, lowered the walls, and demolished the gates. Xerxes destroyed the temples, and with the rest the great temple of Belus; Herod. iii. 159. Arrian. Exp. Alexandri, lib. vii. The building of Seleucia on the Tigris exhausted Babylon by its neighbourhood, as well as by the immediate loss of inhabitants taken away by Seleucus to people his new city: Strabo, lib. xvi. A king of the Parthians soon after carried away into slavery a great number of the inhabitants, and burnt and destroyed the most beautiful parts of the city: Valesii Excerpt. Diodori, p. 377. Strabo (ibid.) says, that in his time great part of it was a mere desert; that the Persians had partly destroyed it; and that time, and the neglect of the Macedonians, while they were masters of it, had nearly completed its destruction. Jerom (in loc.) says, that in his time it was quite in ruins, and that the walls served only for the inclosure of a park or forest for the king's hunting. Modern travellers, who have endeavoured to find the remains of it, have given but a very unsatisfactory account of their success: what Benjamin of Tudela and Pietro della Valle supposed to have been some of its ruins, Tavernier thinks are the remains of some late Arabian building. Upon the whole, Babylon is so utterly annihilated, that even the place where this wonder of the world stood, cannot now be determined with any certainty. See also note on chap. xliii. 14.

We are astonished at the accounts which ancient historians of the best credit give, of the immense extent, height, and thickness of the walls of Nineveh and Babylon: nor are we less astonished when we are assured, by the concurrent testimony of modern travellers, that no remains, not the least traces, of these prodigious works are now to be found. Our wonder will, I think, be moderated in both respects, if we consider the fabric of these celebrated walls, and the nature of the materials of which they consisted. Buildings in the East have always been, and are to this day, made of earth or clay, mixed or beat up with straw, to make the parts cohere, and dried only in the sun. This is their method of making bricks: see note on chap. ix. 9. The walls of the city were built of the earth digged out on the spot, and dried upon the place; by which means both the ditch and the wall were at once formed; the former furnishing materials for the latter. That the walls of Babylon were of this kind is well known; and Berosus expressly says, (apud Joseph. Antiq. x. 11.), that Nebuchadnezzar added three new walls both to the old and new city, partly of brick and bitumen, and partly of brick alone. A wall of this sort must have a great thickness in proportion to its height, otherwise it cannot stand. The thickness of the walls of Babylon is said to have been one-fourth of their height, which seems to have been no more than was absolutely necessary. Maundrell, speaking of the garden walls of Damascus,—"They are," says he, "of a very singular structure. They are built of great pieces of earth, made in the fashion of brick, and hardened in the sun. In their dimensions they are two yards long each, and somewhat more than one broad, and half a yard thick." And afterward, speaking of the walls of the houses:—"From this dirty way of building they have this amongst other inconveniences, that upon any violent rain the whole city becomes, by the washing of the houses, as it were a quagmire," p. 124.; and see note on chap. xxx. 13.

When a wall of this sort comes to be out of repair, and is neglected, it is easy to conceive the necessary consequences; namely, that in no long course of ages it must be totally destroyed by the heavy rains, and at length washed away, and reduced to its original earth.

22. —*in their palaces*] באלמנותיו, a plain mistake, I presume, for בארמנותיו. It is so corrected in one MS.

" Πȣλυποδες δ' εν εμοι θαλαμας, φωκαιτε μελαιναι,
Οικια ποιησονται ακηδεα, χητει λαων." Homer. Hymn. in Apol. 77. Of which the following passage of Milton may be taken for a translation, though not so designed:—

" And in their palaces,
Where luxury late reign'd, sea-monsters whelp'd,
And stabled." P. L. xi. 750.

CHAPTER XIV.

1. *And will yet choose Israel.*] That is, will still regard Israel as his chosen people; however he may seem to desert them, by giving them up to their enemies, and scattering them among the nations. Judah is sometimes called Israel; see Ezek. xiii. 16. Mal. i. 1. ii. 11.; but the name of Jacob and of Israel, used apparently with design in this place, each of which names includes the twelve tribes, and the other circumstances mentioned in this and the next verse, which did not in any complete sense accompany the return from the captivity of Babylon; seem to intimate, that this whole prophecy extends its views beyond that event.

3. —*in that day*] ביום ההוא. The word ההוא is added in two MSS, and was in the copies from which the LXX and Vulg. translated: εν τη 'ημερα εκεινη, *in die illa*, ('η αναπαυσει, MS Pachom. adding *ȧ*). This is a matter of no great consequence: however, it restores the text to the common form almost constantly used on such occasions; and is one among many instances of a word lost out of the printed copies.

4. —*this parable*—] *Mashal.* I take this to be the general name for poetic style among the Hebrews, including every sort of it, as ranging under one, or other, or all of the characters, of sententious, figurative, and sublime; which are all contained in the original notion, or in the use and application of the word *mashal*. Parables or proverbs, such as those of Solomon, are always expressed in short pointed sentences; frequently figurative, being formed on

some comparison; generally forcible and authoritative, both in the matter and the form. And such in general is the style of the Hebrew poetry. The verb *mashal* signifies to rule, to exercise authority; to make equal, to compare one thing with another; to utter parables, or acute, weighty, and powerful speeches, in the form and manner of parables, though not properly such. Thus Balaam's first prophecy, Numb. xxiii. 7—10. is called his *mashal;* though it has hardly any thing figurative in it: but it is beautifully sententious, and, from the very form and manner of it, has great spirit, force, and energy. Thus Job's last speeches, in answer to the three friends, chap. xxvii—xxxi. are called *mashals;* from no one particular character which discriminates them from the rest of the poem, but from the sublime, the figurative, the sententious manner, which equally prevails through the whole poem, and makes it one of the first and most eminent examples extant of the truly great and beautiful in poetic style.

The LXX in this place render the word by θρηνος, *a lamentation.* They plainly consider the speech here introduced as a piece of poetry; and of that species of poetry which we call the elegiac,—either from the subject, it being a poem on the fall and death of the king of Babylon; or from the form of the composition, which is of the longer sort of Hebrew verse, in which the Lamentations of Jeremiah, called by the LXX θρηνοι, are written.

11. —*thy covering*] Twenty-eight MSS (ten ancient) and seven editions, with the LXX and Vulg. read נסככ, in the singular number.

12. *O Lucifer, son of the morning*] See note on xiii. 10.

13. *the mount of the divine presence—*] It appears plainly from Exod. xxv. 22. and xxix. 42, 43. where God appoints the place of meeting with Moses, and promises to meet with him before the ark, to commune with him, and to speak unto him; and to meet the children of Israel at the door of the tabernacle; that the tabernacle, and afterward the temple, and Mount Sion, (or Moriah, which is reckoned a part of Sion), whereon it stood, was called the tabernacle, and the mount, of convention, or of appointment; not from the people's assembling there to perform the services of their religion, (which is what our translation expresses by calling it the tabernacle of the congregation), but because God appointed that for the place where he himself would meet with

Moses, and commune with him, and would meet with the people. Therefore, הר מועד, or אהל מועד, means the place appointed by God, where he would present himself; agreeably to which I have rendered it, in this place, the mount of the divine presence.

19. —*like the tree abominated*] That is, as an object of abomination and detestation; such as the tree is on which a malefactor has been hanged. "It is written," saith St. Paul, Gal. iii. 13. "Cursed is every man that hangeth on a tree;" from Deut. xxi. 23. The Jews therefore held also as accursed and polluted the tree itself on which a malefactor had been executed, or on which he had been hanged after having been put to death by stoning. "Non suspendunt super arbore, quæ radicibus solo adhæreat; sed super ligno eradicato, ut ne sit excisio molesta: nam lignum, super quo fuit aliquis suspensus, cum suspendioso sepelitur; ne maneat illi malum nomen, et dicant homines, Istud est lignum, in quo suspensus est ille, ὁ δεῖνα. Sic lapis, quo aliquis fuit lapidatus; et gladius, quo fuit occisus is qui est occisus; et sudarium sive mantile, quo fuit aliquis strangulatus; omnia hæc cum iis, qui perierunt, sepeliuntur:" Maimonides, apud Casaub. in Baron. Exercitat. xvi. An. 34. Num. 134. "Cum itaque homo suspensus maximæ esset abominationi— Judæi quoque præ cæteris abominabantur lignum quo fuerat suspensus, ita ut illud quoque terra tegerent, tanquam rem abominabilem. Unde Interpres Chaldæus hæc verba transtulit כחט טמיר, sicut virgultum absconditum, sive sepultum:" Kalinski, Vaticinia Observationibus illustrata, p. 342. Agreeably to which, Theodoret, Hist. Ecclesiast. i. 17, 18. in his account of the finding of the cross by Helena, says, that the three crosses were buried in the earth near the place of our Lord's sepulchre.

Ibid. —*Clothed with the slain.*] Thirty-five MSS (ten ancient), and three editions, have the word fully written, לבוש. It is not a noun, but the participle passive: thrown out among the common slain, and covered with the dead bodies. So ver. 11. the earth-worm is said to be his bed-covering.

20. *Because thou hast destroyed thy country; thou hast slain thy people.*] Xenophon gives an instance of this king's wanton cruelty in killing the son of Gobrias, on no other provocation than that, in hunting, he struck a boar and a lion, which the king had missed: Cyrop. iv. p. 309.

23. *I will plunge it—*] I have here very nearly followed the version of the LXX: the reasons for which see in the ast note on De Poesi Hebr. Prælect. xxviii.

25. *To crush the Assyrian—on my mountains*] The Assyrians and Babylonians are the same people: Herod. i. 199, 200. Babylon is reckoned the principal city in Assyria: ibid. 178. Strabo says the same thing; lib. xvi. sub init. The circumstance of this judgment's being to be executed on God's mountains is of importance: it may mean the destruction of Senacherib's army near Jerusalem; and have still a further view: Compare Ezek. xxxix. 4.; and see Lowth on this place of Isaiah.

28. Uzziah had subdued the Philistines, 2 Chron. xxvi. 6, 7.; but taking advantage of the weak reign of Ahaz, they invaded Judea, and took and held in possession some cities in the southern part of the kingdom. On the death of Ahaz, Isaiah delivers this prophecy, threatening them with the destruction that Hezekiah, his son, and great-grandson of Uzziah, should bring upon them: which he effected; for "he smote the Philistines, even unto Gaza, and the borders thereof;" 2 Kings xviii. 8. Uzziah therefore must be meant by the rod that smote them, and by the serpent, from whom should spring the flying fiery serpent; that is, Hezekiah, a much more terrible enemy than even Uzziah had been.

30. — *he will slay*] The LXX read המית, in the third person, ανελει; and so Chald. The Vulgate remedies the confusion of persons in the present text, by reading both the verbs in the first person.

31. *From the north cometh a smoke*] That is, a cloud of dust, raised by the march of Hezekiah's army against Philistia; which lay to the south-west from Jerusalem. A great dust raised has, at a distance, the appearance of smoke: " fumantes pulvere campi :" Virg. Æn. xi. 908.

32. —*to the ambassadors of the nations*] The LXX read גוים, εθνων, plural; and so the Chaldee, and one MS. The ambassadors of the neighbouring nations, that send to congratulate Hezekiah on his success; which in his answer he will ascribe to the protection of God. See 2 Chron. xxxii. 23. Or, if גו, singular, the reading of the text, be preferred, the ambassadors sent by the Philistines to demand peace.

CHAPTER XV.

This and the following chapter, taken together, make one entire prophecy, very improperly divided into two parts. The time of the delivery, and consequently of the completion of it, which was to be in three years from that time, is uncertain; the former not being marked in the prophecy itself, nor the latter recorded in history. But the most probable account is, that it was delivered soon after the foregoing, in the first year of Hezekiah; and that it was accomplished in his fourth year, when Shalmaneser invaded the kingdom of Israel. He might probably march through Moab; and, to secure every thing behind him, possess himself of the whole country, by taking their principal strong places, Ar and Kirhares.

Jeremiah has happily introduced much of this prophecy of Isaiah into his own larger prophecy against the same people in his xlviiith chapter; denouncing God's judgments on Moab, subsequent to the calamity here foretold, and to be executed by Nebuchadnezzar: by which means several mistakes in the present text of both Prophets may be rectified.

1. *Because in the night*—] בליל. That both these cities should be taken in the night, is a circumstance somewhat unusual; and not so material as to deserve to be so strongly insisted upon. Vitringa, by his remark on this word, shews, that he was dissatisfied with it in its plain and obvious meaning; and is forced to have recourse to a very hard metaphorical interpretation of it: "Noctu, vel nocturno impetu; vel metaphorice, repente, subito, inexpectata destructione: placet posterius." Calmet conjectures, and I think it probable, that the true reading is כליל. There are many mistakes in the Hebrew text arising from the very great similitude of the letters ב and כ, which in many MSS, and even in some printed editions, are hardly distinguishable. Admitting this reading, the translation will be:—

"Because Ar is utterly destroyed, Moab is undone!
Because Kir is utterly destroyed, Moab is undone!"

2. *Beth-Dibon* :—] This is the name of one place; and the two words are to be joined together, without the ו intervening: so Chald. and Syr.

Ibid.—*on every head*] For ראשיו, read ראש. So the parallel place, Jer. xlviii. 37. and so three MSS (one ancient). An ancient MS reads על כל ראש.

Ibid. *On every head there is baldness and every beard is shorn.*] Herodotus, ii. 36. speaks of it as a general practice among all men, except the Egyptians, to cut off their hair as a token of mourning. " Cut off thy hair and cast it away," says Jeremiah, vii. 29. " and take up a lamentation."

Τȣτο νυ και γεϱας οιον οἰζυϱοισι βϱοτοισι
Κειϱασθαι τε κομην, βαλεειν τ' απο δακϱυ παϱειων. Hom. Od. iv. 197.

"The rites of woe
Are all, alas! the living can bestow;
O'er the congenial dust enjoin'd to shear
The graceful curl, and drop the tender tear." Pope.

Ibid.—*shorn*—] The printed editions, as well as the MSS, are divided on the reading of this word: some have נדועה, others גרעה. The similitude of the letters ד and ר has likewise occasioned many mistakes. In the present case, the sense is pretty much the same with either reading. The text of Jer. xlviii. 37. has the latter.

4.—*the very loins*—] So the LXX, ἡ οσφυς, and Syr. They cry out violently, with their utmost force.

5. *The heart of Moab crieth within her.*] For לבי, LXX, read לבו, or לב; the Chald. לבי. For בריחיה, Syr. reads ברוחה; and so likewise the LXX, rendering it εν αυτῃ, Edit. Vat. or εν ἑαυτῃ, Edit. Alex. and MS I. D. II.

Ibid— *a young heifer*] Heb. a heifer *three years old*, in full strength; as Horace uses *equa trima*, for a young mare just coming to her prime. Bochart observes from Aristotle, Hist. Animal. lib. iv., that, in this kind of animals alone, the voice of the female is deeper than that of the male; therefore the lowing of the heifer, rather than of the bullock, is chosen by the Prophet as the properer image to express the mourning of Moab. But I must add, that the expression here, is very short and obscure, and the opinions of interpreters are various in regard to the meaning. Compare Jer. xlviii. 34.

Ibid.—*they shall ascend*] For יעלה, LXX and a MS read in the plural יעלו. And from this passage the parallel place in Jer. xlviii. 5. must be corrected; where, for יעלה בכי, which gives no good sense, read יעלה בו.

7—*shall perish*] אבדו, or אבדה. This word seems to have been lost out of the text: it is supplied by the parallel place, Jer. xlviii. 36. Syr. expresses it by עבר, præteriit; and Chald. by יתבזזון, diripientur.

Ibid. *to the valley of willows.*] That is, to Babylon.

Hieron. and Jarchi in loc. both referring to Psal. cxxxvii. 2. So likewise Prideaux, Le Clerc, &c.

9. *Upon the escaped of Moab and Ariel, and the remnant of Admah*] The LXX for אריה read אריאל. Ar Moab was called also Ariel or Areopolis; Hieron. and Theodoret. See Cellarius. They make אדמה also a proper name. Michaelis thinks, that the Moabites might be called the remnant of Admah, as sprung from Lot and his daughters escaped from the destruction of that and the other cities; or metaphorically, as the Jews are called the princes of Sodom and people of Gomorrah, chap. i. 10. Bibliothek Orient. Part. V. p. 195. The reading of this verse is very doubtful; and the sense, in every way in which it can be read, very obscure.

CHAPTER XVI.

1. *I will send forth the son—*] Both the reading and meaning of this verse are still more doubtful than those of the preceding. The LXX and Syr. read אשלח, in the first person sing. future tense: the Vulg. and Talmud Babylon. read שלח, sing. imperative. The Syr. for כר reads בר, which is confirmed by one MS, and perhaps by a second. The two first verses describe the distress of Moab on the Assyrian invasion; in which even the son of the prince of the country is represented as forced to flee for his life through the desert, that he may escape to Judea; and the young women are driven forth, like young birds cast out of the nest, and endeavouring to wade through the fords of the river Arnon.

3. *Impart counsel—*] The Vulg. renders the verbs in the beginning of this verse in the singular number. So the Keri; and so likewise many MSS have it, and some editions, and Syr. The verbs throughout the verse are also in the feminine gender; agreeing with Sion, which I suppose to be understood.

4. *—the outcasts of Moab—*] Setting the points aside, this is by much the most obvious construction of the Hebrew, as well as most agreeable to the context, and the design of the Prophet. And it is confirmed by the LXX, οἱ φυγάδες Μωάβ, et Syr.

Ibid. *—the oppressor—*] Perhaps the Israelites; who in the time of Ahaz invaded Judah, defeated his army, slaying 120,000 men; and brought the kingdom to the brink of destruction. Judah, being now in a more prosperous condition, is represented as able to receive and to protect the fugitive Moabites. And with those former times of distress, the security and flourishing state of the kingdom under the government of Hezekiah is contrasted.

6. *We have heard the pride of Moab*—] For נא, read גאה; two MSS, (one ancient), and Jer. xlviii. 29. Zephaniah, in his prophecy against Moab, the subject of which is the same with that of Jeremiah in his xlviiith chapter, (see above Note on xv. 1.), enlarges much on the pride of Moab, and their insolent behaviour towards the Jews:—

"I have heard the reproach of Moab;
And the revilings of the sons of Ammon:
Who have reproached my people;
And have magnified themselves against their borders.
Therefore, as I live, saith JEHOVAH God of Hosts, the God of Israel,
Surely Moab shall be as Sodom,
And the sons of Ammon as Gomorrah:
A possession of nettles, and pits of salt,
And a desolation forever.
The residue of my people shall spoil them,
And the remnant of my nation shall dispossess them:
This shall they have for their pride;
Because they have raised a reproach, and have magnified themselves,
Against the people of JEHOVAH God of Hosts."
Zeph. ii. 8—10.

7. *For the men of Kirhares*—] A palpable mistake in this place is happily corrected by the parallel text of Jer. xlviii. 31. where, instead of אשישי, *foundations* or *flagons*, we read אנשי, *men*. In the same place of Jeremiah, and in ver. 36., and here in ver. 11., the name of the city is Kirhares, not Kirhareseth.

Ibid. —*are put to shame*] Here the text of Jeremiah leaves us much at a loss, in a place that seems to be greatly corrupted. The LXX join the two last words of this verse with the beginning of the following. Their rendering is; καὶ οὐκ ἐντραπήσῃ τα πεδία Εσεβων. For אך they must have read אל; otherwise, how came they by the negative, which seems not to belong to this place? Neither is it easy to make sense of the rest without a small alteration, by reading, instead of ἐντραπήσῃ τα, ἐντραπήσεται. In a word, the Arabic version taken from the LXX, plainly authorizes this reading of the LXX, and without the negative ; and it is fully confirmed by MSS Pachom. and 1. D. 11. which have both of them ευτραπησεται πεδια Εσεβων, without the negative ; which makes an excellent sense, and, I think, gives us the true reading of the Hebrew text : אך נכלמו שדמות חשבון. They frequently render the verb נכלם by ευτρεπομαι. And נכלמו answers perfectly well to אמלל, the parallel word in the next line. The MSS vary in expressing in the word נכאים, which gives no tolerable sense in this place : one reads נוכאים, two others בכאים, in another the כ is upon a rasure of two letters ; and Vulg. instead of it reads מכותם, *plagas suas.*

8. *Her branches extended themselves*—] For נטשו a MS has נגשו; which may perhaps be right : Compare Jer. xlviii. 32. which has in this part of the sentence the synonymous word נגעו.

The meaning of this verse is, that the wines of Sibmah and Heshbon were greatly celebrated, and in high repute with all the great men and princes of that and the neighbouring countries ; who indulged themselves even to intemperance in the use of them. So that their vines were so much in request, as not only to be propagated all over the country of Moab, to the sea of Sodom ; but to have cions of them sent even beyond the sea into foreign countries.

הלמו, knocked down, demolished ; that is, overpowered, intoxicated. The drunkards of Ephraim are called by the Prophet, chap. xxviii. 1. הלומי יין. See Schultens on Prov. xxiii. 25. Gratius, speaking of the Mareotic wine, says of it,

" Pharios quæ fregit noxia reges." Cyneg. ver. 312.

9. *as with the weeping*—] For בבכי a MS reads כב. In Jer. xlviii. 32. it is מבכי. LXX read כבכי, which I follow.

Ibid. *And upon thy vintage the destroyer hath fallen*] ועל קצירך הידד נפל. In these few words there are two great mistakes ; which the text of Jer. xlviii. 32. rectifies : for קצירך, it has בצירך; and for הידד, שדד : both which corrections the Chaldee in this place confirms. As to the first,

" Hesebon and Eleale, and
The flowery dale of Sibmah clad with vines,"

were never celebrated for their *harvests;* it was the *vintage* that suffered by the irruption of the enemy : and so read LXX and Syr. הידד is the noisy acclamation of the treaders of the grapes: and see what sense this makes in the literal rendering of the Vulgate—super messem tuam " vox calcantium irruit." The reading in Jer. xlvii. 32. is certainly right, שדד נפל, *vastator* irruit. The shout of the treaders does not come in till the next verse; in which the text of Isaiah in its turn mends that of Jeremiah, xlviii. 33. where, instead of the first הידד, *the shout*, we ought undoubtedly to read, as here, הדרך, *the treader.*

10. *An end is put to the shouting*] The LXX read השבת, passive, and in the third person,—rightly; for God is not the speaker in this place. The rendering of LXX is πεπαυται γαρ κελευσμα; which last word, necessary to the rendering of the Hebrew, and to the sense, is supplied by MSS Pachom. and 1. D. 11., having been lost out of the other copies.

12. *when Moab shall see*—] For נראה a MS reads ראה, and so Syr. and Chald. " Perhaps כי נראה is only a various reading of כי נלאה;" SECKER. A very probable conjecture.

14. —*and without strength*] An ancient MS, with LXX, reads ולא.

CHAPTER XVII.

THIS prophecy by its title should relate only to Damascus; but it full as much concerns, and more largely treats of, the kingdom of Samaria and the Israelites, confederate with Damascus and the Syrians against the kingdom of Judah. It was delivered probably soon after the prophecies of the viith and viiith chapters, in the beginning of the reign of Ahaz; and was fulfilled by Tiglath Pileser's taking Damascus, and carrying the people captives to Kir, (2 Kings xvi. 9.); and overrunning great part of the kingdom of Israel, and carrying a great number of the Israelites also captives to Assyria; and still more fully in regard to Israel, by the conquest of the kingdom, and the captivity of the people, effected a few years after by Shalmaneser.

1. —*a ruinous heap*] For כיע the LXX read לעי, Vulg. כיע. I follow the former.

2. *The cities are deserted for ever*] What has Aroer on the river Arnon to do with Damascus? and if there be

another Aroer on the northen border of the tribe of Gad, (as Reland seems to think there might be), this is not much more to the purpose. Besides, the cities of Aroer, if Aroer itself is a city, makes no good sense. The LXX, for ערער, *Aroer*, read ערי עד, εἰς τὸν αἰῶνα, *for ever*, or for a long duration. The Chald. takes the word for a verb from ערה, translating it חרבו, devastabuntur. The Syr. read ערוער. So that the reading is very doubtful. I follow the LXX, as making the plainest sense.

3. —*the pride of Syria*—] For שאר Houbigant reads שאת, *the pride*, answering, as the sentence seems evidently to require, to כבוד, *the glory* of Israel. The conjecture is so very probable, that I venture to follow it.

5. —*as when one gathereth*—] That is, the king of Assyria shall sweep away the whole body of the people, as the reaper strippeth off the whole crop of corn; and the remnant shall be no more, in proportion, than the scattered ears left to the gleaner. The valley of Rephaim near Jerusalem was celebrated for its plentiful harvests; it is here used poetically for any fruitful country.

8. —*the altars dedicated to the work of his hands*] The construction of the words, and the meaning of the sentence, in this place, are not obvious: all the ancient versions, and most of the modern, have mistaken it. The word מעשה stands *in regimine* with מזבחות, not in apposition with it: it means the altars *of* the work of their hands; that is, *of* the idols; not which *are* the work of their hands. Thus Kimchi has explained it, and Le Clerc has followed him.

9. —*the Hivites and the Amorites*—] החורש והאמיר. No one has ever yet been able to make any tolerable sense of these words. The translation of the LXX has happily preserved what seems to be the true reading of the text, as it stood in the copies of their time; though the words are now transposed, either in the text, or in their version: οἱ Ἀμόῤῥαιοι καὶ οἱ Εὐαῖοι. It is remarkable, that many commentators, who never thought of admitting the reading of the LXX, yet understand the passage as referring to that very event which their version expresses: so that it is plain, that nothing can be more suitable to the context. My Father saw the necessity of admitting this variation, at a time when it was not usual to make so free with the Hebrew text. See Lowth on the place.

10. —*shoots from a foreign soil*] The pleasant plants,

and shoots from a foreign soil, are allegorical expressions for strange and idolatrous worship; vicious and abominable practices connected with it; reliance on human aid, and on alliances entered into with the neighbouring nations, especially Egypt: to all which the Israelites were greatly addicted; and in their expectations from which they should be grievously disappointed.

12—14. *Wo to the multitude*—] The three last verses of this chapter seem to have no relation to the foregoing prophecy, to which they are joined. It is a beautiful piece, standing singly and by itself; for neither has it any connexion with what follows: whether it stands in its right place, or not, I cannot say. It is a noble description of the formidable invasion, and of the sudden overthrow, of Senacherib; which is intimated in the strongest terms, and the most expressive images, exactly suitable to the event.

12, 13. *Like the roaring of mighty waters*—] Five words, three at the end of the 12th verse, and two at the beginning of the 13th, are omitted in five MSS; that is, in effect, the repetition, contained in the first line of verse 13, in this translation, is not made. After having observed, that it is equally easy to account for the omission of these words by a transcriber, if they are genuine; or their insertion, if they are not genuine: occasioned by his carrying his eye backwards to the word לאמים, or forwards to ישאון; I shall leave it to the reader's judgment to determine, whether they are genuine, or not.

14. —*and he is no more*] For איננו, ten MSS (three ancient) and two editions, and LXX, Syr. Chald. Vulg. have ואיננו. This particle, authenticated by so many good vouchers, restores the sentence to the true poetical form, implying a repetition of some part of the parallel line preceding, thus:

" At the season of evening, behold terror!
Before the morning, and [behold] he is no more!"
            See Prelim. Dissert. p. xii. note.

CHAPTER XVIII.

This is one of the most obscure prophecies in the whole book of Isaiah. The subject of it, the end and design of it, the people to whom it is addressed, the history to which it belongs, the person who sends the messengers, and the nation to whom the messengers are sent; are all obscure and doubtful.

1. *The winged cymbal*] צלצל כנפים. I adopt this as the most probable of the many interpretations that have been given of these words. It is Bochart's: see Phaleg iv. 2. The Egyptian Sistrum is expressed by a periphrasis; the Hebrews had no name for it in their language, not having in use the instrument itself. The cymbal they had; an instrument in its use and sound not much unlike to the sistrum; and to distinguish from it the sistrum, they called it the cymbal with wings. The cymbal was a round hollow piece of metal, which being struck against another, gave a ringing sound: the sistrum was a round instrument, consisting of a broad rim of metal, through which from side to side ran several loose laminæ, or small rods, of metal, which being shaken, gave a like sound: These projecting on each side, had somewhat of the appearance of wings; or might be very properly expressed by the same word which the Hebrews used for wings, or for the extremity, or a part of any thing projecting. The sistrum is given in a medal of Adrian, as the proper attribute of Egypt. See Addison on Medals, Series iii. No. 4. where the figure of it may be seen.

In opposition to other interpretations of these words which have prevailed, it may be briefly observed, that צלצל is never used to signify *shadow*, nor כנף applied to the sails of ships.

If therefore the words are rightly interpreted *the winged cymbal*, meaning the sistrum, Egypt must be the country to which the prophecy is addressed: And upon this hypothesis the version and explanation must proceed. I further suppose, that the prophecy was delivered before Senacherib's return from his Egyptian expedition, which took up three years; and that it was designed to give to the Jews, and perhaps likewise to the Egyptians, an intimation of God's counsels in regard to the destruction of their great and powerful enemy.

Ibid. *Which borders on the rivers of Cush*] What are the rivers of Cush, whether the eastern branches of the lower Nile, the boundary of Egypt towards Arabia, or the parts of the upper Nile towards Ethiopia, it is not easy to determine. The word מעבר signifies either *on this side* or *on the further side*: I have made use of the same kind of ambiguous expression in the translation.

2. —*in vessels of papyrus*] This circumstance agrees perfectly well with Egypt. It is well known, that the Egyptians commonly used on the Nile a light sort of ships, or boats, made of the reed papyrus. " Ex ipso quidem papyro navigia texunt :" Plin. xiii. 11.

" Conseritur bibula Memphitis cymba papyro." Luc. iv. 136.

Ibid. *Go, ye swift messengers*—] To this nation before mentioned, who, by the Nile, and by their numerous canals, have the means of spreading the report, in the most expeditious manner, through the whole country ; go, ye swift messengers, and carry this notice of God's designs in regard to them. By the swift messengers are meant, not any particular persons specially appointed to this office, but any the usual conveyers of news whatsoever, travellers, merchants, and the like, the instruments and agents of common fame: these are ordered to publish this declaration made by the Prophet throughout Egypt, and to all the world; and to excite their attention to the promised visible interposition of God.

Ibid. —*stretched out in length*—] Egypt, that is, the fruitful part of it, exclusive of the deserts on each side, is one long vale, through the middle of which runs the Nile, bounded on each side to the east and west by a chain of mountains ; seven hundred and fifty miles in length ; in breadth, from one to two or three days' journey : even at the widest part of the Delta, from Pelusium to Alexandria, not above two hundred and fifty miles broad. Egmont and Heyman, and Pococke's Travels.

Ibid. —*smoothed*—] Either relating to the practice of the Egyptian priests, who made their bodies smooth by shaving off their hair ; see Herod. ii. 37.; or rather to the country's being made smooth, perfectly plain and level, by the overflowing of the Nile.

Ibid. —*meted out by line*—] It is generally referred to the frequent necessity of having recourse to mensuration in Egypt, in order to determine the boundaries after the inundations of the Nile ; to which even the origin of the science of geometry is by some ascribed. Strabo, lib. xvii. sub init.

Ibid. —*trodden down*—] Supposed to allude to a peculiar method of tillage in use among the Egyptians. Both Herodotus (lib. ii.) and Diodorus (lib. i.) say, that when the Nile had retired within its banks, and the ground became somewhat dry, they sowed their land, and then sent in their cattle (their hogs, says the former) to tread in the seed; and without any further care expected the harvest.

Ibid. —*the rivers have nourished*] The word בזאו is generally taken to be an irregular form for בזז, *have spoiled*, as an ancient MS has it in this place; and so most of the versions, both ancient and modern, understand it. On which Schultens, Gram. Heb. p. 491. has the following remark: " Ne minimam quidem speciem veri habet בזאו, Esai. xvii. 2. elatum pro בזז, *diripiunt*. Hæc esset anomalia, cui nihil simile in toto linguæ ambitu. In talibus nil finire, vel fateri ex mera agi conjectura, tutius justiusque. Radicem בזא olim extare potuisse, quis neget? Si cognatum quid sectandum erat, ad בזה, *contemsit*, potius decurrendum fuisset: ut בזאו pro בזו sit enuntiatum, vel בזיו. Digna phrasis, *flumina contemnunt terram*, i. e. *inundant*." "בזא, Arab. *extulit se superbius*, item *subjecit sibi:* unde præt. pl. בזאו. *subjecerunt sibi*, i. e. *inundarunt:* " Simonis Lexic. Heb.

A learned friend has suggested to me another explanation of the word. בז, Syr. and בזא, Chald. signifies *uber, mamma;* agreeably to which the verb might signify *to nourish*. This would perfectly well suit with the Nile: whereas nothing can be more discordant than the idea of spoiling and plundering; for to the inundation of the Nile Egypt owed every thing,—the fertility of the soil, and the very soil itself. Besides, the overflowing of the Nile came on by gentle degrees, covering without laying waste the country. "Mira æque natura fluminis, quod cum cæteri omnes abluant terras et eviscerent, Nilus tanto cæteris major adeo nihil exedit, nec abradit, ut contra adjiciat vires; minimumque in eo sit, quod solum temperet. Illato enim limo arenas saturat ac jungit: debetque illi Ægyptus non tantum fertilitatem terrarum, sed ipsas:" Seneca, Nat. Quæst. iv. 2. I take the liberty, therefore, which Schultens seems to think allowable in this place, of hazarding a conjectural interpretation.

3. *When the standard is lifted up—*] I take God to be the agent in this verse; and that by the standard and the trumpet are meant the meteors, the thunder, the lightning, the storm, earthquake, and tempest, by which Senacherib's army shall be destroyed, or by which at least the destruction of it shall be accompanied; as it is described in chap. xxix. 6. and xxx. 30, 31. and x. 16, 17. See also Psal. lxxvi. and the title of it according to LXX, Vulg. and

Æthiop. They are called by a bold metaphor, the standard lifted up, and the trumpet sounded. The latter is used by Homer, I think, with great force, in his introduction to the battle of the gods; though I find it has disgusted some of the minor critics:

Βραχε δ' ευρεια χθων,
Αμφι δε σαλπιγξεν μεγας ϐρανος.   Il. xxi. 388.

"Heaven in loud thunders bids the trumpet sound,
And wide beneath them groans the rending ground." Pope.

4. *For thus hath JEHOVAH said unto me*—] The subject of the remaining part of the chapter is, that God would comfort and support his own people, though threatened with immediate destruction by the Assyrians; that Senacherib's great designs and mighty efforts against them should be frustrated, and that his vast expectations should be rendered abortive, when he thought them mature, and just ready to be crowned with success; that the chief part of his army should be made a prey for the beasts of the field, and the fowls of the air, (for this is the meaning of the allegory continued through the 5th and 6th verses); and that Egypt, being delivered from his oppression, and avenged by the hand of God of the wrongs which she had suffered, should return thanks for the wonderful deliverance, both of herself and of the Jews, from this most powerful adversary.

Ibid. *Like the clear heat*—] The same images are employed by an Arabian poet:—

"Solis more fervens, dum frigus; quumque ardet
   Sirius, tum vero frigus ipse et umbra."

Which is illustrated in the note by a like passage from another Arabian poet:—

"Calor est hyeme, refrigerium æstate."

Excerpta ex Hamasa; published by Schultens, at the end of Erpenius's Arabic Grammar, p. 425.

Ibid. —*after rain*—] "אור hic significat pluviam; juxta illud, *sparget nubes pluviam suam*, Job xxxvii. 11." Kimchi. In which place of Job the Chaldee paraphrast does indeed explain אורו by מטריה; and so again ver. 21.; and chap. xxxvi. 30. This meaning of the word seems to make the best sense in this place; it is to be wished, that it were better supported.

Ibid. —*in the day of harvest.*] For בחם, *in the heat*,

five MSS, (three ancient), LXX, Syr. and Vulg, read בְּיוֹם, *in the day.* The mistake seems to have risen from כֵּהֶם in the line above.

5. *—the blossom—*] Heb. *her* blossom; נִצָּה: that is, the blossom of the vine, גֶפֶן, understood, which is of the common gender. See Gen. xl. 10. Note, that, by the defective punctuation of this word, many interpreters, and our translators among the rest, have been led into a grievous mistake, (for how can the swelling grape become a blossom?) taking the word נִצָּה for the predicate; whereas it is the subject of the proposition, or the nominative case to the verb.

7. *—a gift—*] The Egyptians were in alliance with the kingdom of Judah, and were fellow-sufferers with the Jews under the invasion of their common enemy Senacherib; and so were very nearly interested in the great and miraculous deliverance of that kingdom by the destruction of the Assyrian army. Upon which wonderful event, it is said, 2 Chron. xxxii. 23. that " many brought gifts unto JEHOVAH to Jerusalem, and presents to Hezekiah king of Judah; so that he was magnified of all nations from thenceforth." It is not to be doubted, that among these the Egyptians distinguished themselves in their acknowledgments on this occasion.

Ibid. *—from a people—*] The LXX and Vulg. read מֵעַם; which is confirmed by the repetition of it in the next line. The difference is of importance; for, if this be the true reading, the prediction of the admission of Egypt into the true church of God is not so explicit as it might otherwise seem to be. However, that event is clearly foretold at the end of the next chapter.

CHAPTER XIX.

NOT many years after the destruction of Senacherib's army before Jerusalem, by which the Egyptians were freed from the yoke with which they were threatened by so powerful an enemy, who had carried on a successful war of three years' continuance against them; the affairs of Egypt were again thrown into confusion by intestine broils among themselves; which ended in a perfect anarchy, that lasted some few years. This was followed by an aristocracy, or rather tyranny, of twelve princes, who divided the country between them; and at last by the sole dominion of Psammitichus, which he held for fifty-four years. Not long after that, followed the invasion and conquest of Egypt by Nebuchadnezzar; and then by the Persians under Cambyses, the son of Cyrus. The yoke of the Persians was so grievous, that the conquest of the Persians by Alexander may well be considered as a deliverance to Egypt; especially as he and his successors greatly favoured the people, and improved the country. To all these events the Prophet seems to have had a view in this chapter; and in particular, from ver. 18. the prophecy of the propagation of the true religion in Egypt seems to point to the flourishing state of Judaism in that country, in consequence of the great favour shewn to the Jews by the Ptolemies. Alexander himself settled a great many Jews in his new city Alexandria, granting them privileges equal to those of the Macedonians. The first Ptolemy, called Soter, carried great numbers of them thither, and gave them such encouragement, that still more of them were collected there from different parts; so that Philo reckons, that in his time there were a million of Jews in that country. These worshipped the God of their fathers; and their example and influence must have had a great effect in spreading the knowledge and worship of the true God through the whole country. See Bishop Newton on the Prophecies, Dissert. xii.

4. —*cruel lords*] Nebuchadnezzar in the first place, and afterwards the whole succession of Persian kings, who in general were hard masters, and grievously oppressed the country. Note, that for קשה, a MS reads קשים, agreeable to which is the rendering of LXX, Syr. and Vulg.

6. —*shall become putrid*] האזניחו. This sense of the word, which Simonis gives in his Lexicon from the meaning of it in the Arabic, suits the place much better than any other interpretation hitherto given. And that the word in Hebrew had some such signification is probable from 2 Chron. xxix. 18. where the Vulgate renders it by *polluit*, and the Targum by *profanavit* and *abominabile fecit*, which the context in that place seems plainly to require. The form of the verb here is very irregular; and the rabbins and grammarians seem to give no probable account of it.

8. —*And the fishers*—] There was great plenty of fish in Egypt: see Numb. xi. 5. "The Nile," says Diodorus, lib. 1. "abounds with incredible numbers of all sorts of fish." And much more the lakes; Egmont, Pococke, &c.

10.—*her stores*—] שתתיה, αποθηκαι, Aquila.

Ibid. *all that make a gain of pools for fish*] This obscure line is rendered by different interpreters in very different manners. Kimchi explains אגמי, as if it were the same with עגמי, from Job xxx. 25. In which he is followed by some of the rabbins, and supported by LXX: and שכר, which I translate *gain*, and which some take for *nets*, or *inclosures*, the LXX render by ζυθον, strong drink, or beer, which it is well known was much used in Egypt: and so likewise the Syriac, retaining the Hebrew word שברא. I submit these very different interpretations to the reader's judgment. The version of the LXX is as follows:—και παντες οι ποιουντες τον ζυθον λυπηθησονται, και τας ψυχας πονεσουσι: "And all they that make barley-wine shall mourn, and be grieved in soul."

11.—*have counselled a brutish counsel*] The sentence, as it now stands in the Hebrew, is imperfect; it wants the verb. Archbishop Secker conjectures, that the words יעצי נבערה should be transposed; which would in some degree remove the difficulty. But it is to be observed, that the translator of the Vulgate seems to have found in his copy the verb יעצו added after פרעה: "Sapientes consiliarii Pharaonis *dederunt* consilium insipiens." This is probably the true reading; it is perfectly agreeable to the Hebrew idiom, makes the construction of the sentence clear, and renders the transposition of the above words unnecessary.

12.—*let them come*—] Here too a word seems to have been left out of the text. After חכמיך, two MSS (one ancient) add יבאו, *let them come*. Which, if we consider the form and the construction of the sentence, has very much the appearance of being genuine; otherwise the connective conjunction at the beginning of the next member, is not only superfluous but embarrassing. See also the version of LXX, in which the same deficiency is manifest.

Ibid.—*and let them declare*—] "For ידעו, *let them know*, perhaps we ought to read יודיעו, *let them make known*." SECKER. The LXX and Vulg. favour this reading: ειπατωσαν, *indicent*.

13. *They have caused*—] The text has והתעו, *and they have caused to err*. Fifty MSS, thirteen editions, Vulg. and Chald. omit the ו.

Ibid.—*pillars*—] פנת to be pointed as plural without doubt. So Grotius, and so Chald.

26

14—*in the midst of them*—] "בקרבם, LXX, quod forte rectius:" SECKER. So likewise Chald.

16.—*the Egyptians shall be*—] יהיו, plural, MS Bodl. LXX, and Chald. This is not proposed as an emendation, for either form is proper.

17. *And the land of Judah*—] The threatening hand of God will be held out and shaken over Egypt, from the side of Judea; through which the Assyrians will march to invade it. Five MSS and two editions have לחנה.

18.—*the City of the Sun*] עיר החרס. This passage is attended with much difficulty and obscurity. First, in regard to the true reading. It is well known, that Onias applied it to his own views, either to procure from the king of Egypt permission to build his temple in the Hieropolitan Nome, or to gain credit and authority to it when built; from the notion which he industriously propagated, that Isaiah had in this place prophesied of the building of such a temple. He pretended, that the very place were it should be built was expressly named by the Prophet עיר החרס, the city of the sun. This possibly may have been the original reading. The present text has עיר ההרס, the city of destruction: which some suppose to have been introduced into the text by the Jews of Palestine afterwards; to express their detestation of the place, being much offended with this schismatical temple in Egypt. Some think the latter to have been the true reading, and that the Prophet himself gave this turn to the name out of contempt, and to intimate the demolition of this Hieropolitan temple; which in effect was destroyed by Vespasian's orders after that of Jerusalem. "Videtur Propheta consulto scripsisse הרס pro חרם, ut alibi scribitur א'ש בעל pro א'ש בשת, בית אל pro בית און, &c. Vide Lowth in loc.:" SECKER. But on supposition that עיר ההרס, is the true reading, others understand it differently. The word הרס in Arabic signifies a lion: and Conrad Ikenius has written a dissertation (Dissert. Philol. Theol. xvi.) to prove that the place here mentioned is not Heliopolis, as it is commonly supposed to be, but Leontopolis in the Heliopolitan Nome; as it is indeed called in the letter, whether real or pretended, of Onias to Ptolemy, which Josephus has inserted in his Jewish Antiquities, lib. xiii. cap. 3. And I find, that several persons of great learning and judgment think that Ikenius has proved the point beyond contradiction. See Christian. Muller. Satura. Observ.

Philolog. Michaelis Bibliothek Oriental, Part V. p. 171. But after all, I believe, that neither Onias, nor Heliopolis, nor Leontopolis, has any thing to do with this subject. The application of this place of Isaiah to Onias's purpose seems to have been a mere invention; and, in consequence of it, there may perhaps have been some unfair management to accommodate the text to that purpose; which has been carried even further than the Hebrew text; for the Greek version has here been either translated from a corrupted text, or wilfully mistranslated or corrupted, to serve the same cause. The place is there called πολις Ασεδεκ, the city of righteousness; a name apparently contrived by Onias's party to give credit to their temple, which was to rival that of Jerusalem. Upon the whole, the true reading of the Hebrew text in this place is very uncertain; nine MSS and seven editions have חרס, so likewise Sym. Vulg. Arab. LXX, Compl. On the other hand, Aquila, Theodot. and Syr. read הרס; the Chaldee paraphrase takes in both readings.

The reading of the text being so uncertain, no one can pretend to determine what the city was that is here mentioned by name; much less to determine, what the four other cities were which the Prophet does not name. I take the whole passage, from the 18th verse to the end of the chapter, to contain a general intimation of the future propagation of the knowledge of the true God in Egypt and Syria, under the successors of Alexander; and, in consequence of this propagation, of the early reception of the gospel in the same countries, when it should be published to the world. See further on this subject, Prideaux's Connect. an. 149.; Dr. Owen's Inquiry into the Present State of the LXX Version, p. 41., and Bryant's Observations on Ancient History, p. 124.

CHAPTER XX.

THARTHAN beseiged Ashdod or Azotus, which probably belonged at this time to Hezekiah's dominions: see 2 Kings xviii. 8. The people expected to be relieved by the Cushites of Arabia, and by the Egyptians. Isaiah was ordered to go uncovered, that is, without his upper garment, the rough mantle commonly worn by the prophets, (see Zech. xiii. 4.), probably three days, to shew that within three years the town should be taken, after the defeat of the Cushites and Egyptians by the king of Assyria, which event should make their case desperate, and induce them to surrender. Azotus was a strong place: it afterwards held out twenty-nine years against Psammitichus, king of Egypt, Herod. ii. 157. Tharthan was one of Senacherib's generals, 2 Kings xviii. 17., and Tirhakah king of the Cushites was in alliance with the king of Egypt against Senacherib. These circumstances make it probable, that by Sargon is meant Senacherib. It might be one of the seven names by which Jerom, on this place, says he was called. He is called Sacherdonus and Sacherdan in the book of Tobit. The taking of Azotus must have happened before Senacherib's attempt on Jerusalem; when he boasted of his late conquests, chap. xxxvii. 25. And the warning of the Prophet had a principal respect to the Jews also, who were too much inclined to depend upon the assistance of Egypt. As to the rest, history and chronology affording us no light, it may be impossible to clear either this or any other hypothesis, (which takes Sargon to be Shalmaneser, or Asarhaddon, &c.), from all difficulties.

It is not probable that the Prophet walked uncovered and barefoot for three years: his appearing in that manner was a sign, that within three years the Egyptians and Cushites should be in the same condition, being conquered and made captives by the king of Assyria. The time was denoted, as well as the event; but his appearing in that manner for three whole years, could give no premonition of the time at all. It is probable, therefore, that the Prophet was ordered to walk so for three days, to denote the accomplishment of the event in three years; a day for a year, according to the prophetical rule: Numb. xiv. 34. Ezek. iv. 6. The words ימים שלש, *three days*, may possibly have been lost out of the text, at the end of the second verse, after יחף, *barefoot*; or after the same word in the third verse: where, in the Alexandrine and Vatican copies of LXX, and in MSS Pachom. and I. D. II. the words τρια ετη are twice expressed. Perhaps, instead of שלש ימים, the Greek translator might read שלש שנים, by his own mistake, or by that of his copy, after יחף in the third verse, for which stands the first τρια ετη in the Alexandrine and Vatican LXX, and in the two MSS above-mentioned.

CHAPTER XXI.

The ten first verses of this chapter contain a prediction of the taking of Babylon by the Medes and Persians. It is a passage singular in its kind, for its brevity and force; for the variety and rapidity of the movements; and for the strength and energy of colouring with which the action and event is painted. It opens with the Prophet's seeing at a distance the dreadful storm that is gathering, and ready to burst upon Babylon: The event is intimated in general terms; and God's orders are issued to the Persians and Medes to set forth upon the expedition which he has given them in charge. Upon this the Prophet enters into the midst of the action; and, in the person of Babylon, expresses in the strongest terms the astonishment and horror that seizes her on the sudden surprise of the city, at the very season dedicated to pleasure and festivity, ver. 3, 4.: then in his own person describes the situation of things there; the security of the Babylonians, and in the midst of their feasting the sudden alarm of war, ver. 5. The event is then declared in a very singular manner. God orders the Prophet to set a watchman to look out, and to report what he sees: he sees two companies marching onward, representing by their appearance the two nations that were to execute God's orders, who declare, that Babylon is fallen, ver. 6—9.

But what is this to the Prophet, and to the Jews, the object of his ministry? The application, the end, and design of the prophecy is admirably given in a short expressive address to the Jews, partly in the person of God, partly in that of the Prophet: " O my threshing !"—" O my people, whom for your punishment I shall make subject to the Babylonians, to try and to prove you, and to separate the chaff from the corn, the bad from the good among you; hear this for your consolation: Your punishment, your slavery and oppression, will have an end in the destruction of your oppressors."

1. —*the desert of the sea*] This plainly means Babylon, which is the subject of the prophecy. The country about Babylon, and especially below it towards the sea, was a great flat morass, often overflowed by the Euphrates and Tigris. It became habitable by being drained by the many canals that were made in it.

Herodotus, i. 184. says, that "Semiramis confined the Euphrates within its channel, by raising great dams against it; for before it overflowed the whole country like a sea." And Abydenus, (quoting Megasthenes, apud Euseb. Præp. Evang. ix. 41.), speaking of the building of Babylon by Nebuchadonosor, "It is reported, that all this part was covered with water, and was called the sea; and that Belus drew off the waters, conveying them into proper receptacles, and surrounded Babylon with a wall." When the Euphrates was turned out of its channel by Cyrus, it was suffered still to drown the neighbouring country. The Persian government, which did not favour the place, taking no care to remedy this inconvenience, it became in time a great barren morassy desert; which event the title of the prophecy may perhaps intimate. Such it was originally; such it became after the taking of the city by Cyrus; and such it continues to this day.

Ibid. *Like the southern tempests.*—] The most vehement storms, to which Judea was subject, came from the great desert country to the south of it. "Out of the south cometh the whirlwind;" Job xxxvii. 9. "And there came a great wind from the wilderness, and smote the four corners of the house;" Ibid. i. 19. For the situation of Idumea, the country, as I suppose, of Job, (see Lam. iv. 21. compared with Job i. 1.), was the same in this respect with that of Judea.

"And JEHOVAH shall appear over them,
And his arrow shall go forth as the lightning:
And the Lord JEHOVAH shall sound the trumpet;
And shall march in the whirlwinds of the south." Zech. ix. 14.

2. *The plunderer is plundered, and the destroyer is destroyed.*] הבוגר בוגר והשודד שודד. The MSS vary in expressing or omitting the ו in these four words. Ten MSS are without the ו in the second word, and eight MSS are without the ו in the fourth word; which justifies Symmachus, who has rendered them passively: ὁ ἀθετῶν ἀθετεῖται, καὶ ὁ ταλαιπωρίζων ταλαιπωρεῖ. He read בגור, שדור. Cocceius (Lexicon in voce) observes, that the Chaldee very often renders the verb בגד by בזז, *spoliavit;* and in this place, and in xxxiii. 1. by the equivalent word אנס; and in chap. xxiv. 16. both by אנס and בזז; and Syr. in this place renders it by טלם, *oppressit.*

Ibid. —*her vexations*—] Heb. her sighing; that is, the

sighing caused by her. So Kimchi on the place: " Innuit illos, qui gemebant ob timorem ejus; quia suffixa nom num referuntur ad agentem et ad patientem." " Omnes q i gemebant a facie regis Babylonis, requiescere feci eos;" Chald. And so likewise Ephræm Syr. in loc. edit. Assemani: " Gemitum ejus: dolorem scilicet et lachrymas, quas Chaldæi reliquiæ per orbem gentibus ciere pergunt."

5. *The table is prepared*—] In Heb. the verbs are in the infinitive mode absolute; as in Ezek. i. 14. "And the animals ran and returned, רצוא ושוב, like the appearance of lightning:" just as the Latins say currere et reverti, for currebant et revertebantur. See chap. xxxii. 2. and the note there.

7. *And he saw a chariot with two riders; a rider on an ass, a rider on a camel.*] This passage is extremely obscure, from the ambiguity of the term רכב, which is used three times; and which signifies a chariot, or any other vehicle, or the rider in it; or a rider on a horse, or any other animal; or a company of chariots or riders. The Prophet may possibly mean a cavalry in two parts, with two sorts of riders; riders on asses or mules, and riders on camels: or led on by two riders, one on an ass, and one on a camel. However, so far it is pretty clear, that Darius and Cyrus, the Medes and the Persians, are intended to be distinguished by the two riders, or the two sorts of cattle. It appears from Herodotus, i. 80. that the baggage of Cyrus's army was carried on camels. In his engagement with Crœsus, he took off the baggage from the camels, and mounted his horsemen upon them: the enemy's horses, offended with the smell of the camels, turned back and fled.

8. *he that looked out on the watch*—] The present reading אריה, *a lion,* is so unintelligible, and the mistake so obvious, that I make no doubt that the true reading is הראה, as the Syriac translator manifestly found it in his copy, who renders it by דוקא, speculator.

9. —*a man, one of the two riders*] So the Syriac understands it; and Ephræm Syr.

18. *O my threshing*—] " O thou, the object upon which I shall exercise the severity of my discipline; that shalt lie under my afflicting hand, like corn spread upon the floor to be threshed out and winnowed, to separate the chaff from the wheat!" The image of threshing is frequently used by the Hebrew poets with great elegance, and force, to express

the punishmen of the wicked and the trial of the good, or the utter dispersion and destruction of God's enemies. Of the different ways of threshing in use among the Hebrews, and the manner of performing them, see note on chap. xxviii. 27.

Our translators have taken the liberty of u ing the word *threshing* in a passive sense, to express the object or matter that is threshed: in which I have followed them, not being able to express it more properly, without departing too much from the form and letter of the original. *Son* of my floor, Heb. It is an idiom of the Hebrew language to call the effect, the object, the adjunct, any thing that belongs in almost any way to another, the *son* of it. " O my threshing—" The Prophet abruptly breaks off the speech of God, and, instead of continuing it in the form in which he had begun, and in the person of God, " This I declare unto you by my Prophet ; " be changes the form of address, and adds, in his own person, " This I declare unto you from God."

11, 12. *The oracle concerning Dumah.*] " Pro רומה Codex R. Mèiri habet; ארום et sic LXX. Vid. Kimchi ad h. l. ; " Biblia Michaelis, Halæ 1720, not. ad l.

This prophecy, from the uncertainty of the occasion on which it was uttered, and from the brevity of the expression, is extremely obscure. The Edomites as well as Jews were subdued by the Babylonians. They inquire of the Prophet, how long their subjection is to last? he intimates, th t the Jews should be delivered from their captivity ; not so the Edomites. Thus far the interpretation seems to carry with it some degree of probability. What the meaning of the last line may be, I cannot pretend to divine. In this difficulty the Hebrew MSS give no assistance. The MSS of LXX, and the fragments of the other Greek versions, give some variations, but no light. This being the case, I thought it best to give an exact literal translation of the whole two verses ; which may serve to enable the English reader to judge in some measure of the foundation of the various interpretations that have been given of them.

13. *The oracle concerning Arabia.*] This title is of doubtful authority. In the first place, because it is not in many of the MSS of the LXX ; it is in MSS Pachom. and 1. D. 11. only, as far as I can find with certainty : secondly, from the singularity of the phraseology ; for משא is generally prefixed to its object without a proposition, as משא בבל; and

never but in this place with the preposition ב. Besides, as the word בערב occurs at the very beginning of the prophecy itself, the first word but one, it is much to be suspected that some one, taking it for a proper name and the object of the prophecy, might note it as such by the words משא בערב written in the margin, from whence they might easily get into the text. The LXX did not take it for a proper name, but render it ἑσπέρας; and so Chald. whom I follow: for, otherwise, the forest *in Arabia* is so indeterminate and vague a description, that in effect it means nothing at all. This observation might have been of good use in clearing up the foregoing very obscure prophecy, if any light had arisen from joining the two together by removing the separating title; but I see no connexion between them.

This prophecy was to have been fulfilled within a year of the time of its delivery, see ver. 16.; and it was probably delivered about the same time with the rest in this part of the book, that is, soon before or after the 14th of Hezekiah, the year of Senacherib's invasion. In his first march into Judea, or in his return from the Egyptian expedition, he might perhaps overrun these several clans of Arabians: their distress on some such occasion is the subject of this prophecy.

14. —*the southern country*] Θαιμαν, LXX; Austri, Vulg. They read הימן, which seems to be right; for probably the inhabitants of Tema might be involved in the same calamity with their brethren and neighbours of Kedar, and not in a condition to give them assistance, and to relieve them, in their flight before the enemy, with bread and water. To bring forth bread and water is an instance of common humanity in such cases of distress; especially in these desert countries, in which the common necessaries of life, more particularly water, are not easily to be met with or procured. Moses forbids the Ammonite and Moabite to be admitted into the congregation of the Lord to the tenth generation; one reason which he gives for this reprobation is, their omission of the common offices of humanity towards the Israelites; "because they met them not with bread and water in the way, when they came forth out of Egypt;" Deut. xxiii. 4.

17. —*the mighty bowmen*] Sagittariorum fortium, Vulg. transposing the two words, and reading נבורי קשת; which seems to be right.

Ibid. *For JEHOVAH hath spoken it.*] The prophetic Carmina of Marcius, foretelling the battle of Cannæ, Liv. xxv. 12.

conclude with the same kind of solemn form :—" Nam mihi ita Jupiter fatus est." Observe, that the word נאם, (to pronounce, to declare), is the solemn word appropriated to the delivering of prophecies:—"Behold, I am against the prophets, saith (נאם) JEHOVAH, who use their tongues, וינאמו נאם, and solemnly pronounce, He hath pronounced it;" Jer. xxiii. 31.

CHAPTER XXII.

This prophecy, ending with the 14th verse of this chapter, is entitled, "The Oracle concerning the Valley of Vision," by which is meant Jerusalem, because, says Sal. b. Melech, it was the place of prophecy. Jerusalem, according to Josephus, was built upon two opposite hills, Sion and Acra, separated by a valley in the midst: he speaks of another broad valley between Acra and Moriah, Bell. Jud. v. 13. vi. 6. It was the seat of divine revelation, the place where chiefly prophetic vision was given, and where God manifested himself visibly in the holy place. The prophecy foretells the invasion of Jerusalem by the Assyrians under Senacherib; or by the Chaldeans under Nebuchadnezzar. Vitringa is of opinion, that the Prophet has both in view; that of the Chaldeans in the first part, ver. 1—5. (which he thinks relates to the flight of Zedekiah, 2 Kings xxv. 4, 5.); and that of the Assyrians in the latter part; which agrees with the circumstances of that time, and particularly describes the preparations made by Hezekiah for the defence of the city, ver. 8—11. Compare 2 Chron. xxxii. 2—5.

1. —*are gone up to the house-tops.*] The houses in the East were in ancient times, as they are still generally, built in one and the same uniform manner. The roof or top of the house is always flat, covered with broad stones, or a strong plaster of terrace, and guarded on every side with a low parapet wall: see Deut. xxii. 8. The terrace is frequented as much as any part of the house. On this, as the season favours, they walk, they eat, they sleep, they transact business, (1 Sam. ix. 25. see also the LXX in that place), they perform their devotions, (Acts x. 9.) The house is built with a court within, into which chiefly the windows open; those that open to the street are so obstructed with lattice-work, that no one either without or within can see through them. Whenever therefore any thing is to be seen

or heard in the streets, any public spectacle, any alarm of a public nature, every one immediately goes up to the house-top to satisfy his curiosity. In the same manner, when any one had occasion to make any thing public, the readiest and most effectual way of doing it was to proclaim it from the house-tops to the people in the streets: "What ye hear in the ear, that publish ye on the house-top," saith our Saviour, Matt. x. 27. The people's running all to the tops of their houses gives a lively image of a sudden general alarm. Sir John Chardin's MS note on this place is as follows:—" Dans les festes pour voir passer quelque chose, et dans les maladies pour les annoncer aux voisins en allumant des lumieres, le peuple monte sur les terrasses."

3. —*are gone off together.*] There seems to be somewhat of an inconsistency in the sense, according to the present reading. If the leaders were bound, אסרו, how could they flee away? for their being bound, according to the obvious construction and course of the sentence, is a circumstance prior to their flight. I therefore follow Houbigant, who reads הסרו, remoti sunt, they are gone off. גלו, transmigraverunt, Chald. which seems to confirm this emendation.

6. —*the Syrian*—] It is not easy to say what רכב אדם, *a chariot of men*, can mean. It seems, by the form of the sentence, which consists of three members, the first and the third mentioning a particular people, that the second should do so likewise; thus ברכב ארם ופרשים, "with chariots the Syrian, and with horsemen:" the similitude of the letters ד and ר is so great, and the mistakes arising from it so frequent, that I readily adopt the correction of Houbigant, ארם instead of אדם, which seems to me extremely probable. The conjunction ו prefixed to פרשים seems necessary, in whatever way the sentence is taken; and it is confirmed by five MSS (one ancient) and three editions. Kir was a city belonging to the Medes. The Medes were subject to the Assyrians in Hezekiah's time: see 2 Kings xvi. 9. and xvii. 6.; and so perhaps might Elam (the Persians) likewise be, or auxiliaries to them.

8. —*the arsenal*—] Built by Solomon within the city, and called the House of the forest of Lebanon; probably from the great quantity of cedar from Lebanon which was employed in the building: see 1 Kings vii. 2, 3.

9. *And ye shall collect the waters*—] There were two pools in or near Jerusalem, supplied by springs: the upper

pool, or the old pool, supplied by the spring called Gihon, 2 Chron. xxxii. 30. towards the higher part of the city, near Sion or the city of David; and the lower pool, probably supplied by Siloam, towards the lower part. When Hezekiah was threatened with a siege by Senacherib, he stopped up all the waters of the fountains without the city, and brought them into the city by a conduit, or subterraneous passage cut through the rock; those of the old pool, to the place where he made a double wall, so that the pool was between the two walls. This he did in order to distress the enemy, and to supply the city during the siege. This was so great a work, that not only the historians have made particular mention of it, 2 Kings xx. 20. 2 Chron. xxxii. 2, 3. 5. 30.; but the son of Sirach also has celebrated it in his encomium on Hezekiah: "Hezekiah fortified his city, and brought in water into the midst thereof: he digged the hard rock with iron, and made wells for water:" Eccl'us xlviii. 17.

11. —*to him that hath disposed this*] That is, to God, the author and disposer of this visitation, the invasion with which he now threatens you. The very same expressions are applied to God, and upon the same occasion, chap. xxxvii. 26.

"Hast thou not heard, of old, that I have disposed it;
And, of ancient times, that I have formed it?"

14. *the voice of* JEHOVAH—] The Vulg. has vox Domini; as if in his copy he had read קול יהוה: and, in truth, without the word קול, it is not easy to make out the sense of the passage; as it appears from the strange versions which the rest of the ancients, (except Chald.), and many of the moderns, have given of it; as if the matter were revealed in, or to, the ears of JEHOVAH ; εν τοις ωσι Κυριε, LXX. Vitringa translates it, "revelatus est in auribus meis JEHOVAH;" and refers to 1 Sam. ii. 27. iii. 21.: but the construction in those places is different, and there is no speech of God added; which here seems to want something more than the verb נגלה to introduce it. Compare chap. v. 9. where the text is still more imperfect.

15. *Go unto Shebna*—] The following prophecy concerning Shebna seems to have very little relation to the foregoing; except that it might have been delivered about the same time, and Shebna might be a principal person among those whose luxury and profaneness is severely reprehended by the Prophet in the conclusion of that prophecy, ver. 11—14.

Shebna the scribe, mentioned in the history of Hezekiah, chap. xxxvi. seems to have been a different person from this Shebna, the treasurer or steward of the household, to whom the prophecy relates. The Eliakim here mentioned was probably the person, who, at the time of Senacherib's invasion, was actually treasurer, the son of Hilkiah. If so, this prophecy was delivered, as the preceding, which makes the former part of the chapter, plainly was, some time before the invasion of Senacherib. As to the rest, history affords us no information.

Ibid. —*and say unto him*] Here are two words lost out of the text; which are supplied by two MSS, (one ancient), which read ואמרת אליו; by LXX, και ειπον αυτω; and in the same manner by all the ancient versions. It is to be observed, that this passage is merely historical, and does not admit of that sort of ellipsis by which, in the poetical parts, a person is frequently introduced speaking, without the usual notice that what follows was delivered by him.

16. *thy sepulchre on high—in the rock*] It has been observed before on chap. xiv. that persons of high rank in Judea, and in most parts of the East, were generally buried in large sepulchral vaults hewn out in the rock for the use of themselves and their families. The vanity of Shebna is set forth by his being so studious and careful to have his sepulchre on high; in a lofty vault, and that probably in a high situation, that it might be more conspicuous. Hezekiah was buried למעלה, εν αναβασει, LXX; in the chiefest, says our translation; rather, in the highest part of the sepulchres of the sons of David, to do him the more honour; 2 Chron. xxxii. 33. There are some monuments still remaining in Persia of great antiquity, called Naksi Rustam, which give one a clear idea of Shebna's pompous design for his sepulchre. They consist of several sepulchres, each of them hewn in a high rock near the top; the front of the rock to the valley below is adorned with carved work in relievo, being the outside of the sepulchre. Some of these sepulchres are about thirty feet in the perpendicular from the valley; which is itself raised perhaps above half as much by the accumulation of the earth since they were made. See the description of them in Chardin, Pietro della Valle, Thevenot, and Kempfer. Diodorus Siculus, lib. xvii. mentions these ancient monuments, and calls them the sepulchres of the kings of Persia.

17. *—cover thee*] That is, thy face. This was the condition of mourners in general, and particularly of condemned persons: see Esther vi. 12. vii. 8.

19. *I will drive thee*] אהרסך, in the first person, Syr. Vulg.

21. *—to the inhabitants—*] ליושבי, in the plural number, four MSS, (two ancient), LXX, Syr. Vulg.

22. *—the key upon his shoulder.*] As the robe and the baldric, mentioned in the preceding verse, were the ensigns of power and authority, so likewise was the key the mark of office, either sacred or civil. The priestess of Juno is said to be the key-bearer of the goddess, κλειδȣχος Ηϱας: Æschyl. Suppl. 299. A female high in office under a great queen has the same title:—

Καλλιθοη κλειδȣχος Ολυμπιαδος Βασιλειης.

Auctor Phoronidis ap. Clem. Alex. p. 418. Edit. Potter. This mark of office was likewise among the Greeks, as here in Isaiah, borne on the shoulder: the priestess of Ceres κατωμαδιαν εχε κλαιδα: Callim. Ceres, ver. 45. To comprehend how the key could be borne on the shoulder, it will be necessary to say somewhat of the form of it: but without entering into a long disquisition, and a great deal of obscure learning, concerning the locks and keys of the ancients, it will be sufficient to observe, that one sort of keys, and that probably the most ancient, was of considerable magnitude, and as to the shape very much bent and crooked. Aratus, to give his reader an idea of the form of the constellation Cassiopeia, compares it to a key. It must be owned, that the passage is very obscure; but the learned Huetius has bestowed a great deal of pains in explaining it, Animadvers. in Manilii, lib. i. 355. and I think has succeeded very well in it. Homer, Odyss. xxi. 6. describes the key of Ulysses's storehouse as ευκαμπης, of a large curvature; which Eustathius explains by saying it was δρεπανοειδης, in shape like a reap-hook. Huetius says, the constellation Cassiopeia answers to this description; the stars to the north making the curve part, that is, the principal part of the key; the southern stars, the handle. The curve part was introduced into the key-hole; and, being properly directed by the handle, took hold of the bolts within, and moved them from their places. We may easily collect from this account, that such a key would lie very well upon the shoulder; that it must be of some considerable size and weight, and could hardly be commodiously carried otherwise. Ulysses's key was of brass, and the handle of ivory: but this was a royal key; the more common ones were probably of wood. In Egypt they have no other than wooden locks and keys to this day; even the gates of Cairo have no better: Baumgarten, Peregr. i. 18. Thevenot, Part II. ch. 10.

In allusion to the image of the key as the ensign of power, the unlimited extent of that power is expressed, with great clearness as well as force, by the sole and exclusive authority to open and shut. Our Saviour therefore has upon a similar occasion made use of a like manner of expression, Matt. xvi. 19.; and in Rev. iii. 7. has applied to himself the very words of the Prophet.

23. —*a nail*—] In ancient times, and in the eastern countries, as the way of life, so the houses were much more simple then ours at present. They had not that quantity and variety of furniture, nor those accommodations of all sorts, with which we abound. It was convenient and even necessary for them, and it made an essential part in the building of a house, to furnish the inside of the several apartments with sets of spikes, nails, or large pegs, upon which to dispose of, and to hang up, the several moveables and utensils in common use, and proper to the apartment. These spikes they worked into the walls at the first erection of them—the walls being of such materials, that they could not bear their being driven in afterwards; and they were contrived so as to strengthen the walls, by binding the parts together, as well as to serve for convenience. Sir John Chardin's account of this matter is this: "They do not drive with a hammer the nails that are put into the eastern walls: the walls are too hard, being of brick; or if they are of clay, too mouldering: but they fix them in the brickwork as they are building. They are large nails, with square heads like dice, well made; the ends being bent so as to make them cramp-irons. They commonly place them at the windows and doors, in order to hang upon them, when they like, veils and curtains:" Harmer, Observat. i. p. 191. And we may add, that they were put in other places too, in order to hang up other things of various kinds; as it appears from this place of Isaiah, and from Ezekiel xv. 3. who speaks of a pin, or nail, "to hang any vessel thereon." The word used here for a nail of this sort, is the same by which they express that instrument, the stake,

or large pin of iron, with which they fastened down to the ground the cords of their tents. We see, therefore, that these nails were of necessary and common use, and of no small importance, in all their apartments; conspicuous, and much exposed to observation: and if they seem to us mean and insignificant, it is because we are not acquainted with the thing itself, and have no name to express it by, but what conveys to us a low and contemptible idea. "Grace hath been shewed from the Lord our God, (saith Ezra ix. 8.), to leave us a remnant to escape, and to give us a nail in his holy place:" that is, as the margin of our Bible explains it, "a constant and sure abode."

"He that doth lodge near her [Wisdom's] house,
Shall also fasten a pin in her walls." Eccl'us xiv. 24.

The dignity and propriety of the metaphor appears from the Prophet Zechariah's use of it:

"From him shall be the corner-stone; from him the nail,
From him the battle-bow,
From him every ruler together." Zech. x. 4.

And Mohammed, using the same word, calls Pharaoh the lord or master of the *Nails;* that is, well attended by nobles and officers capable of administering his affairs; Koran Sur. xxxviii. 11. and lxxxix. 9. So some understand this passage of the Koran: Mr. Sale seems to prefer another interpretation.

Taylor, in his Concordance, thinks יתד means the pillar or post that stands in the middle, and supports the tent, in which such pegs are fixed to hang their arms, &c. upon; referring to Shaw's Travels, p. 287. But יתד is never used, as far as it appears to me, in that sense. It was indeed necessary that the pillar of the tent should have such pegs on it for that purpose; but the hanging of such things in this manner upon this pillar, does not prove that יתד was the pillar itself.

23. —*a glorious seat*—] That is, his father's house, and all his own family, shall be gloriously seated, shall flourish in honor and prosperity; and shall depend upon him, and be supported by him.

24. —*all the glory*—] One considerable part of the magnificence of the eastern princes, consisted in the great quantity of gold and silver vessels which they had for various uses. "Solomon's drinking vessels were of gold, and all the vessels

of the House of the forest of Lebanon were of pure gold: none were of silver; it was nothing accounted of in Solomon's days;" 1 Kings x. 21. "The vessels in the House of the forest of Lebanon (the armory of Jerusalem so called) were two hundred targets, and three hundred shields, of beaten gold;" Ibid. ver. 16, 17. These were ranged in order upon the walls of the armoury, (see Cant. iv. 4.) upon pins worked into the walls on purpose, as above mentioned. Eliakim is considered as a principal stake of this sort, immoveably fastened in the wall, for the support of all vessels destined for common or sacred uses: that is, as the principal support of the whole civil and ecclesiastical polity. And the consequence of his continued power will be the promotion and flourishing condition of his family and dependents, from the highest to the lowest.

Ibid. —*meaner vessels*] נבלים seems to mean earthen vessels of common use, brittle, and of little value, (see Lam. iv. 2. Jer. xlviii. 12.), in opposition to אגנות, goblets of gold and silver used in the sacrifices; Exod. xxiv. 6.

25. *The nail fastened*—] This must be understood of Shebna, as a repetition and confirmation of the sentence above denounced against him.

CHAPTER XXIII.

1. *Howl, O ye ships of Tarshish*—] This prophecy denounceth the destruction of Tyre by Nebuchadnezzar. It opens with an address to the Tyrian negociators and sailos at Tarshish, (Tartessus in Spain), a place which, in the course of their trade, they greatly frequented. The news of the destruction of Tyre by Nebuchadnezzar is said to be brought to them from Chittim, the islands and coasts of the Mediterranean: "For the Tyrians, (says Jerom on ver. 6.), when they saw they had no other means of escaping, fled in their ships, and took refuge in Carthage, and the islands of the Ionian and Egean Sea:" from whence the news would spread and reach Tarshish. So also Jarchi on the place. This seems to be the most probable interpretation of this verse.

2. *Be silent*] Silence is a mark of grief and consternation: see chap. xlvii. 5. Jeremiah has finely expressed this image:—

"The elders of the daughter of Sion sit on the ground, they are silent:
They have cast up dust on their heads, they have girded themselves with sackcloth.
The virgins of Jerusalem hang down their heads to the ground." Lam. ii. 10.

3. *And the seed of the Nile*—] The Nile is called here Shichor, as it is Jer. ii. 18. and 1 Chron. xiii. 5. It had this name from the blackness of its waters charged with the mud which it brings down from Ethiopia, when it overflows, " Et viridem Ægyptum nigra fœcundat arena : " as it was called by the Greeks Melas, and by the Latins Melo, for the same reason. See Servius on the above line of Virgil, Georg. iv. 291. It was called Siris by the Ethiopians ; by some supposed to be the same with Shichor. Egypt, by its extraordinary fertility, caused by the overflowing of the Nile, supplied the neighbouring nations with corn ; by which branch of trade the Tyrians gained great wealth.

4. *Be ashamed, O Sidon*—] Tyre is called, ver. 12. the daughter of Sidon. "The Sidonians, (says Justin, xviii. 3.), when their city was taken by the king of Ascalon, betook themsleves to their ships, and landed, and built Tyre." Sidon, as the mother city, is supposed to be deeply affected with the calamity of her daughter.

Ibid. —nor *educated*—] ורוממתי, so an ancient MS, prefixing the ו, which refers to the negative preceding, and is equivalent to ולא. See Deut. xxxiii. 6. Prov. xxx. 3.

7. —*whose antiquity is of the earliest date.*] Justin, in the passage above quoted, had dated the building of Tyre at a certain number of years before the taking of Troy ; but the number is lost in the present copies. Tyre, though not so old as Sidon, yet was of very high antiquity : it was a strong city, even in the time of Joshua : it is called עיר מבצר צר, "the city of the fortress of Sor," Josh. xix. 29. Interpreters raise difficulties in regard to this passage, and will not allow it to have been so ancient: with what good reason, I do not see ; for it is called by the same name, "the fortress of Sor," in the history of David, 2 Sam. xxiv. 7. ; and the circumstances of the history determine the place to be the very same.

10. *O daughter of Tarshish*—] Tyre is called the daughter of Tarshish ; perhaps because, Tyre being ruined, Tarshish was become the superior city, and might be considered as the metropolis of the Tyrian people ; or rather, because of

the close connexion and perpetual intercourse between them; according to that latitude of signification in which the Hebrews use the words *son* and *daughter*, to express any sort of conjunction and dependence whatever. מגה, a girdle, which collects, binds, and keeps together the loose raiment, when applied to a river, may mean a mound, mole, or artificial dam, which contains the waters, and prevents them from spreading abroad. A city, taken by seige, and destroyed, whose walls are demolished, whose policy is dissolved, whose wealth is dissipated, whose people is scattered over the wide country, is compared to a river whose banks are broken down, and its waters, let loose and overflowing all the neghbouring plains, are wasted and lost. This may possibly be the meaning of this very obscure verse; of which I can find no other interpretation that is at all satisfactory.

13. *Behold the land of the Chaldeans*—] This verse is extremely obscure: the obscurity arises from the ambiguity of the agents which belong to the verbs, and of the objects expressed by the pronouns; from the change of number in the verbs, and of gender in the pronouns. The MSS gives us no assistance; and the ancient versions very little. The Chaldee and Vulg. read שמוה in the plural number. I have followed the interpretation, which among many different ones seemed to me most probable, that of Perizonius and Vitringa.

The Chaldeans, Chasdim, are supposed to have had their origin, and to have taken their name, from Chesed the son of Nachor, the brother of Abraham. They were known by that name in the time of Moses; who calls Ur in Mesopotamia, from whence Abraham came, to distinguish it from other places of the same name, Ur of the Chaldeans. And Jeremiah calls them an ancient nation. This is not inconsistent with what Isaiah here says of them: "This people was not;" that is, they were of no account, (see Deut. xxxii. 21.); they were not reckoned among the great and potent nations of the world, till of later times: they were a rude, uncivilized, barbarous people, without laws, without settled habitations; wandering in a wide desert country, ציים, and addicted to rapine, like the wild Arabians. Such they are represented to have been in the time of Job, (i. 16.), and such they continued to be till Assur, some powerful king of Assyria, gathered them together, and settled them in Babylon, and the neighbouring country. This probably was Ninus, whom I suppose to have lived in the time of the Judges. In this, with many eminent chronologers, I follow the authority of Herodotus; who says, that the Assyrian monarchy lasted but five hundred and twenty years. Ninus got possession of Babylon from the Cuthean Arabians, the successors of Nimrod in that empire, collected the Chaldeans, and settled a colony of them there, to secure the possession of the city, which he and his successors greatly enlarged and ornamented. They had perhaps been useful to him in his wars, and might be likely to be further useful in keeping under the old inhabitants of that city, and of the country belonging to it; according to the policy of the Assyrian kings, who generally brought new people into the conquered countries. See Isa. xxxvi. 17. 2 Kings xvii. 6. 24. The testimony of Dicæarchus, a Greek historian contemporary with Alexander, (apud Steph. de Urbibus, in v. Χαλδαιος), in regard to the fact is remarkable, though he is mistaken in the name of the king he speaks of: He says, "That a certain king of Assyria, the fourteenth in succession from Ninus," (as he might be, if Ninus is placed, as in the common chronology, eight hundred years higher than we have above set him), "named as it is said Chaldæus, having gathered together and united all the people called Chaldeans, built the famous city Babylon, upon the Euphrates."

14. *Howl, O ye ships*—] The Prophet Ezekiel hath enlarged upon this part of the same subject with great force and elegance:—

"Thus saith the Lord JEHOVAH concerning Tyre:
At the sound of thy fall, at the cry of the wounded,
At the great slaughter in the midst of thee, shall not the islands tremble?
And shall not all the princes of the sea descend from their thrones,
And lay aside their robes, and strip off their embroidered garments?
They shall clothe themselves with trembling, they shall sit on the ground;
They shall tremble every moment, they shall be astonished at thee.
And they shall utter a lamentation over thee, and shall say unto thee:
How art thou lost, thou that wast inhabited from the seas!
The renowned city, that was strong in the sea, she and her inhabitants!

>   That struck with terror all her neighbours!
>   Now shall the coasts tremble in the day of thy fall,
>   And the isles that are in the sea shall be troubled at thy departure."   Ezek. xxvi. 15—18.

15. *According to the days of one king*—] That is, of one kingdom. See Dan. vii. 17. viii. 20. Nebuchadnezzar began his conquests in the first year of his reign; from thence to the taking of Babylon by Cyrus are seventy years; at which time the nations conquered by Nebuchadnezzar were to be restored to liberty. These seventy years limit the duration of the Babylonish monarchy. Tyre was taken by him, towards the middle of that period; so did not serve the king of Babylon during the whole period, but only for the remaining part of it. This seems to be the meaning of Isaiah: The days allotted to the one king, or kingdom, are seventy years; Tyre, with the rest of the conquered nations, shall continue in a state of subjection and desolation to the end of that period—not from the beginning and through the whole of the period; for, by being one of the latest conquests, the duration of that state of subjection in regard to her was not much more than half of it. "All these nations," saith Jeremiah, (xxv. 11.), "shall serve the king of Babylon seventy years." Some of them were conquered sooner, some later; but the end of this period was the common term for the deliverance of them all.

There is another way of computing the seventy years, from the year in which Tyre was actually taken to the nineteenth of Darius Hystaspis; whom the Phenicians, or Tyrians, assisted against the Ionians, and probably on that account might then be restored to their former liberties and privileges. But I think the former the more probable interpretation.

Ibid. *sing as the harlot singeth*—] "Fidicinam esse meretricum est," says Donatus in Terent. Eunuch. iii. 2. 4.

> "Nec meretrix tibicina, cujus
>   Ad strepitum salias."   Hor. I. Epist. xiv. 25.

Sir John Chardin, in his MS note on this place, says: "C'est que les vieilles prostituées—ne font que chanter quand les jeunes dancet, et les animer par l'instrument et par la voix."

17, 18. *And at the end of seventy years*—] Tyre, after its destruction by Nebuchadnezzar, recovered, as it is here foretold, its ancient trade, wealth, and grandeur; as it did likewise after a second destruction by Alexander. It became Christian early with the rest of the neighbouring countries. St. Paul himself found many Christians there, Acts xxi. 4. It suffered much in the Diocletian persecution. It was an archbishoprick under the patriarchate of Jerusalem, with fourteen bishopricks under its jurisdiction. It continued Christian till it was taken by the Saracens in 639: was recovered by the Christians in 1124. But in 1280 was conquered by the Mamelukes; and afterwards taken from them by the Turks in 1516. Since that time it has sunk into utter decay; is now a mere ruin; a bare rock; "a place to spread nets upon," as the Prophet Ezekiel foretold it should be, chap. xxvi. 14. See Sandys's Travels; Vitringa on the place; Bishop Newton on the Prophecies, Dissert. xi.

CHAPTER XXIV.

From the xiiith chapter to the xxiiid inclusive, the fate of several cities and nations is denounced;—of Babylon, of the Philistines, Moab, Damascus, Egypt, Tyre. After having foretold the destruction of the foreign nations, enemies of Judah, the Prophet declares the judgments impending on the people of God themselves, for their wickedness and apostasy; and the desolation that shall be brought on their whole country.

The xxivth, and the three following chapters, seem to have been delivered about the same time—before the destruction of Moab by Shalmaneser, (see xxv. 10.); consequently before the destruction of Samaria; probably in the beginning of Hezekiah's reign. But concerning the particular subject of the xxivth chapter, interpreters are not at all agreed: some refer it to the desolation caused by the invasion of Shalmaneser; others to the invasion of Nebuchadnezzar; and others to the destruction of the city and nation by the Romans. Vitringa is singular in his opinion, who applies it to the persecution of Antiochus Epiphanes. Perhaps it may have a view to all of the three great desolations of the country, by Shalmaneser, by Nebuchadnezzar, and by the Romans; especially the last, to which some parts of it may seem more peculiarly applicable. However, the Prophet chiefly employs general images; such as set forth the greatness and universality of the ruin and desolation that is to be brought upon the country by these great revolutions, involving all orders and degrees of men, changing entirely the face of things, and destroying the whole polity both religious and civil; without entering into minute circumstances, or necessarily restraining it by particular marks to one great event, exclusive of others of the same kind.

4. *The world languisheth*] The world is the same with the land; that is, the kingdoms of Judah and Israel; orbis Israeliticus. See note on chap. xiii. 11.

5. —*the law*] תורה, singular: so read LXX, Syr. Chald.

6. —*are destroyed*] For חרו, read חרבו: see LXX, Syr. Chald. Sym.

9. —*palm wine*—] This is the proper meaning of the word שכר, σικερα; see note on chap. v. 11. All enjoyment shall cease; the sweetest wine shall become bitter to their taste.

11. —*is passed away*] For ערבה, read עברה; transposing a letter: Houbigant, Secker. Five MSS (two ancient) add כל after שמחה: LXX add the same word before it.

14. *But these*—] That is, they that escaped out of these calamities. The great distresses brought upon Israel and Judah drove the people away, and dispersed them all over the neighbouring countries: they fled to Egypt, to Asia Minor, to the islands and the coasts of Greece. They were to be found in great numbers in most of the principal cities of these countries. Alexandria was in a great measure peopled by them. They had synagogues for their worship in many places; and were greatly instrumental in propagating the knowledge of the true God amongst these heathen nations, and preparing them for the reception of Christianity. This is what the Prophet seems to mean by the celebration of the name of Jehovah in the waters, in the distant coasts, and in the uttermost parts of the land. כְּמַיִם, *the waters;* ύδωρ, LXX; ύδατα, Theod.; not כְּמִי, *from the sea.*

15. *In the distant coasts of the sea*] For באריס, I suppose we ought to read באיים; which is in a great degree justified by the repetition of the word in the next member of the sentence, with the addition of הים to vary the phrase, exactly in the manner of the Prophet. איים is a word chiefly applied to any distant countries, especially those

lying on the Mediterranean Sea. Others conjecture בִּיאָרִים, בָּאוּרִים; בְּחוּרִים, בַּעֲמִים, בְּאָכְלָם, בְּהָרִים, a בְּאֵר, illustrati; Le Clerc. Twenty-three MSS read בָּאוּרִים. The LXX do not acknowledge the reading of the text, expressing here only the word בָּאִיִּים, εν ταις νησοις, and that not repeated. But MSS Pachom. and I, D. II. supply in this place the defect in the other copies of LXX, thus: Διὰ τῦτο ἡ δόξα Κυρίυ ἐσαι ἐν ταις νησοις της θαλασσης· ἐν ταις νησοις τὸ ὄνομα τῦ Κυρίυ Θεῦ Ἰσραηλ ἔνδοξον ἔσται. According to which the LXX had in their Hebrew copy בָּאִיִּים, repeated afterward, not בָּאֻרִים.

16. *But I said*—] The Prophet speaks in the person of the inhabitants of the land still remaining there; who should be pursued by divine vengeance, and suffer repeated distresses from the inroads and depredations of their powerful enemies. Agreeably to what he said before in a general denunciation of these calamities.

"Though there be a tenth part remaining in it;
Even this shall undergo a repeated destruction."
                                Chap. vi. 13. See the note there.

Ibid. *The plunderers plunder*] The note on chap. xxi. 2.
17, 18. *The terror, the pit,*—] If they escape one calamity, another shall overtake them;

"As if a man should flee from a lion, and a bear should overtake him:
Or should betake himself to his house, and lean his hand on the wall,
And a serpent shall bite him."   Amos v. 19.

For, as our Saviour expressed it in a like parabolical manner, "wheresoever the carcass is, there shall the eagles be gathered together;" Matt. xxiv. 28. The images are taken from the different methods of hunting and taking wild beasts, which were anciently in use. The terror was a line strung with feathers of all colours, which fluttering in the air scared and frightened the beasts into the toils, or into the pit, which was prepared for them. "Nec est mirum, cum maximos ferarum greges linea pennis distincta contineat, et in insidias agat, ab ipso effectu dicta Formido:" Seneca de ira, ii. 12. The pit, or pit-fall, Fovea; digged deep in the ground, and covered over with green boughs, turf, &c. in order to deceive them, that they might fall into it unawares. The snare, or toils, Indago; a series of nets, inclosing at first a great space of ground, in which the wild beasts were known to be; and then drawn in by degrees into a narrower compass, till they were at last closely shut up, and entangled in them.

For מקול a MS reads מפני, as it is in Jer. xlviii. 44.; and so the Vulg. and Chald. But perhaps it is only, like the latter, a Hebraism, and means no more than the simple preposition מ. See Psal. cii. 6. For it does not appear, that the terror was intended to scare the wild beasts by its noise. The paronomasia is very remarkable; *pachad pachath pach:* and that it was a common proverbial form, appears from Jeremiah's repeating it in the same words, chap. xlviii. 43, 44.

18. *from the pit*] For מתוך, *from the midst of,* a MS reads מן, *from,* as it is in Jer. xlviii. 44.; and so likewise LXX, Syr. Vulg.

19. *The land*] "הארץ, forte delendum ה, ut ex præcedente ortum. Vid. seqq." SECKER.

20. —*like a lodge for a night.*] See note on chap. i. 8.

21—23. —*on high,* —*on earth*—] That is, the ecclesiastical and civil polity of the Jews; which shall be destroyed: The nation shall continue in a state of depression and dereliction for a long time. The image seems to be taken from the practice of the great monarchs of that time; who, when they had thrown their wretched captives into a dungeon, never gave themselves the trouble of inquiring about them; but let them lie a long time in that miserable condition, wholly destitute of relief, and disregarded. God shall at length revisit and restore his people in the last age; and then the kingdom of God shall be established in such perfection, as wholly to obscure and eclipse the glory of the temporary, typical, preparative kingdom now subsisting.

" The figurative language of the Prophets is taken from the analogy between the world natural, and an empire or kingdom considered as a world politic. Accordingly the whole world natural, consisting of heaven and earth, signifies the whole world politic, consisting of thrones and people, or so much of it as is considered in prophecy; and the things in that world signify the analogous things in this. For the heavens and the things therein signify thrones and dignities, and those who enjoy them; and the earth, with the things thereon, the inferior people; and the lowest parts of the earth, called hades or hell, the lowest or most miserable part of them.—Great earthquakes, and the shaking of heaven and earth, are put for the shaking of kingdoms, so as to distract and overthrow them; the creating a new heaven and earth, and the passing of an old one, or the beginning and end of a world, for the rise and ruin of a body politic signified thereby.—The sun, for the whole species and race of kings, in the kingdoms of the world politic; the moon, for the body of the common people, considered as the king's wife; the stars, for subordinate princes and great men; or for bishops and rulers of the people of God, when the sun is Christ:—setting of the sun, moon, and stars; darkening the sun, turning the moon into blood, and falling of the stars, for the ceasing of a kingdom." Sir I. Newton, Observations on the Prophecies, Part I. chap. ii.

CHAPTER XXV.

It doth not appear to me, that this chapter hath any close and particular connexion with the chapter immediately preceding, taken separately, and by itself. The subject of that was the desolation of the land of Israel and Judah, by the just judgment of God, for the wickedness and disobedience of the people; which, taken by itself, seems not with any propriety to introduce a hymn of thanksgiving to God for his mercies to his people in delivering them from their enemies. But taking the whole course of prophecies, from the xiiith to the xxivth chapter inclusive, in which the Prophet foretells the destruction of several cities and nations, enemies to the Jews, and of the land of Judah itself, yet with intimations of a remnant to be saved, and a restoration to be at length effected by a glorious establishment of the kingdom of God; with a view to this extensive scene of God's providence in all its parts, and in all its consequences, the Prophet may well be supposed to break out into this song of praise; in which his mind seems to be more possessed with the prospect of future mercies than with the recollection of the past.

2. —*the city*—] Nineveh, Babylon, Ar Moab, or any other strong fortress possessed by the enemies of the people of God.

For the first מְעִיר, Syr. Vulg. read הָעִיר; LXX, and Chald. read, in the plural, עָרִים, transposing the letters. After the second עִיר, a MS adds לְגַל.

Ibid. —*the proud ones*—] For זָרִים, *strangers*, MS

Bodl. and another read זדים, *the proud*: so likewise the LXX; for they render it ασεβων here, and in verse 5th, as they do in some other places: see Deut. xviii. 20. 22. Another MS reads צרים, *adversaries;* which also makes a good sense. But זרים and זדים are often confounded by the great similitude of the letters ד and ר. See Mal. iii. 15. iv. 1. Psal. xix. 14. apud LXX; and Psal. liv. 5. (where Chald. reads זדים) compared with Psal. lxxxvi. 14.

4. —*a winter storm.*] For קיר read קור: or as עיר from ערו, so קיר from קור: Capellus.

5. —*the proud*—] The same mistake here as in ver. 2.: see note there. Here זדים, *the proud*, is parallel to עריצים, *the formidable;* as in Psal. liv. 5. and lxxxvi. 14.

Ibid. *As the heat by a thick cloud.*] For חרב, Syr Chald. Vulg. and two MSS, read כחרב; which is a repetition of the beginning of the forgoing parallel line: and the verse taken out of the parallel form, and more fully expressed, would run thus: "As a thick cloud interposing tempers the heat of the sun on the burnt soil, so shalt thou, by the interposition of thy power, bring low and abate the tumult of the proud, and the triumph of the formidable."

6. —*shall make for all the people a feast.*] A feast is a proper and usual expression of joy in consequence of victory, or any other great success. The feast here spoken of is to be celebrated on Mount Sion, and all the peoples without distinction are to be invited to it. This can be no other than the celebration of the establishment of Christ's kingdom, which is frequently represented in the gospel under the image of a feast; where many shall come from the east and west, and shall sit down at table with Abraham, Isaac, and Jacob, in the kingdom of heaven;" Matt. viii. 11. See also Luke xiv. 16. xxii. 29, 30. This sense is fully confirmed by the concomitants of this feast expressed in the next verse; the removing of the veil from the face of the nations, and the abolition of death: the first of which is obviously and clearly explained of the preaching of the gospel; and the second must mean the blessing of immortality procured for us by Christ, "who hath abolished death and through death hath destroyed him that had the power of death."

Ibid. —*of old wines*] Heb. *lees;* that is, of wines kept long on the lees. The word used to express the lees in the original signifies the *preservers;* because they preserve the strength and flavour of the wine. "All recent wines, after the fermentation has ceased, ought to be kept on their lees for a certain time; which greatly contribute to increase their strength and flavour. Whenever this first fermentation has been deficient, they will retain a more rich and sweet taste than is natural to them in a recent true vinous state; and unless further fermentation is promoted by their lying longer on their own lees, they will never attain their genuine strength and flavor, but run into repeated and ineffectual fermentations, and soon degenerate into a liquor of an acetous kind.—All wines of a light and austere kind, by a fermentation too great, or too long continued, certainly degenerate into a weak sort of vinegar; while the stronger not only require, but will safely bear a stronger and often repeated fermentation; and are more apt to degenerate from a defect than excess of fermentation, into a vapid, ropy, and at length into a putrescent state:" Sir Edward Barry, Observations on the Wines of the Ancients, p. 9. 10.

Thevenot observes particularly of the Schiras wine, that, after it is refined from the lees, it is apt to grow sour: "Il a beaucoup de lie; c'est pourquoi il donne puissemment dans la teste; et pour le rendre plus traitable, on le passe par un chausse d'hypocras: après quoi il est fort clair, et moins fumeux. Ils mettent ce vin dans des grandes jarres de terre, qui tiennent dix ou douze jusqu'à quatorse carabas: mais quand l'on a entamé une jarre, il faut la vuider au plutost, et mettre le vin qu'on en tire dans des bouteilles ou carabas; car si l'on y manque en le laissant quelque tems après que la jarre est entamée, il se gâte et s'aigrit:" Voyages, tom. ii. p. 245.

This clearly explains the very elegant comparison, or rather allegory, of Jeremiah; where the reader will find a remarkable example of the mixture of the proper with the allegorical, not uncommon in the Hebrew poets:

> "Moab hath been at ease from his youth,
> And he hath settled upon his lees;
> Nor hath he been drawn off from vessel to vessel,
> Neither hath he gone into captivity:
> Wherefore his taste remaineth in him,
> And his flavor is not changed." Jer. xlviii. 11.

Sir John Chardin's MS note on this place of Jeremiah is as follows: "On change ainsi le vin de cupe en cupe en

Orient; et quand on en entamé une, il faut la vuider en petites cupes ou bouteilles; sans quoy il s'aigrit."

7. —*the face of all*—] MS Bodl. reads על פני כל. The word פני has been removed from its right place into the line above, where it makes no sense; as Houbigant conjectured.

9. —*shall they say*—] So LXX and Vulg. in the plural number. They read ואמרו. Syr. reads ואמרת, Thou shalt say.

10. —*shall give rest*—] "Heb. הנוח, *quiescet*. Annon תניח, *quietem dabit*, ut Græci, αναπαυσιν δωσει, et Copt.?" Mr. WOIDE. That is, "shall give peace and quiet to Sion, by destroying the enemy;" as it follows.

Ibid. *As the straw is threshed*—] "Hoc juxta ritum loquitur Palæstinæ et multarum Orientis provinciarum, quæ ob pratorum et fæni penuriam paleas preparant esui animantium. Sunt autem carpenta ferrata rotis per medium in serrarum modum se volventibus, quæ stipulam conterunt; et comminuunt in paleas. Quomodo igitur plaustris ferratis paleæ conteruntur, sic conteretur Moab sub eo; sive sub Dei potentia, sive in semetipso, ut nihil in eo integri remaneat:" Hieron. in loc. See Note on chap. xxviii. 27.

Ibid. —*under the wheels of the car*.] For מדמנה, LXX, Syr. Vulg. read מרכבה; which I have followed. See Joshua xv. 21. compared with xix. 5. where there is a mistake very nearly the same. The Keri, במו, is confirmed by twenty-eight MSS (seven ancient) and three editions.

11. *As he that sinketh stretcheth out his hands to swim.*] There is great obscurity in this place: some understand God as the agent; others Moab. I have chosen the latter sense, as I cannot conceive that the stretching out of the hands of a swimmer in swimming, can be any illustration of the action of God stretching out his hands over Moab to destroy it. I take הׂשחה, altering the point on the ש on the authority of LXX, to be the participle of שחה, the same with שוח and שחח, *inclinari, deprimi;* and that the Prophet designed a paronomasia here, a figure which he frequently uses, between the similar words שחה and שחות. As תחתי, *in his place*, or *on the spot*, as we say, in the preceding verse, gives us an idea of the sudden and complete destruction of Moab; so בקרבו, *in the midst of him*, means that this destruction shall be open, and exposed to the view of all: The neighbouring nations shall plainly see him strug-

gling against it, as a man in the midst of the deep waters exerts all his efforts, by swimming, to save himself from drowning.

CHAPTER XXVI.

1. —*we have a strong city*] In opposition to the city of the enemy, which God hath destroyed, chap. xxv. 2.; see the note there.

3. —*they have trusted*] So Chald. בטחו. Syr. and Vulg. read בטחנו, *we have trusted*. Schroeder, Gram. Hebr. p. 360. explains the present reading, בטוח, impersonally, *confisum est*.

4. —*in JEHOVAH*] In JAH JEHOVAH, Heb.; but see Houbigant, not. in cap. xii. 2.

8. *We have placed our confidence in thy name*] LXX, Syr. and Chald. read קוינו, without the pronoun annexed.

9. —*have I desired thee*] Forty-one MSS (nine ancient), and five editions, read אויתיך. It is proper to note this; because the second ו being omitted in the text, Vulg. and many others have rendered it in the third person.

16. —*we have sought thee—*] So LXX, and two MSS, בקדנוך, in the first person. And so perhaps it should be נקצ, in the first person: but how LXX read this word is not clear; and this last member of the verse is extremely obscure.

For למו the LXX read לנו, in the first person likewise: a frequent mistake; see note on chap. x. 29.

19. —*we have brought forth wind*] The learned professor Michaelis explains this image in the following manner:—" Rariorem morbum describi, empneumatosin, aut ventosam molam, dictum; quo quæ laborant diu et sibi et peritis medicis gravidæ videntur, tandemque post omnes veræ graviditatis molestias et laboies ventum ex utero emittunt: quem morbum passim describunt medici:" Syntagma Comment. vol. ii. p. 165. The Syriac translator seems to have understood it in this manner: " Enixi sumus, ut illæ, quæ ventos pariunt."

Ibid. —*in the land*) בארץ, so a MS, LXX, Syr. and Vulg.

19. —*my deceased*] All the ancient versions render it in the plural; they read נבלותי, *my* dead bodies. Syr. and Chald. read נבלותיהם, *their* dead bodies.

Ibid. —*of the dawn*] Lucis, Vulg.; so also Syr. and Chald.

The deliverance of the people of God from a state of the lowest depression, is explained by images plainly taken from the resurrection of the dead. In the same manner the Prophet Ezekiel represents the restoration of the Jewish nation from a state of utter dissolution, by the restoring of the dry bones to life, exhibited to him in a vision, chap. xxxvii. which is directly thus applied and explained, ver. 11—13. And this deliverance is expressed with a manifest opposition to what is here said above, ver. 14. of the great lords and tyrants under whom they had groaned;

"They are dead, they shall not live;
They are deceased tyrants, they shall not rise:"

that they should be destroyed utterly, and should never be restored to their former power and glory. It appears from hence that the doctrine of the resurrection of the dead was at that time a popular and common doctrine: for an image which is assumed in order to express or represent any thing in the way of allegory or metaphor, whether poetical or prophetical, must be an image commonly known and understood; otherwise it will not answer the purpose for which it is assumed.

20. *Come O my people; retire*—] An exhortation to patience and resignation under oppression, with a confident expectation of deliverance, by the power of God manifestly to be exerted in the destruction of the oppressor. It seems to be an allusion to the command of Moses to the Israelites, when the destroying angel was to go through the land of Egypt, "not to go out at the door of their houses until the morning;" Exod. xii. 22. And before the passage of the Red Sea: "Fear ye not, stand still, and see the salvation of JEHOVAH:—JEHOVAH shall fight for you, and ye shall hold your peace;" Exod. xiv. 13, 14.

CHAPTER XXVII.

THE subject of this chapter seems to be the nature, the measure, and the design of God's dealings with his people: ver. 1. his judgments inflicted on their great and powerful enemies: ver. 2. his constant care and protection of his favourite vineyard, in the form of a dialogue: ver. 7. the moderation and lenity with which the severity of his judgments have been tempered: ver. 9. the end and design of them, to recover them from idolatry; and, ver. 12. the recalling of them, on their repentance, from their several dispersions. The first verse seems connected with the two last verses of the preceding chapter.

1. *Leviathan, &c.*] The animals here mentioned seem to be,—the crocodile, rigid, by the stiffness of the back-bone, so that he cannot readily turn himself, when he pursues his prey; hence the easiest way of escaping from him is by making frequent and short turnings: the serpent, or dragon, flexible and winding; which coils himself up in a circular form: the sea-monster, or the whale. These are used allegorically, without doubt, for great potentates, enemies and persecutors of the people of God: but to specify the particular persons or states designed by the Prophet under these images is a matter of great difficulty, and comes not necessarily within the design of these notes.

2. —*The beloved vineyard*] For חמר, a great number of MSS, and some printed editions, have חמד; which is confirmed by LXX, and Chald.

Ibid. —*a responsive song*] That ענה, *to answer*, signifies occasionally to sing responsively; and that this mode of singing was frequently practised among the ancient Jews, see De S. Poes. Hebr. Præl. xix. at the beginning.

3. *I will take care of her*] For פן יפקד, Syr. read ואפקד: and fifteen MSS (six ancient), and six editions, read אפקד, in the first person.

4. *I have no wall*] For המה, LXX and Syr. read חומה. An ancient MS has חימה. For בה, two MSS read בם, plural. The vineyard wishes for a wall, and a fence of thorns; human strength and protection; (as the Jews were too apt to apply to their powerful neighbours for assistance, and to trust to the shadow of Eygpt): JEHOVAH replies, that this would not avail her, nor defend her against his wrath: he counsels her therefore to betake herself to his protection. On which she entreats him to make peace with her.

"About Tripoly there are abundance of vineyards and gardens, enclosed for the most part with hedges; which chiefly consist of the rhamnus, paliurus, oxyacantha," &c.: Rawolf, p. 21, 22. A fence of thorns is esteemed equal to a wall for strength, being commonly represented as impenetrable. See Micah vii. 4. Hos. ii. 6.

Ibid. —*of the thorn and brier*] Seven MSS (two ancient), and one edition, and Syr. Vulg. Aquila, read השית, with the conjunction ו prefixed.

5. *Ah!*] For אך, I read און, as it was at first in a MS. The ו was easily lost, being followed by another ו.

6. —*from the root*] For ישרש, I read with the Syr. משרש. And for יציץ ופרח, יציץ פרח, joining the ו to the first word, and taking that into construction with the first part of the sentence. I suppose the dialogue to be continued in this verse, which pursues the same image of the allegory, but in the way of metaphor.

9. *And if—*] ולא, four MSS (two ancient), and LXX.

11. —*her boughs*] קצירה, MS and Vulg.; that is, the boughs of the vineyard, referring still to the subject of the dialogue above.

The scarcity of fuel, especially wood, in most parts of the East is so great, that they supply it with every thing capable of burning; cow dung dried, roots, parings of fruit, withered stalks of herbs and flowers: see Matt. vi. 28—30. Vine-twigs are particularly mentioned, as used for fuel in dressing their food, by D'Arvieux; La Roque, Palestine, p. 198. Ezekiel says, in his parable of the vine, used figuratively for the people of God, as the vineyard is here, " Shall wood be taken thereof to do any work? or will men take a pin of it to hang any vessel thereon? Behold, it is cast into the fire for fuel;" chap. xv. 3, 4. " If a man abide not in me," saith our Lord, " he is cast forth as a branch [of the vine], and is withered; and men gather them, and cast them into the fire, and they are burned;" John xv. 6. They employed women and children to gather these things; and they laid them up in store for use. The dressing and pruning of their vines afforded a good supply of the last sort of fuel: but the Prophet says, that the vines themselves of the beloved vineyard shall be blasted, withered, and broken; and the women shall come, and gather them up, and carry away the whole of them, to make their fires, for domestic uses. See Harmer, Observ. i, p. 254. &c.

CHAPTER XXVIII.

1. *The proud crown—*] " Sebaste, the ancient Samaria, is situated on a long mount of an oval figure; having first

a fruitful valley, and then a ring of hills, running round about it:" Maundrell, p. 58. "E regione horum ruderum mons est peramœnus, planitie admodum frugifera circumseptus, super quem olim Samaria urbs condita fuit:" Fureri Itinerarium, p. 93. The city, beautifully situated on the top of a round hill, and surrounded immediately with a rich valley, and a circle of other hills beyond it, suggested the idea of a chaplet, or wreath of flowers, worn upon their heads on occasions of festivity; expressed by *the proud crown*, and the *fading flower of the drunkards*. That this custom of wearing chaplets in their banquets prevailed among the Jews, as well as among the Greeks and Romans, appears from the following passage of the book of Wisdom:

> "Let us fill ourselves with costly wine and ointments,
> And let no flower of the spring pass by us;
> Let us crown ourselves with rose-buds, before they are withered."   Wisd. ii. 7, 8.

2. —*the exceedingly strong one*] אמיץ לאדני, fortis Domino, *i. e.* fortissimus, a Hebraism. For לאדני, thirty-eight MSS, and two editions, read ליהוה.

3. —*crowns*] I read עטרות, plural, to agree with the verb תרמסנה.

4. *The early fruit before summer*] "No sooner doth the *boccore* [the early fig] draw near to perfection, in the middle or latter end of June, than the *kermez*, or summer fig, begins to be formed, though it rarely ripens before August; about which time the same tree frequently throws out a third crop, or the winter fig, as we may call it. This is usually of a much longer shape and darker complexion than the kermez, hanging and ripening upon the tree even after the leaves are shed; and, provided the winter proves mild and temperate, is gathered as a delicious morsel in the spring:" Shaw, Travels, p. 370. fol. The image was very obvious to the inhabitants of Judea and the neighbouring countries, and is frequently applied by the Prophets to express a desirable object; by none more elegantly than by Hosea, chap. ix. 10.

> "Like grapes in the wilderness, I found Israel;
> Like the first ripe fig in her prime, I saw your fathers."

Ibid. —*he plucketh it*] For יראה, which with הראה makes a miserable tautology, read by a transposition of a letter יארה; a happy conjecture of Houbigant. The image expresses in the strongest manner the great ease with which the Assyrians shall take the city and the whole kingdom, and the avidity with which they shall seize the rich prey without resistance.

5. *In that day*—] Thus far the prophecy relates to the Israelites, and manifestly denounces their approaching destruction by Shalmaneser. Here it turns to the two tribes of Judah and Benjamin, the remnant of God's people, who were to continue a kingdom after the final captivity of the Israelites. It begins with a favourable prognostication of their affairs under Hezekiah; but soon changes to reproofs and threatenings, for their intemperance, disobedience, and profaneness.

6. —to the gate *of the enemy*] That is, who pursue the fleeing enemy even to the very gates of their own city: "But we were upon them even unto the entering of the gate;" 2 Sam. xi. 23.; that is, we drove the enemy back to their own gates: see also 1 Sam. xvii. 52.

9. *Whom [say they] would he teach*—] The scoffers mentioned below, ver. 14. are here introduced as uttering their sententious speeches: they treat God's method of dealing with them, and warning them by his Prophets, with contempt and derision. What, say they, doth he treat us as mere infants just weaned? doth he teach us like little children, perpetually inculcating the same elementary lessons, the mere rudiments of knowledge; precept after precept, line after line, here and there, by little and little? imitating at the same time, and ridiculing, ver. 10. the concise prophetical manner. God by his Prophet retorts upon them, with great severity, their own contemptuous mockery; turning it to a sense quite different from what they intended. Yes, saith he, it shall be in fact as you say: ye shall be taught by a strange tongue, and a stammering lip; in a strange country: ye shall be carried into captivity by a people whose language shall be unintelligible to you, and which ye shall be forced to learn like children: and my dealing with you shall be according to your own words; it shall be command upon command for your punishment; it shall be line upon line, stretched over you to mark out your destruction; (compare 2 Kings xxi. 13.) : it shall come upon you at different times, and by different degrees; till the judgments, with which from time to time I have threatened you, shall have their full accomplishment.

Jerom seems to have rightly understood the general design of this passage, as expressing the manner in which the scoffers, by their sententious speeches, turned into ridicule the warnings of God by his Prophets; though he has not so well explained the meaning of the repetition of their speech in the 13th verse. His words, are, on ver. 9. "Solebant hoc ex persona Prophetarum ludentes dicere:" and on ver. 14. "Quod supra diximus, cum irrisione solitos principes Judæorum Prophetis dicere, *manda, remanda*, et cætera his similia, per, quæ ostenditur, nequaquam eos Prophetarum credidisse sermonibus, sed Prophetiam habuisse despectui, præsens ostendit capitulum, per quod appellantur viri illusores:" Hieron. in loc.

And so Jarchi interprets the word משלים in the next verse: "Qui dicunt verba irrisionis parabolice." And the Chaldee paraphrases the 11th verse to the same purpose, understanding it as spoken not of God, but of the people deriding his prophets: "Quoniam in mutatione loquelæ et in lingua subsannationis irridebant contra Prophetas qui prophetabant populo huic."

12. *This is the true rest—*] The sense of this verse is: God had warned them by his prophets, that their safety and security, their deliverance from their present calamities, and from the apprehensions of still greater approaching, depended wholly on their trust in God, their faith and obedience; but they rejected this gracious warning with contempt and mockery.

15. —*a covenant with death*] To be in covenant with, is a kind of proverbial expression to denote perfect security from evil and mischief of any sort:

" For thou shalt be in league with the stones of the field;
And the beasts of the field shall be at peace with thee."
                                            Job v. 23.

" And I will make a covenant for them with the beasts of the field,
And with the fowls of heaven, and with the creeping things of the ground."   Hos. ii. 18.

That is, none of these shall hurt them. But Lucan, speaking of the Psylli, whose peculiar property it was to be unhurt by the bite of serpents, with which their country abounded, comes still nearer to the expression of Isaiah in this place:—

" Gens unica terras
Incolit a sævo serpentum innoxia morsu
Marmaridæ Psylli.——
Pax illis cum morte data est."   Pharsal. ix. 894.

" Of all who scorching Afric's sun endure,
None like the swarthy Psyllians are secure;
With healing gifts and privileges graced,
Well in the land of serpents were they placed:
Truce with the dreadful tyrant death they have,
And border safely on his realm the grave."   Rowe.

18. —*shall be broken*] For כפר, which seems not to belong to this place, Chald. reads תפר; which is approved by Houbigant and SECKER : see Jer. xxxiii. 21. where the very same phrase is used. See Prelim. Dissert. p. xxxi.

20. —*For the bed is too short*—] A *mashal* or proverbial saying, the meaning of which is, that they will find all means of defence and protection insufficient to secure them, and cover them from the evils coming upon them. מסך, chap. xxii. 8. the *covering*, is used for the outworks of defence, the barrier of the country; and here in the allegorical sense it means much the same thing. Their beds were only mattresses laid on the floor; and the coverlet, a sheet, or in the winter a carpet, laid over it, in which the person wrapt himself. For כהתכנס, it ought probably to be מהתכנס: Houbigant, SECKER.

23. *Listen ye, and hear my voice*—] The foregoing discourse, consisting of severe reproofs, and threatenings of dreadful judgments impending on the Jews for their vices, and their profane contempt of God's warnings by his messengers, the Prophet concludes with an explanation and defence of God's method of dealing with his people in an elegant parable or allegory; in which he employs a variety of images, all taken from the science of agriculture. As the husbandman uses various methods in preparing his land, and adapting it to the several kinds of seed to be sown, with a due observation of times and seasons; and, when he hath gathered in his harvest, employs methods as various in separating the corn from the straw and the chaff by different instruments, according to the nature of the different sorts of grain : so God, with unerring wisdom, and with strict justice, instructs, admonishes, and corrects his people ; chastises and punishes them in various ways, as the exigence of the case requires; now more moderately, now more severely; always tempering justice with mercy; in order to reclaim

the wicked, to improve the good; and finally, to separate the one from the other.

26. *For his God instructeth him*] All nations have agreed in attributing agriculture, the most useful and the most necessary of all sciences, to the invention and to the suggestions of their deities. " The Most High hath ordained husbandry," saith the son of Sirach; Eccl'us vii. 15.

"Namque Ceres fertur fruges, Liberque liquoris
Vitigeni laticem mortalibus instituisse." Lucretius, v. 14.

'Ο δ' ηπιος ανθρωποισι
Δεξια σημαινει, λαους δ' επι εργον εγειρει
Μιμνησκων βιοτοιο· λεγει δ' οτε βωλος αριση
Βουσι τε και μακεληστι· λεγει δ' οτε δεξιαι ωραι
Και φυτα γυρωσαι, και σπερματα παντα βαλεσθαι. Aratus, Phæn. 5.

He (Jupiter) to the human race
Indulgent, prompts to necessary toil
Man provident of life; with kindly signs
The seasons marks, when best to turn the glebe
With spade and plough, to nurse the tender plant,
And cast o'er fostering earth the seeds abroad.

27, 28. Four methods of threshing are here mentioned, by different instruments; the flail, the drag, the wain, and the treading of the cattle. The staff, or flail, was used for the *infirmiora semina*, says Hieron. the grain that was too tender to be treated in the other methods. The drag consisted of a sort of frame of strong planks, made rough at the bottom with hard stones or iron: it was drawn by horses or oxen over the corn-sheaves spread on the floor, the driver sitting upon it. Kempfer has given a print representing the manner of using this instrument: Amœn. Exot. p. 682. fig. 3. The wain was much like the former, but had wheels with iron teeth or edges like a saw. " Ferrata carpenta rotis per medium in serrarum modum se volventibus:" Hieron. in loc.; by which it should seem that the axle was armed with iron teeth, or serrated wheels, throughout. See a description and print of such a machine used at present in Egypt for the same purpose; it moves upon three rollers armed with iron teeth or wheels, to cut the straw; in Niebuhr's Voyage en Arabie, tab. xvii. p. 123. In Syria they make use of the drag, constructed in the very same manner as above described: Niebuhr, Description de l'Arabie, p. 140. This not only forced out the grain, but cut the straw in pieces for fodder for the cattle; for in the eastern countries they have no hay. See Harmer's Observ. i. p. 425. The last method is well known from the law of Moses, which "forbids the ox to be muzzled, when he treadeth out the corn;" Deut. xxv. 4.

28. —*but the bread-corn*—] I read ולחם, on the authority of Vulg. and Symmachus: the former expresses the conjunction ו, omitted in the text, by *autem*; the latter by δε.

Ibid. —*hoofs*—] For פרשיו, *horsemen*, read פרסיו, *hoofs:* so Syr. Sym. Theod. Vulg.

CHAPTER XXIX.

The subject of this and the four following chapters is the invasion of Senacherib; the great distress of the Jews while it continued; their sudden and unexpected deliverance by God's immediate interposition in their favour; the subsequent prosperous state of the kingdom under Hezekiah;—interspersed with severe reproofs, and threats of punishment, for their hypocrisy, stupidity, infidelity, their want of trust in God, and their vain reliance on the assistance of Egypt; and with promises of better times, both immediately to succeed, and to be expected in the future age. The whole making not one continued discourse, but rather a collection of different discourses upon the same subject; which is treated with great elegance and variety: though the matter is various, and the transitions sudden, yet the Prophet seldom goes far from his subject. It is properly enough divided by the chapters in the common translation.

1. *Ariel*—] That Jerusalem is here called by this name is very certain; but the reason of this name, and the meaning of it as applied to Jerusalem, is very obscure and doubtful. Some, with the Chaldee, suppose it to be taken from the hearth of the great altar of burnt-offerings, which Ezekiel plainly calls by the same name; and that Jerusalem is here considered as the seat of the fire of God, אור אל, which should issue from thence to consume his enemies: compare chap. xxxi. 9. Some, according to the common derivation of the word, ארי אל, the lion of God, or the strong lion, suppose it to signify the strength of the place, by which it was enabled to resist and overcome all its enemies. Τινες δε φασι την πολιν ουτως ειρησθαι· επει, δια Θεου, λεοντος δικην εσπαρατ]ε τους

ἀνταίροντας: Procop. in loc. There are other explanations of this name given, but none that seems to be perfectly satisfactory.

Ibid. *Add year to year*—] Ironically: Go on year after year; keep your solemn feasts: yet know, that God will punish you for your hypocritical worship, consisting of mere form destitute of true piety. Probably delivered at the time of some great feast, when they were thus employed.

2. —*mourning and sorrow*—] Instead of your present joy and festivity.

Ibid. —*as the hearth of the great altar*—] That is, it shall be the seat of the fire of God; which shall issue from thence to consume his enemies. See note on ver. 1. Or, perhaps, all on flame, as it was when taken by the Chaldeans; or covered with carcasses and blood, as when taken by the Romans: an intimation of which more distant events, though not immediate subjects of the prophecy, may perhaps be given in this obscure passage.

3. —*like David*] For כדור read כדוד; So LXX, and two MSS, and f. two more.

Ibid. —*towers*—] For מצרות read מצדות; so LXX, and five MSS, one of them ancient.

4. —*a feeble speech*] That the souls of the dead uttered a feeble stridulous sound, very different from the natural human voice, was a popular notion among the heathens as well as among the Jews. This appears from several passages of their poets; Homer, Virgil, Horace. The pretenders to the art of necromancy, who were chiefly women, had an art of speaking with a feigned voice; so as to deceive those who applied to them, by making them believe that it was the voice of the ghost. They had a way of uttering sounds, as if they were formed, not by the organs of speech, but deep in the chest, or in the belly; and were thence called ἐγγαστρίμυθοι, ventriloqui: they could make the voice seem to come from beneath the ground, from a distant part, in another direction, and not from themselves, the better to impose upon those who consulted them. Εξεπίτηδες το γενος τουτο τον αμυδρον ηχον επιτηδευονται, ινα δια την ασαφειαν της φωνης του του ψευδους αποδιδρασκωσιν ελεγχον: Psellus de Dæmonibus, apud Bochart. i. p. 731. "These people studiously acquire, and affect on purpose, this sort of obscure sound, that by the uncertainty of the voice they may the better escape being detected in the cheat." From these arts of the necroman-

5.—*the proud*—] For זריך, *thy strangers*, read זדים, *the proud*, LXX; parallel and synonymous to עריצים *the terrible*, in the next line: the ר was at first ד in a MS. See note on xxv. 2.

5—7. *But the multitude of the proud*—] These verses contain an admirable description of the destruction of Senacherib's army, with a beautiful variety of the most expressive and sublime images; perhaps more adapted to shew the greatness, the suddenness, and horror, of the event, than the means and manner by which it was effected. Compare chap xxx. 30—33.

7.—*like as a dream*—] This is the beginning of the comparison, which is pursued and applied in the next verse. Senacherib and his mighty army are not compared to a dream, because of their sudden disappearance: but the disappointment of their eager hopes is compared to what happens to a hungry and thirsty man, when he awakes from a dream in which fancy had presented to him meat and drink in abundance, and finds it nothing but a vain illusion. The comparison is elegant and beautiful in the highest degree, well wrought up, and perfectly suited to the end proposed: the image is extremely natural, but not obvious; it appeals to our inward feelings, not to our outward senses; and is applied to an event in its concomitant circumstances exactly similar, but in its nature totally different. See De S. Poes. Hebr. Prælect. xii. For beauty and ingenuity it may fairly come in competition with one of the most elegant of Virgil, (greatly improved from Homer, Iliad xxii. 199.), where he has applied to a different purpose, but not so happily, the same image of the ineffectual working of imagination in a dream:—

" Ac veluti in somnis oculos ubi languida pressit
  Nocte quies, necquicquam avidos extendere cursus
  Velle videmur, et in mediis conatibus ægri
  Succidimus; non lingua valet, non corpore notæ
  Sufficiunt vires, nec vox, aut verba sequuntur." Æn. xii. 908.

" And as, when slumber seals the closing sight,
  The sick wild fancy labours in the night;
  Some dreadful visionary foe we shun
  With airy strides, but strive in vain to run;

In vain our baffled limbs their powers essay;
We faint, we struggle, sink, and fall away;
Drain'd of our strength, we neither fight nor fly,
And on the tongue the struggling accents die."   Pitt.

Lucretius expresses the very same image with Isaiah:

"Ac veluti in somnis sitiens quum quurit, et humor
Non datur, ardorem in membris qui stinguere possit:
Sed laticum simulachra petit, frustraque laborat,
In medioque sitit torrenti flumine potans."   iv. 1091.

Ibid. —*their armies and their towers*] For צביה ומצדתה, I read with the Chald. צבאם ומצדתם.

9. *They are drunken, but not with wine.*] See note on chap. li. 21.

11. *I cannot read it—*] An ancient MS and LXX have preserved a word here, lost out of the text, לקרות, (for לקראת), αναγνωναι.

13. JEHOVAH—] For אדני, sixty-three MSS and three editions read יהוה, and five MSS add יהוה.

Ibid. *And vain—*] I read, for ותהי, ותהו with LXX, Matt. xv. 9. Mark vii. 7.; and for מלמדה, מלמדים with Chald.

17. *Ere Lebanon become like Carmel—*] A mashal, or proverbial saying, expressing any great revolution of things; and, when respecting two subjects, an entire reciprocal change: explained here by some interpreters, I think with great probability, as having its principal view beyond the revolutions then near at hand; to the rejection of the Jews, and the calling of the Gentiles. The first were the vineyard of God, כרם אל, (if the Prophet, who loves an allusion to words of like sounds, may be supposed to have intended one here), cultivated and watered by him in vain, to be given up, and to become a wilderness: compare chap. v. 1—7. The last had been hitherto barren, but were, by the grace of God, to be rendered fruitful. See Matt. xxi. 43. Rom. xi. 30, 31. Carmel stands here opposed to Lebanon, and therefore is to be taken as a proper name.

21. —*that pleaded in the gate*] "They are heard by the treasurer, master of the horse, and other principal officers of the regency [of Algiers], who sit constantly in the gate of the palace for that purpose;" [that is, the distribution of justice]: Shaw's Travels, p. 315. fol. He adds, in the note, "That we read of the *elders in the gate*, Deut. xxii. 15. xxv. 7.; and Isa. xxix. 21. Amos. v. 10. of *him*

that reproveth and *rebuketh in the gate.* The Ottoman Court likewise seems to have been called *the Port,* from the distribution of justice, and the despatch of public business, that is carried on in the gates of it."

22. —*the God of the house of Jacob.*] I read אל as a noun, not a preposition: the parallel line favours this sense; and there is no address to the house of Jacob, to justify the other.

Ibid. —*covered with confusion*] "יחור, Chald. ut ὁ [μεταβαλεῖ], Theod. στραπησεται, Syr. נחפרו, videtur legendum יחפרו: hic enim solum legitur verbum חור, nec in linguis affinibus habet pudoris significationem:" SECKER.

23. *When his children shall see*—] For בראתו, I read בראית, with LXX and Syr.

CHAPTER XXX.

1. *Who ratify covenants*—] Heb. "Who pour out a libation." Sacrifice and libation were ceremonies constantly used, in ancient times, by most nations, in the ratifying of covenants: a libation therefore is used for a covenant, as in Greek the word σπονδή, for the same reason, stands for both. This seems to be the most easy explication of the Hebrew phrase; and it has the authority of the LXX, εποιησατε συνθηκας.

4. —*at Hanes*] Six MSS, and perhaps six others, read חנם, in vain, for הנם, Hanes; and so also LXX, who read likewise יגע, laboured, for יגיע, arrived at.

5. —*were ashamed*—] Eight MSS (one ancient) read הביש without א. So Chald. and Vulg.

Ibid. *But proved*—] Four MSS (three ancient) after כי add אם, which seems wanted to complete the phrase in its usual form.

6. *The burthen*—] משא seems here to be taken in its proper sense; the *load,* not the *oracle.* The same subject is continued; and there seems to be no place here for a new title to a distinct prophecy.

Ibid. —*a land of distress*—] The same deserts are here spoken of, which the Israelites passed through when they came out of Egypt; which Moses describes, Deut. viii. 15. as "that great and terrible wilderness, wherein were fiery serpents, and scorpions, and drought; where there was no water." And which was designed to be a kind of barrier between them and Egypt, of which the Lord had said, "Ye shall henceforth return no more that way;" Deut. xvii. 16.

6. —*will not profit them*] A MS adds in the margin the word למו, which seems to have been lost out of the text: it is authorized by LXX and Vulg.

7. *Rahab the Inactive*] The two last words, הם שבת, joined into one, make the participle pihel, המשבת. I find, that the learned professor Doederlein, in his version of Isaiah, and note on this place, has given the same conjecture; which he speaks of as having been formerly published by him. A concurrence of different persons in the same conjecture adds to it a greater degree of probability.

8. *For a testimony*] לעד, so Syr. Chald. Vulg. and LXX, in MSS Pachom. and 1. D. 11. εις μαρτυριον; which two words have been lost out of the other copies of LXX.

12. —*in obliquity*] בעקש, transposing the two last letters of בעשק, *in oppression*, which seems not to belong to this place: a very probable conjecture of Houbigant.

13. —*a swelling in a high wall*] It has been observed before, that the buildings in Asia generally consist of little better than what we call mud-walls. "All the houses at Ispahan," says Thevenot, vol. ii. p. 159. "are built of bricks made of clay and straw, and dried in the sun; and covered with a plaster made of a fine white stone. In other places in Persia, the houses are built with nothing else but such bricks, made with tempered clay and chopped straw, well mingled together, and dried in the sun, and then used: but the least rain dissolves them." Sir John Chardin's MS remark on this place of Isaiah is very apposite: "Murs en Asie etant faits de terre se fendent ainsi par milieu et de haut en bas." This shews clearly how obvious and expressive the image is. The Psalmist has in the same manner made use of it, to express sudden and utter destruction:

"Ye shall be slain all of you;
[Ye shall be] like an inclining wall, like a shattered fence."
Psal. lxii. 4.

14. —*and spareth it not*] Five MSS add the conjunction ו to the negative; ולא.

17. —*ten thousand*—] In the second line of this verse a word is manifestly omitted, which should answer to *one thousand* in the first: LXX supply πολλοι, רבים. But the true word is רבבה; as, I am persuaded, any one will be

convinced, who will compare the following passage with this place:

"How should one chase a thousand:
And two put ten thousand [רבבה] to flight?"
                                Deut. xxxii. 30.

"And five of you shall chase a hundred;
And a hundred of you shall chase [רבבה] ten thousand."
                                Lev. xxvi. 8.

18. —*shall he expect in silence*] For ירם, *he shall be exalted*, which belongs not to this place, Houbigant reads ידם, *he shall be silent:* and so it seems to be in a MS. Another MS instead of it reads ישׁיב, *he shall return*. The mistakes occasioned by the similitude of the letters ד and ר are very frequent, as the reader may have already observed.

19. *When a holy people*—] Λαος ἁγιος, LXX, עם קרוש. The word קרוש, lost out of the text, but happily supplied by LXX, clears up the sense, otherwise extremely obscure.

Ibid. —*shalt implore him with weeping*] The negative particle לא is not acknowledged by LXX. It may perhaps have been written by mistake for לו, of which there are many examples.

20. *Though JEHOVAH*—] For אדני, sixteen MSS and three editions have יהוה.

21. —*to the right, or to the left*] Syr. Chald. Vulg. translate as if, instead of כי—וכי, they read לא—ולא.

22. *And ye shall treat*—] The very prohibition of Moses, Deut. vii. 25. only thrown out of the prose into the poetical form. "The graven images of their gods ye shall burn with fire: thou shalt not desire the silver or the gold that is on them; nor take it unto thee, lest thou be snared therein; for it is an abomination to JEHOVAH thy God."

25. —*the mighty*—] מגדלים, μεγαλους, Sym. μεγαλυνομενους, Aquila; רברבין, Chald.

26. —*shall be sevenfold*] The text adds, כאיר שבעת הימים, "as the light of seven days;" a manifest gloss, taken in from the margin: it is not in most of the copies of LXX; it interrupts the rhythmical construction, and obscures the sense by a false, or at least an unnecessary interpretation.

27. —*the flame*—] משׂאה; this word seems to be rightly rendered in our translation, *the flame*, Judg. xx. 30. 40. &c.; a sign of *fire*, Jer. vi. 1. called properly משׂאה, an *elevation*, from its tending upwards.

28. —*to toss the nations with the van of perdition*] The

word להנפה is in its form very irregular. Kimchi says it is for להניף. Houbigant supposes it to be a mistake, and shews the cause of it; the adjoining it to the ה, which should begin the following word. The true reading is להניף הגוים.

The Vulgate seems to be the only one of the ancient interpreters who has explained rightly the sense: but he has dropped the image: "ad perdendas gentes in nihilum." Kimchi's explanation is to the following effect: "נפה is a van with which they winnow corn; and its use is to cleanse the corn from the chaff and straw: but the van, with which God will winnow the nations, will be the van of emptiness, or perdition; for nothing useful shall remain behind, but all shall come to nothing, and perish. In like manner, a bridle is designed to guide the horse in the right way; but the bridle which God will put in the jaws of the people, shall not direct them aright, but shall make them err, and lead them into destruction." This latter image the Prophet has applied to the same subject afterward, chap. xxxvii. 29.

" I will put my bridle in thy jaws,
And turn thee back by the way in which thou camest."

And as to the former it is to be observed, that the van of the ancients was a large instrument, somewhat like a shovel, with a long handle, with which they tossed the corn mixed with the chaff and chopped straw into the air that the wind might separate them. See Hammond on Matt. iii. 12.

31. *He, that was—*] "Post אשור forte excidit אשר:" SECKER.

32. *—the rod of correction*] For מוסדה, the *grounded* staff, of which no one yet has been able to make any tolerable sense, Le Clerc conjectured מסרה, *of correction;* see Prov. xxii. 15.; and so it is in two MSS (one of them ancient), and seems to be so in the Bodley MS. Syr. has דשועברה, virga domans, vel subjectionis.

Ibid. *—against them*] For כה, fifty-two MSS and five editions read בם.

Ibid. *—with tabrets and harps*] With every demonstration of joy and thanksgiving for the destruction of the enemy in so wonderful a manner: with hymns of praise, accompanied with musical instruments. See ver. 29.

33. *For Tophet is ordained—*] Tophet is a valley very near to Jerusalem, to the south-east, called also the valley of Hinnom, or Gehenna; where the Canaanites, and afterwards the Israelites, sacrificed their children, by making them pass

through the fire—that is, by burning them in the fire—to Moloch. It is therefore used for a place of punishment by fire; and by our blessed Saviour in the gospel for hell-fire; as the Jews themselves had applied it. See Chald. on Isa. xxxiii. 14. where מוקדי עלם is rendered "the Gehenna of everlasting fire." Here the place where the Assyrian army was destroyed is called Tophet by a metonymy; for the Assyrian army was destroyed probably at a greater distance from Jerusalem, and quite on the opposite side of it: for Nob is mentioned as the last station from which the king of Assyria should threaten Jerusalem, chap. x. 32. where the Prophet seems to have given a very exact chorographical description of his march in order to attack the city.

CHAPTER XXXI.

1. *Who trust—*] For על, 1mo, twenty MSS, and LXX and Vulg. read על, without the conjunction.

2. *—his word*] דברו, singular, without י; MS and LXX, and Targ. Hieros.

4. *Like as the lion—*] This comparison is exactly in the spirit and manner, and very nearly approaching to the expression of Homer:—

Βη ρ' ιμεν, ωστε λεων ορεσιτροφος, ος' επιδευης
Δηρον εη κρειων, κελεται δε ε θυμος αγηνωρ,
Μηλων πειρησοντα, και ες πυκινον δομον ελθειν·
Ειπερ γαρ χ' ευρησι παρ' αυτοφι βωτορας ανδρας
Συν κυσι και δυρεσσι φυλασσοντας περι μηλα,
Ου ρα τ' απειρητος μεμονε σταθμοιο διεσθαι·
Αλλ' ο γ' αρ' η 'ηρπαξε μεταλμενος, ηε και αυτος
Εβλητ' εν πρωτοισι θοης απο χειρος ακοντι.   Iliad, xii. 299.

As the bold lion, mountain-bred, now long
Famish'd, with courage and with hunger stung,
Attempts the thronged fold: him nought appals,
Though dogs and armed shepherds stand in guard
Collected; he nathless undaunted springs
O'er the high fence, and rends the trembling prey;
Or rushing onward in his breast receives
The well-aimed spear.

Of metaphors, allegories, and comparisons of the Hebrew poets, in which the divine nature and attributes are represented under images taken from brutes and other low objects; of their effect, their sublimity, and the cause of it; see De S. Poes. Hebr. Prælect. xvi. sub fin.

5. *leaping forward*—] The generality of interpreters observe, in this place, an allusion to the deliverance which God vouchsafed to his people, when he destroyed the first-born of the Egyptians, and exempted those of the Israelites sojourning among them by a peculiar interposition. The same word is made use of here which is used upon that occasion, and which gave the name to the feast which was instituted in commemoration of that deliverance; פסח. But the difficulty is, to reconcile the commonly received meaning of that word with the circumstances of the similitude here used to illustrate the deliverance represented as parallel to the deliverance in Egypt.

" As the mother-birds hovering over their young;
So shall JEHOVAH God of Hosts protect Jerusalem,
Protecting and delivering, *passing over*, and rescuing her."

This difficulty is, I think, well solved by Vitringa; whose remark is the more worthy of observation, as it leads to the true meaning of an important word, which hitherto seems greatly to have been misunderstood; though Vitringa himself, as it appears to me, has not exactly enough defined the precise meaning of it. He says, "פסח signifies to cover, to protect by covering; σκεπασω ὑμας, LXX; JEHOVAH *obteget ostium*:" whereas it means that particular action or motion, by which God at that time placed himself in such a situation as to protect the house of the Israelite against the destroying angel,—to spring forward, to throw one's self in the way, in order to cover and protect. Cocceius comes nearer to the true meaning than Vitringa, by rendering it *gradum facere*, to march, to step forward: Lexicon in v. The common meaning of the word פסח upon other occasions is to halt, to be lame, to leap as in a rude manner of dancing, (as the prophets of Baal did, 1 Kings xviii. 26.); all which agrees very well together; for the motion of a lame person is a perpetual springing forward, by throwing himself from the weaker upon the stronger leg. The common notion of God's passing over the houses of the Israelites is, that in going through the land of Egypt to smite the first-born, seeing the blood on the door of the houses of the Israelites, he passed over, or skipped, those houses, and forbore to smite them. But that this is not the true notion of the thing, will be plain from considering the words of the sacred historian; where he describes very explicitly the action: "For JEHOVAH will pass through, to smite the Egyptians; and when he seeth the blood on the lintels and on the two side-posts, JEHOVAH will spring forward over (or before) the door, ופסח יהוה על הפתח, and will not suffer the destroyer to come into your houses to smite *you;*" Exod. xii. 23. Here are manifestly two distinct agents, with which the notion of *passing over* is not consistent.; for that supposes but one agent: The two agents are the destroying angel passing through to smite every house; and JEHOVAH the protector, keeping pace with him; and who, seeing the door of the Israelite marked with the blood, the token prescribed, leaps forward, throws himself with a sudden motion in the way, opposes the destroying angel; and covers and protects that house against the destroying angel, nor suffers him to smite it. In this way of considering the action, the beautiful similitude of the bird protecting her young, answers exactly to the application by the allusion to the deliverance in Egypt: As the mother-bird spreads her wings to cover her young, throws herself before them, and opposes the rapacious bird that assaults them; so shall JEHOVAH protect, as with a shield, Jerusalem from the enemy, protecting and delivering, *springing forward* and rescuing her; ὑπερϐαινων, as the three other Greek interpreters, Aquila, Symmachus, and Theodotion, render it: LXX, περιποιησεται; instead of which, MS Pachom. has περιϐησεται, *circumeundo proteget*, which I think is the true reading. Homer (Il. viii. 331.) expresses the very same image by this word:—

Αλλα θεων περιϐη, και οἱ σακος αμφεκαλυψε:
——— "But Ajax his broad shield display'd,
And screen'd his brother with a mighty shade." Pope.
——— Ὁς Χρυσην αμφιϐεϐηκας. Il. i. 37.

Which the Scholiast explains by περιϐεϐηκας, ὑπερμαχεις.

6. *ye have so deeply*—] All the ancient versions read תעמיקו, in the second person.

7. *The sin, which their own hands have made*] The construction of the word חטא, *sin*, in this place is not easy. The LXX have omitted it: MSS Pachom. and 1. D. 11. and Cod. Marchal. in margine, supply the omission by the word ἁμαρτιαν, or ἁμαρτημα, said to be from Aquila's version; which I have followed. The learned professor Schroeder, Institut. Ling. Hebr. p. 298. makes it to be *in regimine* with

ידיכם, as an epithet; your *sinful hands*. The LXX render the pronoun in the third person, αἱ χειρες αυτων; and an ancient MS has, agreeably to that rendering, להם, for לכם; which word they have likewise omitted, as not necessary to complete the sense.

CHAPTER XXXII.

1. *And princes*—] ושרים, without ל; so the ancient versions. An ancient MS has ושריו, and *his* princes.

2. *As the shadow of a great rock*] The shadow of a great projecting rock is the most refreshing that is possible in a hot country; not only as most pe.fectly excluding the rays of the sun, but also having in itself a natural coolness, which it reflects and communicates to every thing about it.

" Speluncæque tegant, et saxea procubet umbra."
Virg. Georg. iii. 145.
" Let the cool cave and shady rock protect them."

Επει κεφαλην και γουνατα Σειριος αζει,
Αυαλεος δε τε χρως απο καυματος. αλλα τοτ' ηδη
Ειη πετραιη τε σκιη, και Βιβλινος οινος.   Hesiod. ii. 206.

When Sirius rages, and thine aching head,
Parch'd skin, and feeble knees, refreshment need;
Then to the rock's projected shade retire,
With Biblin wine recruit thy wasted powers.

3. *And him the eyes*] For ולא Le Clerc reads ולו; of which mistake the Masoretes acknowledge there are fifteen instances; and many more are reckoned by others. The removal of the negative restores to the verb its true and usual sense.

6. *The fool will still utter folly*] A sort of proverbial saying; which Euripides (Bacchæ, 369.) has expressed in the very same manner and words: μωρα γαρ μωρος λεγει. Of this kind of simple and unadorned proverb or parable, see De S. Poes. Hebr. Prælect. xxiv.

Ibid. *Against JEHOVAH*] For אל, two MSS read על, more properly.

7. *As for the niggard his instruments*—] His machinations, his designs. The paronomasia, which the Prophet frequently deals in, suggested this expression: וכלי כליו. The first word is expressed with some variety in the MSS: seven MSS read וכילי, one וכל, another וכולי.

Ibid. *And to defeat the assertions*—] A word seems to have been lost here, and two others to have suffered a small alteration; which has made the sentence very obscure. The LXX have happily retained the rendering of the lost word, and restored the sentence in all its parts: και διασκεδασαι λογους ταπεινων εν κρισει· ולהפר דברי אביון במשפט. They frequently render the verb הפר by διασκεδασαι. A MS reads ולדבר; which gives authority for the preposition ל necessary to the sense; and LXX, Syr. Chald. read במשפט.

8. *And he by his generous*—] "Of the four sorts of persons mentioned ver. 5. three are described, ver. 6, 7, and 8. but not the fourth:" SECKER. Perhaps for והוא we ought to read ושוע.

11. *Gird the sackcloth*—] שק, sackcloth, a word necessary to the sense, is here lost, but preserved by LXX, MSS Alex. and Pachom. and 1. D. 11. and Edit. Ald. and Comp. and Arab. and Syr.

Ibid. *Tremble—be disquieted—strip ye*—] פשטה, רגזה, &c. These are infinitives, with a paragogic ה, according to Schultens, Institut. Ling. Hebr. p. 453. and are to be taken in an imperative sense.

12. *Mourn ye for the pleasant field*] The LXX, Syr. and Vulg. read ספדו, *mourn ye*, imperative: twelve MSS (five ancient), two editions, LXX, Aquilla, Sym. Theod. Syr. Vulg. all read שדה, *field*; not שרי, *breasts*.

13. —*And the brier shall come up*] All the ancient versions read ושמיר, with the conjunction. And an ancient MS has תעלה בו, which seems to be right; or rather בה: and there is a rasure in the place of בו in another ancient MS.

Ibid. *Yea over all*—] For כי, the ancient versions, except Vulg. seem to have read ו. כי may perhaps be a mistake for בו or בה above-mentioned. It is not necessary in this place.

13—18. *Over the land of my people*—] This description of impending distress belongs to other times than that of Senacherib's invasion, from which they were so soon delivered. It must at least extend to the ruin of the country and city by the Chaldeans. And the promise of blessings, which follows, was not fulfilled under the Mosaic dispensation; they belong to the kingdom of Messiah. Compare ver. 15. with chap xxix. 17. and see the note there.

14. *Ophel*] It was a part of Mount Sion, rising higher than the rest; at the eastern extremity, near to the temple,

a little to the south of it; called by Micah, iv. 8. "Ophel of the daughter of Sion." It was naturally strong by its situation, and had a wall of its own, by which it was separated from the rest of Sion.

15. *And the fruitful field*] והכרמל, fifteen MSS (six ancient), and two editions; which seems to make the noun an appellative.

10. *The city shall be laid level with the plain*] For ובשפלה, Syr. reads וכשפלה. The city, probably Nineveh, or Babylon: but this verse is very obscure. "Saltus; Assyriorum regnum: civitas: magnifica Assyriorum castra:" Ephræm. Syr. in loc. For וברד, a MS has ויֹרד; and so conjectured Archbishop Secker, referring to Zech. xi. 2

20. *who sow your seed in every watery place*] Sir John Chardin's note on this place is: "This exactly answers the manner of planting rice; for they sow it upon the water: and before sowing, while the earth is covered with water, they cause the ground to be trodden by oxen, horses, and asses, who go mid-leg deep; and this is the way of preparing the ground for sowing. As they sow the rice on the water, they transplant it in the water; Harmer's Observ. i. p. 280. "Rice is the food of two-thirds of mankind:" Dr. Arbuthnot. "It is cultivated in most of the eastern countries:" Miller. "It is good for all, and at all times:" Sir J. Chardin, ibid. "La ris, qui est leur principal aliment et leur froment (*i. e.* des Siamois), n'est jamais assez arrosé; il croit au milieu de l'eau, et les campagnes où on le cultive ressemblent plutôt à de maréts que non pas à des terres qu'on laboure avec la charue. Le ris a bien cette force, que quoy qu'il y ait six ou sept pieds d'eau sur lui, il pousse toujours sa tige au dessus, et le tuyau qui le porte s'eleve et croit à proportion de la hauteur de l'eau qui noye son champ:" Voyage de l'Evêque de Beryte, p. 144.; Paris, 1666.

CHAPTER XXXIII.

The plan of the prophecy, continued in this chapter, and which is manifestly distinct from the foregoing, is peculiarly elegant. To set it in a proper light, it will be necessary to mark the transitions from one part of it to another.

In ver. 1. the Prophet addresses himself to Senacherib, briefly, but strongly and elegantly, expressing the injustice of his ambitious designs, and the sudden disappointment of them.

Ver. 2. the Jews are introduced offering up their earnest supplications to God in their present distressful condition; with expressions of their trust and confidence in his protection.

Ver. 3. and 4. the Prophet, in the name of God, or rather God himself, is introduced addressing himself to Senacherib, and threatening him, that notwithstanding the terror which he had occasioned in the invaded countries, yet he should fall, and become an easy prey to those whom he had intended to subdue.

Ver. 5. and 6. a chorus of Jews is introduced, acknowledging the mercy and power of God, who had undertaken to protect them; extolling it with direct opposition to the boasted power of their enemies; and celebrating the wisdom and piety of their king Hezekiah who had placed his confidence in the favour of God.

Then follows, ver. 7—9. a description of the distress and despair of the Jews, upon the king of Assyria's marching against Jerusalem, and sending his summons to them to surrender, after the treaty he had made with Hezekiah on the conditions of his paying, as he actually did pay to him, three hundred talents of silver, and thirty talents of gold; 2 Kings xviii. 14—16.

Ver. 10. God himself is again introduced, declaring that he will interpose in this critical situation of affairs, and disappoint the vain designs of the enemies of his people, by discomfiting and utterly consuming them.

Then follows, ver. 11—22. still in the person of God, (which however falls at last into that of the Prophet), a description of the dreadful apprehensions of the wicked in those times of distress and imminent danger; finely contrasted with the confidence and security of the righteous, and their trust in the promises of God, that he will be their never-failing strength and protector.

The whole concludes, in the person of the Prophet, with a description of the security of the Jews under the protection of God, and of the wretched state of Senacherib and his army, wholly discomfited, and exposed to be plundered even by the weakest of the enemy.

Much of the beauty of this passage depends on the explanation above given of ver. 3. and 4. as addressed by the

Prophet, or by God himself, to Senacherib; not, as it is usually taken, as addressed by the Jews to God, ver. 3. and then, ver. 4. as addressed to the Assyrians. To set this in a clear light, it may be of use to compare it with a passage of the Prophet Joel; where, speaking of the destruction caused by the locusts, he sets in the same strong light of opposition, as Isaiah does here, the power of the enemy, and the power of JEHOVAH who would destroy that enemy. Thus Isaiah, to Senacherib;

" When thou didst raise thyself up, the nations were dispersed.
                                                            ver. 3.

" But now will I arise, saith JEHOVAH;
Now will I be exalted."   ver. 10.

And thus Joel, ii. 20, 21.

" His stink shall come up, and his ill savour shall ascend;
Though he hath done great things.
Fear not, O land, be glad and rejoice;
For JEHOVAH will do great things."

1. *thou plunderer*—] See note on chap. xxi. 2.

Ibid. —*when thou art weary*—] "כנלתך, alibi non extat in s. s. nisi f. Job. xv. 29. —simplicius est legere ככלתך. Vid. Capell. nec repugnat Vitringa. Vid. Dan. ix. 24. כלה, התם:" SECKER.

2. *our strength*—] For זרעם, Syr. Chald. Vulg. read זרענו, in the first person of the pronoun, not the third: the edition of Felix Pratensis has זרעתינו in the margin.

3. *From thy terrible voice*—] For המון, LXX and Syr. read אמיך; whom I follow.

6. —*thy treasure*—] Ο θησαυρος σου, Sym. He had in his copy אצרך, not אצרו.

7. —*the mighty men raise a grievous cry*] Three MSS read אראלים; that is, lions of God, or strong lions: so they called valiant men, heroes; which appellation the Arabians and Persians still use. See Bochart. Hieroz. Part I. lib. iii. cap. 1. " Mahomet ayant reconnu Hamzeh son oncle pour homme de courage et de valeur, lui donne le titre ou surnom d'Assad Allah, qui signifie, le Lion de Dieu:" D'Herbelot, p. 427. And for חצה, Syr. and Chald. read קשה: whom I follow. Chald. Syr. Aquila, Sym. and Theod. read אראה להם, or יראה ; with what meaning, is not clear.

9. —*are stripped*—] LXX, φανερα εσαι· they read ונערה.

11. *And my spirit*—] "For רוחכם, read רוחי כמו:"

SECKER. Which reading is confirmed by Chald. where מימרי, *my word,* answers to רוחי, *my spirit.*

15. —*the proposal of bloodshed*] A MS reads בדמים.

18. *Where is he that numbered the towers?*] That is, the commander of the enemy's forces, who surveyed the fortifications of the city, and took an account of the height, strength, and situation of the walls and towers, that he might know where to make the assault with the greatest advantage; as Capaneus before Thebes is represented in a passage of the Phœnissæ of Euripides, which Grotius has applied as an illustration of this place:

Εκεινος επτα προσβασεις τεκμαιρεται
Πυργων, ανωτε και κατω τειχη μετρων.   ver. 187.

20. *Thou shalt see*—] For חזה, read תחזה with the Chaldee: Houbigant.

21. *But the glorious name of* JEHOVAH—] I take שם for a noun, with LXX and Syr.: see Psal. xx. 1. Prov. xviii. 10.

23. *Thy mast*—]. For חרנם, *their mast,* Syr. reads תרנך, LXX and Vul. תרנך, ὁ ἱστος σου εκλινεν, *thy mast is fallen aside:* LXX, they seem to have read נטה, or (פנה) תרנך; or rather לא כן, *is not firm,* the negative having been omitted in the present text by mistake. However, I have followed their sense, which seems very probable; as the present reading is to me extremely obscure.

24. *Neither shall the inhabitant say*—] This verse is somewhat obscure: the meaning of it seems to be, that the army of Senacherib shall by the stroke of God be reduced to so shattered and so weak a condition, that the Jews shall fall upon the remains of them, and plunder them without resistance: that the most infirm and disabled of the people of Jerusalem shall come in for their share of the spoil; the lame shall seize the prey; even the sick and the diseased shall throw aside their infirmities, and recover strength enough to hasten to the general plunder.

The last line of the verse is parallel to the first, and expresses the same sense in other words. Sickness being considered as a visitation from God, and a punishment of sin; the forgiveness of sin is equivalent to the removal of a disease. Thus the Psalmist;

"Who forgiveth all thy sin;
And healeth all thine infirmities."   Psal. ciii. 3.

Where the latter line only varies the expression of the former. And our blessed Saviour reasons with the Jews on the same principle: "Whether is it easier to say to the sick of the palsy, Thy sins are forgiven thee; or to say, Arise, and take up thy bed, and walk?" Mark ii. 9. See also Matt. viii. 17. Isa. liii. 4. "Qui locus Isaiæ, 1 Pet. ii. 24. refertur ad remissionem peccatorum: hic vero ad sanationem morborum, quia ejusdem potentiæ et bonitatis est utrumque præstare; et, quia peccatis remissis, et morbi, qui fructus sunt peccatorum, pelluntur:" Wetstein on Matt. viii. 17.

That this prophecy was exactly fulfilled, I think we may gather from the history of this great event given by the Prophet himself. It is plain, that Hezekiah, by his treaty with Senacherib, by which he agreed to pay him three hundred talents of silver and thirty talents of gold, had stripped himself of his whole treasure: he not only gave him all the silver and gold that was in his own treasury, and in that of the temple, but was even forced to cut off the gold from the doors of the temple and from the pillars, with which he had himself overlaid them, to satisfy the demands of the king of Assyria: but after the destruction of the Assyrian army we find, that he "had exceeding much riches, and that he made himself treasuries for silver, and for gold, and for precious stones," &c.; 2 Chron. xxxii. 27. He was so rich, that out of pride and vanity he displayed his wealth to the ambassadors from Babylon. This cannot be otherwise accounted for, than by the prodigious spoil that was taken on the destruction of the Assyrian army.

CHAPTERS XXXIV. & XXXV.

These two chapters make one distinct prophecy; an entire, regular, and beautiful poem, consisting of two parts: the first containing a denunciation of Divine vengeance against the enemies of the people or church of God; the second describing the flourishing state of the church of God, consequent upon the execution of those judgments. The event foretold is represented as of the highest importance, and of universal concern: all nations are called upon to attend to the declaration of it; and the wrath of God is denounced against all the nations; that is, all those that had provoked to anger the defender of the cause of Sion. Among those, Edom is particularly specified. The principal provocation of Edom was their insulting the Jews in their distress, and joining against them with their enemies the Chaldeans: see Amos i. 11. Ezek. xxv. 12. xxxv. 15. Psal. cxxxvii. 7. Accordingly the Edomites were, together with the rest of the neighbouring nations, ravaged and laid waste by Nebuchadnezzar: see Jer. xxv. 15.—26 Mal. i. 3, 4.; and see Marsham. Can. Chron. Sæc. xviii. who calls this the age of the destruction of cities. The general devastation spread through all these countries by Nebuchadnezzar, may be the event which the Prophet has primarily in view in the xxxivth chapter; but this event, as far as we have any account of it in history, seem by no means to come up to the terms of the prophecy, or to justify so highwrought and so terrible a description. And it is not easy to discover what connexion the extremely flourishing state of the church or people of God, described in the next chapter, could have with those events, and how the former could be the consequence of the latter, as it is there represented to be. By a figure very common in the prophetical writings, any city, or people, remarkably distinguished as enemies of the people and kingdom of God, is put for those enemies in general. This seems here to be the case with Edom and Botsra. It seems therefore reasonable to suppose, with many learned expositors, that this prophecy has a further view to events still future; to some great revolutions to be effected in later times, antecedent to that more perfect state of the kingdom of God upon earth, and serving to introduce it, which the Holy Scriptures warrant us to expect.

That the xxxvth chapter has a view beyond any thing that could be the immediate consequence of those events, is plain from every part, especially from the middle of it, ver. 5, 6.; where the miraculous works wrought by our blessed Saviour are so clearly specified, that we cannot avoid making the application. And our Saviour himself has moreover plainly referred to this very passage as speaking of him and his works: Matt. xi. 4, 5. He bids the disciples of John to go and report to their master the things which they heard and saw; that the blind received their sight, the lame walked, and the deaf heard; and leaves it to him to draw the conclusion in answer to his inquiry, whether he who performed the very works which the Prophets foretold should be performed by the Messiah, was not indeed the Messiah himself? And where are these works so distinctly marked by any of the Prophets as in this place; and how could they be marked more distinctly? To these the strictly literal interpretation of the Prophet's words directs us. According to the allegorical interpretation they may have a further view: This part of the prophecy may run parallel with the former, and relate to the future advent of Christ; to the conversion of the Jews, and their restitution to their land; to the extension and purification of the Christian faith;—events predicted in the Holy Scriptures, as preparatory to it.

1. *And attend unto me*—] A MS adds in this line the word אל, *unto me*, after לאמים; which seems to be genuine.

4. *And all the host of heaven*—] See note on chap. xxiv. 21. and De S. Poesi Hebræorum Præl. ix.

5. *For my sword is made bare in the heaven*] There seems to be some impropriety in this, according to the present reading, "my sword is made drunken, or is bathed, in the heavens;" which forestalls, and, expresses not in its proper place, what belongs to the next verse: for the sword of JEHOVAH was not to be bathed or glutted with blood in the heavens, but in Botsra and the land of Edom. In the heavens it was only prepared for slaughter. To remedy this, Archbishop Secker proposes to read, for ברמם, בשמים; referring to Jer. xlvi. 10. But even this is premature, and not in its proper place. The Chaldee, for רותה, has תתגלי, shall be revealed, or disclosed: perhaps he read תראה, or נראתה. Whatever reading, different I presume from the present, he might find in his copy, I follow the sense which he has given of it.

6. *For JEHOVAH celebrateth a sacrifice*] Ezekiel has manifestly imitated this place of Isaiah: he hath set forth the great leaders and princes of the adverse powers under the same emblems of goats, bulls, rams, fatlings, &c. and has added to the boldness of the imagery, by introducing God as summoning all the fowls of the air, and all the beasts of the field, and bidding them to the feast which he has prepared for them by the slaughter of the enemies of his people:—

" And thou, son of man,
Thus saith the Lord JEHOVAH:

Say to the bird of every wing,
And to every beast of the field,
Assemble yourselves, and come ;
Gather together from every side,
To the sacrifice which I make for you,
A great slaughter on the mountains of Israel.
And ye shall eat flesh and drink blood :
The flesh of the mighty shall ye eat,
And the blood of the lofty of the earth shall ye drink;
Of rams, of lambs, and of goats,
Of bullocks, all of them the fat ones of Basan.
And ye shall eat fat, till ye are cloyed,
And drink blood till ye are drunken;
Of my slaughter, which I have slain for you."
                                        Ezek. xxxix. 16. 17.

The sublime author of the Revelation (chap. xix. 17, 18.) has taken this image from Ezekiel, rather than from Isaiah.

7. —*with their blood*] מדמם: so an ancient MS, Syr. and Chald.

8. —*the defender of the cause of Sion*] As from דין, דון, a judge; so from רוב, ריב, an advocate, or defender: *Judici Sionis*, Syr.

11. —*over her scorched plains*] The word חריה, joined to the 12th verse, embarrasses it, and makes it inexplicable. At least I do not know that any one has yet made out the construction, or given any tolerable explication of it. I join it to the 11th verse, and supply a letter or two, which seem to have been lost. Fifteen MSS (five ancient), and two editions, read חוריה. The first printed edition of 1486, I think nearer to the truth, חור חריה. I read כהוריה, or הוריה על : see Jer. xvii. 6. A MS has חריה, and the Syriac reads חדות, *gaudium*, joining it to the two preceding words; which he likewise reads differently, but without improving the sense. However, his authority is clear for dividing the verses, as they are here divided. I read שׂם as a noun. They shall boast, יקראו; see Prov. xx. 6.

13. *And in her palaces shall spring up*—] ועלו בארמנותיה; so read all the ancient versions.

15. *Every one her mate*] A MS adds אל after אשה, which seems necessary to the construction ; and so Syr. and Vulg. Another MS adds in the same place את, which is equivalent.

16. *For the mouth of* JEHOVAH] For הוא, five MSS (three ancient) read יהוה, and another is so corrected: so

likewise LXX. Two editions have ציס, and so LXX and Vulg.; and a MS has קבצם, with the masculine pronoun instead of the feminine: and so in the next verses it is להם, instead of לחן, in fourteen MSS, six of them ancient.

CHAPTER XXXV.

1. —*shall be glad,*] ישׁשׂום: In a MS the ם seems to have been added; and שׁם is upon a rasure in another. None of the ancient versions acknowledge it: it seems to have been a mistake arising from the next word's beginning with the same letter. Sixteen MSS have ישׁושׂום, and five MSS ישׁשׂם.

2. *The well-watered plain of Jordan.*] For ורן, the LXX read ירדן; τα ερημα του Ιορδανου. Four MSS read גלת; see Joshua xv. 19. irrigua Jordani; Houbigant: גידת, ripa Jordani; Kennicott. See De S. Poesi Hebr. Prælect. xx. note,

Ibid. For לה, *to it*, nine MSS read לך, *to thee*. See ibid.

7. —*the glowing sand*] שׁרב: This word is Arabic as well as Hebrew, expressing in both languages the same thing; the glowing sandy plain, which in the hot countries at a distance has the appearance of water. It occurs in the Koran, chap. xxiv. "But as to the unbelievers, their works are like a vapour in a plain; which the thirsty traveller thinketh to be water, until, when he cometh thereto, he findeth it to be nothing." Mr. Sale's note on this place is: —"The Arabic word *serab* signifies that false appearance which in the eastern countries is often seen in sandy plains about noon, resembling a large lake of water in motion, and is occasioned by the reverberation of the sunbeams: ['by the quivering undulating motion of that quick succession of vapours and exhalations, which are extracted by the powerful influence of the sun;' Shaw, Trav. p. 378.] It sometimes tempts thirsty travellers out of their way, but deceives them, when they come near, either going forward, (for it always appears at the same distance), or quite vanishes." Q. Curtius has mentioned it:—"Arenas vapor æstivi solis accendit;—camporumque non alia, quam vasti et profundi æquoris species est;" lib. vii. cap. 5. Dr. Hyde gives us the precise meaning and derivation of the word:—" Dictum nomen [Barca] הברקה, *splendorem* seu *splendentem regio-*

nem notat; cum ea regio radiis solaribus tam copiose collustretur, ut reflexum ab arenis lumen adeo intense fulgens, a longinquo spectantibus, ad instar corporis solaris, aquarum speciem referat; et hinc arenarum splendor et radiatio (ex lingua Persica petito nomine) dicitur *serab*, i. e. aquæ superficies, seu superficialis aquarum species:" Annot, in Peritsol. cap. 2.

Ibid. —*shall spring forth*—] The ה, in רבצה, seems to have been at first ם in MS Bodl.; whence Dr. Kennicott concludes it should be רבצים. But instead of this word, Syr. Vulg. and Chald. read some word signifying to *grow*, *spring up*, or *abound*; perhaps פרצה, or פרצו; or פרץ החציר, as Houbigant reads.

8. *And a highway*] The word ודרך is by mistake added to the first member of the sentence from the beginning of the following member: sixteen MSS (seven ancient) have it but once; so likewise Syr.

Ibid. —*err therein*] A MS adds בו, which seems necessary to the sense: and so Vulg. *per eam*.

Ibid. *But He shall be with them walking*—] That is, God; see ver. 4. "Who shall dwell among them, and set them an example, that they should follow his steps." Our old English versions translated the place to this purpose: our last translators were misled by the authority of the Jews, who have absurdly made a division of the verses in the midst of the sentence, thereby destroying the construction and the sense.

9. *Neither shall he be found there*] Three MSS read ולא, adding the conjunction; and so likewise LXX and Vulg. And four MSS (one ancient) read ימצא, the verb, as it certainly ought to be, in the masculine form.

For further remarks on the two foregoing chapters, see De S. Poesi Hebr. Prælect. xx.

CHAPTER XXXVI.

THE history of the invasion of Senacherib, and of the miraculous destruction of his army, which makes the subject of so many of Isaiah's prophecies, is very properly inserted here, as affording the best light to many parts of those prophecies; and as almost necessary to introduce the prophecy in the xxxviith chapter, being the answer of God to Hezekiah's prayer, which could not be properly understood without it. We find the same narrative in the second book of Kings, chapters xviii. xix. xx.; and these chapters of Isaiah, xxxvi. xxxvii. xxxviii. xxxix. for much the most part, (the account of the sickness of Hezekiah only excepted), are but a different copy of that narration. The difference of the two copies is little more than what has manifestly arisen from the mistakes of transcribers: they mutually correct each other, and most of the mistakes may be perfectly rectified by a collation of the two copies, with the assistance of the ancient versions. Some few sentences, or members of sentences, are omitted in this copy of Isaiah, which are found in the other copy in the book of Kings. Whether these omissions were made by design or by mistake, may be doubted: these therefore I have not inserted in 'the translation; I shall only report them in the notes.

3. *Then came out unto him*] Before these words, the other copy, 2 Kings xviii. 18. adds ויקראו אל המלך, "and they demanded audience of the king."

5. *Thou hast said*] Fourteen MSS (three ancient) have it in the second person, אמרת; and so the other copy, 2 Kings xviii. 20.

6. —*in Egypt*] MS Bodl. adds מלך, *the king* of Egypt: and so perhaps Chald. might read.

7. *But if ye say*] Two ancient MSS have תאמרו in the plural number: so likewise LXX, Chald. and the other copy, 2 Kings xviii. 22.

Ibid. *only before this altar*—] See 2 Chron. xxxii. 12.

12. *destined to eat their own dung*]. לאכל, "that they may eat," as our translation literally renders it. But Syr. reads מאכל, "that they may not eat," perhaps rightly; and afterwards ומשתות, or ושתות, to the same purpose.

17. *and of vineyards*] The other copy, 2 Kings xviii. 32. adds here, "a land of oil-olive, and of honey; that ye may live, and not die; and hearken not unto Hezekiah, when he seduceth you."

19. —*of Sepharvaim*—] The other copy, 2 Kings xviii. 34. adds of "Henah and Ivah."

Ibid. *have they delivered*] וכי, the copulative is not expressed here by LXX, Syr. Vulg. and three MSS; nor is it in the other copy: Ibid. Houbigant reads הכי, with the interrogative particle: a probable conjecture, which the ancient versions, above quoted, seem to favour.

21. *But the people held their peace*] The word הָעָם, *the people*, is supplied from the other copy; and is authorized by a MS, which inserts it after אתו.

CHAPTER XXXVII.

7. *I will infuse a spirit into him*] "נתון בו רוח never signifies any thing but putting a spirit into a person; this was πνευμα δειλιας:" SECKER.

9. *he sent messengers again*] The word וישמע, (*and he heard*), which occurs the second time in this verse, is repeated by mistake from the beginning of the verse. It is omitted in an ancient MS. It is a mere tautology, and embarrasses the sense. The true reading, instead of it, is וישב, which the LXX read in this place απεϛρεψε, and which is preserved in the other copy, 2 Kings xix. 9. "He returned and sent"—that is, according to the Hebrew idiom, "he sent again."

14. *and read them*] ויקראם, so MS Bodl. in this place; and so the other copy; instead of ויקראהו, and read *it*.

Ibid. —*and spread* them] ויפרשהו; הו is upon a rasure in a MS; which probably was at first ם. The same mistake as in the foregoing note.

15. —*before JEHOVAH*] That is, in the sanctuary. For אל, Syr. Chald. and the other copy, 2 Kings xix. 15. read לפני.

18. —*the nations*—] הארצות, *the lands:* instead of this word, which destroys the sense, ten MSS (one ancient) have here גוים, *nations;* which is undoubtedly the true reading, being preserved also in the other copy, 2 Kings xix. 17. Another MS suggests another method of rectifying the sense in this place, by reading מלכם, *their king*, instead of ארצם, *their land;* but it ought to be מלכיהם, "all the countries and their kings."

20. *Save us, we beseech thee*—] The supplicating particle נא is supplied here from eighteen MSS (three ancient), and from the other copy.

Ibid. —*that thou JEHOVAH art the only God*] The word אלהים, *God*, is lost here in the Hebrew text, but preserved in the other copy, 2 Kings xix. 19. Syr. and LXX seem here to have had in their copies אלהים, instead of יהוה.

21. *Then Isaiah sent unto Hezekiah*] Syr. and LXX understand and render the verb passively, *was sent*.

Ibid. —*I have heard*] שמעתי: this word, necessary to the sense, is lost in this place out of the Hebrew text. A MS has it written above the line in a later hand. LXX and Syr. found it in their copies; and it is preserved in the other copy, 2 Kings xix. 20.

23. —*against the Holy One of Israel*] For אל, the other copy has על, rather more properly.

24. —*By thy messengers*—] The text has עבדיך; *thy servants:* but the true reading seems to be מלאכיך, *thy messengers,* as in the other copy, 2 Kings xix. 23.; and as LXX and Syr. found it in their copies in this place.

Ibid. —*his extreme retreats*] The text has מרום, *the highth;* which seems to have been taken by mistake from the line but one above. A MS has here מלון, the *lodge,* or *retreat;* which is the word in the other copy, 2 Kings xix. 23.; and I think is the true reading.

25. —*strange waters*] The word זרים, *strange,* lost out of the Hebrew text in this place, is supplied from the other copy. A MS supplies the word רבים, *many,* instead of it.

Ibid. *all the canals of fenced places*] The principal cities of Egypt, the scene of his late exploits, were chiefly defended by deep moats, canals, or large lakes, made by labour and art, with which they were surrounded. See Harmer's Observ. ii. p. 304. Claudian introduces Alaric boasting of his conquests in the same extravagant manner:

" Subsidere nostris
Sub pedibus montes; arescere vidimus amnes.—
Fregi Alpes, galeisque Padum victricibus hausi."
De Bello Getic. 526.

26. *warlike nations*] גלים נצים. It is not easy to give a satisfactory account of these two words; which have greatly embarrassed all the interpreters, ancient and modern. For גלים, I read גוים, as the LXX do in this place, εθνη. The word נצים, Vulg. renders in this place *compugnantium;* in the parallel place, 2 Kings xix. 25. *pugnantium,* and LXX, μαχιμων, *fighting, warlike.* This rendering is as well authorized as any other that I know of, and, with the reading of LXX, perfectly clears up the construction.

27. *corn blasted*] שרמה. It does not appear that there is any good authority for this word. The true reading seems to be שדפה, as it is in four MSS (two ancient), here, and in the other copy.

29. *I will put my hook in thy nose*] " *Et frænum meum:*

Jonathan vocom מֶתֶג interpretatus est זָמָם, *i. e.* annulum, sive uncum, eumque ferreum, quem infigunt naribus camelæ: coque trahitur, quoniam illa feris motibus agitur: et hoc est, quod discimus in Talmude; et camela cum annulo narium: scilicet, egreditur die Sabbathi:" Jarchi in 2 Reg. xix. 28. " Ponam circulum in naribus tuis:" Hieron. Just as at this day they put a ring into the nose of the bear, the buffalo, and other wild beasts, to lead them, and to govern them when they are unruly.

35. *And the angel*—] Before "the angel," the other copy, 2 Kings xix. 35. adds, " it came to pass the same night, that"——

The Prophet Hosea has given a plain prediction of this miraculous deliverance of the kingdom of Judah:

" And to the house of Judah I will be tenderly merciful:
And I will save them by JEHOVAH their God.
And I will not save them by the bow;
Nor by sword, nor by battle;
By horses, nor by horsemen.   Hosea i. 7.

CHAPTER XXXVIII.

2. *Then Hezekiah turned his face to the wall*] The furniture of an eastern divan, or chamber either for the reception of company or for private use, consists chiefly of carpets spread on the floor in the middle, and of sophas or couches ranged on one or more sides of the room, on a part raised somewhat above the floor. On these they repose themselves in the day, and sleep at night. It is to be observed, that the corner of the room is the place of honour. Dr Pococke, when he was introduced to the Sheik of Furshout, found him sitting in the corner of his room. He describes another Arab Sheik, " as sitting in a corner of a large green tent, pitched in the middle of an encampment of Arabs; and the Bey of Girge as placed on a sopha in a corner to the right as one entered the room:" Harmer's Obs. ii. p. 60. Lady Mary W. Montague, giving an account of a visit which she made to the Kahya's lady at Adrianople, says, " She ordered cushions to be given me, and took care to place me in the corner, which is the place of honour:" Letter xxxiii. The reason of this seems to be, that the person, so placed, is distinguished, and in a manner separated from the

rest of the company, and as it were guarded by the wall on each side. We are to suppose Hezekiah's couch placed in the same situation: in which, turning on either side, he must turn his face to the wall; by which he would withdraw himself from those who were attending upon him in his apartment, in order to address his private prayer to God.

4, 5. The words in the translation included within crotchets are supplied from the parallel place, 2 Kings xx. 4, 5. to make the narration more perfect. I have also taken the liberty, with Houbigant, of bringing forward the two last verses of this chapter, and inserting them in their proper places of the narration with the same mark. Kimchi's note on these two verses is as follows: "This and the following verse belong not to the writing of Hezekiah: and I see no reason why they are written here after the writing; for their right place is above, after *And I will protect this city*, ver. 6. And so they stand in the book of Kings;" 2 Kings xx. 7, 8. The narration of this chapter seems to be in some parts an abridgment of that of 2 Kings xx. The abridger, having finished his extract here with the 11th verse, seems to have observed, that the 7th and 8th verses of 2 Kings xx. were wanted to complete the narration: he therefore added them at the end of the chapter, after he had inserted the song of Hezekiah, probably with marks for their insertion in their proper places; which marks were afterwards neglected by transcribers: or a transcriber might omit them by mistake, and add them at the end of the chapter with such marks. Many transpositions are, with great probability, to be accounted for in the same way.

6. *I will protect this city—*] The other copy, 2 Kings xx. 6. adds, " for mine own sake, and for the sake of David my servant;" and the sentence seems somewhat abrupt without it.

8. *by which the sun is gone down—*] For במעלו, LXX, Syr. Chald. read השמש: Houbigant. In the history of this miracle in the book of Kings, 2 Kings xx. 9—11. there is no mention at all made of the sun, but only of the going backward of the shadow; which might be effected by a supernatural refraction. The first ὁ ἥλιος in this verse is omitted in LXX, MS Pachom.

9. *The writing of Hezekiah.*] Here the book of Kings deserts us, the song of Hezekiah not being inserted in it. Another copy of this very obscure passage (obscure not only

from the concise poetical style, but because it is probably very incorrect) would have been of great service. The MSS and ancient versions, especially the latter, will help us to get through some of the many difficulties which we meet with in it.

11. *JEHOVAH*] יה יה seems to be יהוה in MSS Bodl. and it was so at first written in another; so Syr. See Houbigant.

12. —*a shepherd's tent*—] רעי is put for רעה, say the Rabbins; Sal. b. Melec on the place: but much more probably is written imperfectly for רעים. See note on chap. v. 1.

Ibid. *My life is cut off*—] קפדתי: this verb is rendered passively, and in the third person, by Syr. Chald. Vulg.

13. The last line of the foregoing verse, מיום עד לילה תשלימני, "In the course of the day thou wilt finish my web," is not repeated at the end of this verse in the Syriac version; and a MS omits it. It seems to have been inserted a second time in the Hebrew text by mistake.

Ibid. *I roared*—] For שויתי, the Chaldee has נהמית: he read שאגתי, the proper term for the roaring of a lion; often applied to the deep groaning of men in sickness: see Psal. xxii. 2. xxxii. 4. xxxviii. 9. Job. iii. 24. The Masoretes divide the sentence, as I have done, taking כארי, *like a lion*, into the first member; and so likewise LXX.

14. *Like the swallow*—] כסיס; so read two MSS, Theod. and Hieron.

Ibid. —*mine eyes fail*] For דלו, the LXX read כלו, εξελιπον. Compare Psal. lxix. 4. cxix. 82. 123. Lam. ii. 11. iv. 17. in the Hebrew and in LXX.

Ibid. —*O Lord*—] For יהוה, thirty MSS and eight editions read אדני.

Ibid. —*contend thou*—] עשקה, with שׁ, Jarchi. This sense of the word is established by Gen. xxvi. 20. "he called the name of the well עשק, Esek, because they *strove* with him:" התעשקו, equivalent to יריבו at the beginning of the verse.

15. —*will I reflect*—] אדדה, *recogitabo*, Vulg. *reputabo*, Hieron. in loc.

16. *For this cause shall it be declared*—] Περι αυτης γαρ ανηγγελη σοι, και εξηγειρας μου την πνοην, LXX. They read in their copies, עליה יחוו לך ותחי רוחי; not very different from the present text, from which all the ancient versions vary. They entirely omit two words, ולכל בהן; as to which there is

some variation in the MSS. A MS has ובכל, two others וכל, and ten MSS have כהם.

Ibid. —*hast prolonged my life.*] A MS and the Babylonish Talmud read ותחיני; and so the ancient versions. It must necessarily be in the second person.

17. *My anguish is changed into ease*—] מר לי מר, "mutata mihi est amaritudo." Paronomasia; a figure, which the Prophet frequently admits: I do not always note it, because it cannot ever be preserved in the translation, and the sense seldom depends upon it. But here it perfectly clears up the great obscurity of the passage. See Lowth on the place.

Ibid. *Thou hast rescued*—] חשכת, with כ instead of ק; so LXX and Vulg.: Houbigant. See Chappelow on Job xxxiii. 18.

Ibid. —*from perdition*—] משחת בלי, ἱνα μη απολητάι, LXX; ut non periret, Vulg.; perhaps inverting the order of the words. See Houbigant.

19. —*thy truth*] אל אמתך. A MS omits אל; and instead of אל, an ancient MS and one edition read את. The same mistake as in Psal. ii. 7.

21. *Let them take a lump of figs: and they bruised them*---] God, in effecting this miraculous cure, was pleased to order the use of means not improper for that end. "Folia, et, quæ non maturuere, fici, strumis illinuntur, omnibusque quæ emollienda sunt discutiendave:" Plin. Nat. Hist. xxiii. 7. "Ad discutienda ea, quæ in corporis parte aliqua coierunt, maxime possunt—ficus arida," &c.: Celsus, v. 11.

CHAPTER XXXIX.

Hitherto the copy of this history in the second book of Kings has been much the most correct: in this chapter, that in Isaiah has the advantage. In the two first verses two mistakes in the other copy are to be corrected from this: for חוקיהו, *Hezekiah*, read ויחזק, *and was recovered;* and for ישמע, *he heard,* read וישמח, *he rejoiced.*

1. —*and ambassadors.*] The LXX add here και πρεσβεις; that is, ומלאכים, *and ambassadors;* which word seems necessary to the sense, though omitted in the Hebrew text both here and in the other copy, 2 Kings xx. 12. For the subsequent narration refers to them all along; "these men,

whence came they?" &c. plainly supposing them to have been personally mentioned before. See Houbigant.

6. —*to Babylon*—] בבלה; so two MSS (one ancient); rightly without doubt, as the other copy, 2 Kings xx. 17. has it.

8. *And Hezekiah said*—] The nature of Hezekiah's crime, and his humiliation on the message of God to him by the Prophet, is more expressly declared by the author of the book of Chronicles: "But Hezekiah rendered not again, according to the benefit done unto him; for his heart was lifted up: therefore there was wrath upon him, and upon Judah and Jerusalem. Notwithstanding, Hezekiah humbled himself for the pride of his heart, (both he and the inhabitants of Jerusalem), so that the wrath of the LORD came not upon them in the days of Hezekiah. And Hezekiah prospered in all his works. Howbeit, in the business of the ambassadors of the princes of Babylon, who sent unto him to inquire of the wonder that was done in the land, God left him, to try him, that he might know all that was in his heart;" 2 Chron. 25, 26. 30, 31.

CHAPTER XL.

THE course of prophecies, which follow from hence to the end of the book, and which taken together constitute the most elegant part of the sacred writings of the Old Testament; interspersed also with many passages of the highest sublimity; was probably delivered in the latter part of the reign of Hezekiah. The Prophet in the foregoing chapter had delivered a very explicit declaration of the impending dissolution of the kingdom, and of the captivity of the royal house of David, and of the people, under the kings of Babylon. As the subject of his subsequent prophecies was to be chiefly of the consolatory kind, he opens them with giving a promise of the restoration of the kingdom, and the return of the people from that captivity, by the merciful interposition of God in their favour. But the views of the Prophet are not confined to this event. As the restoration of the royal family, and of the tribe of Judah, which would otherwise have soon become undistinguished, and have been irrecoverably lost, was necessary, in the design and order of Providence, for the fulfilling of God's promises of establishing a more glorious and an everlasting kingdom, under the Messiah to be born of the tribe of Judah, and of the family of David; the Prophet connects these two events together, and hardly ever treats of the former without throwing in some intimations of the latter; and sometimes is so fully possessed with the glories of the future more remote kingdom, that he seems to leave the more immediate subject of his commission almost out of the question.

Indeed this evangelical sense of the prophecy is so apparent, and stands forth in so strong a light, that some interpreters cannot see that it has any other; and will not allow the prophecy to have any relation at all to the return from the captivity of Babylon. It may be useful, therefore, to examine more attentively the train of the Prophet's ideas, and to consider carefully the images under which he displays his subject. He hears a crier giving orders by solemn proclamation to prepare the way of the Lord in the wilderness; to remove all obstructions before JEHOVAH marching through the desert; through the wild, uninhabited, unpassable country. The deliverance of God's people from the Babylonish captivity is considered by him as parallel to the former deliverance of them from the Egyptian bondage. God was then represented as their king, leading them in person through the vast deserts, which lay in their way to the promised land of Canaan. It is not merely for JEHOVAH himself, that in both cases the way was to be prepared, and all obstructions to be removed; but for JEHOVAH marching in person at the head of his people. Let us first see, how this idea is pursued by the sacred poets who treat of the Exodus, which is a favourite subject with them, and affords great choice of examples :—

"When Israel came out of Egypt;
The house of Jacob, from the barbarous people;
Judah was his sanctuary,
Israel his dominion."   Psal. cxiv. 1, 2.

"JEHOVAH his God is with him;
And the shout of a king is among them:
God brought them out of Egypt."   Numb. xxiii. 21, 22.

"Make a highway for him that rideth through the deserts:
O God, when thou wentest forth before thy people;
When thou marchedst through the wilderness,
The heavens dropped."   . Psal. lxviii. 4. 7.

Let us now see how Isaiah treats the subject of the return

of the people from Babylon: they were to march through the wilderness with JEHOVAH at their head, who was to lead them, to smooth the way before them, and to supply them with water in the thirsty desert; with perpetual allusion to the Exodus:

> "Come ye forth from Babylon, flee ye from the land of the Chaldeans with the voice of joy:
> Publish ye this, and make it heard; utter it forth even to the end of the earth:
> Say ye, JEHOVAH hath redeemed his servant Jacob:
> They thirsted not in the deserts, through which he made them go;
> Waters from the rock he caused to flow for them;
> Yea he clave the rock, and forth gushed the waters."
> Chap. xlviii. 20, 21.

> "Remember not the former things;
> And the things of ancient times regard not:"

(That is, the deliverance from Egypt):

> "Behold, I make a new thing;
> Even now shall it spring forth: will ye not regard it?
> Yea I will make in the wilderness a way;
> In the desert, streams of water." Chap. xliii. 18, 19.

> "But he that trusteth in me shall inherit the land,
> And shall possess my holy mountain.
> Then will I say, Cast up, cast up the causeway; make clear the way;
> Remove every obstruction from the road of my people."
> Chap. lvii. 13, 14.

> "How beautiful appear on the mountains
> The feet of the joyful messenger, of him that announceth peace;
> Of the joyful messenger of good tidings, of him that announceth salvation;
> Of him that sayeth to Sion, Thy God reigneth!
> All thy watchmen lift up their voice, they shout together;
> For face to face shall they see, when JEHOVAH returneth to Sion.
> Verily not in haste shall ye go forth;
> And not by flight shall ye march along:
> For JEHOVAH shall march in your front;
> And the God of Israel shall bring up your rear."
> Chap. lii. 7, 8. 12.

Babylon was separated from Judea by an immense tract of country, which was one continued desert; that large part of Arabia called very properly Deserta. It is mentioned in history as a remarkable occurrence, that Nebuchadnezzar, having received the news of the death of his father, in order to make the utmost expedition in his journey to Babylon from Egypt and Phœnicia, set out with a few attendants, and passed through this desert. Berosus, apud Joseph. Antiq. x. 11. This was the nearest way homewards for the Jews; and whether they actually returned by this way or not, the first thing that would occur on the proposal or thought of their return, would be the difficulty of this almost impracticable passage. Accordingly the proclamation for the preparation of the way is the most natural idea, and the most obvious circumstance, by which the Prophet could have opened his subject.

These things considered, I have not the least doubt, that the return of the Jews from the captivity of Babylon is the first, though not the principal, thing in the Prophet's view. The redemption from Babylon is clearly foretold; and at the same time is employed as an image to shadow out a redemption of an infinitely higher and more important nature. I should not have thought it necessary to employ so many words in endeavouring to establish what is called the literal sense of this prophecy, which I think cannot be rightly understood without it, had I not observed, that many interpreters of the first authority, in particular the very learned Vitringa, have excluded it entirely.

Yet obvious and plain as I think this literal sense is, we have nevertheless the irrefragable authority of John the Baptist, and of our blessed Saviour himself, as recorded by all the Evangelists, for explaining this exordium of the prophecy of the opening of the gospel by the preaching of John, and of the introducing of the kingdom of Messiah; who was to effect a much greater deliverance of the people of God, Gentiles as well as Jews, from the captivity of sin and the dominion of death. And this we shall find to be the case in many subsequent parts also of this prophecy, where passages manifestly relating to the deliverance of the Jewish nation, effected by Cyrus, are with good reason, and upon undoubted authority, to be understood of the redemption wrought for mankind by Christ.

If the literal sense of this prophecy, as above explained, cannot be questioned, much less surely can the spiritual; which, I think, is allowed on all hands even by Grotius himself. If both are to be admitted, here is a plain example of the mystical allegory, or double sense, as it is commonly called, of prophecy; which the sacred writers of the New Testament clearly suppose, and according to which they frequently frame their interpretation of passages of the Old Testament. Of the foundation and properties of this sort of allegory, see De S. Poes. Hebr. Prælect. xi.

2. *Blessings double to the punishment*] It does not seem reconcileable to our notions of the divine justice, which always punishes less than our iniquities deserve, to suppose, that God had punished the sins of the Jews in double proportion: and it is more agreeable to the tenor of this consolatory message, to understand it as a promise of ample recompense for the effects of past displeasure, on the reconciliation of God to his returning people. To express this sense of the passage, which the words of the original will very well bear, it was necessary to add a word or two in the version to supply the elliptical expression of the Hebrew. Compare chap. lxi. 7. Job. xlii. 10. Zech. ix. 12. חטאה signifies punishment for sin, Lam. iii. 39. Zech. xiv. 19.

3. *A voice crieth: In the wilderness*—] The idea is taken from the practice of eastern monarchs, who, whenever they entered upon an expedition, or took a journey, especially through desert and unpractised countries, sent harbingers before them to prepare all things for their passage, and pioneers to open the passes, to level the ways, and to remove all impediments. The officers appointed to superintend such preparations the Latins call *Stratores*. "Ipse (Johannes Baptista) se *stratorem* vocat Messiæ, cujus esset alta et elata voce homines in desertis locis habitantes ad itinera et vias Regi mox venturo sternendas et reficiendas hortari:" Mosheim, Instituta Majora, p. 96.

Diodorus's account of Semiramis's marches into Media and Persia, will give us a clear notion of the preparation of the way for a royal expedition: "In her march to Ecbatane she came to the Zarcean mountain; which extending many furlongs, and being full of craggy precipices and deep hollows, could not be passed without taking a great compass about. Being therefore desirous of leaving an everlasting memorial of herself, as well as of shortening the way, she ordered the precipices to be digged down, and the hollows to be filled up; and at a great expense she made a shorter and more expeditious road, which to this day is called from her the Road of Semiramis. Afterward she went into Persia, and all the other countries of Asia subject to her dominion; and wherever she went, she ordered the mountains and precipices to be levelled, raised causeways in the plain country, and at a great expense made the ways passable:" Diod. Sic. lib. ii.

The writer of the apocryphal book called Baruch, expresses the same subject by the same images; either taking them from this place of Isaiah, or from the common notions of his countrymen: " For God hath appointed, that every high hill, and banks of long continuance, should be cast down, and vallies filled up, to make even the ground, that Israel may go safely in the glory of God;" chap. v. 7.

The Jewish church, to which John was sent to announce the coming of Messiah, was at that time in a barren and desert condition, unfit without reformation for the reception of her king. It was in this desert country, destitute at that time of all religious cultivation, in true piety and good works unfruitful, that John was sent to prepare the way of the Lord by preaching repentance. I have distinguished the parts of the sentence according to the punctuation of the Masoretes, which agrees best both with the literal and the spiritual sense; which the construction and parallelism of the distich in the Hebrew plainly favours; and of which the Greek of the LXX and of the Evangelists is equally susceptible.

John was born in the desert of Judea, and passed his whole life in it, till the time of his being manifested to Israel. He preached in the same desert: it was a mountainous country; however, not entirely and properly a desert, for, though less cultivated than other parts of Judea, yet it was not uninhabited: Joshua (chap. xv. 61, 62.) reckons six cities in it. We are so prepossessed with the idea of John's living and preaching in the desert, that we are apt to consider this particular scene of his preaching as a very important and essential part of his history: whereas I apprehend this circumstance to be no otherwise important, than as giving us a strong idea of the rough character of the man, which was answerable to the place of his education; and as affording a proper emblem of the rude state of the Jewish church at that time; which was the true wilderness meant by the Prophet, in which John was to prepare the way for the coming of the Messiah.

4. *The word* עקב *is very generally rendered* crooked *;* but this sense of the word seems not to be supported by any good authority. Ludolphus, Comment. ad Hist. Æthiop. p. 206. says, that in the Æthiopic language it signifies clivus, locus editus *;* and so the Syriac version renders it in this place ערמא, Heb. ערמה, tumulus, acervus. Thus the parallelism would be more perfect: "the hilly country shall be made level, and the precipices a smooth plain."

5. —*the salvation of our God*] These words are added here by LXX: το σωτηριον του Θεου, ישועת אלהינו את, as it is in the parallel place, chap. lii. 10. The sentence is abrupt without it, the verb wanting its object; and I think it is genuine. Our English translation has supplied the word *it*, which is equivalent to this addition from LXX.

This omission in the Hebrew text is ancient, being prior to the Chaldee, Syriac, and Vulgate versions: but the words stand in all the copies of the LXX; and they are acknowledged by Luke, iii. 6.

6. *its glory*—] For חסרו read הדרו; LXX, and Vulg. and 1 Pet. i. 24.

7. *this people*—] So Syr. who perhaps read העם הזה.

6—8. *A voice sayeth, Proclaim*—] To understand rightly this passage is a matter of importance; for it seems designed to give us the true key to the remaining part of Isaiah's prophecies; the general subject of which is the restoration of the people and church of God. The Prophet opens the subject with great clearness and elegance: he declares at once God's command to his messengers, (his Prophets, as the Chaldee rightly explains it,) to comfort his people in captivity, to impart to them the joyful tidings, that their punishment has now satisfied the divine justice, and the time of reconciliation and favour is at hand. He then introduces a harbinger giving orders to prepare the way for God leading his people from Babylon, as he did formerly from Egypt, through the wilderness; to remove all obstacles, and to clear the way for their passage. Thus far nothing more appears to be intended than a return from the Babylonish captivity: but the next words seem to intimate something much greater:

"And the glory of JEHOVAH shall be revealed;
And all flesh shall see together the salvation of our God."

He then introduces a voice commanding him to make a solemn proclamation. And what is the import of it? That the people, the flesh, is of a vain temporary nature; that all its glory fadeth, and is soon gone; but that the word of God endureth for ever. What is this, but a plain opposition of the flesh to the spirit; of the carnal Israel to the spiritual; of the temporary Mosaic economy to the eternal Christian dispensation? You may be ready to conclude, (the Prophet may be supposed to say), by this introduction to my discourse, that my commission is only to comfort you with a promise of the restoration of your religion and polity, of Jerusalem, of the temple, and its services and worship in all its ancient splendour: These are earthly, temporary, shadowy, fading things, which shall soon pass away, and be destroyed for ever; these are not worthy to engage your attention, in comparison of the greater blessings, the spiritual redemption, the eternal inheritance, covered under the veil of the former, which I have it in charge to unfold unto you. The law has only a shadow of good things; the substance is the gospel. I promise you a restoration of the former; which, however, is only for a time, and shall be done away, according to God's original appointment: but under that image I give you a view of the latter; which shall never be done away, but shall endure for ever. This I take to be agreeable to St. Peter's interpretation of this passage of the Prophet, quoted by him 1 Pet. i. 24, 25. "All flesh is as grass, and all the glory of man as the flower of grass. The grass withereth, and the flower thereof falleth away; but the word of the Lord endureth for ever. And this is the word which by the gospel is preached unto you." This is the same word of the Lord of which Isaiah speaks, which hath now been preached unto you by the gospel. The law and the gospel are frequently opposed to one another by St Paul under the images of flesh and spirit: "Having begun in the spirit, are ye now made perfect by the flesh?" Gal. iii. 3.

7. *When the wind of* JEHOVAH—] רוח יהוה, a wind of JEHOVAH, is a Hebraism, meaning no more than a strong wind. It is well known, that a hot wind in the East destroys at once every green thing. Compare Psal. ciii. 16. Two MSS omit the word יהוה, JEHOVAH.

9. *O daughter that bringest glad tidings*] That the true construction of the sentence is this, which makes Sion the receiver, not the publisher, of the glad tidings, (which latter has been the most prevailing interpretation), will, I think,

very clearly appear, if we rightly consider the image itself, and the custom and common practice from which it is taken. I have added the word *daughter*, to express the feminine gender of the Hebrew participle, which I know not how to do otherwise in our language. And this is absolutely necessary in order to ascertain the image; for the office of announcing and celebrating such glad tidings as are here spoken of, belonged peculiarly to the women. On occasion of any great public success, a signal victory, or any other joyful event, it was usual for the women to gather together, and with music, dances, and songs, to [publish and celebrate the happy news. Thus, after the passage of the Red Sea, Miriam, and all the women, with trimbrels in their hands, formed a chorus, and joined the men in their triumphant song, dancing, and throwing in alternately the refrain or burthen of the song:—

Sing ye to JEHOVAH, for he is greatly exalted;
The horse and his rider hath he cast into the sea."
Exod. xv. 20, 21.

So Jephthah's daughter collected a chorus of virgins, and with dances and songs came out to meet her father, and to celebrate his victory; Judg. xi. 34. After David's conquest of Goliah, " all the women came out of the cities of Israel, singing and dancing, to meet Saul, with tabrets, with joy, and with instruments of music:" and forming themselves into two chorusses, they sung alternately,—

" Saul has slain his thousands;
And David his ten thousands."   1 Sam. xviii. 6, 7.

And this gives us the true sense of a passage in the lxviiith Psalm, which has frequently been misunderstood:—

" JEHOVAH gave the word; (that is, the joyful news);
The women, who published the glad tidings, were a great company:
The kings of mighty armies did flee, did flee;
And even the matron, who staid at home, shared the spoil."

The word signifying *the publishers of glad tidings* is the same, and expressed in the same form by the feminine participle, as in this place; and the last distich is the song which they sung. So in this place, JEHOVAH having given the word by his Prophet, the joyful tidings of the restoration of Sion, and of God's returning to Jerusalem, (see chap. lii. 8.), the women are exhorted by the Prophet to publish the joyful news with a loud voice from eminences, whence they might best be heard all over the country; and the matter and burthen of their song was to be, " Behold your God !"

10. —*his reward, and the recompense of his work*] That is, the reward and recompense, which he bestows and which he will pay to his faithful servants : this he has ready at hand with him, and holds it out before him, to encourage those who trust in him, and wait for him.

11. *The nursing ewes shall he gently lead*] A beautiful image, expressing, with the utmost propriety as well as elegance, the tender attention of the shepherd to his flock. That the greatest care in driving the cattle in regard to the dams and their young was necessary, appears clearly from Jacob's apology to his brother Esau, Gen. xxxiii. 13. " The flocks and the herds giving suck to their young are with me ; and if they should be over-driven, all the flock will die." Which is set in a still stronger light by the following remark of Sir John Chardin : " Their flocks, (says he, speaking of those who now live in the East after the patriarchal manner), feed down the places of their encampments so quick, by the great numbers that they have, that they are obliged to remove them too often ; which is very destructive to their flocks on account of the young ones, who have not strength enough to follow:" Harmer's Observ. i. p. 126.

16. *And Lebanon is not sufficient*—] The image is beautiful and uncommon; it has been imitated by an apocryphal writer, who however comes far short of the original :—

" For all sacrifice is too little for a sweet savour unto thee;
And all the fat is not sufficient for thy burnt offering."
Judith xvi. 16.

19. —*and forgeth*—] For צוֹיף, the participle, twenty-seven MSS (five ancient), and three editions, read צף, præt. 3d person.

21. —*understood it from the foundation*—] The true reading seems to be ממוסדות, to answer to מראש in the foregoing line. It follows a word ending with מ; and out of three *mems* concuring, it was an easy mistake to drop the middle one.

22. —*as a thin veil*] " It is usual in the summer season, and upon all occasions, when a large company is to be received, to have the court sheltered from heat, or inclemency of the weather, by a *velu* umbrella, or veil, as I shall call it; which, being expanded on ropes from one side of the parapet-wall to the other, may be folded or unfolded at

pleasure. The Psalmist seems to allude to some covering of this kind in that beautiful expression of spreading out the heavens like a curtain :" Shaw, Trav. p. 274.

24. *If he but blow upon them*] The LXX, Syr. Vulg. and MS Bodl. and another, have גם without the conjunction ו.

28. *And that his understanding*—[Twenty-four MSS, two editions, LXX, and Vulg. read ואין, with the conjunction ו.

31. *They shall put forth fresh feathers.*] It has been a common and popular opinion, that the eagle lives and retains his vigour to a great age; and that, beyond the common lot of other birds, he moults in his old age, and renews his feathers, and with them his youth. " Thou shalt renew thy youth like the eagle," says the Psalmist, ciii. 5.; on which place St. Ambrose notes, " Aquila longam ætatem ducit, dum, vetustis plumis fatiscentibus, nova pennarum successione juvenescit." Phile, de Animalibus, treating of the eagle, and addressing himself to the Emperor Michael Palæologus junior, raises his compliment upon the same notion :—

Τουτου συ, βασιλευ, τον πολυν ζωοις βιον,
Αει νεουργων, και κρατηναν την φυσιν.

Long may'st thou live, O king; still like the eagle
Renew thy youth, and still retain thy vigour.

To this many fabulous and absurd circumstances are added by several ancient writers and commentators on Scripture: see Bochart, Hieroz. II. ii. 1. Whether the notion of the eagle's renewing his youth is in any degree well founded or not, I need not inquire; it is enough for a poet, whether profane or sacred, to have the authority of popular opinion to support an image introduced for illustration or ornament.

CHAPTER XLI.

1.—*repair to me with new sentiments*] Εγκαινιζεσθε, LXX. For החרישו, *be silent*, they certainly read in their copy החדישו, *be renewed;* which is parallel and synonymous with יחליפו כח, *recover their strength;* that is, their strength of mind, their powers of reason; that they may overcome those prejudices by which they have been so long held enslaved to idolatry. A MS has חד upon a rasure. The same mistake seems to have been made in this word, Zeph. iii. 17.: for יחריש באהבתו, "*silebit* in dilectione sua," as the Vulgate renders it, which seems not consistent with what immediately follows, "exultabit super te in laude;" LXX and Syr. read יחריש באהבתו, "*renovabitur* in amore suo."

2. —*the righteous man.*] The Chald. and Vulg. seem to have read צדיק. But Jerom, though his translation has *justum*, appears to have read צדק; for in his comment he expresses it by *justum, sive justitiam*. However, I think [all interpreters understand it of a person. So the LXX, in MS Pachom. εκαλεσεν αυτον, but the other copies have αυτην. They are divided in ascertaining this person: some explain it of Abraham; others of Cyrus. I rather think that the former is meant; because the character of the righteous man, or righteousness, agrees better with Abraham than with Cyrus. Besides, immediately after the description of the success given by God to Abraham and his posterity, (who, I presume, are to be taken into the account), the idolaters are introduced as greatly alarmed at this event. Abraham was called out of the east; and his posterity were introduced into the land of Canaan, in order to destroy the idolaters of that country; and they were established there, on purpose to stand as a barrier against idolatry, then prevailing, and threatening to overrun the whole face of the earth. Cyrus, though not properly an idolater, or worshipper of images, yet had nothing in his character to cause such an alarm among the idolaters, ver. 5—7. Further, after having just touched upon that circumstance, the Prophet with great ease returns to his former subject, and resumes Abraham and the Israelites; and assures them, that as God had called them, and chosen them for this purpose, he would uphold and support them to the utmost, and at length give them victory over all the heathen nations, their enemies; ver. 8—16.

Ibid. —*made them like the dust*—] The image is strong and beautiful; it is often made use of by the sacred poets; see Psal. i. 4. xxxv. 5. Job. xxi. 18. and by Isaiah himself in other places, chap. xvii. 13. xxix. 5. But there is great difficulty in making out the construction. The LXX read חרבם, קשתם, *their sword, their bow*, understanding it of the sword and bow of the conquered kings; but this is not so agreeable to the analogy of the image, as employed in other places. The Chaldee Paraphrast and Kimchi solve the difficulty by supposing an ellipsis of לפני before those words.

It must be owned, that the ellipsis is hard and unusual: but I choose rather to submit to this, than, by adhering with Vitringa to the more obvious construction, to destroy entirely both the image and the sense. But the Vulgate by *gladio ejus*, and *arcui ejus*, seems to express לחרבו and לקשתו; the admission of which reading may perhaps be thought preferable to Kimchi's ellipsis.

3. —*he passeth in safety*] The preposition seems to have been omitted in the text by mistake: LXX and Vulg. seem to have had it in their copies; εν ειρηνη, *in pace*, בשלום.

4. —*and made these things*] A word is here lost out of the text. It is supplied by an ancient MS, אלה, *these things;* and by LXX, ταυτα; and by Vulg. *hæc;* and by Chald. אלין.

5. —*and they were terrified*] Three MSS have ויחרדו, adding the conjunction ו, which restores the second member of the sentence to its true poetical form.

7. —*that it shall not move.*] Five MSS (two ancient), and the ancient versions, add the conjunction ו, reading ולא; which seems to be right.

9. —*from the extremities thereof*] מאצילה : אציל signifies the arm, axilla, ala; and is used like כנף, the wing, for any thing extended from the extremity of another, or joined on to it. It is here parallel and synonomous to מקצות, *from the ends*, in the preceding member.

15. —*a threshing wain,—a corn-drag*] See note on chap. xxviii. 27, 28.

19. *In the wilderness I will give the cedar*] The two preceding verses express God's mercy to them in their passage through the dry deserts, in supplying them with abundant water, when distressed with thirst, in allusion to the Exodus: this verse expresses the relief afforded to them, fainting with heat in their journey through that hot country, destitute of shelter, by causing shady trees, and those of the tallest and most beautiful kinds, to spring up for their defence. The apocryphal Baruch, speaking of the return from Babylon, expresses God's protection of his people by the same image: "Even the woods and every sweet smelling tree shall overshadow Israel by the commandment of God;" chap. v. 8.

20. —*and may consider—*] The verb ישימו, without לב added, cannot signify to apply the heart, or to attend to a thing, as Houbigant has observed: he therefore reads שמו,

they shall *wonder*. The conjecture is ingenious: but it is much more probable that the word לב is lost out of the text; for all the ancient versions render the phrase to the same sense, as if it were fully expressed, ישימו לב; and the Chaldee renders it paraphrastically, yet still retaining the very words in his paraphrase, וישוון דחלתי על לבהון, "ut ponant timorem meum in corde suo." See also ver. 22. where the same phrase is used.

21. *Produce these your mighty powers*] "Accedant, inquit, *idola* vestra, quæ putatis esse fortissima:" Hieron. Com. in loc. I prefer this to all other interpretations of this place, and to Jerom's own translation of it, which he adds immediately after, "Afferte, si quid forte habetis." The false gods are called upon to come forth, and appear in person; and to give evident demonstration of their fore-knowledge and power, by foretelling future events, and exerting their power in doing good or evil.

23. —*and terror*] The word ונרא is written imperfectly in the Hebrew text: the Masoretes supply ה at the end; and so it is read in twenty-two MSS, and four editions: that is, ונראה, and we shall *see*. But the true reading seems to be ונירא, and we shall *fear*, with י supplied, from ירא.

24. —*than nought*] For מאפע, read מאפס; so Chald. and Vulg. A manifest error of the text: compare chap. xl. 17. The Rabbins acknowledge no such error; but say, that the former word signifies the same with the latter, by a change of the two letters ס and ע: Sal. b. Melech in loc.

25. —*he shall trample*—] For יבא, Le Clerc reads יבס, from the Chaldee, who seems to read both words. "Forte legend. יבס, vel וירמם; sequitur ס:" SECKER. See Nahum iii. 14.

27. *I first to Sion*—] This verse is somewhat obscure by the transposition of the parts of the sentence, and the peculiar manner in which it is divided into two parallel lines. The verb at the end of the sentence belongs to both parts; and the phrase, *Behold they are here!* is parallel to *the messenger of glad tidings;* and stands, like it, as the accusative case to the verb. The following paraphrase will explain the form and the sense of it: "I first, by my Prophets, give notice of these events, saying, Behold, they are at hand! and I give to Jerusalem a messenger of glad tidings."

28. *And among the idols*—] For ומאלה, I read ומאלים, with the LXX, και απο των ειδωλων. See Exod. xv. 11. Isa. lvii. 5.

CHAPTER XLII.

The Prophet, having opened his subject with the preparation for the return from captivity at Babylon, and intimated that a much greater deliverance was covered under the veil of that event; proceeded to vindicate the power of God, as creator and disposer of all things; and his infinite knowledge, from his prediction of future events, and in particular of that deliverance. He went still further, and pointed out the instrument by which he should effect the redemption of his people the Jews from slavery, namely, a great conqueror, whom he would call forth from the north and the east to execute his orders. In this chapter he proceeds to the greater deliverance; and at once brings forth into full view, without throwing any veil of allegory over the subject, the Messiah. "Behold, my servant, Messiah," says the Chaldee. St Matthew has applied it directly to Christ; nor can it with any justice or propriety be applied to any other person or character whatever.

1. *And he shall publish judgment*] Four MSS (two ancient) add the conjunction ומשפט. See Matt. xii. 18.

The word משפט, *judgment*, like צדקה, *righteousness*, is taken in a great latitude of signification. It means rule, form, order, model, plan; rule of right, or of religion; an ordinance, institution; judicial process, cause, trial, sentence, condemnation, acquittal, deliverance, mercy, &c. It certainly means in this place the law to be published by Messiah; the institution of the gospel.

4. *His force shall not be abated nor broken*] "Rabbi Meir ita citat locum istum, ut post ירוץ addat כחו, *robur ejus*, ו quod hodie non comparet in textu Hebræo, sed addendum videtur, ut sensus fiat planior:" Capel. Crit. Sac. p. 382. For which reason I had added it in the translation, before I observed this remark of Capellus.

6. *a covenant to the people*] For עם, two MSS read עולם, the covenant *of the age to come*, or *the everlasting* covenant; which seems to give a clearer and better sense.

7. *To open the eyes of the blind*—] In this verse the Prophet seems to set forth the spiritual redemption, under images borrowed from the temporal deliverance.

Ibid. —*and from the dungeon*—] The LXX, Syr. and four MSS (one ancient), add the conjunction ו, ומבית.

10. *Ye that go down upon the sea*] This seems not to belong to this place; it does not well consist with what follows, " and the fulness thereof." They that go down upon the sea, means navigators, sailors, traders, such as do business in great waters: an idea much too confined for the Prophet, who means the sea in general, as it is used by the Hebrews, for the distant nations, the islands, the dwellers on the sea-coasts all over the world. I suspect that some transcriber had the 23d verse of Psal. cvii. running in his head, יורדי הים באניות; and wrote in this place יורדי הים instead of ירעם הים, or יריע, or ירן; "let the sea roar, or shout, or exult." But as this is so different in appearance from the present reading, I do not take the liberty of introducing it into the translation. "Conjeceram legendum יגירו, ut ver. 12.; sed non favent versiones:" SECKER.

11. *Let the desert*—] The most uncultivated countries, and the most rude and uncivilized people, shall confess and celebrate with thanksgiving the blessing of the knowledge of God graciously imparted to them. By the desert is meant Arabia Deserta; by the rocky country, Arabia Petræa: by the mountains, probably those celebrated ones, Paran, Horeb, Sinai, in the same country; to which also belonged Kedar, a clan of Arabians, dwelling for the most part in tents: but there were others of them, who inhabited or frequented cities and villages, as may be collected from this place of the prophet. Pietro della Valle, speaking of the people of Arabia Deserta, says, " There is a sort of Arabs of that country called Maédi, who with their herds, of buffaloes for the most part, sometimes live in the deserts, and sometimes in cities; from whence they have their name, which signifies wandering, going from place to place. They have no professed homes; nor are they properly Bedaui, or Beduui, that is, *Deserticoli*, who are the most noble among them, and never abide within walls, but always go wandering through the open country with their black tents; nor are they properly Hhadesi, as they call those who dwell in cities and lands with fixed houses: these by the latter are esteemed ignoble and base; but by both are considered as of low condition:" Viaggi, Parte III. lett. 2.

14. *shall I keep silence forever?*] After מעולם, in the copy which the LXX had before them, followed the word הלעולם, εσιωπησα απ' αιωνος· μη και αει σιωπησομαι; according to MSS Pachom. and I. D. II. and edition Complut.; which

word הלעולם has been omitted in the text by an easy mistake of a transcriber, because of the similitude of the word preceding.

15. —*dry deserts*] Instead of איים, islands, read ציים; a very probable conjecture of Houbigant.

16. *And through paths*—] The LXX, Syr. Vulg. and nine MSS (two ancient), read ובנתיבות.

Ibid. —*will I do for them*] עשיתם: This word so written, as it is in the text, means, Thou wilt do, in the second person: the Masoretes have indeed pointed it for the first person; but the י in the last syllable is absolutely necessary to distinguish the first person; and so it is written in forty MSS, עשיתים.

Jarchi, Kimchi, Sal. b. Melech, &c. agree, that the past time is here put for the future, עשיתי for אעשה; and indeed the context necessarily requires that interpretation. Further, it is to be observed, that עשיתים is for עשיתי להם, *I have done them*, for *I have done for them*; as עשיתני is for עשיתי לי, *I have made myself*, for *I have made for myself*; Ezek. xxix. 3.: and in the celebrated passage of Jephthah's vow, Judges xi. 31. והעליתיהו עולה, for העליתי לו עולה, *I will offer him a burnt-offering*, for *I will offer unto him* (that is unto JEHOVAH) *a burnt-offering*; by an ellipsis of the preposition, of which Buxtorff gives many other examples, Thes. Grammat. lib. ii. 17. See also note on chap. lxv. 5. A late happy application of this grammatical remark to that much disputed passage, has perfectly cleared up a difficulty which for two thousand years had puzzled all the translators and expositors, had given occasion to dissertations without number, and caused endless disputes among the learned, on the question, whether Jephthah sacrificed his daughter, or not: in which both parties have been equally ignorant of the meaning of the place, of the state of the fact, and of the very terms of the vow; which now at last has been cleared up beyond all doubt by my very learned friend Dr. Randolph, Margaret Professor of Divinity in the university of Oxford, in his sermon on Jephthah's vow; Oxford, 1766.

19. —*as he, to whom I have sent my messengers.*] כמלאכי אשלח, "ut ad quem nuncios meos misi;" Vulg. Chald.; almost the only interpreters who render it rightly, in consistence with the rest of the sentence, and in perfect agreement with the Hebrew idiom; according to which the ellipsis is to be thus supplied, כלאשר מלאכי אשלח.

Ibid. *—as he that is perfectly instructed*] See note on chap. xliv. 2.

Ibid. *And deaf as the servant of* JEHOVAH] For ועור, *and blind*, we must read וחרש, *and deaf*: κωφος, Symmachus; and so MS. The mistake is palpable, and the correction self-evident; and admissible, though there had been no authority for it.

20. *Thou hast seen indeed*] The text has ראית רבות, which the Masoretes in the marginal Keri have corrected to ראות רבות; as indeed a hundred and seven MSS, and five editions, now have it in the text. This was probably the reading of most of the MSS in their time; which, though they approved of it, out of some superstition they would not admit into their standard text. But these wretched critics, though they perceived there was some fault, yet did not know where the fault lay, nor consequently how to amend it; and yet it was open enough to a judicious eye: "רבות, sic veteres; et tamen forte legendum, ראות: vide cap. vi. 9:" SECKER. That is, ראית ראות. I believe no one will doubt of admitting this as the true reading.

Ibid. *—yet thou wilt not hear*] For ישמע, read תשמע, in the second person: so all the ancient versions, and forty MSS (four of them ancient), and perhaps five more. Two others have תשמעו, second person, plural.

21. *—his own praise*] For תורה, the LXX read הודה.

22. *—are taken in the toils*] For הפח, read הופחו, in the plural number, Hophal; as החבאו, which answers to it in the following member of the sentence: Le Clerc, Houbigant. הפה, SECKER.

24. *—they have sinned*] For חטאנו, first person, LXX and Chald. read חטאו, in the third person.

25. *the heat of his wrath*] For חמה, the Bodley MS has חמת, *in regimine*; more regularly.

CHAPTER XLIII.

1. *I have called thee by thy name*] קראתי בשמך. " Sic versiones. Videtur ex versu septimo et reipsa legendum קראתיך בשמי, [vocavi te meo nomine]; nam sæpe usurpatur hæc phrasis, nunquam altera. Nam xlv. 24. de Cyro alia res est. Sed dum Deus Jacobum Israelem vocat, Dei nomine vocat. Vide Exod. xxxi. 2." SECKER.

3. *I have given Egypt for thy ransom*] This is commonly supposed to refer to the time of Senacherib's invasion; who, when he was just ready to fall upon Jerusalem, soon after his entering Judea, was providentially diverted from that design, and turned his arms against the Egyptians, and their allies the Cushean Arabians, with their neighbours the Sabeans probably joined with them, under Tirhakah. See chap. xx. and xxxvii. 9. Or, as there are some reasonable objections to this opinion, perhaps it may mean more generally, that God had often saved his people at the expense of other nations, whom he had, as it were in their stead, given up to destruction. Vitringa explains this of Shalmaneser's designs upon the kingdom of Judea, after he had destroyed that of Samaria; from which he was diverted by carrying the war against the Egyptians, Cusheans, and Sabeans; but of this, I think, he has no clear proof in history. It is not to be wondered, that many things of this kind should remain very obscure for want of the light of history, which in regard to these times is extremely deficient.

"Did not Cyrus overcome these nations? and might they not be given him for releasing the Jews? It seems to have been so from chap. xlv. 14:" SECKER.

7. *Whom for my glory*—] Ten MSS (three ancient), Syr. and Vulg. read לכבודי, without the conjunction ו.

8. *Bring forth the people blind*—] I understand this of the Gentiles, as the verse following, not of the Jews. Their natural faculties, if they had made a proper use of them, must have led them to the knowledge of the being and attributes of the one true God; "for his eternal power and Godhead, if well attended to, are clearly seen in his works;" Rom. i. 20.; and would have preserved them from running into the folly and absurdity of worshipping idols. They are here challenged to produce the evidence of the power and foreknowledge of their idol-gods; and the Jews are just afterward, ver. 10, appealed to as witnesses for God in this cause: therefore these latter cannot here be meant by the people blind with eyes, and deaf with ears.

9. *Who among them*—] Seven MSS (three ancient), and the first edition, 1486, with Syr. and Vulg. read בכם, who among *you*. The present reading is preferable.

14. —*the Chaldeans exulting in their ships*] Babylon was very advantageously situated, both in respect to commerce and as a naval power. It was open to the Persian

Gulf by the Euphrates, which was navigable by large vessels; and being joined to the Tigris above Babylon by the canal called Naharmalca, or the Royal River, supplied the city with the produce of the whole country to the north of it, as far as the Euxine and Caspian Seas: Herod. i. 194. Semiramis was the foundress of this part also of the Babylonian greatness: she improved the navigation of the Euphrates; Herod. i. 184. Strabo, lib. xvi.; and is said to have had a fleet of three thousand gallies: Huet, Hist. du Commerce, chap. xi. We are not to wonder, that in later times we hear little of the commerce and naval power of Babylon; for, after the taking of the city by Cyrus, the Euphrates was not only rendered less fit for navigation, by being on that occasion diverted from its course, and left to spread over the whole country; but the Persian monarchs, residing in their own country, to prevent any invasion by sea on that part of their empire, purposely obstructed the navigation of both the rivers, by making cataracts in them; Strabo, ibid.; that is, by raising dams across the channel, and making artificial falls in them, that no vessel of any size or force could possibly come up. Alexander began to restore the navigation of the rivers by demolishing the cataracts upon the Tigris as far up as Seleucia; Arrian. lib. vii.; but he did not live to finish his great designs; those upon the Euphrates still continued. Ammianus, xxiv. 1. mentions them as subsisting in his time.

The Prophet therefore might very justly speak of the Chaldeans as glorying in their naval power in his time, though afterward they had no foundation for making any such boast.

15. *The Creator of Israel*] For בורא, creator, six MSS (two ancient) have אלהי, God.

20. *The wild beast of the field shall glorify me—*] The image is elegant and highly poetical. God will give such an abundant miraculous supply of water to his people traversing the dry desert, in their return to their country, that even the wild beasts, the serpents, the ostriches, and other animals that haunt those adust regions, shall be sensible of the blessing; and shall break forth into thanksgiving and praises to him for the unusual refreshment, which they receive from his so plentifully watering the sandy wastes of Arabia Deserta, for the benefit of his people passing through them.

22—24. *But thou hast not invoked—*] The connexion

is—But thou, Israel, whom I have chosen, whom I have formed for myself, to be my witness against the false gods of the nations; even thou hast revolted from me, hast neglected my worship, and hast been perpetually running after strange gods. The emphasis of this and the following parts of the sentence, on which the sense depends, seems to lie on the words Me, on My account, &c. The Jews were diligent in performing the external services of religion; in offering prayers, incense, sacrifices, oblations: but their prayers were not offered with faith; and their oblations were made more frequently to their idols than to the God of their fathers. The Hebrew idiom excludes with a general negative, in a comparative sense, one of two objects opposed to one another: thus, "I will have mercy, and *not* sacrifice;" Hosea vi. 6. "For I spake *not* to your fathers, *nor* commanded them—concerning burnt-offerings or sacrifices; but this thing I commanded them, saying, Obey my voice;" Jer. vii. 22, 23. And the meaning of this place of Isaiah seems to be much the same with that of Amos; who however has explained at large both parts of the comparison, and specified the false service opposed to the true:

"Have ye offered unto Me sacrifices and offerings
In the wilderness forty years, O house of Israel?
Nay, but ye have borne the tabernacle of your Moloch,
And Chiun, your images;
The star of your God, which you made to yourselves."
Amos v. 25, 26.

22. *Neither hast thou laboured—*] For כי יגעת, LXX and Vulg. read ויגעת: Houbigant. The negative is repeated, or referred to, by the conjunction ו; as in many other places. See note on chap. xxiii. 4.

20. *And thy princes have profaned—*] Instead of ואחלל שרי, read ויחללו שריך. So Syr. and LXX, καὶ ἐμίαναν οἱ ἄρχοντες τὰ ἅγιά μου, קדש: Houbigant. Οἱ ἄρχοντες σου, MSS Pachom. and 1. D. 11. and Marchal.

Ibid. —*to reproach.*] לנדופח, in the singular number; so an ancient MS, and LXX, Syr. Vulg.

CHAPTER XLIV.

2. *Jeshurun means Israel.* This name was given to that people by Moses, Deut. xxxii. 15. xxxiii. 5. and 26. The

most probable account of it seems to be that in which the Jewish commentators agree; namely, that it is derived from ישר, and signifies *upright*. In the same manner, Israel, as a people, is called משלם, *perfect*, chap. xlii. 19. They were taught of God, and abundantly furnished with the means of rectitude and perfection in his service and worship.

4. —*as the grass among the waters*] כבין חציר, "They shall spring up *in the midst of*, or rather, *in among*, the *grass.*" This cannot be right: ten MSS, and two editions, have כבין, or כבן. Twenty-four MSS read it without the י, כבן; and so reads the Chaldee; the Syriac, מבין. The true reading is in all probability כבין; and the word מים, which should have followed it, is lost out of the text; but it is happily supplied by the LXX: ὡς ἀνα μεσον ὑδατος. "In every place where there is water, there is always grass; for water makes every thing grow in the East:" Sir John Chardin's note on 1 Kings xviii. 5.; Harmer's Observ. i. p. 54.

5. —*shall be called*] Passive, יקרא, κληθησεται, Symmachus.

Ibid. *And this shall inscribe his hand to* JEHOVAH.] Και ἑτερος ἐπιγραψει χειρι (χειρα, Aq. Sym.) αὐτου, του Θεου εἰμι: "And another shall write upon his hand, I belong to God:" LXX. They seem to have read here, as before, ליהוה אני. But the repetition of the same phrase without any variation is not elegant. However, they seem to have understood it rightly as an allusion to the marks which were made, by punctures rendered indelible by fire or by staining, upon the hand or some other part of the body, signifying the state or character of the person, and to whom he belonged: the slave was marked with the name of his master; the soldier, of his commander; the idolater, with the name or ensign of his god: ςεγματα ἐπιγραφομενα, ὁια των ςρατευομενων ἐν ταις χερσιν: Aetius apud Turnebum Advers. xxiv. 12. "Victuris in cute punctis milites scripti et matriculis inserti jurare solent:" Vegetius, ii. 5. And the Christians seem to have imitated this practice, by what Procopius says on this place of Isaiah: Το δε ΤΗι ΧΕΙΡΙ, δια το ςιζειν ἰσως πολλους ἐπι καρπων, η βραχιονων, η του ςαυρου το σημειον, η την Χριςου προσηγοριαν: "Because many marked their wrists, or their arms, with the sign of the cross, or with the name of Christ." See Rev. xx. 4. Spencer, De Leg. Hebr. lib. ii. cap. 20.

7. —*let them declare unto us*] For למו, *unto them*, the Chaldee reads לנו, *unto us*. The LXX read לכם, *unto you*:

which is preferable to the reading of the text. But למו and
לנו are frequently mistaken one for the other: see chap. x.
29. Psal. lxxx. 7. lxiv. 6.

8. *Fear ye not*—] "תרהו nusquam occurrit: forte
תיראו, timete:" SECKER. Two MSS read חירהו.

9, 10. *That every one may be ashamed, that he hath
formed a god*] The Bodleian MS, one of the first extant for its antiquity and authority, instead of מי at the
beginning of the 10th verse has כי, which greatly clears up
the construction of a very obscure passage. The LXX
likewise closely connect in construction the end of ver. 9.
with the beginning of ver. 10. and wholly omit the interrogative מי, which embarrasses the sentence: αισχυνθησονται οι
πλασσοντες Θεον, και γλυφοντες παντες ανωφελη: agreeably to the
reading of the MS above-mentioned.

11. *Even the workmen themselves shall blush*] I do not
know, that any one has ever yet interpreted these words to
any tolerably good sense: וחרשים המה מאדם. The Vulgate, and our translators, have rendered them very fairly,
as they are written and pointed in the text: "Fabri enim
sunt ex hominibus:" "And the workmen, they are of men."
Out of which the commentators have not been able to extract any thing worthy of the Prophet. I have given another explanation of the place; agreeable enough to the
context, if it can be deduced from the words themselves. I
presume, that אדם, *rubuit* may signify *erubuit*, to be red
through shame, as well as from any other cause; though I
cannot produce any example of it in that particular sense:
and the word in the text I would point מֵאָדְפֿם; or if any
one should object to the irregularity of the number, I would
read מאדמים. But I rather think, that the irregularity of
the construction has been the cause of the obscurity, and
has given occasion to the mistaken punctuation. The singular is sometimes put for the plural; see Psal. lxviii. 31.;
and the participle for the future tense; see Isa. lx. 11.

12. —*cutteth off*—] מְעַצֵּד, participium pihel of עצד, to
cut; still used in that sense in the Arabic. See Simonis
Lex. Heb. The LXX and Syr. take the word in this form;
but they render it, *sharpeneth* the iron. See Castell. Lex.
in voce.

The sacred writers are generally large and eloquent upon
the subject of idolatry: they treat it with great severity, and
set forth the absurdity of it in the strongest light. But this

passage of Isaiah, ver. 12—20. far exceeds any thing that ever was written upon the subject, in force of argument, energy of expression, and elegance of composition. One or two of the apocryphal writers have attempted to imitate the Prophet, but with very ill success; Wisd. xiii. 11—19. xv. 7, &c. Baruch, chap. vi.; especially the latter, who, injudiciously dilating his matter, and introducing a number of minute circumstances, has very much weakened the force and effect of his invective. On the contrary, a heathen author, in the ludicrous way, has, in a line or two, given idolatry one of the severest strokes it ever received:—

"Olim truncus eram ficulnus, inutile lignum;
Cum faber, incertus scamnum faceretne Priapum,
Maluit esse Deum." Horat.

14. *He heweth down*—] For לכרת, the LXX and Vulg. read כרת, or יכרת.

16. *And with part*—] Twenty-three MSS, LXX, and Vulg. add the conjunction ו, ועל.

18. *—their eyes are closed up*] The LXX, Chald. and Vulg, for טש read טחו. See note on chap. vi. 10.

20. *He feedeth on ashes*] He feedeth on that which affordeth no nourishment: a proverbial expression for using ineffectual means, and bestowing labour to no purpose. In the same sense Hosea says, "Ephraim feedeth on wind," chap. xii. 1.

22. *I have made thy transgressions vanish away like a cloud, and thy sins like a vapour.*] Longinus admired the sublimity of the sentiment, as well as the harmony of the numbers, in the following sentence of Demosthenes: Τουτο το ψηφισμα τον τοτε τη πολει περιςαν]α κινδυνον παρελθειν εποιησεν ωσπερ νεφος: "This decree made the danger then hanging over the city pass away like a cloud."

24. *by myself*] Thirteen MSS (six ancient), confirm the reading of the Keri, מאתי.

27. *Who sayeth to the deep, Be thou wasted*] Cyrus took Babylon by laying the bed of the Euphrates dry, and leading his army into the city by night through the empty channel of the river. This remarkable circumstance, in which the event so exactly corresponded with the prophecy, was also noted by Jeremiah:

"A drought shall be upon her waters, and they shall be dried up.
I will lay her sea dry;
And I will scorch up her springs." Jer. l. 38. li. 36.

It is proper here to give some account of the means and method by which the stratagem of Cyrus was effected.

The Euphrates in the middle of summer, from the melting of the snows on the mountains of Armenia, like the Nile, overflows the country. In order to diminish the inundation, and to carry off the waters, two canals were made by Nebuchadnezzar a hundred miles above the city; the first on the eastern side, called Naharmalca, or the royal river, by which the Euphrates was let into the Tigris; the other on the western side, called Pallacopas, or Naharaga, (נהר אגם, the river of the pool), by which the redundant waters were carried into a vast lake, forty miles square, contrived not only to lessen the inundation, but for a reservoir, with sluices, to water the barren country on the Arabian side. Cyrus, by turning the whole river into the lake by the Pallacopas, laid the channel, where it ran through the city, almost dry; so that his army entered it, both above and below, by the bed of the river, the water not reaching above the middle of the thigh. By the great quantity of water let into the lake, the sluices and dams were destroyed; and being never repaired afterward, the waters spread over the whole country below, and reduced it to a morass, in which the river is lost. "Ingens modo et navigabilis, inde tenuis rivus, despectus emoritur; et nusquam manifesto exitu effluit, ut alii omnes, sed deficit:" Mela, iii. 8. Herod. i. 185. 190. Xenophon. Cyrop. vii. Arrian. vii.

28. *Who sayeth to Cyrus, Thou art my shepherd*] "Pastor meus *es*:" Vulg. The true reading seems to be רעי אתה; the word אתה has probably been dropt out of the text. The same word is lost out of the text, Psal. cxix. 57. It is supplied in LXX by the word εἶ.

Ibid. *Who sayeth to Jerusalem*] For ולאמר, LXX and Vulg. read האומר.

Ibid. —*and to the temple*] ולהיכל, as לירושלם before: the preposition is necessary; and the Vulgate seems to read so: Houbigant.

CHAPTER XLV.

1. *And ungird the loins of kings*] See note on chap. v. 27. Xenophon gives the following list of the nations conquered by Cyrus: the Syrians, Assyrians, Arabians, Cappadocians, both the Phrygians, Lydians, Carians, Phenicians,

Babylonians. He moreover reigned over the Bactrians, Indians, Cilicians, the Sacæ, Paphlagones, and Mariandyni: Cyrop. lib. i. p. 4. edit. Hutchinson, 4to. All these kingdoms he acknowledges, in his decree for the restoration of the Jews, to have been given to him by JEHOVAH, the God of heaven: Ezra i. 2.

Ibid. *That I may open before him the valves; and the gates shall not be shut.*] The gates of Babylon within the city, leading from the streets to the river, were providentially left open, when Cyrus's forces entered the city in the night through the channel of the river, in the general disorder occasioned by the great feast which was then celebrated; otherwise, says Herodotus, i. 191. the Persians would have been shut up in the bed of the river, and taken as in a net, and all destroyed: And the gates of the palace were opened imprudently by the king's orders, to inquire what was the cause of the tumult without; when the two parties under Gobrias and Gadatas rushed in, got possession of the palace, and slew the king: Xenoph. Cyrop. vii. p. 528.

2. —*the mountains*—] For הררים, a word not easily accounted for in this place, the LXX read הרים, τα ορη. Two MSS have הדרים, without the ו; which is hardly distinguishable from the reading of the LXX. The divine protection which attended Cyrus, and rendered his expedition against Babylon easy and prosperous, is finely expressed by God's going before him, and making the mountains level. The image is highly poetical:

" At vos, qua veniet, tumidi subsidite montes,
　Et faciles curvis vallibus este viæ." Ovid. Amor. ii. 16.

Ibid. *The valves of brass*—] Abydenus, apud Eusch. Præp. Evang. ix. 41. says, that the wall of Babylon had brazen gates. And Herodotus, i. 179. more particularly: " In the wall all round there are a hundred gates, all of brass; and so in like manner are the sides and the lintels." The gates likewise within the city, opening to the river from the several streets, were of brass; as were those also of the temple of Belus: Id. i. 180, 181.

3. *I will give unto thee the treasures of darkness*] Sardes and Babylon, when taken by Cyrus, were the wealthiest cities in the world. Crœsus, celebrated beyond all the kings of that age for his riches, gave up his treasures to Cyrus, with an exact account in writing of the whole, containing the particulars with which each waggon was loaded, when

they were carried away; and they were delivered to Cyrus at the palace of Babylon : Xenoph. Cyrop. lib. vii. p. 503. 515. 540.

Pliny gives the following account of the wealth taken by Cyrus in Asia. "Jam Cyrus devicta Asia, pondo xxxiv millia [auri] invenerat; præter vasa aurea, aurumque factum, et in eo folia, ac platanum, vitemque. Qua victoria argenti quingenta millia talentorum reportavit; et craterem Semiramidis, cujus pondus quindecim talenta colligebat. Talentum autem Ægyptium pondo lxxx patere [l. capere] Varro tradit:" Nat. Hist. xxxiii. 15.

The gold and silver, estimated by weight in this account, being converted into pounds sterling, amount to £. 126,224,000 : Brerewood, De Ponderibus, cap. x.

7. *Forming light, and creating darkness*] It was the great principle of the Magian religion, which prevailed in Persia in the time of Cyrus, and in which probably he was educated, that there are two supreme, co-eternal, and independent Causes, always acting in opposition one to the other; one the author of all good, the other of all evil; the good Being they called Light; the evil Being, Darkness: that, when light had the ascendant, then good and happiness prevailed among men; when darkness had the superiority, then evil and misery abounded:—an opinion that contradicts the clearest evidence of our reason, which plainly leads us to the acknowledgment of one only Supreme Being, infinitely good as well as powerful. With reference to this absurd opinion, held by the person to whom this prophecy is addressed, God by his Prophet, in the most significant terms, asserts his omnipotence and absolute supremacy:

"I am JEHOVAH, and none else;
Forming light, and creating darkness;
Making peace, and creating evil:
I JEHOVAH am the author of all these things."

Declaring, that those Powers whom the Persians held to be the original authors of good and evil to mankind, representing them by light and darkness as their proper emblems, are no other than creatures of God, the instruments which he employs in his government of the world, ordained or permitted by him in order to execute his wise and just decrees; and that there is no Power, either of good or evil, independent of the One Supreme God, infinite in power and in goodness.

There were, however, some among the Persians, whose sentiments were more moderate as to this matter; who held the evil principle to be in some measure subordinate to the good; and that the former would at length be wholly subdued by the latter: See Hyde, De Relig. Vet. Pers. cap. xxii.

That this opinion prevailed among the Persians as early as the time of Cyrus, we may, I think, infer, not only from this passage of Isaiah, which has a manifest reference to it, but likewise from a passage in Xenophon's Cyropædia, where the same doctrine is applied to the human mind. Araspes, a noble young Persian, had fallen in love with the fair captive Panthea, committed to his charge by Cyrus. After all his boasting, that he was superior to the assaults of that passion, he yielded so far to it, as even to threaten violence, if she would not comply with his desires. Awed by the reproof of Cyrus, fearing his displeasure, and having by cool reflection recovered his reason; in his discourse with him on this subject he says, "O Cyrus, I have certainly two souls; and this piece of philosophy I have learned from that wicked sophist Love. For if I had but one soul, it would not be at the same time good and evil; it would not at the same time approve of honourable and base actions; and at once desire to do, and refuse to do, the very same things. But it is plain, that I am animated by two souls; and when the good soul prevails, I do what is virtuous; and when the evil one prevails, I attempt what is vicious. But now the good soul prevails, having gotten you for her assistant, and has clearly gained the superiority:" Lib. vi. p. 424.

8. *Drop down, O ye heavens*—] The eighty-fifth Psalm is a very elegant ode on the same subject with this part of Isaiah's prophecies—the restoration of Judah from captivity; and is, in the most beautiful part of it, a manifest imitation of this passage of the Prophet:—

> "Verily his salvation is nigh unto them that fear him,
> That glory may dwell in our land.
> Mercy and truth have met together;
> Righteousness and peace have kissed each other.
> Truth shall spring from the earth,
> And righteousness shall look down from heaven.
> Even JEHOVAH will give that which is good,
> And our land shall yield her produce.

Righteousness shall go before him,
And shall direct his footsteps in the way."
Psal. lxxxv. 10—14.

These images of the dew and the rain descending from heaven, and making the earth fruitful, employed by the prophet, and some of those nearly of the same kind which are used by the Psalmist, may perhaps be primarily understood as designed to set forth in a splendid manner the happy state of God's people restored to their country, and flourishing in peace and plenty, in piety and virtue: but justice and salvation, mercy and truth, righteousnesss and peace, and glory dwelling in the land, cannot with any sort of propriety, in the one or the other, be interpreted as the consequences of that event; they must mean the blessings of the great redemption by Messiah.

Ibid. —*let salvation produce her fruit*] For ויפרו, the LXX, Vulg. and Syr. read ויפרה; and a MS has a rasure close after the letter ו, which probably was ה at first.

9. *Wo unto him, that contendeth with the power that formed him*] The Prophet answers or prevents the objections and cavils of the unbelieving Jews, disposed to murmur against God, and to arraign the wisdom and justice of his dispensations in regard to them; in permitting them to be oppressed by their enemies, and in promising them deliverance instead of preventing their captivity. St Paul has borrowed the image, and has applied it to the like purpose with equal force and elegance: "Nay, but, O man! who art thou that repliest against God? Shall the thing formed say to him that formed it, Why hast thou made me thus? Hath not the potter power over the clay, out of the same lump to make one vessel to honour, and another to dishonour?" Rom. ix. 20, 21.

Ibid. —*and to the workmen, Thou hast no hands*] The Syr. renders as if he had read ולא היתי פעל ידיך, "Neither am I the work of thy hands;" the LXX, as if they had read, ולא פעלת ואין ידים לך, "Neither hast thou made me; and thou hast no hands." But the fault seems to be in the transposition of the two pronouns: for ופעלך read ופעלו; and for לו read לך. So Houbigant corrects it, reading also ולפעלו; which last correction seems not altogether necessary. The LXX in MSS Pachom. and 1. D. 11. have it thus: και το εργον, ουκ εχεις χειρας; which favours the reading here proposed.

11. *And he that formeth the things which are to come*] I read ויצר, without the ו suffixed, from the LXX, who join it in construction with the following word; ὁ ποιήσας τα επερχομενα.

Ibid. *Do ye question me—*] "תשאלוני, Chald. recte: præcedit ה ; et sic forte legerunt reliqui Intt. :" SECKER.

14. *The wealth of Egypt—*] This seems to relate to the future admission of the Gentiles into the church of God. Compare Psal. lxviii. 32. lxxii. 10. chap. lx. 6—9. And perhaps these particular nations may be named, by a metonymy common in all poetry, for powerful and wealthy nations in general. See note on chap. lx. 1.

Ibid. *The Sabeans tall of stature—*] That the Sabeans were of a more majestic appearance than common, is particularly remarked by Agatharchides, an ancient Greek historian quoted by Bochart, Phaleg. ii. 26. τα σωματα ιστι των χατοικουντων αξιολογωτερα. So also the LXX understand it, rendering it ανδρες υψηλοι. And the same phrase, אנשי מדה, is used for persons of extraordinary stature, Numb. xiii. 32. and 1 Chron. xx. 6.

Ibid. *—and in suppliant guise—*] The conjunction ו is supplied by the ancient versions, and confirmed by fifteen MSS (seven ancient), and six editions, ואליך. Three MSS (two ancient), omit the ו before אליך at the beginning of the line.

16. *They are ashamed—*] The reader cannot but observe the sudden transition from the solemn adoration of the secret and mysterious nature of God's counsels, in regard to his people, to the spirited denunciation of the confusion of idolaters, and the final destruction of idolatry: contrasted with the salvation of Israel, not from temporal captivity, but the *eternal* salvation by Messiah, strongly marked by the repetition and augmentation of the phrase, *to the ages of eternity.* But there is not only a sudden change in the sentiment; the change is equally observable in the construction of the sentences; which from the usual short measure runs out at once into two distichs of the longer sort of verse: See Prelim. Dissert. p. xli. &c. There is another instance of the same kind, and very like to this, of a sudden transition in regard both to the sentiment and construction in chap. xlii. 17.

Ibid. *—his adversaries, all of them.*] This line, to the great diminution of the beauty of the distich, is imperfect in the present text; the subject of the proposition is not particularly expressed, as it is in the line following. The version of the LXX happily supplies the word that is lost; οἱ ἀντικείμενοι αὐτῳ: the original word was צרי.

18. —*for he formeth it to be inhabited*] An ancient MS has כי before לשבת; and so the ancient versions.

19. *I have not spoken in secret, in a dark place of the earth*] In opposition to the manner in which the heathen oracles gave their answers; which were generally delivered from some deep and obscure cavern. Such was the seat of the Cumean Sybil:

"Excisum Euboicæ latus ingens rupis in antrum."
Virg. Æn. vi. 42.

Such was that of the famous oracle at Delphi: of which, says Strabo, lib. 9. φασι δ᾽ ειναι το μαντειον αντρον κοιλον μετα βαθους, ου μαλα ευρυστομον: "The oracle is said to be a hollow cavern of considerable depth, with an opening not very wide." And Diodorus, giving an account of the origin of this oracle, says, "that there was in that place a great chasm, or cleft, in the earth; in which very place is now situated what is called the Adytum of the temple." Ἀδυτον· σπηλαιον; η το αποκρυφον μερος του ιερου: Hesych. "Adytum means a cavern, or the hidden part of the temple."

Ibid. *I am JEHOVAH, who speak truth, who give direct answers.*] This also is said in opposition to the false and ambiguous answers given by the heathen oracles; of which there are many noted examples; none more so than that of the answer given to Crœsus, when he had marched against Cyrus, which piece of history has some connexion with this part of Isaiah's prophecies. Let us hear Cicero's account of the Delphic answers in general, and of this in particular.

"Sed jam ad te venio,
O Sancte Apollo, qui umbilicum certum terrarum obsides,
Unde superstitiosa primum sæva evasit vox fera.

Tuis enim oraculis Chrysippus totum volumen implevit, partim falsis, ut ego opinor; partim casu veris, ut fit in omni oratione sæpissime; partim flexiloquis et obscuris, ut interpres egeat interprete, et sors ipsa ad sortes referenda sit; partim ambiguis, et quæ ad dialecticum deferenda sint. Nam cum sors illa edita est opulentissimo regi Asiæ,

Crœsus Halym penetrans magnam pervertet opum vim:

hostium vim sese perversurum putavit; pervertit autem suam. Utrum igitur eorum accidisset, verum oraculum fuisset:" De Divinat. ii. 56.

21. —*bring them near, and let them consult together*] For ויעצו, let them *consult*, the LXX read ידעו, let them *know*; but an ancient MS has ויעדו, "let them come together by appointment;" which may probably be the true reading.

23. —*truth is gone forth from my mouth; The word*—] So the LXX distinguish the members of the sentence; preserving the elegance of the construction, and the clearness of the sense.

24. *Saying, Only to* J<small>EHOVAH</small>—] A MS omits לי, *unto me*; and instead of לי אמר, *he said* or *shall say unto me*, the LXX read, in the copy which they used, לאמר, *saying*. For יבא, *he* shall come, in the singular, twelve MSS (three ancient) read יבאו, plural; and a letter is erased at the end of the word in two others: and so the Alexandrine copy of the LXX, Syr. and Vulg. read it. For צדקות, plural, two MSS read צדקת, singular; and so LXX, Syr. Chald.

CHAPTER XLVI.

1. *Their burthens are heavy*] For נשאתיכם, *your* burthens, the LXX had in their copy נשאתיהם, *their* burthens.

2. *They could not deliver their own charge*] That is, their worshippers; who ought to have been borne by them. See the two next verses. The Chaldee and Syriac versions render it in effect to the same purpose, *portantes se, those that bear them*, meaning their worshippers; but how they can render משא in an active sense, I do not understand.

Ibid. *Even they themselves*—] For ונפשם, an ancient MS has כי נפשם, with more force.

3—7. *Ye that have been borne by me from the birth*—] The Prophet very ingeniously, and with great force, contrasts the power of God, and his tender goodness effectually exerted towards his people, with the inability of the false gods of the heathen: He like an indulgent father had carried his people in his arms, "as a man carrieth his son;" Deut. i. 31.; he had protected them, and delivered them from their distresses: whereas the idols of the heathen are forced to be carried about themselves, and removed from place to place, with great labour and fatigue, by their worshippers; nor can they answer, or deliver their votaries, when they cry unto them.

Moses, expostulating with God on the weight of the

charge laid upon him as leader of his people, expresses that charge, under the same image of a parent's carrying his children, in very strong terms: "Have I conceived all this people? have I begotten them? that thou shouldest say unto me, Carry them in thy bosom, as a nursing father beareth the sucking child, unto the land which thou swarest unto their fathers;" Numb. xi. 12.

Pindar has treated with a just and very elegant ridicule the work of the statuary, even in comparison with his own poetry, from this circumstance of its being fixed to a certain station. "The friends of Pytheas, says the Scholiast, came to the poet, desiring him to write an ode on his victory. Pindar demanded three drachms (*minæ*, I suppose it should be) for the ode. No, say they, we can have a brazen statue for that money, which will be better than a poem. However, changing their minds afterwards, they came and offered him what he had demanded." This gave him the hint of the following ingenious exordium of his ode:—

Ουκ ανδριαντοποιος ειμ'
'Ως' ελινυσσοντα μ' εργαζεσ-
θαι αγαλματ' επ' αυτας βαθμιδος
Εςαοτ'. Αλλ' επι πασας
Ολκαδος, εν τ' ακατῳ,
Στοιχ' απ' Αιγινας διαγγελ-
λοισ' οτι Λαμπωνος υιος
Πυθεας ευρυσθενης
Νικη Νεμειοις παγκρατιȣ ςεφανον.   Nem. v.

Thus elegantly translated by Mr Francis in a note to Hor. Carm. iv. 2. 19.

"It is not mine with forming hand
To bid a lifeless image stand
For ever on its base:
But fly, my verses, and proclaim
To distant realms, with deathless fame,
That Pytheas conquered in the rapid race."

Jeremiah seems to be indebted to Isaiah for most of the following passage:—

"The practices of the people are altogether vanity;
For they cut down a tree from the forest;
The work of the artificer's hand with the axe:
With silver and with gold it is adorned;
With nails and with hammers it is fastened, that it may not totter.
Like the palm-tree they stand stiff, and cannot speak;

>   They are carried about, for they cannot go:
>   Fear them not, for they cannot do harm,
>   Neither is it in them to do good."   Jer. x. 3—5.

8. —*shew yourselves men*] התאששו. This word is rather of doubtful derivation and signification. It occurs only in this place; and some of the ancient interpreters seem to have had something different in their copies. Vulg. read התבששו, take shame to yourselves; Syr. התבוננו, consider with yourselves; LXX, ςεναξετε; perhaps התאבלו, groan, or mourn, within yourselves.

11. *Calling from the east the eagle*] A very proper emblem for Cyrus, as in other respects, so particularly because the ensign of Cyrus was a golden eagle, ΑΕΤΟΣ χρυσους; the very word עיט, which the Prophet uses here, expressed as near as may be in Greek letters. Xenoph. Cyrop. lib. vii. sub. init.

Ibid. *And from a land*] Two MSS add the conjunction ו, ומארץ; and so LXX, Syr. Vulg.

CHAPTER XLVII.

1. *Descend, and sit on the dust*—] See note on chap. iii. 26, and on chap. lii. 2.

2. *Take the mill, and grind the corn*] It was the work of slaves to grind the corn. They used handmills: watermills were not invented till a little before the time of Augustus; (see the Greek epigram of Antipater, which seems to celebrate it as a new invention: Anthol. Cephalæ, 653.); wind-mills, long after. It was not only the work of slaves, but the hardest work; and often inflicted on them as a severe punishment.

> "Molendum in pistrino; vapulandum: habendæ compedes."
>   Terent. Phormio, ii. 1. 19.
> "Hominem pistrino dignum!"   Id. Heaut. iii. 2. 19.

But in the East it was the work of the female slaves. See Exod. xi. 5. xii. 29. (in the version of the LXX), Matt. xxiv. 41. Homer. Odyss. xx. 105—108. And it is the same to this day: "Women alone are employed to grind their corn;" Shaw, Algiers and Tunis, p. 297. "They are the female slaves that are generally employed in the east at those hand-mills [for grinding corn]: it is extremely laborious, and esteemed the lowest employment in the house:" Sir J. Chardin, Harmer's Observ. i. p. 153.

2. *I will not suffer man to intercede*] The verb should be pointed, or written, אפגיע, in Hiphil.

4. *Our avenger*—]. Here a chorus breaks in upon the midst of the subject ; with a change of construction, as well as sentiment, from the longer to the shorter kind of verse, for one distich only ; after which the former subject and style is resumed. See note on xlv. 16.

6. *I was angry with my people*—] God, in the course of his providence, makes use of great conquerors and tyrants as his instruments to execute his judgments in the earth : he employs one wicked nation to scourge another. The inflictor of the punishment may perhaps be as culpable as the sufferer: and may add to his guilt by indulging his cruelty in executing God's justice. When he has fulfilled the work to which the divine vengeance has ordained him, he will become himself the object of it. See chap. x. 5—12. God charges the Babylonians, though employed by himself to chastise his people, with cruelty in regard to them. They exceeded the bounds of justice and humanity in oppressing and destroying them ; and though they were really executing the righteous decree of God, yet, as far as it regarded themselves, they were only indulging their own ambition and violence. The Prophet Zechariah sets this matter in the same light : " I was but a little angry, and they helped forward the affliction ; " chap. i. 15.

7. *Because thou didst not*—] For עד read עלי ; so two MSS, and one edition. And for אחריתה, the latter end *of it*, read אחריתך, *thy* latter end : so thirteen MSS, and two editions, and Vulg.

9. *On a sudden*—] Instead of כתמם, *in their perfection*, as our translation renders it, the LXX and Syr. read, in the copies from which they translated, פתאם, *suddenly ;* parallel to רגע, *in a moment*, in the preceding alternate member of the sentence. The concurrent testimony of LXX and Syr., favoured by the context, may be safely opposed to the authority of the present text.

Ibid. *Notwithstanding the multitude*—] ברב, for this sense of the particle ב, see Numb. xiv. 11.

11. —*how to deprecate*] שחרה : so the Chaldee renders it ; which is approved by Jarchi on the place, and Michaelis Epim. in Prælect. xix. ; see Psal. lxxviii. 34.

Ibid. " Videtur in fine [hujus commatis] deesse verbum ut hoc membrum prioribus respondeat : " SECKER.

In order to set in a proper light this judicious remark, it is necessary to give the reader an exact verbal translation of the whole verse :—

" And evil shall come upon thee, thou shalt not know how to deprecate it;
And mischief shall fall upon thee, thou shalt not be able to expiate it;
And destruction shall come suddenly upon thee, thou shalt not know "——

What? how to escape, to avoid it, to be delivered from it; (perhaps צאת ממנה, Jer. xi. 11.) I am persuaded, that a phrase is here lost out of the text. But as the ancient versions retain no traces of it, and a wide field lies open to uncertain conjecture, I have not attempted to fill up the chasm; but have in the translation, as others have done before me, palliated and disguised the defect, which I cannot with any assurance pretend to supply.

13. *What are the events*—] For מאשר, read מה אשר; so the LXX.

15. —*to his own business*] לעברו. Expositors give no very good account of this word in this place. In a MS it was at first לעברו, which is probably the true reading. The sense however is pretty much the same with the common interpretation.

CHAPTER XLVIII.

1. *Ye that flow from the fountain of Judah*] ממי, from the *waters*. "Perhaps ממעי, *from the bowels*, [so many others have conjectured], or [יהודה] מני, or מיהודה, *from Judah:*" SECKER. But see Michaelis in Prælect. not. 22. And we have עין יעקב, the fountain of Jacob, Deut. xxxiii. 28. and ממקור ישראל, from the mountain of Israel, Psal. lxviii. 27. Twenty-seven MSS, and three editions, have מימי, from the *days;* which makes no good sense.

6. —*behold, the whole is accomplished*] For חזה, see, a MS has הזה, *this;* thou hast heard the whole of *this:* the Syriac has וחזית, thou hast heard, *and thou hast seen*, the whole. Perhaps it should be הנה, *behold*. In order to express the full sense, I have rendered it somewhat paraphrastically.

9. *And for the sake of my praise*] I read ולמען תהלתי. The word למען, though not absolutely necessary here, for

it may be understood as supplied from the preceding member, yet seems to have been removed from hence to ver. 11.; where it is redundant, and where it is not repeated, in LXX, Syr. and a MS. I have therefore omitted it in the latter place, and added it here.

10. *I have tried thee*—] For בחרתיך, I have *chosen* thee, a MS has בחנתיך, I have *tried* thee. And so perhaps read the Syriac and Chaldee interpreters: they retain the same word בחרתך; but in those languages it signifies, I have *tried* thee. ככסף, *quasi* argentum, Vulg.

11. *for how would my name be blasphemed?*] The word שמי, *my name*, is dropt out of the text: it is supplied by a MS which has שמי; and by LXX, ὅτι τὸ ἐμὸν ὄνομα βεβηλωται. The Syr. and Vulg. get over the difficulty, by making the verb in the first person, that *I may not be blasphemed.*

12. —*O Jacob, my servant*] After יעקב, a MS, and the two old editions of 1486 and 1488, add the word עבדי, which is lost out of the present text; and there is a rasure in its place in another ancient MS. The Jerusalem Talmud has the same word.

Ibid. For אף אני, *even* I, two ancient MSS, and the ancient versions, read ואני, *and* I; more properly.

14. *Who among you*—] For בהם, among *them*, twenty-one MSS (nine ancient), and two editions (one of them that of the year 1488), have בכם, among *you;* and so the Syriac.

Ibid. *He, whom* JEHOVAH *hath loved, will execute*] That is, Cyrus: so Symmachus has well rendered it; Ὃν ὁ Κύριος ἠγάπησε, ποιήσει τὸ θέλημα αὐτοῦ.

Ibid. —*on the Chaldeans*] The preposition is lost; it is supplied in the edition of 1486, which has בכשדים; and so Chald. and Vulg.

16. *Draw near unto me, and hear ye this*] After the word קרבו, *draw near*, a MS adds גוים, *O ye nations;* which, as this and the two preceding verses are plainly addressed to the idolatrous nations, reproaching their gods as unable to predict future events, is probably genuine.

Ibid. —and *hear*—] A MS adds the conjunction, ושמעו; and so LXX, Syr. Vulg.

Ibid. —*I have not spoken in secret*] The Alexandrine copy of LXX adds here, Οὐδὲ ἐν τόπῳ γῆς σκοτεινῷ, *nor in a dark place of the earth*, as in xlv. 19. That it stands rightly, or at least stood very early, in this place of the version of the

LXX, is highly probable; because it is acknowledged by the Arabic version, and by the Coptic, MS St Germain de Prez, Paris, translated likewise from the LXX. But whether it should be inserted as of right belonging to the Hebrew text, may be doubted; for a transcriber of the Greek version might easily add it by memory from the parallel place; and it is not necessary to the sense.

Ibid. —*when it began to exist*] An ancient MS has היותם, *they* began to exist: and so another had it at first.

Ibid. *I had decreed it*] I take שם for a verb, not an adverb.

Ibid. *And now the Lord JEHOVAH hath sent me, and his Spirit*] Τις εςιν ὁ εν τῳ Ηςαιᾳ λεγων; καν νυν Κυριος απεςειλε με και το Πνευμα αυτου· εν ᾡ αμφιβολου οντος του ῥητου, ποτερον ὁ Πατηρ και το Ἁγιον Πνευμα απεςειλαν τον Ιησουν, ἢ ὁ Πατηρ απεςειλε τον τε Χριςον και το Ἁγιον Πνευμα· το δευτερον εςιν αληθες: "Who is it that saith in Isaiah, And now the Lord hath sent me and his Spirit? in which, as the expression is ambiguous, is it the Father and the Holy Spirit who hath sent Jesus; or the Father who hath sent both Christ and the Holy Spirit? The latter is the true interpretation:" Origen. cont. Cels. lib. i. I have kept to the order of the words of the original, on purpose that the ambiguity, which Origen remarks in the version of LXX, and which is the same in the Hebrew, might still remain, and the sense which he gives to it be offered to the reader's judgment; which is wholly excluded in our vulgar translation.

18. *like the river*] That is, the Euphrates.

19. —*like that of the bowels thereof*] והם כצאצאי מעי הים הרגים : "As the issue of the bowels of the sea; that is, the fishes;" Salom. b. Melec. And so likewise Aben Ezra, Jarchi, Kimchi, &c.

Ibid. *Thy name*] For שמו, *his* name, the LXX had in the copy from which they translated שמך, *thy* name.

20. —*and make it heard*—] Twenty-seven MSS (ten ancient), and one edition, prefix to the verb the conjunction ו, והשמיעו.

21. *They thirsted not in the deserts*—] Kimchi has a surprising observation upon this place: "If the prophecy," says he, "relates to the return from the Babylonish captivity, as it seems to do, it is to be wondered how it comes to pass, that in the book of Ezra, in which he gives an account of their return, no mention is made that such miracles were

wrought for them; as, for instance, that God clave the rock for them in the desert." It is really much to be wondered, that one of the most learned and judicious of the Jewish expositors of the Old Testament, having advanced so far in a large comment on Isaiah, should appear to be totally ignorant of the Prophet's manner of writing; of the parabolic style which prevails in the writings of all the Prophets; and more particularly in the Prophecy of Isaiah, which abounds throughout in parabolic images from the beginning to the end; from "Hear, O heavens, and give ear, O earth," to "the worm and the fire" in the last verse. And how came he to keep his wonderment to himself so long? Why did he not expect, that the historian should have related, how, as they passed through the desert, cedars, pines, and olive-trees, shot up at once on the side of the way to shade them; and that, instead of briers and brambles, the accacia and the myrtle sprung up under their feet, according to God's promises, chap. xli. 19. and lv. 13.? These, and a multitude of the like parabolical or poetical images, were never intended to be understood literally: all that the Prophet designed in this place, and which he has executed in the most elegant manner, was an amplification and illustration of the gracious care and protection of God, vouchsafed to his people in their return from Babylon, by an allusion to the miraculous Exodus from Egypt. See De S. Poesi Hebr. Præl. ix.

22 *There is no peace, saith* JEHOVAH, *to the wicked.*] See below, note on chap. lvii. 21.

CHAPTER XLIX.

1. *Hearken unto me, O ye distant lands*—] Hitherto the subject of the prophecy has been chiefly confined to the redemption from the captivity of Babylon; with strong intimations of a more important deliverance sometimes thrown in; to the refutation of idolatry; and the demonstration of the infinite power, wisdom, and foreknowledge of God. The character and office of the Messiah was exhibited in general terms at the beginning of chap. xlii. but here he is introduced in person, declaring the full extent of his commission; which is not only to restore the Israelites, and reconcile them to their Lord and Father, from whom they had

so often revolted; but to be a light to lighten the Gentiles, to call them to the knowledge and obedience of the true God, and to bring them to be one church together with the Israelites, and to partake with them of the same common salvation procured for all by the great Redeemer and Reconciler of man to God.

2. *And he hath made my mouth a sharp sword*—] The servant of God, who speaks in the former part of this chapter, must be the Messiah. If any part of this character can, in any sense, belong to the Prophet, yet in some parts it must belong exclusively to Christ; and, in all parts, to him in a much fuller and more proper sense. Isaiah's mission was to the Jews, not to the distant nations, to whom the speaker in this place addresses himself. "He hath made my mouth a sharp sword," "to reprove the wicked, and to denounce unto them punishment," says Jarchi, understanding it of Isaiah; but how much better does it suit him, who is represented as having "a sharp two-edged sword going out of his mouth," Rev. i. 16. who is himself the Word of God? which "Word is quick and powerful, and sharper than any two-edged sword, piercing even to the dividing asunder of soul and spirit, and of the joints and marrow, and a discerner of the thoughts and intents of the heart;" Heb. iv. 12. This mighty agent and instrument of God, "long laid up in store with him, and sealed up among his treasures," is at last revealed, and produced by his power, and under his protection, to execute his great and holy purposes: he is compared to a polished shaft stored in his quiver for use in his due time. The polished shaft denotes the same efficacious word, which is before represented by the sharp sword. The doctrine of the gospel pierced the hearts of its hearers, "bringing into captivity every thought to the obedience of Christ." The metaphor of the sword and the arrow, applied to powerful speech, is bold, yet just. It has been employed by the most ingenious heathen writers, if with equal elegance, not with equal force. It is said of Pericles by Aristophanes, (see Cicero, Epist. ad Atticum, xii. 6.)—

Ουτως εκηλει, και μονος των ρητορων
Το κεντρον εγκατελειπε τοις ακροωμενοις. Apud Diod. lib. xii.

His powerful speech
Pierced the hearer's soul, and left behind
Deep in his bosom its keen point infixt.

Pindar is particularly fond of this metaphor, and frequently applies it to his own poetry:—

Επεχε νυν σκοπῳ τοξον,
Αγε, θυμε. τινα βαλλομεν
Εκ μαλθακας αυτε φρε-
νος ευκλεας οϊσους
Ιεντες;   Olymp. ii. 160.

" Come on! thy brightest shafts prepare,
And bend, O Muse, thy sounding bow;
Say, through what paths of liquid air
Our arrows shall we throw?"   West.

See also ver. 149. of the same ode, and Olymp. ix. 17.; on the former of which places the Scholiast says, τροπικος ὁ λογος· βελη δε τους λογους ειρηκε, δια το οξυ και καιριον των εγκωμιων: " He calls his verses shafts by a metaphor, signifying the acuteness and the apposite application of his panegyric."

This person who is, ver. 3. called Israel, cannot in any sense be Isaiah. That name, in its original design and full import, can only belong to him who contended powerfully with God in behalf of mankind, and prevailed: Gen. xxxii. 28.

5. *And now thus saith JEHOVAH*] The word כה, before אמר, is dropt out of the text: it is supplied by eight MSS (two ancient), and LXX, Syr. Vulg.

Ibid. *And that Israel unto him may be gathered*] Five MSS (two ancient), confirm the *Keri*, or marginal correction of the Masoretes, לו, *unto him*, instead of לא; *not*, in the text; and so read Aquila and Chald.: LXX and Arab. omit the negative. But LXX, MSS Pachom. and i. D. ii. express also the *Keri* לו by προς αυτον.

6. *And to restore the branches of Israel*] נצירי, or נצורי, as the Masoretes correct it in the marginal reading. This word has been matter of great doubt with interpreters: the Syriac renders it *the branch*, taking it for the same with נצי, chap. xi. l.: see Michaelis, Epim. in Prælect. xix.

7. *The Redeemer of Israel, his Holy One*] " Forte, לקדושׁ;" SECKER: that is, to his Holy One. The preceding word ends with a ל, which might occasion that letter's being lost here. The Talmud of Babylon has וקדושׁ.

Ibid. *To him, whose person is despised*] " Forte, נבזה;" SECKER: or בזוי, Le Clerc: that is, instead of the active, the passive form, which seems here to be required.

9. *And to those that are in darkness*—] Fifteen MSS (five ancient), and the two old editions of 1486 and 1488, add the conjunction ו at the beginning of this member: another MS had it so at first; and two others have a rasure at the place: and it is expressed by LXX, Syr. Chald. Vulg.

12. *Lo! and these shall come from afar*] "Babylon was far, and east, ממזרח; (non sic Vett.); Sinim, Pelusians, to the south:" SECKER.

Ibid. —*the land of Sinim*] Prof. Deoderlein thought of Syene, the southern limit of Egypt; but does not abide by it. Michaelis thinks it is right; and promises to give his reasons for so thinking in the second part of his Specilegium Geographiæ Hebræorum Exteræ. See Biblioth. Oriental. Part XI. p. 176.

13. *Ye mountains burst forth*] Three ancient MSS are without either the י, or the conjunction ו, before the verb: and so LXX, Syr. Vulg.

16. *Behold, on the palms of my hands have I delineated thee*] This is certainly an allusion to some practice, common among the Jews at that time, of making marks on their hands or arms by punctures on the skin, with some sort of sign or representation of the city or temple, to shew their affection and zeal for it. They had a method of making such punctures indelible by fire, or by staining. See note on chap. xliv. 5. It is well known, that the pilgrims at the holy sepulchre get themselves marked in this manner with what are called the ensigns of Jerusalem; Maundrell, p. 75.; where he tells us how it is performed: and this art is practised by travelling Jews all over the world at this day.

17. *They that destroyed thee shall soon become thy builders*] "Auctor Vulgatæ pro בָּנַיִךְ videtur legisse בּוֹנַיִךְ, unde vertit, *structores tui;* cui et LXX fere consentiunt, qui verterunt ῳκοδομηθης, *ædificata es,* prout in Plantiniana editione habetur; in Vaticana sive Romana legitur, οικοδομηθηση, *ædificaberis.* Hisce etiam Targum Jonathanis aliquatenus consentit, ubi, *et ædificabunt.* Confer infra Esai. cap. liv. ver. 13. ad quem locum Rabbini quoque notarunt ex tractatu Talmudico Berachot. cap. ix. quod non legendum sit בָּנַיִךְ, id est, *filii tui;* sed בּוֹנַיִךְ, *ædificatores tui.* Confer not. ad librum Prec. Jud. Part. II. p. 226. ut et D. Wagenseil Sot. p. 253. n. 9.:" Breithaupt. not. ad Jarchi in loc. See also note on this place in De Sac. Poes. Hebr. Prælect. xxxi.

Ibid.—*shall become thine offspring*] ממך יצאו, shall proceed, spring, issue, from thee,—as thy children. The phrase is frequently used in this sense: see chap. xi. 1. Micah v. 2. Nahum i. 11. The accession of the Gentiles to the church of God is considered as an addition made to the number of the family and children of Sion: see ver. 21, 22. and chap. lx. 4. The common rendering, "shall go forth of thee, or depart from thee," is very flat, after their zeal had been expressed by " shall become thy builders; " and as the opposition is kept up in one part of the sentence, one has reason to expect it in the other, which should have been parallel to it.

18. *And bind them about thee, as a bride*—] The end of the sentence is manifestly imperfect. Does a bride bind her children, or her new subjects, about her? Sion clothes herself with her children, as a bride clothes herself—with what? some other thing certainly. The LXX help us out in this difficulty, and supply the lost word: ὡς κοσμον νυμφη· ככליח כלה, or ככלה כליה. The great similitude of the two words has occasioned the omission of one of them. See chap. lxi. 10.

21. —*these then, where were they?*] The conjunction is added before אלה, that is, ואלה, in above thirty MSS (nine ancient).; and so LXX, Chald. Vulg.

23. *With their faces to the earth*—] It is well known, that expressions of submission, homage, and reverence, always have been, and are still, carried to a great degree of extravagance in the eastern countries. When Joseph's brethren were introduced to him, " they bowed down themselves before him with their faces to the earth; " Gen. xlii. 6. The kings of Persia never admitted any one to their presence without exacting this act of adoration; for that was the proper term for it. " Necesse est," says the Persian courtier to Conon, " si in conspectum veneris, venerari te regem ; quod προσκυνειν illi vocant ; " Nepos in Conone. Alexander, intoxicated with success, affected this piece of oriental pride: " Itaque more Persarum Macedonas venerabundos ipsum salutare, prosternentes humi corpora:" Curtius, lib. viii. The insolence of eastern monarchs to conquered princes, and the submission of the latter, is astonishing. Mr. Harmer, Obs. ii. 43. gives the following instance of it from D'Herbelot;—" This prince threw himself one day on the ground, and kissed the prints that his victorious enemy's

horse had made there; reciting some verses in Persian, which he had composed, to this effect:—

"The mark that the foot of your horse has left upon the dust, serves me now for a crown.

"The ring, which I wear as the badge of my slavery, is become my richest ornament.

"While I shall have the happiness to kiss the dust of your feet, I shall think that fortune favours me with its tenderest caresses, and its sweetest kisses."

These expressions, therefore, of the Prophet, are only general poetical images, taken from the manners of the country, to denote great respect and reverence: and such splendid poetical images, which frequently occur in the prophetical writings, were intended only as general amplifications of the subject, not as predictions to be understood and fulfilled precisely according to the letter.

24. *Shall the prey seized by the terrible be rescued?*] For צדיק read עריץ. A palpable mistake, like that in chap. xlii. 19. The correction is self-evident from the very terms of the sentence; from the necessity of the strict correspondence in the expressions between the question and the answer made to it; and it is apparent to the blindest and most prejudiced eye. However, if authority is also necessary, there is that of Syr. and Vulg. for it; who plainly read עריץ in the 24th as well as in the 25th verse, rendering it in the former place by the same word as in the latter.

CHAPTER L.

1. *Where is this bill*—] Husbands, through moroseness or levity of temper, often sent bills of divorcement to their wives on slight occasions, as they were permitted to do by the law of Moses, Deut. xxiv. 1. And fathers, being oppressed with debt, often sold their children; which they might do, for a time, till the year of release: Exod. xxi. 7. That this was frequently practised, appears from many passages of Scripture; and that the persons and the liberty of the children were answerable for the debts of the father. The widow, 2 Kings iv. 1. complains, "that the creditor is come to take unto him her two sons to be bondmen." And in the parable, Matt. xviii. 25. "The lord, forasmuch as his servant had not to pay, commands him to be sold, and

his wife and children, and all that he had, and payment to be made." Sir John Chardin's MSS note on this place of Isaiah is as follows: "En Orient, on paye ses dettes avec ses esclaves, car ils sont des principaux meubles; et en plusieurs lieux on les paye aussi de ses enfans." But this, saith God, cannot be my case: I am not governed by any such motives; neither am I urged by any such necessity: your captivity, therefore, and your afflictions, are to be imputed to yourselves, and to your own folly and wickedness.

2. *Their fish is dried up*] For תבאש, *stinketh*, read תיבש, *is dried up:* so it stands in the Bodleian MS, and it is confirmed by the LXX, ξηρανθήσονται.

5. *Neither did I withdraw*—] Eleven MSS, and the oldest edition, prefix the conjunction ו; and so also LXX and Syr.

6· *And my cheeks to them that plucked off the hair*] The greatest indignity that could possibly be offered. See note on chap. vii. 20.

Ibid. *My face I hid not from shame and spitting*] Another instance of the utmost contempt and detestation. It was ordered by the law of Moses, as a severe punishment, carrying with it a lasting disgrace: Deut. xxv. 9. Among the Medes, it was highly offensive to spit in any one's presence, Herod. i. 99.; and so likewise among the Persians, Xenophon. Cyrop. lib. i. p. 18.

"They abhor me; they flee far from me;
They forbear not to spit in my face." Job. xxx. 10.

And JEHOVAH said unto Moses: "If her father had but spit in her face, should she not be ashamed seven days?" Numb. xii. 14.; on which place Sir John Chardin remarks, "that spitting before any one, or spitting upon the ground in speaking of any one's actions, is through the East an expression of extreme detestation:" Harmer's Observ. ii. 509. See also, of the same notions of the Arabs in this respect, Niebuhr, Description de l'Arabie, p. 26. It so evidently appears, that in those countries spitting has ever been an expression of the utmost detestation, that the learned doubt whether in the passages of Scripture above quoted, any thing more is meant than spitting (not in the face, which perhaps the words do not necessarily imply, but only) in the presence of the person affronted. But in this place it certainly means spitting in the face: so it is understood in St Luke, where our Lord plainly refers to this prophecy:—"All things that are written by the Prophets concerning the Son of Man shall be accomplished; for he shall be delivered to the Gentiles, and shall be mocked and spitefully entreated, and spitted on, εμπτυσθησεται," xviii. 31, 32.; which was in fact fulfilled; και ηρξαντο τινες εμπτυειν αυτω, Mark xiv. 65. xv. 19. If spitting in a person's presence was such an indignity, how much more spitting in his face?

7. *Therefore have I set my face as a flint*—] The Prophet Ezekiel has expressed this with great force, in his bold and vehement manner:

"Behold, I have made thy face strong against their faces,
And thy forehead strong against their foreheads:
As an adamant, harder than a rock, have I made thy forehead.
Fear them not, neither be dismayed at their looks,
Though they be a rebellious house." Ezek. iii. 8. 9.

8. *Who is he that will contend*—] The Bodleian MS, and another, add the word הוא ; מי הוא יריב, as in the like phrase in the next verse: and in the very same phrase, Job xiii. 19., and so likewise in many other places, Job xvii. 3. xli. 1. Sometimes, on the like occasions, it is מי זה, and מי הוא זה. The word has been probably lost out of the present text; and the reading of the MS above-mentioned seems to be genuine.

10. *Let him hearken to the voice of his servant.*] For שמע, pointed as the participle, the LXX and Syr. read ישמע, future or imperative: this gives a much more elegant turn and distribution to the sentence.

11. —*ye who kindle a fire*—] The fire of their own kindling, by the light of which they walk with security and satisfaction, is an image designed to express, in general, human devices, and mere worldly policy, exclusive of faith and trust in God; which, though they flatter them for a while with pleasing expectations and some appearance of success, shall in the end turn to the confusion of the authors. Or, more particularly, as Vitringa explains it, it may mean the designs of the turbulent and factious Jews in the times succeeding those of Christ; who, in pursuit of their own desperate schemes, stirred up the war against the Romans, and kindled a fire which consumed their city and nation.

Ibid. —*who heap the fuel round about*] "מגוזלי, accendentes, Syr. forte legerunt [pro מאזרי] מאירי; nam sequitur אור:" SECKER. Lud. Capellus, in his critical notes on this place, thinks it should be מעורי, from the LXX, κατισχυοντες.

CHAPTER LI.

4. —*O ye people ; O ye nations*] For עמי, *my people*, the Bodley MS, and another, read עמים, *ye peoples;* and for לאומי, *my nation*, the Bodley MS, and eight others (two of them ancient), read לאמים, *ye nations;* and so the Syriac in both words. The difference is very material: for in this case the address is made, not to the Jews, but to the Gentiles, as in all reason it ought to be; for this and the two following verses express the call of the Gentiles, the islands, or the distant lands on the coasts of the Mediterranean and other seas. It is also to be observed, that God in no other place calls his people לאמי. It has been before remarked, that transcribers frequently omitted the final ם of nouns plural, and supplied it, for brevity-sake, and sometimes for want of room at the end of a line, by a small stroke thus, 'עמ; which mark, being effaced or overlooked, has been the occasion of many mistakes of this kind.

5. *My righteousness is at hand*—] The word צדק, *righteousness*, is used in such a great latitude of signification, for justice, truth, faithfulness, goodness, mercy, deliverance, salvation, &c., that it is not easy sometimes to give the precise meaning of it without much circumlocution: it means here the faithful completion of God's promises to deliver his people.

11. —*shall they obtain, and sorrow and sighing shall flee away*] Nineteen MSS, and the two oldest editions, have ישיגו; and forty-six MSS, and the same two editions, and agreeably to them Chald. and Syr. have ונסו: and so both words are expressed, chap. xxxv. 10. of which place this is a repetition. And from comparing both together it appears, that the ו in this place is become by mistake in the present text the final ן of the preceding word.

13. —*of the oppressor, as if he*—] " The כ in כאשר seems clearly to have changed its situation from the end of the preceding word to the beginning of this; or rather, to have been omitted by mistake there, because it was here. That it was there, the LXX shew by rendering המציקך, θλίβοντος σε, of him that oppressed *thee*. And so they render this word in both its places in this verse. The Vulgate also has the pronoun in the first instance: furoris ejus qui *te* tribulabat:" Dr. JUBB. The correction seems well founded. I have not

conformed the translation to it, because it makes very little difference in the sense.

14. *He marcheth on with speed*—] Cyrus, if understood of the temporal redemption from the captivity of Babylon; in the spiritual sense, the Messiah.

16. *To stretch out the heavens*] In the present text it is לנטע, *to plant* the heavens. The phrase is certainly very obscure, and in all probability is a mistake for לנטות. This latter is the word used in ver. 13. just before, in the very same sentence; and this phrase occurs frequently in Isaiah, chap. xl. 22. xlii. 5. xliv. 24. xlv. 12.; the former in no other place. It is also very remarkable, that in the Samaritan text, Numb. xxiv. 6. these two words are twice changed, by mistake, one for the other, in the same verse.

19. *These two things—desolation and destruction, the famine and the sword*] That is, desolation by famine, and destruction by the sword; taking the terms alternately: of which form of construction see other examples, De S. Poesi Heb. Præl. xix. and Prelim. Dissert. p. xix. The Chaldee paraphrast, not rightly understanding this, has had recourse to the following expedient: "Two afflictions are come upon thee,—and when *four* shall come upon thee, *depredation* and *destruction*, and the *famine* and the *sword*—" Five MSS have הרעב, without the conjunction ו; and so LXX and Syr.

Ibid. —*Who shall comfort thee?*] A MS, LXX, Syr. Chald. and Vulg. have it in the third person, ינחמך; which is evidently right.

20. —*in the toils, drenched to the full*—] "Forte מכמרה מלאים:" Secker. The demonstrative ה, prefixed to מלאים, seems improper in this place.

21. *And thou drunken, but not with wine.*] Æschylus has the same expression:

Αοινοις εμμανεις θυμωμασι.   Eumen. 863.
Intoxicate with passion, not with wine.

Schultens thinks, that this circumlocution, as he calls it, "gradum adfert incomparabiliter majorem;" and that it means not simply *without wine*, but *much more than with wine:* Gram. Hebr. p. 182. See his note on Job xxx. 28.

The bold image of the cup of God's wrath, often employed by the sacred writers, (see note on chap. i. 22.), is no where handled with greater force and sublimity than in this passage of Isaiah, ver. 17—23. Jerusalem is represented in person as staggering under the effects of it, destitute of that assistance which she might expect from her children; not one of them being able to support or to lead her. They, abject and amazed, lie at the head of every street, overwhelmed with the greatness of their distress: like the oryx entangled in a net, in vain struggling to rend it, and extricate himself. This is poetry of the first order, sublimity of the highest proof.

Plato had an idea something like this: " Suppose, says he, God had given to men a medicating potion inducing fear; so that the more any one should drink of it, so much the more miserable he should find himself at every draught, and become fearful of every thing both present and future; and at last, though the most courageous of men, should be totally possessed by fear; and afterward, having slept off the effects of it, should become himself again:" De Leg. i. near the end. He pursues at large this hypothesis, applying it to his purpose, which has no relation to the present subject. Homer places two vessels at the threshold of Jupiter, one of good, the other of evil: he gives to some a potion mixed of both, to others from the evil vessel only: these are completely miserable: Iliad. xxvi. 527.

23. —*who oppress thee*] " Videntur, LXX, Chald. Syr. Vulg. legisse מוניך, ut xl. 26.:" Secker. And so it is in edit. Gersom.

Ibid. *That say to thee, Bow down thy body*] A very strong and most expressive description of the insolent pride of eastern conquerors; which, though it may seem greatly exaggerated, yet hardly exceeds the strict truth. An example has already been given of it in note to chap. xlix. 23. I will here add one or two more. " Joshua called for all the men of Israel; and said unto the captains of the men of war that went with him: Come near, put your feet upon the necks of these kings;" Josh. x. 24. " Adonibezek said, Threescore and ten kings, having their thumbs and their great toes cut off, gathered their meat under my table: as I have done, so hath God requited me;" Judg. i. 7. The Emperor Valerianus being through treachery taken prisoner by Sapor king of Persia, was treated by him as the basest and most abject slave: for the Persian monarch commanded the unhappy Roman to bow himself down, and offer him his back, on which he set his foot, in order to mount his chariot or his horse, whenever he had occasion: Lactantius, De Mort. Persec. cap. v.; Aurel. Victor. Epitome, cap. xxxii.

CHAPTER LII.

2. —*ascend thy lofty seat*] The literal rendering here is, according to our English translation, "arise, sit:" on which a very learned person remarks; "So the old versions. But sitting is an expression of mourning in Scripture and the ancients; and doth not well agree with the rising just before." It doth not indeed agree according to our ideas; but considered in an oriental light, it is perfectly consistent. The common manner of sitting in the eastern countries is upon the ground or floor, with the legs crossed. The people of better condition have the floors of their chambers or divans covered with carpets for this purpose; and round the chamber broad couches, raised a little above the floor, spread with mattresses handsomely covered, which are called sophas. When sitting is spoken of as a posture of more than ordinary state, it is quite of a different kind; and means sitting on high, on a chair of state or throne; for which a footstool was necessary, both in order that the person might raise himself up to it, and for supporting the legs when he was placed in it. "Chairs (saith Sir John Chardin) are never used in Persia but at the coronation of their kings. The king is seated in a chair of gold set with jewels, three feet high.—The chairs which are used by the people in the East are always so high as to make a footstool necessary. And this proves the propriety of the style of Scripture, which always joins the footstool to the throne:" (Isa. lxvi. 1. Psal. cx. 1,): Voyages, tom. ix, p. 85. 12mo. Beside the six steps to Solomon's throne, there was a footstool of gold fastened to the seat, 2 Chron. ix. 18. which would otherwise have been too high for the king to reach, or to sit on conveniently.

When Thetis comes to wait on Vulcan to request armour for her son, she is received with great respect, and seated on a silver-studded throne, a chair of ceremony, with a footstool:—

Την μεν επειτα καθεισεν επι θρονου αργυροηλυ,
Καλυ, δαιδαλευ· υπο δε θρηνυς ποσιν ηεν.   Iliad. xviii. 389.

"High on a throne, with stars of silver graced,
 And various artifice, the queen she placed;
 A footstool at her feet."   Pope.

Ο γαρ θρονος αυτος μονον ελευθεριος εςι καθεδρα συν υποποδιω: Athenæus, v. 4.: "A throne is nothing more than a handsome sort of chair, with a footstool."

5. *And they that are lords over them*—] For משלו, singular, in the text, more than a hundred and twenty MSS have משליו, plural, according to the Masoretical correction in the margin : which shews, that the Masoretes often superstitiously retained apparent mistakes in the text, even when they had sufficient evidence to authorize the introduction of the true reading.

Ibid. —*make their boast of it*] For יהלילו; "make them to howl," five MSS (two ancient) have יהללו, "make their boast;" which is confirmed by the Chaldee paraphrast, who renders it משתבחין.

6. *Therefore shall my people*—] The word לכן, occurring the second time in this verse, seems to be repeated by mistake. It has no force or emphasis as a repetition; it only embarrasses the construction and the sense. It was not in the copies from which the LXX, Syr. and Vulg. were translated; it was not in the copy of LXX from which the Arabic was translated: but in the Aldine and Complutensian editions δια τετο is repeated; probably so corrected, in order to make it conformable with the Hebrew text.

Ibid. *For I am He that promised*] For הוא, the Bodley MS, and another, have יהוה; "for I am JEHOVAH that promised:" and another ancient MS adds יהוה after הוא. The addition of JEHOVAH seems to be right, in consequence of what was said in the preceding line, "My people shall know my *name*."

7. *How beautiful*—] The watchmen discover afar off, on the mountains, the messenger bringing the expected and much wished-for news of the deliverance from the Babylonish captivity. They immediately spread the joyful tidings, ver. 8. and with a loud voice proclaim that JEHOVAH is returning to Sion, to resume his residence on his holy mountain, which for some time he seemed to have deserted. This is the literal sense of the place.

"How beautiful on the mountains are the feet of the joyful messenger," is an expression highly poetical; for, how welcome is his arrival! how agreeable are the tidings which he brings!

Nahum, who is generally supposed to have lived after

Isaiah, has manifestly taken from him this very pleasing image; but the imitation does not equal the beauty of the original:

" Behold upon the mountains the feet of the joyful messenger,
Of him that announceth peace:
Celebrate, O Judah, thy festivals; perform thy vows:
For no more shall pass through thee the wicked one;
He is utterly cut off. Nah. i. 15.

But it must at the same time be observed, that Isaiah's subject is infinitely more interesting, and more sublime, than that of Nahum: The latter denounces the destruction of the capital of the Assyrian empire, the most formidable enemy of Judah; the ideas of the former are in their full extent evangelical: and accordingly St Paul has, with the utmost propriety, applied this passage to the preaching of the gospel, Rom. x. 15. The joyful tidings here to be proclaimed, " Thy God, O Sion, reigneth," are the same that John the Baptist, the messenger of Christ, and that Christ himself published, " The kingdom of heaven is at hand."

8. *All thy watchmen*—] There is a difficulty in the construction of this place, which, I think, none of the ancient versions, or modern interpreters, have cleared up to satisfaction. Rendered word for word it stands thus: " The voice of thy watchmen: they lift up their voice." The sense of the first member, considered as elliptical, is variously supplied by various expositors; by none, as it seems to me, in any way that is easy and natural. I am persuaded there is a mistake in the present text, and that the true reading is כל צפיך, "all thy watchmen;" instead of קול צפיך. The mistake was easy from the similitude in sound of the two letters כ and ק. And in one MS the ק is upon a rasure. This correction perfectly rectifies the sense and the construction.

Ibid. —*when JEHOVAH returneth to Sion.*] So the Chaldee: כד יתיב שכנתיה לציון, " when he shall bring back his presence to Sion." God is considered as having deserted his people during the captivity; and, at the restoration, as returning himself with them to Sion his former habitation: See Psal. lx. 1. chap. xl. 9. and note.

9. —*he hath redeemed Israel*] For the word ירושלם, which occurs the second time in this verse, MS Bodley, and another, read ישראל. It is upon a rasure in a third; and left unpointed at first, as suspected, in a fourth. It was an easy mistake, by the transcriber's casting his eye on the line

above; and the propriety of the correction, both in regard to sense and elegance, is evident.

11. *Depart, depart ye; go ye out from thence*] The Prophet Jeremiah seems to have had his eye on this passage of Isaiah, and to have applied it to a subject directly opposite. It is here addressed by the Prophet in the way of encouragement and exhortation to the Jews coming out of Babylon: Jeremiah has given it a different turn, and has thrown it out as a reproach of the heathen upon the Jews, when they were driven from Jerusalem into captivity:

"Depart; ye are polluted, depart; depart ye, forbear to touch:
Yea, they are fled, they are removed: they shall dwell here
    no more."   Lam. iv. 15.

Of the metrical distribution of these lines, see the Prelim. Dissertation, p. xxxvi. note.

13. The subject of Isaiah's prophecy, from the fortieth chapter inclusive, has hitherto been, in general, the deliverance of the people of God. This includes in it three distinct parts; which, however, have a close connexion with one another: that is, the deliverance of the Jews from the captivity of Babylon; the deliverance of the Gentiles from their miserable state of ignorance and idolatry; and the deliverance of mankind from the captivity of sin and death. These three subjects are subordinate to one another; and the two latter are shadowed out under the image of the former. They are covered by it as by a veil; which however is transparent, and suffers them to appear through it. Cyrus is expressly named as the immediate agent of God in effecting the first deliverance: A greater Person is spoken of as the agent who is to effect the two latter deliverances; called the servant, the elect of God, in whom his soul delighteth; Israel, in whom God will be glorified. Now these three subjects have a very near relation to one another; for, as the agent who was to effect the two latter deliverances, that is, the Messiah, was to be born a Jew, with particular limitations of time, family, and other circumstances; the first deliverance was necessary in the order of Providence, and according to the determinate counsel of God, to the accomplishment of the two latter deliverances; and the second deliverance was necessary to the third, or rather, was involved in it, and made an essential part of it. This being the case, Isaiah has not treated the three subjects as quite distinct and separate in a methodical and orderly manner,

like a philosopher or a logician, but has taken them in their connective view: he has handled them as a prophet and a poet; he hath allegorized the former, and under the image of it has shadowed out the two latter; he has thrown them all together; has mixed one with another, has passed from this to that with rapid transitions, and has painted the whole with the strongest and boldest imagery. The restoration of the Jews from captivity, the call of the Gentiles, the redemption by Messiah, have hitherto been handled interchangeably and alternately: Babylon has hitherto been kept pretty much in sight; at the same time that strong intimations of something much greater have frequently been thrown in. But here Babylon is at once dropped; and I think hardly ever comes in sight again; unless perhaps in chap. lv. 12. and lvii. 14. The Prophet's views are almost wholly engrossed by the superior part of his subject. He introduces the Messiah as appearing at first in the lowest state of humiliation, which he had just touched upon before, chap. l. 5, 6. and obviates the offence which would be occasioned by it, by declaring the important and necessary cause of it, and foreshewing the glory which should follow it.

This seems to me to be the nature and the true design of this part of Isaiah's prophecies; and this view of them seems to afford the best method of resolving difficulties in which expositors are frequently engaged, being much divided between what is called the literal and the mystical sense—not very properly; for the mystical or spiritual sense is very often the most literal sense of all.

Abarbanel seems to have had an idea of this kind, as he is quoted by Vitringa on chap. xlix. 1. who thus represents his sentiments: " Censet Abarbanel Prophetam hic *transitum* facere a *liberatione ex exilio Babylonico* ad *liberationem ex exilio Romano*, (for this he takes to be the secondary sense); et, quod hic animadversu dignum est, observat liberationem ex exilio Babylonico esse אות וראיה, signum et argumentum liberationis futuræ; atque adeo orationem Prophetæ de duabus hisce liberationibus in superioribus concionibus sæpe inter se permisceri. Verba ejus: ' Et propterea verba, sive res, in prophetia superiore inter se permixtæ occurrunt; modo de liberatione Babylonica, modo de liberatione extrema accipiendæ, ut orationis necessitas exigit.' Nullum hic vitium, nisi quod redemptionem veram et spiritualem a Messia vero Jesu adductam non agnoscat."

14. —*were astonished at him*] For עליך read עליו: so Syr. Chald. and Vulg. in a MS; and so likewise two ancient MSS.

15. *So shall he sprinkle many nations*] I retain the common rendering, though I am by no means satisfied with it. "יזה, frequent in the law, means only to sprinkle: but the water sprinkled is the accusative case; the thing, on which, has על or אל. Θαυμασονται, ὁ, makes the best apodosis. ינהג would do. ינהרו is used ii. 2. Jer. xxxi. 12. li. 44. but is unlike. Kings shall shut, &c. is good; but seems to want a first part:" SECKER. Munster translates it, "Faciet loqui (de se);" and in his note thus explains it: "יזה proprie significat spargere et stillas disseminare: hic vero capitur pro loqui, et verbum disseminare." This is pretty much as the Rabbins, Kimchi, and Salomo ben Melec, explain it, referring to the expression of "dropping the word." But the same objection lies to this as to the common rendering; it ought to be יזה (דבר) על גוים. Bishop Chandler, Defence, p. 148. says, "that to sprinkle, is used for to surprise and astonish, as people are that have much water thrown upon them. And this sense is followed by the LXX." This is ingenious, but rather too refined. Dr DURELL conjectures, that the true reading may be יחזו, they shall *regard*, which comes near to the θαυμασονται of the LXX; who seem to give the best sense of any to the place.

"I find in my papers the same conjecture which Dr DURELL made from θαυμασονται in LXX. And it may be added, that חזה is used to express "looking on any thing with admiration;" Psal. xi. 7. and xvii. 15. and xxvii. 4. and lxiii. 2. Cant. vi. 13. It is particularly applied to "looking on God," Exod. xxiv. 11. and Job xix. 26. Gisbert Cuper, in Observat. lib. ii. 1. though *aliud agens*, has some observations which shew how nearly ὁραω and θαυμαζω are allied, which (with the peculiar sense of the verb חזה above noted) add to the probability of θαυμασονται being the version of יחזו in the text: οἱ δε νυ λαοι Παντες ες αυτον ὁρωσι. Hesiod. id est, cum veneratione quadam admirantur. Hinc ὁραω et θαυμαζω junxit Themistius Or. 1. Εἶτα παυσονται οἱ ανθρωποι προς σε μονον ὁρωντες, και σε μονον θαυμαζοντες. Theophrastus in Charact. cap. iii. Ενθυμη ὡς αποβλεπουσιν εις σε οἱ ανθρωποι. Hence the rendering of this verse seems to be:—

So many nations shall look on him with admiration;
Kings shall stop their mouths—" Dr JUBB.

CHAPTER LIII.

2. *He hath no form, nor any beauty—*] Ουκ ειδος αυτω, ȣδε αξιωμα, ινα ειδωμεν αυτον· ȣδε θεωρια, ινα επιθυμωμεν αυτον: Symmachus; the only one of the ancients that has translated it rightly.

3. —*and acquainted with grief—*] For וידוע, eight MSS and one edition have וידע; LXX, Syr. and Vulg. read it וידֹע.

Ibid. —*as one that hideth his face*] For וכמסתר, four MSS (two ancient) have וכמסתיר, one MS ומסתיר. For פנים, two MSS have פֽנָיו; and so likewise LXX and Vulg. Mourners covered up the lower part of their faces, and their heads; 2 Sam. xv. 30. Ezek. xxiv. 17.; and lepers were commanded by the law, Lev. xiii. 45. to cover their upper lip. From which circumstance it seems, that Vulg. Aquila, Symmachus, and the Jewish commentators, have taken the word נגוע, *stricken*, in the next verse, as meaning stricken with the *leprosy,* εν αφη ονΊα, Sym ; αφημενον, Aq.; leprosum, Vulg.

4. *Surely our infirmities—*] Seven MSS (two ancient), and three editions, have חליינו, in the plural number.

Ibid. —*he hath carried them*] Fifteen MSS (two ancient), and two editions, have the word הוא before סבלם in the text: four other MSS have it in the margin. This adds force to the sense, and elegance to the construction.

5. —*by which our peace is effected*] Twenty-one MSS and six editions have the word fully and regularly expressed, שלמינו; "pacificationum nostrarum :" Ar. Montan.

6. —*the iniquities of us all*] For עון, the ancient interpreters read עונות, plural ; and so Vulg. in MS Blanchini.

8. *And his manner of life who would declare?*] My learned friend Dr KENNICOTT has communicated to me the following passages from the Mishna, and the Gemara of Babylon, as leading to a satisfactory explication of this difficult place. It is said in the former, that, before any one was punished for a capital crime, proclamation was made before the prisoner by the public crier in these words: כל מי שיודע לו זכות יבא וילמד עליו, "quicunque noverit aliquid de ejus innocentia, veniat et doceat de eo:" Tract. Sanhedrim. Surenhus. Par. IV. p. 233. On which passage the Gemara of Babylon adds, that, "before the death of

Jesus, this proclamation was made for forty days; but no defence could be found." On which words Lardner observes," It is truly surprising to see such falsities, contrary to well known facts:" Testimonies, vol. i. p. 198. The report is certainly false; but this false report is founded on the supposition that there was such a custom, and so far confirms the account above given for the Mishna. The Mishna was composed in the middle of the second century, according to Prideaux; Lardner ascribes it to the year of Christ 180.

Casaubon has a quotation from Maimonides, which further confirms this account: Exercitat. in Baronii Annales, Art. lxxxvi. Ann. 34. Num. 119. "Auctor est Maimonides in Perek xiii. ejus Libri ex opere Jad, solitum fieri, ut cum Reus, sententiam mortis passus, a loco judicii exibat ducendus ad supplicium, præcederet ipsum הכרוז, κηρυξ, præco; et hæc verba diceret: *Ille* exit occidendus morte *illa*, quia transgressus est transgressione *illa*, in loco *illo*, tempore *illo*, et sunt ejus rei testes *ille* et *ille*. Qui noverit aliquid ad ejus innocentiam probandam, veniat, et loquatur pro eo."

Now it is plain from the history of the four Evangelists, that in the trial and condemnation of Jesus no such rule was observed, (though, according to the account of the Mishna, it must have been in practice at that time); no proclamation was made for any person to bear witness to the innocence and character of Jesus; nor did any one voluntarily step forth to give his attestation to it. And our Saviour seems to refer to such a custom, and to claim the benefit of it, by his answer to the High Priest, when he asked him of his disciples and of his doctrine: "I spake openly to the world; I ever taught in the synagogue and in the temple, whither the Jews always resort; and in secret have I said nothing. Why askest thou me? ask them which heard me, what I have said unto them: behold, they know what I said;" John xviii. 20, 21. This therefore was one remarkable instance of hardship and injustice, among others, predicted by the prophet, which our Saviour underwent in his trial and sufferings.

St. Paul likewise, in similar circumstances, standing before the judgment-seat of Festus, seems to complain of the same unjust treatment; that no one was called, or would appear to vindicate his character: "My manner of life (την βιωσιν μου, דור), from my youth, which was at the first among my own nation at Jerusalem, know all the Jews; which knew me from the beginning, if they would testify; that after the straitest sect of our religion I lived a Pharisee;" Acts xxvi. 4, 5.

חיי signifies age, duration, the time which one man or many together pass in this world; in this place, the course, tenor, or manner of life. The verb חיי signifies, according to Castell. " ordinatam vitam sive ætatem egit, ordinavit, ordine constituit." In Arabic. " curavit, administravit."

Ibid. —*he was smitten to death*] The LXX read למות, εις θανατον. And so the Coptic and Sahidic versions from LXX, MSS St. Germain de Prez.

" Origen, (contra Celsum. lib. i. p. 370. edit. 1733), after having quoted at large this prophecy concerning the Messiah, tells us, that having once made use of this passage in a dispute against some that were accounted wise among the Jews; one of them replied, that the words did not mean one man, but one people, the Jews; who were smitten of God, and dispersed among the Gentiles for their conversion: that he then urged many parts of this prophecy, to shew the absurdity of this interpretation; and that he seemed to press them the hardest by this sentence; απο των ανομιων τȣ λαȣ μȣ ηχθη εις θανατον. Now as Origen, the author of the Hexapla, must have understood Hebrew, we cannot suppose that he would have urged this last quotation as so decisive, if the Greek version had not agreed here with the Hebrew text; nor that these wise Jews would have been at all distressed by this quotation, unless their Hebrew text had read agreeably to εις θανατον, on which the argument principally depended: for, by quoting it immediately, they would have triumphed over him, and reprobated his Greek version. This, whenever they could do it, was their constant practice, in their dispute with the Christians. Jerom, in his preface to the Psalms, says. " Nuper cum Hebræo disputans, quædam pro Domino salvatore de Psalmis testimonia protulisti: volensque ille te illudere, per sermones fere singulos asserebat, non ita haberi in Hebræo, ut tu de LXX opponebas." And Origen himself, who laboriously compared the Hebrew text with the LXX has recorded the necessity of arguing with the Jews from such passages only as were in the LXX agreeable to the Hebrew: ινα προς Ιȣδαιοις διαλεγομενοι μη προφερωμεν αυτοις τα μη κειμενα εν τοις αντιγραφοις αυτων, και ινα συγχρησωμεθα τοις φερομενοις παρ' εκεινοις. See Epist. ad African. p. 15. 17.

Wherefore, as Origen had carefully compared the Greek version of LXX with the Hebrew text, and speaks of the contempt with which the Jews treated all appeals to the Greek version, where it differed from their Hebrew text; and as he puzzled and confounded the learned Jews, by urging upon them the reading εις θανατον in this place; it seems almost impossible not to conclude, both from Origen's argument and the silence of his Jewish adversaries, that the Hebrew text at that time actually had למות, agreeably to the version of the LXX:" Dr. KENNICOTT.

7. *But with the rich man was his tomb*] Among the various opinions which have been given on this passage, I have no doubt in giving my assent to that which makes the ב in במותי radical, and renders it *excelsa sua*. This is mentioned by Aben Ezra, as received by some in his time; and has been long since approved by Schindler, Drusius, and many other learned Christian interpreters.

The most simple tombs or monuments of old consisted of hillocks of earth heaped up over the grave: of which we have numerous examples in our own country, generally allowed to be of very high antiquity. The Romans called a monument of this sort very properly *tumulus*; and the Hebrews as properly במות, for that is the form of the noun in the singular number; and sixteen MSS, and the two oldest editions, express the word fully in this place, במותי. " Tumulus et collem et sepulchrum fuisse significat. Potest enim tumulus sine sepulchro interpretatione collis interdum accipi. Nam et terræ congestio super ossa tumulus dicitur:" Servius, in Æneid iii. 22. And to make the tumulus still more elevated and conspicuous, a pillar or some other ornament was often erected upon it:—

> Τυμβον χευαντες, και επι στηλην ερυσαντες,
> Πηξαμεν ακροτατω, τυμβω ευηρες ερετμον.   Odyss. xii. 14.

" A rising tomb, the silent dead to grace,
Fast by the roarings of the main we place:
The rising tomb a lofty column bore,
And high above it rose the tapering oar."   Pope.

The tomb therefore might with great propriety be called the high place. The Hebrews might also call such a tomb במות, from the situation; for they generally chose to erect them on eminences. The sepulchre of Joseph of Arimathea, in which the body of Christ was laid, was upon a hill, Mount Calvary. See chap. xxii. 16. and the note there.

"It should be observed, that the word במותי is not formed from במות, the plural of במה, the feminine noun, but from במותים, the plural of a masculine noun, במות. This is noted, because these two nouns have been negligently confounded with one another, and absurdly reduced to one, by very learned men. So Buxtorff, Lex. in v. במה, represents במותי, though plainly without any pronoun suffixed, as it governs the word ארץ following it, as only another form of במות; whereas the truth is, that במות and במותים are different words, and have through the whole Bible very different significations: במה, whether occurring in the singular or plural number, always signifying "a place, or places, of worship;" and במותים always signifying "heights." Thus in Deut. xxxii. 13. Isa. lviii. 14. Amos iv. 13. and Mic. i. 3. תמותי ארץ signifies "the heights of the earth;" Isa. xiv. 14. במותי עב, "the heights of the clouds;" and in Job ix. 8. במותי ים, "the heights of the sea," i. e. the high waves of the sea, as Virgil calls a wave "præruptus aquæ mons." These being all the places where this word occurs without a suffix, the sense of it seems clearly determined by them. It occurs in other instances with a pronoun suffixed, which confirm this signification. Unluckily our English Bible has not distinguished the feminine noun במה from the masculine singular noun במות; and has consequently always given the signification of the latter to the former, always rendering it "a high place:" whereas the true sense of the word appears plainly to be, in the very numerous passages in which it occurs, "a place of worship," or "a sacred court," or "a sacred inclosure," whether appropriated to the worship of idols, or to that of the true God : for it is used of both *passim*. Now, as the Jewish graves are shewn, from 2 Chron. xxxii. 33. and Isa. xxii. 16. to have been in high situations; to which may be added the custom of another eastern nation from Osbeck's Travels, who says, vol. i. p. 339. "The Chinese graves are made on the side of hills;" "his heights" becomes a very easy metaphor to express his sepulchre :" Dr. JUBB.

The exact completion of this prophecy will be fully shewn, by adding here the several circumstances of the burial of Jesus, collected from the accounts of the Evangelists :—

"There was a rich man of Arimathea, named Joseph, a member of the Sanhedrim, and of a respectable character, who had not consented to their counsel and act: he went to Pilate, and begged the body of Jesus; and he laid it in his own new tomb, which had been hewn out of the rock, near to the place where Jesus was crucified; having first wound it in fine linen with spices, as the manner of the Jews was to bury the rich and great."

10. —*with grief*] For החלי, the verb, the construction of which seems to be hard and inelegant in this place, Vulg. reads כחלי, in infirmitate.

Ibid. *If his soul shall make*—] For תשים, a MS has תשם, which may be taken passively, " If his soul shall be made—," agreeably to some copies of LXX, which have δωται. So likewise Syr.

11. —*and be satisfied*—] LXX, Vulg. Syr. and a MS, add the conjunction to the verb; וישבע.

Ibid. —*shall my servant justify*] Three MSS (two of them ancient), omit the word צדיק; it seems to be only an imperfect repetition, by mistake, of the preceding word. It makes a solecism in this place; for, according to the constant usage of the Hebrew language, the adjective, in a phrase of this kind, ought to follow the substantive; and צדיק עבדי in Hebrew would be as absurd as " shall my *servant righteous* justify," in English. Add to this, that it makes the hemistich too long.

12. *And made intercession*—] For יפגיע, in the future, a MS has הפגיע, preterit; rather better, as agreeable with the other verbs immediately preceding in the sentence.

CHAPTER LIV.

1. *Shout for joy, O thou barren*—] The church of God under the Old Testament, confined within the narrow bounds of the Jewish nation, and still more so in respect of the very small number of true believers, and which sometimes seemed to be deserted of God her husband; is the barren woman, that did not bear, and was desolate. She is exhorted to rejoice, and to express her joy in the strongest manner, on the reconciliation of her husband, see ver. 6. and on the accession of the Gentiles to her family. The converted Gentiles are all along considered by the Prophet as a new accession of adopted children, admitted into the original church of God, and united with it. See chap. xlix. 20, 21.

4. *For thou shalt forget*] "Shame of thy youth; *i. e.* the bondage of Egypt: widowhood, the captivity of Babylon:" SECKER.

7. *In a little anger—*] So the Chald. and Syr. either reading רגז for רגע, or understanding the latter word as meaning the same with the former, which they both make use of. See Psal. xxx. 5. xxxv. 20. in LXX, where they render רגע by οργη.

8. *I hid my face [for a moment] from thee*] The word רגע is omitted by LXX, Syr. and two MSS. It seems to embarrass rather than to help the sentence. "Forte reponi debet pro שצף, quod potest a קצף errore scribæ originem duxisse:" SECKER.

9. —*as in the days of Noah*] כימי, in one word, in a MS, and some editions; and so Syr. Chald. Vulg. Sym. Theod. Abarbanel, Salomo b. Melec, and Kimchi, acknowledge that their copies vary in this place.

11, 12. *Behold, I lay thy stones—*] These seem to be general images to express beauty, magnificence, purity, strength, and solidity, agreeably to the ideas of the eastern nations; and to have never been intended to be strictly scrutinized, or minutely and particularly explained, as if they had each of them some precise moral or spiritual meaning. Tobit, in his prophecy of the final restoration of Israel, describes the New Jerusalem in the same oriental manner: "For Jerusalem shall be built up with sapphires, and emeralds, and precious stones; thy walls, and towers, and battlements, with pure gold. And the streets of Jerusalem shall be paved with beryl, and carbuncle, and stones of Ophir:" Tob. xiii. 16, 17. Compare also Rev. xxi. 18—21.

15. —*shall come over to thy side*] For יבול, twenty-eight MSS (eight ancient) have יבל, in its more common form. For the meaning of the word in this place, see Jer. xxxvii. 13.

CHAPTER LV.

9. *For as the heavens are higher—*] I am persuaded that כ, the particle of comparison, is lost in this place, from the likeness of the particle כי immediately preceding it. So Houbigant, and SECKER. And their remark is confirmed by all the ancient versions, which express it; and by the

following passage of Psalm. ciii. 11. which is almost the same:—

כי כגבה שמים על הארץ
גבר חסדו על יראיו.

" For as the heavens are high above the earth,
So high is his goodness over them that fear him."

Where, by the nature of the sentence, the verb in the second line ought to be the same with that in the first: גבה, not גבר: so Archbishop Secker conjectured; referring however to Psal. cxvii. 2.

12. *The mountains and the hills*—] These are highly poetical images, to express a happy state attended with joy and exultation.

" Ipsi lætitia voces ad sidera jactant
Intonsi montes: ipsæ jam carmina rupes,
Ipsa sonant arbusta."   Virg. Ecl. v.

13. *Instead of the thorny bushes*—] These likewise (see note on the preceding verse, and on chap. liv. 11.) are general poetical images, expressing a great and happy change for the better. The wilderness turned into a paradise, Lebanon into Carmel: the desert of the Gentiles watered with the heavenly snow and rain, which fail not to have their due effect, and becoming fruitful in piety and righteousness; or, as the Chaldee gives the moral sense of the emblem, "Instead of the wicked shall arise the just, and instead of sinners, such as fear to sin." Compare ch. xxxv. 1, 2. xli. 19.

Ibid. *And instead of*—] The conjunction ו is added, ותחת, in forty-five MSS, and five editions; and it is acknowledged by all the ancient versions. The Masoretes therefore might have safely received it into the text, and not have referred us for it to the margin.

CHAPTER LVI.

5. —*will I give them*] For לו in the singular, it is evident that we ought to read למו in the plural: so read LXX, Syr. Chald. and Vulg.

7. —*shall be accepted*] A word is here lost out of the text: it is supplied from the LXX, יהיו, εσονται: Houbigant.

9. *O all ye beasts of the field*—] Here manifestly begins

a new section. The Prophet, in the foregoing chapters, having comforted the faithful Jews with many great promises of God's favour to be extended to them, in the restoration of their ruined state, and of the enlargement of his church by the admission of the Gentiles; here, on a sudden, makes a transition to the more disagreeable part of the prospect: and to a sharp reproof of the wicked and unbelievers, and especially of the negligent and faithless governors and teachers, of the idolators and hypocrites, who would still draw down his judgments upon the nation: probably having in view the destruction of their city and polity by the Chaldeans, and perhaps by the Romans. The same subject is continued in the next chapter; in which the charge of corruption and apostasy becomes more general against the whole Jewish church. Some expositors have made great difficulties in the 9th verse of this chapter, where there seems to be none. It is perfectly well explained by Jeremiah; where, having introduced God declaring his purpose of punishing his people, by giving them up as a prey to their enemies the Chaldeans, a charge to these his agents is given in words very nearly the same with those of Isaiah in this place:—

"I have forsaken my house; I have deserted my heritage;
I have given up the beloved of my soul into the hands of her enemies.—
Come away, be ye gathered together, all ye beasts of the field;
Come away to devour." Jer. xii. 7. 9.

Ibid. —*beasts of the forest*] Instead of ביער, three MSS have יער, without the preposition: which seems to be right; and is confirmed by all the ancient versions.

10. *dumb dogs, they cannot bark*] See below, note on chap. lxii. 6.

Ibid. *Dreamers*] הזים, ενυπνιαζομενοι, LXX. This seems to be the best authority for the meaning of this word, which occurs only in this place: but it is to be observed, that three MSS, and three editions, have חזים; and so Vulg. seems to have read, *videntes vana*.

12. —*let us provide wine*] For אקחה, first person singular, an ancient MS has נקחה, first person plural; and another ancient MS has אק upon a rasure. So Syr. Chald. and Vulg. render it.

CHAPTER LVII.

2. *He shall go in peace*] יבוא שלום: the expression is elliptical, such as the Prophet frequently uses. The same sense is expressed at large and in full terms, Gen. xv. 15. ואתה תבוא אל אבותיך בשלום, "And thou shalt go to thy fathers in peace."

Ibid. —*he shall rest in his bed; even the perfect man*] This obscure sentence is reduced to a perfectly good sense, and easy construction, by an ingenious remark of Dr DURELL. He reads ינוח על משכבו תם. Two MSS (one of them ancient) have ינוח, singular; and so Vulg. renders it, *requiescat*. The verb was probably altered to make it plural, and so consistent with what follows, after the mistake had be en made in the following words, by uniting משכבו and תם into one word. See Merrick's Annotations on the Psalms, Addenda; where the reader will find, that J. S. Moerlius, by the same sort of correction, and by rescuing the adjective תם, which had been swallowed up in another word in the same manner, has restored to a clear sense a passage before absolutely unintelligible :—

כי אין חרצבות למו
תם ובריא אולם:

"For no distresses happen to them;
Perfect and firm is their strength." Psal. lxxiii. 4.

6. *Among the smooth stones of the valley*—] The Jews were extremely addicted to the practice of many superstitious and idolatrous rites, which the Prophet here inveighs against with great vehemence. Of the worship of rude stones consecrated, there are many testimonies of the ancients. They were called Βαιτυλοι and Βαιτυλια; probably from the stone which Jacob erected at Bethel, pouring oil upon the top of it. The practice was very common in different ages and places. Arnobius, lib. i. gives an account of his own practice in this respect, before he became a Christian: "Si quando conspexeram lubricatum lapidem, et ex olivi unguine sordidatum; tanquam inesset vis præsens, adulabar, affabar, et beneficia poscebam nihil sentiente de trunco." Clemens Alex. Strom. lib. vii. speaks of a worshipper of every smooth stone in a proverbial way, to denote one given up to superstition. And accordingly Theophrastus has marked this as one strong feature in the character

of the superstitious man: Καὶ τῶν λιπαρῶν λίθων τῶν ἐν ταῖς τριόδοις παριών, ἐκ τῆς ληκύθου ἔλαιον καταχεῖν, καὶ ἐπὶ γόνατα πεσὼν καὶ προσκυνήσας ἀπαλλάττεσθαι: "Passing by the anointed stones in the streets, he takes out his phial of oil, and pours it on them; and having fallen on his knees, and made his adorations, he departs."

8. *Behind the door, and the door-posts, hast thou set thy memorial*] That is, the image of their tutelary gods, or something dedicated to them; in direct opposition to the law of God, which commanded them to write upon the door-posts of their house, and upon their gates, the words of God's law; Deut. vi. 9. xi. 20. If they chose for them such a situation as more private, it was in defiance of a particular curse denounced in the law against the man who should make a graven or a molten image, and put it in a secret place; Deut. xxvii. 15. An ancient MS, with another, has אחר, without the conjunction ו.

9. *And thou hast visited the king with a present of oil.*] That is, the king of Assyria, or Egypt. Hosea reproaches the Israelites for the same practice:—

"They make a covenant with Assyria,
And oil is carried to Egypt."   Hosea xii. 1.

It is well known, that in all parts of the East, whoever visits a great person must carry him a present. "It is counted uncivil," says Maundrell, p. 26. "to visit in this country without an offering in hand. All great men expect it as a tribute due to their character and authority; and look upon themselves as affronted, and indeed defrauded, when the compliment is omitted." Hence שׁור, to *visit* a person, is equivalent to making him a present: and תשׁורה signifies a *present* made on such occasions; as our translators have rightly rendered it, 1 Sam. ix. 7.: on which Jarchi says, "Menachem exponit תשׁורה quod significet oblationem sive munus, ut aliquis aspiciat faciem regis, aut alicujus magnatis."

10. *Thou hast said, There is no hope*] In one of the MSS at Koningsberg, collated by Lilienthal, the words לא אמרת are left in the text unpointed, as suspected; and in the margin the corrector has written ותאמרי. Now, if we compare Jer. ii. 25. and xviii. 12. we shall find, that the subject is in both places quite the same with this of Isaiah, and the sentiment expressed, that of a desperate resolution to continue at all hazard in their idolatrous practices; the very thing that in all reason we might expect here. Probably therefore the latter is the true reading in this place.

11. —*nor revolved it*—] Eight MSS (four ancient), and the two oldest editions, with another, add the conjunction ו, ולא: which is confirmed by all the ancient versions.

Ibid. —*and winked*] For ומעולם, which makes no good sense or construction in this place, twenty-three MSS (seven ancient), and three editions, have מעלם, (to be thus pointed מַעְלִם); παροραω, LXX; *quasi non videns*, Vulg. : see Psal. x. 1. The truth of this reading so confirmed admits of no doubt.

12. —*my righteousness*] For צדקתך, *thy* righteousness, Syr. LXX, MSS Alex. and Pachom. and 1. D. 11., and Marchal. and ὁ Γ, and Arab, read צדקתי, *my* righteousness.

13. —*let thine associates deliver thee*] Thirty-nine MSS (ten ancient), and the two oldest editions, have יצילוך, plural.

14. *then will I say*] ואמר, to be pointed as the first person future : they are the words of God, as it is plain from the conclusion of the verse ; *my* people, עמי.

15. *For thus saith* JEHOVAH] A MS adds יהוה after אמר, and edition Prag. 1518. So LXX, Alex. and Arab. An ancient MS adds יה.

Ibid. *And with the contrite*—] Twelve MSS have את, without the conjunction ו. " Pro ואת, forte legendum ואראה : confer Psal. cxiii. 5. et cxxxviii. 6. : " SECKER.

16. *For I will not alway*—] The learned have taken a great deal of pains to little purpose on the latter part of this verse, which they suppose to be very obscure. After all their labours upon it, I think the best and easiest explication of it is given in the two following elegant passages of the Psalms, which I presume are exactly parallel to it, and very clearly express the same sentiment.

" But He in his tender mercy will forgive their sin,
 And will not destroy them;
 Yea oftentimes will he turn away his wrath,
 And will not rouse up all his indignation:
 For he remembereth that they are but flesh,
 A breath that passeth, and returneth not."   lxxviii. 38. 39.

" He will not always contend,
 Neither will he for ever hold his wrath:
 As a father yearneth towards his children,
 So is JEHOVAH tenderly compassionate towards them that fear him:
 For he knoweth our frame;
 He remembereth that we are but dust."   ciii. 9. 13, 14.

In the former of these two passages, the second line seems to be defective both in measure and sense: I suppose the word אותם, *them*, is lost at the end; which seems to be acknowledged by Chald. and Vulg. who render as if they had read, ולא ישחית אותם.

17. *Because of his iniquity for a short time I was wroth*] For בצעו, I read בצע, paululum, à בצע, abscidit; as LXX read and render it, βραχυ τι. "Propter iniquitatem *avaritiæ ejus*," the rendering of Vulg., which our translators, and I believe all others follow, is surely quite beside the purpose.

19. *I create the fruit of the lips;*—] "The sacrifice of praise," saith St Paul, Heb. xiii. 15. "is the fruit of the lips." God creates this fruit of the lips, by giving new subject and cause of thanksgiving, by his mercies conferred on those among his people who acknowledge and bewail their transgressions, and return to him. The great subject of thanksgiving is peace; reconciliation and pardon offered to them that are nigh, and to them that are afar off; not only to the Jew, but also to the Gentile, as St Paul more than once applies these terms, Eph. ii. 13. 17.: see also Acts ii. 39.

21. *There is no peace, saith my God*—] For אלהי, twenty-two MSS (five ancient) read יהוה. Vulg. LXX Alex. Arab. and three MSS, have both. This verse has reference to the 19th. The wicked and impenitent are excluded from all share in that peace above-mentioned, that reconcilement and pardon, which is promised to the penitent only. The xlviiith chapter ends with the same declaration; to express the exclusion of the unbelievers and impenitent from the benefit of the foregoing promises.

CHAPTER LVIII.

3. —*afflicted our souls*—] Twenty-seven MSS (six ancient), and the old edition of 1488, have the noun in the plural number, נפשינו: and so LXX, Chald. Vulg.

4. *And to smite with the fist the poor. Wherefore fast ye unto me*—] I follow the version of the LXX, which gives a much better sense than the present reading of the Hebrew. Instead of רשע לא, they seem to have read in their copy רש על מה לי: the four first letters are the same, but otherwise divided in regard to the words; the four last are lost, and א added in their place, in order to make some sort of sense with רשע ל. The version of the LXX is και τυπτετε πυγμαις ταπεινον· ινα τι μοι νηστευετε——.

7. *—the wandering poor—*] πλωχους αςεγους, LXX ; egenos *vagosque*, Vulg. ; and מטלטלין, Chald. They read, instead of הנודים, מרודים. מר is upon a rasure in the Bodleian MS. The same MS reads ביתה, *in domum*.

8. *And thy wounds shall speedily be healed*] "Et cicatrix vulneris tui cito obducetur." Aquila's version, as reported by Jerom ; with which agrees that of the Chaldee.

Ibid. *And the glory—*] Sixteen MSS (five ancient), and LXX, Syr. Vulg. add the conjunction ו, וכבוד.

10. *If thou bring forth thy bread—*] "To draw out thy soul to the hungry," as our translators rightly enough express the present Hebrew text, is an obscure phrase, and without example in any other place. But instead of נפשך, *thy soul*, eight MSS (three ancient) read לחמך, *thy bread ;* and so the Syriac renders it. The LXX express both words, τον αρτον εκ της ψυχης σου, *thy bread from thy soul*.

11. *And he shall renew thy strength*] "Chaldæus forte legit יחליף עצמתך. Confer cap. xl. 29. 31. et xli. 1. :" Secker. Chald. has וגופך יחיי כחיי עלמא, "et corpus tuum vivificabit in vita æterna." The rest of the ancients seem not to know what to make of יחליץ ; and the rendering of the Vulgate, which seems to be the only proper one, *ossa tua liberabit*, makes no sense. I follow this excellent emendation ; to favour which, it is still further to be observed, that three MSS, instead of עצמתיך, have עצמתך, singular.

12. *—to be frequented by inhabitants*] To this purpose it is rendered by Syr. Sym. and Theod.

13. *From doing thy pleasure*] The LXX, Syr. and Chald. for עשות manifestly express מעשות. So likewise a MS has it ; but with the omission of the words שבת רגליך.

Ibid. *And the holy feast*] Twenty-eight MSS (seven ancient) add the conjunction ו, ולקדוש: and so Syr. and Chald.

Ibid. *—and from speaking vain words*] It is necessary to add some epithet to make out the sense : the LXX say *angry* words ; Chald. words of *violence*. If any such epithet is lost here, the safest way is to supply it by the Prophet's own expression, ver. 9. ודבר און, *vain* words ; that is, profane, impious, injurious, &c.

"The additional epithet seems unnecessary. The Vulg. and Syr. have it not. And the sense is good without it ; two ways, first by taking ודבר for a noun, and דבר for the participle pahul, and rendering,

" From pursuing thy pleasure, and the thing resolved on: "

Or, secondly, by supposing the force of the preposition מ to be continued from the verb ממצוא to the verb ודבר immediately following, and rendering.

"From executing thy pleasure, and from speaking words concerning it."

But the first seems the easier rendering." Dr. JUBB.

CHAPTER LIX.

THE foregoing elegant chapter contained a severe reproof of the Jews, in particular for their hypocrisy in pretending to make themselves accepted with God by fasting and outward humiliation without true repentance, while they still continued to oppress the poor, and to indulge their own passions and vices; with great promises, however, of God's favour on condition of their reformation. This chapter contains a more general reproof of their wickedness; bloodshed, violence, falsehood, injustice. At ver. 9. they are introduced as making themselves an ample confession of their sins, and deploring their wretched state in consequence of them. On this act of humiliation a promise is given, that God, in his mercy and zeal for his people, will rescue them from this miserable condition; that the Redeemer will come like a mighty hero to deliver them: he will destroy his enemies, convert both Jews and Gentiles to himself, and give them a new covenant, and a law, which shall never be abolished.

As this chapter is remarkable for the beauty, strength, and variety of the images with which it abounds; so is it peculiarly distinguished by the elegance of the composition, and the exact construction of the sentences: from the first verse to the two last, it falls regularly into stanzas of four lines, (see Prel. Dissert. p. xiii.), which I have endeavoured to express as nearly as possible in the form of the original.

2. *His face*—] For פנים, *faces*, I read פניו, *his face*. So Syr. LXX, Alex. Arab. Vulg. פני, MS. " Forte legendum פני; nam מ sequitur, et loquitur Deus: confer lviii. 14.:" SECKER. I rather think that the speech of God was closed with the last chapter; and that this chapter is delivered in the person of the Prophet.

3. *And your tongue*—] An ancient MS, and LXX and Vulg. add the conjunction.

8. *Whoever goeth in them*—] For בה singular, read בם plural, with LXX, Syr. Vulg. Chald. The ה is upon a rasure in MS. Or for נתיכתיהם plural, we must read נתיבתם singular,

as it is in an ancient MS, to preserve the grammatical concord.

10. *And we wander*—] I adopt here an emendation of Houbigant, נשגה, instead of the second נגשה, the repetition of which has a poverty and inelegance extremely unworthy of the Prophet, and unlike his manner. The mistake is of long standing, being prior to all the ancient versions: it was a very easy and obvious mistake; and I have little doubt of our having recovered the true reading in this ingenious correction.

11. —*and it is far distant from us.*] The conjunction ו must necessarily be prefixed to the verb, as Syr. Chald. Vulg. found it in their copies, ורחפה.

15. *And* JEHOVAH *saw it,* ....] This third line of the stanza appears manifestly to me to be imperfect by the loss of a phrase. The reader will perhaps more perfectly conceive my idea of the matter, if I endeavour to supply the supposed defect. I imagine it might have stood originally in this manner:

וירא יהוה [ויחר לו]
וירע בעיניו כי אין משפט:

" And JEHOVAH saw it, [and he was wroth]:
And it displeased him, that there was no judgment."

We have had already many examples of mistakes of omission: this, if it be such, is very ancient, being prior to all the versions.

17. —*for his clothing*] תלבשת. "I cannot but think that תלבשת is an interpolation. 1. It is in no one ancient version. 2. It is redundant in the sense, as it is before expressed in בגדי. 3. It makes the hemistich just so much longer than it ought to be, if it is compared with the others adjoining. 4. It makes a form of construction in this clause less elegant than that in the others. 5. It might probably be in some margin a various reading for בגדי, and thence taken into the text. This is the more probable, as its form is such as it would be if it were *in regimine*, as it must be before נקם:" Dr. JUBB.

18. *He is mighty*—] The former part of this verse, as it stands at present in the Hebrew text, seems to me to be very imperfect, and absolutely unintelligible. The learned Vitringa has taken a great deal of pains upon it, after Cocceius; who, he says, is the only one of all the interpreters, ancient or modern, who has at all understood it, and has opened the way for him. He thinks, that both of them

together have clearly made out the sense: I do not expect that any third person will ever be of that opinion. He says, "Videtur sententia ad verbum sonare: quasi propter facta [adversariorum] quasi propter rependet; excandescentiam, &c. et sic reddidit Pagninus." This he converts, by a process which will not much edify my reader, into "Secundum summe merita, secundum summe [merita] rependet;" which is his translation. They that hold the present Hebrew text to be absolutely infallible, must make their way through it as they can; but they ought surely to give us somewhat that has at least the appearance of sense. However, I hope the case here is not quite desperate: the Chaldee leads us very fairly to the correction of the text, which is both corrupted and defective. The paraphrase runs thus: מרי גמליא הוא גמלא ישלם, "Dominus retributionum ipse retributionem reddet." He manifestly read בעל, instead of כעל. בעל גמליא is מרי גמלות; as מרי מרימרותא, is כעל אף, Prov. xxii. 24. And so in the same Chaldee paraphrase on Isaiah xxxv. 4. מרי גמליא יי הוא יתגלי, "Dominus retributionum Jehovah ipse revelabitur." Words very near to those of the Prophet in this place. The second כעל, which the Chaldee has omitted, must be read בעל likewise. With this only addition to the Chaldee, which the Hebrew text justifies, we are supplied with the following clear reading of the passage:—

בעל גמולות הוא
בעל גמולות ישלם.

The כ in כעל twice seems to have been at first ב in MS. This verse in LXX is very imperfect. In the first part of it they give us no assistance; the last part is wholly omitted in the printed copies; but it is thus supplied in MSS Pachom. and 1. D. 11.—τοις υπεναντιοις αυτου· αμυναν τοις εχθροις αυτου· ταις νησοις αποδομα αποτιδει.

19.—*which a strong wind driveth along*] "Quam spiritus Domini cogit;" Vulg. נוססה, pihel a נוס fugit. Kimchi says, his father thus explained this word: "נוססה interpretatur in significatione fugæ; et ait, Spiritus Domini *fugabit* hostem;—nam secundum eum נוססה est ex conjugatione quadrata, ejusque radix est נוס." The object of this action I explain otherwise. The conjunction ו prefixed to רוח seems necessary to the sense: it is added by the corrector in one of the Koningsberg MSS collated by Lilienthal.

20. *And shall turn away iniquity from Jacob*] So LXX, and St. Paul, Rom. xi. 26.; reading, instead of לשבי, and

בְּיַעֲקֹב, וְהֵשִׁיב and מִיַעֲקֹב. Syr. likewise reads וְהֵשִׁיב; and Chald. to the same sense, וּלְהָשִׁיב. Our translators have expressed the sense of the present reading of the Hebrew text: "And unto them that turn from transgression in Jacob."

21. —*which I make with them*] For אוֹתָם, *them* twenty-four MSS (four ancient) and nine editions have אִתָּם, *with them.*

CHAPTER LX.

The subject of this chapter is the great increase and flourishing state of the church of God, by the conversion and accession of the heathen nations to it; which is set forth in such ample and exalted terms as plainly shew, that the full completion of this prophecy is reserved for future times. This subject is displayed in the most splendid colours, under a great variety of images highly poetical, designed to give a general idea of the glories of that perfect state of the church of God which we are taught to expect in the latter times; when the fulness of the Gentiles shall come in, and the Jews shall be converted and gathered from their dispersions; and the kingdoms of this world shall become the kingdoms of our Lord, and of his Christ.

Of the use in prophecy of general or common poetical images, in setting forth the greatness and importance of a future event universally, without descending to particulars, or too minutely explaining circumstances, I have already pretty largely treated in the xxth Prelection on the Hebrew Poetry; and have more than once observed in these notes, that such images are not always to be applied particularly to persons and things, and were never intended to be minutely explained. I shall add here the opinion of a very learned and judicious person upon this subject: "It is, I think, a mark of right understanding in the language of prophecy, and in the design of prophecy too, to keep to what appears the design and meaning of the prophecy in general, and what the whole of it, laid together, points out to us; and not to suffer a warm imagination to mislead us from the real intention of the spirit of prophecy, by following uncertain applications of the parts of it:" Lowman on the Revelation, note on chap. xix. 21.

4. —*shall be carried at the side*] For תֵּאָמַנָה, *shall be nursed,* LXX and Chald. read תִּנָּשֶׂאנָה, *shall be carried.* A MS has עַל כָּתֵף תִּנָּשֶׂאנָה, instead of עַל צַד תֵּאָמַנָה; *shall*

be carried on the shoulder, instead of *shall be nursed on the side*. Another MS has both כתף and צד. Another MS has it thus: תנשאנה: תאלנה, with a line drawn over the first word. Sir John Chardin says, that it is the general custom in the East to carry their children astride upon the hip, with the arm round their body. His MS note on this place is as follows: " Coutume en Orient de porter les enfans sur le coste à califourchon sur la hanche: cette façon est generale aux Indes; les enfans se tiennent comme cela, et la personne qui les porte les embrasse et serre par le corps; parceque sont [ni] emmaillottés, ni en robes qui les embrassent."

" Non brachiis occidentalium more, sed humeris, divaricatis tibiis, impositos circumferunt:" Cotovic. Iter Syr. cap. xiv. This last quotation seems to favour the reading על כתף; as the LXX likewise do: but upon the whole I think that על צד תנשאנה is the true reading, which the Chaldee favours; and I have accordingly followed it. See chap. lxvi. 12.

5. *Then shalt thou fear*—] For תראי, *thou shalt see*, as ours, and much the greater number of the translators, ancient and modern, render it; forty MSS (ten ancient), and the old edition of 1488. have תיראי, *thou shalt fear;* the true reading, confirmed by the perfect parallelism of the sentences: the heart *ruffled* and *dilated* in the second line answering to the *fear* and *joy* expressed in the first. The Prophet Jeremiah (chap. xxxiii. 9.) has the same natural and elegant sentiment :—

" And [this city] shall become to me a name of joy;
A praise and an honour for all the nations of the earth;
Which shall hear all the good that I do unto them;
And they shall fear, and they shall tremble, at ؛all the goodness,
And at all the prosperity, that I procure unto her."

And David, (Psal. cxxxix. 14.)

" I will praise thee, for I am fearfully and wonderfully made."
" His tibi me rebus quædam divina voluptas
Percipit atque horror." Lucret. iii. 28.
        " Recenti mens trepidat metu,
Plenoque Bacchi pectore turbidum
Lætatur." Hor. Carm. ii. 19.

6. *And the praise of* JEHOVAH—] Thirty-three MSS and three editions have ותהלת, in the singular number; and so read the ancient versions.

7. *Unto thee shall the rams of Nebaioth minister*] Vitringa (on the place) understands their ministering, and ascending, or going up on the altar, as offering themselves voluntarily: " Ipsi se, non expectato sacerdote alio, gloriæ et sanctificationi Divini nominis ultro ac libenter oblaturi." This gives a very elegant and poetical turn to the image. It was a general notion that prevailed with sacrificers among the heathen, that the victim's being brought without reluctance to the altar was a good omen; and the contrary a bad one. " Sabinos petit aliquanto tristior; quod sacrificanti hostia aufugerat:" Sueton. Titus, cap. x. " Accessit dirum omen, profugus altaribus taurus:" Tacit. Hist. iii. 56.

8.. *And like doves upon the wing*] Instead of אל, *to*, forty-two MSS have על, *upon*. For ארבתיהם, *their windows*, read אברתיהם, *their wings*, transposing a letter: Houbigant. The LXX render it συν νεοσσοις, *with their young*: they read אפרחיהם; nearer to the latter, than to the present reading.

9. —*among the first*—] For בראשנה, twenty-five MSS and Syr. read כבראשנה, *as at the first*.

13. —*the place whereon I rest my feet*] The temple of Jerusalem was called the house of God, and the place of his rest or residence: the visible symbolical appearance of God, called by the Jews the Shechinah, was in the most holy place, between the wings of the cherubim above the ark. This is considered as the throne of God, presiding as king over the Jewish state; and as a footstool is a necessary appendage of a throne, (see note on chap. lii. 2.), the ark is considered as the footstool of God; and is so called, Psal. xcix. 5. 1 Chron. xxviii. 2.

Ibid. *The glory of Lebanon*] That is, the cedar.

19. *Nor by night shall the brightness of the moon enlighten thee*] This line, as it stands in the present text, seems to be defective. The LXX and Chald. both express *the night*, which is almost necessary to answer to *day* in the preceding line, as well as to perfect the sense here. I therefore think that we ought, upon the authority of LXX and Chald. to read either ולילה, *and by night*, instead of ולנגה, *and for brightness:* or ולנגה בלילה, adding the word בלילה, *by night*.

21. —*of my planting*] מטעי, so with the *Keri* read forty-four MSS (seven ancient) and six editions; with which agree Syr. Chald. Vulg.

CHAPTER LXI.

1. *The Spirit of JEHOVAH*—] The LXX, Vulg. and St Luke iv. 18. and MS, and two old editions, omit the word אדני, *the Lord;* which was probably added to the text through the superstition of the Jews, to prevent the pronunciation of the word יהוה following. See Kennicott on the State of the Printed Heb. Text, i. p. 510.

Ibid. —*perfect liberty*] Ten MSS and one edition have פקחקוח in one word; and so the LXX and Vulg. appear to have taken it.

The proclaiming of perfect liberty to the bounden, and the year of acceptance with JEHOVAH, is a manifest allusion to the proclaiming of the year of jubilee by sound of trumpet: see Lev. xxv. 9. &c. This was a year of general release— of debts and obligations; of bond men and women; of lands and possessions, which had been sold from the families and tribes to which they belonged. Our Saviour, by applying this text to himself, Luke iv. 18, 19. a text so manifestly relating to the institution above-mentioned, plainly declares the typical design of that institution.

3. *To impart [gladness] to the mourners*] A word necessary to the sense is certainly lost in this place; of which the ancient versions have preserved no traces. Houbigant, by conjecture, inserts the word ששון, *gladness*, taken from the line next but one below, where it stands opposed to אבל, *sorrow*, or *mourning*; as the word lost here was to אבלי, *mourners;* I follow him.

Ibid. —*a beautiful crown, instead of ashes*] In times of mourning the Jews put on sackcloth, or coarse and sordid raiment; and spread dust and ashes on their heads: on the contrary, splendid clothing, and ointment poured on the head, were the signs of joy. "Feign thyself to be a mourner," says Joab to the woman of Tekoah, "and put on now mourning apparel, and anoint not thyself with oil;" 2 Sam. xiv. 2. These customs are at large expressed in the book of Judith: "She pulled off the sackcloth which she had on, and put off the garments of her widowhood, and washed her body all over with water, and anointed herself with precious ointment, and braided the hair of her head, and put on a tire [mitre, marg.] upon it; and put on her garments of gladness;" chap. x. 3.

Phear, instead of *apher;* a paronomasia, which the Prophet often uses: a chaplet, crown, or other ornament of the head, (for so the Vulgate renders the word here, and in the 10th verse; in which last place the LXX agree in the same rendering), instead of dust and ashes, which before covered it; and the costly ointments used on occasion of festivity, instead of the ensigns of sorrow.

Ibid.—*trees approved*] Heb. *oaks of righteousness*, or *truth;* that is, such as by their flourishing condition should shew that they were indeed "the cion of God's planting, and the work of his hands:" under which images, in the preceding chap. ver. 21. the true servants of God, in a highly improved state of the church, were represented; that is, says Vitringa on that place, "commendable for the strength of their faith, their durability, and firmness."

4. *And they that spring from thee*] A word is lost here likewise. After ובנו, *they shall build,* add ממך, they that spring *from thee.* Four MSS have it so, (two of them ancient), and it is confirmed by chap. lviii. 12. where the sentence is the very same, this word being here added. Kimchi makes the same remark: "the word ממך is omitted here; but is found in chap. lviii. 12."

7. *Instead of your shame—*] The translation of this verse, which is very confused, and probably corrupted in the Hebrew, is taken from the Syriac version; except that the latter has not expressed the word משנה, *double,* in the first place. Five MSS add the conjunction ו to שמחת. Syr. reads תירשו and תרנו in the second person, "*ye* shall rejoice, *ye* shall inherit." And for להם, *to them,* two MSS (one of them ancient), and Syr. read לכם, *to you,* in the second person likewise.

The version of the LXX is imperfect in this place: the first half of the verse is entirely omitted in all the printed copies. It is supplied by MSS Pachom. and 1. D. 11. in the following manner:

Αντι της αισχυνης υμων της διπλης,
Και αντι της εντροπης αγαλλιασεται η μερις αυτων·
Δια τουτο την γην αυτων εκ δευτερου——

In which the two MSS agree, except that 1. D. 11. has by mistake ημερας for η μερις. And Cod. Marchal. in the margin, has pretty nearly the same supplement as from Theodotion.

8. —*and iniquity*] Syr. and Chald. prefix the conjunction ו, instead of the preposition ב, to עולה; which they render iniquity or oppression; and so the LXX, αδικιας.

10. *As the bridegroom decketh himself with a priestly crown*] An allusion to the magnificent dress of the High Priest, when performing his functions; and particularly to the mitre, and crown, or plate of gold on the front of it; Exod. xxix. 6. The bonnet or mitre of the priests also was made, as Moses expresses it, "for glory and for beauty;" Exod. xxviii. 40. It is difficult to give its full force to the Prophet's metaphor in another language; the version of Aquila and Symmachus comes nearest to it: ὡς νυμφιον ἱερατευομενον στεφανῳ.

11. *The Lord JEHOVAH*—] "ארנ, *the Lord*, makes the line longer than the preceding and following: and LXX Alex. [and MSS Pachom. and 1. D. 11.] and Arab. do not render it. Hence it seems to be interpolated:" Dr. JUBB. Three MSS have it not: See note on ver. 1. of this chapter.

CHAPTER LXII.

5. *For as a young man—so—*] The particles of comparison are not at present in the Hebrew text; but the LXX, Syr. and Chald. seem to have read in their copies כ prefixed to the verb כי כיבעל, which seems to have been omitted by mistake of a transcriber, occasioned by the repetition of the same two letters. And before the verb in the second line a MS adds כן, *so;* which the LXX, Syr. and Chald. seem also to have had in their copies. In the third line of this verse the same MS has in like manner וכמשש, and two MSS and the Babylonish Talmud כמשש, adding the כ: and in the fourth line, the Babylonish Talmud likewise adds כן, *so,* before the verb.

Sir John Chardin, in his note on this place, tells us, "that it is the custom in the East for youths, that were never married, always to marry virgins; and widowers, however young, to marry widows:" Harmer, Observ. ii. p. 482.

Ibid. —*thy restorer*—] בֹּנָיִךְ; see note on chap. xlix. 17.

6. *O ye that proclaim*—] The faithful, and in particular the priests and Levites, are exhorted by the Prophet to beseech God, with unremitted importunity, (compare Luke xviii. 1. &c.), to hasten the redemption of Sion. The image in this place is taken from the temple service: in which there was appointed a constant watch, day and night, by the Levites: and among them this service seems to have belonged particularly to the singers; see 1 Chron. ix. 33, Now the watches in the East, even to this day, are performed by a loud cry from time to time of the watchmen, to mark the time, and that very frequently, and in order to show that they themselves are constantly attentive to their duty. Hence the watchmen are said by the Prophet, chap. lii. 8. *to lift up their voice;* and here they are commanded, *not to keep silence;* and the greatest reproach to them is, *that they are dumb dogs; they cannot bark; dreamers, sluggards, loving to slumber:* chap. lvi. 10. " The watchmen in the camp of the caravans go their rounds, crying one after another, ' God is One, He is merciful;' and often add, ' Take heed to yourselves:'" Tavernier, Voyage de Perse, liv. i. chap. x. The cxxxivth Psalm gives us an example of the temple watch. The whole Psalm is nothing more than the alternate cry of two different divisions of the watch. The first watch addresses the second, reminding them of their duty; the second answers by a solemn blessing: the address and the answer seem both to be a set form, which each division proclaimed, or sung aloud, at stated intervals, to notify the time of the night: —

First Chorus.
" Come on now, bless ye JEHOVAH, all ye servants of JEHOVAH;
Ye that stand in the house of JEHOVAH in the nights:
Lift up your hands towards the sanctuary,
And bless ye JEHOVAH."

Second Chorus.
" JEHOVAH bless thee out of Sion;
He that made heaven and earth."

" Qui statis *in loco custodiæ* domus sanctuarii JEHOVÆ, et laudatis per noctes;" says the Chaldee paraphrase on the second line. And this explains what is here particularly meant by proclaiming, or making remembrance of, the name of JEHOVAH. The form which the watch made use of on these occasions was always a short sentence, expressing some pious sentiment, of which JEHOVAH was the subject: and it is remarkable, that the custom in the East in this respect also still continues the very same; as it appears by the example above given from Tavernier.

And this observation leads to the explanation of an obscure passage in the Prophet Malachi, ii. 12.

" JEHOVAH will cut off the man that doeth this;
  The watchman and the answerer, from the tabernacles of
    Jacob;
  And him that presenteth an offering to JEHOVAH God of
    Hosts."

עֵר וְעֹנֶה, *the master and the scholar,* says our translation after Vulg. ; *the son and the grandson,* says Syr. and Chald. as little to the purpose : Arias Montanus has given it, *vigilantem et respondentem, the watchman and the answerer ;* that is, the Levite : and *him that presenteth an offering to Jehovah ;* that is, the priest.

9. *But they that reap the harvest shall eat it, and praise* JEHOVAH—] This and the following line have reference to the law of Moses : " Thou mayest not eat within thy gates the tithe of thy corn, or of thy wine, or of thy oil ;—but thou must eat them before the Lord thy God, in the place which the Lord thy God shall choose ; " Deut. xii. 17, 18. " And when ye shall come into the land, and shall have planted all manner of trees for food, then ye shall count the fruit thereof as uncircumcised : three years it shall be as uncircumcised unto you ; it shall not be eaten of. But in the fourth year all the fruit thereof shall be holy to praise the Lord withal. And in the fifth year ye shall eat the fruit thereof : " Lev. xix. 23—25. This clearly explains the force of the expressions, " shall praise JEHOVAH," and " shall drink it in my sacred courts."

Five MSS (one ancient) have יאכלוהו, fully expressed : and so likewise ישתוהו is found in nineteen MSS, three of them ancient.

10—*for the people*] Before the word הָעָם, *the people,* two MSS insert יהוה, *Jehovah ;* one MS adds the same word after it ; and eight MSS (three ancient), instead of הָעָם have יהוה, and so likewise one edition. But though it makes a good sense either way, I believe it to be an interpolation, as the ancient versions do not favour it. The LXX indeed read עַמִּי, *my people.*

11. —*Lo ! thy Saviour*—] So all the ancient versions render the word יִשְׁעֵךְ.

Ibid. *Lo ! his reward*—] See note on chap. xl. 10.

CHAPTER LXIII.

THE very remarkable passage with which this chapter begins, seems to me to be in a manner detached from the rest, and to stand singly by itself ; having no immediate connection with what goes before, or with what follows ; otherwise than as it may pursue the general design, and stand in its proper place in the order of prophecy. It is by many learned interpreters supposed, that Judas Maccabeus and his victories make the subject of it. What claim Judas can have to so great an honour, will, I think, be very difficult to make out; or how the attributes of the great person introduced can possibly suit him. Could Judas call himself the announcer of righteousness, mighty to save? Could he talk of the day of vengeance being in his heart, and the year of his redeemed being come? or that his own arm wrought salvation for him? Besides, what were the great exploits of Judas in regard to the Idumeans? he overcame them in battle, and slew twenty thousand of them: and John Hyrcanus, his brother Simon's son and successor, who is called in to help out the accomplishment of the prophecy, gave them another defeat some time afterward, and compelled them by force to become proselytes to the Jewish religion, and to submit to circumcision; after which they were incorporated with the Jews, and became one people with them. Are these events adequate to the Prophet's lofty prediction? Was it so great an action to win a battle with considerable slaughter of the enemy; or to force a whole nation by dint of the sword into Judaism? or was the conversion of the Idumeans, however effected, and their admission into the church of God, equivalent to a most grievous judgment and destruction threatened in the severest terms?—But here is another very material circumstance to be considered, which, I presume, entirely excludes Judas Maccabeus, and even the Idumeans properly so called: The Idumea of the Prophet's time was quite a different country from that which Judas conquered; for, during the Babylonish captivity, the Nabatheans had driven the Edomites out of their country, who upon that took possession of the southern parts of Judea, and settled themselves there; that is, in the country of the whole tribe of Simeon, and in half of that of Judah: See Prideaux, ad An. 740 et 165.: And the metropolis of the Edomites, and of the country thence called Idumea, which Judas took, was Hebron, 1 Macc. v. 65. not Botsra.

I conclude therefore, that this prophecy has not the least relation to Judas Maccabeus. It may be asked, To whom, and to what event does it relate? I can only answer, that I know of no event in history to which, from its importance and circumstances, it can be applied; unless perhaps to the destruction of Jerusalem and the Jewish polity, which in the gospel is called the coming of Christ, and the days of vengeance; Matt. xvi. 28. Luke xxi. 22. But, though this prophecy must have its accomplishment, there is no necessity of supposing that it has been already accomplished. There are prophecies, which intimate a great slaughter of the enemies of God and his people, which remain to be fulfilled. Those in Ezekiel, chap. xxxviii. and in the Revelation of St. John, chap. xx. are called Gog and Magog. This prophecy of Isaiah may possibly refer to the same or the like event. We need not be at a loss to determine the person who is here introduced as stained with treading the wine-press, if we consider how St. John in the Revelation has applied this image of the Prophet; Rev. xix. 13. 15, 16.: compare chap. xxxiv.

1. *I who announce righteousness, and*—] A MS has המדבר, with the demonstrative article added, with greater force and emphasis, *The announcer* of righteousness. A MS has צדקה, without ב prefixed; and so LXX and Vulg. And thirty-eight MSS (seven ancient) add the conjunction ו to רב; which the LXX Syr. and Vulg. confirm.

2. *Wherefore is thine apparel red*—] For ללבוש, twenty-nine MSS (nine ancient), and one edition, have ללבושיך in the plural: so LXX and Syr. And all the ancient versions read it with מ instead of the first ל. But the true reading is probably מלבוש in the singular, as in ver. 3.

3. *And I have stained*—] For אגאלת, a verb of very irregular formation, compounded, as they say, of the two forms of the preterite and future, a MS has אגאלהו, the regular future with a pleonastic pronoun added to it, according to the Hebrew idiom: "And all my raiment, I have stained it." The necessity of the verb's being in the past time, seems to have given occasion to the alteration made in the end of the word. The conversive ו at the beginning of the sentence affects the verb, though not joined to it; of which there are many examples —:

ומקרני רמים עניתני

"And thou wilt hear me, (or hear thou me), from among the horns of the unicorns." Psal. xxii. 22.

7. *And mine indignation*—] For וחמתי, nineteen MSS (three ancient), and four editions, have וצדקתי, *and my righteousness*; from chap. lix. 16. which, I suppose, the transcriber retained in his memory.

6. *And I crushed them*] For ואשכרם, "and I made them drunken," twenty-seven MSS (three ancient), and

the old edition of 1488, have ואשכרם, " and I crushed them :" and so Syr. and Chald. The LXX have omitted this whole line.

7. The remaining part of this chapter, with the whole chapter following, contains a penitential confession and supplication of the Israelites in their present state of dispersion, in which they have so long marvellously subsisted, and still continue to subsist, as a people; cast out of their country; without any proper form of civil polity, or religious worship; their temple destroyed, their city desolated and lost to them; and their whole nation scattered over the face of the earth; apparently deserted and cast off by the God of their fathers, as no longer his peculiar people.

They begin with acknowledging God's great mercies and favours to their nation, and the ungrateful returns made to them on their part; that by their disobedience they had forfeited the protection of God, and had caused him to become their adversary. And now the Prophet represents them, induced by the memory of the great things that God had done for them, as addressing their humble supplication for the renewal of his mercies: They beseech him to regard them in consideration of his former loving-kindness; they acknowledge him for their Father and Creator; they confess their wickedness and hardness of heart; they entreat his forgiveness; and deplore their present miserable condition under which they have so long suffered. It seems designed as a formulary of humiliation for the Israelites, in order to their conversion.

The whole passage is in the elegiac form, pathetic and elegant; but it has suffered much in our present copy by the mistakes of transcribers.

Ibid. —*the praise of* JEHOVAH] For תהלות, plural, twenty-nine MSS (three ancient), and two editions, have תהלת, in the singular number: and so the Vulgate renders it; and one of the Greek versions, in the margin of Cod. Marchal. and in the text of MSS Pachom. and 1. D. 11. $την$ $αινεσιν$ $κυριου$.

8, 9. *And he became their saviour in all their distress*—] I have followed the translation of the LXX in the latter part of the 8th and the former part of the 9th verse; which agrees with the present text, a little differently divided, as to the members of the sentence. They read מכל, *out of all*, instead of בכל, *in all*, which makes no difference in the sense; and צר they understand as ציר. $Και$ $εγενετο$ $αυτοις$ $εις$

σωτηριαν εκ πασης θλιψεως αυτων· ου πρεσβυς, ουδε αγγελος—
An angel of his presence means an angel of superior order, in immediate attendance upon God. So the angel of the Lord says to Zacharias, "I am Gabriel, that stand in the presence of God;" Luke i. 19. The presence of JEHOVAH, Exod. xxxiii. 14, 15. and the angel, Exod. xxiii. 20, 21. is JEHOVAH himself: here, an angel of his presence is opposed to JEHOVAH himself; as an angel is in the following passages of the same book of Exodus. After their idolatrous worshipping of the golden calf, " when God had said to Moses, I will send an angel before thee—I will not go up in the midst of thee—the people mourned," Exod. xxxiii. 2—4. God afterwards comforts Moses by saying, " My presence (that is, I myself in person, and not by an angel) will go with thee," ver. 14. αυτος προπορευσομαι σου, as the LXX render it.

The MSS and editions are much divided between the two readings of the text and margin in the common copies, לא and לו. All the ancient versions express the chetib לא.

Ibid. *And he took them up, and he bare them*] See the note on chap. xlvi. 3.

10. *And he fought against them*] Twenty-six MSS (ten ancient), and the first edition, with another, add the conjunction ו, והוא.

11. *How he brought them up from the sea with the shepherd of his flock; How—*] For איה, *how*, interrogative, twice, the Syriac version reads אי, *how*, without interrogation; as that particle is used in the Syriac language, and sometimes in the Hebrew. See Ruth iii. 18. Eccles. ii. 16.

Ibid. *Moses his servant—*] For עמו, *his people*, two MSS (one of them ancient), and the old edition of 1488, and Syr. read עבדו, *his servant*. These two words have been mistaken one for the other in other places: Psal. lxxviii. 71. and lxxx. 5. for עמו and עמך, the LXX read עבדו and עבדך.

Ibid. *—the shepherd of his flock*] That is, Moses. The MSS and editions vary in this word: some have it רעה in the singular number; so LXX, Syr. Chald.; others רעי, plural.

14. *The spirit of Jehovah conducted them*] For תניחנו, *caused him to rest*, the LXX have ὡδηγησεν αυτους, *conducted them*. They read תנחם: Syr. Chald. Vulg. read תנהגו, *conducted him*. Two MSS have the word without the י in the middle.

15. *—and thy mighty power*] For גבורתיך, plural, thirty-

two MSS (seven ancient), and seven editions, have נבורתך, singular.

Ibid. —*are they restrained from us*] For אלי, *from (or in regard to) me*, LXX and Syr. read אלינו, *from us*.

16. *O deliver us for the sake of thy name*] The present text reads, as our translation has rendered it, "Our Redeemer, thy name is from everlasting." But instead of מעולם, *from everlasting*, an ancient MS has למען, *for the sake of*, which gives a much better sense. To shew the impropriety of the present reading, it is sufficient to observe, that the LXX and Syriac translators thought it necessary to add עלינו, *upon us*, to make out the sense; that is, "Thy name is *upon us*, or we are called by thy name, from of old." And the LXX have rendered גאלנו in the imperative mood, ῥῦσαι ἡμᾶς.

13. *It is little that they have taken possession of thy holy mountain*] The difficulty of the construction in this place is acknowledged on all hands. Vitringa prefers that sense as the least exceptionable, which our translation has expressed; in which however there seems to me to be a great defect; that is, the want of what in the speaker's view must have been the principal part of the proposition, the object of the verb, *the land*, or *it*, as our translators supply it; which surely ought to have been expressed, and not to have been left to be supplied by the reader. In a word, I believe, there is some mistake in the text. And here the LXX help us out: they had in their copy הר, *mountain*, instead of עם, *people;* Τοῦ ὄρους τοῦ ἁγίου σου. "Not only our enemies have taken possession of Mount Sion, and trodden down thy sanctuary; even far worse than this has befallen us: Thou hast long since utterly cast us off; and dost not consider us as thy peculiar people."

CHAPTER LXIV.

2. —*the dry fuel*—] המסים. "It means *dry stubble*, and the root is המם," says Rabbi Jonah, apud Sal. ben Melech in loc. Which is approved by Schultens, Orig. Hebr. p. 30.

"The fire kindling the stubble does not seem like enough to the melting of the mountains to be brought as a simile to it. Quid si sic?

That the mountains might flow down at thy presence!
As the fire of things smelted burneth,
As the fire causeth the waters to boil—

There is no doubt of the Hebrew words of the second line bearing that version:" DR JUBB.

I submit these different interpretations to the reader's judgment. For my own part, I am inclined to think that the text is much corrupted in this place. The ancient versions have not the least traces of either of the above interpretations. The LXX and Syr. agree exactly together in rendering this line by, "As the wax melted before the fire," which can by no means be reconciled with the present text. Vulg. for המסים reads ימסו.

Ibid. *That the nations*—] For גוים, *the nations*, four MSS (one of them ancient) have הרים, *the mountains*.

4. *For never have men heard*—] St. Paul is generally supposed to have quoted this passage of Isaiah, 1 Cor. ii. 9.; and Clemens Romanus, in his first epistle, has made the same quotation, very nearly in the same words with the apostle. But the citation is so very different both from the Hebrew text and the version of LXX, that it seems very difficult, if not impossible, to reconcile them by any literal emendation, without going beyond the bounds of temperate criticism. One clause, "neither hath it entered into the heart of man," (which, by the way, is a phrase purely Hebrew, עלה על לב, and should seem to belong to the Prophet), is wholly left out; and another is repeated without force or propriety, viz. "nor perceived by the ear," after "never have heard:" and the sense and expression of the apostle is far preferable to that of the Hebrew text. Under these difficulties, I am at a loss what to do better than to offer to the reader this, perhaps disagreeable, alternative; Either to consider the Hebrew text and LXX in this place as wilfully disguised and corrupted by the Jews; of which practice, in regard to other quotations in the New Testament from the Old, they lie under strong suspicions; (see Dr. Owen on the Version of the Seventy, sect. vi.—ix.); or to look upon St. Paul's quotation as not made from Isaiah, but from one or other of the two apocryphal books entitled, The Ascension of Esaiah, and The Apocalyps of Elias, in both of which this passage was found; and the apostle is by some supposed in other places to have quoted such apocryphal writings. As the first of these conclusions will perhaps not easily be admitted by many; so I must fairly warn my readers, that the second is treated by Jerom as little better than heresy. See his comment on this place of Isaiah.

The variations on this place are as follows: for שמעו, *they have heard*, a MS and LXX read שמענו, *we have heard*: for the second לא, sixty-nine MSS and four editions have ולא; and Syr. Chald. Vulg.; and so ויען, LXX Syr. את is added before אלהים in MS Bodl. למחכי, plural, two MSS, and all the ancient versions.

5. *Thou meetest with joy those—*] Syr. reads—פוגע אתה שש בעשי.

Ibid. *Because of our deeds, for we have been rebellious.*] בהם עולם ונושע. I am fully persuaded, that these words, as they stand in the present Hebrew text, are utterly unintelligible: there is no doubt of the meaning of each word separately, but put together they make no sense at all. I conclude, therefore, that the copy has suffered by mistakes of transcribers in this place. The corruption is of long standing; for the ancient interpreters were as much at a loss for the meaning as the moderns, and give nothing satisfactory. The LXX render these words by διὰ τουτο ἐπλανήθημεν: they seem to have read עליהם נפשע, without helping the sense. In this difficulty, what remains but to have recourse to conjecture? Archbishop SECKER was dissatisfied with the present reading: he proposes, הבט עלינו ונושע; "look upon us; and we shall, or that we may, be saved;" which gives a very good sense, but seems to have no sufficient foundation. Besides, the word ונושע, which is attended with great difficulties, seems to be corrupted, as well as the two preceding; and the true reading of it is, I think, given by the LXX, ונפשע, ἐπλανήθημεν, (so they render the verb פשע, chap. xlvi. 8. and Ezek. xxxiii. 12), parallel to ונחטא, ἡμαρτομεν. For בהם עולם, which mean nothing, I would propose המעללינו; which I presume was first altered to במעלליהם, an easy and common mistake of the third person plural of the pronoun for the first, (see note on chap. xxxiii. 2.), and then with some further alteration to בהם עולם. The עליהם, which the LXX probably found in their copy, seems to be a remnant of במעלליהם.

This, it may be said, is imposing your sense upon the Prophet. It may be so; for perhaps these may not be the very words of the Prophet: but however it is better than to impose upon him what makes no sense at all; as they generally do who pretend to render such corrupted passages. For instance, our own translators: "In *those* is continuance, and we shall be saved:" In those—in whom, or what?

There is no antecedent to the relative. *In the ways of God*, say some: *with our fathers*, says Vitringa, joining it in construction with the verb קצפת, *thou hast been angry with them, our fathers;* and putting ונחטא, *for we have sinned*, in a parenthesis. But there has not been any mention of *our fathers:* and the whole sentence, thus disposed, is utterly discordant from the Hebrew idiom and construction. In those is *continuance:* עולם means a destined, but hidden and unknown, portion of time; but cannot mean continuation of time, or *continuance*, as it is here rendered. Such forced interpretations are equally conjectural with the boldest critical emendation; and generally have this further disadvantage,' that they are altogether unworthy of the sacred writers.

6. *There is no one—*] Twelve MSS have אין, without the conjunction ו prefixed: and so read Chald. and Vulg.

Ibid. *And hast delivered us up—*] For ותמוגנו, *hast dissolved us*, LXX, Syr. Chald. had in their copies תמגננו, *hast delivered us up:* Houbigant; SECKER.

7. *But Thou, O JEHOVAH, Thou—*] For ועתה, *and now*, five MSS (one of them ancient), and the two oldest editions of 1486 and 1488, have ואתה, *and thou;* and so Chald. seems to have read. The repetition has great force. The other word may be well spared.

Ibid. *We are all of us the work of thy hands.*] Three MSS (two of them ancient), and LXX, read מעשה, without the conjunction ו prefixed. And for יד, the Bodl. and two other MSS, LXX, Syr. Vulg. read ידיך, in the plural number.

CHAPTER LXV.

THIS chapter contains a defence of God's proceedings in regard to the Jews, with reference to their complaint in the chapter preceding. God is introduced declaring, that he had called the Gentiles, though they had not sought him; and had rejected his own people, for their refusal to attend to his repeated call; for their obstinate disobedience, their idolatrous practices, and detestable hypocrisy. That nevertheless he would not destroy them all; but would preserve a remnant, to whom he would make good his ancient promises. Severe punishments are threatened to the apostates; and great rewards are promised to the obedient in a future flourishing state of the church.

1. *I am made known to those that asked not for me*] נדרשתי,

ἐμφανὴς ἐγενόμην, LXX, Alex. and St Paul. Rom. x. 20.; who has however inverted the order of the phrases, ἐμφανὴς ἐγενόμην, and εὑρέθην, from that which they have in LXX. נדרשתי means, "quæsitus sum cum effectu—I am sought, so as to be found:" Vitring. If this be the true meaning of the word, then שאלו, *that asked*, which follows, should seem to be defective, the verb wanting its object; but two MSS (one of them ancient) have שאלוני, asked *me ;* and another MS שאלו לי, asked *for me ;* one or other of which seems to be right. But Cocceius in Lex. and Vitringa in his translation. render נדרשתי by "I have answered;" and so the word s rendered by all the ancient versions in Ezek. xx. 3. 31. If this be right, the translation will be, "I have answered those that asked not." I leave this to the reader's judgment; but have followed in my translation the LXX, and St Paul, and the MSS above mentioned. בקשני is written regularly and fully in above a hundred MSS, and in the oldest edition, בקשוני.

3, 4. *Sacrificing in the gardens, and*—] These are instances of heathenish superstition, and idolatrous practices. to which the Jews were immoderately addicted before the Babylonish captivity. The heathen worshipped their idols in groves; whereas God, in opposition to this species of idolatry, commanded his people, when they should come into the promised land, to destroy all the places wherein the Canaanites had served their gods, and in particular to burn their groves with fire; Deut. xii. 2, 3. These apostate Jews sacrificed upon altars built of bricks, in opposition to the command of God in regard to his altar, which was to be of unhewn stone; Exod. xx. 25. "—et pro uno altari, quod impolitis lapidibus Dei erat lege constructum, coctos lateres et agrorum cespites hostiarum sanguine cruentabant:" Hieron. in loc. Or it means, perhaps, that they sacrificed upon the roofs of their houses, which were always flat, and paved with brick, or tile, or plaster of terrace. An instance of this idolatrous practice we find in 2 Kings xxiii. 12. where it is said, that Josiah "beat down the altars that were on the top of the upper chamber of Ahaz, which the kings of Judah had made." See also Zeph. i. 5. Sir John Chardin's MS note on this place of Isaiah is as follows: "Ainsi font tous les Gentiles, sur les lieux elevés, et sur les terrasses; appellez *lateres,* parceque sont faits de briq."—" *Who dwell in the sepulchres, and lodge in the caverns,*" for the purposes of necromancy and divination; to obtain dreams and revelations. Another instance of heathenish superstition :—

"Huc dona sacerdos
Cum tulit, et cæsarum ovium sub nocte silenti
Pellibus incubuit stratis, somnosque petivit;
Multa modis simulacra videt volitantia miris,
Et varias audit voces, fruiturque deorum
Colloquio, atque imis Acheronta affatur Avernis."
Virg. Æn. vii. 86.

"Here in distress the Italian nations come,
Anxious to clear their doubts, and learn their doom:
First, on the fleeces of the slaughtered sheep,
By night the sacred priest dissolves in sleep;
When, in a train, before his slumbering eye,
Thin airy forms and wondrous visions fly:
He calls the Powers who guard the infernal floods,
And talks, inspired, familiar with the gods." Pitt.

—"*Who eat swine's flesh*," which was expressly forbidden by the law, Lev. xi. 7.; but among the heathen was in principal request in their sacrifices and feasts. Antiochus Epiphanes compelled the Jews to eat swine's flesh, as a full proof of their renouncing their religion, 2 Macc. vi. 18. and vii. 1.—"*And the broth of abominable meats*," for lustrations, magical arts, and other superstitious and abominable practices.

Ibid. —*in the caverns.*] בנצורים, a word of doubtful signification. An ancient MS has בצורים, another בצרים, *in the rocks;* and Le Clerc thinks the LXX had it so in their copy. They render it by εν τοις σπηλαιοις.

Ibid. —*in their vessels.*] For כליהם, a MS had at first בכליהם : so Vulg. and Chald.; and the preposition seems necessary to the sense.

5. —*For I am holier than thou*] So the Chaldee renders it. קדשתיך is the same with קדשתי ממך. In the same manner חזקתני, Jer. xx. 7. is used for חזקת ממני, *thou art stronger than I*.

7. —*into their bosom*] For על, ten MSS and five editions have אל. So again, at the end of this verse, seventeen MSS and four editions have אל.

6, 7. —*their iniquities and the iniquities of their fathers*] For the pronoun affixed of the second person בם, *your*, twice. read הם, *their*, in the third person; with LXX, and Houbigant.

8. —*for the sake of my servants*] It is to be observed, that one of the Koningsberg MSS collated by Lilienthal points the word עבדי, singular; that is, *my servant*, meaning

the Messiah; and so read the LXX; which gives a very good sense.

9. —*inheritor of my mountain*] הרי, in the singular number; so LXX and Syr.; that is, of Mount Sion. See ver. 11. and chap. lvi. 7.; to which Sion, the pronoun feminine singular, added to the verb in the next line, refers; ירשוה, *shall inherit her.*

10. —*Sharon, and the valley of Achor*—] Two of the most fertile parts of Judea, famous for their rich pastures: the former to the west, not far from Joppa; the latter north of Jericho, near Gilgal.

11. *Who set in order a table for Gad*—] The disquisitions and conjectures of the learned concerning Gad and Meni are infinite and uncertain: perhaps the most probable may be, that Gad means good fortune, and Meni the moon. "But why should we be solicitous about it?" says Schmidius. "It appears sufficiently, from the circumstance, that they were false gods, either stars or some other natural object, or a mere fiction. The Holy Scriptures did not deign to explain more clearly what these objects of idolatrous worship were; but chose rather that the memory of the knowlledge of them should be utterly abolished. And God be praised that they are so totally abolished, that we are now quite at a loss to know what and what sort of things they were:" Schmidius on the place, and on Judg. ii. 13. Bibl. Hallensia.

Jerom, on the place, gives an account of this idolatrous practice of the apostate Jews, of making a feast, or a lectisternium, as the Romans called it, for these pretended deities. "Est in cunctis urbibus, et maxime in Ægypto, et in Alexandria, idololatriæ vetus consuetudo, ut ultimo die anni, et mensis ejus qui extremus est, ponant mensam refertam varii generis epulis, et poculum mulso mixtum; vel præteriti anni vel futuri fertilitatem auspicantes. Hoc autem faciebant et Israelitæ, omnium simulacrorum portenta venerantes; et nequaquam altari victimas, sed hujusmodi mensæ liba fundebant." See also Le Clerc on the place; and on lxvi. 17. and Dav. Millii Dissert. v.

The allusion to Meni, which signifies *number*, is obvious. If there had been the like allusion to Gad, which might have been expected, it might perhaps have helped to let us into the meaning of that word. It appears from Jerom's version of this place, that the words τῳ δαιμονίῳ, (or δαίμονι, as some copies have it), and τῇ τύχῃ stood in his time in the

Greek version in an inverted order from that which they have in the present copies; the latter then answering to גד, the former to מנ: by which some difficulty would be avoided; for it is commonly supposed that גד signifies τυχη. See Gen. xxx. 11. apud LXX. This matter is so far well cleared up by MSS Pachom. and 1. D. 11.; which agree in placing these two words in that order which Jerom's version supposes.

15. —*shall slay you.*] For והמיתך, *shall slay thee*, LXX and Chald. read והמיתכם, *shall slay you*, plural.

17. —*I create new heavens, and a new earth*] Concerning this image and the application of it, see De S. Poes. Hebr. Præl. ix.

18. —*in the age to come, which I create*] So in chap. ix. 5. אבי־עד, πατηρ του μελλοντος αιωνος, LXX. See Bishop Chandler, Defence of Christianity, p. 136.

20. For משם, *thence*, LXX, Syr. Vulg. read שם, *there*.

21. *They shall not build, and another inhabit*] The reverse of the curse denounced on the disobedient, Deut. xxviii. 30. "Thou shalt build a house, and thou shalt not dwell therein; thou shalt plant a vineyard, and shalt not gather the grapes thereof."

22. *For as the days of a tree—*] It is commonly supposed, that the oak, one of the most long-lived of the trees, lasts about a thousand years; being five hundred years growing to full perfection, and as many decaying; which seems to be a moderate and probable computation: See Evelyn, Sylva, B. iii. ch. 3. The present Emperor of China, in his very ingenious and sensible poem, entituled, Eloge de Moukden, a translation of which in French was published at Paris, 1770, speaks of a tree in his country which lives more than a hundred ages; and of another, which after fourscore ages is only in its prime, p. 37, 38. But his imperial majesty's commentators, in their note on the place, carry the matter much further; and quote authority which affirms, that the tree last mentioned by the Emperor, the immortal tree, after having lived ten thousand years, is still only in its prime. I suspect that the Chinese enlarge somewhat in their national chronology, as well as in that of their trees: See Chou King, Preface, by Mons. De Guignes. The Prophet's idea seems to be, that they shall live to the age of the antediluvians; which seems to be very justly expressed by the days of a tree, according to our notions.

23. *My chosen shall not labour in vain*] I remove בחירי from the end of the 22d to the beginning of the 23d verse, on the authority of LXX, Syr. Vulg. and a MS; contrary to the division in the Masoretic text.

Ibid. *Neither shall they generate a short-lived race*] לבהלה, *in festinationem*, what shall soon hasten away. Εις καταραν, *for a curse*, LXX. They seem to have read לאלה; Grotius. But Psal. lxxviii. 33. both justifies and explains the word here.

ויכל בהבל ימיהם
ושנותם בבהלה:

"And he consumed their days in vanity;
And their years in haste."

Μετα σπουδης, say the LXX. Jerom on this place of Isaiah, explains it to the same purpose: " εις ανυπαρξιαν, hoc est, *ut esse desistant.*"

25. —*shall feed together*] For כאחד, *as one*, an ancient MS has יחדו, *together;* the usual word, to the same sense, but very different in the letters. LXX, Syr. and Vulg. seem to agree with the MS.

CHAPTER LXVI.

This chapter is a continuation of the subject of the foregoing. The Jews valued themselves much upon their temple, and the pompous system of services performed in it, which they supposed were to be of perpetual duration; and they assumed great confidence and merit to themselves for their strict observance of all the externals of their religion. And at the very time when the judgments, denounced in ver. 6th and 12th of the preceding chapter, were hanging over their heads, they were rebuilding, by Herod's munificence, the temple in a most magnificent manner. God admonishes them, that the Most High dwelleth not in temples made with hands; and that a mere external worship, how diligently soever attended, when accompanied with wicked and idolatrous practices in the worshippers, would never be accepted by him. This their hypocrisy is set forth in strong colours; which brings the Prophet again to the subject of the former chapter; and he pursues it in a different manner, with more express declaration of the new economy, and of the flourishing state of the church under it. The increase of the church is to be sudden and astonishing. They that escape of the Jews, that is, that become converts to the Christian faith, are to be employed in the divine mission to the Gentiles, and are to act as priests in presenting the Gentiles as an offering to God: see Rom. xv. 16.: And both, now collected into one body, shall be witnesses of the final perdition of the obstinate and irreclaimable.

These two chapters manifestly relate to the calling of the Gentiles, the establishment of the Christian dispensation, and the reprobation of the apostate Jews, and their destruction executed by the Romans.

2. —*all these things are mine*] A word, absolutely necessary to the sense, is here lost out of the text; לי, *mine;* it is preserved by LXX, and Syr.

3. *He that slayeth an ox, killeth a man;*—] These are instances of extreme wickedness joined with hypocrisy, of the most flagitious crimes, committed by those who at the same time affected great strictness in the performance of all the external services of religion. God, by the Prophet Ezekiel, upbraids the Jews with the same practices: "When they had slain their children to their idols, then they came the same day into my sanctuary to profane it;" chap. xxiii. 39. Of the same kind was the hypocrisy of the Pharisees in our Saviour's time; "who devoured widows' houses, and for a pretence made long prayers;" Matt. xxiii. 14.

The generality of interpreters, by departing from the literal rendering of the text, have totally lost the true sense of it, and have substituted in its place what makes no good sense at all; for it is not easy to shew, how in any circumstances sacrifice and murder, the presenting of legal offerings and idolatrous worship, can possibly be of the same account in the sight of God.

Ibid. —*that maketh an oblation [offereth] swine's blood*] A word here likewise, necessary to complete the sense, is perhaps irrecoverably lost out of the text. The Vulg. and Chald. add the word *offereth*, to make out the sense; not, as I imagine, from any different reading, (for the word wanted seems to have been lost before the time of the oldest of them, as the LXX had it not in their copy), but from mere necessity.

Le Clerc thinks, that כלה is to be repeated from the beginning of this member; but that is not the case in the parallel members, which have another and a different verb in the second place. "דם, sic versiones: putarem tamen legendum participium aliquod, et quidem זבח, cum sequatur

ר, nisi jam præcesserat:" SECKER. Houbigant supplies אכל, *eateth*. After all, I think the most probable word is that which Chald. and Vulg. seem to have designed to represent; that is, מקריב.

5. *Say ye to your brethren—*] The Syr. reads אמרו לאחיכם; and so the LXX, edit. Comp. ειπατε αδελφοις υμων; and MS Marchal. has αδελφοις; and so Cyril and Procopius read and explain it. It is not easy to make sense of the reading of LXX in the other editions: ειπατε αδελφοι ημων τοις μισουσιν υμας—but for ημων, MS 1. D. 11. also has υμων.

8. *—and who hath seen*] Twenty MSS (four ancient), and the two oldest editions, with two others, have ומי, adding the conjunction ו: and so read all the ancient versions.

11. *—from her abundant stores*] For מזיו, two MSS, and the old edition of 1488, have מזיז; and the latter ז is upon a rasure in three other MSS. It is remarkable, that Kimchi and Sal. ben Melec, not being able to make any thing of the word as it stands in the text, says it means the same with מזיו: that is, in effect, they admit of a various reading, or an error, in the text. But, as Vitringa observes, what sense is there in sucking nourishment from the *splendour* of her glory? He therefore endeavours to deduce another sense from the word זיו; but, as far as it appears to me, without any authority. I am more inclined to accede to the opinion of those learned Rabbins, and to think that there is some mistake in the word; for that in truth is their opinion, though they disguise it by saying, that the corrupted word means the very same with that which they believe to be genuine. So in chap. xli. 24. they say, that אפעה, *a viper*, means the same with אפס, *nothing*; instead of acknowledging that one is written by mistake instead of the other. I would propose to read in this place מזון, or מזן, (instead of מזיו), *from the stores*; from זון, *to nourish, to feed*: see Gen. xlv. 23. 2 Chron. xi. 23. Psal. cxliv. 13. And this perhaps may be meant by Aquila, who renders the word by απο πανδαπιας: with which that of the Vulgate, " ab omnimoda gloria," and of Symmachus and Theodotion, nearly agree. The Chaldee follows a different reading, without improving the sense; מיין, *from the wine*.

12. *—like the great river, and like the overflowing stream—*] That is, the Euphrates, (it ought to have been pointed כנהר, *ut fluvius ille*, as The River), and the Nile.

Ibid. *And ye shall suck at the breast*] These two words על שד, *at the breast*, seem to have been omitted in the present text, from their likeness to the two words following; עַל צַר, *at the side.* A very probable conjecture of Houbigant. Chald. and Vulg. have omitted the two latter words instead of the two former. See note on chap. lx. 4.

15. —*shall come as a fire*] For באש, *in fire,* the LXX had in their copy כאש, *as a fire;* ὡς πυρ.

Ibid. *To breathe forth his anger*] Instead of לְהָשִׁיב, as pointed by the Masoretes, *to render,* I understand it as לְהַשִּׁיב, *to breathe,* from נשב.

17. *after the rites of Achad*—] The Syrians worshipped a god called Adad: Plin. Nat. Hist. xxxvii. 11. Macrob. Sat. i. 23. They held him to be the highest and greatest of the gods, and to be the same with Jupiter and the Sun: and the name Adad, says Macrobius, signifies *One;* as likewise does the word Achad in Isaiah. Many learned men therefore have supposed, and with some probability, that the Prophet means the same pretended deity. אחר, in the Syrian and Chaldean dialects is חר; and perhaps by reduplication of the last letter, to express perfect unity, it may have become חדר, not improperly expressed in Latin by Macrobius Adad, without the aspirate. It was also pronounced by the Syrians themselves, with a weaker aspirate הדר; as in Benhaded, Hadadezer, names of their kings, which were certainly taken from their chief object of worship. This seems to me to be a probable account of this name.

But the Masoretes correct the text in this place: their marginal reading is אחת, which is the same word, only in the feminine form; and so read thirty MSS (six ancient) and the two oldest editions. This Le Clerc approves, and supposes it to mean Hecate, or the Moon; and he supports his hypothesis by arguments not at all improbable. See his note on the place.

Whatever the particular mode of idolatry which the Prophet refers to might be, the general sense of the place is perfectly clear. But Chald. and Syr. and after them Symmachus and Theodotion, cut off at once all these difficulties, by taking the word אחר in its common meaning, not as a proper name; the two latter rendering the sentence thus: οπισω αλληλων εν μεσω εσθιοντων το κρεας το χοιρειον, *one after another, in the midst of those that eat swine's flesh.* I suppose, they all read in their copies אחר אחר, *one by one,* or perhaps אחר אחר, *one after another.* See a large Dissertation on this subject in Davidis Millii Dissertationes Selectæ, Dissert. vi.

18. *For I know their deeds* —] A word is here lost out of the present text, leaving the sense quite imperfect. The word is ידע, *knowing*, supplied from the Syriac. The Chald. had the same word in the copy before him, which he paraphrases by קדמי גלן, their deeds *are manifest before me :* and the Aldine and Complutensian editions of LXX acknowledge the same word, επισαμαι; which is verified by MS Pachom. and the Arabic version. I think there can be little doubt of its being genuine.

Ibid. *And I come*—] For באה, which will not accord with any thing in the sentence, I read בא, with a MS; the participle answering to יודע; with which agree LXX, Syr. Vulg. Perhaps it ought to be ובא, Syr. *quando* veniam : and so LXX, according to edit. Ald. and Complut. and Cod. Marchal.

19. —*who draw the bow*] I much suspect, that the words משכי קשת, *who draw the bow*, are a corruption of the word משך, Moschi, the name of a nation situated between the Euxine and Caspian Seas; and properly joined with תבל, the Tibareni : see Bochart, Phaleg. iii. 12. The LXX have μοσοχ, without any thing of the *drawers of the bow:* the word being once taken for a participle, *the bow* was added to make sense of it. קשת, *the bow*, is omitted in a MS.

Ibid. —*who never heard my name*] For שמעי, *my fame*, I read with LXX and Syr. שמי, *my name.*

20. —*and in counes*] There is a sort of vehicle, much used in the East, consisting of a pair of hampers, or cradles, thrown across a camel's back, one on each side ; in each of which a person is carried. They have a covering to defend them from the rain and the sun. Thevenot calls them Counes, i. p. 356. Maillet describes them as covered cages hanging on both sides of a camel. "At Aleppo," says Dr Russell, "women of inferior condition, in longer journies, are commonly stowed, one on each side of a mule, in a sort of covered cradles : " Nat. Hist. of Aleppo, p. 89. These seem to be what the Prophet means by the word צבים : See Harmer, Observ. i. p. 445.

21. —*and for Levites*] For ללוים, fifty-nine MSS (eight ancient) have וללוים, adding the conjunction ו, as the sense seems necessarily to require ; and so read all the ancient versions. See Josh. iii. 3. and the various readings on that place in Kennicott's Bible.

24. *For their worm shall not die*—] These words of the Prophet are applied by our blessed Saviour, Mark ix. 44.

to express the everlasting punishment of the wicked in Gehenna, or in Hell. Gehenna, or the Valley of Hinnom, was very near to Jerusalem, to the south-east: it was the place where the idolatrous Jews celebrated that horrible rite of making their children pass through the fire—that is, of burning them in sacrifice—to Moloch. To put a stop to this abominable practice, Josiah defiled, or desecrated, the place, by filling it with human bones; 2 Kings xxiii. 10. 14.; and probably it was the custom afterwards to throw out the carcasses of animals there; and it became the common burying-place for the poorer people of Jerusalem. Our Saviour expressed the state of the blessed by sensible images; such as Paradise, Abraham's bosom, or, which is the same thing, a place to recline next to Abraham at table in the kingdom of heaven: see Matt. viii. 11. ("Cænabat Nerva cum paucis. Veiento *proximus*, atque etiam *in sinu* recumbebat;" Plin. Epist. iv. 22.: compare John xiii. 23.); for we could not possibly have any conception of it, but by analogy from worldly objects. In like manner, he expressed the place of torment under the image of Gehenna; and the punishment of the wicked, by the worm which there preyed on the carcasses, and the fire which consumed the wretched victims:— marking however, in the strongest manner, the difference between Gehenna and the invisible place of torment; namely, that in the former the suffering is transient—the worm itself, that preys on the body, dies; and the fire, which totally consumes it, is soon extinguished;—whereas in the figurative Gehenna the instruments of punishment shall be everlasting, and the suffering without end; for there "the worm dieth not, and the fire is not quenched."

These emblematical images, expressing heaven and hell, were in use among the Jews before our Saviour's time; and in using them he complied with their notions. "Blessed is he that shall eat bread in the kingdom of God," says the Jew to our Saviour, Luke xiv. 15. And in regard to Gehenna, the Chaldee paraphrast, as I observed before on chap. xxx. 33. renders everlasting, or continual, burnings, by "the Gehenna of everlasting fire." And before his time the Son of Sirach, vii. 17. had said, "the vengeance of the ungodly is fire and worms." So likewise the author of the book of Judith: "Wo to the nations rising up against my kindred: the Lord Almighty will take vengeance of them in the day of judgment, in putting fire and worms in their flesh," chap. xvi. 17.; manifestly referring to the same emblem.

INDEX OF TEXTS

OCCASIONALLY ILLUSTRATED.

The small Numeral Letters refer to the pages of the DISSERTATION; the Figures, to the pages of the Notes.

	Page		Page
GENESIS.		xxviii. 40.	386
ii. 10.	145	xxix. 6.	386
xiii. 10.	145	—— 42, 43.	224
xxiv. 47.	163	xxxiii. 2—4. 14.	392
xxvi. 20.	307	—— 14, 15.	392
xxx. 11.	400	xxxviii. 8.	195
xxxi. 34.	152	xl. 34—38.	158
—— 42, 53.	198	— 38.	169
xxxiii. 13.	318		
xl. 11.	172	LEVITICUS.	
xlii. 6.	351	iv.	138
xlix. 11.	172	vi. 12, 13.	184
EXODUS.		ix. 24.	184
iv. 10.	184	xi. 7.	398
v.	204	xiii. 45.	364
vi. 12.	184	xiv. 42.	184
x. 21.	201	xix. 23—25.	388
xi. 5.	342	xxi. 18.	177
xii. 22.	271	xxii. 23.	177
— 23.	289	xxiii. 36.	139
— 29.	342	xxv. 9, &c.	384
xiii. 21.	169	xxvi. 8.	285
xiv. 13, 14.	271		
—— 21.	213	NUMBERS.	
—— 27.	190	vi. 4.	174
xv. 17.	169,170	xi. 5.	137, 240
— 20,21.	xli, 183,317	— 12.	341
xvi. 9. 10.	158	xii. 14.	353
xx. 25.	397	xiii. 22, 23.	171
xxi. 7.	352	xiv. 34.	244
— 10.	167	xvi. 41, 42.	158
xxiii. 20,21.	392	xxi. 17, 18.	xxxv
—— 28.	179	xxii. 4.	178
xxiv. 6.	257	xxiii. 7—10.	224
xxv. 22.	224	—— 21, 22.	310

INDEX OF TEXTS.

	Page		Page
xxiv. 6.	356	**1 Samuel.**	
xxix. 35.	139	ii. 27.	252
		iii. 21.	252
Deuteronomy.		ix. 7.	374
i. 31.	340	— 15.	176
— 44.	179	— 25.	250
iii. 25.	171	xiii. 6.	156
vii. 25.	285	xiv. 4, 5.	210
viii. 15.	285	xv. 27.	157
xii. 2, 3.	397	xvii. 52.	275
— 17, 18.	388	xviii. 6, 7.	xli, 317
xvi. 8.	139	xix. 13.	152
xvii. 16.	284	xxiv.	155
—— 16, 17.	151		
xxi. 23.	225	**2 Samuel.**	
xxii. 15.	282	vi. 14. 16.	xli
— 8.	250	x. 4, 5.	193
xxiii. 4.	249	xi. 23.	275
xxiv. 1.	352	xiv. 2.	384
xxv. 4.	279	xv. 30.	364
—— 7.	282	xxii. 41.	xii
—— 9.	353	xxiv. 7.	258
xxvii. 15.	374		
xxviii. 30.	400	**1 Kings.**	
xxx. 19.	133	iv. 22, 23.	158
xxxi. 21.	132	vii. 2, 3.	251
xxxii.	xxxv, xxxix	x. 16, 17, 21.	257
—— 1.	132	— 26—29.	151
—— 13.	368	— 27.	204
—— 15.	329	xviii. 26.	288
—— 16.	xxxix	—— 38.	178
—— 21.	259	xx. 11.	179
—— 30.	285	xxii. 48.	154
—— 32, 33.	175	—— 49.	154
xxxiii. 5. 26.	329		
—— 6.	258	**2 Kings.**	
—— 28.	344	iv. 1.	352
		— 39—41.	174
Joshua.		v. 23.	196
iii. 3.	405	ix. 30.	160
v. 6.	190	xv. 3, 4. 34, 35.	152
x. 24.	357	— 29.	196, 201
xi. 6.	202	— 37.	136, 136
xv. 2. 5.	214	xvi. 9.	196, 232, 251
xviii. 19.	214	xvii. 6.	251
xix. 29.	258	— 6. 24.	260
xxii. 14.	157	xviii, xix, xx.	302
		xviii. 8.	226, 243
Judges.		—— 14—16.	293
i. 7.	357	—— 17.	214
vi. 2.	156	—— 18.	302
xi. 31.	325	xviii. 20.	302
— 34.	317	—— 22.	302
xvi. 3, 4.	171	—— 32.	302
xx. 38. 40.	285	—— 34.	302
Ruth.		xix. 9.	303
ii. 14.	190	— 15.	303
iii. 18.	392		

INDEX OF TEXTS.

	Page		Page
xix 17.	303		
— 19.	303	NEHEMIAH.	
— 20.	304	v. 17, 18.	158
— 23.	304	xii. 24.	xli
— 25.	304		
— 35.	305	ESTHER.	
xx. 4, 5.	306	ii. 12.	165
— 6.	306	vi. 12. and vii. 8.	254
— 7, 8.	306		
— 9. 11.	306	JOB.	
— 12.	308	i. 1.	246
— 17.	309	— 17.	257
— 20.	252	— 19.	246
xxi. 13.	275	iii. 4. 6. 9.	xiii
xxiii. 10. 14.	406	— 24.	307
—— 12.	397	v. 23.	276
—— 19, 20.	187	viii. 5, 6.	xiv
xxiv. 14.	157	ix. 8.	368
xxv. 4, 5.	250	xii. 13—16.	xviii
—— 12. 22.	185	xiii. 19.	354
		xvii. 3.	354
		xx. 24.	220
1 CHRONICLES.		xxi. 18.	320
v. 26.	196, 201	xxvi. 2, 3.	207
ix. 33	386	xxvi. 5.	xii
xiii. 5.	258	xxvii—xxxi.	224
xxviii. 2.	383	xxvii. 18.	137
		xxx. 7.	151
2 CHRONICLES.		— 10.	353
i. 15.	152	— 30.	199
vii. i.	184	xxxiii. 18.	308
viii. 17, 18.	154	xxxvii. 9.	246
ix. 18.	358	—— 11.	238
— 21.	154	xxxviii. 6.	135
xx. 20.	189	xli. 1.	354
— 36.	154	xlii. 10.	313
xxvi. 6, 7.	226		
—— 22.	181	PSALMS.	
xxix. 19.	240	i. 3.	146
xxxii. 2—5.	250	— 4.	145, 320
—— 2, 3. 5. 30.	252	ii. 7.	308
—— 10.	135	x. 1.	375
—— 23.	226, 239	xviii. 35.	220
—— 25, 26. 30, 31.	309	xix. 7—10.	xxiv
—— 27.	296	— 14.	267
—— 30.	252	xx. 1.	295
—— 32.	131	— 7, 8.	xvi
—— 33.	253, 368	xxi. 1, 2.	x
xxxiii. 11.	188	xxii. 2.	307
—— 17.	152	— 22.	390
xxxiv. 6, 7. 33.	187	— 29.	149
xxxv. 18.	187	xxv.	iv, v
		xxx. 5.	xvi, 370
EZRA.		xxxi, 19, 20.	xxiv
i. 2.	334	xxxii. 3.	307
iii. 11.	xli, 183	xxxiv.	iv, v.
iv. 2.	188	— 1—3.	xl
ix. 8.	256		

410 INDEX OF TEXTS.

	Page		Page
xxxv. 5.	320	cxvii. 2.	371
—— 20.	370	cxviii. 12.	179. 205
xxxvii.	v	cxix.	iv, v
—— 1, 2.	xiii	—— 57.	333
—— 10, 11.	xvii	cxx. 1. 6.	xxi
xxxviii. 9.	307	cxxvii. 4.	xxix
—— 19.	xxxii.	cxxxiv.	387
—— 20.	xxi	cxxxv. 6, 7.	xviii
xlii, xliii.	xxv	cxxxvii. 1.	167
xlv. 1.	170	—— 2.	229
xlvi. 9.	202	cxxxix. 14.	382
l. 3. 4.	132	cxliv. 5, 6.	xi
lviii. 9.	205	—— 12—14.	xxiv
lx. 1.	360	cxlv.	iv, v
lxii. 4.	284	cxlvi. 2, 3. 10.	xxix
lxiv. 6.	210, 331	cxlviii. 7—13.	xvii
lxviii. 4. 7.	310		
—— 11, 12.	317	PROVERBS.	
—— 27.	344	i. 24—32.	x
—— 31.	331	iii. 8.	136
—— 32.	338	—— 9.	xi
lxix. 5.	xxxii	vi. 16—19.	
—— 28.	168	—— 20.	199
lxxii. 10.	338	vii. 2.	199
lxxiii. 4.	373	—— 22, 23.	162
lxxv. 9.	142	x. 1. 7.	xv
lxxvi, title,	237	xi. 22.	164
lxxviii. 33.	401	—— 24.	xv
—— 34.	342	xvi. 33.	xvi
—— 38, 39.	375	xviii. 10.	295
—— 47.	172	xxi. 1.	147
—— 71.	292	xxiii. 30.	141
lxxx. 5.	392	xxv. 26.	135
—— 7.	210, 331	xxix. 26.	xvi
lxxxv. 10—14.	337	xxx.	xix
lxxxvi. 14.	267	—— 3.	258
lxxxvii. 6.	168	xxxi. 10—31.	iv
xcix. 5.	383		
ci.	xxvi	ECCLESIASTES.	
cii. 6.	265	ii. 5, 5.	147
ciii. 3.	295	—— 8.	157
—— 5.	319	—— 16.	392
—— 9. 13, 14.	375	xi. 2.	xix
—— 11.	371	CANTICLES.	
—— 11, 12.	xv	i. 5.	xix
ciii. 16.	316	ii. 15.	137
cv. 33.	172	iv. 4.	257
cviii. 4, 5.	xxxviii	—— 10, 11.	165
cx. 1.	358	viii. 2.	141
cxi.	iv, v		
—— 4.	xxix	ISAIAH.	
cxii.	iv, v	i. 3.	xiii
—— 1.	x	—— 8.	173
—— 10.	xiii	iii. 1.	157
cxiv. 1—4.	xxviii	iv. 1.	157
—— 1, 2.	310	—— 5.	175
cxvi. 1. 9. 12. 14, 15.	xxi	—— 22.	141

INDEX OF TEXTS. 411

	Page		Page
vi. 13.	264	xlvi. 3.	xi
viii. 10.	xxxii	—— 9.	xiv
—— 22.	181	xlvii. 5.	257
ix. 10.	xvii, 204	xlviii. 20, 21.	311
— 20.	xiii	xlix. 4.	xiv
x. 5—12.	334	—- 20, 21.	369
— 32.	287	l. 5, 6.	xix
xiii. 4, 5.	xxiv	-- 10.	xv
—— 6.	175	li. 7, 8.	xi
—— 10.	xxi	-- 17.	142
xiv. 4—27.	xxvi	-- 19.	xix
— 14.	368	-- 20.	xlii
— 28.	181	lii. 7, 8. 12.	311
xv. 3.	xix	— 8.	317
xvi. 10.	173	liii. 4.	149, 296
xvii. 9.	xxi	liv. 4.	x
—— 13.	320	— 4, 5.	167
xx.	327	— 10.	xvii
xxii. 6 .	220	lv. 2.	207
——14.	175	— 3.	xi
—— 16.	367, 368	— 6, 7.	x
xxiv. 17.	175	--- 13.	347
xxvi. 5, 6.	xii	lvii. 6.	175
xxvii. 7.	175	----- 13, 14.	311
xxviii. 14, 15. 18.	xxx	lviii. 5---8.	xviii
xxix. 5.	320	----- 14.	368
—— 21.	282	lx. 4.	351
xxx. 16.	xv	--- 6---9.	338
—— 26.	218	--- 11.	331
——30—33.	281	lxi. 3.	175
xxxi. 8.	207	--- 7.	313
—— 9.	279	lxv. 11, 12.	175
xxxii. 11.	247	----- 21, 22.	xi
xxxiii. 1.	175	lxvi. 1.	358
—— 12.	205		
—— 21.	xxi	JEREMIAH.	
xxxiv.	390	i. 6.	184
xxxv. 1, 2,	371	-- 10.	184
xxxvi, xxxvii, xxxviii, xxxix	302	ii. 18.	258
xxxvi. 17.	260	ii. 21.	174
xxxvii. 9.	327	-- 25.	374
—— 22, &c.	xxvi	-- 27.	135
—— 25.	244	iv. 30.	160
—— 26.	252	vi. 1.	285
—- 29.	286	vii. 22, 23.	329
xl. 2.	xxi	— 24.	135
xli. 19.	347, 371	— 29.	228
— 24.	403	viii. 7.	133
— 28.	xii	x. 3—5.	342
xliii. 17.	xxiv, 338	-- 9.	154
xliii. 18, 19.	311	xii. 7. 9.	372
xliv. 7.	210	xvii. 8	145, 146
—— 18.	184	—-- 12.	182
—— 26.	xiv	xviii. 12.	374
xlv. 1.	179	xix. 9.	206
—-- 8.	168	xx. 7.	398
—-- 16, 17.	xxiv	xxiii. 31.	250

INDEX OF TEXTS.

	Page		Page
xxv. 11.	261	xxii. 18—22.	168
xxxiii. 9.	382	xxiii. 30.	402
xxxvii. 13.	370	—— 40.	160
xl. 12.	185	xxiv. 17.	364
xli. 9.	156	xxvi. 14.	262
xlviii.	227	—— 15—18.	261
—— 5.	228	xxvii. 12.	154
—— 11.	268	xxix. 3.	325
—— 12.	257	—— 18—20.	193
—— 29.	230	xxxii. 27.	217
—— 31.	230	xxxvii. 11—13.	271
—— 32.	231	xxxviii.	390
—— 33.	232	xxxix. 4.	226
—— 34.	228	—— 8—10.	203
—— 36.	228, 230	—— 16, 17.	299
—— 37.	227, 228	xliii. 3.	184
—— 43, 44.	265	—— 5, 6.	182
xlix. 35.	220	—— 7.	182
l. 9.	218		
—— 38.	332	**DANIEL.**	
li. 27, 28.	218	vii. 17.	261
—— 36.	332	viii. 20.	261

LAMENTATIONS.

		HOSEA.	
i.	v	i. 7.	305
—— 1, 2.	xxiii	ii. 6.	272
ii.	v	—— 18.	276
—— 4.	xxv	iv. 13.	144
—— 10.	166, 258	v. 7.	151
—— 15.	xxxvi	vi. 4.	xii
iii.	iv, v	—— 6.	329
—— 1—6	xxiii	ix. 10.	274
—— 14.	169	x. 8.	156
—— 31.	xxv	xi. 4.	133
—— 39.	313	—— 9.	207
—— 66.	169	xii. 1.	332, 374
iv.	iv, v	xiii. 4.	206
iv. 2.	257	xiv. 9.	xiv.
—— 8.	199		
—— 15.	xxxvi, 361	**JOEL.**	
—— 17.	307	i. 14.	139
—— 21.	246	ii. 2.	199
		—— 7.	xi
EZEKIEL.		—— 10.	219
i. 14.	247	—— 15.	139
iii. 8, 9.	354	—— 20. 22.	294
iv. 6.	244	—— 25.	179
v. 13.	142	iii. 10.	150
xiii. 9.	168	—— 13.	xiii, 173
—— 16.	223	—— 15, 16.	219
xv. 3.	255	—— 16.	xiv
—— 3, 4.	273		
xvi. 11, 12.	163	**AMOS.**	
xvii. 22—24.	150	i. 1.	178
xx. 3. 31.	397	—— 2.	xiv
—— 38.	144	iv. 11.	208
—— 47.	305, 208	—— 13.	368

INDEX OF TEXTS. 413

	Page		Page
v. 10.	282	**Tobit.**	
— 19.	264	xiii. 16, 17.	370
— 21—24.	139		
— 25, 26.	329	**Judith.**	
vi. 3—6.	176	iv. 7.	210
— 12.	180	x. 3.	384
— 13.	207	xvi. 16.	318
viii. 9.	219	— 17.	406
Micah:		**Wisdom.**	
i. 3.	368	ii. 7, 8.	274
iii. 1—3.	159	xiii. 11—19.	332
iv. 1—4.	149	xv. 7.	332
— 8.	292		
v. 2.	351	**Ecclesiasticus.**	
— 3.	192	vii. 15.	278
vi. 1, 2.	132	— 17.	406
— 15.	xix	xiv. 24.	256
— 16.	169	xxiv. 30, 31.	147
vii. 4.	272	xlviii. 17.	252
Nahum.		**Baruch.**	
i. 11.	351	v. 7.	314
— 15.	360	— 8.	321
ii. 13.	202	vi.	332
iii. 5, 6.	162		
— 14.	322	**1 Maccabees.**	
Habakkuk.		v. 65.	389
ii. 5.	177	**2 Maccabees.**	
		vi. 18.	398
Zephaniah.		vii. 1.	393
i. 5.	397		
ii. 8—11.	230	**Matthew.**	
iii. 17.	320	iii. 3.	314
		vi. 28—30.	273
Haggai.		viii. 11.	267, 406
ii. 17.	173	— 17.	296
		x. 27.	251
Zechariah.		xi. 4, 5.	297
i. 15.	343	xii. 18.	323
ii. 5.	169	xiii. 14.	182, 185
viii. 23.	157	xv. 9.	282
ix. 12.	313	xvi. 19.	255
— 14.	246	— 28.	390
x. 4.	256	xviii. 25.	352
xiii. 4.	243	xxi. 33.	173
xiv. 5.	178	— 43.	282
— 10.	173	xxiii. 14.	403
— 19.	313	xxiv. 28.	264
		— 29.	219
Malachi.		— 41.	342
i. 1.	223		
ii. 11.	223	**Mark.**	
— 12.	387	i. 3.	216
iii. 2, 3.	168	ii. 9.	292
— 15.	267	vii. 7.	235
iv. 1.	267	ix. 44	40

	Page
xii. 1.	173
xiv. 65.	354
xv. 19.	354

LUKE.

	Page
i. 19.	392
ii. 1.	219
iii. 4.	219
iv. 18, 19.	384
x. 34.	136, 214
xiv. 15.	406
—— 16.	267
xv. 22.	202
xviii. 1.	386
—— 31, 32.	354
xxi. 22.	390
xxii. 29, 30.	267

JOHN.

	Page
i. 23.	214
vii. 37. 39.	215
xii. 40.	182, 185
— 41.	182
xiii. 23.	406
xv. 6.	273
xviii. 20, 21.	365

ACTS.

	Page
ii. 3.	178
— 39.	376
x. 9.	250
xi. 28.	219
xii. 8.	202
xxi. 4.	262
xxvi. 4, 5.	366
xxviii. 26.	182
—— 27.	185

ROMANS.

	Page
i. 20.	327
vi. 17.	215
ix. 20, 21.	337

	Page
ix. 28.	208
x. 15.	360
——20.	397
xi. 8.	182
— 26.	380
— 30, 31.	282
xv. 4, 5.	138
— 12.	211
— 12, 13.	138

1 CORINTHIANS.

	Page
ii. 9.	394
iii. 15.	208

GALATIANS.

	Page
iii. 3.	316
— 13.	225

EPHESIANS.

	Page
ii. 13. 17.	376

HEBREWS.

	Page
iv. 12.	348
xiii. 15.	376

1 PETER.

	Page
i. 24.	315
— 24, 25.	316

REVELATION.

	Page
i. 16.	348
iii. 7.	255
iv. 73.	182
v. 5.	213
vi. 15, 16.	156
xiv. 10.	142
xix. 13. 15, 16.	390
—— 17, 18.	299
xx.	390
— 4.	330
xxi. 18—21.	370
xxii. 16.	213

INDEX OF PERSONS.

Abarbanel, 362, 370
Abendana, 135, 137
Aben-Ezra, 129, 137, 163, 209, 346, 367
Aben Tybbon, xxxv
Abraham, 320
Abydenus, 246, 334
Addison, 167, 202, 235
Æschylus, 254, 356
Ætius, 330
Agatharchides, 338
Ahaz, 130, 136
Alexander, 240, 262
Ambrose, 319
Ammianus, 328
Antiochus Epiph. liii.
Antipater, 342
Aquila, xliii, lvi, 134, 144, 177, 377
Aratus, 254, 278
Arbuthnot, 292
Arias Montanus, 364, 388
Aristophanes, 161, 348
Aristotle, his Treatise on Poetry, xlviii.
—— Hist. Animal. 228.
Arnobius, 373
Arrian, 221, 328, 333
Athenæus, 359
Aurelius Victor, 358
Azarias, Rab. xxxiii, &c.

Bagot, 208
Balkis, Queen of Sheba, 148
Barry, 268
Baumgarten, 255
Benjamin of Tudela, 222
Berosus, 222, 312
Beryte, l'Evêque de, 292
Blanchini, 364
Bochart, 140, 154, 171, 228, 235, 280, 294, 319, 338, 405
Breithaupt, 350
Brentius, 151
Brerewood, 335
Bruns, lvii.
Bryant, 243
Buxtorff, 325, 368
Buxtorff, junior, xxxiii.

Cælius Antipater, 154
Callimachus, 191, 254
Calmet, 227
Cambyses, 240
Camden, 170
Capellus, 267, 323, 354
Casaubon, 365
Castell, 331, 366
Castellio, xxviii, xlix.
Cellarius, 229
Celsius, 144
Celsus, 308
Chandler, Bp. 199, 363, 400
Chappelow, 142, 157, 308
Chardin, 136, 158, 172, 173, 183, 204, 217, 251, 253, 255, 261, 268, 284, 292, 318, 330, 342, 353, 358, 382, 386, 397
Chrysostom, 176
Cicero, iii, 339, 348
Claudian, 304
Clemens Alexand. 161, 254, 373
—— Rom. 394
Cocceius, 246, 288, 379, 397
Columella, 171
Cotovicus, 382
Crœsus, 334, 339
Cuper, 363
Curtius, 300, 351
Cyril, 178, 403
Cyrus, 214, 220, 246, 247, 320, 332, 333, 334, 335, 336, 361

Darius Hystaspis, 221
D'Arvieux, 193, 273
De Guignes, 400
De Lisle, 171
Demosthenes, iii, 332
Deschamps, 200
D'Herbelot, 205, 294, 351
Dicæarchus, 260
Diodorus, 236, 240, 253, 314, 339
Doederlein, 284, 350
Donatus, 261
Drusius, 367
Durell, lvi, 143, 153, 166, 177, 189, 363, 373

INDEX OF PERSONS.

Egmont and Heyman, 171, 236, 240
Ephræm Syr. 145, 247, 292
Esarhaddon, 187
Eudoxus, 154
Evelyn, 400
Eugene Roger, 162, 171
Euripides, 135, 290, 295
Eusebius, 210, 334
Eustathius, 254

Festus, 365
Furer, 274

Gibson, 170
Glassius, 135
Grabe, ii, lv.
Gratius, 231
Gregory Naz. 183
Grotius, 241, 295, 312, 401

Hadrian, 185
Hammond, 286
Hanno, 154
Hare, viii, xxxii.
Harmer, 136, 137, 156, 158, 173, 174, 184, 190, 205, 255, 273, 279, 292, 304, 305, 318, 330, 342, 351, 353, 386, 405
Hasselquist, 137, 172, 175
Herman von der Hardt, ii.
Herodotus, 154, 172, 214, 220, 221, 226, 228, 236, 244, 247, 260, 328, 330, 333, 334, 353
Hesiod, 290, 363
Hesychius, 339
Hezekiah, 130, 230, 251, 252, 293, 296, 302, 309
Homer, 141, 180, 191, 223, 228, 238, 254, 280, 281, 287, 289, 342, 343, 357, 358, 367
Horace, 212, 261, 280, 332, 382
Houbigant, xxxi, 139, 151, 157, 175, 177, 192, 204, 211, 215, 233, 251, 263, 269, 274, 277, 284, 285, 286, 295, 300, 302, 306, 308, 309, 321, 325, 326, 329, 337, 370, 371, 379, 383, 384, 396, 398, 403, 404
Huet, 154, 179, 254, 328
Hunt, 162
Hyde, 300, 336

Jarchi, xxxi, 159, 181, 191, 229, 257, 276, 305, 307, 325, 343, 346, 348, 374
Jephthah, his vow, 325
Jerom, ii, lvi. 173, 182, 204, 210, 221, 229, 244, 257, 269, 276, 278, 287, 305, 307, 320, 366, 377, 394, 397, 399, 400.

Ikenius, 242
John the Baptist, 313—315
John Hyrcanus, 389
Jonathan Ben Uziel, lv.
Jones, 213
Josephus, 155, 210, 222
Jotham, 129
Isaiah, 129
Jubb, 140, 151, 154, 159, 166, 187, 188, 355, 363, 368, 378, 379, 386, 394
Judas Maccabeus, 389
Julius Pollux, 161
Justin, 258
Juvenal, 160, 165, 197

Kalinski, 225
Kempfer, 141, 146, 173, 183, 253, 278
Kennicott, 1, lvii. 203, 215, 300, 301, 364, 367, 384, 405
Kimchi, 135, 137, 143, 149, 170, 177, 180, 188, 197, 206, 207, 209, 212, 233, 238, 241, 246, 248, 286, 306, 320, 325, 346, 364, 370, 380, 385, 403

Labid, 200
Lactantius, 357
Lardner, 365
La Roque, 273
Le Clerc, 143, 229, 233, 286, 290, 322, 326, 349, 398, 399, 402, 404
Lilienthal, 374, 380, 398
Livy, 249
Locke, 138
Longinus, 135, 332
Lowman, 381
Lowth, 140, 213, 226, 233, 242, 306
Lucan, 167, 170, 214, 236, 276
Lucretius, 278, 282, 382
Ludolphus, 315

Macrobius, 404
Maillet, 405
Maimonides, 225, 365
Martial, 150
Maundrell, 145, 146, 147, 155, 171, 204, 217, 222, 274, 350, 374
Megasthenes, 246
Meir, Rabbi, 248, 323
Mela, 333
Merrick, 373
Michaelis, 148, 151, 168, 170, 171, 175, 200, 229, 243, 270, 343, 344, 349, 350
Miller, 140, 292
Millius, Dav. 399, 304
Milton, 223

INDEX OF PERSONS. 417

Moerlius, 208, 373
Mohammed, 148, 155, 200, 256
Montagu, L. Mary, 305
Mosheim, 313
Montfaucon, lvi.
Muller, 200, 242
Munster, 363

Nau, 171
Nebuchadnezzar, 227, 240, 246, 257, 261, 262, 297, 333
Nepos, 351
Newton, Sir I. 187, 266
———Bp. 240, 262
Niebuhr, 148, 193, 278, 353
Ninus, 259
Nonnus, 174

Onkelos, xxxv.
Origen, viii, 346, 366, 377
Osbeck, 368
Ovid, 135, 150, 219, 334
Owen, 243, 394

Pachomius, liv.
Palladius, 171
Paul Lucas, 156, 164
Pausanias, 179
Pekah, 130
Perizonius, 259
Persius, 171
Phile, 319
Philo, xli. 240
Pietro della Valle, 160, 164, 222, 253, 324
Pindar. 341, 349
Plato, 357
Pliny, 140, 146, 154, 160, 176, 236, 308, 335, 404, 406
Pococke, 236, 240, 305
Prideaux, 229, 243, 365, 389
Procopius, xliii. 199, 280, 403
Prodiucs, 165
Psammitichus, 239, 244
Psellus, 280
Ptolemy Philometer, 242
——— Soter, 240
Publius, Syr. 165

Randolph, 325
Rauwolf, 272
Reland, 171, 233
Retsin, 130, 185, 194
Russell, 161, 405

Sal. ben Melee, 134, 137, 169, 178, 184, 207, 209, 250, 307, 322, 325, 346, 363, 370, 393, 403

Sale, 148, 256, 300
Salmasius, 140, 161
Salvian, 219
Sanctius, 161, 166
Sandys, 160, 172, 262
Sardanapalus, 215
Scaliger, ii.
Schindler, 137, 201, 270, 367
Schmidius, 387
Schroeder, 161, 195, 289
Schultens, 137, 157, 200, 231, 237, 233, 356, 393
Secker, xxxi, lvi, 143, 159. 169, 177, 189, 192, 197, 198, 204, 206, 207, 209, 213, 232, 241, 242, 263, 265, 277, 283, 286, 291, 292, 294, 298, 303, 322, 324, 326, 327, 331, 338, 343, 344, 349, 354, 356, 357, 363, 370, 371, 375, 377, 378, 395, 396, 403
Semiramis, 246, 313, 328
Senacherib, 131, 206, 209, 210, 234, 237, 244, 279, 293, 294, 301, 327
Seneca, 237, 264
Servius, 258, 367
Shalmaneser, 131, 187, 206, 227, 232, 262, 275, 327
Shaw, 160, 204, 256, 274, 282, 300, 319, 342
Shebna, 252, 253
Sherlock, 152
Simonis, 205, 211, 237, 240, 331
Solinus, 170
Solomon, 147, 148, 151, 158, 204, 251, 256
Spencer, 330
Strabo, 146, 155, 170, 221, 226, 236, 328, 339
Suetonius, 383
Surenhusius, 364
Symmachus, xliii, lvi, 144, 177, 246, 326, 330, 345, 364

Tacitus, 883
Tavernier, 136, 138, 155, 222, 387
Taylor, Concord. 137, 256
Terence, 262, 342
Tharthan, 243
Themistius, 363
Theocritus, 212
Theodoret, xlii, 176, 168, 225
Theodotion, xliii, lvi, 134, 144, 177, 385
Theophrastus, 363, 373
Thevenot, 141, 171, 193, 253, 255, 268, 284, 405
Tiglath Pileser, 130, 187, 196, 201, 204, 232

Tirhakah, 244, 327
Trallian, 171

Valesius, 221
Vasco de Gama, 155
Vegetius, 330
Virgil, l. 147, 150, 170, 178, 180, 197, 202, 212, 220, 226, 258, 280, 281, 290, 339, 368, 371, 398
Vitringa, ii, xxxi, 130, 213, 215, 218, 227, 250, 252, 259, 262, 288, 312, 321, 327, 354, 362, 379, 383, 385, 393, 396, 397, 403

Ulloa, 140
Vossius, 145
Usher, 187
Uzziah, 129, 226

Wetstein, xlix, 296
Woide, lv, 269
Wolfius, ii, xxxiii, 215

Xenophon, 160, 165, 180, 214, 218, 220, 225, 333, 334, 335, 336, 342, 353
Xerxes, 221

INDEX OF THINGS.

Acrostic; see *Alphabetical*.
Abraham, 320
——— his bosom, 406
Additions, Hebrew text, xxxv, 192, 218, 286, 306, 344, 345, 369, 379, 384
Æneid, xlviii.
Africa, 154
Agriculture, 277
Alcahol, 160
Alexandria, Jewish church there, liii.
——— many Jews there, 240, 263
Allegory, mystical, 313
Alphabetical, twelve Hebrew poems, iv.
——— their cause and use, iv.
Alternate members, xix.
——— singing; see *Responsive*.
Anomalies, probably corruptions, 145, 170, 355, 390
Anthropopathia, 142, 287
Ancient versions, lii, 343
——— confirmed by Hebrew MSS, lii, liii.
——— some examples of it, 145, 153, 157, 223, 239, 280, 282, 283, 291, 320, 321, 325, 326, 331, 343, 345, 349, 353, 355, 356, 364, 370, 372, 375, 377, 382, 386, 390, 396, 405
Apocalyps of Elias, 394
Arabic version, liv, 230
Arabs, different sorts of them, 324
Armour, burning of, emblem of peace, 202
Ascension of Esaiah, 394
Assyrians and Babylonians the same, 236
Azotus; 244

Babylon, 245, 259
——— its naval power, 327
——— greatness and ruin, 220, 221

Babylon, the total annihilation of its walls accounted for, 221
——— how taken, 245, 332, 334
——— Prophecy on it, beautiful, 215
——— deliverance from it, a shadow of deliverance by Christ, 315, 316
Balaam's prophecies, xxii.
Beard, highly honoured in the East, 193
Botsra, 297, 389
Buildings, eastern, 204, 221, 284

Cape of Good Hope passed, 154
Cassiterides, 154
Caverns large, for refuge, 155
Chaldee Paraphrase, xxxi, xxxv, lv, 140, 204, 207, 231, 282, 298, 320, 321, 325, 345, 380
Chambers, eastern, 305
Chapters, not in order of time, 181
——— not rightly divided, 167, 203, 215, 227, 272
Chasdim, Chaldeans, 259
Chinese chronology, 400
Chittim, 257
Chorus, 216, 293, 343, 387
Collation of MSS necessary, xlix.
——— Heb. MSS, how far useful, l, li, liv, lvii.
——— requires long examination, lvii.
——— MSS of LXX very desirable, lv.
Comparison, particles of, omitted, 386
Conjectures, concurrent 284
——— in correcting, xxxi.
——— in translating, lii.
——— the latter as hazardous as the former, lii, 396
Construct state for absolute, probably a mistake, 169, 307.
Construction of sentences, suddenly changed, 388, 343.
——— alternate, xix.

INDEX OF THINGS.

Coptic version, lv, 181, 269, 346 366
Copyists, Jewish, fallible, xlvii, lii.
────────── their customs in writing, xlvii, 170
Corner, the place of honour in the East, 305
Corruptions, perhaps wilful, liii, 395
Counes, an eastern vehicle, 405
Cymbal, 235
Cup of God's wrath, 142, 356

Damascus, 145, 232
Delphi, oracle there, 339
Dream, similitude from, 281

Eagle, 319
────── Cyrus's ensign, 342
Edomites, 297
────── settled in Judea, 389
Egypt, 234—236, 239, 243
Eluth, port, 129
Elegiac verses, in Hebrew, xxv.
Ellipsis, 138, 209, 253, 320, 325, 373
English version, vulgar, xxix, xli, lviii.
────── revision of it expedient, lvi, lix.
────── versions old, sometimes better, 302
Eshcol, 171
Euphrates, 328, 333
Eziongeber, 154
Expedition of eastern monarchs, the manner of it, 313

Fathers, Christian, generally bad commentators on the prophecies, xliii.
Figs, 274
Flocks, great care in driving them necessary, 318
Footstool, 357, 383
Fuel, 273

Gardens in the East, 145
Garments, transparent, 165
Gate, the place of judicature, 282
Gehenna, 286, 406
Gemara of Babylon, 364
Gentiles called by Christ, 355, 369, 381, 396, 402
Girdle, 179, 212
Glosses, from margin into text, 192, 285
Gog and Magog, 390
Golden age, 212
Gourd-kind, fruits of the, much in request in the East, 137

Greek New Test. its non-integrity, xlv, xlvi.
────── version of the Old Testament, its importance, liii, 139, 185, 192, 213, 233, 282, 284, 291, 300, 304, 308, 315, 330, 392
────────── interpolated, 181
────────── altered, perhaps wilfully, liii, 243
────────── MSS of LXX very useful, 166, 230, 232, 244, 264, 284, 289, 329, 330, 380, 385, 392
────────── collation of them now necessary, liv.
────────── MS Pachom. and MS I. D. II. Br. Mus. liv, 166, 181, 209, 219, 231, 232, 248, 284, 289, 324, 329, 337, 349, 380, 385
Groves, sacred, 143

Hades, image of, 177, 216
Halle Bible, lvi.
Half-pause, in long verses, xxv, xxvii.
Hands, marks on, 330, 350
Harbinger of eastern monarchs, 313
Harian metre confuted, viii.
Hebraisms, 274, 316
Heb. alphabet, only consonants, vii.
────── Bible, left complete by Ezra,
────── mistakes in it early, xxxiii, 315, 395
────── now incorrect, xlvii.
────── its integrity strangely believed, xlv.
────── its true readings how recoverable, liii.
────── letters similar, the sources of error, xlvi, xlvii.
────── MSS, now extant, how old, 1, lviii.
────── the present collation of them, l, li, lv.
────── poetry, its characteristic, xl.
────── verses not in rhyme, vii, viii.
────── longer and shorter, xxii—xxvii.
────── words single, require many English, xxxvi.
Homage, eastern modes of, 351, 357
Horites, 155
Hosts, for God of Hosts, 138
Houses in the East, 250
Hunting, ancient, 264

Jackal, 137
Idolatry exposed, 331
Idolatrous practices among the Jews, 397, 399

INDEX OF THINGS. 421

Idumea, 389
Jerusalem, the Valley of Vision, 250
Jeshurun, 329
Jewels of the feet, nostrils, &c. 162
Jews, great destructions of them, 185
—— present dispersion, with a confession for them, 391
Iliad, xlviii.
Images poetical, from nature, &c. 153, 337
—— emblematical of heaven and hell, 406
Infinitives absolute, for tenses past, 247
—— signify imperatively, 291
Intercalary stanza, xxvi.
Interpolation; see *Additions*.
Job, book, already allowed poetical, ii, xxii.
Isaiah, book, lii.
—— history of its time, 129
—— Notes here, their design, lx.
Israel sometimes means the Messiah, 349
—— people, carried away, in 6th Hezekiah, 131
———————————— finally, 22d Manasseh, 187
Judea called the Mountain, 170
—— wilderness of, 314

Keys, ancient, 254
—— mark of office, 254
Kingdom of Christ, under the image of a feast, 267, 406
Koran, 155, 200, 256, 300

Lake, below the wine-press, 173
Latter days, 149
Lebanon, House of the Forest of, 257
—— and Carmel, 282
Leviathan, the crocodile, and the serpent, 272
Libation, 283
Literal sense, the necessary foundation of all interpretations, xli, xlii, lx.
—— may be the mystical, or spiritual, 362
—— is so; see *Messiah*.
London Polyglott, lii.
Magian religion, 335.
Marks on the hands, 330, 350
Mashal, its nature, xxx, 184, 223, 277, 282
Masoretes, their pauses and punctuation, viii, xx, xliii.

Masoretes, wretched critics, 326
Medicean MS of Virgil, li.
Medicine and surgery, 136
Messiah himself, 168, 182, 186, 192, 195, 211, 291, 310, 323, 337, 347, 348, 349, 353, 361, 365, 368, 369, 378, 389
—— his kingdom, 148, 182, 186, 195, 201, 211, 214, 266, 267, 291, 310 312, 316, 338, 355, 369, 378, 381, 389, 396, 401
Metre of things; see *Rhythmus*.
Mills, grinding at, the work of females, 342
Mirrors of metal, 195
Mishna, 364
Moukden, present Emperor of China's poem, 400
Mizmor, its nature, xl.

Naharaga, 333
Naharmalca, 328, 333
Nails, ancient, 255
Necromancy, 280
Negative, understood as if repeated, 258, 320
Nile, 237, 240, 258
—— Shichor, 258
Nose-jewels, 163

Ode on K. Babylon, most excellent, 216—218
Old Testament, defective method of studying it, xliii.
Omissions, Heb. Text, xxv, lii, 134, 151, 153, 157, 166, 175, 180, 181, 198, 213, 219, 223, 228, 241, 252, 253, 282, 283, 285, 291, 299, 301, 303, 308, 321, 322, 325, 330, 333, 344, 345, 349, 351, 354, 364, 370, 371, 374, 376, 377, 379, 384, 385, 402, 403, 405.
Onias's temple, 242
Ophel, 291.
Ophir, 154.

Pallacopas, 333.
Palm-wine, 176, 263.
Parabolic style, 153, 218, 265, 272, 320, 323, 347, 352, 370, 371, 381.
Parallelism of verses or lines, ix, xxxii.
—— attention to, useful in interpreting poetical parts of Scripture, xxx.
Parallel lines, synonymous, ix.
—— antithetic, ix, xv.
—— synthetic, ix, xvii.
—— places, useful in correcting,

INDEX OF THINGS.

227, 228, 230—232, 302, 306, 309, 315.
Paronomasia, 175, 265, 290, 308, 384.
Participle, for future tense, 331.
Passover, the manner of that deliverance, 288.
Perfumes, eastern, 165.
Personification, iv.
Port, the, whence the name, 283.
Presents to the great in the East necessary, 374.
Prophecies of Isaiah, not prose, ii.
——————— not now in order of time, 136, 181.
Prosopopœia, 217.
Proverbs of Solomon, xvi, xxii.
——————— allowed poetical, ii.
Psalms, already allowed poetical, ii, xxii.
—————— ill-divided, xxvi.

Rabbinical evasion, 403.
Responsive song, xli, 183, 272, 316, 317.
Resurrection, a common doctrine, 271.
Rhythmus of things, xxxiii—xli.
Rice, how planted, 292.
Romans, destruction of Jerusalem by, 262.

Saba, reservoir of, 148.
Sahidic version, 366.
Samaria, 273.
Scoffers, 275.
Seder Olam, 187.
Separation of Psalms, xxvi.
—————— words, 284, 373.
Sepulchres, 253, 367, 368.
Sickness and sin considered as equivalent, 295.
Sidon, mother-city of Tyre, 258.
Siloah, 196, 252.
Singulars sometimes for plurals, 331.
Sitting in the East, common manner of, 358.
—————— in state, 358.
Sistrum, 235.
Sorek, in Judah, vines of, 171.
Spanish version, 139, 161.
Speech of ghosts supposed feeble, 280.
Spitting, an expression of detestation, 353.
Standard copy, none infallible, liii.
Strong drink, 176, 263.
Supreme Beings, two, Persian, 335.
Syriac version, lv, 213, 247, 355, 392.

Tabor, Mount, 171.
Talmud, Babylonish, 158, 349.
Tarshish, where, 154, 257.
—————— ships, 154, 257.
Teraphim consulted, 152.
Threshing, 247, 269, 278.
Tophet, 286.
Transcribers; see *Copyists*.
Translations, modern, whether in Latin, or for the use of the Protestant Churches, all from the pointed Hebrew text, xliii.
Translator's duty, xxviii, xxix, xlii.
Transpositions, Hebrew text, 186, 198, 307.
Treasures of Cyrus, 335.
Trees, long-lived, 400.
Troglodytes, 155.
Tyre, 257—262.

Van, ancient, 285.
Various readings, Hebrew, publication of commended, xlix.
Veil, to shade the court, 318.
Ventriloqui, 280.
Verse, its characteristics, iv—viii, xx. xli.
Verses, ill-divided, 139, 218, 299, 401.
—————— long or short. xxii.
Versions of versions useful, lv, 180, 230.
Vineyard-tower, 173.
Vines, large trunks of, 172.
—————— poisonous fruit of, 174.
Vowel points, not original, nor by Ezra, xliv.
Vulgate, xxviii, lvi, 135, 175, 185, 198, 218, 252, 285, 301, 321, 322, 325.
—————— authentic, by Council of Trent, xlv.

Wardrobes, Eastern, 158.
Watchmen in the Temple, 387.
Water, in gardens, 145.
Wine mixed, 141.
Wine-press, 173.
Wines, 267.
Women celebrate great events, 317.
Words, many now lost in the text of Isaiah, lii.
—————— wrongly divided, 153, 273.
World, sometimes for land or country, 219, 263,

INDEX OF THINGS. 423

אדני for יהוה, 183, 203, 205, 207, 213, 285, 307.
איה and אין, 392.
איים and ציים, 259, 262, 325.
ב and כ mistaken, 177, 189, 209, 228, 380, 404.
Βαιτυλοι, 373.
במות, 368.
ד and ר mistaken, 197, 198, 204, 228, 251, 267, 281, 285, 326.
גליון, 195.
ו omitted at the half-pause, xxv.
ו for ולא, 258.
זדים and זרים changed, 266, 267.
י necessary, 1st person preterite, 270, 325.

חטאה, punishment for sin, 313.
לא and לו changed, 285, 290.
למו and לנו changed, 210, 270, 330.
ם, plural termination, frequently omitted, 170, 355.
מזמור, xl.
מקול, as מ, 265.
משל, xxx, 223, 277, 282.
משפט, 323.
נאם, solemn delivery of prophecy, 250.
פסח, 288.
צדקה, 323, 355.
שרב, the glowing sand in the East, 300.

Remarkable Variations in the Text of Isaiah, where there is little Similitude between the Words.

Text.	Variations.	Chapter.
וידעו	ויגבהו	ix. 8. Chald.
מפני	מקול	xxiv. 18. MS, Chald. Vulg.
וישכע	וישב	xxxvii. 9. LXX and parallel place.
הארצות	גוים	xxxvii. 18. ten MSS.
עבדיך	כלאכיך	xxxvii. 24. LXX, Syr.
ועור	וחרש	xlii. 19. MS, Sym.
כתמם	פתאם	xlvii. 9. LXX, Syr.
צדיק	עריץ	xlix. 24. Syr. Vulg.
ירושלם, 2do.	ישראל	lii. 9. two MSS.
נפשך	לחמך	lviii. 10. eight MSS, Syr.
צד תאמנה	כתף הנשאנה	lx. 4. MS.
עמו	עבדו	lxiii. 11. two MSS, vet. edit. Syr.
מעולם	למען	lxiii. 16. MS.
עם	הר	lxiii. 18. LXX.
גוים	הוים	xliv. 2. four MSS.
יחדי	כאחד	lxv. 25. MS, LXX, Syr. Vulg.

THE END.